Post-Reformation Reformed Dogmatics

Post-Reformation Reformed Dogmatics

Volume 2
Holy Scripture:
The Cognitive Foundation
of Theology

Richard A. Muller

 Baker Books

A Division of Baker Book House Co.
Grand Rapids, Michigan 49516

© 1993 by Richard Muller

Published by Baker Books
a division of Baker Book House Company
P.O. Box 6287, Grand Rapids, MI 49516-6287

Printed in the United States of America

ISBN: 0-8010-6299-3

For
Karen
and
Kieth

in celebration of their marriage

27 November 1992

Contents

Preface

This study of the Reformed orthodox doctrine of Scripture is intended as a continuation of my earlier essay on the theological prolegomena of the orthodox or scholastic Reformed systems. As in the case of the previous volume, the present essay is a historical study that attempts to set forth in some detail the theology of the sixteenth and seventeenth centuries. Here, the subject is the doctrine of Scripture as it developed in the theology of post-Reformation Protestantism, specifically in the Reformed churches. Attention has been paid to the roots of the doctrine in the thought of the medieval scholastics and in the teaching of the Reformers and to the way in which these diverse roots were drawn upon in and for the creation of a distinctly Protestant dogmatics. In attempting to argue the continuities and discontinuities between the post-Reformation dogmatics and the thought of earlier eras, I have consistently avoided language of praise and blame and I have also avoided contemporary theological commentary.

I remain convinced that the only fruitful approach to the theological development of the old Protestant dogmatics is one that takes no theological sides, that refuses to muddy the historical waters with claims about the doctrinal rectitude or usefulness of one view or another, and that refrains as much as is humanly possible from reading the concerns of various schools of twentieth century theology into the thought of the Reformers or the orthodox for the sake finding either antecedents or foils for a contemporary opinion. It is certainly true that the contemporary study of Reformation and post-Reformation Protestantism owes much to the efforts of nineteenth-century theologians and historians like Alexander Schweizer, Matthias Schneckenburger, Heinrich Heppe and Albrecht Ritschl, just to name a few; to early twentieth-century scholars like Karl Holl, Adolf von Harnack, Hans Emil Weber, and Otto Ritschl; and to the host of neo-orthodox and conservative Reformed and Lutheran writers who have looked with deep respect and strong theological interest at the documents of sixteenth and seventeenth-century Protestantism. It is also the case, however, that all too many of these writers have embedded in their historical scholarship large components of theological argumentation, designed to manifest the relationship of their own theologies either to the Reformation and to Protestant orthodoxy in an integral line of development or, by way of contrast, to the "dynamic" and even "existential" approach of the Reformers as distinct from the "rigid," "dry," and "excessively formalized" theology of the orthodox. These theological approaches to historical materials have been most evident—and most in danger of obscuring the history itself—in the cases of the doctrine of predestination and the doctrine of Scripture. Unfortunately, the result of such a mingling of history and theology has typically been a portrait of the Reformation and of orthodoxy that looks more like the painter than the original subject. My own hope in the following essay, as in the preceding volume, is to present the ideas of the sixteenth and seventeenth centuries without any consideration of or reference to my own theological position, if indeed I can be said to have one.

Despite the length of the study, I have been continually aware that it barely scratches the surface of the subject. The variety of formulations and patterns of argument in the may Reformed orthodox treatises and systems, together with the vast number of commentaries and exegetical studies written during the period prevents exhaustive treatment in a single volume. Individual theologians, particularly those who worked in more than one genre and who moved from dogmatics to exegesis and to preaching require monographic study, if only in order to demonstrate the elements of originality that belong to their work and which tend to be submerged under the weight of materials in a more synthetic presentation of Reformed doctrine. Exegetical method in the seventeenth century could be the subject of a large monograph.

Some comment ought also to be made about my approach to translation, both of the theological treatises and systems cited and of the text of Scripture. Most of the citations have simply been translated out of the original Latin. Others—like those from Bullinger's *Decades,* Calvin's *Institutes,* and Vermigli's *Loci communes*—have been drawn from extant translations with consistent reference to and emendation on the basis of the Latin original. The sixteenth-century translations, in particular, are usually excellent and I have not noted minor emendations. The citations from Scripture translate Latin quotations in sixteenth and seventeenth-century documents directly into English from the Latin, frequently after consultation with the Geneva Bible and the King James Version. Citations from sixteenth and seventeenth-century English documents retain the version given in the original.

In response to some queries about the availability of sources used in volume one, I am pleased to note the increased accessibility of many of the documents cited through the efforts of the Inter-Documentation Corporation of Geneva which has produced an excellent microfiche collection of Reformed sources and has begun to make Lutheran materials similarly available. Many works, both of theologians of the British Isles and of continental authors in British editions and/or English translations are available through the University Microfilms "Early English Books, 1475–1640" and "Early English Books, 1641–1700" series, based on the Pollard-Redgrave and Wing short title catalogues, respectively.

Finally, a word of thanks must be offered to a series of colleagues and institutions. First, to the Mellon Foundation, which generously provided an initial year-long research grant that enabled me to do the basic research for the entire project of my *Post-Reformation Reformed Dogmatics*, I offer my continued thanks. I am also indebted to the H. Henry Meeter Center for Calvin Studies at Calvin College and Seminary in Grand Rapids, Michigan, for a summer fellowship crucial to the concluding stages of the present volume. The research contained in this volume has depended on the resources of a score of libraries, most notably the libraries of Duke University and the Duke Divinity School, Fuller Theological Seminary, and Calvin College and Seminary, and the Huntington Library in San Marino. I owe these libraries and their librarians a profound debt. To Dr. Susan Schreiner of the Divinity School, University of Chicago, I owe thanks for a careful and insightful reading of the manuscript and for lengthy discussion of her own research on the history of hermeneutics and the problem of certainty in the sixteenth century. Dr. John Thompson of Fuller Theological Seminary also performed yeoman service in his reading of portions of the manuscript. A word of thanks is also due to Diane Bradley who transformed a handwritten manuscript into fine electronic form at the word processor, to Maria denBoer whose copy-editing rectified many a problem, and to David Sielaff, whose skills produced the camera -ready copy.

Finally, to my wife, Gloria, I offer my thanks for support and love throughout the many months and years of teaching, research, and writing. Without her my work would be impossible.

Richard A. Muller
October 1992

Abbreviations

BRK — Heinrich Heppe, *Die Bekenntnisschriften der reformirten Kirche Deutschlands.* [*Schriften zur reformirten Theologie, Band I*] Elberfeld: R. L. Friederichs, 1860.

BTT — *Bible de tous les temps.* 8 vols. Collection dirigée par Charles Kannengiesser. Paris: Beauchesne, 1984–.

CC — Schaff, Philip. *The Creeds of Christendom, with a History and Critical Notes.* 3 vols. Sixth edition. N.Y., 1931; repr. Grand Rapids: Baker Book House, 1983.

CHB I, II, or III — *The Cambridge History of the Bible.* 3 vols. Edited by P. R. Ackroyd and C. F. Evans (I), G. W. H. Lampe (II), and S. L. Greenslade (III). Cambridge: Cambridge University Press, 1963–70.

CR — *Corpus Reformatorum.* Edited by Karl G. Bretschneider, et al. 101 vols. Halle, Berlin, Leipzig and Zürich, 1834–1962.

CO — John Calvin. *Opera quae supersunt omnia.* Edited by Baum, Cunitz, and Reuss. Brunswick, 1863-1900.

DDP — Heinrich Heppe, *Die Dogmatik des Protestantismus im 16. Jahrhundert.* 3 vols. Gotha, 1857.

DTC — *Dictionnaire de théologie catholique.* Edited by A. Vacant et al. 23 vols. Paris, 1923-50.

DB — *Dictionnaire de la Bible, contenant tous les noms de personnes, de lieux, de plantes, d'animaux mentionnés dans les Saintes Écritures, les questions théologiques, archéologiques* ... Ed. F. Vigouroux, et al. 5 vols. Paris: Letouzey et Ané, 1907–1912.

DLGT — Richard A. Muller, *Dictionary of Latin and Greek Theological Terms: Drawn Principally from Protestant Scholastic Theology.* Grand Rapids: Baker Book House, 1985.

LW — Martin Luther. *Luther's Works: American Edition.* Edited by Jaroslav Pelikan and Helmut Lehmann. 55 vols. St. Louis and Philadelphia: Concordia/Fortress, 1955-1986.

PL — *Patrologia cursus completus.* Series Latina. Ed. J.-P. Migne. 221 vols. Paris, 1844–55.

PRRD, I — Richard A. Muller, *Post Reformation Reformed Dogmatics: Volume 1, Prolegomena to Theology.* Grand Rapids: Baker Book House, 1985.

RD — Heinrich Heppe, *Reformed Dogmatics Set Out and Illustrated from the Sources.* Revised and edited by Ernst Bizer. Trans. G. T. Thomson. London, 1950; repr. Grand Rapids: Baker Book House, 1978.

RED — *A Religious Encyclopedia or Dictionary of Biblical, Historical, Doctrinal and Practical Theology.* Based on the Realencyklopädie of Herzog, Plitt, and Hauck. Edited by Philip Schaff. Associate Editors, Samuel M. Jackson and D. S. Schaff. Revised edition. 3 vols. New York: The Christian Literature Company, 1888.

SCG — Thomas Aquinas, *Summa contra gentiles.* Rome: Leonine Commission/Vatican Library, 1934.

WA — D. *Martin Luthers Werke: Kritische Gesamtausgabe.* Weimar: Hermann Böhlaus, 1883–.

PART 1

Introduction

1

The Doctrine of Scripture in Medieval Scholastic Theology: Documents and Issues from the Rise of Scholasticism to the End of the Fifteenth Century

1.1 Scholarship and Perspectives on the History of the Doctrine of Scripture

The theological or intellectual movement from the question of theological prolegomena to the issue of the doctrine of Scripture is very slight, if it can be called a movement at all. The doctrine of Scripture was, after all, not an independent *locus* or *quaestio* in theological system until the second half of the sixteenth century, and even then it remained closely linked to its systematic place of origin, the prolegomena. There is also a near contradiction in the phrase "doctrine of Scripture," granting that Scripture itself is *doctrina,* teaching, and that a doctrine of Scripture is a doctrine concerning doctrine, a teaching about teaching. Such a doctrine is, by nature, propaedeutic and not precisely of a piece with the rest of the doctrines belonging to theology. The formulation of a doctrine of Scripture virtually presupposes the formulation of the other doctrines in the theological system and assumes an exegetical, hermeneutical, and methodological analysis of those doctrines from the perspective of their relationship to and use of the text of Scripture. To state the matter in another way, the creation of a doctrine of Scripture assumes a distinction between Scripture as source and doctrine as result—and such a distinction itself took centuries to arise. The rise and development of the doctrinal discussion of Scripture, then, parallel and in a sense belong to the development of theological prolegomena and, therefore, not merely to the era of the Reformation but, instead, to the development of theology as a discipline from the twelfth through the seventeenth centuries.

The Protestant doctrine of Scripture and its relationship to the movement from Reformation to orthodoxy have received more attention than virtually any other theological issues in the early history of Protestantism. The implications of the Reformers' views on Scripture for theology and church have been subjected to intense scrutiny and the character of both the Reformation and Protestant orthodoxy has been assessed by numerous authors in the light of comparisons and contrasts between sixteenth- and seventeenth-century approaches to Scripture. Despite all of this attention, however, historians and theologians have come no closer to a convincing presentation and analysis of the Protestant orthodox formulation of this doctrinal point than they have to a clear and balanced discussion of other elements of seventeenth-century theological system. Altogether too much of the discussion of the Reformation and Protestant orthodox doctrines of Scripture has approached the subject from theologically biased perspectives and with the specific intention of justifying one or another twentieth-century view of Scripture. Of course, a discontinuity between the Reformers and the Protestant orthodox on the doctrine of Scripture ought not to give theologians an excuse for rejecting one view and adopting the other as a basis for their present-day theological musings—any more than a continuity between the teachings of the Reformers and the doctrines of Protestant orthodoxy can become a legitimate reason for accepting the doctrines of older Protestantism in and for the present without any further ado. *The historical and the theological task must remain separate.*

As I argued in the general introduction to this study of prolegomena and *principia,* the movement of Protestant theology from the Reformation into the era of orthodoxy cannot be described either as a radical alteration of perspective and a distortion of theology or as a purely continuous development of doctrine. Both of these models are simplistic and erroneous. Instead, the development of Protestant orthodoxy must be described against the background of both later medieval and Reformation theology and in terms of a spectrum of continuities and discontinuities with these antecedents. In addition, the development of post-Reformation dogmatics has to be set into the context of the bitter polemics of the age, of the rise of a new and renewed Aristotelianism in the Renaissance, and of the recovery, by Protestants as well as by Catholics, of the theology of the great medieval doctors, particularly those of the *via antiqua*.[1] The need for this more complex description is nowhere more pressing than in the discussion of the Reformed orthodox doctrine of Scripture.

Scripture, variously understood, as the canon was developed and defined, has been the foundation of Christian doctrine throughout all ages of the church. From the writings of the earliest fathers to the vast systematic efforts of dogmaticians like Barth and Brunner in the present century, the identifying characteristic of Christian teaching has been a direct reliance on Scripture for the basic issues and materials of theological formulation. Nonetheless, the explicit examination of Scripture as the proper basis for theology—an exercise quite distinct from the use of Scripture in theology and from the basic work of the exposition of Scripture—is an issue only scantily addressed before the rise of fully developed theological systems. It is quite true that the fathers of the church frequently acknowledged Scripture as the primary foundation of their thinking and that they identified orthodox Christian teaching as resting on the canonical books of the Old Testament (with occasional queries, as in the case of Jerome, concerning the differences between the Hebrew and the Septuagint lists) together with the apostolic witness. The fathers also devoted, particularly in the fourth and fifth centuries (the close of the patristic period), considerable space to discussions of the principles of interpretation: Jerome's prefaces to the various books of the Bible and Augustine's *De doctrina christiana* are preeminent examples of this kind of meditation.

Nonetheless, the fathers do not provide us with a formal doctrine of Scripture—only with a consistent appeal to the inspiration and authority of Scripture throughout their writings and an occasional discussion of their principles of interpretation. Of course, elements of a "doctrine of Scripture" could be elicited or compiled from the writings of the fathers, but it would be something other than a patristic doctrine, granting that the impulse to such formulation and the organizing principles used in the task would not be patristic.

---

[1]Cf. Richard A. Muller, *Post-Reformation Reformed Dogmatics,* vol. 1: *Prolegomena* (Grand Rapids: Baker Book House, 1987), 1.1, 1.3, with idem, *God, Creation, and Providence in the Thought of Jacob Arminius: Sources and Directions of Scholastic Protestantism in the Era of Early Orthodoxy* (Grand Rapids: Baker Book House, 1991), pp. 15–49, 269–85.

Very much as noted concerning theological prolegomena,[2] the doctrine of Scripture represents a theological reflection on the presuppositions of an extant body of doctrine. The church fathers devoted virtually all of their theological energies to the exposition of the central issues in that body of doctrine—Trinity, Christology, soteriology. Whereas a high view of Scripture is implied in all of their efforts, the development of an explicit doctrine of Scripture was, like the problem of theological prolegomena, left to later ages, specifically to the high scholastic era of the Middle Ages and to the Reformation and post-Reformation eras.[3] Beginning in the late twelfth century, coincident with the development of concepts that would shortly coalesce into theological prolegomena, theologians began to inquire into the way in which Scripture is the presupposition of the body of Christian doctrine. In the later Middle Ages, the debate over the relation of Scripture to tradition brought about further development of the doctrinal language concerning Scripture. The Reformation, with its pronouncement of *sola Scriptura* as the foundational principle of theology, brought this development to a climax and, in addition, assured the separate elaboration of formal prolegomena and of a doctrine of Scripture in the orthodox Protestant systems of the post-Reformation era.

Whereas the analysis of Protestant orthodox theological prolegomena is complicated by the absence of definition and discussion of preliminary topics from the writings of the Reformers, analysis of the Protestant orthodox doctrine of Scripture encounters a very different problem: there was a great body of material written during the Reformation in which Scripture was discussed. The presence of these writings intensifies the problem of continuity and discontinuity, particularly when the rather kerygmatic, discursive, and even "existential" style of the Reformers is compared with the dogmatic, scholastic, and objective style of their orthodox successors. The basic issue remains the same, however: the continuity and discontinuity of doctrine and method in the development of Christian thought from the later Middle Ages through the Reformation and into the seventeenth century. The question, by way of contrast, is no longer whether the theology of the Reformers can be drawn out into a theological topic not found in the writings of the Reformers, but

[2]Cf. *PRRD,* I, 2, introduction.

[3]Cf. the discussion in Herman Sasse, "The Rise of the Dogma of Holy Scripture in the Middle Ages," in *Reformed Theological Review* 18/2 (June 1959): 45–54.

whether a particular topic of discussion found in the writings of the Reformers is substantively altered when it is exposited not only in a new form but also in the context of doctrinal issues not fully addressed or even recognized by the Reformers.

The doctrine of Scripture, particularly in its later medieval, Reformation, and post-Reformation development, has not received any great attention in the more recent histories of Christian thought, with the notable exceptions of the magisterial *Handbuch der Dogmengeschichte* edited by Grillmeier, Schmaus and Scheffczyk and *The Christian Tradition* by Jaroslav Pelikan.[4] Protestant histories have, since the time of Harnack, tended away from the so-called *lokale-methode* or general-special pattern of presentation and, as a result, have emphasized the doctrines or doctrinal discussions characteristic of the most pointed dogmatic debates of the church in each particular era, rather than attempting to elicit from the materials of each age an entire body of doctrine. Since the doctrine of Scripture, conceived as a formal *locus* in theological system, is a comparatively recent development, histories organized according to the modern pattern inaugurated by Harnack have tended to omit the discussion. Older histories of doctrine—like the works of Neander and Hagenbach—do, however, provide overviews of the doctrine of Scripture throughout history as a primary element in the "special history" of each period.[5] Roman Catholic histories, moreover, continue to present doctrine by *locus,* and, as witnessed by the *Handbuch,* provide a valuable resource in the present inquiry.

There are, of course, a large number of historical surveys of the doctrine and interpretation of Scripture and monographs emphasizing eras important to the development and alteration of the doctrine. Many of these treatises, from the older works of Pesch, Holzhey, Rohnert, and Farrar,[6] to more recent efforts like the essays by Preus,

---

[4]Johannes Beumer, *Die Inspiration der Heiligen Schrift,* in *Handbuch der Dogmengeschichte,* ed. A. Grillmeier, M. Schmaus and L. Scheffczyk, part I, fasc. 3b (Freiburg: Herder, 1968); Jaroslav Pelikan, *The Christian Tradition: A History of the Development of Doctrine,* 5 vols. (Chicago: University of Chicago Press, 1971–), IV:336–50.

[5]Johann August Wilhelm Neander, *Lectures on the History of Christian Dogmas,* trans. J. E. Ryland, 2 vols. (London: Bohn, 1858), II:492–94, 606–8, 620–42; Karl R. Hagenbach, *A History of Christian Doctrines,* trans. E. H. Plumptre, 3 vols. (Edinburgh: T. & T. Clark, 1880-81), II:151–74; III:39–70, 306–21.

[6]Chr. Pesch, *De inspiratione sacrae Scripturae* (Freiburg-im-Breisgau, 1906); Karl Holzhey, *Die Inspiration der heiligen Schrift in der Anschauung des Mittelalters: von Karl der Grosser bis zum Konzil von Trient* (Munich:

Gerstner, and Rogers and McKim,[7] fall into the category of theological treatises that offer a particular construction of the history as a basis for the formulation of doctrine in the present. None of these works ought to be overlooked—but all must be examined in the realization that they frequently miss the issues and problems of the past in their quest for or advocacy of present-day doctrinal and interpretive positions.

Covering the entire history of these issues but from a wholly different perspective, namely, the text and interpretation of Scripture, are works like the classic essays of Mangenot and Mandonnet,[8] *The Cambridge History of the Bible*,[9] the highly detailed, but somewhat uneven series *Bible de tous les temps*,[10] two volumes by G. R. Evans,[11] and the finely researched and argued works of Kropatscheck, Spicq, de Vooght, de Lubac, Smalley, J. S. Preus, and

1895); W. Rohnert, *Die Inspiration der heiligen Schrift und ihre Bestreiter. Eine biblisch-dogmengeschichtliche Studie* (Leipzig: Böhme/Ungleich, 1889); Frederic W. Farrar, *History of Interpretation* (New York: Dutton, 1886; repr. Grand Rapids: Baker Book House, 1961).

[7]Cf. Robert Preus, "The View of the Bible Held by the Church: The Early Church through Luther," and John Gerstner, "The View of the Bible Held by the Church: Calvin and the Westminster Divines," in *Inerrancy,* ed. Norman L. Geisler (Grand Rapids: Zondervan, 1979), pp. 357–82, 385–410, with Jack B. Rogers and Donald K. McKim, *The Authority and Interpretation of the Bible: An Historical Approach* (San Francisco: Harper and Row, 1979); and note John D. Woodbridge, *Biblical Authority: A Critique of the Rogers/McKim Proposal* (Grand Rapids: Zondervan, 1982).

[8]Eugene Mangenot, "Allégories bibliques," in *DTC,* 1/1, cols. 833–36; "Inspiration de l'Écriture," in *DTC,* 7/2, cols. 2068-2266; "Concordances," in *DB,* 2/1, cols. 892–905; "Correctoires de la Bible," in *DB,* 2/1, cols. 1022–26; "Hugues de St Cher," in *DTC,* 7/1, cols. 221–39; with J. Rivière, "Interprétation de l'Écriture," in *DTC,* 7/2, cols. 2290-2343; Pierre Mandonnet, "Chronologie des écrits scriptuaires de Saint Thomas d'Aquin," in *Revue Thomiste* 33 (1928):25–45, 116–66, 211–45; 34 (1929):53–66, 132–45, 489–519; "Dominicains, travaux sur les Saintes Écritures," in *DB,* 2/2, cols. 1463–82; and "L'enseignement de la Bible selon l'usage de Paris," in *Revue Thomiste,* NS 12 (1929):489–519.

[9]*The Cambridge History of the Bible,* ed. P. R. Ackroyd and C. F. Evans [I], G. W. H. Lampe [II], and S. L. Greenslade [III], 3 vols. (Cambridge: Cambridge University Press, 1963–70).

[10]*Bible de tous les temps,* 8 vols. Collection dirigée par Charles Kannengiesser (Paris: Beauchesne, 1984–).

[11]G. R. Evans, *The Language and Logic of the Bible: the Earlier Middle Ages* (Cambridge: Cambridge University Press, 1984); idem. *The Language and Logic of the Bible: the Road to Reformation* (Cambridge: Cambridge University Press, 1985).

Reventlow.[12] These latter essays stand as historical investigations of the history of hermeneutics with little or no desire to argue modern theological issues and are, therefore, more useful to the understanding of the historical travail of the doctrine of Scripture in the sixteenth and seventeenth centuries. Inasmuch, moreover, as the doctrinal question of the nature and authority of Scripture is inseparable from the hermeneutical question of the methods to be employed in the exegesis of Scripture, the history of exegesis is as important to the present inquiry as the history of the doctrine of Scripture. After all, it is one thing to argue the infallibility of the text in all matters of faith and practice and then to interpret the text following the fourfold "allegorical" exegesis typical of the medieval commentators and to do so before any creed or confession of the church had defined the canon of Scripture in the strictest terms—and quite another thing to make the same statement of the infallibility of the text in the context of a literal method of exegesis and a strict definition of the books included in the normative canon of Scripture.

Indeed, the stresses and strains placed upon the doctrine of Scripture throughout its Reformation and post-Reformation history are to be traced less to changes in the doctrine itself than to alterations of the interpretive context into which the doctrine of Scripture—as the doctrine concerning doctrine—and into which the rest of theological system, hermeneutically understood, had been placed. The problem of the doctrine of Scripture in the age of the Reformation and the era of orthodoxy was, in other words, not so much a problem of a new view of inspiration and authority as it was a problem of a very traditional view of inspiration and authority in the context of an altered approach to exegesis and hermeneutics. And the fundamental problem, therefore, was not so much the doctrine of

---

[12]Friedrich Kropatscheck, *Das Schriftprinzip der lutherischen Kirche. Geschichte und dogmatische Untersuchungen. I. Die Vorgeschichte. Das Erbe des Mittelalters* (Leipzig: Deichert, 1904); Ceslaus Spicq, *Esquisse d'une histoire de l'exégèse latine au moyen âge* (Paris: J. Vrin, 1944) and idem, "Saint Thomas d'Aquin: VI. Saint Thomas d'Aquin exégète," in *DTC*, 15/1, cols. 694–738; Paul de Vooght, *Les sources de la doctrine chrétienne d'après les théologiens du XIVᵉ siècle et du début du XVᵉ* (Paris: Desclée, 1954); Henri de Lubac, *Exégèse mediaevale: les quatre sens de l'Ecriture,* 4 vols. (Paris: Aubier, 1959-64); Beryl Smalley, *The Study of the Bible in the Middle Ages* (Notre Dame: University of Notre Dame Press, 1964); James S. Preus, *From Shadow to Promise: Old Testament Interpretation from Augustine to the Young Luther* (Cambridge, Mass.: Harvard University Press, 1969); Henning Graf Reventlow, *The Authority of the Bible and the Rise of the Modern World,* trans. John Bowden (Philadelphia: Fortress, 1985).

Scripture itself as the way in which exegesis and interpretation led from an authoritative Scripture to authoritative doctrinal statement—granting that neither the fundamental doctrinal assumptions about the scriptural point of origin nor the dogmatic and confessional conclusions about the systematic theological result had changed, but only the hermeneutical path that lay between them.[13]

Granting this fundamental hermeneutical problem and the massive alteration of perspective brought about in the seventeenth and eighteenth centuries by the development of text-critical and historical-critical methodology, the various histories of the modern interpretation of Scripture and its theology are also of some importance to this investigation, notably the works of Diestel,[14] Farrar,[15] Fullerton,[16] Kraus,[17] Kümmel,[18] Hayes and Prussner,[19] and the recent survey by Rogerson, Rowland, and Lindars.[20] Whereas Diestel's, Kraus', and Kümmel's studies are works of carefully designed and exhaustively researched scholarship, the latter two essays not only tend to devalue "precritical" exegesis and to evidence a certain unwillingness to deal in a more or less neutral fashion with the exegetical methods of earlier periods, they also evidence a failure to address the truly important exegetical and hermeneutical works of the sixteenth and seventeenth centuries—although only Hayes and Prussner descend to the intensely negative and polemical style of Farrar. These works are all useful, however,

---

[13]Cf. Gerhard Ebeling's comments in "The Word of God and Hermeneutics," in *Word and Faith,* trans. James W. Leitch (Philadelphia: Fortress; London: S.C.M., 1963), pp. 305–32.

[14]Ludwig Diestel, *Geschichte des Alten Testamentes in der christlichen Kirche* (Jena: Mauke, 1869).

[15]Frederick W. Farrar, *The History of Interpretation* (1886; repr. Grand Rapids: Baker Book House, 1961).

[16]Kemper Fullerton, *Prophecy and Authority: A Study in the History of the Doctrine and Interpretation of Scripture* (New York: Macmillan, 1919).

[17]Hans-Joachim Kraus, *Geschichte der historisch-kritischen Erforschung des Alten Testaments,* 2d ed. (Neukirchen: Neukirchner Verlag, 1969); and idem, *Die biblische Theologie: Ihre Geschichte und Problematik* (Neukirchen: Neukirchner Verlag, 1970).

[18]Werner Georg Kümmel, *The New Testament: The History of the Investigation of Its Problems,* trans. S. McLean Gilmour and Howard C. Kee (Nashville: Abingdon, 1972).

[19]John H. Hayes and Frederick C. Prussner, *Old Testament Theology: Its History and Development* (Atlanta: John Knox, 1985).

[20]John Rogerson, Christopher Rowland, and Barnabas Lindars, *The History of Christian Theology,* vol. 2: *The Study and Use of the Bible,* ed. Paul Avis (Grand Rapids: Eerdmans, 1988).

in tracing the beginnings of critical method and in framing the problem faced by theology at and immediately after the close of the era of Protestant orthodoxy. Diestel's *Geschichte des Alten Testamentes* remains the magisterial study in its field, unfortunately without parallel in the realm of New Testament study.

1.2 Canon, Inspiration, and the Interpretation of the Bible in Medieval Scholastic Theology

A large part of the modern difficulty in coming to terms with the post-Reformation development of a Protestant doctrine of Scripture arises from a general misapprehension of the medieval view of Scripture and its positive relationship to later Protestant teaching both in the Reformation and beyond. In particular, many of the discussions of the history of Scripture—its text and interpretation as well as the formal doctrine concerning it—have subscribed to the erroneous assumption that the medieval scholastics devalued or ignored the biblical foundation of theology or, at the very least, approached the text so uncritically that theological and philosophical considerations consistently overrode textual and exegetical concerns.[21] (A parallel misconception concerning Protestant orthodoxy leaves the Reformation looking like a scriptural island in the midst of an uncritically dogmatic sea!) When the argument is stated this starkly, the Reformation appears in radical discontinuity with its past and the post-Reformation rise of a scholastic Protestantism appears discontinuous with the issues raised by the Reformers. A more careful and critical look at the materials of history manifests a rather different picture. The problem of the text and canon of Scripture debated by Reformers and humanists alike is rooted firmly in medieval discussion. The importance of the original languages to the interpretation of the text of Scripture, including the need to retranslate the Old Testament from Hebrew into a literal Latin version, was recognized as clearly by Robert Grosseteste, bishop of Lincoln (d. 1253), as it was by the humanist-trained scholars of the sixteenth century.[22] Similarly, critique of the Vulgate text can be cited as easily from Roger Bacon (ca. 1214-94) as from the Reformers. It cannot, of course be claimed that the medieval writers had either the expertise or the incentive characteristic of the Hebraists and classi-

---

[21]E.g., Farrar, *History of Interpretation,* pp. 245–46; Kümmel, *New Testament,* pp. 19–20.

[22]Cf. Ralph Loewe, "The Medieval Christian Hebraists of England," in *CHB,* II:211–14.

cists of the sixteenth century, but it must also be recognized that we are dealing with a long history of approach to the text rather than with a sudden and historically discontinuous biblicism. The history of text and canon, like the history of hermeneutics, does not oblige the desire to create neat boxes called "Middle Ages," "Reformation," and "Post-Reformation Orthodoxy."[23]

Medieval theologians and, indeed, early medieval Bibles manifest a relative fluidity of the canon. Perhaps the most prominent examples of the openness of the medieval canon are the occurrences in medieval Bibles and in the works of medieval commentators and theologians of the text and of references to the Shepherd of Hermas and the Epistle to the Laodicenes. The seventh-century Codex Claromontanus offers, for example, a final grouping of books including (in order) James, 1, 2, and 3 John, Jude, Barnabas, the Revelation of John, the Acts of the Apostles, the Shepherd of Hermas, the Acts of Paul, and the Revelation of Peter.[24] Among these books, the Revelation or Apocalypse of Peter occupies an important place in the larger realm of medieval theology and popular religion. Where the Revelation of John lacks detail on such matters as the geography of hell, Peter supplies a storehouse of information. The medieval mind, as witnessed by Dante's *Inferno* and its various predecessors, was profoundly influenced by such deuterocanonical literature.[25] Similarly, the Epistle to the Laodicenes was viewed by a medieval commentator like Haimo of Halberstadt as a useful or edifying work and quite a few of the bibles of the later Middle Ages, both in Latin and in the vernacular (English and German), include a brief Epistle to the Laodicenes usually after Galatians or Colossians and sometimes just before the Pastorals.[26]

---

[23]See Eduard Reuss, *History of the Canon of the Holy Scriptures in the Christian Church,* trans. David Hunter (Edinburgh: R. W. Hunter, 1891); idem, *History of the Sacred Scriptures of the New Testament,* 5th ed., trans. E. L. Houghton (Edinburgh: T. & T. Clark, 1884); and Brooke Foss Westcott, *A General Survey of the History of the Canon of the New Testament,* 6th ed. (1889; repr. Grand Rapids: Baker Book House, 1980).

[24]Reuss, *History of the Canon,* pp. 159–60.

[25]Cf. Marcus Dods, *Forerunners of Dante: An Account of Some of the More Important Visions of the Unseen World, from the Earliest Times* (Edinburgh: T. & T. Clark, 1903), pp. 126–27; R. E. McNally, "Exegesis, Medieval," in *New Catholic Encyclopedia* (New York: McGraw-Hill, 1967), V:710.

[26]Cf. Haimo of Halberstadt, *In divi Pauli epistolas expositio* (Col. 4), in *PL* 117, col. 765; with Reuss, *History of the Canon,* pp. 254, 264 and Westcott, *General Survey,* pp. 458–62, 465 (text on pp. 580–84).

As for the apocryphal books, so hotly disputed by Protestants and Roman Catholics in the sixteenth century, they were quite commonly singled out by medieval teachers as deuterocanonical. Thus Hugh of St. Victor noted that the these books do not belong to the canon but ought to be read for edification while John of Salisbury not only distinguished between the canonical and apocryphal books but also listed the Shepherd of Hermas among the Old Testament Apocrypha.[27] Hugh could also understand as Old Testament all sacred books written before Christ and as the New Testament all churchly books written after Christ, so that "New Testament" referred to all subsequent writings of the church, with the four Gospels standing in the first rank *(in primo ordine),* the Acts, the Pauline and the catholic epistles, and the Apocalypse on the second rank, and the Decretals on the third, followed by "the writings of the holy Fathers ... which are numberless" occupying the place of a final link in the historical chain of witnesses. The harmony of the whole was so obvious to Hugh that he could state "no one of [these writings] is superfluous."[28] The fourfold exegesis, with its powerful emphasis on the unity and analogy of the faith, made such statements possible and rendered a strictly defined canon unnecessary.

The reading and study of Scripture were central to the theological enterprise of the Middle Ages. Indeed, before the late twelfth century, the Bible was the only "set text" in the medieval schools.[29] In the late twelfth century, with the differentiation between study of *sacra pagina* and the science of theology, the study of Scripture was, typically, followed by a course on Christian doctrine organized topically into groupings of statements or *sententia.*[30] The examination of the method and form of theological exposition that led to the medieval practice of elaborating on and augmenting Lombard's standard *Sententiae in IV libris distinctae* with more texts, further arguments, and preliminary discussion of the nature of theology also

[27]Hugh of St. Victor, *De scripturis et scriptoribus sacris, praenotatiunculae,* cap.6–7, in *PL* 175, cols. 15–17; John of Salisbury, *Epistola* 143, in *PL* 199, col. 126.

[28]Hugh of St. Victor, *De scripturis et scriptoribus, praenot.,* cap.6 in *PL* 175, cols. 16–17.

[29]Cf. Beryl Smalley, "Bible in the Medieval Schools," in *CHB,* II:197–98.

[30]Cf. Yves M.-J. Congar, *A History of Theology* trans. Hunter Guthrie (Garden City: Doubleday, 1968), pp. 79–80; Johannes Beumer, *Die theologische Methode,* in *Handbuch der Dogmengeschichte,* ed. A. Grillmeier, M. Schmaus, and L. Scheffczyk (Freiburg-im-Breisgau: Herder, 1972), pp. 72–73; J. Van der Ploeg, "The Place of Holy Scripture in the Theology of St. Thomas," in *Thomist* 10 (1947):404–7; and *PRRD,* I, 2.1

led to the more cohesive organization of the study of Scripture. In the case of biblical study, the early scholastics had a stronger foundation on which to build their exegetical edifice than did the builders of the *sententia:* they had the tradition of the gloss or, as it later came to be called, the *Glossa ordinaria.*[31]

Although certain elements of the *Gloss* were derived from commentaries written in the ninth and tenth centuries, the actual production of a running commentary on the whole text of Scripture belonged to the twelfth century and was the work of Anselm of Laon and his assistants. Between 1100 and 1130, the scholars of Laon gathered together all of Jerome's prologues, joined them to other prefatory material, and copied out the whole together with the text of Scripture and with a composite, running commentary consisting in marginal and interlinear discussion of the text. Both the marginal and the interlinear comments draw on earlier medieval and patristic materials in, to borrow Smalley's words, "varying degrees of thickness"[32]: important doctrinal or moral passages receive lengthier comments. Later in the twelfth century, Gilbert de la Porrée and Peter Lombard expanded Anselm's *Gloss.* It also became the practice, at least from Anselm of Laon onward, not only to lecture in the form and on the basis of the *Gloss* but to introduce *quaestiones* on important doctrinal topics into the lectures. Thus, Lombard's expansion of the *Gloss* on the Pauline epistles draws out doctrinal themes at length in the form of carefully argued *quaestiones.*[33]

The development of these various levels of gloss was intimately related to the common assumption of the medieval writers that Scripture and tradition spoke with one voice and that the meaning of the text had been embodied in the interpretations of the fathers. The text of Scripture, as in the case of the great Paris Bibles of the second quarter of the thirteenth century, was frequently copied out, together with the *Gloss,* for use as a text-book for theological study. In many cases, the text itself was accommodated to the *Gloss* on the assumption of the correctness of patristic interpretation.[34] Loewe observes that "it is possible to illustrate the organic interdependence of the text in its twelfth-century form, and the *gloss,* and to point to

[31]See the discussion of the gloss in Evans, *The Earlier Middle Ages,* pp. 37–47.

[32]Smalley, *Study of the Bible,* p. 56.

[33]Smalley, *Study of the Bible,* p. 73.

[34]Cf. Smalley, *Study of the Bible,* pp. 334–35; Glunz, *Vulgate in England,* pp. 259–65; and Loewe, "Medieval History of the Latin Vulgate," in *CHB,* II:147.

the dependence of the *sentences* on both."[35] The gloss developed in the first half of the twelfth century by Anselm of Laon and his school became, through the efforts of Anselm's pupil, Gilbert de la Porrée, and of Peter Lombard, the standard or ordinary gloss *(Glossa ordinaria)* used in basic biblical instruction from the twelfth century onward. Lombard also took the Anselmic gloss as the basis of his own lengthy exposition of the Psalter and the Pauline epistles, the *Magna glosatura,* which eventually became the standard exposition of these particular biblical books. In his compilation of the *Sentences,* Lombard drew on both the *Glossa ordinaria* and his own *magna glosatura,*[36] with the result that the biblical-traditional amalgam of the various levels of gloss became the authoritative basis for doctrinal exposition in the basic medieval course in theology.

This mutual interdependence of text and tradition as evidenced in Scripture, the *Gloss* and the new theological science serves to identify and define the issue of the relationship and relative authority of Scripture and tradition as found in the Middle Ages and to distinguish it both formally and materially from the issue of the relative authority of Scripture and tradition as encountered in subsequent periods. Perhaps even more important, this intimate relationship of text, gloss, and *sententia* points toward the context and significance of medieval references to the inspiration and authority of Scripture in theology: the line between text and theology was drawn only with difficulty—just as the scholastic identification of *sacra pagina* and *sacra theologia* was a distinction, hardly a separation. The terms *theologia* and *sacra scriptura* were virtually synonymous.[37] Both hermeneutically and linguistically, the Vulgate text and the work of theological formulation were so profoundly interwoven that the language of Scripture and the language of theology flowed into one another. Indeed, in the Middle Ages, one cannot distinguish firmly between biblical and theological language, but only between the fundamental elements of theological language learned from Scripture and the other aspects and elements of

[35]Loewe, "The Medieval History of the Latin Vulgate," in *CHB,* II:145.

[36]Smalley, *The Study of the Bible,* pp. 63–64.

[37]Cf. Bonaventure, *Opera omnia,* 10 vols. (Quaracchi: Collegium S. Bonaventurae, 1882-1902): *Breviloquium,* in vol. 5, prooem., 1; with Thomas of Strasburg, *Scripta super quattuor libros Sententiarum* (Strasburg, 1490), prol., q.4, a.2; and see De Vooght, *Les sources,* pp. 40–42, 70, 80–81, 88–89, 103; Smalley, "Bible in the Medieval Schools," pp. 198–99; and idem, *Study of the Bible,* pp. 271, 275–76.

theological language learned from the larger tradition and used to interpret Scripture and to formulate doctrine.

The issue of text and interpretation was further defined and complicated by the many popular Bibles of the Middle Ages, both Latin and vernacular, prose and verse, and by the interrelationship of Scripture, tradition, and legend with the medieval identification of the literal meaning of the text and the temporal sojourn of the people of God as *historia*. Works like the *Speculum historiale* of Vincent of Beauvais and the *Speculum humanae salvationis* of Ludolph of Saxony functioned as biblical paraphrases that mediated the sacred history of the Scriptures together with legendary additions and augmentations, some of which, in the case of the latter work, come from ancient secular history, and virtually all of which serve the underlying hermeneutical purpose of manifesting the movement through history from obscurely promised salvation under the Old Testament to clearly offered redemption under the New. The typological interpretation of the entirety of history by means of the New Testament fulfillment not only is characteristic of these works and others of their type, it is also the basis, by way of these popular Bibles, of much of the art of the Middle Ages.

This gradual accommodation of the text to its interpretation and the "corruption" of the text through scribal errors did not pass unnoticed during the scholastic era. Virtually at the same point that the Paris text, the *Glossa ordinaria,* and Lombard's *Sententia* became standard components of a highly organized and interrelated program of theological study, the text of the Vulgate itself became the subject of debate. Even in the twelfth century a few theologians had raised questions about the relationship of the Vulgate to the Hebrew Old Testament: at the beginning of the century (1109), Stephen Harding, abbot of Citeaux, had excised, with the help of a convert from Judaism, passages in the Vulgate not found in the original Hebrew.[38] Similar efforts characterize the work of another Cistercian of the twelfth century, Nicholas Manjacoria. Nicholas had studied Hebrew and worked to remove additions that had been made to the text of the Vulgate. He specifically singled out for criticism the idea that the most elaborate version of a text was the best and he spelled out his approach to the text at length in a treatise, the *Libellus de corruptione et correptione Psalmorum* (ca. 1145).[39] Hugh of St. Victor

---

[38]Loewe, "Medieval History of the Latin Vulgate," in *CHB,* II:143.

[39]Loewe, "Medieval History of the Latin Vulgate," in *CHB,* II:143; and see A. Wilmart, "Nicolas Manjacoria, Cistercien à Trois-Fontaines," in *Revue*

(d. 1141) had also noted textual corruptions in the Vulgate.[40]

In the thirteenth century, particularly in the great teaching orders, there was a concerted effort to disentangle text and gloss and even to correct the text on the basis of the Hebrew and Greek originals. Thus, Hugh of St. Cher tested the text of the Vulgate against Jerome's commentaries, several pre-Carolingian codices, and the Hebrew text. So extensive was this effort that Hugh and his associates produced a supplement to the *Gloss*—in effect, "a new apparatus to the whole Bible."[41] On the one hand, Hugh superintended the production of a massive concordance organized alphabetically; on the other he developed a new set of postils or annotations on the entire Bible in which he emphasized parallels between texts and stressed, as did his contemporaries Albert the Great and Thomas Aquinas, the priority of the literal sense as the basis for the examination of the other three senses of Scripture.[42] The thirteenth century was, moreover, responsible for the standardization of the text and its chapter divisions in the so-called Paris text, begun by Stephen Langton and carried forward in the corrections of Hugh of St. Cher and in the adept edition of William de la Mare, who knew both Hebrew and Greek.[43]

The *quadriga* or fourfold exegesis was neatly defined for the high Middle Ages in the *Glossa ordinaria*. There we read that the four senses of the text are "*historia,* which tells what happened *(res gestae); allegoria,* in which one thing is understood through another; *tropologia,* which is moral declaration, and which deals with the ordering of behavior; *anagoge,* through which we are led to higher things that we might be drawn to the highest and heavenly."[44] The three latter or spiritual meanings reflect the three Christian virtues, faith, love, and hope: allegory teaches "things to be believed"

Benedictine 33 (1921):139–42.

[40]Hugh of St. Victor, *De scripturis et scriptoribus,* 9, in *PL* 175, col. 18A.

[41]See Smalley, "Bible in the Medieval Schools," in *CHB,* II:206–7; Mangenot, "Correctoires de la Bible," cols. 1023–25; and idem, "Hugues de St. Cher," cols. 228–34.

[42]Hugh of St. Cher, *Postillae in universa Biblia juxta quadruplicem sensum, literalem, allegoricum, moralem, anagogicum* (Venice and Basel, 1487); cf. Mandonnet, "Dominicains, travaux sur les Saintes Écritures," cols. 1464, 1465.

[43]Loewe, "Medieval History of the Latin Vulgate," pp. 146–50. William, it should be noted, did not make major corrections in the text of the Vulgate, because he doubted that contemporary Hebrew manuscripts were more accurate than the Latin text. Cf. Spicq, *Histoire de l'exégèse latine,* pp. 159–72.

[44]*Prothemata glossae ordinariae,* in *PL* 113, col 63B; cf. McNally, "Exegesis, Medieval," pp. 708–9.

(credenda), tropology "things to be loved" or "done" *(diligenda* or *agenda),* and *anagoge* "things to be hoped for" *(speranda).* The *speranda,* it should be noted, could be understood either in a mystical or in an eschatological sense.

As the history of exegesis in the Middle Ages amply demonstrates, this approach to the text could result either in a movement away from or a gravitation toward the literal sense. At the beginning of the scholastic era, Hugh of St. Victor could dispute with those among his contemporaries who ignored the letter for the spiritual meanings. This procedure, Hugh contended, was self-defeating inasmuch as the Spirit had given the literal sense as the starting-point for all other meanings: the word of the text or "letter" is, after all, the sign of the initial "thing" *(res)* that, in its own function as "sign" *(signum),* directs our attention toward other things. In other words, if the "thing" literally signified by any given word is not understood, the spiritual meanings of the text—which arise not from the words of the text but from the things that they signify—cannot be grasped.[45] Hugh's disciple, Andrew of St. Victor, coupled his teacher's emphasis on the literal meaning of the text with a firm grounding in Hebrew and a profound use of Jewish exegesis of the Old Testament—even to the point of identifying non-messianic readings of the text as the literal sense, without, however, attempting any revision of the *quadriga.*[46]

In the next century, Albert the Great and Thomas Aquinas were largely responsible for a major shift in the emphasis of medieval exegesis away from Gregorian allegorism toward a greater emphasis on the letter.[47] Albert assumed that "that there was but one genuine exegesis worthy of the name; that which explains the sense intended by the author and is indicated by the text itself": the literal sense, therefore, provided the basis for the three spiritual senses, which

[45]Hugh of St. Victor, *De scripturis et scriptoribus,* cap.5, in *PL* 175, cols. 13–14; cf. de Lubac, *Exégèse médiévale,* II/2, pp. 288–97 with Evans, *Earlier Middle Ages,* pp. 67–68.

[46]Smalley, *The Study of the Bible,* pp. 155–72.

[47]Spicq, *Histoire de l'exégèse latine,* pp. 204–12, 288; Smalley, *Study of the Bible,* pp. 300–301, 365; Raymond Brown, *The Sensus Plenior of Sacred Scripture* (Baltimore: St. Mary's University, 1955), p. 61; see also F. A. Blanche, "Le sens littéral des Écritures d'apres saint Thomas d'Aquin," in *Revue Thomiste* (1906):192–212, and Paul Synave, "La doctrine de St. Thomas d'Aquin sur le sens littéral des Écritures," in *Revue biblique* 35 (1926):40–65; also note Spicq, "Pourquoi le Moyen Age n'a-t-il pas practiqué davantage l'exégèse littérale," in *Revue des Sciences Philosophiques et Théologiques* 30 (1941–42):169–79.

Albert understood as pedagogical extensions of the letter.[48] Aquinas built on this assumption and moved away from the method of the postils or annotations toward an analysis of the text in terms of its logical divisions and their relationship to one another. Mandonnet argues that he originated the basic exegetical procedure of analyzing words and phrases in their context, seeking out units of meaning in the text, and thereby stressing the literal sense as the foundation of theology. Aquinas' commentaries are "almost exclusively occupied" with the exposition of the literal sense, which he also identified as the *fundamentum historiae*. Indeed, Aquinas commented with some frequency that the *primus sensus* and *prima expositio* of Scripture was *magis litteralis,* and that the purpose of exegesis was to identify the "intention" of the words, of the book, or of the writer.[49]

Aquinas resolved the questions raised by the Victorine exegetes concerning the relationship of the literal to the other senses by emphasizing the connection between the "thing" *(res)* signified by the word of the text and the *res* of the spiritual meanings and by insisting that any word in a given text could mean only one thing. It was not as if a multiplicity of spiritual meanings could be elicited by finding a series of significations for a particular word: each word of the text, given the grammatical context in which it stands, must speak univocally. The "historical or literal" sense is rooted directly in the "things" that the words signify and is the sense intended by the human author of the text. All of the senses, therefore, are founded directly on the literal sense—not because the words of the text themselves have multiple meanings, but because the writer and his words belong to a "sacred history" that offers a broader context for understanding the spiritual significance of the text:[50] Aquinas concludes that the literal sense alone is ground for argument and insists that every truth necessary for salvation is offered somewhere in Scripture in the literal sense of the text.[51] Thus the spiritual senses, although useful and highly enlightening are not absolutely necessary. It must be noted in this connection, however, that while

[48]Spicq, *Histoire de l'exégèse latine,* p. 210; cf. pp. 271–72.

[49]Mandonnet, "Dominicains travaux des sur les saintes Écritures," col. 1465; cf. Spicq, *Histoire de l'exégèse latine,* pp. 209, 273–85; and see Maximino Arias Reyero, *Thomas von Aquinsa als Exeget: Die Prinzipien seiner Schriftdeutung und seine Lehre von den Schriftsinnen* (Münster: Johannes Verlag, 1971), pp. 155–61.

[50]Smalley, *Study of the Bible,* p. 300.

[51]Aquinas, *Summa theologiae cura fratrum in eiusdem ordinis,* 5 vols. (Madrid: Biblioteca de Autores Cristianos, 1962-65), Ia, q.1, art. 1.

Aquinas considered the various figures and symbols of Christ in the Old Testament as belonging to the spiritual sense, he understood the messianic prophecies as references to Christ in the literal sense. The literal sense, thus, was gleaned from the text in the larger context of sacred history. Albeit a given text could have only one literal sense, granting that each word must have a single correct significance, that single sense could have a fairly broad frame of reference.[52] Indeed, Aquinas clearly understood that the "intention" of the author of a text extended beyond the bare letter to figures of speech: his exegesis abounds in discussions of the signs, figures, similitudes, types, and symbols in the text which belong to the broader literal sense construed according to authorial intention.[53]

The methodological contribution of Roger Bacon also demands mention. Bacon argued strongly for the mastery of the original languages of the text as a general principle of study. Both Scripture and the works of the great philosophers were written in ancient languages—and translations fail to convey the character of the original, the *proprietas linguae.* The original languages are necessary, Bacon argued, for careful philological interpretation—and are even significant for the understanding of later languages like Latin, the letters and grammar of which are derivative from Greek and Hebrew.[54]

Just as the medieval view of text, canon, and exegesis is the proper background against which the Reformation and the subsequent development of Protestant approaches to Scripture must be understood, so also is the medieval doctrine of Scripture the necessary background to an understanding of the development of an orthodox Protestant doctrine of Scripture. With striking uniformity the medieval doctors declare the authority of Scripture as the divinely given source of all doctrines of the faith. They deal, for the most part, quite carefully and precisely with the concept of inspiration, recognizing the need to balance the divine and human authorship of the text and, with surprising frequency, noting the relationship between the diversity of genre and literary style within the canon and the form taken by the doctrine of inspiration.[55]

[52]Cf. Synave, "La doctrine de St. Thomas d'Aquin sur le sens littéral," pp. 45, 60–61.

[53]Arias Reyero, *Thomas von Aquinsa als Exeget,* pp. 160–71.

[54]Roger Bacon, *The Opus Maius of Roger Bacon,* ed. J. H. Bridges, 2 vols. (Oxford: Clarendon, 1897), I:81; cf. Spicq, *Histoire de l'exégèse latine,* pp. 182–83.

[55]Cf., e.g, Johannes Beumer, *Die Inspiration der Heiligen Schrift,* in *Handbuch der Dogmengeschichte,* I/3b (Freiburg: Herder, 1968); P. Dausch, *Die*

This connection between the doctrine of Scripture (specifically of the inspiration of Scripture), the concept of theology as a science, and the development of theological prolegomena, was hardly fortuitous. The majority of the great scholastic doctors—Alexander of Hales, Bonaventure, Albert the Great, Thomas Aquinas, Giles of Rome, Henry of Ghent, Duns Scotus—chose to formulate their doctrine of Scripture in the context of theological prolegomena. At least, the key elements of their doctrine of Scripture were formulated at this point. Just as the presuppositional issues and definitions of theology that belong to prolegomena are, arguably, among the last elements of theological system to receive formal discussion,[56] so also are the enumeration of *principia* and sources, and the methodological development of interpretive paradigms aspects of this final effort in codification. Only when *sacra pagina, sacra doctrina,* and *theologia* or, more precisely, the *scientia theologiae,* had been distinguished could a doctrine of Scripture—in effect, a *doctrina doctrinae*—emerge.[57]

The greater part of the first question of Alexander of Hales' *Summa,* the question *"De doctrina theologiae,"* is devoted to the discussion of Scripture. Alexander, observing a basic distinction between the "sacred page" itself and the formulation of theology, identifies theology as a "manner or mode of technique" *(modus ... artis)* for dealing with the "arrangement of divine wisdom" given in the text of Scripture "for the sake of informing the soul of those things that pertain to salvation."[58] Alexander's comment indicates, thus, his sense of both the priority of Scripture as a source of Christian doctrine and the sufficiency of the biblical record for the salvation of human beings. This biblical record and the truths it

---

Schriftinspiration, eine biblischgeschichtliche Studie Freiburg-im-Breisgau, 1891); Josef Finkenzeller, *Offenbarung und Theologie nach der Lehre des Johannes Duns Skotus,* in *Beiträge zur Geschichte der Philosophie und Theologie des Mittelalters,* XXXVIII/5 (Münster: Aschendorff, 1961); Paul de Vooght, *Les sources de la doctrine Chrétienne d'après les théologiens du XIVe siècle* (Paris, 1954); and idem, "Le rapport écriture-tradition d'après saint Thomas d'Aquin et les théologiens du XIII siècle," in *Istina* 8 (1962):499–510; John F. Johnson, "Biblical Authority and Scholastic Theology" in *Inerrancy and the Church,* pp. 67–97.

[56]Cf. *PRRD,* I, Ch. 2.

[57]Cf. Smalley, "Bible in the Medieval Schools," pp. 198–99, with de Vooght, *Les sources,* pp. 40–42.

[58]Alexander of Hales, *Summa theologica,* 4 vols. (Quaracchi: Collegium S. Bonaventurae, 1924-58), lib.I, q.1; cf. Preus, "View of the Bible Held by the Church," in *Inerrancy,* p. 367.

contains partake of a higher certainty than do human reason and human experience.[59] Significantly, Alexander identifies this biblical *dispositio* of divine wisdom as taking the form of *historia* and, as one would expect from his comment concerning the higher certainty of theology, a *historia* not only more correct but also having a higher purpose than other histories. This identification of the biblical record as *historia* set at the beginning of Alexander's *Summa* testifies to the character of the relationship between medieval exegesis and medieval theology, between *sacra pagina* and *sacra theologia*. The text of Scripture in its fundamental meaning is a *historia salvationis* from which teaching can be drawn to address Christian faith, love, and hope. The history of the text itself, its literal meaning, together with its doctrinal implications, correspond with the four elements of the *quadriga*—while the *quadriga* or fourfold exegesis, in turn, corresponds with the fundamental needs and interests of theological formulation.

Like the majority of the scholastic teachers of the thirteenth and fourteenth centuries, Thomas Aquinas did not develop a separate question or article dealing with the doctrine of Scripture. He did, however, make a major contribution to the medieval doctrine of Scripture and included an extended comment on the sources and grounds of sacred theology in the first question of the *Summa*.[60] There, he clearly argues what Alexander stated by implication: that Scripture by its very nature is the ground or foundation of necessary argument in theology—whereas other sources, such as the church's normative tradition, yield up only "probable" arguments.[61]

Aquinas accepted, as did his predecessors and successors, the truth of Jerome's observation that the inspiration of Scripture is in no way opposed to the individuality of the various human authors. "God," he wrote, "is the principal author of Scripture, man however is the instrument." In stressing the literal sense of the text, moreover, Aquinas could reiterate the issue of primary authorship in its relation to theological meaning: "the literal sense is that which the author

[59]Alexander of Hales, *Summa theologica,* I, q.5.

[60]But cf. the extended comments on the interpretation of Scripture in Aquinas' *Scriptum super primum librum sententiarum,* prol., q.1, art.5; idem, *Quodlibetum* VII, q.6, art.14–16; and idem, *Super epistolam ad Galatas lectura,* IV, lect.vii (all three texts are offered in Arias Reyero, *Thomas von Aquin als Exeget,* pp. 263–72).

[61]Aquinas, *Summa theologiae,* Ia, q.1, art.10, ad 2; and see Van der Ploeg, "Place of Holy Scripture in the Theology of St. Thomas," pp. 417–19.

intends, and the author of Scripture is God."[62] True to his demonstrative method, Thomas proceeded to develop this principle inductively, based on his study of Scripture, rather than deductively from the doctrinal point itself. His analysis led him to distinguish among various forms of prophetic vision, between inspiration and revelation, and between the forms of inspiration found in the prophetic books and in the hagiographa.[63]

In the first place, Aquinas recognized that prophecy was founded on several different kinds of vision. These he identified as imaginative, intellective, spiritual, and ecstatic.[64] Whatever the visionary foundation of particular prophecies, however, Aquinas was convinced that prophecy itself belongs to the province of knowledge and is, therefore, a matter of revelation: "in prophecy it is required that the attention of the mind *(intentio mentis)* be elevated toward the perception of the divine" so that the initial elevation of the mind by the movement of the Spirit falls under the category of inspiration, while the perception of divine things, by the removal of obscurity and ignorance from the mind, is the act of revelation itself.[65] Thus, "inspiration" refers to the work of movement of the Spirit elevating the mind toward and giving it the capacity for divine knowledge, whereas "revelation" refers to the actual presentation to the intellect of otherwise inaccessible knowledge. Inspiration and revelation are, thus, separable both conceptually and in fact. In particular, inspiration can occur without revelation—there can be a spiritually given elevation of the intellect without the impartation of new knowledge. This distinction, together with a distinction between "express revelation" and an inward inclination or *instinctus,* enabled Aquinas to identify two basic kinds of prophecy and to explain the difference between prophecy and the writings or hagiographa.

On the one hand, a distinction between inspiration and revelation can be made with reference to prophecy itself—granting that prophecy "consists primarily and principally in knowledge" and is, therefore, essentially constituted by the fact of revelation rather than by the presence of inspiration.[66] At its most simple level, inspiration can result in an inward gift of knowledge or discernment without

---

[62]Aquinas, *Summa theologiae,* Ia, q.1, art.10; IIa–IIae, q.171–74; cf. Kropatschek, *Das Schriftprinzip,* pp. 424–25.

[63]Aquinas, *Summa theologiae,* IIa–IIae, q.171, art.5; cf. Mangenot, "Inspiration de l'Écriture," cols. 2121–22.

[64]Aquinas, *Summa theologiae,* IIa–IIae, qq.171–74.

[65]Aquinas, *Summa theologiae,* IIa–IIae, q.171, art.1, ad obj.4.

[66]Cf. Mangenot, "Inspiration de l'Écriture," col. 2121.

clear representation of its source—so that the human subject neither knows that the knowledge comes directly from God nor knows with certainty that it is true. Prophecy, however, more typically consists in a revelation that is clearly recognized by the prophet to be a word from God and therefore both true and a rule or foundation for judgment.[67] True prophecy, according to Aquinas, consists both in the acceptance or vivid presentation in the mind of new knowledge *(acceptatio seu repraesentatio rerum)* and a judgment concerning the truth of the knowledge presented to the mind *(judicium de rebus repraesentatis)*.[68] "In making this judgment, the mind of the prophet operates under the influence of divine light."[69]

The identification of prophecy as consisting essentially in revelation and in a judgment concerning the truth of the revelation leads to a basic distinction between the prophets and the holy writers of historical books and wisdom literature. The prophets are recipients of an imaginative and intellectual vision not simply for the sake of knowing divine truth but "for the sake of judging rational truths according to the certitude of divine truth."[70] The holy writers do not receive revelation as such—rather they are inspired, their minds are elevated by the movement of the Spirit to the end that they can write rational truths with the aid of the divine light.[71] Of course, prophets are inspired and holy writers both have knowledge and make judgments concerning it, but revelation is the essence of prophecy while inspiration or divine assistance is the essence of hagiography—the former belongs primarily to the intellect, the latter more fully to the affections.

The distinction between inspiration and revelation led both Albert the Great and Thomas Aquinas away from a theory of simple verbal dictation.[72] Since inspiration is the elevation of the mind, not the impartation of words, the hagiographa cannot be described as dictated in the usual sense of the term. What is more, in the case of prophetic revelation, the issue for Albert and for Thomas is the gift of otherwise unknowable truths to the spiritually elevated intellect of

---

[67]See Aquinas, *Summa theologiae,* IIa–IIae, q.171, art.5.

[68]Cf. Aquinas, *Summa theolgiae,* IIa–IIae, q.173, art.2 with idem, *SCG,* II.154 and *De veritate,* q.12, art.7.

[69]Mangenot, "Inspiration de l'Écriture," col. 2121.

[70]Mangenot, "Inspiration de l'Écriture," col. 2122.

[71]Mangenot, "Inspiration de l'Écriture," col. 2122; cf. Aquinas, *Summa theologiae,* IIa–IIae, q.171, art.5; Holzhey, *Die Inspiration,* pp. 89–93.

[72]Cf. Manegnot, "Inspiration de l'Écriture," cols. 2200–2201, with Kropatscheck, *Das Schriftprinzip,* p. 430.

the prophet. The way in which this knowledge moves from perception to expression is different from the usual pattern of human perception and expression. According to Aquinas, knowledge arises from sense perception: what the senses perceive is subjected to the power of the active intellect which abstracts from perceptions universals or "intelligible species" and brings about an inward or mental identification *(verbum mentis)* of the concept in the passive intellect—which is to say the universal ideas of things are known to the mind by a process of abstraction from things that results in the impress of the idea on mind by nature receptive to such ideas. The passive intellect is, thus, the potency of the intellect for ideas.[73] Our speech, in turn, arises from the expression of these ideas.

Aquinas recognized, on the basis of this theory of knowledge, that truths given by revelation not only have a different source from truths known through the senses but also, as a result of their different source, stand in a very different relation to our words than do the truths that we learn through experience. (We have already noted this problem in the discussion of theological prolegomena. Aquinas himself recognized the limitation of theology *in via* and the later medieval doctors, followed by the Protestant orthodox, distinguished between the absolute or archetypal truth known to God and its accommodated or ectypal forms.[74]) We are enabled by God to know of spiritual things inasmuch as God teaches us by means of analogies drawn from corporeal things. Our words are accommodated to revealed truths and take on, by analogy, a dimension of meaning not previously associated with the word.[75]

Aquinas could use the traditional metaphor taken from the fathers that the Holy Spirit uses the language of the biblical writers as a scribe uses a reed pen *(calamus):* the Spirit is principal author, the human writer is his instrument. Nonetheless, as Mangenot rather nicely argues, this is not a process that reduces the human mind to nothing:

> the Spirit writes rapidly in the heart of men. Those who have knowledge by divine revelation are subtly filled with wisdom. The psalmist has first thought in his heart, then he has spoken and finally he has written. The inspiration of the psalmist thus consists

[73]Cf. Copleston, *A History of Philosophy,* 9 vols. (Westminster, Md.: Newman, 1946-74; repr. Garden City: Image Books, 1985), II:389–90.
[74]Cf. *PRRD*, I, pp. 59–63, 132–33, 153–66.
[75]Aquinas, *Summa theologiae,* Ia, q.1, art.9 and 10.

primarily in the revelation of ideas that he must then propound
both in speech and in writing.[76]

Even so, according to Aquinas, the Holy Spirit has not dictated the
various expressions used to indicate the divine in Scripture—rather
the Spirit has influenced, by inspiration, the judgment of the human
writer in using certain terms rather than others.[77] By implication, the
words themselves already belonged to the vocabulary of the writer
and the process of inspiration is integral to his own thought process.

Although his doctrine of Scripture and its inspiration is not laid
out in the detail or with as subtle attention to the relationship of the
divine and the human in the work of composition as the doctrine of
Aquinas, Bonaventure does provide a distinctive view of the inspiration and authority of Scripture based on his essentially Augustinian
concept of divine illumination. This marks a significant point of contrast with Aquinas whose intellectualistic emphasis on the *acceptio
rerum* and the rational *judicium* of the prophet and whose distinction
between inspiration as an elevation of the mind and revelation as a
gift of knowledge were linked, most certainly, to his epistemological
assumption that truth is not, typically, learned by illumination.[78]
Bonaventure by way of contrast, taught that "Holy Scripture does
not proceed by rational argumentation, definition and division, as
the other sciences do, but, inasmuch as it arises from a supernatural
light, it teaches truths superior to the things of this world."[79]

The language of divine illumination appears clearly in the
Breviloquium where Bonaventure rests the authority of Scripture on
divine revelation, arguing a distinction between *revelatio divina* and
investigatio humana: the Holy Spirit, the true author of Scripture,
illuminated the hearts of the prophets with his revelations.[80] Even
so, in direct contrast with the line of Aquinas' argument, Bonaventure could argue that prophets do not accept what they predict as
true in and of itself but rather they accept it as true according to the
truth of their illumination and enlightenment, that is, prophecy does
not require a rational movement in the mind of the prophet but
rather takes its entire rationale from the inspiration of the Spirit.[81]

[76]Mangenot, "Inspiration de l'Écriture," col. 2200, citing Aquinas, *In Ps.*
44:2.
[77]Aquinas, *Summa theologiae,* IIIa, q. 60, art. 5, ad obj. 1.
[78]Cf. Copleston, *History of Philosophy,* II, pp. 389–390.
[79]Mangenot, "Inspiration de l'Écriture," col. 2123.
[80]Bonaventure, *Breviloquium,* prooem., 5–6.
[81]Bonaventure, *In Sent.,* II, d.24, art.1, q.2, ad obj.5; cf. Mangenot,

Bonaventure does not, however, intend to reduce the human authors of Scripture to the status of unthinking instruments. The Spirit does not inspire in such a way as to place the biblical writers in a trance or deprive them of their senses.[82]

The doctrine of the inspiration of Scripture stood, in the systems of the great thirteenth-century scholastics, Alexander of Hales, Bonaventure, Albert the Great, and Thomas Aquinas, in a profound and crucial relationship to the emerging concept of theology as a science.[83] Inasmuch as a science consists in a knowledge of first principles and of the conclusions that can be drawn from them, the issue of certainty in theology is crucial to the conduct of the discipline. Logically derived conclusions, no matter how expert and precise the logic, cannot be endowed with certainty unless certainty is known to reside in the principles from which they have been drawn. But theology, as Aquinas in particular recognized, is a sub-alternate science the first principles of which are not self-evident but are derived from a higher science—the *scientia Dei*—that is not immediately known to us.[84] If theology is to have the certainty that must belong to any legitimate or genuine *scientia,* that certainty must be inherent in its first principles and in the source of those principles. If theology is to be a divine *scientia,* it must rest on revelation.[85]

Thus, Alexander of Hales could argue, "what is known by divine inspiration is recognized as more true *(verius)* than what is known by human reason, inasmuch as it is impossible for falsehood to be in inspiration while reason is infected with many. Therefore, when knowledge of theology *(cognitio theologiae)* is elevated by divine inspiration it is a truer science *(verius scientia)* than other sciences."[86] Scripture, the foundation of theological science, is always true and is to be discussed for the sake of manifesting its truth or for the sake of defending it against charges of falsehood—but never for the sake of finding faults in it![87] In Scripture we encounter a

"Inspiration de l'Écriture," col. 2123.

[82]Cf. Mangenot, "Inspiration de l'Écriture," col. 2123.

[83]Cf. *PRRD,* I, 2.1, 6.2.

[84]Aquinas, *Summa theologiae,* Ia, q.1, art.2.

[85]Cf. Aquinas, *Summa theologiae,* Ia, q.1, art.1; art.8, ad2; with Charles A. Callan, "The Bible in the *Summa Theologica* of St. Thomas Aquinas," in *Catholic Biblical Quarterly* 9/1 (1947):36–37.

[86]Alexander of Hales, *Summa theologica,* II, q.1, n.1; cited in Mangenot, "Inspiration de l'Écriture," col. 2219.

[87]Alexander of Hales, *Summa theologica,* II, q.124, n.1, 4.

narrative concerned with good and evil, truths and falsehoods, in order that we be encouraged to imitate the good and the true, to avoid the evil and the false. Thus, the existence of *recorded* false-hoods in Scripture is no indication of falsification. Indeed, Alexander can go so far as to claim that the human authors of Scripture were preserved from the taint of mortal sin in the moment of their inspiration.[88]

Alexander recognized also that a major objection to his view of theology as *scientia* could be raised on the basis of the historical character of the greater part of Scripture. Historical events are not normally to be considered as first principles from which conclusions can be drawn and are, therefore, not to be viewed as proper objects of a science. To this Alexander replied by arguing a distinction between Scripture and other books: the historical events recorded in Scripture are recorded not for the sake of their particularity (as are the events recorded in historical chronicles) but rather because of their universality. The events in Scripture instruct us in matters concerning human existence and the mysteries of God.[89]

Albert the Great similarly argued the higher certainty of theo-logical science on the ground of the inspiration of Scripture: theol-ogy and theologians derive their authority from the books inspired by "the Spirit of truth." Even so, it is not possible to doubt a single word of Scripture. Reason itself may fall into contradiction but Scripture stands against error as a foundation of truth higher than anything present within the human soul.[90] Bonaventure, somewhat more simply, declares that the authority of Scripture arises "not by human investigation but by divine revelation"; the Spirit, who is the author of Scripture, speaks neither falsehood nor superfluity.[91] Anyone who contradicts Scripture therefore contradicts uncreated truth itself.[92] The scholastics' testimony to the infallibility of Scrip-ture was, moreover, intimately bound up with literal and gram-matical foundation of the medieval fourfold exegesis. Albert the Great could state categorically that the literal or historical sense of

---

[88]Alexander of Hales, *Summa theologica,* II, q.123, n.6.

[89]Alexander of Hales, *Summa theologica,* II, q.1, n.1; as cited in Mangenot, "Inspiration de l'Écriture," col. 2219.

[90]Albert the Great, *Summa theologiae,* in *Opera omnia,* ed. Borgnet, 38 vols. (Paris, 1890–99), V:Ia, tr.1, q.5, n.2–3; cf. Holzhey, *Die Inspiration,* p. 88.

[91]Bonaventure, *Breviloquium,* prol., v.3–4.

[92]Bonaventure, *In Sent.,* III, dist.24, art.1, q.2, ad obj.4; cf. Mangenot, "Inspiration de l'Écriture," col. 2219–2220.

Scripture was the foundation for the allegorical, tropological, and anagogical meanings: *unde litteralis sensus primus est, et in ipso fundantur tres alii sensus spirituales.*[93]

This intimate relationship among the doctrine of inspiration, the problem of authority, the definition of theology as *scientia,* and the insufficiency of reason to deal with divine mysteries brought about, as Callan has noted of Thomas Aquinas, an enormous emphasis on Scripture in medieval theological system.[94] Granting, moreover, that the typical progress of the medieval doctor was from *cursor Biblicus,* responsible for the basic course on the Bible; to *baccalaureus sententiarum,* responsible for the introductory theology course; and from there to commentator and doctor, the amount of biblical knowledge available to virtually all of the major medieval formulators of theology was considerable.

Thus, Callan comments, all of Scripture is dealt with in the *Summa* except for the books of Obadiah and Zephanaiah—and the books that are dealt with are cited both extensively and intensively: "as to the New Testament," he writes, "the *Summa* contains a magnificent commentary on the Gospels, the Acts of the Apostles, and the Epistles of St. Paul."[95] What is more, Aquinas' use of Scripture in the *Summa* must be set against the background of his extensive knowledge of the text as a commentator on numerous books of the Bible, namely, Isaiah, the Song of Songs, Lamentations, Jeremiah, Job, Psalms, the Gospels of Matthew and John, the Pauline epistles, and the famous *Catena Aurea* or *glossae in quatuor evangelica,* a running comment on the harmony of the Gospels. Aquinas also had, most probably, a rudimentary knowledge of Greek.[96] His work as commentator is characterized by an emphasis on the literal meaning of texts, by an interest in the relation of the original context of a

---

[93]Cited in Holzhey, *Die Inspiration,* p. 88.

[94]Callan, "Bible in the *Summa,*" p. 39.

[95]Callan, "Bible in the *Summa,*" p. 38, and cf. Paul Synave, "Les commentaires scriptuaires de saint Thomas d'Aquin," in *La Vie Spirituelle* 8 (1923): 455–69; idem,"Le canon scriptuaire de saint Thomas d'Aquin," in *Revue Biblique* 33 (1924): pp. 522–33; and the exhaustive essay by Pierre Mandonnet, "Chronologie des écrits scriptuaires de Saint Thomas d'Aquin," in *Revue Thomiste* 33 (1928):25–45, 116–66, 211–45; 34 (1929):53–66, 132–45, 489–519.

[96]Cf. Callan, "Bible in the *Summa,*" pp. 39–40, with Synave, "Le canon scriptuaire de saint Thomas d'Aquin," pp. 522–33; idem, "Les commentaires scriptuaires de saint Thomas d'Aquin," pp. 455–69; and Spicq, "Saint Thomas d'Aquin: VI. Saint Thomas d'Aquin exégète," in *DTC* 15/1, cols. 694–738.

passage to its meaning,[97] and by a recognition of basic text-critical issues, such as the problem of variations in the text of the Vulgate.[98]

1.3 Developments in the Doctrine of Inspiration and Authority in the Later Middle Ages

Theologians of the late thirteenth and fourteenth centuries, like Giles of Rome, Hervaeus Natalis, Henry of Ghent, and Alphonsus Vargas carried forward the causal line of argument adumbrated by Aquinas' maxim, *Deus est auctor principalis Scripturae, homo autem instrumentum.* Giles of Rome, the great doctor of the Augustinian Order, could argue that God, who is the creator of all things, ought also to be understood as the creator, by inspiration, of the Scriptures. God is, in other words "the principal efficient cause" of the entirety of inspired Scripture.[99] Hervaeus did not write a lengthy prolegomenon but he did argue a distinction between simple faith and the *scientia theologiae:* the latter is an exposition of doctrine resting on the authority of Scripture. The conclusions drawn from Scripture, moreover, are certain inasmuch as "whatever things are in Scripture are spoken by God *(sunt dicta a Deo)"* and "it is certain that God cannot speak falsehood."[100] Vargas held as a basic maxim that all theological statements on rested either "a proposition of sacred scripture or were deduced from statements in sacred scripture."[101] Indeed, it was the assumption of the theologians of the thirteenth and fourteenth centuries that Scripture was the materially sufficient "source and norm" for all theological formulation, granting the inspiration and resulting authority of the text. The language of these thinkers, although not precisely the meaning and application, looks directly toward the Reformation and particularly toward the Protestant orthodox assumption of a positive biblical *principium* for theological formulation.[102]

[97]E.g., Thomas Aquinas, *Commentaria in epistolas Pauli* (Venice, 1498), fol.45v, col. 2.

[98]Cf. Callan, "Bible in the *Summa,"* pp. 39–40, with Van der Ploeg, "Place of Holy Scripture in the Theology of St. Thomas," pp. 400–402.

[99]Giles of Rome, *Primum sententiarum* (Venice, 1521), prol.

[100]Hervaeus Natalis, *In quattuor Petri Lombardi Sententiarum* (Venice, 1505), prol., q.1, as cited in de Vooght, *Les sources,* p. 62.

[101]Cited in J. Kürtzinger, *Alfonsus Vargas Toletanus und seine theologische Einleitungslehre. Ein Beitrag zur Geschichte der Scholastik in 14. Jahrhundert* (Munich, 1930), p. 36.

[102]Hermann Schüssler, *Der Primat der heiligen Schrift als theologisches und kanonistisches Problem in Spätmittelalter* (Wiesbaden: Franz Steiner

A particularly subtle view of inspiration and authority was developed at the close of the thirteenth century by Henry of Ghent.[103] In great works of art, noted Henry, it is possible to distinguish between the artist who designs and directs the work and the apprentice whose task is to realize the plan of the artist. Even so, in the sciences, a distinction can be drawn between the founder or creator of a way of knowing and the subsequent practitioners of the science. In theology, God alone knows in and of himself the fundamental supernatural truths of the discipline. No creature can gain this knowledge without the assistance of divine inspiration. God is thus the primary author of theology—and, specifically, the primary author of Scripture who has assisted the human writers by inspiration in their task of writing.[104]

Granting this relationship between the divine and the human authors of Scripture, Henry can argue that the truth of Scripture—like the ultimate authority of Scripture—does not rest entirely upon the efforts of the human authors who wrote under the inspiration of the Spirit. The human authors are analogous to the apprentice artists who pass on to others the gift that they have been given by the primary author, the artist. Thus the prophets teach not their own thoughts but rather they act as ministers, teaching others what they have learned from the Spirit. Nonetheless, the authority and truth of Scripture also rest on the words and the style of the human authors —as Henry notes, the words and the linguistic expression in Scripture are no different from the common forms of human expression or from the language of secular writings.[105] Henry also adumbrates what Oberman calls "Tradition I" by indicating the priority of Scripture over church, if there were to be a disagreement.[106]

Verlag, 1977), pp. 73–74; cf. Albert Lang, *Die theologische Prinzipienlehre der mittelalterlichen Scholastik* (Freiburg, 1964), pp. 196–216.

[103]Henry of Ghent, *Summa quaestionum ordinariarum theologi recepto praeconio solennis Henrici a Gandavo, cum duplici repertorio, tomos prior-posterior* (Paris, 1520; repr. 2 vols. St. Bonaventure, N.Y.: Franciscan Institute, 1953), Lib.I, art.9, q.11; cf. Mangenot, "Inspiration de l'Écriture," cols. 2122–23.

[104]Henry of Ghent, *Summa,* Lib.I, art.9, q.11.

[105]Henry of Ghent, *Summa,* Lib.I, art.9, q.11.

[106]Cf. Michael Schmaus, "Die Schrift und die Kirche nach Heinrich von Gent," in *Kirche und Überlieferung,* ed. J. Beta and H. Fries (Freiburg: 1960), pp. 211–71 with A. N. S. Lane, "Scripture, Tradition and Church: An Historical Survey," in *Vox Evangelica,* 9, p. 42, and Oberman, *The Harvest of Medieval Theology: Gabriel Biel and Late Medieval Nominalism,* rev. ed. (Grand Rapids: Eerdmans, 1967), pp. 365–75.

Even more than Henry, Duns Scotus must be credited with the development of a clearly defined doctrine of Scripture, the basic divisions and arguments of which provided a structural and doctrinal foundation for the arguments of later theologians, including the Protestant orthodox.[107] Scotus assumed that knowledge of the heavenly goal and of the means necessary to its attainment was beyond the grasp of the *viator* in his natural condition. Natural reason could not attain to saving truth. Revelation is, therefore, necessary. Scotus located these truths of revelation in Scripture and in the tradition grounded upon Scripture and the apostolic faith.[108]

Scotus begins by asking whether human nature necessitates the gift of a "special doctrine supernaturally inspired" such as cannot be attained by the natural light of the mind.[109] An interpolation in the text at this point describes the divisions of the prologue: Scotus' first question raises the issue of the necessity of the doctrine and thereby shows the connection between the prologue and the discussion that follows it at the beginning of the four books of the *Sentences*. The second question—of the sufficiency of Scripture—deals with the category of formal causes *(genus causae formalis)* in relation to theology; the third deals with the material cause, the subject of theology. The fourth and fifth sections—theology as practical science—deal with the issue of the final cause of theology.[110] This structure of argument is important for several reasons. In the first place, it demonstrates the connection between Scotus and several of his immediate predecessors in the scholastic tradition, including writers like Robert Kilwardby and Henry of Ghent, whose philosophical and theological teachings he often disagreed with: at a formal level at least, he echoes them in the use of fourfold causality as a heuristic device in the explanation of the logic and grounds of

[107]On Scotus' theology, cf. P. Raymond, "Duns Scot" in DTC, vol. 4, cols. 1865–1947; P. Parthenius Minges, *Ioannis Duns Scoti Doctrina Philosophica et Theologica,* 2 vols. (Quaracchi, 1930); and Bernardine M. Bonansea, *Man and His Approach to God in John Duns Scotus* (Lanham, Md.: University Press of America, 1983); the significance of the *prologus* to Scotus' *Ordinatio* is discussed in Finkenzeller, *Offenbarung und Theologie nach der Lehre des Johannes Duns Skotus,* pp. 66–77 and Antonellus G. Ostdiek, *Scotus and Fundamental Theology* (Teutopolis, Ill.: 1967).

[108]Scotus, *Ordinatio,* in *Opera Omnia,* ed. Charles Balic (Vatican City: Typis Polyglottis Vaticanis, 1950–), Lib.I, prol., q.1, nn.6–8, 22. The older complete edition, *Opera Omnia,* edito nova iuxta editonem Waddingi, 26 vols. (Paris: Vives, 1891–95), is also serviceable.

[109]Scotus, *Ordinatio,* I, prol., q.1, n.a.

[110]Scotus, *Ordinatio,* prol., I, q.i.

theology. Second, it manifests the growing interest in the doctrine of Scripture as an element in theological prolegomena—another point of formal similarity between Scotus and Henry.[111] And, finally, it offers a significant point of comparison with the Protestant orthodox systems, which not only press the issue of fourfold causality as a heuristic device, but develop the issue further by adapting the causal models of the medieval systems not only to their prolegomena but also to their separate doctrine of Scripture: in the latter adaptation, moreover, the Protestant scholastics parallel in the discussion of Scripture as ground of theology the pattern of causality noted by the medieval doctors in and for theology as a whole.[112]

After listing arguments against the necessity of revelation drawn from Avicenna and Aristotle and arguments in favor of its necessity from Scripture, Scotus notes,

> In this question we see a controversy between philosophers and theologians. While the philosophers hold to the perfection of nature and deny supernatural perfection, the theologians truly understand the defect of nature, and the necessity of grace and supernatural perfection.[113]

The philosophers raise the issue of the perfection of nature from an epistemological viewpoint: for if nature is perfect, then all knowledge may be attained through the examination of the activity of natural causality.[114] The problem of necessity of revelation and therefore of *fides acquisita* can now be related to the order of the universe: given the nature of human beings and of the world, is revelation necessary?

Scotus argues that God might, according to his *potentia absoluta,* save certain individuals and even make them meritorious of glory apart from an infusion of faith if he gave them a certain grace to reform their wills in the light of natural reason and of the acquired knowledge of divine truth *(fides acquisita)* which they already possessed. But according to God's *potentia ordinata* this grace is not given without the infused habit of faith preceding it: this is not to say that God's grace is insufficient, but only that the gracious will of God reforms the whole man, in both his knowing and his willing.[115]

---

[111]Cf. *PRRD,* I, p. 21.
[112]See below, 4.1.
[113]Scotus, *Ordinatio,* prol., I, q.1, §3.
[114]Scotus, *Ordinatio,* prol., I, q.1, §4.
[115]Scotus, *Ordinatio,* prol., I, q.1 (n.55); cf. Heiko A. Oberman, *The*

Similarly, says Scotus, the *habitus theologiae*—which in its perfection includes both *fides infusa* and *fides acquisita*—belongs in its fullness to the ordained pattern of salvation. Theology is necessary, therefore, and with it the acquired articles of faith revealed by God in Scripture.116

Scotus distinguishes, finally, between two possible modes of supernaturally revealed knowledge: we might be given to know natural objects by supernatural revelation, but this is unnecessary, in view of our God-given natural capacities. Revelation is not needed to duplicate natural, rational knowledge. The arguments of the philosophers concerning knowledge of nature, therefore, can be accorded a place in theological system. According to the second mode of understanding the problem, however, it is clearly necessary to be given supernatural knowledge of those things which cannot be known naturally.117 Granting this, it only remains to be shown that the articles of faith revealed in Scripture are true, necessary to salvation, and inaccessible to the natural reason.

The sufficiency of the revelation contained in Scripture is stated very succinctly by Scotus and with a minimum of debate. He asks whether "the supernatural knowledge necessary for the *viatores* is sufficiently conveyed in sacred Scripture."118 It seems not, since first the law of nature, then the law of Moses needed to be replaced by further writings—nor is the Old Testament the entirety of sacred Scripture. The historical progress of revelation through these successive stages would indicate, it seems, the need for continuing addition to the body of knowledge. Further, it seems that scripture is insufficient because it contains many superfluous ceremonies and histories. Finally, Scripture lacks information concerning many things, whether they be sinful or not and therefore is also insufficient.119 Against these objections Scotus poses simply the statement of Augustine, that the canonical Scriptures are authoritative for faith in "those things of which we must not be ignorant, but which we cannot know of our selves."120

We need to recognize the three stated objections, the authority of

Harvest of Medieval Theology: Gabriel Biel and Late Medieval Nominalism, rev. ed. (Grand Rapids: Eerdmans, 1967), p. 33.

116Scotus, *Ordinatio,* prol., I, q.1 (n.56).

117Scotus, *Ordinatio,* prol., I, q.i (n.65).

118Scotus, *Ordinatio,* prol., II, q.1.

119Scotus, *Ordinatio,* prol., II, q.1, n.95–97.

120Scotus, *Ordinatio,* prol., II, q.1, n.98, citing Augustine, *De civitate Dei.* XI.iii.

Augustine, and Scotus' eventual *"responsio principalis ad quaestionum"* as all arising within the context of the church. None of the objections belongs to the category of heresy, nor does the *responsio* section of Scotus' argument treat them as such. But Scotus does recognize the existence of objections to Scripture from outside the church which strike of a deeper problem than the sufficiency of the revelation in Scripture: pagans and heretics who, like Christians, recognize the "necessity of revealed doctrine," nevertheless deny the identity of Scripture with that doctrine. Therefore, as a formal ground to his response on the issue of sufficiency, Scotus first argues the truth of Scripture. In other words, Scotus argues first that Scripture does in fact contain the necessary and true revelation of God and only then proceeds to the proof of the sufficiency of the scriptural revelation.[121]

In a fashion similar to that adopted by Calvin and the later Protestant orthodox, Scotus sets forth a series of arguments demonstrating objectively the truth and, therefore, the sufficiency of the Scriptures. Biblical prophecy is validated by its fulfillment and Scripture is self-consistent, everywhere agreeing with itself. The writers of Scripture, moreover, state that they write with divine authority—to disagree is to claim that the writers themselves are guilty of falsehood, despite the evidence from prophecy and self-consistency. The careful reception of the canon by the church and the strength or stability of the church on the ground of Scripture also argue the truth of the text, as do the perfection and of the teachings of Scripture. Similarly the miracles attested by the text indicate its divinity. And, in a subsidiary manner, the foolishness and irrationality of the teachings of "Jews, Manicheans, and other heretics" only serve to confirm the wholeness and rectitude of biblical teaching as contained in both Old and New Testament.[122]

These arguments on the divine origin and truth of Scripture serve first to confirm, against the heretics, that the doctrine of the canon is true; from which it follows—in confirmation of Scotus' original point—that Scripture is necessary and sufficient to draw the Christian pilgrims toward their goal.[123] The unity of Scotus' prologue is, moreover, made clear in this conclusion since the revelation in Scripture as the ground of *theologia nostra aut viatorem* appears

[121]Cf. Ostdiek, *Scotus and Fundamental Theology,* pp. 22–23.
[122]Cf. the discussion in Preus, "View of the Bible Held by the Church," in *Inerrancy,* pp. 370–71.
[123]Scotus, *Ordinatio,* prol., n.120.

also and with emphasis in the later discussion of the object of theology[124] and also in the analysis of theology as a science.[125] And in what is by far the longest part of the *prologus,* Scotus argues that theology is practical rather than speculative—again focusing his argument on the theology of the *viator* rather than on the speculative or contemplative theology that exists in the mind of God.

As Minges carefully noted, Scotus' dictum *"Sacra scriptura sufficienter continent doctrinam necessariam viatori"* [126] should not be taken as an indication that Scotus viewed Scripture as sufficiently clear to be interpreted apart from the church's tradition or that he believed that the entire sum of doctrine could be elicited from Scripture alone.[127] Nor did Scotus not intend to set up Scripture as the sole norm of doctrine: he could argue that the ancient symbols of the church summarize the truth of revelation and even that, beside the authority of Scripture and creeds, stands that of the "authentic Fathers" and the "Church of Rome."[128] Even so, he held that the "substance of the faith" derives equally from Scripture and the declarations and determinations of the church—a view resembling that of Oberman's "Tradition II."[129]

A further development of the concept of inspiration along the lines adumbrated by Aquinas occurred in the fifteenth century. Alphonse Tostat argued that the Spirit implanted in the minds of the prophets and the apostles "the meaning of the things" about which they would subsequently speak and write, "but once they had understood what had been revealed to them, they spoke of it in their accustomed manner of speech."[130] The differences in style among the various biblical writers are to be understood as differences resident in the individuals themselves. Tostat denied that God literally moved the vocal organs of the prophets and apostles—this, he noted, was the form of demonic possession, not of divine inspiration. Rather, God raises the mind of the prophet or apostle to a higher level of understanding, by speaking or dictating to the soul truths that the individual prophet or apostle will formulate into inward or mental words and subsequently either write or speak: all Scripture, therefore, is a divine revelation by the agency of the Spirit

[124]Scotus, *Ordinatio,* prol., n.210.
[125]Scotus, *Ordinatio,* prol., n.204.
[126]Scotus, *Ordinatio,* prol., q.2, n.14.
[127]Minges, *Scoti doctrina,* I:534.
[128]Scotus, *Ordinatio,* I, d.26; cf. III, d.25, q.i.4; I.d.26.
[129]Scotus, *Ordinatio,* IV, d.2, q.3.5; cf. Oberman, *Harvest,* pp. 365–85.
[130]Mangenot, "Inspiration de l'Écriture," col. 2201.

who not only inspires but also preserves the writer from error.[131] Such theorizations did not, however, rule out or even ultimately conflict with the more traditional concept of a dictation by the Holy Spirit to an amanuensis, secretary, or "penman" *(calamus)* found in such diverse theologians of the later Middle Ages as Wyclif, Biel, and D'Ailly, but rather reinforced the understanding given to the traditional language of dictation by Aquinas—namely, an inward elevation of mind and spirit rather than use of the prophets and apostles as mindless instruments.[132]

1.4 Questions concerning Scripture, Tradition, and Hermeneutics in the Later Middle Ages and the Renaissance

The preceding volume of this study, the investigation of theological prolegomena, recognized the fundamental continuity between Luther's declaration at Worms, "Unless I am convicted by Scripture and plain reason ... I cannot and will not recant," and the doctrinal presuppositions of both medieval scholasticism and Protestant orthodoxy.[133] The point is relevant to the present discussion also. As Kropatscheck argues, *ratio* in this particular context cannot be restricted to the exercise of logic or dialectic, but indicates also "the inner consistency of individual dogmatic statements" and therefore stands in a crucial relation to Scripture which, as divine Word, is the certain foundation for all acknowledged truth. The great question addressed by scholasticism was the nature of this relationship between rational and supernatural truth.[134] The resolution of this question, in turn, points toward the problem of authority.

Dogmatic statements about the character of Scripture must also, of course, be read in the context of prevailing models of biblical interpretation. The doctrinal question of the nature and authority of Scripture is inseparable from the hermeneutical question of the methods to be employed in the exegesis of Scripture. Crucial to the understanding of the meaning of the medieval view of the inspiration and authority of Scripture and to what these doctrinal concepts, so

---

[131]Mangenot, "Inspiration de l'Écriture," cols. 2128, 2201, citing Alphonse Tostast, *In Matthaeum,* praef., q.2; c.10, q.104.

[132]Kropatscheck, *Das Schriftprinzip,* pp. 424–29.

[133]*PRRD,* I, p. 64.

[134]Kropatscheck, *Das Schriftprinzip,* I, p. 454; cf. the comments in Martin Brecht, *Martin Luther: His Road to Reformation, 1483–1521,* trans. James Schaaf (Philadelphia: Fortress, 1985), p. 460.

similar at times to the teachings of Protestantism, implied for their formulators, therefore, is the hermeneutical and exegetical context of the doctrine. The later Middle Ages, in particular, saw the rise of new hermeneutical currents and of a fundamental question concerning the way in which the authority of Scripture functioned in the context of churchly interpretation.

As Kropatschek, de Vooght, and Oberman have demonstrated, the typical procedure of contrasting the *sola Scriptura* of the Reformers and various select forerunners with an emphasis on tradition or on the twin authorities of Scripture and tradition held by various late medieval theologians falls, for lack of subtlety and sensitivity to detail, far short of an accurate view of the contrast between the late Middle Ages and the Reformation or of the character of the late medieval discussion leading toward the Reformation.[135] The theologians of the late Middle Ages did not pose Scripture and tradition against one another neatly as competing norms in theology. Instead, together with the exegetes of the age, they asked questions about pattern and meaning in interpretation that had direct implications for their view of the relationship of Scripture to tradition and their conception of the doctrinal authority of Scripture. On these points there is a clear continuity of discussion between the fifteenth and sixteenth centuries.

Kropatscheck showed that the medieval background, both religious and theological, to the Reformers' understanding of Scripture was the necessary context within which to understand the Reformation itself—without this history, the motivation of the Reformation itself, the biblical foundations of the movement, would be utterly obscured for lack of a doctrine of Scripture.[136] "Neither the formula *'sola Scriptura,'* nor the emphasis on the literal sense of the text, nor the doctrine of inspiration, was the achievement of the Reformation, nor, beyond that, was the demand for a purely biblical teaching," wrote Kropatscheck. Nonetheless, "not a single one of the medieval biblicists became a Reformer of the church"—a detail that must be balanced against the fact "that neither Wyclif nor Luther said anything particularly new when they proclaimed Scripture to be the 'Word of God.' " If the doctrine was no different, the origins of the Reformation must be found, not in the declaration of a new principle

---

[135]Kropatscheck, *Das Schriftprinzip,* especially pp. 382–445; de Vooght, *Les sources,* pp. 254–64; Heiko Oberman, "Scripture and Tradition: Introduction," in *Forerunners of the Reformation* (New York: Holt, Rinehart and Winston, 1966), p. 54; idem, *Harvest,* pp. 361–412.

[136]Kropatscheck, *Das Schriftprinzip,* I, p. iii.

but rather in the way in which that principle was set forth.[137] Just how Kropatscheck would have resolved this problem and developed his thesis is unclear, inasmuch as the projected second volume of his study never appeared.

A similar perspective, differing primarily in its more nuanced approach to late medieval debate over the relation of Scripture, tradition, and magisterium, may be found in de Vooght's essay on the "sources of Christian doctrine" in the late Middle Ages. De Vooght notes that the condemnations of Wyclif and Hus at the Council of Constance concerned their doctrine of the church, not their theological method and its presuppositions. With considerably more refinement than Kropatschek, moreover, de Vooght shows that Wyclif's conception of the priority of Scripture was not so much a doctrine of *sola Scriptura* as an identification of the norm of doctrinal truth with "Scripture and its traditional and catholic interpretation."[138] Wyclif was able to reject contemporary churchly teachings without rejecting a close association of Scripture with tradition—indeed, on the assumption of a coherence of traditionary interpretation with its theologically and soteriologically sufficient scriptural foundation. This in itself ought to give pause to anyone who would distinguish between Catholics and proto-Protestants in the fourteenth century on the ground that the former insisted on both written and unwritten, traditionary sources of revealed truth whereas the latter held forth for Scripture alone as the authoritative source for Christian doctrine.[139]

For Oberman, the question of authority in the later Middle Ages rests not so much on differing views of Scripture as on differing views of tradition. There was, in fact, an "encounter," according to Oberman, "of two general notions about tradition."[140] In one view, Scripture is identified as the unique source of revealed truth and, therefore, as the sole norm for the understanding of Christian doctrine, but is viewed as standing in accord with rather than in contrast to an interpretive tradition. In the other view, tradition is more than the ongoing churchly interpretation of the biblical revelation—it contains truths handed down orally in the church from the time of Christ and the apostles but never placed in written form. In particular, this view of tradition assumed that the apostles had written down

[137]Kropatscheck, *Das Schriftprinzip,* I, pp. 425, 459.

[138]De Vooght, *Les sources,* p. 199.

[139]Paul de Vooght, *Les sources,* pp. 10, 180–88; and cf. idem, "Wyclif et la *Scriptura Sola,*" in *Ephemerides theologiae lovaniensis* 39 (1963): 50–86.

[140]Oberman, *Forerunners,* p. 54.

all of the teachings of Jesus belonging to his earthly ministry between baptism and crucifixion but had not reported fully Jesus' teachings between the resurrection and ascension. "In the first case," Oberman writes, "tradition was seen as the instrumental vehicle of Scripture which brings the contents of Holy Scripture to life in constant dialogue between the doctors of Scripture and the Church; in the second case, tradition was seen as the authoritative vehicle of divine truth, embedded in Scripture but overflowing in extrascriptural apostolic tradition handed down through episcopal succession."[141]

Whereas medieval theologians tended to view *sacra theologia* as distinct but inseparable from *sacra pagina* and universally understood Scripture as the normative foundation for theology, the canon lawyers tended to argue a "two-source theory": "canon law stands on the two pillars of Scripture and Tradition."[142] Oberman argues that this two-source theory is evident as early as Ivo of Chartres (d. 1116) and Gratian of Bologna (d. 1158) and that they rested their view on an argument made by Basil the Great in his treatise *On the Holy Spirit* that "equal respect and obedience" be given "to the written and to the unwritten ecclesiastical traditions."[143] The approach of the canon lawyers was buttressed by appeal to Augustine's famous saying, "I would not have believed the gospel, unless the authority of the catholic church had moved me."[144] Oberman points out that the "practical authority" granted to the church by Augustine was viewed by some late medieval thinkers as a statement of the "metaphysical priority" of the authority of the church over that of Scripture.[145] Augustine had, in fact, assumed the authority of extrascriptural tradition in many matters. Jerome, likewise, had declared that the church speaks in the silence of Scripture.[146]

Late medieval theologians like Occam, D'Ailly, and Biel, then, were able to balance the authority of Scripture and tradition at the same time that they identified Scripture as the sole ultimate source of divine revelation. Occam and Biel assumed, categorically, that the

---

[141]Oberman, *Forerunners,* p. 55; cf. Oberman, *Harvest,* pp. 371–93.

[142]Oberman, *Forerunners,* p. 55.

[143]Oberman, *Forerunners,* p. 55.

[144]Augustine, *Contra epistolam Manichaei quam vocant Fundamentum,* I.v: *"Ego vero evangelio non crederem, nisi me catholicae ecclesiae commoveret auctoritas" (PL).*

[145]Oberman, *Forerunners,* p. 56.

[146]Jerome, *Dialogus contra luciferianos* 8, in *PL* 23, cols. 163–64.

entire content of the Old and New Testaments was to be received as true—and that anyone who denied the authority of so much as a single point of doctrine was a heretic. D'Ailly could insist, even more strongly, that an assertion of Scripture was of higher authority than any assertion of the church. Nonetheless, Occam insisted that doctrines like transubstantiation were to be believed because they had received the sanction of the fathers and of the Roman Catholic Church, and Biel clearly viewed the tradition. as encapsulated in the ecumenical creeds, both as in accord with Scripture and as authoritative.[147] All three writers held, moreover, "two main categories of truths," those which derive from the express statements of Scripture and those which arise out of the judgments of the church.[148] Beyond this basic twofold distinction of Scripture and tradition, theologians of the fifteenth century could offer a detailed *ordo* for authoritative "catholic truths"—beginning with truths found in the Old and New Testaments and moving on through a descending series of categories: truths elicited as necessary conclusions from Scripture, truths not set down in Scripture but nevertheless belonging to the apostolic tradition, truths defined by plenary councils or by papal decree, truths belonging to the accepted teachings of the church, and truths capable of being inferred from the councils, decrees, or accepted teachings of the church.[149]

Among the late medieval commentaries on Lombard's *Sentences,* Jan Hus' *Super IV sententiarum,* perhaps most clearly enunciates a principle of the primacy of Scripture[150]—but even here, as de Vooght remarks, there is little that is revolutionary. Hus consistently assumes that Scripture supports traditional churchly formulations and that theology is to be formulated in the sense and context of the

---

[147]Cf. William of Occam, *Tractatus de corpore Christi,* cap.8, in *Opera theologica* (St. Bonaventure, N.Y.: Franciscan Institute, 1967–), X:106–7; cf. idem, *The 'De sacramento altaris' of William of Ockham,* ed. Thomas B. Birch (Burlington, Iowa: Lutheran Literary Board, 1930), cap.3; Gabriel Biel, *Collectorium circa quattuor libros sententiarum* (Tübingen, 1501), III, d.24, q.1, dubium 3; d.25, q.1, art.3, dubium 3; and Pierre D'Ailly, as cited in Tschakert, *Petrus von Ailli: Zur Geschichte des grossen abendländisschen schisma und der Reformconcilien von Pisa und Constanz* (Gotha: Perthes, 1877), appendix, p. 10.

[148]Oberman, *Harvest,* p. 383; cf. pp. 381, 397–98.

[149]Schüssler, *Der Primat der Heiligen Schrift,* p. 80, citing Torquemada.

[150]Jan Hus, *Mag. Joannis Hus Super IV Sententiarum.* Nach handschriften zum Erstenmal herausgegeben von Wenzel Flájshans & Dr. Marie Komínková. *Opera omnia,* vol. II (Osnabrück, 1966).

catholic church.[151] When Hus approaches the first distinction of Book I of the *Sentences*—Lombard's own brief prologue on the knowledge conveyed by signs and things—he is constrained to note the source of all doctrine in Scripture, Scripture being the sum of knowledge concerning signs and things.[152] This in itself does not move far beyond the terms of Lombard's first distinction, but it manifests a change of emphasis, a shift of authority on Hus' part. He views Scripture alone as that which directs us toward the wisdom of God.[153] There can be no movement from *signa* to *res significata* apart from the guidance of Scripture as the revelation of God's Word. Hus' *Inceptio* to the second book of the *Sentences* provided him with the opportunity to return to his theme of the authority of Scripture. It is Scripture that testifies to the wisdom of Christ and which witnesses to us his coming for the sake of our salvation.[154] Scripture conveys to us the divine wisdom apart from which all human knowledge would be vain: indeed it is infinite wisdom, the "thesaurus of human wisdom," which brings about in man the love of divine wisdom.

> In brief, [divine] wisdom and thus sacred scripture, defeats evil, casts out sin, frees [men] from the devil, opens the mind, leads back the erring, raises up the oppressed, blesses those who follow it, leads down just paths, and reveals to them finally the kingdom of God. From this it appears, that wisdom is to be praised and, therefore, also in a formal sense, the sacred scriptures, by which [this wisdom] perfects humanity.[155]

Gregory of Rimini had similarly placed a strong emphasis on Scripture as the source of theology and had assumed that churchly doctrine, when not grounded on direct statements of Scripture, must be capable of being drawn from Scripture as a proper logical conclusion. Gregory also could state, somewhat radically, that a theologian could reason from Scripture toward a truth previously unknown to the church.[156] Yet Gregory had "a highly developed consciousness

---

[151]De Vooght, *Les sources,* pp. 224–25.

[152]Hus, *Super IV sententiarum,* I, dist.1, 4.

[153]Cf. Hus, *Super IV sententiarum,* II, *Inceptio* I.7.

[154]Hus, *Super IV Sent.* II, *Inceptio* I.6.

[155]Hus, *Super IV Sent.* II, *Inceptio* I.8.

[156]Gregory of Rimini, *Super primum et secundum sententiarum* (Venice, 1521; repr. St. Bonaventure, N.Y.: Franciscan Institute, 1955), prol., q.1, art.2; cf. John W. O'Malley, "A Note on Gregory of Rimini: Church, Scripture, Tradition," in *Augustinianum* (1965):366; and de Vooght, *Les sources,* pp. 104–8.

of continuity with the Christian past" that led him to interpret Scripture in the light of the authority of the "catholic and holy teachers *(doctores)*" of the church and in the light of the creeds or "articles of the faith." What Gregory proposed, in short, was not a rejection of tradition in favor of Scripture, but a priority of Scripture over the other sources of theology in a churchly context of interpretation.[157]

Not only the late medieval debate framed by Oberman's language of "Tradition I" and "Tradition II," but also the late medieval development of new and in many cases increasingly "literal" or textually unitary patterns of interpretation created pressure on the text and began to offer grounds for a methodological separation of Scripture from tradition. We remember that the radical statements of earlier medieval doctors concerning the ultimate normative authority of Scripture virtually all implied the essential agreement of Scripture with tradition. This agreement was most obvious in the work of interpretation, where the model of the *quadriga,* inherited in its basic outlines from the fathers of the early church, had long assured the intimate relationship between the results of exegesis and the traditional definitions of doctrine—if only because those definitions had all been elicited and argued on the basis of a virtually identical exegetical method. As Congar aptly comments, for the Middle Ages,

> Everything was found in Scripture, all the more easily because the processes of interpretation included the use of symbolism, obligingly accommodating to all needs; and also, more seriously, because extending by reasoned argument the field of application of a statement was not looked upon as overstepping the limits of the original statement. It was generally held that Scripture contained all the truths of faith necessary for salvation. If a question was put concerning a non-scriptural doctrinal formulation, attempts were made to provide some scriptural reference which was at least equivalent or indirect.[158]

Movement away from the *quadriga* toward various forms of "literal" exegesis offered, as one of its incidental results, an increasing separation between the canonical text and the postcanonical tradition.

---

[157]O'Malley, "Note on Gregory of Rimini," pp. 368–70, 373.

[158]Yves M.–J. Congar, *Tradition and Traditions: An Historical and a Theological Essay,* trans. M. Naseby and T. Rainborough (New York: Macmillan, 1967), p. 87.

On this issue as well as in the development of two ways of understanding the normative value of tradition ("Tradition I" and
"Tradition II"), the later Middle Ages prepared the way for the great
debates of the sixteenth century and, indeed, for the hermeneutical
difficulties experienced by seventeenth-century scholastic orthodoxy
in its attempt to maintain a traditional doctrine of Scripture and a
traditional structure of theological system and its dogmas. The
emphasis given by Thomas Aquinas to the literal meaning of the text
as the foundation of all other meaning gradually led to a parting of
the ways among late medieval exegetes—some clinging to the
essentially Gregorian model of the *quadriga* and, specifically, to the
doctrinal use of its three spiritual meanings; others seeking out other
patterns for the interpretation of the text that would gravitate even
more toward the literal sense as the foundation not only of theological argumentation, but also of theological formulation.

Most notable among those who followed out the Victorine and
Thomist emphasis on the literal sense was Nicholas of Lyra (d.
1349).[159] Although it can be argued that the Franciscan Lyra
follows the theology of his own order on some points—such as his
refusal to follow Aquinas in granting Moses higher prophetic status
than David on the grounds of Moses' vision of God and his interest
in prophecy as giving knowledge of future contingencies—it is clear
that his emphasis, even in and through these differences, is upon the
literal sense of the text as history. Lyra cited Aquinas regularly and
at some length and, in search of the literal or historical reading of
the text also looked to rabbinical exegesis of the Old Testament,
in particular to the work of Rashi, who had placed a particular
emphasis on literal exegesis.[160] He is also to be singled out for his
pronounced interest in the original languages of the text. Very much
like Aquinas and like Hugh of St. Victor before him, Lyra com-
plained of tendencies toward spiritual and mystical exegesis that
ignore the letter. As an antidote to the problem, he proposed a
"double literal sense" *(duplex sensus literalis)* according to which
the letter of the text is the "foundation" *(fundamentum)* of all
meaning—indeed, Lyra argued that the literal fulfillment of Old

[159]Cf. de Lubac, *Exégèse médiévale,* II/2, pp. 348–50, and Smalley, "Bible
in the Middle Ages," p. 66.

[160]Preus, *From Shadow to Promise,* pp. 65–66; cf. Eugene H. Merrill,
"Rashi, Nicholas de Lyra and Christian Exegesis," in *Westminster Theological
Journal* 38 (1975–76):66–79; Herman Hailperin, *Rashi and the Christian
Scholars* (Pittsburg: University of Pittsburg Press, 1963); and de Lubac *Exégèse
médievale,* II/2, pp. 342, 352–53.

Testament prophecies in the New Testament indicated that the fulfillment was a spiritual but also second literal sense of the Old Testament text.[161] Lyra, thus, attempted to effect a renewal of interest in the historical meaning of the text, but he also sought to retain the christological reading of the Old Testament, now as the second part of a twofold literal sense.

Many of the doctrinal and hermeneutical issues raised by the development of later medieval exegesis had a direct impact on dogmatic formulation, as is seen in the *quaestio de sacra scriptura* in Heinrich Totting of Oyta's commentary on the *Sentences*. Henry (d. 1397) proposed as the second question of his commentary, "Whether all of the books of our Bible, specifically, in the literal sense of all their assertions are divine, i.e, are written by divine inspiration."[162] Jerome had, after all, distinguished between the Hebrew of the larger part of the Old Testament and the Greek text of the apocrypha and had argued the exclusion of Sirach, Judith, and Tobit from the canon. Jerome had also offered corrections of the Septuagint—and in many places, Henry notes, the Septuagint falls short of the literal sense of the Hebrew. Henry also indicates that doubt might be raised concerning the veracity of the writings of Mark and Luke, neither of whom were present during the ministry of Jesus and who both wrote long after the events they recorded.[163]

Henry proceeds to address these problems in three articles: (1) the authenticity and security of the books of the Bible; (2) the truth of the various senses of Scripture; and (3) the catholic truths not contained in the books of Scripture. He argues at length, resting on the declaration of Isidore of Seville, that all seventy-two of the biblical books are canonical, pronouncing the Vulgate to be the preferred translation, that the entire canon is inspired and authoritative.[164] To objections such as the problem of Marcan and Lucan authorship, he responds that these writers were disciples of Peter and of Peter and Paul respectively and that both were surely guided by

[161]Cf. Nicholas of Lyra *Prologus primus de commendatione sacrae scripturae in generali* (Basel, 1502), fol.3–4; with Preus, *From Shadow to Promise,* pp. 67–68.

[162]Henry Totting of Oyta, *Quaestio de sacra scriptura et de veritatibus catholicis,* ed. Albert Lang (Münster: Aschendorff, 1953), p. 10; on Henry's theology and its significance, see Albert Lang, *Heinrich Totting von Oyta. Ein Beitrag zur Entstehungsgeschichte der ersten deutschen Universitäten und zur Problemgeschichte der Spätscholastik* (Münster: Aschendorff, 1937).

[163]Henry Totting, *Quaestio de sacra scriptura,* pp. 10–11, 24.

[164]Henry Totting, *Quaestio de sacra scriptura,* pp. 13–14ff., 19ff.

the Holy Spirit in recording what they had learned from the apostles.

Scripture is also entirely true—despite the inclusion of certain untrue assertions in it, such as the serpent's assertion, in Genesis 3, "You shall not die." This assertion, Henry comments, was not the assertion of Moses, the editor or compiler of the Pentateuch, who correctly recorded what was said, albeit the statement was an untruth. Similarly, the fact that the text refers to Moses in the third person, does not undermine Mosaic authorship: this is a proper mode of speech for a compiler such as Moses—even as Baruch, the secretary of Jeremiah, wrote (Jer. 36:27) "Baruch wrote all the words of the Lord from the mouth of Jeremiah." These and other examples, then, can be explained so as to demonstrate the truth of the literal sense.[165] Nor does the presence of more than one sense undermine the truthfulness of the text—as if each text had more than one author—granting that it is not the case that the literal sense arises from the human author and the spiritual sense from the divine, as is written in 2 Peter 1:21, "For prophecy does not arise from the will of man, but holy men of God spoke as they were inspired by the Holy Spirit." The literal sense is the primary sense and represents the primary intention of the author of Scripture, the Holy Spirit. The literal sense, then, is also the basis of all further argument.[166] In his final question, following out the pattern of "Tradition II," Henry notes other sources for catholic truth—such as the decisions of councils and of the pope and the truths found in the writings of the "holy doctors" of the church—but comments that these sources are not equal in authority. The primary truths necessary for salvation are given by divine revelation in the canon of Scripture. Christ, and faith in him is the foundation of our salvation, while the church, as Augustine himself taught, is the necessary authority that moves us to belief and that teaches truths of Christ not found in the text of Scripture. It is therefore the case, Henry concludes, that all catholic truth is given for belief unto salvation, although all sources are not of equal authority.[167]

After Nicholas of Lyra's time, from the middle of the fourteenth century onward, there was, in Verger's words, a "quantitative and qualitative" collapse of exegetical labor in the universities, even as "the prestige of Lombard's *Sentences* as the basis of all theological instruction" continued to rise. This did not indicate, however, a total

---

[165]Henry Totting, *Quaestio de sacra scriptura*, pp. 43–46.
[166]Henry Totting, *Quaestio de sacra scriptura*, pp. 46–52.
[167]Henry Totting, *Quaestio de sacra scriptura*, pp. 61–68.

loss of Thomas' or Lyra's insight—the fundamental hermeneutical patterns "continued to attempt to hold the religious necessity of spiritual interpretation and the theological primacy of literal exposition together," often resulting in a mingling of "allegorization with ultra-literalism."[168] Exegetes of the fifteenth century, such as Gerson (d. 1429), Tostat (d. 1455), and Denis the Carthusian (d. 1471), placed their emphasis on the spiritual sense, especially on allegorical and tropological interpretation. De Lubac says of Tostat that he "lost himself in allegories all the while proclaiming that he desired to hold fast to the letter."[169]

On the eve of the Reformation, at least in part in reaction to this mingling of styles, the humanist exegete, Lefèvre d'Étaples, introduced yet another approach to the exegetical problem of the "letter." Lyra's approach had raised a problem for the interpretation of the Old Testament inasmuch as it had opened the way to a strictly historical, literal sense that did not easily yield up traditional Christian readings—while at the same time it offered a second literal sense that opened the Old Testament to the New. Lefèvre cut through the problem of the double literal sense and did away with the shift from letter to spirit characteristic of the fourfold exegesis by posing a single literal sense expressing the "intention of the prophet and of the Holy Spirit speaking in him."[170] In effect, Lefèvre had concentrated on the second of Nicholas of Lyra's literal senses and had excluded the historical sense of the text: the meaning of the Old Testament is understood as *literally* identical with its fulfillment in the New.

If the rhetorical, literary, and philological development known as "humanism" and traditionally associated with the revival of arts, philosophy, and classical study in the Renaissance can no longer be thoroughly separated from the scholasticism of the later Middle Ages,[171] it remains the case that the philological emphasis of Renaissance humanism marks a significant departure in the history

---

[168]Jacques Verger, "L'exégèse de l'université," in *Bible de tous les temps,* IV:225–26; de Lubac, *Exégèse médievale,* II/2, pp. 369–91.

[169]De Lubac, *Exégèse médiévale,* II/2, pp. 363–367, 386.

[170]Lefèvre d'Étaples, *Quincuplex psalterium,* as cited in Preus, *From Shadow to Promise,* p. 137; cf. Guy Bedouelle, "L'humanisme et la Bible," in *BTT* 5, pp. 103–7.

[171]Cf. James H. Overfield, "Scholastic Opposition to Humanism in Pre-Reformation Germany," in *Viator* 7 (1976):419–20; and idem, *Humanism and Scholasticism in Late Medieval Germany* (Princeton, N.J.: Princeton University Press, 1984), pp. 59–60, 94–100, 329–30.

of exegesis and hermeneutics and, in recognizable continuity with the increased interest in the "letter" of the text characteristic of at least one tendency in later medieval exegesis, a source both of the exegetical methods of the Reformation and of the sixteenth- and seventeenth-century problem of authority and certainty.[172] The close, text-critical scrutiny of Valla, Reuchlin, and Erasmus resulted not only in the establishment of a far more accurate text of the Bible but also in a considerably greater degree of freedom for the individual exegete. In addition, the humanists brought to their study of the text not only an increased linguistic capability—particularly in Greek, which the medieval exegetes had lacked—but also a strong antischolastic sentiment. They assumed that their expertise as grammarians and philologists placed them far in advance of all forms of medieval exegesis and of the logical niceties of scholasticism. As a result, they seldom delved deeply into the medieval exegetical tradition and tended to prefer textual annotations to lengthy theological analysis in their commentaries. Erasmus, for example, knew little of the work of Hugh of St. Cher and Nicholas of Lyra, even less of the commentaries of Aquinas, and nothing at all of the Victorines: in his case, in particular, the exegesis of the New Testament was "a fresh endeavour ... almost completely ignorant" of the medieval period, a philological task immersed in the text itself and in the works of the patristic era.[173]

[172]Cf. Kristeller's identification of humanism as primarily a study of *grammatica, rhetorica, poetica, historia,* and *philosophia moralis,* rather than of the medieval university disciplines of "theology, jurisprudence, medicine, and the philosophical disciplines other than ethics, such as logic, natural philosophy and metaphysics," in Kristeller, "Humanism," in *The Cambridge History of Renaissance Philosophy,* pp. 113–14; and note idem, *Renaissance Thought: The Classic, Scholastic, and Humanist Strains* (New York: Harper and Row, 1961); also note H. Schlingensiepen, "Erasmus als Exeget auf grund seiner Schriften zu Matthäus," in *Zeitschrift für Kirchengeschichte,* 48 (1929), pp. 16–57; John William Aldridge, *The Hermeneutic of Erasmus* (Richmond: John Knox, 1966) and the magisterial essays of John B. Payne, "Erasmus: Interpreter of Romans," in *Sixteenth Century Studies and Essays* II, ed. Carl S. Meyer, (St Louis: Foundation for Reformation Research, 1971), pp. 1–35; "Erasmus and Lefèvre d'Étaples as Interpreters of Paul," in *Archiv für Reformationsgeschichte,* 65 (1974), pp. 54–83; and "Toward the Hermeneutics of Erasmus," in *Scrinium Erasminianum: Mélanges historiques,* ed. Joseph Coppens, 2 vols. (Leiden: E. J. Brill, 1969), 2:12–49.
[173]Cf. Louis Bouyer, "Erasmus in Relation to the Medieval Biblical Tradition," in *CHB,* II: 492–93 with Bedouelle, "L'humanisme et la Bible," in *BTT* 5, pp. 53–54, 57, and Jeremy Bentley, *Humanists and Holy Writ: New Testament Scholarship in the Renaissance* (Princeton, N.J.: Princeton University Press,

Such works as Valla's *Adnotationes* on the New Testament (1505), Reuchlin's *De rudimentis hebraicis* (1506), and Erasmus' *Novum instrumentum* (1516; 2d ed., with Erasmus' own Latin translation, 1519) demonstrated the number and significance of the problems in the Vulgate and marked a turning point in the history of exegesis and interpretation. Reuchlin, in particular, represented a profound emphasis on the Hebrew text—to the point of identifying Hebrew as "a holy language, the source of all other languages, free from impurity" and of viewing all translations as inferior.[174] This assumption led Reuchlin to adopt a highly literalistic word-for-word method of translation designed to lead the reader back to the Hebrew rather than to please the reader's sensibilities.

This sense of the holiness of the language of Scripture, linked explicitly to the identification of Scripture as the revealed Word of God, indeed, the language of God, focused on Christ who is the essential Word, is found also in the work of Levèfre d'Étaples. Rather than arguing a doctrine of *sola Scriptura* like that of the Reformers, Lefèvre held, arguably, to a doctrine of *Christus solus* —Christ alone as the center and meaning of Scripture.[175] At a hermeneutical level, however, this assumption, together with his doctrine that there is a broad internal agreement or *concordantia scripturarum* brought about by the revelatory work of the Spirit in the production of the text, Lefèvre clearly stands in continuity with the development of theological interpretation in the work of the Reformers and the orthodox.[176]

Some comment is therefore in order about the relationship of the doctrine and interpretation of Scripture in the centuries before the Reformation to the Reformation and to Protestant orthodoxy. Several points of broad continuity and specific discontinuity emerge: the doctrine of inspiration, as such, replete with medieval refinements concerning the illumination and elevation of the mind of the

---

1983), p. 218.

[174]Schwarz, *Principles and Problems,* p. 84; cf. Thomas F. Torrance, "The Hermeneutics of John Reuchlin, 1455–1522," in *Church, Word, and Spirit: Historical and Theological Essays in Honor of Geoffrey W. Bromiley,* ed. James E. Bradley and Richard A. Muller (Grand Rapids: Eerdmans, 1987), pp. 107–21.

[175]Cf. Jean–Pierre Massaut, "Lefèvre d'Étaples et l'exégèse au XVIᵉ siècle," in *Revue d'Histoire Ecclésiastique* 78 (1983): 75, with Richard Cameron, "The Charges of Lutheranism Brought Against Jacques Lefèvre d'Etaples (1520–1529)," in *Harvard Theological Review* 63 (1970): 119–49.

[176]Massaut, "Lefèvre d'Étaples et l'exégèse au XVIᵉ siècle," pp. 75, 78.

author would pass over, virtually untouched by revision, into the sixteenth and seventeenth centuries. Similarly, the problem of the canon and of its authority over against tradition and church was mediated to the sixteenth and seventeenth centuries—exacerbated by the opposition of the Tridentine decrees to the Protestant confessions, but with the Protestants finding it necessary to wrestle with the importance of tradition and with its relation as a subsidiary norm and, more important, a bearer of meaning, to the sole prior authority of Scripture. This question of authority was all the more pressing in view of the work of the humanist philologists of the early sixteenth century and their successors: the wedge that they drove between the Vulgate and the Greek and Hebrew texts not only became foundational to the Reformers' revisions of faith and practice, it also sowed the seeds of the major hermeneutical problem of the era of orthodoxy—the maintenance of traditional doctrines in the face of changing views of the text and altered patterns of exegesis. For if, as Bentley has argued, the Reformation in some sense derailed the movement toward pure philology and textual criticism by drawing the study and revision of the text of Scripture into the theological battles of the age, it is also the case that the humanistic interests in philology and criticism grew and expanded toward the great age of text criticism and orientalism that was to come, together with a whole series of new battles between philologists and theologians, in the seventeenth century.[177] Similarly, the drive toward the letter of the text and its grammatical or even grammatical-historical meaning, begun in the twelfth and thirteenth centuries by the Victorines and Thomas Aquinas, reinforced by Nicholas of Lyra and by the exegetes and philologists of the Renaissance, exerted enormous pressure on exegesis and theology in the late sixteenth and seventeenth centuries when the theologians of the orthodox era, unlike the early Renaissance philologists, attempted to carry forward the churchly tradition of theological exegesis as well as the critical labors of the textual scholar. In these several elements of continuity and discontinuity we have encapsulated the problem of Reformation and orthodoxy.

[177]Cf. Bentley, *Humanism and Holy Writ,* pp. 213–19.

2

The Doctrine of Scripture in its Protestant Development:
Documents and Issues from the Beginning of the Reformation to the End of the Seventeenth Century

2.1 Scripture and the Reformation

a. From Luther to Calvin

Although early Reformation view of Scripture arose in the midst of conflict with the churchly tradition of the later Middle Ages, it nonetheless stands in strong continuity with the issues raised in the theological debates of the fourteenth and fifteenth centuries. The late medieval debate over tradition and the late medieval and Renaissance approach to the literal sense of the text of Scripture in its original languages had together raised questions about the relationships between Scripture and churchly theology, between the individual exegete and the text, and between the exegete and established doctrine that looked directly toward the issues and problems addressed by the early Reformers. It is, thus, entirely anachronistic to view the *sola Scriptura* of Luther and his contemporaries as a declaration that all of theology ought to be constructed anew, without reference to the church's tradition of interpretation, by the lonely exegete confronting the naked text. It is equally anachronistic to assume that Scripture functioned for the Reformers like a set of numbered facts or propositions suitable for use as ready-made solutions to any and all questions capable of arising in the course of human history. Both the language of *sola Scriptura* and the actual use of the text of Scripture by the Reformers can be explained only in terms of the questions of authority and interpretation posed by the developments of the late fifteenth and early sixteenth centuries. Even so, close study of the actual exegetical results of the Reformers manifests strong interpretive and doctrinal continuities with the exegetical results of the fathers and the medieval doctors.[1]

This approach to the context of the Reformation view of Scripture also indicates continuity between the medieval conception of Scripture and the high doctrine of the inspiration and authority of Scripture held by the Reformers. Like their medieval predecessors and, indeed, like their Protestant orthodox followers, they affirmed the divine origin of Scripture and its character as infallible rule for theological judgments. But, over against many of the writers of the preceding centuries, the Reformers were in a position to press in a radical way the point of how that scriptural rule functioned in the context of other claims of authority—whether of tradition or churchly *magisterium;* and they pressed the question of exegetical method and hermeneutics on text and doctrine with a consistent emphasis on the problematic character of virtually all of the late medieval exegetical patterns. From the earliest reformatory arguments of Luther and the first of Swiss disputations and theses, the point was made that Scripture judged tradition and church, rather than tradition and church judged Scripture. And, at the same time, the increasingly textual approach of their theology raised rather pointedly the problem of the establishment of churchly dogmas.

Whereas it is certainly true that the Protestant orthodox returned with some emphasis to a churchly, dogmatic, and confessional

---

[1]Cf. James S. Preus, *From Shadow to Promise: Old Testament Interpretation from Augustine to the Young Luther* (Cambridge, Mass.: Harvard University Press, 1969); David C. Steinmetz, *Luther and Staupitz* (Durham, N.C.: Duke University Press, 1981); idem, "John Calvin on Isaiah 6: A Problem in the History of Exegesis," in *Interpretation* 36 (1982):156–70; and Susan E. Schreiner, "Exegesis and Double Justice in Calvin's Sermons on Job," in *Church History* 58 (1989):322–38; on the study and use of Hebrew in the era of the Reformation, see Ludwig Geiger, *Das Studium der Hebräischen Sprache in Deutschland vom Ende des XV. bis zur Mitte des XVI. Jahrhunderts* (Breslau, 1870); also see *The Cambridge History of the Bible: vol. 3, The West from the Reformation to the Present Day,* ed. S. L. Greenslade (Cambridge: Cambridge University Press, 1963); *The Bible in the Sixteenth Century,* ed., with an introduction, by David C. Steinmetz, (Durham, N.C.: Duke University Press, 1990); the relevant sections in Diestel, *Geschichte des Alten Testamentes,* pp. 230–554; and Charles S. Carter, *The Reformers and Holy Scripture* (London, 1928).

model of theology, it is also the case that they retained the Reformers' interest in the text, the original languages, and a literal-grammatical method of exegesis. Indeed, the exegetical works of late sixteenth- and seventeenth-century Protestantism, with the exception of the typological interests characteristic of the federal theology, were increasingly literal, grammatical, text-critical, and less reminiscent of medieval exegetical works than the writings of the Reformers. At the same time, the orthodox retained the high view of inspiration and authority characteristic of both the Middle Ages and the Reformation and continued—in the context of their increasingly literal, grammatical, and text-critical exegesis—to argue for the priority of Scripture in the formulation of Christian doctrine.

Scholarship has generally ignored the continuities between the view of Scripture held during the later Middle Ages and the Reformers' view of Scripture and, by extension, has tended to ignore the way in which both medieval scholastic and Reformation Protestant formulations concerning the character, authority, and interpretation of Scripture combine to produce the later Protestant scholastic doctrine of Scripture. A major exception to this generalization is Seeberg's discerning statement that

> Calvin establishes the authority of the Scriptures partly upon their divine dictation, and partly upon the testimony of the Holy Spirit working through them. Historically considered, he thereby combines the later medieval conception of inspiration with the theory of Luther. Calvin is therefore the author of the so-called inspiration theory of the older [i.e., the Protestant orthodox] dogmaticians.[2]

A similar perception of Calvin's role in the development of orthodoxy is voiced by Wendel, despite his rather different view of Calvin's doctrine of Scripture. The character and impact of the final version of the *Institutes,* Wendel argues, "was indubitably one of the causes of the very rapid rise of a Calvinist orthodoxy, strictly adherent to the formulas of the *Institutes,* which even the later controversies have only with difficulty managed to modify."[3] Whether Calvin ultimately appears as the great mediating figure in the history of the doctrine of Scripture, it is certain that he bears witness to the

[2]Reinhold Seeberg, *Text-book of the History of Doctrines,* trans. Charles E. Hay, 2 vols. (Grand Rapids: Baker Book House, 1977), II:395–96.
[3]François Wendel, *Calvin: The Origins and Development of His Religious Thought,* trans. Philip Mairet (New York: Harper and Row, 1963), p. 122.

continuity of thought between the Middle Ages and the seventeenth century.

The great difficulty in assessing Luther's theology lies not so much in the analysis of what he says on a topic as in what he leaves unsaid about the larger dogmatic structure within which he operates. The wrong approach to this seeming paradox or contradiction—an approach followed by far too many contemporary writers—is to select one of these approaches to Scripture as the "true Luther" and to explain the other away. Rather we must take both sides of the paradox as equally genuine and then proceed to ask just how these rather opposite perspectives that seem mutually exclusive in our own time can in fact belong to the teaching of one theologian in another time. The fact is that Luther—and, indeed, the later writers of the Reformation and the Protestant orthodox of the next century —are not easily wedged into the exegetical, hermeneutical, and doctrinal patterns of the nineteenth and twentieth centuries.[4] Luther retained, for example, a profound tendency toward tropological exegesis, and his interest in Old Testament history was rooted in a sense of the divine work in the history of the world and in Christ as the center or "scope" of all Scripture.[5]

[4]For Luther's views on the interpretation and authority of Scripture, see Julius Köstlin, *The Theology of Luther in Its Historical Development and Inner Harmony,* 2 vols., trans. Charles E. Hay (Philadelphia: Lutheran Publication Society, 1897; repr. St. Louis: Concordia, 1986); Otto Scheel, *Luthers Stellung zur Heiligen Schrift* (Tübingen: J. C. B. Mohr, 1902); Heinrich Bornkamm, *Luther and the Old Testament,* trans. Eric W. and Ruth C. Gritsch (Philadelphia: Fortress, 1969); Kenneth Hagen, *A Theology of Testament in the Young Luther: The Lectures on Hebrews* (Leiden: E. J. Brill, 1974); Brian Gerrish, "Biblical Authority and the Continental Reformation," in *Scottish Journal of Theology* 10 (1957):337–60; J. Theodore Mueller, "Luther and the Bible," in *Inspiration and Interpretation,* ed. John Walvoord (Grand Rapids: Eerdmans, 1957), pp. 87–114; Willem Jan Kooiman, *Luther and the Bible,* trans. John Schmidt (Philadelphia: Muhlenberg Press, 1961); David W. Lotz, "Sola Scriptura: Luther on Authority," in *Interpretation* 35 (1981):258–73; Jaroslav Pelikan, *Luther the Expositor: Luther's Works Companion Volume* (St. Louis: Concordia Publishing House, 1959); Robert D. Preus, "Luther and Biblical Infallibility," in *Inerrancy and the Church,* pp. 99–142; idem, "The View of the Bible Held by the Church: The Early Church through Luther," in *Inerrancy,* pp. 357–82; Michael Reu, *Luther and the Scriptures* (Columbus, Ohio: Wartburg Press, 1944); idem, *Luther's German Bible* (Columbus, Ohio: Lutheran Book Concern, 1934); Pieter A. Verhoef, "Luther and Calvin's Exegetical Library," in *Calvin Theological Journal* 3 (1968):5–20.

[5]Cf. Bornkamm, *Luther and the Old Testament,* pp. 89–114, 199–207, with Heinrich Karpp, "Zur Geschichte der Bibel in der Kirche des 16. und 17.

Luther's teaching concerning Scripture was multifaceted—and we certainly cannot settle contemporary debate over his doctrine in a few paragraphs of survey. Nonetheless, we must recognize in Luther's teaching both a certain continuity and discontinuity with the medieval doctrine of Scripture and, again, both a measure of continuity and discontinuity with the later Protestant doctrine as codified during the era of orthodoxy. On the one hand, Luther's teaching manifests a dynamic, existential encounter with "Word" that defies dogmatic codification and, in addition, an emphasis on the preaching of Christ at the heart of Scripture that gave to Luther a high degree of freedom on such issues as the seeming contradictions in the text of Scripture and the identification of the canonical books. All of this sets Luther and, to a certain extent, other early Reformers, somewhat apart from their more dogmatic predecessors and followers. On the other hand, Luther clearly identifies Scripture itself, in the words of the text, as the authoritative Word of God, making no distinction like that found in the neo-orthodox writers of this century, between Christ alone as Word and Scripture as derived Word or witness to the Word. Of course, like Calvin, Bullinger, and later orthodox thinkers, both Lutheran and Reformed, Luther understood Word as having several referents: the eternal, hypostatic Word; the Word incarnate; and the proclamation of the Gospel. And Luther, equally clearly, can speak of Scripture as free from error.[6]

Gerrish is certainly correct when he notes that these two foundations of biblical authority in Luther's thought—the witness of Scripture to Christ and the inspired, infallible character of the text—ought not to be viewed as contradictory tendencies.[7] It is not accurate, however, to equate Luther's sense of the whole of Scripture as bearing and witnessing to Christ with the Barthian concept of Scripture as a witness to the Word or to revelation.[8] Luther understood all of Scripture to bear witness to Christ precisely because he

Jahrhunderts," in *Theologische Rundschau,* N.F., 40 (1983):132–33; and on the "scope" of Scripture, see below, §3.5.

[6]See Jaroslav Pelikan, *Luther the Expositor: Luther's Works Companion Volume* (St. Louis: Concordia Publishing House, 1959), pp. 48–70; and cf. Rohnert, *Die Inspiration der Heiligen Schrift,* pp. 144–46; with Mueller, "Luther and the Bible," pp. 94–99; Gerrish, "Biblical Authority," pp. 343–44; and Klaas Runia, "The Hermeneutics of the Reformers," in *Calvin Theological Journal* 19 (1984):129–32; and E. Gordon Rupp, "Word and Spirit in the Early Years of the Reformation," in *Archiv für Reformationsgeschichte,* 49 (1958): 13–26.

[7]Gerrish, "Biblical Authority," pp. 344–45.

[8]Cf. Gerrish, "Biblical Authority," p. 342.

viewed Scripture as God's revelatory Word and Christ as the fulfillment of God's revelation. Barth understood Scripture as witness
to Christ because he viewed Christ as the Word and as God's revelation in an ultimate and ultimately restrictive sense and Scripture as
Word only in a derivative sense, and not as revelation. For Barth,
Scripture can be said to *become* God's Word in the event of God
speaking through it to believers concerning the revelation that is
Jesus Christ.[9] The difference between the two perspectives is
frequently overlooked by theologians who would relate the Reformation to neo-orthodoxy and drive a wedge between the Reformation and post-Reformation Protestantism.

The frequently uttered comment that Luther was not a "systematic thinker" cannot, moreover, be allowed to create a barrier to the
study of Luther's thought in relation to later systematic developments or to provide an excuse for avoiding systematic questions. As
Karl Holl long ago argued in refutation of the comment, Luther may
not have presented doctrine in a scholastic or dogmatic manner but
he had an incredible grasp of the interrelationship of theological
ideas—and, in view of this latter characteristic of his thought, ranks
higher as a "systematic" thinker than Calvin or Melanchthon.[10] Even
so, it is a mistake to view as contradictory tendencies in Luther's
thought the contrast between his statements on the infallibility of
Scripture and his relatively open approach to the problem of canon
—as in the case of his frequently noted negative comments on the
Epistle of James. However Luther defined the canon by distinguishing between homologoumena and antilegomena even within the
New Testament, he was nonetheless certain of the infallibility of all
of the books that were in the canon of Scripture.[11]

This point, of course, does not exactly resolve the problem—
since some of the books identified by Luther as antilegomena (and,
therefore, presumably, less than infallible) were viewed by later
Protestantism, both Lutheran and Reformed, as canonical and infallible. We come closer to resolving the seeming paradox of Luther's
position by taking fuller account of his historical context. The affirmation of the infallible and sufficient character of Scripture in the

[9]On Luther, cf. the numerous citations in Reu, *Luther and the Scriptures,*
pp. 49–64, with Barth, *Church Dogmatics,* I/1, pp. 98–140, esp. pp. 123–24,
134–35.

[10]Karl Holl, "Die Rechtfertigungslehre in Luthers Vorlesung über den
Römerbrief mit besonderer Rücksicht auf die Frage der Heilsgewissheit," in
Gesammelte Aufsätze, 3 vols. (Tübingen: J. C. B. Mohr, 1928), I, p. 117, n.2.

[11]Cf. Mueller, "Luther and the Bible," p. 101.

context of a rather loosely defined canon was, as we have already seen, typical of the Middle Ages. Luther was simply holding a view of Scripture that he had inherited and that was, in a historical sense, understandable, prior to the solidification of the canon at the Council of Trent and, subsequently, in the Protestant confessions. It is worth noting that Luther and Cajetan were in substantial agreement on this point.[12] As in the case of the hermeneutical question of the way in which Scripture, as a whole, teaches or conveys Christ, the problem is not so much a difference in the basic doctrine of Scripture as infallible, sufficient, authoritative, and so forth, between Luther and the late sixteenth-century Protestant theologians, as a difference in understanding the text itself and the boundaries of interpretation.

Scholars have often drawn a strong contrast between Zwingli and Luther on the assumption that Luther approached Paul from an Augustinian perspective and Scripture from a Pauline perspective, while Zwingli interpreted the text in a more humanistic fashion, aided by Erasmus and by a greater variety of church fathers.[13] Zwingli, far more than Luther, owed an intellectual debt to Erasmus. Nevertheless, despite this contrast—and despite the similar contrast frequently drawn between Luther the theologian and Zwingli the philosopher—there is good evidence that Zwingli viewed himself as a preacher and an exegete whose primary guide to the interpretation of Scripture was Scripture itself. His theology, moreover, has been shown to have an evangelical and christological focus, to have strong roots in the scholastic past, and to follow typological interpretations of Scripture far more than Erasmus.[14] Zwingli's doctrine of Scripture—or, as it might better be expressed, his view of the power and perspicuity of Scripture as the basis of faith and doctrine—is found in the treatise *De certitudine et claritate verbi Dei* and clearly implied by the use of Scripture in his *De vera et falsa religione*

---

[12]See Westcott, *General Survey of the History of the Canon,* pp. 475–76.

[13]See especially Walther Köhler, *Ulrich Zwingli: Zum Gedächtnis der Zürcher Reformation, 1515–1919* (Zürich, 1919), pp. 45–70, and H. A. Enno van Gelder, *The Two Reformations of the Sixteenth Century* (The Hague: De Graaf, 1961). Cf. Seeberg, *History,* II:307–9.

[14]Jean Rilliet, *Zwingli: Third Man of the Reformation,* trans. H. Knight (Philadelphia: Westminster, 1964), p. 43; and W. P. Stephens, *The Theology of Huldrych Zwingli* (Oxford: Clarendon Press, 1986), pp. 12–17. On Zwingli's tendency toward allegorical and typological exegesis, see Edwin Künzli, "Quellenproblem und mystischer Schriftsinn in Zwinglis Genesis- und Exoduskommentar," *Zwingliana* 9 (1950–51): 185–207, 253–307; and idem, "Zwingli als Ausleger des Alten Testament," in *Huldreich Zwinglis Sämtliche Werke,* ed. Emil Egli, Georg Finsler, et al., 14 vols. (Zürich: Berichthaus, 1959) 14:871–99.

commentarius.[15] Like virtually all of the Reformers, Zwingli spoke
of Scripture as inspired and as given by the dictation of the Spirit.
Scripture therefore is the Word of God and provides an absolute
standard in doctrine that overrules all human words. Nonetheless,
like both Luther and Calvin, Zwingli also noted differences among
the various Gospel accounts and held a doctrine of divine accommodation to human patterns of speech. Although his denial of ultimate
authority to the Apocrypha and the Book of Revelation indicates
some of the fluidity of the canon typical of his time, Zwingli was far
less ready than Luther to create a "canon within the canon."[16]

Zwingli approached the interpretation of Scripture with both a
stress on the immediate context of a passage and the recognition that
the meaning of the more difficult passages was to be gathered from
the larger scope of Scripture and from comparison with other
passages. Similarly, the Old Testament, which received considerable
stress in Zwingli's theology, was to be interpreted in terms of its fulfillment in the New. There is, in other words, a promise-fulfillment
or, as Stephens terms it, a "shadow"-"light" hermeneutic in
Zwingli's theology. This is not to say that Zwingli abandoned the
letter—far from it. He insisted on a mastery of the biblical languages
for the sake of grasping the literal meaning of the text, but he also
recognized that the sense of the text was frequently bound up with
types and figures and, in addition, that the living voice of God in
Scripture directed the text beyond its ancient context toward contemporary meaning in both a moral and a mystical sense.[17] Strong
elements of continuity can be seen, therefore, between Zwingli's
approach to the text and the later Middle Ages—and between it and
later Reformed exegesis as well.

Among Zwingli's early Reformed contemporaries, Martin Bucer
ought to be remembered for his profound interest in the relationship of Scripture and its right exposition to preaching—as argued

[15]Ulrich Zwingli, *De certitudine et claritate verbi dei liber,* vol. 1; trans. as
On the Clarity and Certainty of the Word, in *Zwingli and Bullinger,* trans. and
ed. Geoffrey W. Bromiley (Philadelphia: Westminster, 1953); *De vera et falsa
religione commentarius,* in *Sämtliche Werke,* vol. 3; trans. as *Commentary on
True and False Religion,* ed. Samuel Macauley Jackson and Clarence Nevin
Heller (Philadelphia, 1929; repr. Durham, N.C.: Labyrinth Press, 1981).

[16]Cf. Zwingli, *On the Clarity and Certainty of the Word,* pp. 68–93, with
idem, *Commentary on True and False Religion,* pp. 91, 224, 283, 287; also note
Stephens, *Theology of Zwingli,* pp. 55–57, and Samuel Berger, *La Bible en
seizième siècle; étude sur les origines de la critique* (Paris: Sandoz & Fischbacher, 1879), p. 110.

[17]Stephens, *Theology of Zwingli,* pp. 64–66, 72–75.

eloquently in the *Tetrapolitan Confession*—and for his brief but nonetheless significant treatise on interpretation.[18] The treatise divides into two parts of unequal length. In the first and shorter section of his treatise, Bucer discusses "the books [of the Bible] which ought to be set forth in the church" and the proper order of their exposition: thus, he comments that Matthew, Mark, and Luke ought to receive first consideration, and the Gospel of John ought to be examined only after the study of the history in the first three Evangelists. Next in order, study and preaching ought to emphasize the Epistles to the Romans and the Galatians. After noting specifically the other Pauline epistles and the Acts, Bucer passes to the Old Testament, expressing a preference for Psalms, Deuteronomy, Genesis, and Isaiah, respectively. He concludes that prudence ought to be exercised in the occasional explication of the sacrificial rites in Leviticus and Numbers, the Song of Songs, and the visions of Ezekiel and Zechariah.[19] What follows is a lengthy discussion of rules and patterns of interpretation that proceeds from the most general rules for resolving differences of interpretation, to a critique of allegorical exegesis, to an approach to preaching about Jesus' life and work, to the longest of the subdivisions of the treatise—the discussion of the content of the Pauline epistles as it relates to the preaching and needs of the church.[20]

Zwingli's successor, Heinrich Bullinger, also produced several important treatments of the doctrine of Scripture: his *De scripturae sanctae authoritate, certitudine, firmitate, et absoluta perfectione* (1538), subsequently incorporated into the *Decades,* is one of the earliest Reformed treatises dealing with the subject. Bullinger also composed three works in which he surveyed what his English contemporaries would have termed a "complete body of divinity." The most famous of these is his personal statement of faith, which became the *Confessio Helvetica Posterior.* It was written in 1562

---

[18]Martin Bucer, *Quomodo S. Literae pro Concionibus tractandae sint Instructio,* text, with intro. and trans. by François Wendel and Pierre Scherding, in *Revue d'histoire et de philosophie religieuses* 26 (1946):32–75; on Bucer's methods of interpretation also see Johannes Müller, *Martin Bucers Hermeneutik* (Gütersloh, 1965); and Henri Strohl, "La méthode exégétique des Réformateurs," in *Le problème biblique dans le Protestantisme,* ed. J. Boisset (Paris, 1955).

[19]Bucer, *Quomodo S. literae pro concionibus tractandae sint instructio,* §3–4 (pp. 50–52).

[20]Bucer, *Quomodo S. literae pro concionibus tractandae sint instructio,* §5–19 (pp. 54–74).

but only published in 1566. Next in the order of eminence is the series of sermons commonly called the *Decades,* the first volume of which appeared in 1549. This is by far Bullinger's largest systematic essay. Least known but most interesting from the point of view of order and emphasis is his *Compendium christianae religionis* of 1556.[21] Here Bullinger sets forth a system of doctrine from a covenantal perspective.

Bullinger begins the entire series of *Decades* with a sermon on "The Word of God; the cause of it; and how, and by whom, it was revealed to the world."[22] The second sermon continues this theme, dealing with the hearing of the Word and the fact "that it doth fully teach the whole doctrine of godliness."[23] Next, Bullinger treats of the right exposition of the Word and defines faith as "an assured belief of the mind, whose only stay is upon God and his Word."[24] In continuity with the later *Compendium* and *Confessio,* Bullinger sets forth the objective ground of the doctrines he will subsequently expound. This extended treatment of Scripture as Word parallels the order of Calvin's *Institutio* and would prove normative for later Reformed thought. Bullinger also includes here an element which is absent from his other systematic works: faith as the faculty or capacity of receiving the Word. Thus, in the earliest systematic structure he produced, Bullinger presents Word and faith as the twofold ground of doctrine—the objective and subjective foundations. There is nothing of Christian knowledge that is not "drawn, taught, or ... soundly confirmed ... out of the word of God."[25]

---

[21]Heinrich Bullinger, *Confessio et expositio simplex orthodoxae fidei ...* (Zürich, 1566), text in Schaff, *The Creeds of Christendom,* III:233–306; *Sermonum decades quinque* (Zürich, 1552), trans. as *The Decades of Henry Bullinger,* ed. Thomas Harding, trans. H. I., 4 vols. (Cambridge University Press, 1849–52); *Compendium christianae religionis* (Zürich, 1556), trans. as *Commonplaces of Christian Religion, compendiously written, by Master Henry Bullinger* (London, 1575). On the doctrine of Scripture, Bullinger also wrote *De scripturae sanctae authoritate* (Zürich, 1538); on the relation of the *Decades* to the *Compendium* see Carl Pestalozzi, *Heinrich Bullinger: Leben und ausgewählte Schriften. Nach handschriftlichen und gleichzeitigen Quellen* (Elberfeld: Friedrichs, 1858), pp. 386, 469, and 505ff. Pestalozzi views the *Compendium* as an abridgment of the *Decades.* This certainly is so in view of its content; but Pestalozzi does not do justice to the *Compendium* as an independent essay with its own argumentative integrity.

[22]Bullinger, *Decades,* I.i (p. 36).

[23]Bullinger, *Decades,* I.ii (p. 57).

[24]Bullinger, *Decades,* I.iii and iv (pp. 70, 81).

[25]Bullinger, *Decades,* I.i (p. 36).

In his *Compendium* where, more than in the *Decades,* Bullinger was concerned to show the underlying rationale of the Reformed theology and to manifest the interconnection of doctrines, he devotes the beginning of his second book, "of God and his most excellent works," to an analysis of the transition from the prolegomenon on Scripture to the doctrine of God: in short, he adumbrates the later discussion of the *principia theologiae,* their order and relationship. His argument also parallels very closely Calvin's initial discussion of the true knowledge of God and of man in the *Institutes.*[26] The Scriptures, he begins, have a definite goal and end toward which they "lead the godly reader"—the knowledge of God and of man, "which is unto God's honor and man's salvation."[27] This dictum leads Bullinger to state in brief, the contents of his system and to manifest again the evangelical tone of the whole.[28]

Bullinger's expositions of doctrine manifest both a close attention to the scriptural ground of his formulations and a careful use of the tradition. Bullinger has read the fathers closely. He views their interpretation of doctrine as of greatest importance to Christian doctrine—and he frequently dwells on ancient heresies and their refutation as essential to the understanding of the dynamics of correct doctrinal formulation. The issue of the use and abuse of tradition was, therefore, a basic issue to be dealt with among one's doctrinal presuppositions.[29] Moreover, in all three of his more or less systematic works Bullinger was intent upon demonstrating in both principle and specific doctrinal argument the continuity of the Reformation with the tradition of patristic interpretation and theology and, therefore, the catholicity of the Reformation. To that end he prefaced his *Decades* with an essay on the four general councils of the ancient church and with full quotations of their credal formulations and the rules of faith of several church fathers.[30] Similarly the *Confessio* is prefaced by a quotation from the Imperial edict of A.D. 380—the code of Justinian—which defines orthodoxy and heresy in terms of adherence to and departure from the apostolic faith and the Nicene symbol.[31]

---

[26]Cf. Bullinger, *Decades,* I.i, with John Calvin, *Institutes of the Christian Religion,* ed. John T. McNeill, trans. F. L. Battles, 2 vols. (Philadelphia: Westminster, 1950), I.i.

[27]Bullinger, *Commonplaces,* II.i (fol. 32r–v).

[28]Bullinger, *Commonplaces,* II.i (fol. 32v–33r).

[29]Bullinger, *Decades,* I.viii (pp. 150–51).

[30]Bullinger, *Decades,* I.1 (pp. 12–35).

[31]Schaff, *Creeds,* III:235. Bullinger also includes here, as in the *Decades,*

Calvin, surely the foremost exegete among the major theologians of his generation, devoted considerable space in his *Institutes* to the doctrine of Scripture, its authority and certainty, and he offered a series of comments, largely in his exegetical works, on the interpretation of the text and the relation of the text to Christian doctrine.[32] As in the case of Luther's teaching, Calvin's also has been subjected to close historical and theological scrutiny in recent times, with rather diverse conclusions. Doumergue, Niesel, Reid, and McNeill, for example, can hold Calvin forth as teaching a dynamic doctrine of Scripture in which Christ alone is truly Word and Scripture Word only because it is the revelation of Christ.[33] Studies such as those by Warfield, Dowey, Gerrish, Kantzer, Johnson, and Forstman, however, offer a view of Calvin more in continuity with later Reformed theories of Scripture as Word on grounds of the direct revelatory activity of God, understood in terms of a theory of verbal inspiration.[34] As I hope subsequent discussion will demonstrate, the

the so-called creed of Damascus.

[32]See the discussions of Calvin's method and principles in Hans Joachim Kraus, "Calvin's Exegetical Principles," in *Interpretation* 31 (1977):8–18; T. H. L. Parker, *Calvin's New Testament Commentaries* (Grand Rapids: Eerdmans, 1971); idem, *Calvin's Old Testament Commentaries* (Edinburgh: T. & T. Clark, 1986); Alexandre Ganoczy and Stefan Scheld, *Die Hermeneutik Calvins: Geistesgeschichtliche Voraussetzungen und Grundzüge* (Wiesbaden, 1983); T. H. L. Parker, "Calvin the Exegete: Change and Development," in *Calvinus Ecclesiae Doctor,* Die Referate des Internationalen Kongresses für Calvinforschung vom 25 bis 28 September 1978 in Amsterdam, ed. W. H. Neuser (Kampen, 1978), pp. 33–46; Richard Gamble, *"Brevitas et facilitas:* Toward an Understanding of Calvin's Hermeneutic," in *Westminster Theological Journal* 47 (1985):1–17; idem, "Exposition and Method in Calvin," in *Westminster Theological Journal* 49 (1987):153–65; and on Calvin's interpretation of Romans, see Girardin, *Rhetorique et théologie;* for an examination of his comments on Romans 13:1–7, see David C. Steinmetz, "Calvin and Melanchthon on Romans 13:1–7," in *Ex Auditu* 2 (1986):74–81; and Richard A. Muller, "The Hermeneutics of Promise and Fulfillment in Calvin's Exegesis of the Old Testament Prophecies of the Kingdom," in *The Bible in the Sixteenth Century,* ed., with an introduction, by David C. Steinmetz (Durham, N.C.: Duke University Press, 1990), pp. 67–82.

[33]Emile Doumergue, *Jean Calvin, les hommes et les choses de son temps,* 7 vols. (Lausanne, 1899–1917), IV:70–82; Wilhelm Niesel, *Theology of Calvin,* trans. Harold Knight (London, 1956; repr. Grand Rapids: Baker, 1980), pp. 26–30, 35–37; J. K. S. Reid, *The Authority of Scripture: A Study of Reformation and Post-Reformation Understanding of the Bible* (London: Methuen, 1962), pp. 36–45; John T. McNeill, "The Significance of the Word for Calvin," in *Church History* 28/2 (June 1959):140–45.

[34]Benjamin Breckenridge Warfield, "Calvin's Doctrine of the Knowledge of

dynamic elements in Calvin's doctrine in no way undermine but perhaps even rest on his identification of Scripture as verbally inspired Word of God—and that, although the balance between the dynamic statement of the power of the biblical Word and the dogmatic identification of Scripture as inspired and revelatory Word and, therefore, as the source of doctrinal truths about God, shifted somewhat between the time of Calvin's *Institutes* and the high orthodox era, substantial continuity can be argued in the development of the Reformed doctrine of Scripture.[35]

A similar case for continuity within a developing tradition and in the context of a series of shared problems can be made for Calvin's hermeneutics. With Calvin's work, as with that of his contemporaries, came an increasing movement away from the *quadriga* and the other forms of medieval exegesis and, consequently, an increasing difficulty in establishing the relationship between certain of the traditional *dicta probantia* and the dogmas of the church.[36] Whereas many Protestant exegetes of the sixteenth and seventeenth centuries maintained the older trinitarian and christological patterns for interpreting the Old Testament, Calvin showed himself to be ill at ease with some of the traditional results: Thus he could deny the trinitarian use of the plural of *Elohim* or the story of Abraham's three angelic visitors, and he denied that Psalm 33:6 could be used as a proof of the divinity of the Spirit. He retained, however, the traditional trinitarian intimation in Genesis 1:26, "let us make man," and he accepted the essentialist reading of Exodus 3:14.[37] This erosion

God," in *Calvin and Augustine,* ed. Samuel Craig (Philadelphia: Presbyterian and Reformed, 1956), pp. 60–67; Edward A. Dowey, *The Knowledge of God in Calvin's Theology* (New York: Columbia University Press, 1952), pp. 90–94; Kenneth Kantzer, "Calvin and the Holy Scriptures," in *Inspiration and Interpretation,* ed. John Walvoord (Grand Rapids: Eerdmans, 1957), pp. 115–55; Brian Gerrish, "Biblical Authority and the Continental Reformation," in *Scottish Journal of Theology* 10 (1957):337–60; Robert Clyde Johnson, *Authority in Protestant Theology* (Philadelphia: Westminster, 1959), pp. 49–51; H. J. Forstman, *Word and Spirit: Calvin's Doctrine of Biblical Authority* (Stanford University Press, 1962), pp. 52–60.

[35]Cf. Richard A. Muller, "The Foundation of Calvin's Theology: Scripture as Revealing God's Word," in *Duke Divinity School Review* 44/1 (1979):14–23 with the discussions, below, §4.2.

[36]On the relationship of Calvin's hermeneutics to late medieval and early Reformation patterns, see Richard A. Muller, "The Hermeneutic of Promise and Fulfillment," pp. 68–82.

[37]Cf. Calvin, *Commentary on Genesis,* Gen. 1:1, 26, with 18:2 (CTS, I, pp. 70–71, 92–93); idem, *Harmony of the Four Last Books of Moses,* Ex. 3:14

of the *dicta probantia,* far from being unique to Calvin, was typical of the travail of theology in the sixteenth and seventeenth centuries and was part and parcel of the problem of the authority of Scripture as debated with Roman Catholics and various Radical Reformers during the Reformation and the era of orthodoxy.

Wolfgang Musculus' lengthy analysis of the doctrine of Scripture must be placed together with Calvin's discussions of the doctrine as one of the major treatments belonging to the works of the early codifiers of the Reform. Musculus' doctrine appears not as part of a preliminary discussion but as part of the exposition of the means and dispensation of salvation. The presentation of the doctrine of the covenant leads to discussions of the distinction and unity of the Testaments, grace, incarnation, the gospel, the Scriptures as a whole, the ministry, faith, election, and the *ordo salutis*.[38] Musculus explains this ordering as a result of the fact that "the certainty of the Christian faith" rests on the Old Testament as well as the New, since the gospel of Christ begins in the ancient word of promise.[39] Calvin too had spoken of faith as "une certaine et ferme cognoissance" or, in the more familiar form given in the 1559 *Institutio,* "divinae erga nos benevolentiae firmam certamque cognitionem."[40] Indeed, it has been argued that the concept of "certainty" is central to Calvin's teaching on faith, although the qualifier must be added from the *Institutes,* "as for its certainty, so long as your mind is at war with itself, the Word will be of doubtful and weak authority, or rather of none."[41]

This emphasis on the "certainty" of the faith thus parallels and reflects the discussion of *authoritas,* specifically of the *authoritas sacrae Scripturae,* granting particularly the issue of the internal self-consistency and self-evidencing character of the text raised already by the Reformers in their debates with the Roman Catholics, with the Radical or Spiritual Reformers, and with the rationalists and

---

(CTS, I, pp. 73–74); and idem, *Commentary on the Psalms,* Ps. 33:6 (CTS, I, p. 543).

[38]Wolfgang Musculus, *Loci communes sacrae theologiae* (Basel, 1560; 3d ed., 1573), trans. as *Commonplaces of Christian Religion,* 2d ed. (London, 1578): *Loci communes,* xiv–xxvi (*Commonplaces,* pp. 283–558).

[39]Musculus, *Loci communes,* xxi (*Commonplaces,* p. 349, col. 2).

[40]John Calvin, *Catechisme* (1541), in *CR,* vol. 34, col. 43; cf. Calvin, *Institutes,* III.ii.7.

[41]Heribert Schützeichel, *Die Glaubenstheologie Calvins* (Munich: Max Hueber, 1972), pp. 133–44; cf. Calvin, *Institutes,* III.ii.6.

early Deist thinkers of the sixteenth century.[42] Underlying the question of authority, particularly in view of the magisterial Reformation's emphasis on *sola Scriptura,* lay the question of how this authority is known—if not through the churchly tradition and *magisterium* or the wisdom of the individual exegete or, indeed, the revelation of new truths by the Spirit.[43] This desire for certainty is surely reflected also in the Reformers' recourse to a discussion of evidences of the divine hand in Scripture despite their declarations of the primacy of the *testimonium internum Spiritus Sancti.* (Thus, Calvin's often-cited comments on certainty point out the difficulty, not the resolution, of the question: He affirms, strongly, against Roman Catholic approaches to the problem of authority and certainty that "the testimony of the Spirit is more excellent than all reason" and that "the highest proof of Scripture derives ... from the fact that God in person speaks in it," and that, therefore, Scripture is "self-authenticating." But he then devotes an entire chapter of the 1559 *Institutes*—longer and more detailed than his discussion of the self-authenticating character of the text—to his discussion of rational evidences of the divinity and "credibility" of Scripture.[44] Indeed, Calvin discusses these evidences of divinity at greater length than either Bullinger or Musculus.)

Musculus' doctrine of Scripture, moreover, occupies a place of preeminent importance in the first codification of the teaching of the Reformation. As noted previously,[45] Calvin cannot be viewed as the most influential writer of his generation on all points of doctrine.

---

[42]Cf. the discussions of the problem of skepticism and unbelief in the sixteenth century in Lucien Febvre, *The Problem of Unbelief in the Sixteenth Century: The Religion of Rabelais,* trans. Beatrice Gottlieb (Cambridge, Mass.: Harvard University Press, 1982); Richard H. Popkin, *The History of Scepticism from Erasmus to Spinoza,* 2d ed. (Berkeley: University of California Press, 1979); idem, "Theories of Knowledge," in *The Cambridge History of Renaissance Philosophy,* pp. 668–84; and C. Constantin, "Rationalisme," in *DTC,* vol. 13/2, cols. 1688–1788.

[43]Cf. Musculus, *Loci communes,* xxi, with Bullinger, *Decades,* I (pp. 62, 64, 75) and with Calvin, *Institutes,* I.vii.1–4; IV.viii.5–9.

[44]Calvin, *Institutes,* I.vii.4–5; viii.13. The problem, here, is not unlike that of the *syllogismus practicus,* where Calvin stresses the grounding of assurance in Christ through faith, but still feels constrained to deal with "latter signs" of election: cf. Calvin, *Institutes,* III.xiv.16, 18; xxiv.1–6; and cf. the discussion in Niesel, *Theology of Calvin,* pp. 178–79, with Muller, *Christ and the Decree,* pp. 25–27.

[45]*PRRD,* I, pp. 68–71, 170, 231–33, 252–53; cf. Muller, *Christ and the Decree,* pp. 39, 71–73.

Just as the development of the Reformed doctrine of covenant rests
on the work of other writers, so also do many of the more formal
elements of the doctrine of Scripture. Musculus was trained in the
older theology and its technical statement, as Calvin was not. He
was profoundly aware not only of the biblical norms of the Reformation but also of earlier formulations of the doctrine of Scripture. His
own formulations in the *Loci communes* both draw on the medieval
language of the sufficiency of Scripture and point toward the orthodox or scholastic Reformed teaching, particularly on such issues as
the necessity of a written Word, the identification of that Word as
"scripture"—in a special sense, distinct from other "scriptures"—
and the historical character of the distinction between unwritten and
written Word.[46]

Indeed, the subtopics within Musculus' *locus de Scriptura* are so
clear an indicator of later discussion that they stand directly in the
way of the notion that the orthodox doctrine is in discontinuity with
the teaching of the Reformers. Musculus begins by identifying the
Old Testament as a firm foundation of the Christian faith and, on the
basis of this assumption, discusses the "origin of sacred writings"
(de origine sacrarum scripturarum) with Moses. Next, Musculus
notes the suitability of the division of Scripture into Old and New
Testaments, rules the Apocrypha out of the canon, and makes a
distinction between the homologoumena and antilegomena of the
New Testament. He then passes on to the issue of the prior authority
of the canonical Scriptures over the church's magisterium and over
the writings of the fathers—in what is the longest subsection of his
locus. There follow discussions of the languages of the Scriptures,
of the right of Christians to read and hear the Scriptures, of the right
use of the Scriptures, and "of the truth and fullness of the Holy
Scriptures."[47]

Most contemporary theologians and historians have emphasized
the discontinuity between the dynamic and seemingly "existential"
declarations of the Reformers concerning the Word of God and the
generally static, objective doctrine of the orthodox concerning
Scripture as Word. Although this contrast can be made, and rather
pointedly, when comparing the occasional or homiletical statements
of Luther with the strictly dogmatic argumentation of the Protestant
orthodox, the conclusion of discontinuity drawn from the linguistic
and attitudinal contrast fails to consider either the underlying genetic

[46]See below, §3.2 and §3.3
[47]Musculus, *Loci communes,* xxi.

reasons for the contrast or the nature of the doctrine being stated. In the first place, a dictum concerning the power of the Word stated homiletically or polemically—as is the case with Luther's assertions —will be phrased differently from a statement concerning the nature of Scripture presented in a system of doctrine. The issue of genre is of considerable importance. In the second place, the subjective or "existential" statements of the Reformers concerning the Word ought not to be separated from their objective dogmatic basis—any more than the sometimes lengthy presentations of the objective authority and divinity of Scripture made by the orthodox ought to be separated from their frequent subjective assertions concerning the necessity of the *testimonium internum Spiritus Sancti.*

In other words, the context in which the Reformers wrote and the genre of their writings account easily for the dynamic, "existential," or subjective emphasis of their doctrine of the Word—just as the context of orthodoxy and the genre of orthodox writings, that is, fully developed theological system, in particular, account for their emphasis on the objective authority of the text. Nevertheless, the Reformers assume the objective ground of their pronouncements and the orthodox assume the subjective reality of the impact of the Word alongside of their objective doctrinal declarations. Nowhere do the Reformers reject the long-established tradition of the objective authority of the text and nowhere do the orthodox reject the Reformers' insight into the personal and subjective power of the Word. The problem of the development of the Protestant doctrine of Scripture, therefore, must be framed both in terms of a movement from kerygma to dogma in the thought of the Reformers and their successors and in terms of the long-standing objective dogma of the authority of Scripture in its history from the time of the medieval doctors to the end of the seventeenth century.

In tracing this development, particular attention needs to be given to literary genre. Thus, despite the absence of a doctrine of *sola Scriptura,* the declarations concerning the authority, perfection, soteriological necessity, and redemptive sufficiency of Scripture found in medieval theological *systems* provide significant antecedents for the doctrinal declarations concerning Scripture in Protestant scholastic *systems.* There is a historical continuity of scholastic models and, indeed, a historical continuity in certain instances of the language of theological system. On the other hand, the presence of declarations of *sola Scriptura,* the so-called scriptural principle of Protestantism, in sermons, commentaries, and tracts of the Reformation era does not necessarily make these writings genuine antecedents of Protestant system. Kerygmatic or "existential" pronouncement contributes little to the language of system. At best, we can raise questions concerning the relationship of the implicit doctrinal underpinnings of such pronouncements to the explicitly doctrinal statements of system. The documents of the Reformation era that provide the clearest antecedents of Protestant orthodox system are the explicitly dogmatic and systematic statements of the Reformers, particularly their confessional writings.

The systems and confessions of the Reformation, moreover, must be examined in their proper historical relationship to the theological systems of Protestant orthodoxy. Systematic essays like Calvin's *Institutes,* Bullinger's *Compendium,* and Musculus' *Loci communes* all belong to the early Protestant effort to state the body of Christian doctrine in a Reformation perspective, as resting on the primary foundation of Scripture, over against the doctrinal assumptions of various adversaries—and, as such, belong to a process of systematic development that eventuated in Protestant scholastic system. Indeed, the exegetical method used by Reformers like Bucer and Musculus included a movement from textual study to doctrinal statement in the construction of theological *loci* as a final step in the work of exegesis. These *loci* pointed directly from an exegetically grounded theological formulation to the gathering of doctrinal topics into theological compendia and systems.[48] In a very real sense, the Reformation systems provide the doctrinal basis, though not always the linguistic foundation and only seldom the methodological ground of Protestant scholastic theology. As I have argued elsewhere, there is a strong element of doctrinal continuity between the Reformers and the Protestant scholastics coupled with an equally strong element of methodological continuity between the medieval and the Protestant scholastics—with, however, doctrine affecting method and method affecting doctrine.[49] In addition, the *locus de Scriptura,* like the other *loci* of scholastic system, participates in the alterations of

---

[48]Cf. Robert Kolb, "Teaching the Text: The Commonplace Method in Sixteenth Century Lutheran Biblical Commentary," in *Bibliothèque d'Humanisme et Renaissance* 49 (1987):571–85, with J. N. Bakhuizen Van Den Brink, "Bible and Biblical Theology in the Early Reformation," in *Scottish Journal of Theology* 14 (1961):337–52; 15 (1962):50–65.

[49]Richard A. Muller, *"Vera philosophia cum sacra theologia nusquam pugnat:* Keckerman on Philosophy, Theology, and the Problem of the Double Truth," in *Sixteenth Century Journal* 15/3 (1984):361–65, and idem, "Scholasticism Protestant and Catholic: Francis Turretin on the Object and Principles of Theology," in *Church History* 55/2 (1986):194–95, 200, 204–5.

method and logic that took place during the fifteenth and sixteenth centuries, as witnessed by the *locus* method itself.

Once we have made this set of important distinctions concerning genre and attitude, we are in a position to recognize both the continuity of the scholastic view of Scripture as *principium* of theology from the thirteenth through the seventeenth centuries and the discontinuity in the approach to Scripture between the late Middle Ages and the Reformation. This discontinuity, moreover, can be seen at the root of both the Reformers' kerygmatic appeal to *sola Scriptura* and the Protestant orthodox theologians' massive development of a distinctively Protestant *locus de Scriptura* separate from the prolegomena (where the medieval doctors had placed it) and far more elaborate than the discussions of Scripture available to the orthodox in medieval systems. In other words, some elements of the medieval discussion of the doctrine of Scripture pass over into the Reformation as the doctrinal presuppositions of the teaching of the Reformers while other elements are modified. Those elements of the discussion accepted at a presuppositional level by the Reformers reappeared, virtually unchanged, when Protestantism moved to formulate its own orthodox theological system, while the modifications brought about by the Reformation together with new elements and emphases pressed by the Reformers become formal elements in the orthodox doctrinal synthesis that distinguish it from the patterns already present in the medieval scholastic doctrine of Scripture.

b. The Development of Doctrine in the Reformed Confessions

The great Protestant confessions of the sixteenth century together with the several later and more elaborate confessional documents of the seventeenth century are both a major source of the orthodox Reformed doctrine of Scripture and a highly important ongoing context for the statement and elaboration of that doctrine. On the one hand a fairly direct line of doctrinal development can be drawn from the earliest Reformed confessional statements concerning Scripture through the more expanded discussions of Scripture in works like the *Second Helvetic Confession* to the doctrinal *loci* on Scripture found in the early orthodox systems. On the other hand, the confessions did not pass out of use—so that confessional declarations concerning Scripture form the theological context within which even the late orthodox systematic exposition of the doctrine of Scripture must be understood.

The confessions of the Reformation era stand in a somewhat different relation to Protestant orthodoxy than the systematic essays of the Reformers. In their fundamental intention, confessions transcend individuals and provide ecclesial statement. From the earliest stages of the Reformation, therefore, the confessions provide a source of more objectively stated doctrinal principles and a source of churchly, standardized norms *(norma normata)* within the bounds and under the guidance of which orthodox theological system could develop. In both form and substance the great confessions of the Reformation provide the necessary framework for large-scale, systematic statement of "right teaching." This is particularly true in the case of the doctrine of Scripture, where the confessions, early on in the Reformation, move from declaration of principle to formalized statement. This is, of course, a notable point of contrast between the Lutheran and the Reformed confessions; whereas the latter moved quickly toward the identification of the doctrine of Scripture as a first topic in the confessional body of doctrine, the former maintained the model of the *Augsburg Confession,* where the *sola Scriptura* was assumed but not elaborated. Only with the *Formula of Concord* did the scriptural *principium* appear fully enunciated—and even then not in the detail of the Reformed documents.

In enunciating this scriptural *principium,* the Reformed confessions performed a major dogmatic service for developing Reformed theology. Scripture became the preliminary confessional article for the Reformed before it became the first *locus* of theological system. It provided, in other words, a model for the structural development of system in an age of confessional theology and Protestant orthodoxy. In addition, the confessions effectively established the doctrine of Scripture as a distinct *locus* over against the prolegomena to theological system. The medieval models used by the Protestant orthodox in their reconstruction of dogmatic system and its prolegomena almost invariably discuss Scripture as a topic belonging to the prolegomena themselves: Scripture stood as the primary source of the doctrinal *principia* from which Christian theology was to be constructed. The confessions served to identify Scripture as the sole ground, in dogmatic language, as the *principium unicum* of theology —and to identify the doctrine of Scripture as a topic for dogmatic discussion in its own right.

The Swiss confessional documents moved in this direction early on. Zwingli's *Sixty-Seven Articles* (1523) raises the issue of a *fundamentum* or *centrum theologicum* that we have already noted as an element of several of the later Reformed prolegomena.[50] Zwingli begins by setting the authority of the gospel prior to the authority of the church and by arguing that the sum or foundational message of the gospel is that Christ, the "true Son of God," has accomplished for us the "will of his heavenly Father" and, by his innocence, has redeemed us from death and reconciled us to God.[51] A similar foundational statement that points even more in the direction of a confessional doctrine of Scripture appears in the *Ten Theses of Bern* (1528). There we read that "the holy Christian church, whose sole head is Christ, is born of the Word of God, stands firm in the same, and listens to no alien voice."[52] The issue here, as in Zwingli's principial statement, is one of authority. The authority of the Word stands prior to the authority of church even though—as the debate recognized—the actual canon of Scripture arose after the establishment of the church. In some form, the Word that we now receive from the text was the foundation of the church, calling it into existence. There can, therefore, be no legitimate laws or commands addressed to the church *extra Dei verbum*, nor can there be any authoritative traditions within the church that are not founded directly on the Word.[53]

Also of considerable importance to the early Reformed doctrine of Scripture is the first section of Bucer's *Tetrapolitan Confession*. Here the crucial connection between the authority of the text and the preaching of the Word is explicitly made at a confessional level.

The so-called *First Helvetic Confession* or *Second Confession of Basel* (1536), written by Bullinger, Gryaneus, and Myconius, carries forward this doctrinal and principial stress on Scripture in a manner that is both more formal and more elaborate than the earlier Swiss Reformed confession. The transition from kerygmatic declaration to formal doctrinal *locus* has been made and the confession points directly toward the systematic formulations of the doctrine of Scripture in early orthodoxy. The simple declaration of Scripture as Word of God and foundation of the church and all its teaching has been developed into a series of five topics: a definition of *Scriptura sacra,* the interpretation of Scripture, the relationship of the patristic authors to Scripture, "human traditions," and the "scope" of Scripture *(scopus Scripturae).*[54]

---

[50]*PRRD,* I, pp. 283–84.
[51]*Articuli sive conclusiones* xvii, i–ii, in Schaff, *Creeds,* III, p. 197.
[52]*Theses Bernenses,* i, in Schaff, *Creeds,* III, p. 208.
[53]*Theses Bernenses,* ii, in Schaff, *Creeds,* III, p. 208.
[54]*Confessio Helvetica Prior,* i–v, in Schaff, *Creeds,* III, pp. 211–13; on the

Shortly after the middle of the sixteenth century there was a flowering of Reformed confessional documents. In very short order there
appeared the *Gallican Confession* (1559), the *Scots Confession*
(1560), the *Belgic Confession* (1561), the *Thirty-Nine Articles of the
Church of England* (1563), the *Heidelberg Catechism* (1563), and
the *Second Helvetic Confession* (1566). The catechetical form of the
Heidelberg Catechism did not require an exposition of a doctrine of
Scripture,[55] but the other documents all contain a statement of the
Reformed doctrine of Scripture and, in the cases of the Gallican and
Belgic confessions and the *Thirty-Nine Articles,* a full identification
of the canon of Scripture in response to the Council of Trent.

The *Second Helvetic Confession,* originally a personal confession
and religious testament of Heinrich Bullinger written during an
illness in 1562, contains a lengthy statement of its author's doctrine
of Scripture that is notable not only for its fullness but also for its
religiosity. Bullinger's confession lacks the prepositional character
of the Gallican and Belgic confessions even when it surpasses them
in detail and breadth of exposition. The document begins with a
clear testimony to the identity of Scripture as Word, its inspiration,
and its authority:

> We believe and confess the Canonical Scriptures of the Holy
> prophets and apostles of both Testaments to be the true Word of
> God, and to have sufficient authority of themselves, not of men.
> For God himself spake to the fathers, prophets, apostles, and still
> speaks to us through the Holy Scripture.[56]

One dimension of the early Reformed view that is powerfully maintained here is the sense of the Word as living Word, *viva vox Dei:*

---

scopus Scripturae, see below, §3.5.

[55]The doctrine of Scripture typically does not appear in catechisms—
although it is added to the structure of the Heidelberger in various editions of
Ursinus' lectures. The Westminster catechisms differ because of their clear
intention to follow a dogmatic or systematic rather than a traditional catechetical outline. See Zacharias Ursinus, *Loci theologici,* in *Opera theologica,* ed.
Quirinius Reuter, 3 vols. (Heidelberg, 1612), I, cols. 426–55 as interpolated
and translated in the catechetical lectures: *The Summe of Christian Religion*
(Oxford, 1591), pp. 5–44, and the *Westminster Shorter Catechism* in Schaff,
Creeds, III, p. 676; note the *Larger Catechism* in H. A. Niemeyer, ed., *Collectio
confessionum in ecclesiis reformatis publicatarum* (Leipzig: J. Klinkhardt,
1840), appendix, p. 47.

[56]*Confessio Helvetica Posterior* (in Schaff, *Creeds,* III, pp. 233–306), I.i
(hereinafter, *Conf. helv. post.*).

Scripture is Word because it records and contains the speech of God which still lives in its pages and in the life of the church—in the preaching of the gospel—still addresses us as Word.[57]

This Word of God provides the *universalis Christi ecclesia* with "all things fully expounded which belong to a saving faith, and also to the framing of a life acceptable to God."[58] For this reason, the text itself commands that nothing be taken away and nothing added to its message (cf. Deut. 4:2; Rev. 22:18–19). Scripture, therefore, provides a standard for "true wisdom and piety, the reformation and government of churches, instruction in all duties of piety, and, finally, the confirmation and condemnation of doctrines and the confutation of all errors."[59]

Having presented Scripture as the foundation of Christian faith and practice, Bullinger moves on to what is a virtually unique series of paragraphs in the Reformed confessional literature: the role of the Word preached in the life of the church. When the biblical Word is preached, Bullinger argues, "the Word of God itself is announced and received by the faithful"—or as the marginal summaries given in Niemeyer read, "Scriptura verbum Dei est.... Praedicatio verbi Dei est verbum Dei."[60] No other Word of God is to be expected by Christians and this Word, as preached, is to be regarded as authoritative despite limitations inherent in the means. Echoing Augustine on the sacraments, Bullinger insists that the Word, not the minister, ought to be our proper object: "even if he is evil and a sinner, the Word of God remains nonetheless good and true."[61]

The importance of this relation of Scripture as living Word to preaching, albeit unique in the confessional literature, was not lost on later Reformed dogmaticians. Indeed, Bullinger's discussion of the issue in a confession that enjoyed such broad and continued use in the Reformed churches seems to have guaranteed the dogmatic importance of the topic. The later theological systems remained in contact with the confessional norms and—despite their technical and disputative character—with the life of the church. Both the living character of the inscripturated Word and the importance of lively

---

[57]*Conf. helv. post.,* I.i, cf. iv.

[58]*Conf. helv. post.,* I.ii.

[59]*Conf. helv. post.,* I.iii.

[60]*Conf. helv. post.,* I. See the marginal heading in Niemeyer, *Collectio,* p. 467.

[61]*Conf. helv. post.,* I.4; cf. Augustine, *De baptismo contra Donatistas,* v. 21.29, in *PL* 43, cols. 191–92.

exposition remain topics dealt with in theological system even during the high and late orthodox eras.[62]

Bullinger also takes pains to state that this "outward preaching" should not be opposed to or devalued by a doctrine of the inward illumination of the Spirit. It is true that effective "instruction in true religion" depends on the inward working of the Spirit, but that inward working is usually conjoined with appointed, external means. Thus, the teaching of Paul that "faith comes by hearing, and hearing by the Word of God" (Rom. 10:17), provides a normative statement for Christian practice, despite the possible exception of a purely inward and spiritual work of God. "We recognize," writes Bullinger, "that God can sometimes also illuminate human beings, whomever and whenever he chooses, without an external ministry, for such is his power. We speak, however, of the usual practice of instruction, bestowed on us by God both by commandment and by example."[63] The point draws on the scholastic distinction between absolute and ordained power: *de potentia absoluta* God may work without means, but *de potentia ordinata* God covenants to work through means that he has appointed.

There are several confessions belonging to the era of early orthodoxy—the confession of Frederick III of the Palatinate (1577), the *Consensus ministri Bremensis ecclesiae* (1595), Jerome Zanchi's personal confession (1585), a *Confession of the Reformed Churches in Germany* (1607) prepared by the Heidelberg theologians, the Brandenburg confessions of 1614–15, and the *Irish Articles of Religion* (1615). Of these documents, the confession of Frederick III, the Bremen, Heidelberg, and Brandenburg confessions, say very little of Scripture—far less than the great confessions of the mid-sixteenth century. Frederick simply states that what he believes must be conformable with the prophetic and apostolic writings.[64] Similarly, the Bremen confession points to the prophetic and apostolic writings as the source of true doctrine and the standard to which all human writings and creeds must be subject.[65] The Heidelberg confession of 1607 contains no statement concerning the norm of doctrine.[66] The

[62]See below, §§3.3 and 7.1.

[63]*Conf. helv. post.*, I.7.

[64]*Bekenntnis des Kurfürsten Friedrich III*, in Heinrich Heppe, *Die Bekenntnisschriften der reformierten Kirche Deutschlands, Schriften zur reformierten Theologie,* Band I (Elberfeld: R. L. Friederichs, 1860), p. 4 (hereinafter, Heppe, *BRKD*).

[65]*Consensus ministerii Bremensis,* I, in Heppe, *BRKD*, p. 147.

[66]*Bekenntnis der heidelberger Theologen,* in Heppe, *BRKD*, pp. 250–61.

Brandenburg confessions declare the scriptural norm at several points. It is a foundation of the Christian religion that no one can rightly understand the Word of God apart from the illumination of the Holy Spirit,[67] that true worship of God must be constituted upon the holy Scripture as its *Form und Norm,* and that all of the teachings of the faith must be grounded on the Word of God: "the Scripture alone is the true teacher and master over all writing and teaching on earth."[68] Taken as a group, these confessions do little to advance the doctrine.

Quite different, however, is the case of Zanchi's personal confession and the *Irish Articles of Religion.* Zanchi's work stands out as a finely tooled systematic work, fully as long and well-developed as Bullinger's *Compendium* and far exceeding the detail of most confessions. With these documents, Reformed confessional theology enters the early orthodox era and evidences the beginnings of scholastic Protestantism.[69] Zanchi's confession follows the order of doctrine typical of the later Reformed confessions and of Reformed orthodoxy, moving from a doctrine of Scripture to the doctrine of God. Since God is inaccessible and unknowable, Zanchi writes, he has revealed himself in Christ and in the Scriptures that testify to his work and its fulfillment in Christ.[70] Zanchi also addresses the problem of Scripture and tradition at greater length than is typical of the Reformed confessions: he identifies the church as the place where the Scriptures are known, but he very clearly and forcefully asserts the priority of Scripture over church. The tradition of the church functions as an aid to the interpretation of Scripture but it cannot replace exegesis or stand as the rule of doctrine.[71]

The doctrine of Scripture in the *Irish Articles* is gathered under six heads to which a seventh, on the ecumenical creeds, is subjoined. Like the early orthodox theology that the *Articles* reflect, they maintain a distinction (but no separation) between Scripture and the

[67]*Glaubens Bekenntnis der reformierten Evangelischen Kirchen,* I.ii, in Heppe, *BRKD,* p. 265.

[68]*Bekenntnis des Kurfürst Joh. Sigismund,* in Heppe, *BRKD,* pp. 285–86.

[69]On Zanchi's confession, see Muller, *Christ and the Decree,* pp. 115–21; on the relationship between the *Irish Articles* and the *Westminster Confession* see Schaff, *Creeds,* I, pp. 665, 761–65; Benjamin B. Warfield, *The Westminster Assembly and Its Work* (New York: Oxford University Press, 1931; repr. Grand Rapids: Baker Book House, 1981), pp. 169–75; and Alexander Mitchell, *Minutes of the Westminster Assembly of Divines* (Edinburgh, 1874), pp. xlviff.

[70]Zanchi, *De religione christiana fides,* I.i–ii, in *Operum theologicorum,* 8 vols. (Geneva, 1617), VIII, col. 453ff.

[71]Zanchi, *De religione christiana fides,* I.xii–xiv.

Word of God: "The ground of our religion and the rule of faith and all saving truth is the Word of God, contained in the Holy Scripture."[72] Clearly, no access to the Word is available apart from Scripture—nonetheless Word is the basic category of revelation and Scripture, though inseparable from it, is the vehicle or means by which the revelation is conveyed to the church. The canonical books are "given by the inspiration of God, and in that regard ... of most certain credit and highest authority."[73] The apocryphal books, by way of contrast, "did not proceed from such inspiration, and therefore are not of sufficient authority to establish any point of doctrine." They can be read, however, inasmuch as they contain "many worthy things for example of life and instruction of manners."[74] The *Irish Articles* also continue the pattern established by the Gallican and Belgic confessions by enumerating the books in the canon and the Apocrypha.[75]

The *Articles* also contain a declaration concerning the need to translate Scripture into the vernacular and to exhort all people to read the Scripture "with great humility and reverence" as an instruction in right "knowledge of God" and personal "duty."[76] This is the case because the Bible clearly teaches "all things necessary to salvation" in a way that is suited "to the capacity both of learned and unlearned."[77] In these and the foregoing statements, early Reformed orthodoxy arrived at a model for its dogmatics—a confessional statement paralleling the shape and structure of argument found in the theological systems of writers like Junius, Arminius, Polanus, Trelcatius, and Scharpius, yet stated at a level of detail suitable to a confession. The date of the *Articles,* 1615, is significant in this regard: it follows the early orthodox systematic development and states the results of a ground gained by the dogmaticians. The actual content is little different from that of the Second Helvetic and the Belgic confessions, but it is set forth in a clearer, more prepositional fashion with more emphasis given to the issue of the clarity and sufficiency of Scripture in things necessary to salvation.

In the years intervening between the publication of the *Irish Articles* and the seating of the Westminster Assembly, Reformed

---

[72]*Irish Articles,* I, in Schaff, *Creeds,* III, pp. 526ff.; cf. James Ussher, *A Body of Divinitie* (London, 1670), pp. 6–7.

[73]*Irish Articles,* 2.

[74]*Irish Articles,* 3; cf. Ussher, *A Body of Divinitie,* pp. 14–16.

[75]*Irish Articles,* 2–3.

[76]*Irish Articles,* 4.

[77]*Irish Articles,* 5–6.

theology underwent considerable development. The early orthodox codification of Reformed theology was elaborated both polemically and positively, and the doctrine of Scripture received considerable augmentation in and through the rise of covenant theology and the increased attention brought by that movement to the relation between the two Testaments and related hermeneutical issues. In addition, between the publication of the two confessions the debate over the origin of the vowel points and the implication of their late dating for textual criticism had begun in earnest. Expansion and clarification of the doctrine of Scripture was to be one of the foremost tasks of the *Westminster Confession.*

The *Westminster Confession* (1647), although written with a retrospective glance at the *Thirty-Nine Articles,* most clearly echoes the order and contents of the *Irish Articles.* It represents, in confessional form, the codification into a rule or norm of faith of the ground gained for English Reformed theology by Perkins, Ames, Rollock, Whittaker, and Reynolds and interpreted in the first half of the seventeenth century by Usher, Fisher, Featley, Leigh, and others. Westminster is, undoubtedly, the greatest confessional document written during the age of Protestant scholasticism.[78] It would also provide the basis of fuller systematic theologies in the form of catechetical lectures—following the pattern of the Dutch Reformed meditations on the *Heidelberg Catechism*—such as the systems of Watson and Ridgley.[79]

Records of the Westminster Assembly manifest no great debate over the subject of the first chapter of the proposed confession. Several of the most important predecessors of the confession—both Helvetic confessions, the *Genevan Harmony,* and the *Irish Articles* —as well as many of the major systems of Reformed theology began with a discussion of the source of theology in the Scriptures. The other option, which became increasingly the model for fullscale systems, was to define "theology" and to speak of the knowledge of

[78]Cf. the comments of John T. McNeill, *The History and Character of Calvinism,* p. 325; it is simply a misreading of history to claim that the *Westminster Confession* is not scholastic and that the beginnings of Protestant scholasticism in England can be marked in the slightly later work of John Owen. Scholastic Protestantism was in full flower in England in the time of Perkins, and the *Westminster Confession* is one of its contributions to the Reformed tradition: contra Rogers and McKim, *Interpretation and Authority of Scripture,* pp. 202–3, 218–23.

[79]See Schaff, *Creeds,* I, pp. 701–804; text of the *Westminster Confession,* III, pp. 600–673; of the *Shorter Catechism,* III, pp. 676–704.

God in general before moving on to the scriptural revelation.[80] Westminster does, in fact, note this latter order by commentary on natural knowledge of God briefly by way of showing its insufficiency and pointing to the necessity of the Scriptures. The inability of humanity to attain right knowledge and true worship of God through the light of nature led God to "reveal himself and to declare his will unto his Church."[81]

The confession, like many of the systems we will examine, distinguishes between the direct revelation of God by various means to the faithful in ancient times and the inscripturation of that revelation. Not only continuing "corruption of the flesh, and the malice of Satan and of the world" but also the cessation of immediate revelations necessitated the careful compilation of God's Word. Scripture consists of the books of the Old and New Testaments, "All of which are given by inspiration of God, to be the rule of faith and life."[82] The apocryphal books are to be excluded from this characterization, since they are not "of divine inspiration ... and therefore as of no authority in the Church of God."[83] Westminster enumerates the books in the canon but—in contrast to earlier post-Tridentine Reformed confessions—does not list the apocryphal books by name. The identification of the canonical books as "the Word of God written" maintains the larger sense of "Word of God" found in the earlier confessions, as does the concluding statement of the confession that "the Supreme Judge of all controversies" in religion is "the Holy Spirit speaking in Scripture."[84] The canon and the text of the canon is genuinely Word, but it is also true that Word and Spirit work through Scripture.[85]

Clearly drawing upon the debate between Protestant and Roman

---

[80]E.g., the Gallican (1559) and Belgic (1561) confessions; and note Johannes Wollebius, *Compendium theologiae christianae,* new edition (Neukirchen, 1935); William Ames, *Medulla ss. theologiae* (Amsterdam, 1623; London, 1630); also, *The Marrow of Theology,* trans. with intro. by John Dykstra Eusden (Boston: Pilgrim, 1966; repr. Durham, N.C.: Labyrinth Press, 1984); Lucas Trelcatius, Jr., *Scholastica et methodica locorum communium institutio* (London, 1604) trans. as *A Briefe Institution of the Commonplaces of Sacred Divinitie* (London, 1610); Amandus Polanus von Polansdorf, *Syntagma theologiae christianae* (Geneva, 1617), and idem, *The Substance of the Christian Religion* (London, 1595).

[81]*Westminster Confession,* I.i; in Schaff, *Creeds,* III, pp. 600ff.

[82]*Westminster Confession,* I.i–ii.

[83]*Westminster Confession,* I.iii.

[84]*Westminster Confession,* I.ii–iii, x.

[85]See further, below, §§3.3 and 3.4.

theologians over the role of the church in determining the authority of Scripture, Westminster asserts:

> The authority of the Holy Scripture, for which it ought to be believed and obeyed, dependeth not upon the testimony of any man or church, but wholly upon God (who is truth itself), the Author thereof; and therefore it is to be received, because it is the Word of God.[86]

It is indeed true that the church testifies to the great value of the Scriptures while the style and contents, the scope and consistency, together with the obvious perfection of the Bible testify to its divine origin.

> yet, notwithstanding, our full persuasion and assurance of the infallible truth, and divine authority thereof, is from the inward work of the Holy Spirit, bearing witness by and with the Word in our hearts.[87]

Significant, here, is the reversal of the point made by the *Irish Articles:* the authority of Scripture is not grounded by Westminster on the concept of inspiration but rather on its nature as Word. The Westminster standards, thus, contradict Heppe's thesis that orthodoxy moved away from the Reformation stress on Word toward a view of biblical authority grounded on the doctrine of inspiration.[88] The confession also maintains the Reformers' emphasis on the internal testimony of the Spirit over the external or empirical evidences of the divinity of Scripture.

Having made the basic point concerning the divinity and authority of the canonical Scriptures, the *Westminster Confession* moves on to address the content and the interpretation of the Bible. The sufficiency and fullness of the biblical revelation for the salvation of the world is stated and qualified with more precision and clarity than can be found in any earlier Reformed confession—"The whole counsel of God, concerning all things necessary for his own glory, man's salvation, faith and life, is either expressly set down in Scripture, or by good and necessary consequence may be deduced

[86]*Westminster Confession,* I.iv.

[87]*Westminster Confession,* I.v.

[88]Cf. Heinrich Heppe, *Reformed Dogmatics Set Out and Illustrated from the Sources,* rev. and ed. Ernst Bizer, trans. G. T. Thomson (1950; repr. Grand Rapids: Baker, 1978), pp. 16–17 (hereinafter, Heppe, *RD*).

from Scripture: unto which nothing at any time is to be added, whether by new revelations of the Spirit, or traditions of men."[89] The basic truths of Christianity are, thus, readily available either directly or by inference. Nonetheless, the mere address of reason to the text does not produce salvation, and there are some issues in the life of the church not directly addressed by Scripture. The confession assumes that a "saving understanding" of the Word, as distinct from a historical and rational understanding, rests on the inward illumination of the Spirit, and it acknowledges that issues of worship and church government must be inferred in a general way from Scripture in concert with "the light of nature and Christian precedence."[90] The doctrine of Scripture is thus safeguarded from a wooden rationalism and, in the life of the church, the realm of *adiaphora* is carefully marked out and preserved from a rigoristic biblicism.

The confession also qualifies its doctrine of the sufficiency and fullness of Scripture with the traditional caveat that not all places in Scripture are clear and plain in their meaning. Nonetheless, it continues, all things "necessary to be known, believed, and observed for salvation" are stated clearly if not in one place in Scripture, then in another and are stated so clearly that "not only the learned, but the unlearned, in a due use of ordinary means, may attain unto a sufficient understanding of them."[91] This relationship between the clarity, sufficiency, and fullness of Scripture and the right of laity to own and read translations of the Bible is central to the orthodox Protestant doctrine of Scripture. The declaration of clarity and sufficiency is in fact a declaration of the openness of Scripture to Christians generally set against the Roman Catholic reservation of interpretation to the church hierarchy.

In setting aside the hierarchy and, indeed, the tradition, as norms for the interpretation of Scripture, the *Westminster Confession* declares that Scripture itself is the guide to its own interpretation. This point is implied in the declaration that Scripture is the ultimate norm of doctrine and that it states clearly in one place what is unclear in another, but it had not been stated explicitly in any of the great Reformed confessions prior to Westminster. Here, the hermeneutical principle of the *analogia fidei*, previously developed only in theological systems, attains confessional status. Scripture is the infallible rule of faith and life—and "the infallible rule of inter-

---

[89]*Westminster Confession,* I.vi.
[90]*Westminster Confession,* I.vi.
[91]*Westminster Confession,* I.vii.

pretation of Scripture is the Scripture itself."[92] This pattern for interpretation can be justified, moreover, by the fact that Scripture, governed as it is by "the whole counsel of God," has a single fundamental meaning: its "full sense ... is not manifold but one."[93]

If the Westminster confession argues the necessity of translation and the propriety of the use of Scripture by the unlearned, it also insists upon the priority of the Hebrew and Greek originals of the books of the Bible and ultimately lodges all authority in the text as preserved in the ancient languages. The Hebrew and Greek texts are the "authentic" Scriptures that were "immediately inspired by God, and by his singular care and providence kept pure in all ages."[94] "Final appeal" in all religious controversy, therefore, must be to the text in the original languages rather than to translations. The detail, here, is once again greater than that of previous confessions, but it cannot be claimed that we have entered the realm of dogmatic system. There is no elaboration or discussion distinguishing between "words" *(verba)* and "substance" *(res)* such as appears in the systems of the day and no discussion of the *autographa*.[95] The emphasis of the confession is simply upon the original-language texts currently known to the church.

As John Leith notes in his admirable study of the confession, this first chapter—like all that follow—is remarkably concise and entirely devoid of unnecessary or tendentious argument. We encounter here a simple statement of the contents of the canon of Scripture and no debate on problems of authorship; we find a strong statement of the inspiration and authority of Scripture but no attempt to formulate a particular theory of inspiration.[96] This is a pointed contrast with the *Formula Consensus Helvetica,* which attempted to make normative among the Reformed churches the most rigid of verbal inspiration theories. As with the *Irish Articles,* Westminster marks a formal development of the Reformed doctrine of Scripture without any abandonment of the basic premises of early Reformed doctrine.

The Westminster standards also well illustrate the path of doctrinal exposition taken by Protestant scholasticism, and stand in relation to the confessions of the preceding century much as the

[92]*Westminster Confession,* I.ix.
[93]*Westminster Confession,* cf. I.vi with ix.
[94]*Westminster Confession,* I.viii.
[95]See below, §4.2.
[96]Cf. John H. Leith, *Assembly of Westminster: Reformed Theology in the Making* (Richmond: John Knox Press, 1973), pp. 75–76.

theological systems of the era of orthodoxy stand to the more systematic efforts of the Reformers. The two catechisms of the assembly follow a logical and systematic form based on earlier documents of the scholastic era, notably Ussher's *A Body of Divinity* and, according to some, Wollebius' *Compendium,* which had gone through a series of Latin editions around the time of the assembly and which was translated into English shortly afterward.[97] As for the confession, its reliance on the earlier work of Ussher, its intellectual and spiritual kinship to the theological works of various members of the assembly,[98] and its subsequent elaboration into a large-scale scholastic system, probably by David Dickson, all point to its place at the center of the development of an English Reformed version of Protestant scholastic theology.[99] Indeed, there is little difference in doctrine and perspective between the divines of the Westminster Assembly and their continental Reformed orthodox counterparts.[100]

[97]Johannes Wollebius, *Compendium theologiae* (London, 1642), 47, 48, 54, 55, 57, 61); translated by Alexander Ross as *the Abridgement of Christian Divinity* (London, 1650), 56, 60; and cf. the comments of Schaff, *Creeds,* I, p. 756.

[98]E.g., John Arrowsmith, *Armilla Catechetica; A Chain of Principles: Or, An Orderly Concatenation of Theological Aphorisms and Exercitations* (Cambridge, 1659); William Gouge, *A Short Catechisme* (London, 1615); Thomas Gataker, *A Short Catechism* (London, 1624); William Twisse, *A Brief Catecheticall Exposition* (London, 1645); and idem, *The Scriptures Sufficiency* (London, 1656); and note the *Annotations upon all the Books of the Old and New Testament, Wherein the Text Is Explained, Doubts Resolved, Scriptures Parallelled, and Various Readings Observed. By the Joynt-Labour of certain Learned Divines* ... (London, 1645), compiled by John Ley (the Pentateuch and the four Gospels), William Gouge (1 Kings through Esther), Merle Casaubon (Psalms), Francis Taylor (Proverbs), Edward Reynolds (Ecclesiastes), Smallwood (Song of Solomon), Thomas Gataker (Isaiah, Jeremiah, and Lamentations), Pemberton (Ezekiel, Daniel, and the Minor Prophets, in the first edition), Richardson (Ezekiel, Daniel, and the Minor Prophets, in the second edition), Daniel Featley (the Pauline epistles), John Downame, and J. Reading: Ley, Gouge, Taylor, Reynolds, Gataker, and Featley were members of the Westminster Assembly. The commentary has been referred to as the "Westminster Annotations" or the "Assembly's Annotations" not only because of the number of Westminster divines who participated in its compilation but also because the commentary was, in part, a response to the so-called *Dutch Annotations,* translated by Theodore Haak, and received unfavorably by the assembly. A set of additional annotations, augmenting the second enlarged edition of 1651, was published under the auspices of Parliament in 1658.

[99]David Dickson, *The Summe of Saving Knowledge* (Edinburgh, 1671).

[100]Contra the conclusions of Jack B. Rogers, *Scripture in the Westminster Confession: A Problem of Historical Interpretation for American Presbyterian-*

The *Declaratio thoruniensis* (1645) was one of three confessions produced and read at the Colloquy of Thorn in West Prussia. The other two—a Roman and a Lutheran—never attained great importance in their respective denominations but the Reformed declaration, or as it was more fully titled, *Professio Doctrinae Ecclesiarum Reformatarum in Regno Polaniae,* was adopted as one of the confessional standards of Brandenburg. The *Declaratio* is unique in structure, being divided into a *generalis professio* and a *specialis professio.* Only in the latter part does the divergence in doctrine among Reformed, Lutheran, and Roman receive attention. The *generalis professio* accepts the scriptures of the Old and New Testaments as the sole and sufficient rule of faith. It contains, following the articles on Scripture, the most lengthy discussion of the teachings of the early church, both the councils and the fathers individually, to appear in any confession of the sixteenth and seventeenth centuries. Finally, it accepts the Augsburg *Variata* (1540) and the Polish *Consensus of Sendomir* (1570), in Schaff's words, "as correct statements of the Scripture doctrines, differing in form, but agreeing in essence."[101] The *Declaratio* breathes much the same air as the *Westminster Confession:* it was crafted by Reformed orthodox scholastics and it evidences the form of the doctrine of Scripture and authority taken by the confessional, as distinct from the dogmatic, writings of the mid-seventeenth century.

The *Formula Consensus Helvetica* (1675) is the last of the orthodox Reformed confessions, occupying a place in the Reformed churches similar to the place occupied by Calovius' *Consensus repetitus fidei vere Lutheranae* (1664). It is a late orthodox essay that, in many of its points, steps beyond the bounds usually assigned to confessional documents and elevates fine points of theological system to the level of fundamental articles of the faith. The level of dogmatic detail and the confessional precision indicated in the *Formula* point toward the difficulties encountered by high orthodoxy at

---

ism (Grand Rapids: Eerdmans, 1967), where the author assumes that a priority of faith over reason is characteristic of a Platonic approach and then, without documentation, argues that the continental theologians of the era, as Aristotelians, must have placed reason before faith—as if the relation between faith and reason could be settled by appeal to these broad philosophical perspectives; cf. the far more accurate comments of Schaff in *Creeds,* I, p. 760: "the Westminster Confession sets forth the Calvinistic system in its scholastic maturity.... The confession had the benefit of the Continental theology." And note Warfield, *The Westminster Assembly and Its Work,* pp. 159–69.

[101]Schaff, *Creeds,* I, p. 562; Latin text in Niemeyer, *Collectio,* pp. 669–89.

the end of the seventeenth century. Specifically, the extension of the doctrine of inspiration to the vowel points of the Masoretic Text manifests, if nothing else, the profound trauma experienced by the orthodox theories of the inspiration, interpretation, and authority of Scripture in the face of a rising tide of textual and historical criticism of the Bible. Arguments which, given the state of the problem in the late seventeenth century, would understandably be debated in the pages of theological systems and polemical tracts, have here become confessional issues. Nor ought it to be forgotten that the *Formula,* for all its advocacy of a very strict doctrine of inspiration against the rising tide of text-critical exegesis, did not brand the Saumur theologians heretical, but referred to them as "revered brethren" whose teachings on a limited set of topics were to be disapproved.[102] Thus, the critical Reformed exegesis of the age, even in the view of the *Formula Consensus Helvetica,* remained within the pale of Reformed orthodoxy, albeit uneasily. Neither did the authors of the *Formula* see fit to condemn the Cocceian school or the Cartesians.

The *Formula* begins with a summary statement of the divine gift of the biblical word and its providential preservation:

> God, the supreme Judge, not only took care to have his word, which is the "power of God unto salvation to everyone that believes" (Rom. 1:16), committed to writing by Moses, the Prophets, and the Apostles, but has also watched and cherished it with paternal care ever since it was written up to the present time, so that it could not be corrupted by the craft of Satan or fraud of man.[103]

The position is very similar to the one taken at the beginning of the *Westminster Confession,* although more detailed,[104] and it is little different from statements concerning the gift and preservation of the Scriptures in Reformed dogmatics as early as Calvin's *Institutes* and Bullinger's *Decades.*[105] Nonetheless, when compared to the great Reformed confessions of earlier eras, the *Formula* even here has the appearance more of high orthodox dogmatics than of a confessional document: The point at issue is somewhat removed from churchly piety or root issues that can be identified as necessary articles or

[102]*Formula Consensus Helvetica,* praefatio, in Niemeyer, *Collectio,* p. 730: cf. Schaff, *Creeds,* I, p. 486.
[103]*Formula Consensus Helvetica,* I, in Niemeyer, *Collectio,* p. 730.
[104]Cf. *Westminster Confession,* I.i and above, this section.
[105]Cf. Calvin, *Institutes,* I.vi.2; vii.10; Bullinger, *Decades,* I.i (p. 55).

fundamental articles of the faith.

The purpose of this initial declaration is to give rational or doctrinal foundation to the church's belief that God by "his singular grace and goodness" has given to his church for all time a "sure word of 'prophecy' and 'Holy Scriptures' (2 Tim. 3:15), from which, though heaven and earth perish, 'neither one jot nor one tittle shall pass away' (Matt. 5:18)."[106] This interest in maintaining the integrity of the inspired text in every jot and tittle leads the framers of the *Formula,* in their next canon, to argue the absolute purity of the "Hebrew original of the Old Testament ... not only in its consonants, but in its vowels, either the vowel points themselves, or at least the power of the points, not only in its matter, but in its words inspired of God."[107] This language grows out of the great controversy over the origin of the vowel points—a controversy which seemed to many theologians, both Protestant and Catholic, to raise the specter of an uninspired, human element embedded in the Masoretic Text of the Old Testament as a primary determinant of meaning. If the points were in fact invented by the Masoretes after A.D. 600, then they could hardly be regarded as a necessary, canonical reading of the text. Not only did this leave the Hebrew text open to emendation based on early versions, including the Vulgate, but it also stood in the way of the fundamental juxtaposition demanded by Protestant theology between the biblical norm and the church's tradition of interpretation. If the vowel points were in fact a late invention, then tradition had invaded Scripture![108]

The only way open to the authors of the *Formula Consensus Helvetica,* as far as they were able to determine, was to argue that the "Hebrew original of the Old Testament ... together with the original of the New Testament" were "the sole and complete rule of our faith and life" to which "as to a Lydian stone, all extant versions, oriental and occidental, ought to be applied, and wherever they differ, be conformed."[109] The insistence on the inspiration and integrity of the vowel points meant that even the finest differences of reading between the Masoretic Text and the ancient versions would necessarily be decided by the Masoretic Text. Those who

[106]*Formula Consensus,* I.

[107]*Formula Consensus,* II.

[108]Cf. Richard A. Muller, "The Debate over the Vowel Points and the Crisis in Orthodox Hermeneutics," in *Journal of Medieval and Renaissance Studies* 10/1 (1980): 53–72, with Diestel, *Geschichte,* p. 335; and note the discussion, below, §6.3.

[109]*Formula Consensus,* II.

propose such emendations of the Hebrew "bring the foundation of our faith and its inviolable authority into perilous hazard."[110] Significantly, none of the Reformed confessions, not even the strictly defined *Formula Consensus Helvetica,* saw fit to draw a detailed doctrine of the inspiration of Scripture into the realm of confession. Discussion of the mode or manner of inspiration was left to dogmatic system.

2.2 Developments, Issues, and Documents of the Early Orthodox Era

a. Reformation and Orthodoxy: A Matter of Perspective

The development of the Protestant doctrine of Scripture during the early orthodox era (ca. 1565–1640) was influenced by internal, positive forces of confessional and doctrinal development as well as external, negative forces of polemic, principally with Roman Catholicism. In the former case, the language of the confessions provided a positive ground of formulation, while the success of the Reformation in establishing new ecclesiastical institutions with their own universities and programs of theological education fostered the creation of increasingly formal and elaborate theological systems in which a doctrine of Scripture, along with the other *loci* of Protestant dogmatics, received explicit attention. This side of the development looked back to the well-springs of the Reformation, to the declaration of *sola Scriptura,* and to the tendency, noted in the previous section, of the Reformed confessions to present a doctrine of Scripture. In the latter case, and surely, as important for the content and character of the early orthodox development, the angry debate with Roman Catholic theologians provided a negative and polemical ground of development, according to which the outlines of the major polemical treatises—like Bellarmine's *De verbo Dei*—provided the topics and, sometimes, even the outlines for Protestant dogmatic discussion. It was typical not only of the Protestant polemics of the day but also of many of the early orthodox theological systems to include point for point refutations of the more eminent Roman Catholic treatises.[111]

[110]*Formula Consensus,* III.

[111]Cf., e.g., Johannes Scharpius, *Cursus theologicus in quo controversia omnes de fide dogmatibus hoc seculo exagitate,* 2 vols. (Geneva, 1620), col. 8ff; Trelcatius, *Scholastica methodus,* cap. ii; Festus Hommius, *LXX disputationes theologicae,* 2d ed. (Oxford, 1630), i–vi.

What is more, for all that can be said about the existence and development of a doctrine of Scripture in the Middle Ages and the Reformation, it is clear that the doctrine first came into its own as an independent dogmatic *locus* during the era of early Protestant orthodoxy. The Roman Catholic polemic itself did not arise out of an already extant dogmatic locus but rather took the shape of a negatively argued theological topic in the hands of polemical writers like Bellarmine. Bellarmine's great *De verbo Dei,* thus has no positive analogue in medieval theology apart from subsections of various theological prolegomena, perhaps most notably the prologue to Henry of Ghent's *Summa.* Even so, Protestant responses to the polemic, as they moved toward the inclusion of point for point rebuttal in larger, well-ordered systematic treatises on Scripture, had virtually no formal precedent, either from the Middle Ages or from the Reformation apart from the extended discussion in Calvin's *Institutes* and the short doctrinal expositions that had appeared in the Reformed confessions of the mid-sixteenth century.

In other words, the early orthodox development of an independent *locus de sacra Scriptura* represented in large part the development of a new theological form into which a series of issues and concerns—some deriving from patristic and medieval sources, others from the Protestant Reformation itself or from patristic and medieval sources via the writings of the Reformers, and still others from post-Reformation debate primarily with Roman Catholics—could be placed in an organized and dogmatically convincing manner. Few of the doctrinal statements found in these loci were new, original, or independent of earlier theological arguments, but the idea of the locus itself and of its placement and standing as an independent theological topic immediately following the prolegomena and before the doctrine of God was new to the era of early orthodoxy—as was the identification of Scripture as the *principium unicum cognoscendi theologiae.*[112]

As will be argued at length below, this development of an independent *locus* parallels and supplements the assimilation of a distinctly Protestant approach to the language of theological *principia* present in the first Protestant theological prolegomena. The early orthodox theologians inherited the preliminary discussion of *principia* or foundations of theology from the medieval doctors, but they inherited from the Reformers a principial concentration on Scripture as the sole, ultimate source of teaching about God. The medieval

---

[112]Cf. *PRRD,* I, 9.3, with the discussion below, §3.1.

conception of fundamental doctrines as the *principia theologiae* gave way to a conception of the source of those doctrines as the *principium theologiae* or *principium unicum theologiae*. This transformation of an issue in the prolegomena pointed directly toward the establishment of a discussion of the doctrine of Scripture, the *principium cognoscendi theologiae* after the prolegomena and before the doctrine of God as *principium essendi theologiae*. This development marks the use of scholastic categories not merely as a way of stating clearly and argumentatively a Reformation issue, but as a way of drawing out the implications of that issue for formal theological system, in continuity with the basic teachings of the Reformers but in a manner never envisioned by them.

It has been typical of earlier scholarship to portray the theology of Protestant orthodoxy—and, in particular the doctrine of Scripture—either as a simple development of the theology of the Reformers that can be evaluated by an equally simple comparison with the theology of Luther or Calvin or as a radical distortion of the theology of the Reformation that resulted in a rigid orthodoxy in discontinuity with the theology of the Reformers.[113] As we have seen in the preceding volume—and as should be clear from the foregoing comments about the character of the early orthodox doctrine of Scripture—neither of these approaches to the theology of the Protestant orthodox is particularly fruitful.[114] On the one hand it is clear from the sources that later Protestant theologians intended to state their doctrines as a theological development of the insights of the Reformers: their teaching, generally construed, contains no intentional deviation from the doctrines of the Reformation. On the other hand, the Reformed orthodox theologians, as individuals, felt no particular obligation to duplicate the teaching of one or another individual theologian of the early sixteenth century. If they fail on

[113]E.g., Ernst Bizer, *Frühorthodoxie und Rationalismus* (Zurich: EVZ, 1963); Walter Kickel, *Vernunft und Offenbarung bei Theodor Beza* (Neukirchen: Neukirchner Verlag, 1967); Holmes Rolston III, *John Calvin versus the Westminster Confession* (Richmond: John Knox, 1972); R. T. Kendall, *Calvin and English Calvinism to 1649* (Oxford: Oxford University Press, 1979); J. K. S. Reid, *The Authority of Scripture: A Study of Reformation and Post-Reformation Understanding of the Bible* (London: Methuen, 1962); Jack B. Rogers, *Scripture in the Westminster Confession: A Problem of Historical Interpretation for American Presbyterianism* (Grand Rapids: Eerdmans, 1967); Jack B. Rogers and Donald K. McKim, *The Authority and Interpretation of the Bible: An Historical Approach* (San Francisco: Harper and Row, 1979).

[114]Cf. *PRRD*, I, 2.4–2.5, with Muller, *Christ and the Decree*, pp. 1–14, 79, 95–96, 175–82.

some points to be perfect Calvinians, they also fail to be pure Musculusians, Vermiglians, or Bullingerians. And, indeed, the differences between the formulations of later Reformed theologians and exegetes are often as great and as significant to Reformed theology as are the differences between the formulations offered by the initial codifiers of Reformed theology.

In the case of the doctrine of Scripture, the simple fact of a formal dogmatic *locus* marks a point of difference between the orthodox statement of belief concerning Scripture and the early Reformation statement. Orthodoxy intended, in its systematization of the doctrines of the Reformation, to maintain the substance while altering the form—and, in instances of issues either not fully discussed or not discussed at all by the Reformers, to add new material, in substantial agreement with the teaching of both the Reformers and the Reformed confessions.[115] Beyond this intention, the orthodox also intended to state theology in and for their own time and in a manner suitable to the institutional and intentionally catholic Protestant church, which now claimed all that was good in the tradition of the church for Protestantism.

Nor is it correct to view the orthodox theological systems as identical in their form and content. The shorter compendia—from Ames' *Medulla* and Wollebius' *Compendium* on to later works like Marckius' *Medulla* and *Medulla medullae* and Van Til's *Compendium*—simply line out the doctrine with concern to state no more than basic premises, and even at this level manifest differences in formulation, emphasis, and placement of doctrine. Ames, by way of example, postpones his doctrine of Scripture until he comes to the *loci* concerned with church and ministry.[116] By way of contrast, the larger systematic efforts like Polanus' *Syntagma,* or Maccovius' *Loci communes,* and high orthodox works like Turretin's *Institutio theologicae* or Mastricht's *Theoretico-practica theologia,* include

---

[115]Cf. Richard A. Muller, "The Debate over the Vowel Points and the Crisis in Orthodox Hermeneutics," 53–72; idem, *"Duplex cognitio dei* in the Theology of Early Reformed Orthodoxy," in *Sixteenth Century Journal* 10/2 (1979): 51–61; idem, "Perkins' *A Golden Chaine:* Predestinarian System or Schematized *Ordo Salutis?"* in *Sixteenth Century Journal* 9/1 (1978):69–81; idem, "Scholasticism Protestant and Catholic: Francis Turretin on the Object and Principles of Theology," in *Church History* 55/2 (1986):193–205; and W. Robert Godfrey, "Biblical Authority in the Sixteenth and Seventeenth Centuries: A Question of Transition," in *Scripture and Truth,* ed. D. A. Carson and John D. Woodbridge (Grand Rapids: Zondervan, 1983), pp. 225–43.

[116]Ames, *Medulla theologica,* I.xxxiv.

not only statements of the basic doctrine but elements of the polemic with Rome and, in the cases of Maccovius and Mastricht in particular, elements of hermeneutical discussion paralleling those found in treatises on Scripture and exegesis. In addition, it becomes apparent from both an examination of the more systematic or doctrinal works and a review of exegetical writings, that approaches to exegesis and interpretation varied considerably from writer to writer—with some, like Cartwright, Perkins, Chamier, and the eminent exegete and biblical scholar, Rivetus, following—in evident continuity with Calvin's pronouncements concerning interpretation—a more literal-grammatical approach to the text and others, like Piscator and Cocceius, allowing for a high degree of allegory and arguing a highly typological pattern of biblical interpretation.[117] It is also clear that the orthodox and their theology were neither ignorant of nor immune from the advances and alterations in exegetical method and in hermeneutics that took place during the sixteenth and seventeenth centuries, and that some of the variety and diversity of theological argument arose from variations in exegesis and hermeneutics. This is certainly the case in the distinction between Cocceian federalism and Voetian orthodoxy, where the former rested its theology on typological and allegorical exegesis, strongly rooted in the medieval tradition, while the latter held to a more literal, grammatical pattern of exegesis.

Much of the contemporary discussion of the orthodox Protestant doctrine of Scripture and revelation reflects both a lack of awareness of the variety of formulations and, in addition, a neo-orthodox assessment of the older dogmatics—like Emil Brunner's judgment that the orthodox made a "fatal equation of revelation with the inspiration of Scripture" with the result that, no matter "how much or how little emphasis was laid on a 'general' or 'natural' revelation," "the ecclesiastical doctrine of revelation was and remained identical with her doctrine of Scripture."[118] Instead of viewing revelation as

---

[117]Cf. Diestel, *Geschichte,* p. 380 (on the continuity of later Reformed hermeneutics with Calvin) and p. 531 (on typological exegesis among the federalists) with Muller, "William Perkins and the Protestant Exegetical Tradition," pp. 75, 90, n. 35 and with the discussion below, §§7.2 and 7.3.

[118]Emil Brunner, *Revelation and Reason: The Christian Doctrine of Faith and Knowledge,* trans. Olive Wyon (Philadelphia: Westminster, 1946), p. 7; cf. J. K. S. Reid, *The Authority of Scripture,* p. 86; Brunner's approach to this problem involved what may be called a "fatal" reliance on Heppe and Schmid and a partial understanding of the orthodox materials. See Richard A. Muller, "Christ—the Revelation or the Revealer? Brunner and Reformed Orthodoxy on

"something that happens, the living history of God in His dealings with the human race," orthodoxy identified revelation as "supernaturally revealed doctrine" and the Bible as the sole source of that doctrine.[119] The Reformers, by way of contrast, held a "biblical" view of faith as "obedient trust" and therefore taught an equally biblical view of "revelation ... as God's action in Jesus Christ" but this perception was rapidly "falsified" as Protestantism sought after a doctrinal norm to pose against the papacy.[120] As Reid argues, summarizing Brunner's claims, orthodoxy is characterized by a "neglect" of the "idea of revelation."[121]

The force of this argument, such as it is, arises almost exclusively from the fact that Protestant orthodoxy did not and, of course, historically could not reflect the neo-orthodox interpretation of the Reformation and/or the neo-orthodox view of revelation as "event." The Protestant orthodox systems are certainly not wanting in discussions of revelation—nor do they restrict revelation to Scripture. Not only do they acknowledge the category of natural revelation, they also recognize that revelation can take the form of a direct divine "word" or of a dream or vision. Direct words, dreams, and visions, however, are not ecclesiastically normative in the way that Scripture is.[122] Quite contrary, moreover, to Brunner's and Reid's claim that they equated revelation with inspiration, the Protestant orthodox almost invariably assume the clear distinction, already made by the medieval doctors, between revelation and inspiration.[123] In addition, the orthodox quite clearly recognize that the divine Word spoken to the prophets and incarnate in Christ has the character of an event and was part of a living, sacred history. These events, however, as far as the present church is concerned are not "something that *happens,*" but instead, and necessarily so, *something that happened.* It was, after all the Protestant orthodox who inherited from Melanchthon and Hyperius the idea of a historical series of revelatory moments as

the Doctrine of the Word of God," in *Journal of the Evangelical Theological Society* 26/3 (Sept. 1983):307–19.

[119]Brunner, *Revelation and Reason,* pp. 8–9.

[120]Brunner, *Revelation and Reason,* pp. 10–11.

[121]Reid, *Authority of Scripture,* p. 86.

[122]E.g., Polanus, *Syntagma theol.,* I.x–xi; Francis Turretin, *Instutio theologiae elencticae,* 3 vols. (Geneva, 1679–85; a new edition, Edinburgh, 1847), I.ii.7; II.i.1–6; Benedict Pictet, *Theologia christiana ex puris ss. literarum fontibus hausta* (Geneva, 1696), I.iii.1–5; iv.1–3; Salomon Van Til, *Theologiae utriusque compendium cum naturalis tum revelatae* (Leiden, 1719), I.iii; cf. the discussion below, §§3.2 and 3.3, with *PRRD,* I, 5.1–3.

[123]See above, §1.3 and further, below, §4.2.

a *methodus* for theology and who began to employ the concept of covenant as a structural device in theological system.[124] In the present of the church, both the prophetic Word and the preaching—indeed, the person!—of Christ are mediated by the scriptural testimony: the living biblical Word provides the necessary access to the message of salvation and to the covenantal history in which it is lodged.[125] The orthodox systems, in their discussions of revelation and Scripture, simply gravitate to the form of Word that the church presently possesses, and they discuss that form in terms of its dogmatic use. Treatises on the interpretation of Scripture and sermons written by the same theologians echo the more "dynamic" or "existential" language of the Reformers. And it is certainly the case that *neither* the Reformers *nor* their orthodox successors understood revelation as an "event" or as a "personal encounter." Brunner's and Reid's interpretations of the documents, far from being genuine historical analyses, rest on a theological program of the twentieth century intended to establish a relationship between the Reformation and neo-orthodoxy at the expense of the historical development of Christian doctrine and biblical interpretation.

A virtually identical wedge, based on a dichotomy between kerygma and dogma, is driven between the Reformation and orthodoxy by Diem in his discussion of "the post-Reformation deviation from the unity of Scriptural proclamation to the unity of doctrine."[126] One is left wondering precisely what this "unity of Scriptural proclamation" is—granting, among other things, Luther's famous comments about the problematic character of the Epistle of James; and wondering also why it should bother a twentieth-century theologian, who ought to be aware of the present difficulty of identifying a "unity of the Bible" or a "theology of the Bible," that the orthodox, writing at a time of hermeneutical change pointing increasingly toward modern critical and textual exegesis, should seek the unity of theological thinking in broad doctrinal categories rather than in "proclamation." It is also the case that both the Reformers and the Protestant orthodox would probably question the

[124]Cf. the discussion in *PRRD,* I, pp. 251–67.

[125]See, e.g., Robert Rollock, *A Treatise of Effectual Calling,* (London, 1603); new edition, in *Select Works of Robert Rollock,* ed. William M. Gunn, 2 vols. (Edinburgh, 1844–49), I, pp. 65–66; Turretin, *Inst. theol. elencticae,* I.v.4; II.i.5–6; Petrus van Mastricht, *Theoretico-practica theologia* (Utrecht, 1724), II.i.11, 12, 14, 15.

[126]Hermann Diem, *Dogmatics,* trans. H. Knight (Edinburgh: Oliver & Boyd, 1959), pp. 225–29.

viability of a distinction between the unity of scriptural proclamation and the unity of doctrine—as if it were possible to have the one without the other—and would insist that the unity of Scripture and the unity of the doctrines drawn from it were both grounded on Christ, who is the *scopus* and *fundamentum* of the text considered as a whole.[127]

The underlying problem with all of these statements concerning the character of the Protestant orthodox view of Scripture, a problem most apparent in those treatments where the orthodox doctrine is compared, unfavorably, with the doctrine of the Reformers, is that these statements, whether, Brunner's, or Reid's, or Diem's, tell us more about the theology of their authors than they do about the history of Protestant doctrine. And all of them commit the fallacy of identifying a "Golden Age" of Protestant theology that not only offers historical precedent for their own theology but that also is somehow recoverable in the present. All of them, moreover, seem unwilling to admit the amount of hermeneutical water that has passed under the bridge since the Reformation.[128] The powerfully existential thrust of much of the Reformation language of the *verbum Dei* or, indeed, the *viva vox Dei* speaking in Scripture arose out of a conviction that (despite the loss of the *quadriga* and the various other forms of medieval exegesis as such) the text spoke directly to the *agenda, credenda,* and *speranda* of the contemporary church. By way of contrast, the somewhat less existential character of much of the seventeenth-century language of Scripture as Word arose more from the hermeneutical changes that had taken place than from the "rigid scholasticism" to which the orthodox form of the Protestant doctrine of Scripture is attributed. The farther that hermeneutics moved away from the *quadriga* toward a strict literal, grammatical, linguistic, and contextual analysis of the text itself, the less tenable did the interpretive concept of *viva vox Dei*—and related concepts, like the christological *scopus scripturae*—become. And it was the age of orthodoxy in the seventeenth century that saw the further flowering of textual criticism and of the study of the cognate languages of the Bible. If existential language of the *viva vox Dei* became more difficult to maintain hermeneutically in the seventeenth century, it would become impossible in the eighteenth

[127]See below, §3.5.

[128]Cf. the comments of Marten H. Woudstra, "Calvin Interprets 'What Moses Reports': Observations on Calvin's Commentary on Exodus 1–19," in *Calvin Theological Journal* 21 (1986):157, n. 20.

and nineteenth. Critique of the Protestant orthodox for the (partial!) loss of this dimension of the Reformation view of Scripture amounts to little more than an unrequited and unrequitable theological nostalgia.

In a similar vein, the frequently heard characterization of the orthodox view of Scripture that Protestantism rejected an infallible Roman pope only to replace him with an infallible "paper pope" is, at best, a catchily worded misunderstanding of the history of the doctrine of Scripture. On the one hand, it ignores the continuity of Christian doctrine on the point. Catholic teaching before the Reformation assumed the infallibility of Scripture, as did the Reformers —the Protestant orthodox did not invent the concept. What is more, the catholic teachers of the Middle Ages and of the sixteenth and seventeenth centuries were hardly vociferous in declaring the infallibility of the pope! The issue is really a far more complex one of the interrelationship and ranking of different authorities. Thus, on the other hand, the characterization ignores the crucial role played by tradition and churchly confessions in the formulation of Protestant doctrine. The doctrine of the infallible authority of Scripture, in other words, remained a constant while the framework of interpretation shifted away from a strong emphasis on churchly magisterium and tradition to an equally powerful emphasis on confessional norms and on a more closely defined tradition of interpretation. The central debate was not over the infallibility of Scripture—that was taken for granted by both sides—rather the debate was centered on the question of authority—specifically on the authority of interpretation.

It is also worth noting, particularly in view of the topical approach taken by the larger and more detailed portions of this study, that Reformed orthodoxy, for all that it formulated its theology within relatively clearly marked confessional boundaries, was hardly a monolith. As noted in volume 1, there was considerable variety in the discussions of such issues as the forms taken by knowledge of God or the character of theology as speculative or practical, synthetic or analytic. There was also considerable variety in the organization and exposition of theological system as a whole.[129]

Similarly, within the context of the universal Protestant declaration that Scripture is the infallible rule of faith and practice and the sole norm for Christian doctrine, prior in authority to the church, and so forth, there is considerable variety among the post-Reformation Reformed theologians on such issues as the definition of *analogia*

[129]Cf. *PRRD*, I, 5.3; 6.2–3; 8.1.

fidei, the use of typological and other figurative patterns of interpretation, the extent to which such concepts as the "scope" or "foundation" of Scripture can become definitive of the doctrine of Scripture as a whole, the logic and arrangement of the dogmatic *locus de Scriptura,* and the relationship of the *locus* to the system as a whole —is it part of the prolegomena or is the first *locus* of the system proper? In attempting to redefine the relationship among Reformation and orthodoxy, then, we must not replace the notion of a predestinarian or decretal monolith with the idea of another kind of monolith: the variety within confessional boundaries found in the comparison and contrast among Reformation era thinkers like Calvin, Hyperius, Musculus, Bullinger, and Vermigli is echoed still in the era of scholastic orthodoxy.

And although it may be impossible to identify in detail various "national" styles in theology, it remains the case that the various trajectories of Reformed thought engendered by the Reformation—a French and French-speaking Swiss, a German and German-speaking Swiss, a Dutch, and an English trajectory—all continued to exist and to develop their own confessional identities and theological styles, despite the consistent communication and cross-fertilization of ideas characteristic of Reformed Protestantism. It is one thing, in other words, to recognize characteristics of Reformed orthodoxy in, for example, both Dutch and English theology in the seventeenth century—and quite another not to identify differences, such as the stronger interest of the Dutch Reformed in theological system, the less systematic, more homiletical interest of the English, and the enormous contribution of the English to textual, linguistic, and critical study. English interest in the continental theologians is evidenced by the marginalia of Leigh's *A Body of Divinity* and continental interest in English piety and linguistic scholarship is evidenced by the frequent reference to writers like Perkins, Ames, Whitaker, Rainolds, Gataker, and Willett by continental Reformed theologians and exegetes. By way of example, Gataker's philological works, *De stilo novi instrumenti, De nomine tetragrammato,* the *Opera critica,* and the so-called *Adversaria miscellanea* were renowned in their day. In the first treatise he identified the distinctive style of New Testament Greek in comparison with Classical Greek. In the second he addressed the etymology of the divine name, and was attacked by no less a continental philologist than Louis Cappel, to whom he responded at length.[130] The latter two volumes gathered his many

---

[130]Thomas Gataker, *De nomine tetragrammato dissertatio* (London, 1645);

classical and biblical reflections, the *Opera critica* being a collection
edited by Witsius and published in Leiden in 1698. The rise of
scholastic orthodoxy, as evidenced in the Reformed doctrine of
Scripture, implied, then, not only the large-scale development of
theological system within confessional bounds, but also a highly
variegated attempt to grapple systematically and dogmatically with a
series of textual and interpretive issues some barely touched on by
the Reformers.

b. The Early Orthodox and the Trajectory of Reformed Teaching on Scripture

By the end of the sixteenth century, Reformed theologians had
recognized that, underlying the doctrinal differences separating them
from Rome and from Wittenberg, were a series of hermeneutical
problems. Not only had they recognized these problems, they had
also begun to state them explicitly in treatises on the subjects of
scriptural interpretation and of the means of eliciting doctrinal
determinations or conclusions from Scripture—as they sometimes
identified the problem, of "rightly dividing" the text and its doctrines. The Heidelberg theologians, Ursinus and Zanchius, had paid
particular attention to these issues, Ursinus in the *locus de Scriptura
sacra* that he placed at the head of his fragmentary *Loci theologici*
(later excerpted as part of the "prolegomena" to many editions of his
Doctrinae christianae compendium) and in the series of theses on
holy Scripture contained in his *Miscellanea catechetica,*[131] and
Zanchius in his confession of faith and in his lengthy *Praefatiuncula
in locos communes.*[132]

The ordering and arrangement of Ursinus' catechetical lectures,
as they appear in the earliest editions, before the editorial expansion
that took place at the hands of Paraeus and Reuter, offer insight into
the early orthodox approach to theological system, especially to the
logic of the initial placement of the doctrine of Scripture in the early

and idem, *Dissertatio de tetragrammato suae vindicatio adversus Capellum*
(London, 1652).

[131]Zacharias Ursinus, *Loci theologici,* in *Opera,* I, cols. 426–55; idem, *Doctrinae christianae compendium sive commentarii catechetici* (Neustadt, Leiden,
and Geneva, 1584; Cambridge, 1585); idem, *Miscellanea catechetica, seu
collectio eorum quae catecheticic explicationibus prius sparsa in texta fuerunt*
(Heidelberg, 1612).

[132]Jerome Zanchi, *De religione christiana fides* (Neustadt, 1585); idem,
*Praefatiuncula in locos communes: cum priore loco de sacris Scripturis
agendum sit: & quae methodus servanda,* in *Operum theologicorum,* 8 vols.
(Geneva, 1617), VIII, cols. 297–452.

orthodox system. Of course, the medieval summas and the Reformed confessions both provided precedent for the initial placement of the doctrine—either as a source of *principia* or as the *principium unicum theologiae*—but it was still possible either to omit the doctrine or to give it an alternative placement, as demonstrated by Beza's *Quaestionum et responsionum Christianarum libellus* and the Genevan academy's *Theses theologicae* of 1586, respectively.[133] Ursinus' lectures show very clearly the logic of transition between certain elements of what were to become the prolegomena to theology to the doctrine of Scripture—specifically, between the discussion of religion and the necessity of revelation in Christ and the doctrine of Scripture as a form of divine Word. This transition, already found in Calvin's *Institutes* and Bullinger's *Compendium* and *Decades,* becomes more explicit still in Ursinus' lectures, underlining not only the importance of Scripture to Protestant theology but also the importance of the concept of *religio* at the foundation of Reformed dogmatics.[134]

In his *locus de Scriptura sacra* Ursinus presents a fully developed discussion of the doctrinal identity of Scripture, the scriptural basis of true religion, the priority of Scripture over all human authority including that of the church, the grounds of our acceptance of Scripture as certain—both the internal testimony of the Spirit and the marks of divinity, the authority of Scripture as the necessary and sufficient *regula fidei,* and the right interpretation of Scripture, all in the form of scholastic *quaestiones* that move from basic argument to objections and resolutions. Ursinus provides a clear definition of the *sola Scriptura* of the Reformation as "Scripture alone is worthy of faith *(autopistos)* and the rule of faith." This is so inasmuch as faith "rests on the word alone" and inasmuch as Scripture alone is

---

[133]Theodore Beza, *Quaestionum et responsionum christianarum libellus, in quo praecipua christianae religionis capita kat epitome proponunter* (Geneva, 1570; second part, Geneva, 1576); *Theses theologicae in schola Genevensi ab aliquot sacrarum literarum studiosus sub DD Theod. Beza & Antonio Fayo* (Geneva, 1586) also available as *Propositions and Principles of Divinitie Propounded and Disputed in the University of Geneva under M. Theod. Beza and M. Anthonie Faius.* Translated by John Penry. Edinburgh, 1595.

[134]There are editorial problems with Ursinus' lectures. Numerous alterations were made by his students and followers to fill out the unedited text posthumously. At this particular point in the catechetical lectures, an entire prolegomenon has been added to the form of the catechism either by Ursinus himself or by an editor using materials from another work of Ursinus. The basic point, however, remains unchanged: that Ursinus' lectures, as published, were highly influential on this particular issue in the development of early orthodoxy.

sufficient for salvation. There are, Ursinus comments, degrees or gradations of authority in the community of belief, with the prophets and apostles standing "far superior" to the ministers of the church.[135]

Zanchi's *Praefatiuncula in locos communes* points, in greater detail than Ursinus' two efforts, toward the form and contents of the Protestant orthodox *locus de Scriptura sacra*. It is, moreover, only by comparison with Zanchi's other massive efforts in the realm of theological *loci* that this 155 folio columns in small print begins to merit the diminutive ending provided by its author. Zanchi begins his *Praefatiuncula* by asserting the theological priority of the Scriptures: They are, he comments, to be the first topic treated in theology inasmuch as "the Holy Scriptures are the foundation of all theology, upon which the entire body of Christian doctrine is founded and constructed."[136] Theology rightly consists, Zanchi continues, of the doctrines concerning God taken out of the Word of God—with the result that the problem of our knowledge of God must be dealt with first and foremost in theology, "since neither can God himself be truly and savingly known to us without the Scriptures, which are his word *(sermo),* John 1:18, 'No one has ever seen God: the Son, who is in the bosom of the Father, he has revealed him to us.'"[137] These comments are significant for several reasons. They indicate the continuance of the priority of the epistemological ordering of theology over a fully ontological ordering into the era of early orthodoxy, indeed, in the thought of one of the more important initiators of scholastic Protestantism. They indicate the profound connection registered by the Protestant orthodox between the identity of the second person of the Trinity as Word and the normative character of Scripture as Word. Indeed, Zanchi can identify the humble study of the teachings of God in Scripture with reverent subjection of all thoughts to Christ—granting that the goal of the study of Scripture *(finis Scripturae)* is not merely knowledge but action, both belief in Christ and holy life made possible by Christ.[138] Thus, the *scopus* or center "toward which all the Scriptures tend ... is Jesus Christ."[139] We see here a series of methodological and theological presuppositions that serves to both codify and systematize the Reformers' assumption of the scriptural ground of theology and to

[135]Ursinus, *Loci theologici,* in *Opera,* I, cols. 445–46.
[136]Zanchi, *Praefatiuncula,* col. 319.
[137]Zanchi, *Praefatiuncula,* col. 319.
[138]Cf. Zanchi *Praefatiuncula,* col. 319, with cols. 416 and 418.
[139]Zanchi, *In Mosen et universa Biblia, Prolegomena,* in *Opera,* VIII, col. 16.

carry forward, as methodological principles, central theological concerns of the Reformation.

Matthias Flacius Illyricus' *Clavis scripturae sacrae* (1567) also belongs to the very beginnings of Protestant orthodoxy. And although Flacius was a Lutheran, the treatise is so comprehensive, so generally influential in Protestant circles,[140] and so characteristic of the movement of Protestantism toward its early orthodox synthesis that it deserves mention here. The second part of the treatise, in particular, is crucial for its discussion of the interpretation of Scripture. Flacius argues for the priority and, in most cases, the sole validity of the grammatical meaning of the text as discerned by careful exegesis in the original languages. Multiple meanings are rejected and a figurative or symbolical meaning allowed only when the text itself demands it by failing to make good sense in its literal meaning. In other words, a figurative meaning must be resident in the text itself and not imposed on the text at the whim of the interpreter. Even more important, Flacius recognized that this basic literal or grammatical sense was the sense intended by the original author in addressing his ancient audience in the Hebrew or Greek of the day. This is not, of course, a historical or historical-critical method in exegesis—but it is an exegetical method that roots the meaning of the text in the text itself and in the context provided by the larger framework of the book or passage in which the text appears and by the "purpose of the speaker" of the text.[141]

At the same time—without the sense of contradiction claimed at this point by several modern writers[142]—Flacius argued the unity of Scripture in its doctrinal truth, the absence of genuine contradictions in the text, and the necessity on both the small and the large scale of using Scripture to elucidate Scripture. Not only does Flacius argue the basic exegetical *analogia Scripturae* for the interpretation of difficult or vague passages by means of clear passages dealing with

[140]See Rudolf Keller, *Der Schlüssel zur Schrift, Die Lehre vom Wort Gottes bei Matthias Flacius Illyricus* (Hannover: Luther Verlagshaus, 1984); and Günther Moldaenke, *Schriftverständnis und Schriftdeutung im Zeitalter der Reformation* (Stuttgart, 1936); also note Perkins, *The Art of Prophesying*, in *Workes*, II, p. 669, citing Flacius; and cf. Breward, "Life and Theology of William Perkins," p. 47.

[141]Matthias Flacius Illyricus, *Clavis scripturae seu de sermone sacrorum literarum, plurimas generales regulas continentis* (Wittenberg, 1567; repr. Leipzig, 1965), II, cols. 72, 82–83; cf. Kümmel, *History*, pp. 27–29, with Berger, *La Bible au seizième siècle*, pp. 169–74.

[142]Cf. Kümmel, *History*, pp. 29–30.

the same subject, he also argues an extended *analogia fidei:* "Every understanding and exposition of Scripture is to be in agreement with the faith.... For everything that is said concerning Scripture or on the basis of Scripture must be in agreement with all that the catechism declares or that is taught by the articles of the faith."[143] Flacius, in other words, understands Scripture as the *norma normans theologiae* and the creeds and confessional writings of the church as *norma normata:* the creeds and confessions express the contents and general theological sense of Scripture and, this being the case, any interpretation that differs from that offered in the creeds and confessions must be a denial of the true sense of Scripture.

Clearly, the interest in the grammar of the text and in the textual and historical context of particular passages registered by Flacius' *Clavis* has little to do with modern historical-critical understanding. Rather it sprang from the earlier Renaissance and Reformation desire to move away from the patterns of medieval exegesis toward more grammatically and linguistically controlled interpretation, while (as Flacius' comments on the *analogia Scripturae* and *analogia fidei* make obvious) at the same time respecting the positive relationship between the teaching of Scripture and the doctrine of the church.

This relationship between the teaching of Scripture and the doctrine of the church, in connection with the problem of authority, was the great burden of early Protestant orthodoxy as it strove to create a distinctively Protestant and yet thoroughly catholic dogmatics for the church at the end of the sixteenth century. Since, moreover, the relationship, as it had existed in the pre-Reformation church from the time of the fathers to the late fifteenth century, had depended on particular patterns of interpretation now being set aside, the comments of Flacius and his contemporaries concerning the central meaning or "scope" of Scripture and the relationship between Scripture and the new, eminently biblical confessions of Protestantism point not only toward the central work but also toward the central problem confronted by orthodoxy. The balance indicated by Flacius between grammatical and historical exegesis and the confessional documents of the church would become harder and harder to maintain during the course of the seventeenth century.

The development of the early orthodox doctrine of Scripture also owed much to Martin Chemnitz' vast and masterful *Examination of the Council of Trent* (1565–73). Of fundamental importance to the

---

[143]Flacius, *Clavis,* as cited in Kümmel, *History,* p. 30.

formation of Lutheran orthodoxy, Chemnitz' treatise provides a crystallization of Protestant theology at a level of detail and technical expertise virtually unequaled in its time. Only Zanchi is his equal. Chemnitz' work is certainly the most impressive Protestant refutation of Trent and, as such, one of the preeminent polemical sources for the "elenctical" elements of the relevant *loci* in subsequent Protestant dogmatic systems. The importance of Chemnitz' work to the Reformed as well as the Lutheran orthodox can be inferred from the readiness of Reformed writers of the late sixteenth and early seventeenth centuries not only to draw in its arguments with polite and often glowing acknowledgment, but also to single out Chemnitz for defense against the attacks and rebuttals of Bellarmine and others.[144] In particular, the Reformed gravitated toward Chemnitz' refutation of the third and fourth sessions of Trent in which the issue of traditional, churchly and biblical authority, had been addressed.

A similarly influential work, from the Reformed side, respected and consistently used by Protestant theologians on the Continent throughout the era of orthodoxy was William Whitaker's *Disputatio de sacra scriptura* (1588).[145] Whitaker's treatise singles out two of the most eminent Roman Catholic polemicists—Bellarmine and Stapleton—for lengthy refutation and refers to numerous other thinkers and documents, from the canons of the Council of Trent to the work of the "Rhemists," to Melchior Cano's dogmatic and polemical writings. The importance of Whitaker's work to the Protestant cause, signaled by the posthumous publication of his works in Geneva in 1610 in two large folio volumes, surely stems from his grasp of arguments, sources, and materials. The *Disputatio* evidences a detailed and broad knowledge of patristic, some medieval, and a vast array of sixteenth-century works. Whitaker was particularly adept, like Fulke before him, at turning the Roman Catholic stress on tradition against itself by finding patristic views

[144]Cf. John Rainolds, *The Summe of the Conference between Iohn Rainolds and Iohn Hart: Touching the Head and Faith of the Church. Wherein are handled sundry points, of the sufficiency and right expounding of the Scriptures, the ministrie of the church* ... (London, 1598), p. 29; William Whitaker, *A Disputation on Holy Scripture, against the Papists, especially Bellarmine and Stapleton*. trans. and ed. by William Fitzgerald (Cambridge: Cambridge University Press, 1849), pp. 380, 511.

[145]I have followed the Parker Society edition: William Whitaker, *A Disputation on Holy Scripture, against the Papists, especially Bellarmine and Stapleton* (1849).

contradictory to the claims of late sixteenth-century Roman Catholic theology.[146] Whitaker is also notable for his reading and defense of earlier Protestant writers like Calvin, as well as eminent Lutheran thinkers like Brenz and Chemnitz against Roman Catholic attack.[147]

Whitaker demonstrates a grasp of the text-critical work of biblical scholars and linguists, both Protestant and Catholic. He can, for example, not only cite Roman Catholic biblical scholars like Erasmus and Arias Montanus with approval, but also—with obvious irony—bring their conclusions to bear in defense of Protestantism against Catholic polemicists and dogmaticians. It is, surely, one of the great ironies of early orthodox theological debate that the hermeneutical and confessional changes of the sixteenth century were such that early sixteenth-century Roman Catholic scholars could be found to disagree with post-Tridentine theological teachings and that the Reformers could at times be cited against their own successors, as on such problems as the dating and emendation of the vowel points in the Masoretic Text of the Old Testament.

Whitaker also addresses a series of more strictly dogmatic topics in his *Disputatio,* all of which would be integrated directly into the Reformed orthodox system. He argues, first and foremost, the question of the canon of Scripture and the identification of the number of canonical books to the exclusion of the Apocrypha. This question was, of course, by Whitaker's time, already a confessional issue[148] —so that his argument represents a defense of a point that was a positive element in early Protestant orthodox system by reason of the dogmatic conclusions of the second generation of Reformers. A similar statement may be made concerning Whitaker's second and fifth topics—the authority and interpretation of Scripture—which had received basic positive doctrinal statement in several major Reformed confessions.[149] Whitaker's other topics—the authentic editions and versions, the perspicuity, and the perfection of Scripture —were more a part of the polemic than of the initial and confessional formulation of positive doctrine. In both cases, however, the

[146]Cf., e.g., Whitaker, *Disputation,* pp. 370–79, 393–400.

[147]Cf., e.g., Whitaker, *Disputation,* pp. 277 (Bullinger and Calvin), pp. 340–50 (defending Calvin against Stapleton), p. 351 (Musculus), pp. 380–82 (defending Luther, Brenz, Chemnitz, and "the Lutherans" generally), and pp. 385, 511, 514 (using Brenz).

[148]Cf. above, §1.4 and note *Thirty-Nine Articles,* vi–vii; *Confessio Gallicana,* iii–iv; *Confession Belgica,* iv–vi; *Confessio Helvetica posterior,* i.

[149]*Confession Helvetica prior,* i–ii; *Confessio Helvetica posterior,* i–ii; *Confessio Belgica,* vii.

detail of Whitaker's arguments (and of the arguments of his Protestant contemporaries) passed over into theological system, providing both new substance for extant *loci* and, as polemic passed over into positive doctrine, new *loci* or divisions of *loci*. As late as the publication of Mastricht's *Theoretico-practica theologia* (1714), Whitaker's *Disputation* was recognized as a definitive work.[150]

Beyond the issue of the development of the formal dogmatic *locus de Scriptura Sacra,* there is the related issue of the development of Protestant hermeneutics, of a distinctly Protestant exegetical tradition, and of the field of critical linguistic study. Concurrent with the development of the doctrinal *locus* both positively and polemically, the Protestant approach to Scripture itself changed during the era of early orthodoxy and would change still more during the high orthodox era. Polemical defense of the text reflected, however, the massive positive effort of the early orthodox writers to produce both a definitive, critically acceptable text of Scripture based on the best of the extant codices and a definitive interpretation of the whole of Scripture by carefully comparing text with text and by interpreting the obscure passages in the light of related but clearly stated texts. Oriental studies brought to Protestantism a stronger sense of the importance of collateral languages to the establishment and interpretation of the text—while textual study, spurred on by the Protestant assumption of the radical priority of the literal-grammatical meaning and of the interpretation of difficult passages by the *analogia Scripturae,* yielded consistently better texts.

On the technical and textual side of this effort stood Beza's *Annotationes in Novum Testamentum,* Tremellius' original Latin translation based on a study of Hebrew and Syriac codices, the Stephanus Polyglott of 1569, the highly learned albeit polemical *Confutation of the Rhemists* by Thomas Cartwright, and de Dieu's several critical works collected posthumously under the title *Critica sacra,* in which the author's skills as an orientalist were brought to bear on the text.[151] Beza's *Annotationes,* in particular, provided Protestants of the late sixteenth and seventeenth centuries with a

---

[150]Cf. Mastricht, *Theoretico-practica theol.,* I.ii.9; cf. the use of Whitaker's *Disputation* in Johannes Maccovius, *Loci communes theologici* (Amsterdam, 1658), III (pp. 21, 22)

[151]Thomas Cartwright, *A Confutation of the rhemists Translation, Glosses, and Annotations on the New Testament* (Leiden, 1618); Ludovicus de Dieu, *Critica sacra sive animadversiones in loca quaedam difficiliora Veteris et Novi Testamenti* (Amsterdam, 1693). The annotations on the Old Testament were published originally in 1636, those on the New Testament in 1648.

detailed collation of codices and a careful comparison of translations of the New Testament. And although Beza was far less interested than Calvin in problems of the authorship of books like Hebrews, 2 Peter, and 2 John, his textual work achieved a high critical standard.[152] Commentaries like Ainsworth's annotations on the Pentateuch and the Psalms and Willet's series of "hexapla" on Genesis, Exodus, Leviticus, Daniel, and Romans offered a painstaking approach to the work of translation and comment by way of comparison of texts and collation of ancient versions.[153] On the more popular side are works like Diodati's *Pious and Learned Annotations upon the Holy Bible* and Tossanus' *Biblia ... mit ... ausgegangenen Glossen und Auslegungen.*[154] Continuity with the work of previous ages can be noted in a formal way in Tossanus' work, which follows typographically the pattern of the medieval glosses and of the sixteenth-century printings of the *Glossa ordinaria* with Lyra's *Postilla.*

The exegetical methods of the early orthodox period are as varied as those of the Reformation—ranging from brief theological and linguistic annotation as in the works of Beza, Ainsworth, Tossanus, Diodati, the writers of the so-called Dutch *Annotations,*[155] Gataker

---

[152]Theodore Beza, *Jesu Christi Nostri Novum Testamentum, sine Novum Foedus, cuius Graeco contextui respondent interpretationes duae.... eiusdem Theod. Bezae annotationes* (Cambridge, 1642); the first edition was published in 1556, a second in 1565, and a thoroughly revised third edition in 1580 and 1589, and a fourth edition in 1598, this latter being reprinted as the Cambridge edition in 1642; cf. the somewhat disparaging comments on Beza's discussions of authorship in Berger, *La Bible au seizième siècle,* pp. 133–35.

[153]Henry Ainsworth, *Annotations upon the Five Books of Moses, the Book of Psalms, and the Song of Songs,* 7 vols. (London, 1626–27); also, idem, *The Book of Psalmes: Englished both in Prose and Metre. With Annotations, opening the Words and Sentences, by Conference with Other Scriptures* (Amsterdam, 1612); Andrew Willet, *Hexapla in Genesin* (Cambridge, 1605; 2d ed., enlarged, 1608); *Hexapla in Exodum* (London, 1608); *Hexapla in Leviticum* (London, 1631); *Hexapla in Danielem* (Cambridge, 1610); *Hexapla: That is, a Six Fold Commentarie upon the Epistle to the Romans* (Cambridge, 1620).

[154]Jean Diodati, *Pious and Learned Annotations upon the Holy Bible, plainly Expounding the Most Difficult Places Thereof,* 2d ed. (London, 1648); Paulus Tossanus, *Biblia, das ist die gantze Heilige Schrifft durch D. Martin Luther verteutscht: mit D. Pauli Tossani hiebevor ausgegangenen Glossen und Auslegungen,* 4 vols. (Frankfurt, 1668).

[155]A work compiled by order of the Synod of Dort: *The Dutch Annotations upon the Whole Bible: Or, All the holy canonical Scriptures of the Old and New Testament ... as ... appointed by the Synod of Dort, 1618, and published by authority, 1637,* trans. Theodore Haak, 2 vols. (London, 1657).

and the other compilers of Westminster *Annotations*, Christopher Cartwright, and the authors collected in the famous *Critici Sacri* of 1660;[156] to extended theological commentary, often immersed in the tradition of exegesis and interpretation, evidenced by such writers as Daneau, Perkins, Piscator, Marlorat, Davenant, Mayer, and Downham;[157] to commentaries combining textual, grammatical, and theological interests as evidenced in the works of Willet; to logical analyses of biblical books, like those produced by Piscator and Temple.[158] Not only is there variety and, in the variety, no clearly

[156]Cf. Gataker's annotations on Isaiah, Jeremiah, and Lamentations in *Annotations upon all the Books of the Old and New Testament, wherein the Text is Explained, Doubts Resolved, Scriptures Parallelled, and Various Readings observed. By the Joynt-Labour of certain Learned Divines* ... (London, 1645); Christopher Cartwright, *Electa thargumico-rabbinica; sive Annotationes in Genesin* (London, 1648) and *Electa thargumico-rabbinica; sive Annotationes in Exodum* (London, 1658); *Critici Sacri: sive doctissimorum virorum in SS. Biblia annotationes, & tractatus,* 9 vols. (London, 1660).

[157]Lambert Daneau, *A Fruitfull Commentarie upon the Twelve small Prophets* (Cambridge, 1594); William Perkins, *A Commentarie or Exposition upon the Five first Chapters of the Epistle to the Galatians: With the Continuation of the Commentary Upon the Sixth Chapter* (Cambridge, 1604); idem, *An Exposition Upon Christs Sermon in the Mount* (Cambridge, 1608); idem, *A Clowd of Faithfull Witnesses ... a Commentarie Upon the Eleventh Chapter to the Hebrews* with *A Commentarie Upon Part of the Twelfth Chapter to the Hebrews* (Cambridge, 1607); Johannes Piscator, *Commentarii in omnes libros Novi Testamenti* (Herborn, 1613; 1658); Augustin Marlorat, *A Catholike and Ecclesiasticall Exposition of the Holy Gospell after S. Matthew* (London, 1570); idem, *A Catholike and Ecclesiasticall Exposition of the Holy Gospell after S. Iohn* (London, 1575); idem, *A Catholike and Ecclesiasticall Exposition of St. Marke and Luke* (London, 1583); idem, *A Catholike Exposition upon the Revelation of Sainct Iohn* (London, 1574); John Davenant, *Expositio epistolae ad Colossenses* (Cambridge, 1627); John Mayer, *A Commentary upon all the Prophets both Great and Small: wherein the divers Translations and Expositions both Literal and Mystical of all the most famous Commentators both Ancient and Modern are propounded* (London, 1652); idem, *A Commentarie upon the New Testament. Representing the divers expositions thereof, out of the workes of the most learned, both ancient Fathers, and moderne Writers,* 3 vols. (London, 1631); John Downham, *Lectures upon the Foure First Chapters of Hosea* (London, 1608).

[158]Johannes Piscator, *Analysis logica evangelii secundum Lucam* (London, 1596); idem, *Analysis logica evangelii secundum Marcum* (London, 1595); idem, *Analysis logica evangelii secundum Mattheum* (London, 1594); idem, *Analysis logica in epistolarum Pauli* (London, 1591); idem, *Analysis logica libri S. Lucae qui inscribitur Acta Apostolorum* (London, 1597); idem, *Analysis logica septem epistolarum apostolicarum* (London, 1593); William Temple, *A Logicall Analysis of Twentie Select Psalms* (London, 1605; Latin ed., 1611).

identifiable tendency toward the "dogmatic exegesis" with which the age is typically associated, there is also, in those commentaries that emphasized philological and linguistic issues, a concern for language, criticism, and the establishment of text that looks to the concerns of Renaissance exegetes like Reuchlin, Valla, and Erasmus as much as it does to the work of the Reformers. Ainsworth's approach to translation and annotation, for example, draws more on what Schwarz has called the "philological view" of Reuchlin than it does on the "inspirational view" of Luther—although in its doctrinal aspects, Ainsworth merges philological with traditionary, particularly rabbinic, concerns.[159] In addition, the linguistic skills of the commentators have, in many cases, gone far beyond those of the early humanists. Whereas Hebrew was initially a language in which it was difficult to obtain instruction, the exegetes of the early orthodox era assumed its availability and moved on to Aramaic, Syriac, Arabic, and Persian.[160]

The relationship between exegetical and textual study, polemics, the doctrine of Scripture, and the formulation of Christian doctrine that is evidenced in Whitaker's *Disputation* remained characteristic of Protestant orthodox theology, as did the "locus method" of theological construction found in the doctrinal works of Musculus and Zanchi. Considerable continuity between exegesis, theology, and piety can be observed in a comparison of the works written by the Westminster divines, the *Westminster Confession* and catechisms, and the *Annotations upon all the Books of the Old and New Testament* compiled by members of the assembly and several others. The work of high orthodox theologians like Johannes Marckius and Petrus van Mastricht illustrates the point well: Marckius' several compendia of dogmatics all cite texts heavily, not in the sense of an uncritical prooftexting, but rather following a life-work of detailed

---

[159]Cf. Schwarz, *Principles and Problems of Biblical Interpretation,* pp. 71–76, 169–72; and note the discussion in Richard A. Muller, "Henry Ainsworth and the Development of Protestant Exegesis in the Seventeenth Century," in Henry Ainsworth, *The Book of Psalms,* ed. Gerald T. Sheppard, *Pilgrim Classic Commentaries,* vol. 5 (New York: Pilgrim Press, 1993).

[160]Cf. Ainsworth, *Psalmes,* preface, fol. 2 verso on the use of the Chaldee Paraphrase; and N. B. Johannes Buxtorf, *Manuale Hebraicum et Chaldaicum* (Basel, 1602); idem, *Lexicon Hebraicae et Chaldaicae* (Basel, 1607); and idem., *Biblic Hebraica cum paraphr. Chaldaicum et commentarius rabbinorum,* 4 vols. (Basel, 1618–19); Jacob Golius, *Lexicon Arabico-Latinum contextum ex probatioribus orientis lexicographis* (Leiden, 1653); Ludovicus de Dieu, *Rudimenta linguae persicae* (Leiden, 1639); cf. Diestel, *Geschichte des Alten Testamentes,* pp. 443–50.

exegesis of text;[161] van Mastricht's entire system follows a pattern of careful exegesis of *loci classici* prior to the statement of dogmatic conclusions.[162] It becomes quite impossible to argue, as one recent writer has done, that there was "a tendency within later Calvinism to treat theology and scriptural exegesis as unrelated matters,"[163] given the extent of the evidence to the contrary. What can be noted, however, in accord with the foregoing discussion of polemic surrounding the doctrine of Scripture is the increasing pressure placed on traditional dogmatics, throughout the late sixteenth and seventeenth centuries, by polemics and by the changing patterns of text criticism, exegesis, and hermeneutics.[164] In addition, there may be noted a distinction quite similar to that made by Calvin, in the preface to his *Institutes,* between the work of the commentator and the development of "dogmatic disputations"—with a difference or an appearance of discontinuity being caused by the rise of full theological system and the resulting difference in literary genre between a work like the *Institutes* and, for example, Polanus' *Syntagma theologiae.*

Franciscus Junius of Leiden also plays a crucial role in the development of the Reformed doctrine of Scripture, much as he did in the creation of Reformed theological prolegomena. Although most of the basic doctrinal issues had already been stated by the time that Junius wrote his *Theses theologicae* (ca. 1584–92), it was Junius who gave the doctrine clear scholastic form and who neatly divided the preliminary discussions in theology into the prolegomena and *locus de Scriptura* and then divided both topics into carefully ordered theses. Junius applied to the discussion of Scripture the same interest in efficient, material, formal, and final causality that he had used as a heuristic device in his *De vera theologia,* imparting a clarity of arrangement and order to the *locus.* The topics chosen by Junius for his exposition, taken from both the positive resources of the Reformers and the confessions and the debates of his immediate

---

[161]Johannes Marckius, *Christianae theologiae medulla didactico elenctica* (Amsterdam, 1690); idem, *Compendium theologiae christianae didactico-elencticum* (Groeningen, 1686).

[162]Cf., e.g., Mastricht, *Theoretico-practica theol.,* I.ii, *De Scriptura,* beginning with an examination of 2 Tim. 3:16–17 ("All Scripture is given by inspiration of God...") with idem, II.ii, *De existentia et cognitione Dei,* beginning with an exegesis of Heb. 11:6 ("But without faith it is impossible to please him: for he that cometh to God must believe that he is..."). On the problem of *dicta probantia,* see below, §7.3c.

[163]Alister McGrath, *A Life of John Calvin: A Study in the Shaping of Western Culture* (Oxford: Blackwell, 1990), p. 298, n. 2.

[164]Cf. Diestel, *Geschichte des Alten Testamentes,* pp. 475–76.

predecessors, moreover, continued to be with some minor rearrangement, the basic topics of the *locus:* Scripture considered causally, the authority of Scripture, the perfection of Scripture as Word, the problem of traditions, and the attributes of Scripture.[165] If these topics are not new with Junius—they have roots in the thought of Calvin, Bullinger, and Ursinus and in the Reformed confessional tradition—the methodological care with which they are enunciated, defined, and arranged is a distinct development.

The Protestant orthodox system does frame its statements about Scripture differently—more dogmatically, more technically, and in more strictly defined terms—than the Reformers' writings, but this element of discontinuity must be understood in the larger context of a development of the terminology of theological system in which the confessions and doctrinal writings of the Reformation had an enormous impact. The Protestant scholastics took hold of the medieval systematic models but altered their definitions and structures significantly on the basis of the arguments of the Reformers. They were also pressed, far more than in either the prolegomena or the *locus de Deo* to deal with an intense polemic with Roman Catholic theologians, most notably with Robert Bellarmine, over the doctrine of Scripture in its relation to the question of authority in the church.

The contents of the early orthodox Protestant *loci de scriptura sacra* vary from system to system, with some, like Polanus' *Syntagma theologiae* offering a highly detailed outline with a fine division of topics, and others, like Scharpius' *Cursus theologicus* or Walaeus' *Loci theologici* following a more abbreviated order. Maccovius' *Loci communes* emphasizes the instrumental causality of Scripture and interpretation and the problem of the two Testaments, law, and gospel, whereas the famous Leiden *Synopsis purioris theologiae* balances nicely the dogmatic and hermeneutical concerns of the early orthodox. In all cases, however, the underlying issues addressed are the nature, canonical identity, authority, and interpretation of Scripture—frequently with direct reference to the alternative views of Roman Catholic opponents. Scharpius, by way of example, develops a very brief prolegomena, with scarcely a hint of controversy, and then proceeds to a lengthy, almost entirely controversial, doctrine of Scripture, posed almost exclusively against Bellarmine's *De verbo Dei.* Scharpius distinguishes ten basic contro-

---

[165]Cf. Junius, *Theses theologicae leydenses,* II–VI; *Theses theologicae heidelbergenses,* II–X in *Opuscula theologica selecta,* ed. Abraham Kuyper (Amsterdam: F. Muller, 1882).

versies that are to be treated in the Protestant doctrine of Scripture: 1. the canon; 2. the authentic editions; 3. the versions; 4. the right to read Scripture; 5. the public use of Scripture; 6. the authority of Scripture; 7. the perspicuity of Scripture; 8. right interpretation; 9. the necessity of Scripture; 10. the perfection of Scripture against unwritten traditions.[166] A similar, but more elaborate pattern is found in Rollock's *A Treatise of Effectual Calling,* where the author develops a full doctrine of Scripture against Bellarmine, enumerating ten "controversies" to be dealt with in the establishment of the Protestant position on the nature and character of Scripture. These are, Rollock indicates, "essential" controversies in the sense that they "concern the very essence ... or being of Scripture":

> The first is, "Whether the Scripture, prophetical and apostolical, be the word of God?" The second is, "How may it appear that this Scripture is God's word?" The third is "Of the antiquity of it." The fourth is "Of the perspicuity and clearness of it." The fifth is, Of the simplicity or plainness of it." The sixth is, "Of the vivacity, quickening power or life of it." The seventh is, "Of the simple and evident necessity of it." The eighth is, "Of the perfection and sufficiency thereof, that it is sufficient and perfect in itself, without all unwritten verities or traditions whatsoever." The ninth is, "Whether Scripture may be the judge to determine all controversies?" The tenth is "Whether the Scriptures, prophetical and apostolical must have the chief place of excellency, and be in authority above the church?"[167]

To his discussion of these "controversies" Rollock appends several chapters that not only complete a survey of the debated or controverted points between Protestants and Roman Catholics but that also round out the topics typically included in the Protestant orthodox doctrine of Scripture: the problem of the canon; the "authentic edition" of Scripture; the use and value of translations; public reading of Scripture; and, finally, the use of Scripture by the laity.[168]

Rollock also makes a distinction between the "essence" and the attributes or "properties" of Scripture that was of considerable importance to the order and arrangement of the Protestant orthodox discussion of the doctrine of Scripture:

---

[166]Scharpius, *Cursus theologicus,* col. 8.
[167]Rollock, *A Treatise of Effectual Calling,* ch. vii (pp. 63–64).
[168]Rollock, *A Treatise of Effectual Calling,* chs. xvii–xxii.

As for those eight controversies which follow the two first, they are touching the properties *(proprietas)* of the Holy Scripture; and these, when we shall have proved that Scripture is God's word, will appear evidently, for they are necessary consequents of that theorem. For we grant this, that Scripture is God's word, then these things must follow necessarily; first, that it is most ancient; secondly, most clear; thirdly, most simple and pure; fourthly, most powerful; fifthly, most necessary; sixthly, most perfect; seventhly, the greatest and best judge of all controversies without exception; eighthly, most excellent. But forasmuch as our adversaries deny these eight properties (as is aforesaid) there is of every one of them a special controversy.[169]

The influence of polemics on system is easily seen from the fact that these topics of the polemic were taken over directly into the *locus de Scriptura*. Rollock, even more than Scharpius, provides a view of the logic of early orthodoxy in its development of an objective approach to the authority of Scripture based upon the nature of Scripture as divine Word, given by inspiration, and self-evidencing. The objective authority of the text rather than the subjective authority of its witness to the individual becomes the fundamental premise of the doctrine inasmuch as a subjectivizing approach was not only unsuitable to the argument with Rome but, in addition, altogether too much like the claims of a normative inner light found among the radicals of the Reformation era. The Protestant orthodox claim of an ultimate normative status for Scripture, more formally stated than the Reformers' similar claim, echoed the Reformers in its assumption that God had taken the human words of the text and used them in such a way that they had become his words.[170] The derivation of "properties," not without its parallels among the Reformers, is in the main a formalization resting on the polemic—where, for example, against the Roman Catholic claim of the unclarity of the text and the necessity of a churchly magisterium the orthodox argued an inherent perspicuity; or against the claim of a necessary collateral tradition, the orthodox—echoing both a great number of medieval doctors as well as the Reformers—could argue the sufficiency of Scripture.[171] In addition, the inviolability and integrity of the text itself became, largely due to Roman Catholic polemic against the purity of the text—a doctrinal as well as a text-critical issue.[172]

[169]Rollock, *A Treatise of Effectual Calling,* p. 64.
[170]See below, §4.2.
[171]See below, §5.3–5.4.
[172]See below, §§5.3, 6.2, and 6.3.

Thus, a major, positive system like Polanus' *Syntagma theologiae* begins its *locus de Scriptura* with a definition of the forms of "Word" and then, having identified Scripture as Word, proceeds to a discussion of the divinity of Scripture. This Polanus follows with a discussion of the relative authority of Scripture and church, a definition of the canonical authority of Scripture, and a discussion of the books in the normative canon. He then moves on to deal with the necessity, the authentic editions, and the translations of Scripture; the right of laity to read Scripture; the perspicuity, interpretation, and perfection of Scripture; and, finally, the problem of unwritten traditions.[173] The order represents a slight rationalization of the arrangement of the polemic—but it still manifests the outlines of Bellarmine's *De verbo Dei*. What Polanus has done, by way of positive systematization, is to draw together the issues of the identity of Scripture as Word and the divinity of Scripture, the issues of authority, canon, necessity, and authentic editions, and then, on the basis of those principial discussions, he passes on to the related issues of translation, reading, perspicuity, and interpretation—where the nature of the text, even as translated, makes possible the salvific study by laity. Then, finally, he juxtaposes the perfection of the text in all things necessary to salvation with the imperfection of unwritten traditions. The result is a fairly cohesive *locus,* related to both the concerns of the Reformers and the development of Reformed polemic against Rome.

If most of the orthodox chose to consider Scripture as the *principium cognoscendi* and as the major topic of the formal systematic prolegomena, there were certain exceptions to this rule which illustrate other dimensions of the doctrine of Scripture. Rollock felt so strongly that the principal attribute of Scripture as Word was its efficacy that he placed his doctrine of Scripture prior to his treatment of effectual calling. Both Ames and the Beza-Faius *theses theologicae* consider Word, together with the sacraments, under the doctrine of the church. Together with varieties in structure, organization, and topical emphasis, these variations in placement offer evidence that the Reformed theology of the early orthodox era was—contrary to the impression often given in discussions of Protestant orthodoxy—no theological monolith.

It is also important to recognize both the hermeneutical interest of dogmatics and the dogmatic nature of Protestant hermeneutics evidenced by the parallels between the *locus de Scriptura Sacra* in

---

[173]Polanus, *Syntagma theol.,* synopsis Lib. I.

the early orthodox systems and the structure and contents of introductions to the study of the Bible like Andreas Rivetus' *Isagoge, seu
introductio generalis, ad Scripturam Sacram V. & N.T.,* Weemes'
The Christian Synagogue and *Exercitations Divine,* and Salomon
Glassius' *Philologia sacra.*[174] Rivetus' work stands strongly in the
tradition of Calvin's emphasis on the clarity of the grammatical
meaning of the text and against any excessive attempt to distinguish
a "spiritual" from the "literal" meaning of the text. Indeed, Rivetus
argued against the use of typological interpretations in the Old
Testament on the ground that the historical sense of the text was
thereby endangered—although he did allow a typological reading of
select messianic Psalms.[175] Weemes' studies combine the interest in
Judaica characteristic of the age and a strongly textual approach to
exegesis and interpretation with a clear interest in the movement
from exegesis to doctrinal formulation.

Glassius' *Philologia sacra* combines the task of offering a historical and text-critical introduction to the Bible with the task of providing the outline of a hermeneutics. Glassius' linguistic proficiency
and balanced exegesis were broadly respected, and he is frequently
cited as an authority by the Reformed although, confessionally, he
was an orthodox Lutheran. If the irenic and nondoctrinaire tone of
his work has led scholars to view Glassius as a transitional figure
between "the old orthodoxy and the pietism of Spener,"[176] it is also
to be recognized that many of the orthodox, Lutheran and Reformed
alike, could match Spener in warmth of piety and that if Glassius'
approach, like that of Rivetus, breaks with the modern stereotype of
a rigid, dry orthodoxy, it is more likely that the stereotype lacks
justification than that Glassius and others like him should be placed
outside the bounds of "old orthodoxy."[177]

---

[174]Andreas Rivetus, *Isagoge, seu introductio generalis, ad Scripturam
Sacram V. & N.T.,* in *Opera theologicorum* (Rotterdam, 1651–60), II, pp. 841–
1040; John Weemes, *The Christian Synagogue, wherein is contained the
diverse reading, the right poynting, translation and collation of Scripture with
Scripture* (London, 1623; 2d ed., 1633); and idem, *Exercitations Divine. Containing diverse Questions and Solutions for the right understanding of the
Scriptures. Proving the necessitie, majestie, integritie, perspicuitie, and sense
thereof* (London, 1632); Salomon Glassius' *Philologia sacra* (Jena, 1625).

[175]Cf. Rivetus, *Isagoge,* xiv.17, with Diestel, *Geschichte,* pp. 380, 422.

[176]Friedrich A. G. Tholuck, "Glassius, Salomo," s.v. in *RED*.

[177]Cf. the popularization of portions of Glassius' work in Benjamin Keach,
Tropologia: A Key to Open Scripture Metaphors, 3 parts (London, 1682); on
Keach and his use of Glassius, see Donald R. Dickson, "The Complex-
ities of Biblical Typology in the Seventeenth Century," in *Renaissance and*

Orthodoxy did provide Protestantism with an increasingly lengthy and detailed doctrine of Scripture that maintained the fundamental principles of the Reformers in an increasingly technical and scholastic form. The orthodox firmly maintained Reformation era assumptions: the authority of Scripture stands prior to that of tradition and church; this authority rests on the work of God whose Word and Spirit both ground the authority of the text and presently witness through the text rendering it *autopistos,* capable in and by itself of belief; Scripture is, of itself, sufficient in its revelation for the salvation of the church; and all other authority in doctrine, whether that of creed and confession or of tradition or of the church in the present, derives from and is to be tested by Scripture. On all of these topics, whether those instigated by polemic or those brought about by text-critical study, increase of detail and development of full-scale system bred formalization—but the doctrine itself, as will be shown at length in subsequent chapters, was substantially unchanged from the teaching set forth by Calvin and his contemporaries.

Continuity with the theology of the Reformers was maintained on the central issue of the foundation of authority in faith and in practice. Specifically, the orthodox writers maintained the balance established by the Reformers between the declaration of the objective value of Scripture as Word and the confession of the subjective work of the Spirit necessary for the faithful apprehension of the scriptural Word. Thus the orthodox systems elaborate at length on the divinely given contents of Scripture and on the various historical evidences of the divine work in the production of Scripture, but they insist, at the same time, that all such objective evidence cannot bring about faith if the same Spirit who worked in the prophets and apostles in the production of Scripture does not also testify to his work in the hearts and minds of the faithful.[178]

It is also the case that the positive confessional development contributed a somewhat different set of topics to the scholastic Protestant doctrine of Scripture than were provided in the development of

---

Reformation/Renaissance et Réforme, n.s. 3 (1987):253–72.

[178]Cf. Calvin, *Institutes,* I.vii.4–5; viii.1–13, with Wollebius, *Compendium,* praecognita, viii–ix; Polanus, *Syntagma theol.,* Synopsis libri I; Antionis Walaeus, *Loci communes s. theologiae,* in *Opera omnia* (Leiden, 1643), II (p. 126, col. 2); *Synopsis purioris theologiae, disputationibus quinquaginta duabus comprehensa ac conscripta per Johannem Polyandrum, Andream Rivetum, Antonium Walaeum, Antonium Thysium* (1626), ed. H. Bavinck, 6th ed. (Leiden: Donner, 1881), II.xxxi; and see the discussion, below, §4.3

polemics. The topics of authority and interpretation, which we have already identified as the central issues addressed by the theology of the Reformation, belong to both polemics and positive doctrine. Discussions of the necessity of revelation, of the character of Scripture as Word of God, of the inspiration of Scripture, and of the marks of divinity in Scripture were less a part of debate than of the general churchly confession concerning Scripture —and they tend, therefore, to be absent from or of diminished emphasis in polemical treatises. Discussion of the canon, of the authentic editions and versions, and of attributes like perfection and perspicuity, however, lay at the heart of the debate and were developed polemically before their large-scale positive exposition in dogmatics. Subsidiary issues like the priority of an unwritten to the written Word, particularly as they touch on questions of the tradition and its relation to Scripture, tend to link together the two sets of issues, the positive and the polemical, and to facilitate in the early seventeenth century the creation of a cohesive *locus de Scriptura* covering all of the topics. Reformed orthodox theologians also accepted the confessional conclusions of the second-generation Reformers concerning the canon of Scripture and elaborated those conclusions largely in the context of detailed polemic against Rome. Early orthodox theology, in other words, did not create a theory of the canon but maintained the theory set forth by Calvin, Bullinger, Musculus, Vermigli, de Bres, and other contributors to the Reformed confessional codification.[179]

The problem of the canon—defined as including the Apocrypha by the Council of Trent and as excluding the Apocrypha by the Protestant confessions—became a major issue for the early orthodox not because their teaching on the issue was any different from that of the generation of Calvin and Bullinger, but because the confessional shift away from the late medieval and early Reformation perspective that occurred in the generation of Calvin and Bullinger in response to Trent raised an issue well-suited to the polemics of the age. Alteration of the canon, as all theologians of the time recognized, was a trademark of heresy since the time of the early church. The question was, who had altered the canon!

Gregory Martin, one of the "readers in Divinity in the English College of Rhemes (Rheims)" and a principal translator of the Rheims New Testament, argued that heretics generally "abused" the Bible in order to argue and propagate their errors and that these abuses could be reduced to five basic problems, all of which could

---

[179]Cf. Reuss, *History of the Canon,* p. 343.

be identified in the Protestant approach to Scripture. Heretics deny individual books of the Bible or parts of books: the Alogoi rejected the Gospel of John while Marcion removed materials from the Gospel of Luke and the Pauline epistles. Similarly, heretics deny the authority of certain books.[180] Heretics also "expound the scripture after their own private conceit and fantasy, not according to the approved sense of the holy ancient fathers and catholic church."[181] Not content with erroneous exposition, heretics will also "alter the very original text of the holy scripture, by adding, taking away, or changing it ... for their purpose," or make "false translations ... for the maintenance of error and heresy."[182]

It is not important, at this point, to elaborate the Protestant orthodox answers to these accusations, but only to note their importance for the negative development of the Protestant doctrine of Scripture. The first and second accusations—denial of books or parts of books and denial of the authority of certain books—led directly to the clear identification by Protestants of the canon of Scripture and to a confessional and dogmatic exclusion of the Apocrypha.[183] The third accusation—arbitrary interpretation of Scripture—led to the statement of rules of interpretation and the relation of Scripture to tradition, coupled frequently with attacks on the arbitrary nature of the allegorical method practiced by the fathers and the medieval doctors.[184] The fourth and fifth accusations—alteration of original texts and production of false translations—led to a doctrinal interest in the Hebrew and Greek texts of Scripture and in the relation of the authority of the originals to the authority of translations.[185]

Protestants became sharply aware of the relationship between such issues and progress in linguistic study when, early in the seventeenth century, Louis Cappel raised both the issue of the late origin of the vowel points and the related methodological premise of the correction of the Masoretic Text on the basis of ancient versions.[186] The doctrinal implications of his work were explosive,

---

[180]Martin, *A Discoverie*, cited in William Fulke, *A Defense of the Sincere and True Translations of the Holy scriptures in the English Tongue, against the Cavils of Gregory Martin* (London, 1583; reissued by the Parker Society, Cambridge, 1843), pp. 7–8.

[181]Fulke, *Defense,* p. 9.

[182]Fulke, *Defense,* pp. 11, 12.

[183]See below, §§6.1 and 6.2.

[184]See below, §§7.1–7.2.

[185]See below, §§6.3–6.4

[186]Cf. Muller, "The Debate over the Vowel Points," pp. 57–62, with Diestel,

granting the Protestant insistence on the authority of the text in its original languages and the way in which the text itself guaranteed the certainty of theological knowing. In a similar way, Grotius' learned *Annotationes ad Vetus Testamentum* (1644) and *Annotationes in Novum Testamentum* (1646) caused considerable debate over their application of a highly developed humanistic approach, replete with citations of ancient pagan authors, to the interpretation of Scripture. His variant translations, his tendency toward historical exegesis, and particularly his views on inspiration troubled orthodox Protestants. Grotius argued, for example, a lesser degree of inspiration for the authors of the historical books than for the prophets.[187] In addition, some of Grotius' annotations, notably his denial of a primary messianic significance to Isaiah 53 and his identification of Jeremiah as the "man of sorrows," led to the charge that he aided and abetted the Socinians.[188] Each of the issues raised by Martin, Stapleton, Bellarmine, and other Roman polemicists and, later, those raised by the textual criticism of the seventeenth century, became a part of the Protestant dogmatic *locus de sacra Scriptura* and an issue to be addressed in the work of exegesis. In the early orthodox era, in such systems as Scharpius' *Cursus theologiae,* Trelcatius' *Loci communes,* and Hommius' *Disputationes,* as polemical sections were appended to positive *loci,* but eventually, as witnessed by the systems of Polanus, Alsted,[189] Maccovius, Cocceius, Burmann, Maresius,[190] and virtually all of the high orthodox writers, as an

Geschichte, pp. 334–41; and see below, §6.3

[187]Henning Graf Reventlow, "L'exégèse de Hugo Grotius," in *BTT,* 6, pp. 143, 146–47.

[188]Cf. Grotius, *Annotationes ad Vetus Testamentum,* in *Opera omnia theologica,* 3 vols. (Amsterdam, 1679), I, pp. 323–25, with John Owen, *Vindiciae evangelicae; or, the Mystery of the Gospel Vindicated and Socinianism Examined ... with the Vindication of the Testimonies of Scripture concerning the Deity and Satisfaction of Jesus Christ from the perverse Expositions and Interpretations of them by Hugo Grotius,* in *The Works of John Owen,* 17 vols. (London and Edinburgh: Johnstone and Hunter, 1850–53), XII, pp. 457–58, 475–81.

[189]Johann Heinrich Alsted, *Methodus sacrosanctae theologiae octo libri tradita* (Hanoviae, 1614).

[190]Johannes Cocceius, *Summa theologiae ex Scriptura repetita,* in *Opera omnia theologica, exegetica, didactica, polemica, philologica,* 12 vols. (Amsterdam, 1701–6), VII, pp. 131–403; Franz Burmann, *Synopsis theologiae et speciatim oeconomiae foederum Dei* (Geneva, 1678); Samuel Maresius, *Collegium theologicum sive systema breve universae theologiae comprehensum octodecim disputationibus* (Groningen, 1645, 1659).

integral part of the doctrinal argument of the *locus de sacra Scriptura* itself. The polemic also appears in large-scale exegetical works, like those of Willet and Mayer, in their reviews of exegetical and theological opinion.

These points of polemic, moreover, maintain the emphasis of the later Middle Ages and the Reformation on the issues of authority and interpretation. The points at issue are somewhat more focused and are determined now by later debate and specifically by the controversy over the identity of the true church occasioned by the formal separation of Protestantism from Rome, but beneath this superficial alteration of the terms of the debate, there is, clearly, a continuity of issues and argumentation. The relationship of Scripture, tradition, and churchly magisterium is still primary to the debate. The division of Christendom has merely identified the opposing parties along clear ecclesial lines, while the relation of the individual interpreter to the old norms of authority has been heightened by both the flowering of humanism and the Anabaptist alternative to the magisterial Reformation. Similarly, the method and pattern of interpretation remain a focus of debate, with the traditional tension between the grammatical letter of the text and the churchly need for figurative, symbolical, and doctrinal readings of the text. The poles of the debate are, once again, ecclesially identifiable although the boundaries are much more vague than in the debate over authority. The Protestant writers continue to see the need for some figurative and typological exegesis while the Catholic authors move toward a stronger focus on the grammar of the text. On both sides, humanistic training in the ancient languages has had considerable impact. Among the Protestant authors, however, there is a more direct appeal to the Hebrew and Greek text—as would be expected after the Tridentine assertion of the authority of the Vulgate. This appeal to the ancient languages carried over, on the Protestant side, into dogmatic system itself as the systems arose out of exegetical *loci* and as the appeal to Scripture was pressed into every element of the body of Christian doctrine.

2.3 Scripture, Hermeneutics and the Federal Theology

Although the so-called federal school within Reformed orthodoxy developed only in the mid-seventeenth century under the influence of the teachings of Johannes Cocceius, the hermeneutical impact of the doctrine of covenant was obvious already in the Reformation and in the era of early orthodoxy. Both Calvin and Bullinger expressed a concern to explain the similarity and difference between the Old Testament and the New, based on their assumption of the unity of the covenant of grace. Calvin in particular had emphasized the equivalent doctrinal authority of the Old Testament, granting such interpretive issues as the movement of revelation from promise to fulfillment and the abrogation of the ceremonial law in Christ.[191] And although no fully covenantal system of doctrine appeared in the sixteenth century, or even in the first quarter of the seventeenth century, the architectonic potential of the doctrine was clearly noted by Ursinus and covenant appears as one of several unifying motifs in theology in the works Olevian and of English theologians like Fenner and Perkins.[192]

The issue of covenant theology and its hermeneutical significance also directs our attention to a formal question concerning the contents of the *locus de Scriptura* in Reformed theological systems and, indeed, the boundaries and extent of the Reformed orthodox discussion of Scripture. It ought already to be clear that, neither in the Reformation nor in the era of orthodoxy, can the doctrine of Scripture be separated from the exposition and interpretation of Scripture. Similarly, the great hermeneutical question of the relationship of the two Testaments and of law and gospel, belongs as much to the discussion of the doctrine of Scripture as it does to the analysis of origins and import of Reformed covenant theology. Thus, in Bullinger's presentation of the doctrine of Scripture, there

[191]See further, Diestel, *Geschichte,* pp. 278–96. On Bullinger's covenantal theology see Ernst Koch, *Die Theologie der Confessio Helvetica Posterior* (Neukirchen: Neukirchner Verlag, 1968); also see J. Wayne Baker, *Heinrich Bullinger and the Covenant: The Other Reformed Tradition* (Athens, Ohio, 1980); Charles S. McCoy and J. Wayne Baker, *Fountainhead of Federalism: Heinrich Bullinger and the Covenantal Tradition* (Louisville, KY: Westminster/ John Knox Press, 1991). Baker and McCoy's views of the development of federalism should be balanced against the critique of Lyle D. Bierma, "Federal Theology in the Sixteenth Century: Two Traditions?" in *Westminster Theological Journal* 45 (1983):304–21. On Calvin's contribution to covenantal thought see: Anthony Hoekema, "The Covenant of Grace in Calvin's Teaching," in *Calvin Theological Journal* 2 (1967): 133-61.

[192]Cf. Zacharias Ursinus, *Catechesis, Summa theologiae per quaestiones et responsiones exposita: sive capita religionis Christianae continens* (1562), in August Lang, *Die Heidelberger Katechismus und vier verwandte Katechismen* (Leipzig: Deichert, 1907), pp. 151–99; also in Ursinus, *Opera,* I, cols. with Caspar Olevianus, *De substantia foederis gratuiti inter Deum et electos* (Geneva, 1585); Dudley Fenner, *Sacra theologia sive veritas quae est secundum pietatem* (London, 1585); and William Perkins, *A Golden Chaine,* in *Workes,* I, pp. 9–113.

is considerable discussion of the law and the problem of the Testaments—and in the early orthodox era both Rollock and Maccovius were led to introduce a lengthy discussion of the two Testaments and of law and gospel into their *locus* on Scripture.[193] And it is certainly the case that the problems of the relationship of the Testaments, of the hermeneutics of law and gospel, and of the implications of one covenant of grace under several dispensations continued to have major implications for the Reformed doctrine of Scripture and for the Reformed use of Scripture, particularly of the Old Testament, throughout the era of orthodoxy. It was, of course, characteristic of the period to assume a relationship of promise and fulfillment between the Old and New Testaments and to interpret certain issues typologically, in view of assumptions concerning the validity of Christian doctrine, the larger or broader sense of the whole of Scripture, and the focus of Scripture on Christ as *fundamentum* or *scopus,* but these assumptions all draw attention to the continuity between orthodoxy and the tradition of exegesis and interpretation from the Middle Ages through the Reformation.[194]

The theology of Johannes Cocceius occupies an important position in the development of the Reformed orthodox theological system, particularly with reference to the interrelated topics of Scripture and covenant and to the way in which these topics contribute to the discussion of theological methodology. Cocceius is remembered not only for his doctrine of the covenants of grace and works and for the impetus he gave to the historical model for theological system, but also for the heated controversy generated by the differences between his covenantal schema and the doctrine of covenants held by his Dutch Reformed contemporaries.[195] One of the ironies of the debate—and of the historiography that has taken

[193]Cf. Bullinger, *Decades,* I.i and I.vi, pp. 45–52, 113–16, with Maccovius, *Loci communes,* xii–xiii; and Rollock, *Treatise,* pp. 62–63. Despite considerable temptation, this variant of the doctrinal pattern of Reformed system has not been introduced into the larger outline of the present study, but will appear in a subsequent essay on the Reformation and post-Reformation doctrine of the covenants.

[194]Contra Hayes, *Old Testament Theology,* p. 18; but cf. Diestel, *Geschichte,* pp. 480–82; and see below, §3.5.

[195]On Cocceius' theology and controversies, see Gottlob Schrenck, *Gottesreich und Bund im älteren Protestantismus* (Gütersloh: Bertelmann, 1923); Charles McCoy, "The Covenant Theology of Johannes Cocceius, 1603–1669" (Ph.D. diss. Yale University, 1956); and Heiner Faulenbach, *Weg und Ziel der Erkenntnis Christi: Eine Untersuchung zur Theologie des Johannes Coccejus* (Neukirchen: Neukirchner Verlag, 1973).

its accusations literally—is Cocceius' assault on the "scholasticism" of his adversaries. His most scholastic opponent, Gisbert Voetius, had also criticized scholasticism,[196] and a fair assessment of the theology and method of both writers reveals not only their mutual reluctance to associate their own work with the methods of the medieval doctors but also their mutual acceptance of the expository and polemical style now known as Protestant scholasticism.

Cocceius' theology, for all its biblicism and exegetical interest, is thoroughly scholastic in its approach to the dogmatic and systematic task. Apart from his identification of theology as a thoroughly practical discipline (which was the view of a minority of Reformed orthodox writers although typical of the federal school),[197] Cocceius' preliminary discussion of the presuppositions and principles of theology is congruent with the views of his orthodox contemporaries. He reiterates the standard bifurcation of theology into its archetypal and ectypal forms; he identifies Christian theology as ectypal theology *in via;* and he adopts standard scholastic definitions of Scripture as the *principium cognoscendi theologiae* and of the instrumental use of reason.[198] Even his definition of theology as practical stands in continuity with earlier Reformed orthodox thought—Perkins, Ames, and Keckermann—and has parallels not only in later federal theology but in the fully orthodox covenant system of J. H. Heidegger at the very end of the seventeenth century.[199] What is more, Cocceius' doctrine of God maintains a traditional emphasis on essence and attributes and, accordingly, is indistinguishable from the thought of his orthodox and scholastic Reformed contemporaries.[200]

Cocceius' most original effort, the *Summa doctrinae de foedere et testamento Dei,* is frequently viewed as a rebellion against "scholasticism" in theology and an attempt to write "biblical dogmatics" or at least to introduce *Helisgeschichte* as a fundamental organiza-

---

[196]Voetius, *Selectarum disputationum theologicarum,* 5 vols. (Utrecht, 1648–69), pars. I, disp. 2.

[197]Cf. Cocceius, *Aphorismi per universam theologiam breviores,* I.7 (in *Opera,* vol. 7); idem, *Summa theol.,* I.i.8; Burmann, *Synopsis theologiae,* I.ii.51; Abraham Heidanus, *Corpus theologiae christianae in quindecim locos,* 2 vols. (Leiden, 1686), I.7; and the discussion in *PRRD,* I, 6.3.

[198]Cocceius, *Summa theol.,* I.i.3, 5, 9–10; idem, *Aphorismi ... breviores,* I.2, 4, 16.

[199]See *PRRD,* I, pp. 219–22.

[200]Cf. Cocceius, *Summa theol.,* II.viii–x; and idem, *Aphorismi ... breviores,* IV–V, with *RD,* pp. 57–104.

tional and interpretive motif into Reformed dogmatics.[201] Such characterizations of Cocceius' theology fall somewhat short of the mark, granting that Cocceius' federalism and biblicism did not produce a "biblical theology" in the usual sense of the term—Cocceius' and his followers do not adumbrate the distinction, later posed by Johann Philipp Gabler, between a historically conceived biblical theology and a contemporary dogmatics. Cocceius and the federal theologians intended to produce (as, indeed, did their Reformed orthodox contemporaries and opponents) a biblically grounded contemporary dogmatics. In addition, Cocceius' declamations against "scholastic theology" use the term in a very strict and narrow seventeenth-century sense—as a prolix and disputative elaboration of theological points found in such works as Voetius' *Disputationes*.[202] If, however, by "scholasticism" one indicates the more general phenomenon of a logically argued theology, resting on traditional distinctions and definitions and stated in the form of propositions, then Cocceius' theology is as representative of Protestant scholasticism as the theology of his opponents.

This much is true: Cocceius did attack his opponents as "scholastics" and the *Summa theologiae* does combine a biblical-historical model with the a priori or synthetic pattern of organization typical of the theological systems of the day. It remains the case, however, that the particular doctrines Cocceius found at the heart of Scripture, the *foedus operum* and *foedus gratiae,* had been mediated to him by Reformed orthodoxy and his most original doctrinal structure, the *pactum salutis* forged in eternity between the Father and the Son, is the height of scholastic speculation and a direct outgrowth of earlier Reformed scholastic trinitarian thought.[203] The juxtaposition of "biblical theology" with scholastic or dogmatic theology that appears in many of the discussions of Cocceius' thought and also in discussions of the theology of later federal thinkers like Witsius, can only be viewed as an anachronistic application of Gabler's distinction in the hope of finding a seventeenth-century link between the Reformation and modern biblical theology and exegesis.[204]

---

[201]Cf. Hayes, *Old Testament Theology,* pp. 19–23, with the more balanced remarks of Diestel, "Studien zur Föderaltheologie," pp. 209, 216–17; note also Albertus van der Flier, *Specimen historico-theologicum de Johanne Cocceijo anti-scholastico* (Utrecht, 1859); and Charles C. McCoy, "Johannes Cocceius: Federal Theologian," in *Scottish Journal of Theology* 16 (1963):352–70.

[202]Cf. *PRRD,* I, pp. 258–67.

[203]See Muller, *Christ and the Decree,* pp. 164–71.

[204]This is especially true of Hayes, *Old Testament Theology,* pp. 19–23; cf.

Cocceius did, however, make a significant contribution to the Reformed doctrine of Scripture as well as exert a major influence on the development of continental Reformed covenant theology. Not only did he write a weighty *locus de Scriptura,* he also produced an important discussion of the method of dogmatics from a biblical-exegetical perspective, and he did apply the historical models that he elicited from Scripture to the orthodox system, albeit in a way unacceptable to his orthodox contemporaries.[205] Whereas Cocceius' methodological arguments had a direct relevance to and impact on orthodox dogmatics, his historical-covenantal model had an indirect impact by way of the modified (and therefore hermeneutically and theologically more orthodox) covenantal schema developed by Burmann, Heidanus, Witsius, Heidegger, Vitringa, and de Moor.[206]

McCoy, "Johannes Cocceius: Federal Theologian," pp. 354, 356, 365–70, and McCoy and Baker, *Fountainhead of Federalism,* pp. 74–7; with Van der Flier, *De Johanne Cocceijo anti-scholastico,* pp. 33–35, 76, 117–18; S. P. Heringa, *Specimen historico-theologicum de Hermanno Witsio, theologo biblico* (Amsterdam, 1861), p. 76; and J. van Genderen, *Herman Witsius: Bijdrage tot de Kennis der Gereformeerde Theologie* ('s-Gravenhage: Guido de Bres, 1953), pp. 209–15.

[205]On Cocceius' covenant theology in its relation to the hermeneutical problem of the Old and New Testaments, see Schrenk, *Gottesreich und Bund,* pp. 96–104; McCoy, "Covenant Theology of Johannes Cocceius," pp. 360–64; Diestel, *Geschichte,* pp. 528–30; and idem, "Studien zur Föderaltheologie," pp. 239–48.

[206]Cf. Gass, *Geschichte der protestantischen Dogmatik,* pp. 308–23, with Burmann, *Synopsis theol.,* Lib. II, "De oeconomia foederis naturae, seu operum, & foederis gratiae in genere"; III, "De oeconomia foederis gratiae sub promissione"; Heidanus, *Corpus theol.,* VIII, "De foedere gratiae, eiusque dispensatione sub Vet. & Nov. Testamentum"; Herman Witsius, *The Oeconomy of the Covenants between God and Man. Comprehending a Complete Body of Divinity,* 3 vols. (London, 1775), III.iii: "Of the different oeconomies or dispensations of the covenant of grace"; IV.i: "Of the doctrine of salvation in the first age of the world"; IV.2: "Of the doctrine of grace under Noah"; IV.iii: "Of the doctrine of grace from Abraham to Moses" etc.; Johann Heinrich Heidegger, *Corpus theologiae* (Zürich, 1700), Locus XI: "De foedere gratiae"; XII: "De oeconomia foederis gratiae sub patriarcho"; XIII "De oeconomia foederis gratiae sub lege Mosis" etc.; XX: "De oeconomia foederis gratiae sub evangelio"; Campegius Vitringa, *Doctrina christianae religionis, per aphorismos summatim descripta,* 8 vols. (Arnheim, 1761–86), IV.xix, "De foedere gratiae, quod Testamento Aeterno superstructum est, & variis illius dispensationibus"; xx, "De tempore promissionis bonorum Testamenti Gratiae; cuius tria statuuntur intervalla"; Bernhard de Moor, *Commentarius perpetuus in Joh. Marckii compendium theologiae christianae didactico-elencticum,* 6 vols. (Leiden, 1761–71), III.xvii, "De foedere gratiae, evangelio, & varia huius oeconomia."

2.4 The High Orthodox Doctrine of Scripture

It is a considerable, although quite typical, distortion of the data to claim that "the last great dogmatic systems in Protestantism ... were important, yet futile, attempts to secure the Scriptures as Word of God."[207] The rise and progress of Protestant orthodoxy can hardly be reduced to a last-ditch attempt to save one particular doctrine from destruction at the hands of historical criticism. Far more than the doctrine of Scripture was discussed in the twenty-one volumes just noted, and much of the exposition, particularly in Gerhard's work, was positive rather than polemical and apologetic. The same point can easily be made for the Reformed orthodox.

The high orthodox doctrine of Scripture formulated by Protestant orthodox writers of the latter part of the seventeenth century (ca. 1640–1700) arguably represents both the culmination and the conclusion of the scholastic approach to the authority and interpretation of Scripture—at least on the historical trajectory identified as "Tradition I" by Obermann. The high orthodox writers spell out in full the implications of the language of the sole ultimate authority of Scripture in all matters of faith and practice in the context of a detailed doctrine of the inspiration, the attributes, and the interpretation of Scripture. Their formulas retain and amalgamate features of the doctrine taught by the medieval scholastics, the Reformers, and the early orthodox while at the same time accommodating their doctrine to some of the hermeneutical changes that had occurred in the sixteenth and early seventeenth centuries and fortifying their position against others. The scholastic doctrine of Scripture could be pressed no further—beyond the high orthodox formulation lay the corrosive critiques of the eighteenth century and the demise of scholastic method.

In the high orthodox period the doctrine of Scripture takes on a tone rather different from that of the early orthodox era. Whereas then the doctrine was organized often around polemical lines—at least after the appearance of Bellarmine's *De verbo Dei*—now the doctrine returns to the more positive pattern of doctrinal exposition, usually subsuming polemical issues under the various heads of doctrine. We see this particularly in the systems of Burmann, Mastricht,

---

[207]Edgar Krentz, *Historical-Critical Method,* (Philadelphia: Fortress, 1975) p. 15, citing Johann Gerhard, *Loci communes theologici,* 9 vols. (1610–22; new ed., Berlin, 1863–75); Abraham Calovius, *Systema locorum theologicorum,* 12 vols. (Wittenberg, 1655–72).

and Riissen. This represents a return to the form and method of those founding fathers of orthodoxy, Ursinus and Zanchius—but, in terms of the depth and detail of analysis brought on at least in part by the polemic, a considerable advance in content. The high orthodox doctrine, then, has consistently moved to rationalize the polemic into positive doctrine. What in the earlier period was a *locus* formulated in large part around a series of disputes has become, in the later period, a self-sustaining *locus* containing some polemical elements but, as a whole, integrated into the larger structure of theological system.

The placement of the doctrine has not, of course, been subject to any change. The doctrine of Scripture remains, in the high orthodox era, in the confessionally determined position, following the prolegomena but standing prior to the doctrine of God. In a very real sense, the Reformed orthodox continued to view the doctrine of Scripture as a preliminary statement, an enunciation of principle, set prior to the system proper—virtually an extension of the prolegomena. Like the prolegomena, the doctrine of Scripture contains methodological and hermeneutical statements necessary to the conduct of theological system rather than purely dogmatic statements belonging to system.

One of the most accurate contemporary statements concerning the character of the Reformed orthodox doctrine of Scripture appears in Beardslee's introduction to his translation of Turretin's *locus* on Scripture. Beardslee argues that "much of Turretin's scholasticism can be read as an academic program for accomplishing" one of the crucial demands of the Reformers, the placement of Scripture, in sound vernacular translation, "into the hands of the laity." This concern, notes Beardslee, was "not peculiar to later pietists, but was integral to the movement," that is, to the theological program of the orthodox or scholastic successors of the Reformers.[208] We do Turretin and the other Reformed orthodox a great injustice if we overlook the pastoral and practical implications of their work.

Internal changes have also occurred in the orthodox *locus de Scriptura sacra*. The polemic of high orthodoxy, now codified and frequently subsumed under the positive dogmatic topics, has changed considerably in tone from the polemics of the early orthodox with its Reformation emphasis on the doctrine of scriptural

---

[208]Francis Turretin, *The Doctrine of Scripture: Locus 2 of Institutio Theologiae Elencticae*, ed. and trans. by John W. Beardslee (Grand Rapids: Baker Book House, 1981), p. 11.

authority over against Roman claims of co-equal authority for tradition and the *magisterium* and its related insistence on the integrity of the Hebrew and Greek texts over against the Vulgate. In the high orthodox systems, the polemic with Rome has become formalized: it is no longer a new battle, but rather a long-established battle with clearly defined lines and even more clearly set answers. This older polemic is retained in virtually all of the high orthodox systems, but a new current in debate has become more and more focused on text-critical and hermeneutical issues, particularly as they relate to the authenticity, inspiration, and integrity of the text. This polemic addresses both the problems raised by textual critics like Cappel, Walton, and Simon and the issues drawn into the fray by Socinian and Arminian revision of both the exegetical tradition and the doctrine of inspiration.[209]

Here, too, as in the early orthodox theological systems, a strong emphasis on Word as the living agency and form of revelation remains central to the doctrine of Scripture.[210] Turretin and Riissen begin their doctrine of Scripture with a multifaceted definition of Word and with a statement of the necessity of revelation by means of Word—prior to their approach to Scripture as the form of Word given to the church.[211] They also, with others of their generation, continue to balance their language concerning the objective authority of Scripture with their doctrine of the internal testimony of the Spirit, with the result that the rather lengthy list of divine marks present in the text and the discussion of the divinity of Scripture are somewhat relativized. Like the Reformers, the orthodox continue to recognize that the objective evidences of the divinity and authority of the text will not be acknowledged by those who remain unmoved by the *testimonium internum Spiritus Sancti*.[212] Indeed, Turretin would argue that "the work of the Holy Spirit in our hearts is absolutely necessary to the inward persuasion of the divinity of

---

[209]Cf. Helmut Echternach, "The Lutheran Doctrine of the Autopistia of Holy Scripture," in *Concordia Theological Monthly* (April 1952):254.

[210]Cf. *Synopsis purioris theologiae,* II.ii; cf. iv, vi, xi with Pictet, *Theol. chr.*, I.iv; v.1; vi.1, and see below, §3.1.

[211]Turretin, *Inst. theol. elencticae*, II.i; Leonhard Riissen, *Summa theologiae didactico-elencticae* (Frankfurt and Leipzig, 1731), II.i–ii, and below, §§3.2 and 3.3.

[212]Cf., e.g., Burmann, *Synopsis theologiae,* I.v.xv; Heidanus, *Corpus theologiae,* I (p. 24); Maresius, *Collegium theologicum*, I.xxxiii; Pictet, *Theol. chr.*, I.x.1–8; and Heidegger, *Corpus theologiae*, II.xiv–xv.

Scripture."[213] Nonetheless, although the *testimonium internum Spiritus Sancti* still holds first place in the theological argument for the authority of the text, a relative shift in emphasis to the attributes of Scripture and to the evidences of divinity in the text can be identified in the writings of many of the high orthodox, evidencing the crisis of theological certainty caused by both the hermeneutical changes characteristic of the age and the rise of rationalism.

It remains the case, however, that the various seventeenth-century critiques of the orthodox or scholastic use of Scripture, whether philosophical, scientific, historical, or text-critical, were not self-evidently correct in the seventeenth century. Descartes, for example, argued that reason was the ultimate criterion of truth and the sole ground of certainty, much to the dismay of theologians, who understood Scripture (or, in the case of Roman Catholics, Scripture, tradition, and the magisterium) to be the foundation of theological knowledge. Then, Descartes went on to prove by reason, at least to his own satisfaction, that there was no empty space anywhere in the universe and that the connection between soul and body was the pineal gland at the base of the brain. So much for the utterly independent exercise of unfettered reason! Indeed, the orthodox theologians of the day hardly held a monopoly on the rejection of Cartesian philosophy.[214] From the theological perspective, the large-scale quest for certainty characteristic of the antiskeptical theorizings of the age had not yet—surely not in Descartes—offered a ground of certainty capable of competing with Scripture despite the hermeneutical and magisterial difficulties entailed on the affirmation of a certain knowing grounded on the text.

On a somewhat less humorous note, it can easily be shown that the theologians of the seventeenth century did not simply reject the Copernican and Galilean cosmology as contrary to the biblical story of Joshua making the sun stand still—any more than they rejected the classical and medieval geographers' assumption of a spherical earth on supposed biblical grounds. Many seventeenth-century theologians were quite willing to acknowledge that the language of the story of the sun standing still was not scientific but was simply a figure of speech based on appearances. Nonetheless, like the philosophers and scientists of the day, they recognized what seemed

[213]Francis Turretin, *Disputatio theologica, de Scripturae Sacrae authoritate adversus pontificos*, I.xi (*Opera*, vol. 4, p. 237); contra Rogers and McKim, *Interpretation and Authority of Scripture*, pp. 178–79.

[214]E.g., note the lengthy debate over whether the universe is a *plenum* or a vacuum in the Leibniz-Clarke debate: Clarke, *Works*, IV, pp. 592–93.

to be the mathematical impossibility of the speeds assigned by the Copernican system to the revolution and rotation of the earth—or as Leigh commented, "some think that there is a greater probability the earth should move around once a day, than that the heavens should move with such an incredible swiftnesse, scarce compatible with any natural body." Leigh neither settles the issue nor allows it to disturb his assumption of the infallibility of Scripture.[215]

What is more important still, is that the advances in textual analysis, linguistic study, and historical-contextual reading of the text of Scripture that took place in the seventeenth century cannot be associated, simplistically, with a group of radical thinkers dissociated from the orthodox schools of the day. Quite to the contrary, it was the Protestant orthodox exegetes themselves who raised and resolved many of these issues. Of course, some of the Protestant exegetes who raised critical issues—most notably, Louis Cappel— were immediately viewed as enemies of orthodoxy. But their case is perhaps more the exception than the rule. Examination of the documents of the seventeenth century leads us ineluctably to the conclusion that normative Protestantism itself, because of its theological rootedness in the text of Scripture, was as much responsible for the rise of critical method as it was for the eventual dogmatic opposition to that method. Indeed, the seventeenth century witnessed an "orthodox" development of critical tools and, accordingly, an increasing worry on the part of those same orthodox over the connection between text and doctrine—whereas only in the eighteenth century, with the increasing dominance of rationalism and deism, do we find a crystallization of orthodox opposition to the results of textual and what eventually became historical criticism.

Thus, the great critical and textual endeavors of the age, like the London Polyglott Bible and its massive *Prolegomena* (1654–57), edited by Brian Walton, the nine-volume *Critici Sacri* (1660) of Pearson, Scattergood, and Gouldman, and the application of Talmudic researches to the exegesis of the New Testament in Lightfoot's *Horae hebraicae et talmudicae* (1658–74) all stand in the tradition of Protestant exegesis and theology, not outside of it. And if Walton's efforts, particularly his resolution of the problem of the vowel points disturbed orthodox dogmaticians like Owen,[216] the

---

[215]Cf. Edward Leigh, *A Systeme or Body of Divinity* (London, 1664), III.iii (p. 300).

[216]Cf. John Owen, *Of the Integrity and Purity of the Hebrew and Greek Text of the Scripture; with Considerations on the Prolegomena and the Appendix to the Late "Biblia Polyglotta,"* in *Works,* vol. 16, pp. 345–421, with the

Critici Sacri and Lightfoot's exegetical labors stood directly in the trajectory of orthodox Protestant theology. The *Critici Sacri* gathered together the results of the antiquarian and exegetical labors of the seventeenth century—and the table of its contributors testifies to the consistent interrelationship of text-critical study and the biblical commitment of orthodox Protestantism.

2.5 Doctrinal and Critical Problems of High and Late Orthodoxy

As in the greater part of the seventeenth century, the development of critical method in the work of the scholars and exegetes of the late seventeenth and the eighteenth centuries does not appear, on close scrutiny, to be a work undertaken with the primary intention of undermining traditional theology. The opposition between orthodoxy and biblical criticism and the problems of theological formulation were considerably more subtle—and the distinction between "late orthodox theologians" and "textual critics" cannot be drawn with absolute clarity. Nor can all of the "transitional" and late orthodox theologians be identified unequivocally as rationalists.

In addition to providing Protestantism with a formalized, systematically or dogmatically stated doctrine of Scripture, the orthodox were forced to develop that doctrine under the pressure of text-critical argumentation unknown in the era of the Reformation. The seventeenth century was, after all, the great age of Protestant linguistics, "oriental," Talmudic, and rabbinic studies, and critical comparison of the ancient texts and versions. The presence of discussions of the various ancient texts and versions in theological systems only serves to underscore the importance of this study to Protestant theologians. Indeed, the increasing linguistic capabilities of Protestant exegetes, including the strictly orthodox writers, must be counted as a source of increasing pressure upon the orthodox theological system certainly equal to and perhaps surpassing in intensity the philosophical and scientific revolution of the seventeenth century.

As Laplanche has shown, the exegetes of the school of Saumur, most notably Louis Cappel, identified both a historical development

discussions of his doctrine in Donald K. McKim, "John Owen's Doctrine of Scripture in Historical Perspective," in *Evangelical Quarterly* 45/4 (Oct.–Dec. 1973):195–207; Rogers and McKim, *Interpretation and Authority of Scripture*, pp. 218–23; and Stanley N. Gundry, "John Owen on Authority and Scripture," in *Inerrancy and the Church*, pp. 189–221.

of the Hebrew language and, consequently, a history of the text of the Old Testament. By close examination of the text, moreover, Cappel and his colleagues were able to point out indications of later editing throughout the Pentateuch and the historical books—such as references to the permanence of place names "until this day"—and to argue editing of the text as late as the time of Ezra.[217] In addition, the seventeenth-century debate over the origin of the vowel points in the Masoretic Text, brought on in large part by Cappel's refutation of Buxtorff's *Tiberias,* indicated a mutability of the text that both threatened the orthodox Protestant view of biblical authority and indicated an increasingly rational approach to exegesis and interpretation that offered a higher authority to the individual exegete than had previously been envisioned by Protestant exegesis.[218]

Whereas Laplanche views Cappel's unwillingness to deny the Mosaic authorship of the Pentateuch as an accommodation to his own dogmatic premises concerning the relation of the historical veracity of the text to the theological veracity of Christian doctrine, it is important, also, to add that the conclusion of textual criticism concerning the composite nature of the Pentateuch cut so strongly against received exegetical opinion that it did not appear immediately, bluntly, and in full from the kind of evidence that Cappel had amassed.[219] The textual conclusions of Cappel and his Salmurian colleagues demanded not only a new approach to the relationship between Scripture and theological certainty, but also to the idea of a religious text—such as finally came to light in a developed form in the nearly three decades from the time of the *Critica sacra* (1650) to Richard Simon's *Histoire critique du Vieux Testament* (1678).[220] When, before Simon, Peyrère and Spinoza made the point that Moses was not the author of the Pentateuch, they not only were viewed as assaulting religion and theology, but also as holding an indefensible view of the text of Scripture. In the case of Peyrère's work, which appeared in 1655, five years after the appearance of Cappel's *Critica sacra,* text-critical insights were mingled with theo-

---

[217]François Laplanche, *L'écriture, le sacré et l'histoire: Érudits politiques protestants devant la bible en France au XVIIe siècle* (Amsterdam and Maarssen: APA-Holland University Press/Lille: Presses Universitaires, 1986), pp. 368–70.

[218]Cf. Muller, "Debate over the Vowel-Points," pp. 59–63, 70–72.

[219]Laplanche, *L'écriture,* pp. 370–71.

[220]Cf. John D. Woodbridge, "Richard Simon le 'père de la critique biblique,'" in *BTT* 6, pp. 193–206, with the studies of Simon cited below, n. 240.

logically and exegetically unacceptable theories—such as the existence of pre-Adamites, the imminent gathering of the Jews and appearance of the Messiah, and the universal salvation of all human beings.[221]

Spinoza's *Tractatus-theologico politicus,* published anonymously in 1670, argued a strict separation of theology and philosophy. The subject of theology is faith and obedience, whereas that of philosophy is rational truth. Religion begins in Scripture and seeks the end of man in communion with God: the issue is never knowledge but faith and obedience. Spinoza, thus, stood against the prevailing view of orthodoxy—the doctrine of Scripture as the source of revealed knowledge.[222] The result of Spinoza's division of the subject was to restrict religion to piety, albeit revealed piety, and to place the doctrines of God, creation, providence, and the soul within the bounds of philosophy as distinct from theology and to declare them the products of rational rather than revealed knowledge—and, on the side of theology, to free faith entirely from accountability to and criticism from philosophical reason. Spinoza's motives are clear from his preface to the *Tractatus* and from the argument of the chapter on the interpretation of Scripture. He is deeply oppressed by the intolerance of the so-called religious men particularly in so far as intolerance rests on ideas arbitrarily imported to religion from without. Piety and religion, he comments "are become a tissue of

---

[221]Isaac de la Peyrère, *Prae-Adamitae. sive exercitaio super versibus duodecimus, decimotertio, & decimoquarto, capitis quinti epistolae Pauli ad Romanos. Quibus inducuntur primi homines ante Adamum conditi* (Amsterdam, 1655), translated as *Men Before Adam, or, a discourse upon the twelfth, thirteenth, and fourteenth verses of the Epistle of Paul to the Romans* (London, 1656); and idem, *A Theological System upon that presupposition that men were before Adam,* part I (London, 1655); and cf. Richard Popkin, "The Development of Religious Scepticism and the Influence of Isaac La Peyrère's Pre-Adamism and Bible Criticism," in *Classical Influences on European Culture A.D. 1500–1700,* ed. R. R. Bolgar (Cambridge: Cambridge University Press, 1976), pp. 271–80; and idem, *Isaac La Peyrère (1596–1676): His Life, Work, and Influence* (Leiden: Brill, 1987). Also note the rapidity and rage of orthodox Protestant response: Antoinus Hulsius, *Non-ens prae-adamiticum, sive confutatio vani & sicinizantis cujusdam somnii, quo S. Scripturae praetextu incuatioribus nuper imponere conatus est quidam anonymus, fingens ante Adamum primum homines fuisse in mundo* (Leiden, 1656) and Samuel Maresius, *Refutation fabulae prae-adamiticae, absoluta septem primariis quaestionibus, cum praefatione apologetica pro authentia Scripturarum* (Groningen, 1656).

[222]On Spinoza's place in the history of interpretation, see Jacqueline Lagrée and Pierre François Moreau, "La lecture de la Bible dans le cercle de Spinoza," in *BTT* 6, pp. 97–115.

ridiculous mysteries" which are not at all founded on Scripture but on "speculations of Platonists and Aristotelians." Proponents of this "religion,"

> not content to rave with the Greeks themselves, they want to make the prophets rave also; showing conclusively, that never even in sleep have they caught a glimpse of Scripture's Divine nature. The very vehemence of their admiration for the mysteries plainly attests, that their belief in the Bible is a formal assent rather than a living faith.[223]

The complaint is very much like that leveled against the orthodox by the pietists. Spinoza rails against those who defend "human commentaries" and persist "in the investigation of absurdities" rather than respect "the writings of the Holy Ghost." The text must be addressed on its own grounds—Scripture must be allowed to interpret Scripture—rather than upon grounds imported to the task of interpretation from rational philosophy. What Scripture teaches about God, that he is omnipotent, worthy of worship, loves mankind, and so forth, is not the basis of philosophical truth but rather a guide "to the general conduct of life."[224]

The exact impact of Spinoza's *Tractatus* on biblical criticism is difficult to assess.[225] His critical-historical argumentation was in advance of scholarly consensus but was certainly not unique: Louis Cappell's argument on the Massorah and the exegetical principles elaborated in Brian Walton's critical prefaces to the London Polyglott Bible preceded Spinoza by several years. Spinoza was also aware of the critical work of Isaac de la Peyrère, in which considerable doubt had been shed on the doctrinal continuity of the text and which had pointed to the probability of Moses' use of earlier sources in his composition of the Pentateuch.[226] In addition, the argument of

[223]Baruch Spinoza, *A Theologico-Political Treatise and a Political Treatise,* trans. R. H. M. Elwes (New York: Dover, 1951), pp. 6–7.

[224]Spinoza, *Theologico-Political Treatise,* pp. 98–99, 104; cf. Leo Strauss, *Spinoza's Critique of Religion* (New York: Schocken, 1982), pp. 113–21.

[225]See P. C. Craigie, "The Influence of Spinoza in the Higher Criticism of the Old Testament," in *Evangelical Quarterly* 50 (1978):23–32; and John Sandys-Wunsch, "Spinoza—The First Biblical Theologian," in *Zeitschrift für dir alttestamentliche Wissenschaft* 93 (1981):327–41.

[226]See the discussion of Peyrère and his place in the development of criticism toward Astruc's proto-documentary hypothesis in Adolphe Lods, "Astruc et la critique biblique de son temps," in *Revue d'histoire et de philosophie religieuses* 4 (1924):109–39, 201–27; cf. Strauss, *Spinoza's Critique of*

the *Tractatus* that religion was a matter of obedience, philosophy a matter of knowledge, and that each was inviolable from the criticism of the other, was not taken up by later rationalist exegetes like Semler. Nevertheless, similarities between Spinoza's observations concerning the historical interpretation of the text and the grammatical determination of meaning are found in major exegetical and interpretive projects of the day like Richard Simon's *Histoire critique du Vieux Testament*. It may also be pointed out that a major flaw of eighteenth-century rationalist exegesis lay in its failure to follow Spinoza more closely. He categorically forbid the use of rational and philosophical categories in the elucidation of texts!

Spinoza's views on Scripture, philosophy, and theology were met by a tide of protest from orthodox theologians both Lutheran and Reformed which, on the "Richter scale" of dogmatic dispute, exceeded the bitterness of the polemic leveled against Descartes. Cartesian theologians, like Wittich, were even induced to write anti-Spinozist tracts denying any logical or philosophical relationship between the two philosophies. The *Tractatus theologico-politicus* was attacked in the very year of its publication by Friedrich Rappoltus (1615–76), professor of theology in Leipzig, by Wilhelm Van Blyenburg (fl. 1670–85) and Johannes Musaeus (1613–81) of Jena.[227] The dogmatic treatises by these writers did not attempt to unravel and refute the logic of Spinoza's arguments, but instead, rather superficially, pounced upon Spinoza's identification of the Scriptures as essentially moral and upon the view of inspiration which underlay Spinoza's views on interpretation. The *Tractatus theologico-politicus* militated against the entire orthodox view of the Scriptures: Spinoza would deny that the text conveyed real knowledge of God and thus would attack the nature of revelation itself—he would reduce faith to morality and turn the doctrine of God over to unredeemed philosophy! Musaeus added to the charges the point that Spinoza did not recognize that faith itself is an assent to knowledge and failed to see the essential soteriological message of Scripture—not merely obedience but a gift of grace and a gospel of atonement for sin.[228]

The most notable achievement in the fields of seventeenth-

Religion, pp. 64–85; and the comments in Crehan, "The Bible in the Roman Catholic Church," *CHB,* III:220; also Hayes, *Old Testament Theology,* pp. 26–27.

[227]Cf. Bernhard Pünjer, *History of the Christian Philosophy of Religion from the Reformation to Kant,* trans. W. Hastie (Edinburgh, 1887), pp. 434–35.

[228]Cf. Pünjer, *History of the Christian Philosophy of Religion,* p. 435.

century Protestant linguistics and text-criticism was surely the great
London Polyglott Bible (1654–57) edited by Brian Walton (1600–
61) and its companion, the *Lexicon heptaglotton* (1669) by Walton's
colleague, Edmund Castell (1606–85). The Bible itself has been
called "the most important, the most comprehensive, the most valuable (critically speaking), and the most widely spread of the
Polyglots,"[229] and when augmented by Castell's comparative lexicon, it is surely the most technically advanced textual study and
apparatus of its time, never superseded *in toto.* Involved in the
production of the work, in addition to Walton and Castell, were
others of the most eminent Orientalists of the age—Samuel Clark,
Thomas Graves, Thomas Hyde, John Lightfoot, Dudley Loftus,
Edward Pocock, and Abraham Wheelock.

The *Polyglott* is in six folio volumes, four of which contain the
text of the Old Testament, one the text of the New, and a final volume a prolegomenon and analytical apparatus. Included in the Old
Testament are the Masoretic Text of the Hebrew, the Samaritan
Pentateuch, the Septuagint, fragments of the Itala, the Vulgate, and
the Peshitta, the Arabic version, Buxtorf's text of the Targums, and
the Ethiopic version of the Psalms and Song of Songs, together with
literal translations of each of the ancient non-Latin originals into
Latin. The New Testament includes a carefully collated Greek text
based on Stephanus, the Vulgate, the Peshitta, the Ethiopic, and
Arabic versions, plus a Persian text of the Gospels—and, as in the
Old Testament, a literal translation into Latin of all non-Latin
originals.

While on the one hand the collated texts and versions made possible a far more critical and literal rendition of the text further from
the traditional dogmatic interests even of the exegetes of the
Reformation era than ever before possible, it was Walton's *Prolegomena,* on the other hand, that roused the storm of exegetical,
hermeneutical and theological protest. Both Owen and the noted
Hebraist, Lightfoot (whose work is noted in Poole's *Synopsis,*[230] in
Castell's *Lexicon heptaglotton,* and is represented in the *Polyglott*
itself, particularly in the edition and analysis of the Samaritan
Pentateuch) took exception to some of Walton's own critical

[229]Samuel M. Jackson, s.v. "Polyglot Bibles," in *RED.*

[230]Matthew Poole, *Synopsis criticorum aliorumque sacrae scripturae inter-
pretum et commentatorum, summo studio et fide adornata,* 5 vols. (London,
1669–76). Poole also produced, on the basis of this larger work, *Annotations on
the Holy Bible,* 2 vols. (London, 1683–85; reissued in 3 vols., London: Banner
of Truth, 1962).

conclusions, particularly his late dating of the vowel pointing system in the Masoretic Text.

Although it is impossible to separate totally the purely doctrinal from the explicitly textual aspects of this developing view of Scripture, some distinction and differentiation are in order—inasmuch as the text-critical innovations of the seventeenth century drove the orthodox doctrine of Scripture toward conclusions that did not rest on its own internal and primary theological implications. A particularly striking instance of the impact of text-critical issues on theology is the debate over the "vowel points." The Reformers had, almost universally, assumed the pointing of the Hebrew text to be a late invention and had never noted any problems caused by this assumption for their doctrine of the authority of Scripture or their hermeneutic of the analogy of faith; the orthodox, however, when pressed by the implications of the new criticism for the authority of Scripture and the analogy of faith, found themselves arguing the Mosaic origin of the vowel points primarily for the sake of preserving the Reformers' doctrine, or at least a doctrine very much like it, of the authority and interpretation of Scripture.[231] Thus, the problem of the vowel points provides yet another example of the continuities and discontinuities between the Reformation and orthodoxy.

In addition, the rationalizing character of the orthodox treatment of the vowel points—more problematic for the further development of doctrine in the case of Owen than in the case of Turretin and the *Formula Consensus Helvetica*—left the orthodox system easy prey to the inroads of rationalism in the next century. Owen, in particular, had indicated against Cappel a direct relationship between the revelatory character of the text and its perfect preservation in the smallest jot and tittle. He had not, it is true, predicated his doctrine of Scripture as Word on his ability to prove the perfection of the text. Rather, like Turretin and the other orthodox, he had done precisely the opposite: he assumed the authority, infallibility, and integrity of the text on doctrinal grounds and then had predicated his attack on the new text-criticism of Cappel and Walton on his doctrine.[232] Nevertheless, his close linkage of the two issues, particularly his linkage of the doctrine of authority to the Mosaic origin of the vowel points, not only would provide a source of profound difficulty and

---

[231]Cf. Muller, "Debate Over the Vowel-Points," pp. 61–63, 70–72.

[232]Cf. John Owen, *Of the Divine Original, Authority, Self-evidencing Light, and Power of the Scriptures,* in *Works,* vol. 16; and see the discussion, below, §6.3.a.

embarrassment for orthodoxy in the next two centuries, but also would mark a shift in the basic character and implication of his doctrine.

Lightfoot's role in this debate points out, as noted previously with reference to the work of Matthew Poole, that the advance of "critical" study and the exegetical work of Protestant orthodoxy (despite the problems ultimately caused by the one for the other) cannot be easily separated, either historically or personally. Lightfoot continues—and rightly so—to be noted as one of the leading critical scholars and linguists of his time, particularly in view of his vast Talmudic learning and his ability to draw upon the Talmud and Midrash in order to reconstruct the historical, religious, and cultural context of the New Testament.[233] Nonetheless, in the same work in which he presented these insights to the scholarly community, the *Horae hebraicae et talmudicae,* Lightfoot also took up the philological cudgel against Walton and Cappel over the issue of the origin of the vowel points.[234]

An index to the increasingly textual and critical character of the orthodox Protestant study of Scripture and to the positive impact of the work of à Lapide, Cappel, Simon, and others on the orthodox theologians is the work of the Puritan scholar Matthew Poole (1624–79), as found in his eminent gathering of scholarly analyses of the text, the *Synopsis criticorum* (1669) in five folio volumes and his somewhat less weighty digest of that massive effort, the *Annotations on the Holy Bible* (1683–85). Poole's work is noteworthy not only for its massive grasp of the critical and textual work done by his predecessors and contemporaries throughout the Christian world, but also for its ability and willingness to raise questions about the composition and authorship of the biblical books. Poole recognized, for instance, that some of the statements in the Pentateuch could not have been written by Moses and were probably additions made by later prophets and, in the case of the account of the death of Moses, he could state quite categorically that the problem of authorship was "no more impeachment to the Divine authority of this chapter, that the penman is unknown, which is also the lot of some other books of Scripture, than it is to the authority of the acts of the king or parliament, that they are written or printed by some unknown

[233]Cf. Rogerson et al., *Study and Use of the Bible,* p. 323.

[234]Lightfoot, *Horae hebraicae et talmudicae,* I.lxxxi; cf. John Lightfoot, *A Commentary on the New Testament from the Talmud and Hebraica: Matthew —I Corinthians,* 4 vols. (Oxford: Oxford University Press, 1859; repr. Grand Rapids: Baker Book House, 1979), vol. 1, p. 160.

person."[235] Indeed, this relative openness to questions of authorship and, indeed, to the conclusion that the author or authors of a biblical book are unknown, is evidenced throughout Poole's work. Of 1 and 2 Samuel, he notes that "it is not certainly known who was the penman of this Book, or whether it was written by one or more hands."[236] He notes that Solomon's authorship of Proverbs ends with chapter 24 and that the remainder, by its own testimony, was gathered by others.[237] And he rather pointedly denies apostolic authorship to the Gospel of Mark, and expresses reservations about the ancient identification of the author as John Mark and about the theory that the Gospel was dictated by Peter to Mark. He even goes so far as to comment that the author of the Gospel "seemeth to have compared notes with Matthew, and hath very few things which Matthew hath not."[238] What Poole's work demonstrates is that there is no clear or sudden division between "precritical" and "critical exegesis" and that the Protestant orthodox themselves often contributed positively to the development of exegesis and hermeneutics, even when some of their results would eventually have a somewhat negative effect upon traditional dogmatics.

Perhaps even more surprising to the modern reader than Poole's critical reading of the text is Matthew Henry's lengthy note on the unknown authorship and composite character of the history running from Joshua through 2 Kings. He assumes that, although "the substance of the several histories was written when the events were fresh in memory," they "were put into the form in which we now have them, by some other hand, long afterward."[239] In support of this hypothesis, Henry notes sources like the Book of Jasher, the Chronicles of the Kings of Israel and Judah, and the Books of Gad, Nathan, and Iddo, and assigns authorship to an unknown compiler. He hypothesizes late editorial work perhaps by Jeremiah or even a post exilic effort by Ezra, granting that phrases like "the kings of Judah" (1 Sam. 27:6) could only arise "after Solomon" and granting that the theological judgments made throughout the history resemble the work of the prophet. Significantly, this sense of many anonymous hands at work in no way prejudiced for Henry the inspired

---

[235]Poole, *Commentary,* I, p. 407; cf. the citation and comment on this text in Rogerson et al., *Study and Use of the Bible,* p. 98.

[236]Poole, *Commentary,* I, p. 513.

[237]Poole, *Commentary,* II, p. 213.

[238]Poole, *Commentary,* III, p. 147.

[239]Matthew Henry, *Commentary on the Whole Bible,* 3 vols. (London: Fisher, 1840), I, p. 518.

character of the text.[240]

No textual scholar, exegete, or theologian, however, attempted to explain the historical work of these many anonymous writers of Scripture until Richard Simon published his *Histoire critique du Vieux Testament* in 1678—and his efforts aroused a furious controversy. Simon, a Roman Catholic and member of the Oratory until the publication of his work, proposed a view hinted at previously in Andreas Masius' commentary on Joshua (1574) and implied by the critical labors of Cornelius á Lapide and Cappel. He argued the gradual collection of sources and the gradual writing of the ancient history of Israel by generations of now anonymous "public scribes."[241] Moses, in Simon's view, was the author only of the laws ascribed to him in the Pentateuch and not of the Pentateuch as a whole. He further argued that the order of the biblical books and, indeed, portions of various books in the Old Testament ought to be rearranged on the grounds of historical and philological considerations. Despite his assertions of the importance of tradition in interpreting Scripture, his work found little favor among Roman Catholics. Protestants, notably Isaac Vossius and Jacques Basnage among the Reformed, produced numerous refutations. There was, in other words, a point beyond which the orthodox would not go in their acceptance of critical discoveries; and, indeed, it was left to a follower of Simon, Jean Astruc, in the middle of the eighteenth century to hypothesize the theory of two basic sources for the Pentateuch.

Another indication of the extent of the text-critical problem faced by orthodoxy in the late seventeenth and early eighteenth centuries is found in the work of Richard Bentley (1662–1742), one of the founding fathers of modern textual criticism—the scholar often credited with proving, finally and irrevocably, that the so-called Johannine comma, the trinitarian reference in 1 John 5:7, was a late

---

[240]Matthew Henry, *Commentary on the Whole Bible,* I, p. 518.

[241]On Simon, see Auguste Bernus, *Richard Simon et son Histoire critique du Vieux Testament: la critique biblique au siècle de Louis XIV* (1869; Geneva: Slatkine Reprints, 1969); Jean Steinmann, *Richard Simon et les origines de l'exegèse biblique* (Paris: Desclée de Brouwer, 1960); Paul Auvray, *Richard Simon (1638–1712)* (Paris: Presses Universitaires de France, 1974); Jacques Le Brun, "Meaning and Scope of the Return to Origins in Richard Simon's Work," in *Trinity Journal,* n.s. 3 (1982):57–70; and John D. Woodbridge, "German Responses to the Biblical Critic Richard Simon: From Leibniz to J. S. Semler," in *Historische Kritik und biblischer Kanon in der deutschen Aufklärung, Wolfenbütteler Forschungen,* Band 41 (Göttingen: Hubert, 1988), pp. 65–87.

addition to the text. Bentley should also be remembered as a defender of the integrity of the text as established by critical methods and as a defender of traditional dogmas. It was Bentley who compared the extant manuscripts of the New Testament and recognized that the text of verse 7, "For there are three that bear record in heaven, the Father, the Word and the Holy Ghost: and these three are one," could be found only in the Vulgate and in a late Greek manuscript and was probably a post-Nicene patristic interpolation in the text.[242] The obvious intention of the redactor or scribe who made the addition was to develop the doctrine of the Trinity as a gloss in parallel with the following verse, "And there are three that bear witness in earth, the spirit, and the water, and the blood: and these three agree in one." In discovering what has since become a universally recognized problem in the text, Bentley came to be viewed as an exegetical ally of the antitrinitarians of the day—particularly granting their rapid espousal of the results of his exegesis. Similarly, Bentley is remembered, together with Campegius Vitringa, as one of the first exegetes to argue that the examination of the circumstances of the text—a characteristic of Protestant exegesis noted in the works of Hyperius and Whitaker—ought to include the analysis of contradictions and stylistic inconsistencies. Within decades of Vitringa's and Bentley's observations, this approach had led to the recognition of two distinct creation narratives in Genesis 1–2 and it must be regarded as a clear antecedent of Astruc's and Eichhorn's development of a documentary hypothesis concerning the Pentateuch.[243] Yet Bentley himself did not intend for his work to undermine traditional trinitarian orthodoxy.

Indeed, Bentley's comments on the implications of textual criticism serve as a salutary reminder that the critical method, however it must have appeared to the proponents of late orthodoxy, was not intended as a counter to either the theology and or the piety of the church in that time. What is remarkable about Bentley's comments about the effect of textual criticism on the theological use of the text is that they echo the intentions of the Protestant orthodox view by arguing the establishment of the text by the collation of variants:

[242]The text of the interpolation is found in the KJV and in earlier English Bibles, like the Bishop's Bible and the Geneva Bible, but it has been utterly removed from virtually all modern versions, frequently, as in the RSV, without notation, verse 6 having been divided into two parts to maintain the traditional division of the text.

[243]Samuel Terrien, "History of the Interpretation of the Bible: III. Modern Period," in *The Interpreters Bible* (Nashville: Abingdon, 19), I, p. 103.

In Profane Authors (as they are call'd) whereof One Manuscript only had the luck to be preserv'd, as *Velleius Paterculus* among the *Latins,* and *Hesychius* among the *Greeks;* the Faults of the Scribes are found so numerous, and the Defects beyond all redress; that notwithstanding the Pains of the Learned'st and acutest Critics ... those Books are still and are like to continue a mere Heap of Errors. On the contrary, where the Copies of any Author are numerous, though the *Various Readings* always increase in Proportion; there the Text, by an accurate Collation of them made by skilful and judicious Hands is ever the more correct, and comes nearer the true words of the Author.[244]

In response to the complaint that the collation of texts had produced some thirty thousand variants in the New Testament alone, Bentley continued,

Not frighted therefore with the present 30,000, I for my part, and (as I believe) many others would not lament, if out of the Old Manuscripts yet untouch'd 10,000 more were faithfully collected: some of which without question would render the Text more beautiful, just, and exact; *though of no consequence to the main of Religion; nay perhaps wholy Synonymous in the view of Common Readers, and quite insensible in any modern Version.*[245]

A similar and related point can be made concerning the work of Johann Jacob Wetstein (1693–1754), the great continental biblical critic of his day, nephew of the theologian J. R. Wetstein and a pupil of the last of the great Buxtorfs, whose critical New Testament saw the light of day in a series of volumes beginning in 1749 and concluding in 1752. He possessed by both birth and training a Protestant orthodox pedigree. From the first, however, he had an interest in exegetical and textual study and an eye for critical problems or as he called them "variations" in the text. He traveled widely during his student years, visiting Richard Bentley at Trinity College, Cambridge, in 1715. There Wetstein had access to the *Codex Alexandrinus,* which he examined carefully, with the aid of magnification, coming to the conclusion, radical for his day, that the manuscript of 1 Timothy 3:16 was not written "theos" ($\overline{\Theta\Sigma}$) but

---

[244]Richard Bentley, *Remarks on a late Discourse of Free-Thinking* (London, 1713), pp. 65–66; note that Bentley's treatise was directed against Anthony Collins, *A Discourse of Free-Thinking, Occasion'd by the Rise and Growth of a Sect call'd Free-Thinkers* (London, 1713).

[245]Bentley, *Remarks on a late Discourse of Free-Thinking,* p. 72, my italics.

"hos" (ΟΣ) so that the text would read not "*God* was manifested in the flesh" but "*who* was manifested in the flesh." Not only was Wetstein's career as a critical scholar launched—in addition, the rumor of his heterodoxy was begun. Since Bentley had, in 1715, announced his conclusion that 1 John 5:7–8, the most explicitly trinitarian text in Scripture, was spurious, Wetstein's reading of 1 Timothy 3:16 looked suspiciously contrived. Indeed, just as, in the previous century, Cappel's espousal of a view of the text associated with doctrinal adversaries had led to suspicions regarding his orthodoxy, so now Wetstein's acceptance of a reading of 1 Timothy 3:16 associated with antitrinitarians brought a storm of protest.

A significant example of the attitude of the transitional era is the effort of J.-A. Turretin to produce an irenic theology, more attuned to the demands of reason but also more in touch with the needs of piety than that of the seventeenth-century orthodox. Very much after the manner of his more orthodox father, the younger Turretin shunned the attempt to endue religion and theological argument with a "mathematical" certainty—but unlike his father, he rested his point on the nature of religion rather than on the revealed character of the *principium cognoscendi theologiae*.[246] The younger Turretin was intent on arguing the truth of the Christian religion both rationally and *religiously*. Indeed, he stated rather bluntly, "either no religion is true, (which assertion runs clearly against the goodness and wisdom of God) or the Christian religion is true." And the divinity of the Christian religion is demonstrated by its efficacy against idolatry and immorality—as Chrysostom taught, after the miracles of Christ and the apostles, the propagation of Christianity is the greatest of miracles. In other words, true religion is known by its fruits.[247] And, even so, the divinity of Scripture is clearly seen from its teachings about God and from its referring of all things to the glory of God. The Psalms, by way of example, are unequaled in pagan literature, whether religious or philosophical, in their "sublime conceptions" and their pious reflections on God, which are such that no human pen could express.[248] And echoing his orthodox forbears, Turretin could state that, despite the expected obscurity of so ancient

---

[246]Cf. F. Turretin, *Inst. theol. elencticae,* with J.-A. Turretin, *Cogitationes de variis theologiae capitibus,* §41 in vol. I of *Cogitationes et dissertationes theologicae. Quibus principia religionis, cum naturalis, tum revelatae, adstruuntur & defenditur; animique ad veritatis, pietatis, & pacis studium excitantur,* 2 vols. (Geneva, 1737); and cf. the discussion, below, p. 140.

[247]J.-A. Turretin, *Cogitationes de variis theologiae capitibus,* §§37–39, 43.

[248]J.-A. Turretin, *Cogitationes de variis theologiae capitibus,* §§44–45.

a text, "all things necessary are presented plainly and understandably *(faciles)*, and all are accommodated to our understanding."[249]

Despite the echo of his father's strict orthodoxy, the tendency of the argument and the underlying sense of the conformity of Scripture and Christian doctrine to the light of reason both draw profoundly on the more rationalistic, apologetic, but nonetheless genuinely pious theology of Tronchin.[250] The more rationalistic side of the younger Turretin's approach to the text is seen, in addition, in his hermeneutics and in his theory of accommodation—which is a rather different view of accommodation than that offered by Calvin or by the orthodox writers of the seventeenth century, and occupies what might be characterized as a position half-way toward the view proposed later in his own century by Semler. The younger Turretin, for example, did not hold the first eleven chapters of Genesis to be a precise history or a scientific account: he was able to argue a valid theological and religious meaning to the stories of creation, fall, the flood, and the tower of Babel without feeling constrained to debate either matters of historical detail or of scientific cosmology. He saw, in other words, no need to reconcile the narrative of Genesis with a post-Copernican view of the world.[251] And, very much like Spinoza, Turretin could argue that Scripture was intended to lead people toward faith and obedience rather than to rational or scientific knowledge of the world order.[252]

The effects of these developments in exegesis and criticism on orthodox dogmatics were significant. Wolffian dogmaticians, like Wyttenbach and Stapfer,[253] evidence a major shift in emphasis away

---

[249]J.-A. Turretin, *Cogitationes de variis theologiae capitibus,* §47.

[250]Cf. Jacques Solé, "Ratonalisme chrétien et foi réformée à Genève autour de 1700: les derniers sermons de Louis Tronchin," in *Bulletin de la Société de l'Histoire du Protestantisme français* 128 (1982):28–43; Martin I. Klauber, "Reason, Revelation, and Cartesianism: Louis Tronchin and Enlightened Orthodoxy in Late Seventeenth-Century Geneva," in *Church History* 59 (1990): 326–39; and idem, "The Drive Toward Protestant Union in Early Eighteenth-Century Geneva: Jean-Alphonse Turretini on the 'Fundamental Articles' of Faith," in *Church History* 61 (1992):334–49.

[251]Cf. Martin I. Klauber and Glenn Sunshine, "Jean-Alphonse Turrettini on Biblical Accommodation: Calvinist or Socinian?" in *Calvin Theological Journal* 25 (1990):7–27.

[252]J.-A. Turretin, *Delucidationes,* 2.287, as cited in Klauber and Sunshine, "Jean-Alphonse Turrettini on Biblical Accommodation," pp. 19–20.

[253]Daniel Wyttenbach, *Tentamen theologiae dogmaticae methodo scientifico pertractatae,* 3 vols. (Frankfurt, 1747–49); Johann Friedrich Stapfer, *Institutiones theologiae polemicae universae, ordine scientifico dispositae,* 5 vols., 4th ed. (Zurich, 1756–57).

from the positive declaration of divinity in terms of the causality and attributes of Scripture and, in addition, an equally pronounced shift toward the discussion of critical and exegetical issues in the *locus de Scriptura sacra*. The basic doctrine—Scripture as divine by inspiration and as possessing attributes of sufficiency, perfection, perspicuity, and so forth—remains largely unchanged in its basic statement and in its prior position in the *locus*. But the interpretive or hermeneutical context of the doctrine has altered considerably. Far greater space is devoted to problems of interpretation, to the identification of the canonicity of the books of Scripture, to the style and character of the biblical writings, and to the integrity of the text of the Old and New Testaments.

Another way of making the point is to note that—despite the devastating effects of a rationalistic and deistic use of the results of the critical method in the eighteenth century upon the theological system of late orthodoxy, the method itself was not intended, by a large number of its seventeenth-century forbears and eighteenth-century users, as a negative approach or as a threat to orthodox system. If the historical and critical method eventually prevented Protestant theologians from constructing their view of Scripture and theology precisely the way in which their sixteenth- and seventeenth-century forbears did, the seventeenth-century work of textual criticism did not intentionally prevent them from reconstructing their view of Scripture and their theological system with a clearer perception of meaning and implication of the biblical materials than was available in previous ages.

The theological problem faced by late orthodoxy, including those late orthodox writers who accepted many of the results of textual criticism, was that the path from exegesis to doctrine had taken a methodological turn that removed many of the traditional *dicta probantia* from the realm of legitimate use. This process had, of course, begun already in the sixteenth century, but it had increased exponentially in the seventeenth. The problem is most obvious in cases like that of the Johannine comma and 1 Timothy 3:16, but it is also quite evident in the inability of later exegetes to apply the text of the Old Testament either to christological uses or to the direct instruction of the church in the present. In addition, given the increasingly rationalistic approach not only to the text and its problems, but also—as evidenced by J. A. Turretin's concept of accommodation—to the question of religious truth, the identification of multiple sources of biblical books, of unnamed authors and redactors, an exercise not at all theologically problematic to Poole, Henry, and other orthodox exegetes, became increasingly difficult to reconcile with an orthodox approach to doctrine.

Rather than argue a major shift in doctrinal and philosophical presuppositions within Protestantism between the time of the Reformation and the final codification of Protestant orthodoxy in the late seventeenth century,[254] we ought to identify an underlying doctrinal and philosophical continuity while, at the same time, noting an increasing emphasis on correct dogmatic statement and a fundamental change in hermeneutics from late medieval allegorical and spiritual patterns to an increasingly literal, grammatical, and critical model. The several adumbrations of the modern "critical" reading of the text just noted in the writings of Poole, Henry, and Lightfoot, ought not to be understood as stray insights pointing toward a later age and not at all of a piece with the orthodox dogmatics. The problems of authorship, linguistic and cultural context, and date identified and, from the perspective of the time, resolved by these writers were not merely reflected in the highly biblical and even biblicistic systems of theology written by the Protestant scholastics, these problems were in large part generated by the consistent interaction of exegesis and theology characteristic of the sixteenth and seventeenth centuries. The travail of orthodox theological system as it met critical problems and balanced the results of exegesis off against its doctrine of the authority of Scripture was an integral part of the development of critical, textual method—just as the development of the method was an integral part of the struggle of orthodoxy with its own doctrine of Scripture. In other words, the history of these problems as evidenced in the exegetical work of Poole, Henry, and Lightfoot and also in the dogmatic efforts of theologians like Leigh, Wendelin, and Cloppenburg, was not a history in which problems and issues noted by exegetes were then taken up and beaten about in obscurantistic and anticritical theological systems. Rather it was a history in which the ongoing effort of an increasingly textual and literalistic Protestant exegesis confronted theological formulation with textual and exegetical problems—all within the context of churchly orthodoxy and its polemic with various adversaries, particularly the Roman Catholics and the Socinians; and in which the ongoing theological formulation of the dogmaticians attempted to incorporate exegetical results, in both the form of problems and proposed solutions from the exegetes.

[254]As, e.g., in Jack B. Rogers and Donald McKim, *Interpretation and Authority of Scripture,* pp. 187–88.

Accordingly, the doctrine of Scripture found in the orthodox systems typically had two *foci* in both positive and polemical exposition: the doctrine of the authority of Scripture and the doctrine of the interpretation of Scripture. These *foci* were not fundamental principles or primary definitions from which all else in the *locus* derived; rather they were the issues around which the argument coalesced and, on the polemical side of the development of Protestant doctrine, the reasons for the shape taken by the doctrine of Scripture. Both *foci,* moreover, offer evidence of the pressures placed on the doctrine of Scripture by the course of Reformation and post-Reformation hermeneutics and textual criticism.

In many of the theological systems, the results of critical and textual study are taken up in lengthy doctrinal discourses. Thus, an English writer like Leigh and his Dutch scholastic contemporary, Cloppenburg, both discuss textual variants at some length, address the problem of the canon from the point of view of lost, spurious, and apocryphal books, and argue the character and trustworthiness of the available texts and codices.[255] Leigh even goes so far as to offer a chapter-long excursus on the best available commentaries on each of the books of the Old and New Testaments.[256] And as will be noted throughout the discussion in the present and subsequent volumes, the arguments offered by the dogmaticians stand in clear continuity with the exegetical efforts of the time and attempt to deal with the problems raised by the development of an increasingly textual and critical exegetical style.

The details of this development[257] provide evidence of a shift in emphasis that took place during the era of high orthodoxy. Although the high orthodox theologians still uniformly assert the basic principle that the historical and empirical evidences of the authority, inspiration, and divinity of Scripture are insufficient to convince the heart without the inward testimony of the Spirit, their expositions of doctrine appear to give more and more weight to the discussion of historical and empirical evidences. This shift in emphasis cannot be credited simply to polemic. It must also be understood as a reflection of the shift in hermeneutics from the spiritual, typological, and generally theological methods in vogue during the Reformation despite the Reformers' insistence on the grammar of the original

---

[255]Cf. Leigh, *A Treatise of Divinity* (London, 1646), I.vi–vii with Cloppenburg, *Exercitationes super locos communes,* I.ii–v, in *Opera Theologica,* (Amsterdam, 1684), vol. I.

[256]Leigh, *Treatise,* I.viii.

[257]See below, §§6.2 and 6.3.

languages, to the increasingly historical and critical methods of the late seventeenth and eighteenth centuries.

In other words, the emphasis on the theological determination of canon and on the internal testimony of the Spirit accorded well with the precritical exegesis of the early sixteenth century but was less in accord with the new historical understanding of the text that was dawning in the late seventeenth century and that had its impact even on the exegetical practices of the Protestant orthodox theologians. What is in fact remarkable is that the theologians of high orthodoxy, who were influenced by the new study of collateral "oriental" languages and who were far more adept at text-critical methods than the Reformers and early humanists, managed to hold as closely as they did to the Reformation emphasis on the priority of the testimony of the Spirit over historical and empirical arguments in the determination of the canon of Scripture and its authority.

PART 2

The Reformed Orthodox
Doctrine of Scripture

3

Scripture as Word of God and *principium cognoscendi theologiae*

3.1 Scripture as *principium* or Foundation of Theology

The foundation of our theology is the Word of God *(principium theologiae nostrae est Verbum Dei).*

That Word, the thing and its substance, is one and simple, but the mode of revelation *(revelationis modo)* is twofold: *endiatheton* and *prophorikon,* which is to say, internal *(internum)* and external *(externum).*

Wherefore the Word of God is called scripture: the internal Word is indeed the scripture of the heart *(scriptura cordis);* the external is the scripture of both testaments *(scriptura utriusque Testamenti).*

This scripture is considered either according to essence *(secundum essentiam)* or according to incidental properties *(secundum accidens).*[1]

These definitions and divisions stated by Polanus at the beginning of his *Syntagma* provide a convenient point of departure for a discussion of the Reformed orthodox doctrine of Scripture, both in its content and its structure. The doctrine of Scripture typically appears as the first topic of the theological system following the prolegomena, frequently linked in an organic way to the basic

[1]Polanus, *Syntagma, Synopsis libri I.*

149

definitions of theology. In order to indicate that Scripture is in fact the first doctrinal topic of the system, several of the orthodox theologians, including Cocceius, refrained from identifying the prolegomena as a *locus* of the system and designated Scripture as the *locus primus* of their theology, despite the lengthy discussions of definition and method set prior to the doctrine of Scripture.[2] The beginning of the system proper is, in other words, the exposition of the two *principia,* Scripture and God, as identified, but not fully defined or exposited, in the prolegomena.

The question of order arises immediately upon the identification of the two *principia* or foundations: should the system proceed from its ontic to its noetic foundation, or should it proceed from its noetic to its ontic *principium?* The noetic or cognitive foundation depends for its existence upon the existence and activity of the ontic or essential foundation: there could be no Word of God without God. But the essential foundation could not be known if it were not for the cognitive foundation: There could be no knowledge of God without God's self-revelation. Either order has its justification. There was also the option, favored by some of the Lutheran orthodox and present, among the Reformed in Beza's *Confessio,* and in Ames' *Medulla,* of discussing Word under the *locus* of the church and its ministry, in connection with the doctrine of the sacraments.[3]

Nonetheless, the Protestant orthodox almost invariably adopted the noetic or epistemological pattern and moved from Scripture, the *principium cognoscendi,* to God, the *principium essendi.*[4] It is simply not the case, as one writer has commented, that the Reformed scholastics began their systems with the doctrine of God or that they began "with the Eternal Decree of predestination" and from it "deduced their systems."[5] Nor is it the case that any major difference in initial order and statement of *principia* can be identified between Cocceius' reputed assault on scholastic system and the

[2]Cocceius, *Summa theol.,* cap. i, *De theologia; locus II,* beginning with cap. ii, in *Opera,* VII, pp. 133, 137.

[3]Cf. Beza, *Confessio christianae fidei,* IV.xxii–xxix, in *Tractationes theologicae,* 3 vols. (Geneva, 1582), vol. I; with Ames, *Medulla theologica,* I.xxiv.

[4]Cf., e.g., Polanus, *Syntagma,* II–III; Scharpius, *Cursus theol.,* I.ii, iii; Maccovius, *Loci communes,* iii–xiii (on Scripture), xiv–xxxv (on divine unity and trinity); Cocceius, *Summa theol.,* loci II–III; Turretin, *Inst. theol. elencticae,* II–III; Mastricht, *Theoretico-practica theol.,* I.ii, II.ii ff.; Pictet, *Theol. chr.,* I.iv–xx; II.

[5]Charles S. McCoy, "Johannes Cocceius: Federal Theologian," in *Scottish Journal of Theology* 16 (1963): 369.

scholastic systems that he attacked. Cocceius moved from prolegomena to the doctrines of Scripture and God and he developed a traditional and thoroughly "scholastic" view of both Scripture and the divine essence and attributes.[6] Similarly, there is little point in trying to argue that Calvin followed an *ordo cognoscendi* in the construction of the *Institutes* while later Reformed thinkers adopted an *ordo essendi*.[7]

The cognitive emphasis of Calvin's theology was not lost on the orthodox, and the movement from the problem of theological knowing to the doctrine of Scripture and only then to the doctrine of God, typical of Calvin's thought, is mirrored in most of the orthodox Reformed theological systems. Thus, Gomarus links his prolegomena to the doctrine of Scripture by introducing the topic of holy Scripture in the *locus de theologia* with the identification of Scripture as the proper ground of the *theologia viatorum & peregrinantium*.[8] Of the two kinds of knowledge of God available to the *viator,* the self-authenticating revelation given by God and the knowledge acquired by man for himself, only the former is certain and sure, the suitable ground of theology.[9] Gomarus, moreover, can state, by way of introduction to his *locus* on Scripture, that just as the good architect provides a good foundation for his proposed edifice, so must the theologian place his teaching concerning Scripture first in the discussion of theology: Scripture is the *basis & principium organicum* of theology.[10] Maccovius, with much the same intention, moved from his chapter on theology to a second chapter in which he identified the Word of God as "the internal principle of theology."[11]

Similarly, the Leiden *Synopsis* notes, at the beginning of its second disputation, that once the "nature of theology" has been identified, "it follows" that "the principal instrument" of revelation, Scripture, must be discussed as "the foundation and ground of all Christian doctrine."[12] The three terms used here, instrument

---

[6]Cf. Cocceius, *Summa theol.,* I–II.

[7]Dowey, *Knowledge of God in Calvin's Theology,* p. 218.

[8]Gomarus, *Disputationes,* I.1, in *Opera theologica omnia* (Amsterdam, 1644); and cf. the discussion of *theologia viatorum* in *PRRD,* I, 4.4.

[9]Gomarus, *Disputationes,* I.lii–lv.

[10]Gomarus, *Disputationes,* II, praef.

[11]Maccovius, *Loci communes,* i–ii (cf. pp. 3, 11–12).

[12]*Synopsis purioris theologiae,* II.1: "de revelatione eius praecipuo instrumento, nempe S. Scriptura, agamus; quae est omnium Christianorum dogmatum principium et fundamentum."

(instrumentum), foundation *(principium)*, and ground *(fundamentum)*, are all of significance to the Reformed scholastic understanding of the identification and use of Scripture as the basis for theology. The first of the terms indicates, as in Junius' and Maccovius' theology, the primary function of Scripture in conveying knowledge of God. In Junius' view, Scripture is the divine "instrument" by which the *principia* or *axiomata* of theology are offered to believers.[13] The second term points toward the primary dogmatic declaration of the orthodox, that all rests on Scripture. And the third term raises the issue of ultimate foundation, in relation to both the dogmatic question of the "fundamental articles" of theology and the hermeneutical question of the foundation or scope of all theological argument.[14] A central element in the development of the orthodox or scholastic teaching concerning prolegomena and *principia* was the definition of theology resting on the clear identification and distinction of these terms.

By Scripture, moreover, "we understand, not the external characters, but the Word signified by and expressed in them," which Word is the foundation of the church until the end of the age and the necessary norm of all theology.[15] At the close of the high orthodox era, Pictet marks the point of transition from his discussion of the difference between natural and supernatural revelation to his doctrine of Scripture by noting that "the Word was the most suitable means of revealing God"—being given first in direct, unwritten form and then later, as necessitated by the corruption of humanity, in written form.[16] The point could be cited in various forms—typically either as part of a distinction between natural and supernatural theology or as the simple enunciation of the *principium cognoscendi*—from virtually any of the orthodox systems.[17]

This cognitive ordering of the first two *loci* of the system had, moreover, a series of important precedents. Quite a few of the medieval doctors had developed extended discussions of Scripture and revelation in their theological prolegomena. The crucial distinction made by the medieval scholastics between *sacra doctrina* and the science of theology, moreover, not only involved a recognition

---

[13]Junius, *Theses theologicae* (Leiden), II.i, (Heidelberg), "De definitione et materia scripturae sacrae, i, iii; Maccovius, *Loci communes*, I (pp. 3–4).

[14]Cf. the discussions in *PRRD*, I, 5.2, 5.3, and 9.3 and below, §3.4.

[15]*Synopsis purioris theologiae*, II.ii; cf. iv, vi, xi.

[16]Pictet, *Theol. chr.*, I.iii.5; iv.1–2.

[17]Cf. Hottinger, *Cursus theologicus methodo Altingiana expositus* (Duisburg, 1660), II.ii, canon; Mastricht, *Theoretico-practica theol.*, I.ii.6, 48.

of the difference between exposition of the sacred page with a view to its teaching and the rigorous formulation of the theological definitions in scholastic disputation; it also involved a recognition of the connection that remained between the *sacra pagina,* the *doctrina* based on it, and the theological *scientia,* indeed, of the path that led from the one to the other.

Once theology was identified, in a technical sense, as *scientia* or *sapientia,* it was recognized as having a knowledge of first principles or *principia* by the medieval scholastics as truths known by revelation, primarily the revelation given in Scripture, clarified the relationship between the sacred page and theological science while, at the same time manifesting the reason for inclusion of a discussion of Scripture in the prolegomena prior to the doctrine of God.[18] Both *scientia* and *sapientia* draw on a knowledge of first principles for a particular purpose—*scientia* in order to draw conclusions from the *principia, sapientia* in order to set forth a knowledge of the goals or ends indicated by its *principia.* In each case, the nature of the *principia* and of their source, Scripture, not only becomes crucial to the conduct of the system as a whole but also establishes the fundamental model of the system as it draws conclusions in and for a particular direction of argument. In other words, the revealed truths or *principia* are first identified and then, inasmuch as *theologia* is both *scientia* and *sapientia,* conclusions are drawn and ends are enunciated as the fundamental work of constructing theological system.

Another precedent, already noted,[19] was the confessional embodiment of the *sola Scriptura* of the Reformers. Insofar as confessional theology offered a primary basis for doctrinal development, the tendency of the Reformed confessions to begin with a doctrine of Scripture bore immediate fruit in the structure of the Protestant orthodox systems. This confessional pattern, moreover, was echoed in several of the early Reformed systems—notably, Calvin's *Institutes* and Bullinger's *Decades* and *Compendium*—in which the movement from a declaration of *sola Scriptura* to a full *locus de Scriptura sacra,* if not completed, was certainly confirmed and expedited. Debate with Roman Catholics, moreover, was not over the question of the definition and method of theology. As we have already seen, that issue was taken up only at the end of the sixteenth century and then as an institutional and didactic topic, not as a polemical one.[20]

---

[18]De Vooght, *Les sources,* pp. 235–36, 254–56.
[19]See above, §2.1.b.
[20]*PRRD,* I, 2.3, and the introductory comments to chapters 3 and 4.

Rather, debate was over the question of authority, with specific reference to the interpretation of Scripture and to the relationship of Scripture to the church and its traditions. The result of the debate, in both confession and system, was the early development of a Protestant doctrine of Scripture that could serve, in fact, as a prolegomenon to theology in a formal sense, granting absence of actual prolegomena.

This confessional emphasis on *sola Scriptura* both maintained and transformed the medieval emphasis on a preliminary identification of *principia*. The *sola Scriptura* maintained, in both the Reformed confessions and the early orthodox systems, the logical priority of the discussion of Scripture over the doctrine of God but, because of the Reformation's radical emphasis on Scripture over against other sources of doctrine, transformed the doctrine of Scripture into a separate *locus* no longer included in the general theological prolegomena. Similarly, the confessional *sola Scriptura* maintained the dynamic of drawing conclusions and identifying ends on the basis of revealed truths but transformed the language of a multitude of *principia* elicited exegetically from Scripture into a language of Scripture broadly understood as *principium unicum theologiae,* the sole foundation of theology and, hence, the source of the exegetically elicited truths from which theological conclusions and soteriological goals could be drawn.[21]

The development from a language of multiple dogmatic *principia,* all found in the text of Scripture, to the concept of Scripture as *principium unicum theologiae,* moreover, can be identified as having taken place in the work of the Reformed theologians of the last three decades of the sixteenth century. It was typical of thinkers like Chandieu, Junius, and Lubbertus to maintain the medieval language of many biblical *principia* or *axiomata* as a foundational element in their discussions of the use of scholastic logic in Protestant theological argument.[22] Without denying that use of the term, several of their contemporaries, notably Trelcatius, Polanus, Gomarus, and the other writers of large-scale theological systems, dealt with the question inherent in the logical argumentation from biblical *principia:* when both Scripture and logic are used in the elicitation of doctrine, does the doctrine rest solely on Scripture, or

[21]Cf. *Westminster Confession,* I.vi.

[22]Cf. Chandieu, *De vera methodo,* in *Opera theologica* (Geneva, 1593), pp. 9–10, with Junius, *De vera theologia,* xi, thesis 21, in *Opuscula theologica selecta,* ed. Abraham Kuyper (Amsterdam: F. Muller, 1882); Lubbertus, *De principiis Christianorum dogmatum libri VII* (Franecker, 1591), I.i.

has reason become the foundation of theological argumentation? In positing Scripture as *principium unicum theologiae,* they presented a solution to the scholastic problem of revelation and reason that looked to the Reformation and to the Reformed confessions for its answer.[23] In the language of scholastic argumentation, Scripture is the ultimate *principium* or foundation of theology, from which the individual *principia,* more clearly identified as *axiomata,* of any given theological argument are to be drawn. This view is clearly present as the basic presupposition in the claim, typical of the Protestant scholastics, that specifically theological syllogisms can present a universal truth of reason as the major premise, but must use a truth of revelation as the minor—on the ground that revelation alone can press the conclusion, while reason functions as the instrument of argumentation.[24]

There is, therefore, an underlying continuity of development on this point from the later Middle Ages into the seventeenth century. The Protestant orthodox system does state its language of Scripture differently—more dogmatically, more technically, and in more strictly forged definitions—from the Reformers' writings, but this element of discontinuity must be understood in the context of a larger development of the terminology of theological system in which the confessions and doctrinal writings of the Reformation had an enormous impact. Thus, the Protestant orthodox did take hold here, as elsewhere in theological system, of medieval systematic models and methods, but they alter their definitions and structures significantly—an alteration that can only be explained on the basis of the Reformation and its impact on the questions of authority, canon, and exegetical method. It would be expecting too much of the Protestant orthodox to require them to set aside the whole tradition of exegetical theology on the ground of the Reformers' work, too little to require them to be "scholastic" in a medieval sense without following out the directions indicated by the Reformation, and

[23]Trelcatius, *Schol. meth.,* I.ii; Polanus, *Syntagma,* Synopsis, libri I; Gomarus, *Disputationes,* II, praef.; Johann Heinrich Alsted, *Methodus sacrosanctae theologiae octo libri tradita* (Hanoviae, 1614), I.ix,; idem, *Theologia naturalis, exhibens augustissimam naturae scholam, in qua creaturi Dei communi sermone ad omnes pariter docendos utuntur: adversus Atheos, Epicureos et Sophistas huius temporis* (Hanover, 1623), I.i; Maresius, *Collegium theol.,* I.xxiii; Cocceius, *Aphorismi ... breviores,* i.16.

[24]Cf. Chandieu, *De vera methodo,* p. 10; Turretin, *Inst. theol. elencticae,* I.vii.14; and Pictet, *Theol. chr.,* I.xiv.7, obs.3, 4 with the discussion in *PRRD,* I, 7.3.

too little on another front to expect them to imitate either the Reformation of the Middle Ages rather than moving theology toward new patterns of formulation demanded by the exigencies of exegesis, hermeneutics, and philosophical debate characteristic of their own times.

3.2 The Necessity of Revelation by the Word and the Necessity of Scripture

As a final argument of their theological prolegomena, many of the Reformed orthodox argued that theology has two *principia* or foundations, the essential foundation *(principium essendi)* and the cognitive foundation *(principium cognoscendi)*—God and Scripture. These two foundations are both necessary. Without God, there can be no word concerning God, no theology; without the scriptural revelation, there can be no genuine or authoritative word concerning God and, again, no theology. The first of these assertions is indisputable. If God did not exist, a word concerning God would be gibberish. The second assertion, however, requires supportive argumentation, inasmuch as pagan religion and rational philosophy both claim knowledge of God. In addition, the form of biblical revelation, understood as "Word," demands if not justification at least explanation and discussion of its suitability. Turretin—quite typical on this point of high orthodox dogmatics—thus moves from his prolegomena to his doctrine of Scripture with the declaration, "Inasmuch as the Word of God is the sole foundation *(principium)* of theology, even so should the issue of its necessity be raised prior to all others."[25] Maresius had, earlier, made the same transition by noting that reason is the *principium* of natural theology whereas the Word of God must be the *principium* of Christian or revealed theology inasmuch as "faith comes by hearing and hearing by the Word of God, Rom. 10:17."[26] His point, quite simply, was that theology, understood as faith *(fides quae creditur),* necessarily rests on the Word. As Whitaker pointed out, "God does not teach us now by visions, dreams, revelations, oracles, as of old, but by the scriptures alone; and therefore, if we will be saved, we must of necessity know the scriptures."[27]

Even among the transitional theologians and the late orthodox, in

[25]Turretin, *Inst. theol. elencticae,* II.i.1.
[26]Maresius, *Collegium theologicum,* I.xxiii.
[27]Whitaker, *Disputation,* VI.viii (p. 521).

whose systems a strong element of rationalist philosophy had pene-
trated, the claim of the necessity of a special, scriptural revelation
remains at the foundation of dogmatic theology proper. Thus, J.-A.
Turretin can argue, in a highly rationalistic manner, that revelation is
necessary, inasmuch as "many things can be known about the divine
by the light of nature, but not all" as is evidenced by the defects in
pagan religion and philosophy: "Thus [the apostle] Paul teaches, that
the mystery of salvation is something that the eye has not seen nor
the ear heard"—something that requires the renewal of the Spirit in
the inmost recesses of human willing.[28] What is significant here is
not only the more rationalistic tone of the argument, which is clearly
present, but the intimate blending of rationalism with religious
sentiment such as is typically associated with pietism. Even so,
Turretin writes that "those who would prove the fundamental teachings of religion *(Religionis fundamenta)* in the same manner that the
truths of mathematics are proven, have not rightly attended to the
scope and the inherent qualities of religion."[29]

The second disputation in Turretin's *De veritate religionis
judaicae et christianae* takes up the issue of the necessity of revelation. Once again, he notes that there are "many truths about God and
divine matters" that the natural light teaches, but that God is best
and most fully known through his revelations, given at various times
to various people. These revelations both confirmed and illuminated
the revelation in nature and offered necessary assistance to human
beings in their increasingly degenerate condition—and it is for this
reason, Turretin adds, that revelation must be defended against the
"Deists and other adversaries of revelation."[30]

[28]J.-A. Turretin, *Cogitationes de variis theologiae capitibus,* §34–36.

[29]J.-A. Turretin, *Cogitationes de variis theologiae capitibus,* §41.

[30]J.-A. Turretin, *De veritate religionis judaicae et christianae,* II.v, in
Cogitationes et dissertationes, vol. II. There are strong similarities between the
younger Turretin's approach to the New Testament revelation and the approach
found in Locke's *The Reasonableness of Christianity.* The point should probably be made that the distinction between constructive, rationalistic Christianity
and deism is as evident in Locke's thought as it is in J.-A. Turretin's. The tendency of some older scholarship, such as Stephen's *History of English Thought
in the Eighteenth Century,* to identify Locke's position as a "constructive
deism" must be rejected. See S. G. Hefelbower, *The Relation of John Locke to
English Deism* (Chicago: University of Chicago Press, 1918), pp. 172–78; and
note the comment of H. McLachlan: "One of the main objects of Locke and
Newton was to meet the attacks upon Christianity by Deists and skeptics. In this
they signally failed. Voltaire, and Deists like Toland, Tindal and Collins, carried
to an extreme, even irrational, length the biblical criticism of Locke, whilst they

Thus, if all that we know of "divine things" rested on the "light of reason and philosophy," we would know less and know it less accurately than we are able to discern from revelation. What is more, as Lactantius taught, the lacks and weaknesses of philosophy are supplied by revelation.[31] If religion is founded only on the light of reason, human ignorance and weakness intrudes and the sublime and spiritual truths of religion are obscured: both the fullness of God's law and the offer of salvation are available only through revelation.[32] It is also the case that the divine attributes of goodness and mercy, wisdom, holiness, majesty, and glory are not clearly discerned by reason alone and require revelation for their full understanding; so also the right worship of God, the right understanding of our duties in life, the way of approaching the anger of God, and the path to true blessedness are known only through revelation.[33] Against the deists, it must be pointed out that even Cicero lamented the obscurity of the natural light and the extent of human depravity. Neither the pagan philosophers nor the pagan religions understand the truth of God or rescue human beings from their ignorance.[34]

Wyttenbach, who had taken the Wolffian position that natural theology necessarily preceded Christian or revealed theology, went so far as to remove natural or rational theology from the realm of revelation strictly so-called: "when God makes known to human beings certain necessary things, that man cannot know by the power of his intellect or by the nature of his soul, this is called revelation."[35] Revelation is therefore necessary in order that human beings might be freed from their sins—and for the sake of the right teaching of theology. Natural theology, as known to the heathen, can identify the divine attributes, but, writes Wyttenbach, it lacks the practical truths and high morality of the New Testament revelation,[36] and it cannot lead to the right worship of God by a pure and sanctified

---

brought out more clearly, and separate from his doctrine of revelation, the materialism and skepticism inherent in his philosophy" (*The Religious opinions of Milton, Locke and Newton* [Manchester: Manchester University Press, 1941], p. 206).

[31]J.-A. Turretin, *De veritate religionis judaicae et christianae,* II.vi–vii.

[32]J.-A. Turretin, *De veritate religionis judaicae et christianae,* II.x–xi.

[33]J.-A. Turretin, *De veritate religionis judaicae et christianae,* II.xxiii–xxiv.

[34]J.-A. Turretin, *De veritate religionis judaicae et christianae,* II.xxxi–xxxiii.

[35]Wyttenbach, *Tentamen theologiae dogmaticae,* I.94.

[36]Wyttenbach, *Tentamen theologiae dogmaticae,* I.96, scholion 2, citing Clarke's *Natural Theology* and Locke's *Reasonableness of Christianity.*

mind.[37] Revelation, argues Wyttenbach—in a far more rationalistic vein than his predecessors—is given in order than human beings "might be led clearly and surely *(clarè et certò)* toward their heavenly reward."[38]

There is a profound theological link, therefore, preserved even in the era of late orthodoxy, between the declaration of the Word of God as one of the *principia theologiae* and the discussion of the necessity of revelation by means of Scripture. Indeed, the statement of *principia,* which itself appeared relatively late in the development of sixteenth-century Protestant thought,[39] must be viewed as a highly formalized outgrowth of the early Reformed declarations of the necessity of a written Word of God, at the same time that it is also an outgrowth and natural result of the medieval discussion of theology as a science with identifiable first principles.[40] We recognize immediately, therefore, the issue of multiple lines of continuity as well as various elements of discontinuity between medieval, Reformation, and post-Reformation language of the Word written as the necessary foundation of Christian doctrine. The medieval form of the doctrine was intimately bound up with the transition, found in the writings of late twelfth- and thirteenth-century doctors, from a view of theology as the holy writ *(sacra pagina)* to a distinction between the theology that is Scripture and the theology that is a ratiocinative discipline, a *scientia.*[41]

The Reformation and post-Reformation forms of the doctrine did not at all set aside this basic development. A distinction between Scripture as source and theology as discipline is arguably present in the writings of even the earliest and least systematic of the Reformers. What distinguishes the Reformers and the medieval doctors is the radical biblicism of the Reformation—the *sola Scriptura* was initially argued in the context of a theology based on commentaries and constructed from *loci* drawn out of commentaries, as over against a theology that drew its *loci* and what later came to be called *sedes doctrinae* out of the tradition as well as out of Scripture. Understood in this way, the debate over Scripture and authority can easily be seen, for example, in Melanchthon's initial reluctance to construct his *Loci communes* around such traditionary dogmatic topics as the Trinity and the two natures of Christ and in Calvin's

---

[37]Wyttenbach, *Tentamen theologiae dogmaticae,* I.97.
[38]Wyttenbach, *Tentamen theologiae dogmaticae,* I.98.
[39]Cf. *PRRD,* I, 2.3.
[40]Cf. *PRRD,* I, 2.1, 9.3.
[41]Cf. *PRRD,* I, 2.1.

cautious advocacy of the traditional trinitarian language of person and hypostasis, substance and essence.[42]

Of course, the view of the necessity of Scripture found in the writings of the Reformers—notably in Bullinger's *Decades* and *Compendium christianae religionis* and in Calvin's *Institutes*—is immediately related to their biblical reconstruction of theology and only in a more remote sense to the older language of theology as a science with its own *principia*. The development and clarification of that latter connection was the work of Protestant orthodoxy. The Refomers' immediate interest was in the status of Scripture not merely as authoritative but as bound up with the work of salvation. Granting their strong emphasis on original sin and salvation by grace alone, they emphasized the necessity of the biblical Word over against the use of reason and the examination of God's handiwork in the natural order.[43] In addition, the Reformers' clear sense of the self-authenticating character of Scripture—the a priori character of Scripture as a self-evidencing norm—flowed directly into the ortho-dox identification of Scripture as the *principium cognoscendi theologiae principia,* of their very nature, stand prior to and provide the grounds for a form of knowledge. In the case of the late orthodox, notably Wyttenbach and Van Til,[44] this sense of the necessity of revelation over against reason was modified and became a sense of the necessity of revelation in addition to reason —but this modifica-tion is clearly the work of the early eighteenth century, after the so-called era of the "transitional theologians." An element of change, discontinuity, and most probably a sign of rationalism is evident in the lack of discussion of the character of Scripture as Word or of the concept of revelation as Word from the theologies of Van Til and Wyttenbach. The issue is not that these theologians ignore the iden-tification of Scripture as *verbum Dei*—they simply do not elaborate at any length on the concept, with the result that the mode of revela-tion, specifically, the "lively" dynamic of divine communication. And here, on this specific point, the interest of the Reformation finally disappears—not in the era of early or high orthodoxy, but in the early eighteenth century.[45]

---

[42]Cf. Melanchthon, *Loci communes* (1521), in CR, 21, cols. 84–85 with Calvin, *Institutes*, I.xiii. See *PRRD,* III, 2.2, 6.2.

[43]Cf. Calvin, *Institutes,* I.v–vi.

[44]Cf. Wyttenbach, *Tentamen theologiae dogmaticae,* I.93–100, with Van Til, *Theologiae utriusque compendium ... revelatae,* I.i.

[45]Cf. Wyttenbach, *Tentamen theologiae dogmaticae,* II.101ff., with Van Til, *Theologiae utriusque compendium ... revelatae, principium,* I–IV.

There is also, therefore, a profound connection between this portion of the *locus de Scriptura* and the discussion of natural and supernatural revelation in the Reformed theological prolegomena. There the point was made that the revelation of God in nature was sufficient to provide a rudimentary knowledge of the existence and attributes of God and of the law—sufficient, at least, to ground a kind natural theology that would leave sinners without excuse before God, but insufficient for salvation.[46] Here, too, the Protestant orthodox stand in substantial continuity with the Reformers: Calvin's doctrine of Scripture, arising as it does out of his discussion of the *duplex cognitio Dei,* emphasizes the necessity of a scriptural record of special, saving revelation over against the knowledge of God the creator available in both the natural order and Scripture itself.[47]

There are several basic patterns in Reformed theological system for integrating the concept of the necessity of the written word with the doctrine concerning the way in which Scripture is to be understood as Word. One approach, found in Calvin's *Institutes* and in several of the high orthodox systems—notably those of Burmann, Turretin, and Heidegger—places an initial, formal emphasis on the necessity of Scripture as the basis for developing an entire doctrine of Scripture. This pattern, which would place the *necessitas Scripturae* first in order in the various topics of the *locus de Scriptura sacra,* was not followed by the major codifiers of the early orthodox period, with the important exception of Ursinus. A related pattern of argument, found in Bullinger's *Decades* and *Compendium* and developed into a fully scholastic form by Polanus, that begins the *locus* with a discussion and definition of Word and of the activity or work of Word is more characteristic of early orthodoxy. Both Calvin and Bullinger, moreover, and after them Ursinus, stress the relationship between religion and revelation. This one aspect of their ordering of the discussion would pass over into almost all of the orthodox systems, whether early or high orthodox, regardless of other patterns and arrangements of doctrine.

A third pattern, not altogether different from the definition of *verbum Dei* used by Bullinger and by Polanus, Scharpius, and Maccovius to begin their *locus de Scriptura,* is followed by orthodox dogmaticians like Gomarus, Walaeus (in both his own *Loci communes* and the Leiden *Synopsis*), and Mastricht, where the *locus* is introduced by a definition of *Scriptura sacra.* In the case of the

---

[46]Cf. *PRRD,* I, ch. 5.
[47]Cf. Kantzer, "Calvin and the Holy Scriptures," pp. 116–17.

Leiden *Synopsis,* this pattern leads directly to the discussion of the necessity and, then, the authority of Scripture.

A fourth pattern that can be identified in the work of late orthodox writers like Venema, Vitringa, Van Til, Wyttenbach, and Stapfer, whose theology was influenced by the rationalist climate of the time, acknowledges three *principia theologiae*—God, the *principium essendi,* reason, the *principium cognoscendi primum,* and revelation, the *principium cognoscendi alterum.*[48] Even here, however, despite the acknowledgment of the validity of reason as a foundation of theological knowing that, even after the fall, offers knowledge that is useful to the church, there is a clear pronouncement of the necessity of revelation: granting the blindness of fallen humanity, Vitringa writes, "some praeternatural revelation, i.e., another kind of foundation for theological doctrine, was therefore necessary, if sinful human beings were to know and to attain to God in his true glory, and in order that people might be lifted up in new hope."[49] In introducing his doctrine of the sufficiency and perspicuity of Scripture, Vitringa also, in a highly rationalistic manner, argues that if there is indeed revelation in this world, it will be known by certain marks or evidences *(notas)*—such as divine origin and absence of falsehood—and from the positive consequences of its use in religion.[50] The pattern of these systems is, therefore, to move from the definitions of theology, through the identification of *principia,* to the argument concerning the insufficiency of reason for salvation and the necessity of revelation, and finally to the doctrine of Scripture as the vehicle of the necessary revelation. The result, of course, is a somewhat altered form of "orthodoxy"—the impact of reason as a foundation remains considerable after the fall and, if not the overt cause of major alterations in actual dogmatic statement, this more foundational entrance of reason did have an impact on the

[48]Herman Venema, *Institutes of Theology,* part I, trans. Alexander Brown (Edinburgh: T. & T. Clark, 1850), pp. 8–20, 31; Vitringa, *Doctrina christianae religionis,* vol. I (analysis), p. 44; I.16; Wyttenbach, *Tentamen theologiae dogmaticae,* I, §6, 96–100; Van Til, *Theologiae utriusque compendium ... naturalis,* I, prooem., ii.1; Van Til, *Theologiae utriusque compendium ... revelatae,* I.i (pp. 3–4); and cf. Stackhouse, *A Complete Body of Speculative and Practical Divinity,* 3 vols. (Dumfries, 1776), I.iii (p. 26); Johann Friedrich Stapfer, *Institutiones theologiae polemicae universae, ordine scientifico dispositae,* 4th ed., 5 vols. (Zurich, 1756-57), I, I.i, vi–xiii.

[49]Vitringa, *Doctrina christianae religionis,* I.34; Wyttenbach, *Tentamen theologiae dogmaticae,* I, §96–100.

[50]Vitringa, *Doctrina christianae religionis,* II.1–3.

underlying patterns of hermeneutics, by opening the system of theology increasingly to the results of a more rationalistic, historical, and critical method of interpretation.

The problem confronting this cognitive ordering of theology during the later years of orthodoxy can be seen even more clearly in the pattern of a nominally orthodox English system like Stackhouse's *Body of Divinity*. Here the system begins not with a prolegomenon on the meaning of theology and the identification of its *principia,* but with discussions of religion in general and of the rational knowledge available to all people of the existence and the goodness of God. In a third chapter, Stackhouse comes to the problem of divine revelation as the basis of a distinctively Christian theology and, prior to discussing its necessity, engages in a discussion of its "possibility" and "expediency."[51] Only following these principial discussions conducted on the basis of reason does Stackhouse approach the traditionally prior argument that sin has made necessary a salvific revelation. He also rehearses the forms of Mosaic and prophetic revelation, the revelation in Christ and that given to the apostles, arguing rationally that they are to be valued, before arriving at his statement concerning Scripture itself and the necessity of Scripture as the written form of revelation.[52] A similar pattern is to be found in Wyttenbach's thought.[53]

Virtually all of the orthodox systems, therefore, begin the *locus de Scriptura sacra* with a complex of definitions that focus on the character and necessity for salvation of the Judaeo-Christian revelation as given in the Old and New Testaments: Word and Scripture are defined in relation to one another and the necessity of both revelation by the Word and the embodiment of Word in Scripture are presented as a basis for understanding subsequent topics like the divinity, authority, canon, and interpretation of Scripture. Within this larger consensus, we also detect, however, a diversity of patterns of exposition and, in the late seventeenth and eighteenth centuries, an increasing reliance on the powers of reason that allows for an increasingly large body of theological argumentation to precede the discussion of Scripture and of revealed, "praeternatural" or "supernatural" doctrine. The pattern of exposition adopted in this study moves from the necessity of revelation by the Word, to the necessity of the scriptural Word, followed by a definition of

[51]Cf. Stackhouse, *Complete Body of Divinity,* I, pp. 26–29.
[52]Stackhouse, *Complete Body of Divinity,* I, pp. 38–70.
[53]Wyttenbach, *Tentamen theologiae dogmaticae,* II, §101ff.

Scripture (3.2), to the definition of "Word" in its several forms, as that definition develops out of the logic of the preceding discussions (3.3; 3.4)—with the intention of manifesting both the diversity and the broad agreement of the Reformed systems in their historical development.

The necessity of an embodiment of God's revelation in Scripture over against the inability of fallen creatures to learn rightly of God through the exercise of their own natural powers provides Calvin with the basic impulse to formulate his view of Scripture in the *Institutes*.[54] The sinfulness of humanity acts as an impediment even to our knowledge of God as Creator, so that a further revelation than that present in the natural order must be given if human beings are to understand rightly even the relation of the one true God to the order of nature. The biblical Word comes as a light to people who walk in darkness: "Scripture, gathering up the otherwise confused knowledge of God in our minds, having dispersed our dullness, clearly shows us the true God." Scripture, therefore, first teaches of God as Creator, only afterwards drawing our spirits onward through the law and the prophets to a knowledge of God as Redeemer. If we neglect or turn aside from this "rule of eternal truth" our attempt to know God involves us in an "inexplicable labyrinth" of our own error.[55]

Thus, Calvin would write in his commentary on 2 Peter 1:19, "Without the Word, there is nothing left but darkness." Calvin never wished to deny the existence of a general knowledge of God "naturally implanted in the minds of men," or that religion in general —pagan religion—was devoid of a fundamental sense of the divine.[56] Rather, Calvin sought to emphasize the inability and unwillingness of human beings to take advantage of this knowledge:

> As experience shows, God has sown a seed of religion in all men. But scarcely one man in a hundred is met with who fosters it, once received, in his heart, and none in whom it ripens—much less shows fruit in season.[57]

In "proud vanity and obstinacy," fallen human beings refuse to avail themselves of this natural revelation and construct superstition and idolatry until "no real piety remains in the world." Into this

---

[54]Calvin, *Institutes,* I.vi.1.
[55]Calvin, *Institutes,* I.vi.1–4.
[56]Calvin, *Institutes,* I.xiii, title and 2; cf. the discussion in *PRRD,* I, 5.1–2.
[57]Calvin, *Institutes,* I.iv.1.

darkness, God shines the light of his Word, "another and better help ... to direct us aright to the very creator of the universe."[58]

Calvin understands, moreover, that there is a historical, perhaps a covenantal, dimension to this new, firm ground of the knowledge of God given through the Word. God, according to Calvin, saw the confusion of fallen humanity and, in drawing a particular people, Israel, to himself also determined to provide them with a revelation capable of grounding and sustaining their faith and obedience in a way that natural revelation was not.

> Not only does he teach the elect to look upon a god, but also shows himself as the God upon whom they are to look. He has from the beginning maintained this plan for his church, so that besides these common proofs he has also put forth his word, which is a more direct and certain mark whereby he is to be recognized.[59]

This emphasis on the economy of salvation is evidenced also in the parallel between the introductory logic of Calvin's doctrine of Scripture and that of his Christology. In both places, Calvin brings his readers to a recognition of the problem of human sinfulness and of the absence of saving knowledge. In the former place, a sense of man's inability to find God in a saving way through natural revelation leads to a statement of the necessity of the special revelation given in Scripture; in the latter, the unfulfilled prophecies of the old covenant and man's inability to come to God of his own will lead to a statement of the necessity of mediation in and by means of the God-man. The necessity of Scripture is grounded on the necessity of revelation as a form of mediated knowledge—and the Scripture, once given, reveals the necessity of a mediated salvation.[60]

If the study of the Scriptures leads to a right understanding of God and his will, it is also true that a reverent consideration of the problem of the knowledge of God leads back to the Scriptures. Bullinger argues this on the premise that the inward intentions of human beings are learned from the human beings themselves:

> For as no one knows what is in a man, but the spirit of man that is within him; so also can no one declare what God is, except God in his Word. For whoever feigns other opinions and attempts to

---

[58]Calvin, *Institutes,* I.vi.1.
[59]Calvin, *Institutes,* I.vi.1.
[60]Cf. Calvin, *Institutes,* I.vi.i, with II.xii.1.

obtain this knowledge of God by other means, beguiles himself
and worships idols of his own heart.[61]

The dogmatic assertion of Scripture alone finds its foundation in the
identity of Scripture as the "Word" of the divine speaker, with the
implication, by way of reference to "the spirit of man" that, in
Scripture, there is a profound association of Word and Spirit.

Among the major works of transition from the Reformation style
to the style of early orthodoxy are Ursinus' *Doctrinae christianae
compendium* or, as it was called in later editions, *Explicationes catecheseos,* and his *Loci theologici.* Ursinus' work was particularly
important for the establishment of the connection, so typical of
orthodoxy, between the concept of religion and the argument for the
necessity of revelation, specifically, the necessity of revelation by
means of the scriptural Word as presented in the *locus de Scriptura
sacra.* Ursinus made the connection in his *Loci* and his editors
adapted the locus for use as a prolegomenon to some of the later
editions of the catechetical lectures.

Ursinus began his discussion of Scripture and its interpretation
by noting that our very humanity is predicated on religion. All
human beings "embrace and profess some opinion of God and his
will, as also some manner of worshipping him, partly drawn from
nature itself, partly received by persuasion: this is called religion."[62]
What is more, these same people will all grant that true religion
comes from God and that they must yield to God's revealed will.
Despite this general agreement, resting on natural or innate and on
acquired knowledge of God, Ursinus quickly adds, there has been
perpetual controversy in matters of religion. Indeed, debate will not
end "until our Lord Jesus Christ, returning to judge the living and
the dead, decides the controversy."[63] Since there is only one true
religion and, consequently, only one path to salvation, it is necessary
to establish and discuss the source of that religion before any presentation of doctrine can be offered. That doctrine is true that "God
himself, even from the creation of man, delivered by his own voice
to our first fathers, and afterwards conveyed in the Scriptures by the
prophets and the apostles."[64] Granting the historical premise that
God no longer speaks to mankind as he once did, but that revelation

---

[61]Heinrich Bullinger, *Compendium christianae religionis* (Zurich, 1556), I.ii
(fol. 33).
[62]Ursinus, *Loci theologici,* col. 426.
[63]Ursinus, *Loci theologici,* col. 426.
[64]Ursinus, *Loci theologici,* col. 426.

has moved forward historically in forms suited to the needs of the human race, all affirmations concerning "God and the salvation of man ... depend on the written word," the Scriptures. It is worth noting that this view of Scripture, as found in Ursinus' writings and in many of the early orthodox systems, echoes the model of *historica series* proposed by Ursinus' teacher, Melanchthon, and the historical movement from the revealing voice of God to the written word noted briefly in Calvin's *Institutes*,[65] and points toward federal elements of the Reformed system, particularly as they impinge on the doctrine of Scripture and the basic hermeneutical questions of moving from exegesis to doctrine.

This necessary interrelationship between Scripture and true religion carries over into the four questions that Ursinus poses as the basic structure of his subsequent argument:

1. What Holy Scripture teaches.

2. How the religion delivered in Scripture differs from other religion.

3. How it may be known that this religion alone is true and divine, and all others are false.

4. Why no doctrine is to be received in the church apart from Holy Scripture.[66]

What is more, Ursinus' questions indicate also several of the crucial connections made by orthodoxy between the doctrine of Scripture and the other *loci* of theological system. Thus, the question of the interpretation of Scripture points toward the construction of a body of doctrine; the Scriptures themselves and their religion must somehow be identified as the basis of *theologia vera* as over against *theologia falsa*—reflecting, once again, an issue that would be discussed in the prolegomena of early orthodoxy as well as the concept of Scripture as self-evidencing and capable of being shown intrinsically and extrinsically to be divine; and why Scripture provides not just one foundation among others, but the sole foundation of churchly doctrine.

Beginning in the era of early orthodoxy, and building on these distinctions between the past and present, inward and outward forms of Word, and between the various kinds of evidence available to identify Scripture as the foundation of true doctrine, Protestant

[65]Calvin, *Institutes,* IV.viii.5–6.
[66]Ursinus, *Loci theologici,* col. 426.

theologians presented this historical view of the production of
Scripture—the movement, as they understood it, from immediate
divine speech to the written forms of revelation—as an aspect of the
history of sin and salvation and as an indication of the corporate
nature of the covenant, thereby giving a doctrinal interpretation to
the historical problem of Word and its "inscripturation" and providing a basis for the incorporation of the doctrinal issue of the
necessity of Scripture into theological system. The doctrinal discussion of the necessity of Scripture, thus, amounts to a historical and
soteriological "proof" that the *principium cognoscendi theologiae,*
the Word of God, cannot merely be embodied in an oral tradition
but—contrary to the assertions of post-Tridentine theologians like
Cano—must be given in written form.[67] The movement from the
oral tradition of the patriarchs to the written form of the Mosaic
Torah becomes a historical and soteriological argument against the
claims of unwritten revelation and oral tradition in the sixteenth
century. What was accomplished by divine purpose in the time of
Moses—the beginnings of the written Word—has become the normative form for the maintenance and proclamation of the truths of
God's revelation in the church of all ages.

A further variation on this theme, in which the historical dynamic
is even more evident, is taken up by the Protestant orthodox in their
discussion of the unwritten and written forms of Word.[68] The issues
raised by these historical and economic arguments, moreover, point
toward the increasing importance of covenant theology in Reformed
dogmatics and, specifically, toward the interest of covenant theology
in the relationship of the Old and New Testaments within the
covenant of grace. Of particular importance, given the cumulative,
historical development of the canon of Scripture is the question of
the retention and abrogation of various elements of the Old Testament revelation—a problem debated in both the doctrine of Scripture itself and the doctrine of the covenant of grace.[69]

---

[67]Melchior Cano, *De locis theologicis* (1564), in J.-P. Migne (ed.)
Theologiae cursus completus, vol. 1 (Paris, 1837), III.3 (cols 244, 250).

[68]Cf. below §3.3.

[69]Cf., for example, Maccovius, *Loci communes,* ix–xiii; on the problem of
the two Testaments in relation to the doctrine of covenant, see in particular
Johannes Cocceius, *Summa doctrinae de foedere et testamento Dei* (1648) and
Summa theologiae ex sacris scripturis repetita (1662). Cocceius' approach had
a major impact on the theologies of Franz Burmann, Francis Turretin, and J. H.
Heidegger, as well as a clear successor in the great *De oeconomia foederum Dei
cum hominibus libri quattuor* (1677) of Hermann Witsius. On the history and

In addition, this historical pattern was taken up into the logical structure of the doctrine of Scripture, preeminently by Polanus, who presents the topic in a series of neat logical divisions:

> The necessity of Holy Scripture is considered either in terms of its being written or in terms of its continued existence, especially if one views the goal of Scripture *(Scripturae finem),* which is two-fold, theoretical and practical, the former pertaining to knowledge, the latter to action.
>
> The theoretical goal, similarly, is twofold: doctrinal or judicial.
>
> And the judicial goal is also twofold: directive and definitive *(directivus & definitivus).*[70]

As both the logical partitions of Polanus' *Synopsis* and the arrangement of the actual chapters of the *Syntagma* make clear, Polanus understands the *necessitas Scripturae* to be one of the attributes of the extant text—alongside of authority, authenticity, perspicuity, and so forth—a topic which he can treat only after he has discussed the divinity of Scripture, its authority, and the contents of the canon of Scripture.[71]

Polanus' basic theorem or thesis in disputation with the "heretics"—in his mind, both the Roman Catholics with their emphasis on oral tradition and various Anabaptist or Spiritualist groups with their insistence on present-day revelations—is the "Holy Scripture, from the time that it was given by God to the church, was, is, and will be necessary, not only to the well-being *(bene esse)* but also to the very existence *(esse)* of the church."[72] The necessity of Scripture, therefore, takes on a historical dimension and is directly related to the economy of salvation. The books of Moses, Polanus insists, were necessary to the church in the time of Moses, but the books of the New Testament were not then

---

development of the Reformed federal theology and the various controversies over the doctrine of covenant, see Gottlob Schrenck, *Gottesreich und Bund im älteren Protestantismus vornehmlich bei Johannes Cocceius: Zugleich ein Beitrag zur Geschichte des Pietismus und der heilsgeschichtlichen Theologie* (Gütersloh: Bertelsmann, 1923); Gass, *Geschichte der protestantischen Dogmatik,* II, pp. 253–323; and Charles S. McCoy, "The Covenant Theology of Johannes Cocceius" (Ph.D. diss., Yale University, 1956).

[70]Polanus, *Syntagma, Synopsis libri I.*

[71]Polanus, *Syntagma theol.,* I.xxxv (pp. 69–74).

[72]Polanus, *Syntagma,* I.xxxv (p. 69, col. 2).

necessary—whereas now, inasmuch as both the Old and the New Testaments have been graciously given by God to the church, both are necessary to its existence. It is the height of impiety, comments Polanus, to claim that the Scriptures are not necessary—as if what God has given to his church could easily be dispensed with! Scripture is necessary to the *bene esse* of the church because it is useful to the establishment of both the faith and the true worship of God. It is necessary to the *esse* of the church for the sake of the conservation of true doctrine in the face of heresy.[73]

Polanus' British contemporary, Robert Rollock, had similarly identified "necessity" as one of the "properties" of Scripture. If, he argued, the Scripture is rightly understood as the "very writing and form of revelation," it appears that there could be no church without Scripture. The point, we note, reflects the early Reformed confessional declaration that the church is born of the Word of God,[74] but adds, in response to Roman Catholic polemic, that Scripture is indeed the living Word:

> For the lively voice of God is simply necessary. The Scripture, after a sort, is the lively voice of God: therefore [it is] simply necessary.[75]

There was, indeed, Rollock adds, a time when God spoke directly to his people, "but when God did cease to speak, and that Scripture came in place of God's own voice, then the Scripture was no less necessary than the lively voice of God." The history of God's revelation manifests this pattern: From Adam to Moses God spoke directly, but thereafter—at least, generally—in the writings of Moses and the prophets. When Christ came, the lively voice of God was again present in Christ's own person and in the spoken words of the apostolic preaching. But now, once more, in the "apostolical Scripture" of the New Testament, the voice of God is again provided in written form.[76] The necessity of a historical development from unwritten to written Word, precisely for the sake of maintaining the *viva vox Dei* in the hearts of believers, is thus posed against Cano's

---

[73]Polanus, *Syntagma theol.,* I.xxxv (p. 69, col. 2).

[74]*Theses Bernenses,* I (in Schaff, Creeds, III, p. 208).

[75]Rollock, *Treatise of Effectual Calling,* p. 88; cf. Cano, *De locis theologicis,* III.3 (col. 349), and Tavard, "Tradition in Early Post-Tridentine Theology," p. 383.

[76]Rollock, *Treatise of Effectual Calling,* pp. 89–90.

claim of an ongoing tradition of the spirit, rather than the letter or scriptural Word, in the hearts of the faithful.[77]

In disagreement with Rollock's conclusion that this necessity was absolute or simple,[78] Polanus argues that God is not absolutely bound to the scriptural form of revelation—as if he were unable to teach his church in another manner. Indeed, from the beginning of the world to Moses, God did teach his church in other ways. What appears, here, is that reasoning like that of Rollock made a clear enough historical distinction between the living voice and the written word but failed to apply that distinction logically either to the problem of the necessity of Scripture or to the problem of the meaning of "Word." Polanus moved toward a more precise definition. Scripture, he notes, has been ordained by God and commended to the church as the foundation of right teaching. To develop a simile—Scripture is not only necessary in the way that the power of life *(ops vitae)* is necessary to corporeal existence, but it is also necessary as daily bread is necessary. The Word of God is both power and nourishment and is, therefore, necessary. Since, however, this necessity rests on the divine ordination, of a particular means of empowering and nourishing, it is technically "a necessity in consequence of a divine disposition" *(necessitas ex hypothesi dispositio divinae),* rather than an absolute necessity.[79] Polanus' somewhat more subtle definition rather than Rollock's became the position of Reformed orthodoxy.

Thus, we find in the theology of the English writer, Edward Leigh, the argument that Scripture is necessary.

> In respect of the substance thereof, it was always necessary; in respect of the manner of revealing it is necessary since the time that it pleased God after that manner to deliver his word, and shall be to the world's end. It is not then absolutely and simply necessary, that the word of God should be delivered to us in writing, but only conditionally and upon supposition.[80]

Virtually identical arguments appear in the Leiden *Synopsis* and in systems of Turretin, Riissen, and Mastricht.[81] Weemes makes the

---

[77]Cano, *De locis theologicis,* III.3 (cols. 244, 249); cf. Tavard, "Tradition in Early Post-Tridentine Theology," p. 383.

[78]Rollock, *Treatise of Effectual Calling,* p. 90.

[79]Polanus, *Syntagma,* I.xxxv (p. 69, col. 2).

[80]Leigh, *Treatise,* I.viii (pp. 135–36).

[81]Cf. *Synopsis purioris theologiae,* II.vii; Turretin, *Inst. theol. elencticae,*

point that God's Word, as such, was absolutely necessary granting that it reveals the will of God to humanity, while "his written word was necessary as an instrumentall cause."[82]

The necessity may be further understood as a necessity of writing *(necessitas scriptionis)* or as a necessity of the continued existence of Scripture *(necessitas perpetuae existentiae Scripturae)* in the church. The former necessity can be inferred both from the divine command to Moses and the prophets that they write what was revealed to them (Exod. 17:14; 34:27; Jer. 30:2: Ezek. 43:11) and from the command of Christ to the apostles that they teach all nations (Matt. 28:19). The apostles, Polanus continues, carried out the command of Christ in two ways: they preached the gospel with a living voice *(viva vox)* and, when they could not be present in person, they evangelized the world through their writings. Inasmuch as the apostles are now absent, those living after them must, by necessity, use their written word until the end of the world.[83] Even so, after the ascension of Christ, the apostolic council began its work with a letter written under the guidance of the Spirit—and Paul himself testifies to the inspiration of Scripture, thereby indicating its origin according to the will of God and giving warrant to the claim of its necessity. Polanus concludes syllogistically: "Whatsoever scripture is of divine inspiration, is written by the divine will: But the entire prophetic and apostolic scripture is inspired: Ergo, & c."[84] Scripture, in other words, is necessary *ex hypothesi dispositio divinae,* granting that it has been willed by God. At the close of the orthodox era, Mastricht will still argue that the necessity of Scripture can be inferred from the divine motive in inspiring the amanuenses, the prophets, and the apostles.[85]

In one place, moreover, Scripture itself states the necessity of writing. Jude, the brother of James, writes to the church, "I found it necessary to write to you"—"Necesse habui vobis scribere."[86] This statement and the broader inference of a necessity of writing, finally, are consistent with the apostolic office *(munus)*—it was given to the

---

II.ii.3; Riissen, *Summa theol.,* II.vii; Mastricht, *Theoretico-practica theol.,* I.ii.20.

[82]Weemes, *Exercitations Divine,* p. 61.

[83]Polanus, *Syntagma,* I.xxxv (p. 69, col. 2); cf. Whitaker, Disputation, VI.viii (pp. 521–22).

[84]Polanus, *Syntagma theol.,* I.xxxv (p. 70, col. 1), citing Acts 15:23–29 and 2 Tim. 3:16.

[85]Mastricht, *Theoretico-practica theol.,* I.ii.20.

[86]Polanus, *Syntagma,* I.xxxv (p. 70, col. 1), citing Jude 3.

apostles to be universal teachers of the church *(doctores universales)* in both time and place and not merely for their own time and place. Their mandate was to bring the gospel into all of the world until the end of the age. Their teaching, therefore, needed to be preserved in such a way that it could be transmitted without corruption to future generations.[87]

The nature of the apostolic mission serves Polanus as the point of transition to his next argument—the "necessity of the continued existence of Scripture." In the first place, we are commanded by God to search and to become deeply acquainted with Scripture. Scripture must exist until the end of the world for the fulfillment of this divine command in each generation of the church. Thus, too, Mastricht notes, the general command of Christ to the disciples to "teach all nations" is modified by the extension of that teaching *ad consummationem saeculi.*[88] Second, Scripture contains the teaching necessary to the work of the church, without which the church could not function. Third, Scripture has been put into writing as "the firm and certain cause of faith"—as Luke says of his own writing (Luke 1:4) and Paul also indicates (Phil. 3:1). Scripture is, then, with reference to the text from Luke, the *asphaleias fidei causa,* the secure or certain cause of faith.[89] Even so, Christ himself, after his resurrection, directed his disciples to the Scriptures in order to make their faith more firm and certain (Luke 24:26–27). Fourth, the perpetual existence of Scripture is necessary since, without Scripture, we could neither know the truth of heavenly doctrine *(vertias coelestis doctrinae),* nor preserve ourselves from error, from barbarism or from sin, nor instruct ourselves in holy living, nor have any firm consolation in this life.[90]

With his fifth reason for the necessity of the preservation of Scripture, Polanus comes to the *finis proximus sacrae Scripturae.* The proximate goal of Scripture, Polanus asserts, is "utterly necessary," granting that this goal is the existence of the church universal and its work of instruction in faith and piety, its teaching of the truth, and its adjudication of doctrinal controversy.[91] The *finis proximus* of Scripture, therefore, is twofold—doctrinal and judicial. It is doctrinal inasmuch as Scripture has been written down for the sake of teaching *(doctrina);* it is judicial inasmuch as Scripture has

---

[87]Polanus, *Syntagma,* I.xxxv (p. 70, col. 1).
[88]Mastricht, *Theoretico-practica theol.,* I.ii.20.
[89]Polanus, *Syntagma,* I.xxxv (p. 70, col. 1).
[90]Polanus, *Syntagma,* I.xxxv (p. 70, col. 1).
[91]Polanus, *Syntagma,* I.xxxv (p. 70, col. 1).

been given by God "as an infallible and perfect norm and rule" for dogmatic decisions.[92]

This judicial goal of Scripture is also twofold: directive *(directivus)* and definitive *(definitivus)*. The goal is directive since the church is to be guided by Scripture as its sole infallible rule *(regula infallibile atque unica);* definitive since the church accepts Scripture as its basis for decision *(indicium)* amid the doubts or dangers *(dubia)* and disputes *(lites)* of religion. (Without pressing the point of technical language too far, it is at least worth noting that Polanus' choice of the word *dubia* reflects the language of late medieval scholastic debate, in which *dubia* were frequently set, together with various *notae,* into the extended discussions of distinctions and questions in commentaries on Lombard's *Sententia.)* Polanus comments, by way of conclusion, that Christ himself used the Scriptures as the basis for such definitive judgments and the apostle Paul regularly cited Scripture as the proof of his arguments —and even so the apostolic council itself (Acts 15) resolved a most pressing controversy on the basis of Scripture. In a similar manner, the directive function of Scripture applies to the laity and to private matters as a guide to truth and a preventive to error.[93] In sum, an unalterable rule of faith is necessary to conserve divine truth in the fact of the "weakness of memory, the perversity of human beings and the brevity of life," not to mention the fraud and corruption of Satan.[94]

With the return to the consideration of theology as a *scientia* or *sapientia* typical of the Reformed writers of the late sixteenth and seventeenth centuries, the medieval quest for theological *principia* and the Reformation emphasis on the necessity of revelation by the Word conjoined in a clearer enunciation of Word as *principium cognoscendi* than can be found in the writings of the medieval doctors and in a more "scientific" view of the necessity of Scripture to the discipline of theology than can be found in the writings of the Reformers. Indeed, it was the work of the Protestant orthodox to draw the Reformers' language of the necessity of revelation by the word into theological system by joining it to the extant systematic or technical language of theological *principia* and to an extended meditation on the nature of Scripture as Word.

The issue of the necessity of revelation by the word is nowhere more clearly and succinctly stated than in the high orthodox summa-

---

[92]Polanus, *Syntagma,* I.xxxv (p. 70, col. 1).
[93]Polanus, *Syntagma,* I.xxxv (p. 70, col. 2).
[94]Turretin, *Inst. theol. elencticae,* II.ii.6.

tion of theology in the *Institutio theologiae elencticae* of Francis Turretin. Both in times past and in the present, declares Turretin, there have been individuals who have argued the sufficiency of human reason as the foundation of the good and blessed life and who have claimed that the "light of nature" is sufficient "for the direction of life and the attainment of felicity."[95] The church, however, Turretin continues, has "always believed that revelation by the Word of God stands absolutely and simply necessary to man for his salvation." The revealed Word, thus, is called the seed by which we are regenerated (1 Pet. 1:23), the light by which we are directed (Ps. 119:105), the nourishment on which we are fed (Heb. 5:13–14), and the foundation on which we rest (Eph. 2:20).[96]

A distinction must be made at this point between the notion of the necessity of revelation by the Word and the concept of the necessity of Scripture as the definitive form of that revelation. Turretin's initial question is not whether revelation is necessary—that issue had been addressed and answered in the prolegomena—but "whether revelation by the Word is necessary."[97] In their theological prolegomena, the Reformed orthodox had recognized that revelation was the necessary mode of communication of the knowledge of divine things to finite creatures in a fallen world, in their incapacity to know God either by union or by direct intellectual vision.[98]

Beyond the testimony of Scripture and the church to the necessity of the Word for salvation, Turretin recognizes a series of arguments pointing toward the same truth. First, the ultimate goodness of God is self-communicative *(sui communicativa)* and draws human beings toward itself as their supernatural and blessed goal. This blessedness and the way leading to it, however, are unknown to reason. Both are declared by the Word. Similarly the utter fallenness and corruption of human beings is such that they could have no inkling of divine and heavenly things unless God revealed them—as stated in 1 Corinthians 2:14 and Ephesians 5:8. Finally, Turretin turns to "right reason" which teaches that God cannot be known and worshiped apart from God's own light any more than we can know of the sun apart from its brightness and radiance, as is also testified in Psalm 36:9. Even religious impostors like Numa Pompilius and

[95]Turretin, *Inst. theol. elencticae,* II.i.
[96]Turretin, *Inst. theol. elencticae,* II.ii.
[97]Turretin, *Inst. theol. elencticae,* II.i.
[98]Cf. *PRRD,* I, 4.4.

Mohammed, together with the barbarian pagans and various other false religions spread throughout the world, recognize that human reason is insufficient and some supernatural revelation is necessary for salvation![99]

These arguments are confirmed, continues Turretin, by the "two-fold desire naturally implanted in man" *(duplex appetitus homini naturaliter insitus)* for truth and immortality: all people desire to know the truth and to enjoy the ultimate good, satisfying the desires of both intellect and will in the blessed life. The "school of nature" *(schola naturae)* leads neither to the true knowledge of God nor to a way of salvation capable of drawing sinners into a condition of perfect blessedness *(status perfectae beatitatis)* in union with God. It is therefore necessary that there be a "higher school of grace" *(schola superior gratiae)* in which God, through his Word, teaches "true religion," inculcates genuine knowledge and worship of himself, and draws human beings toward the goal *(fruitio)* of eternal salvation and communion with God.[100] (It is worth noting the continuity of this argument with the views of the Reformers on the subject: where Turretin differs from the Reformers is not in the substance of his teaching but in the scholastic method and forms, the highly technical and somewhat rationalizing character of his theological language and argumentation.[101])

This point was previously made, from a somewhat different perspective, on the prolegomena in the discussion of natural and supernatural theology, but the Reformed orthodox reiterate it specifically in the *locus de Scriptura.* Turretin notes that the works of creation and providence continue to function admirably as divine revelation —as we learn from Romans 1:19–20, *to gnōston tou theou,* what can be known of God, has been made manifest to mankind, specifically, the invisible things of God *(invisibilia eius)* have been made known in creation. In the wake of sin *(post peccatum),* however, such revelation is not sufficient for salvation. Indeed, it falls short subjectively inasmuch as it does not convey a power of the spirit capable of correcting the vileness of humanity, and objectively inasmuch as it does not teach the mystery of salvation, the mercy of God in Christ. The works of God, concludes Turretin, manifest *to gnōston tou theou,* but not *tou pistou*—what can be known, but not what can

---

[99]Turretin, *Inst. theol. elencticae,* II.i.3.

[100]Turretin, *Inst. theol. elencticae,* II.i.4.

[101]Cf. the discussion of natural revelation and natural theology in *PRRD*, I, ch. 5.

(and must be!) believed. The works of God manifest the *Deus creator,* comments Turretin in a direct reflection of both Giles of Rome and John Calvin, but not the *Deus Redemptor;* they manifest the infinite power and deity, but not the grace and saving mercy of God. The Word is therefore necessary to supply the lack in natural revelation, to manifest "the mystery of his will for our salvation."[102]

In his discussion of the cognitive foundation of theology, therefore, Turretin continues to observe the Reformers' concept of a *duplex cognitio Dei.*[103] A distinction must be made between the *opera creationis et providentiae* and the *opera redemptionis et gratiae:* the former reveals what God is *(quod sit Deus)* and the way God is *(qualis sit),* that is, the unity of essence and various divine attributes, but, Turretin continues, the latter alone identifies who God is *(quis sit)* and the manner of God's personal subsistence. This work of grace and redemption, centered on "the mystery of the gospel" *(mysterium evangelii)* is "capable of being known by us through the word alone."[104]

It is worth noting the form of Turretin's *quaestio* and the priorities of his argument—not only because the same pattern appears throughout his *Institutio,* but also because the pattern illustrates in practice the relationship between revelation and reason outlined in theory in Turretin's theological prolegomenon. The arguments from Scripture and from theology are stated first and the arguments based on *recta ratio* follow second in order. Turretin *never* begins with the natural or rational and then builds his theology upon it, even though his system is intentionally polemical or apologetical rather than positive or didactic; he unfailingly sets his rational arguments second in order to his biblical and theological foundations in order to show that reason serves the theological point. The system is, therefore, rational but not rationalist; reason does not compete with Scripture for the title *principium cognoscendi.*[105] What is more, Turretin's

---

[102]Turretin, *Inst. theol. elencticae,* II.i.5; cf. *PRRD,* I, 5.3.

[103]On the importance of the *duplex cognitio Dei* to Calvin's theology, see Edward Dowey, *The Knowledge of God in Calvin's Theology* (New York: Columbia University Press, 1952); on the use of the concept by other Reformed theologians of the sixteenth century and its fairly continuous movement into early orthodoxy, see Richard A. Muller "'Duplex cognitio dei' in the Theology of Early Reformed Orthodoxy," in *Sixteenth Century Journal* 10 (1979):51–61.

[104]Turretin, *Inst. theol. elencticae,* II.i.6

[105]Cf. Turretin, *Inst. theol. elencticae,* II.i.3, with the argument for the oneness of God in ibid., III.iii.5–6; and cf. Rogers and McKim, *Interpretation and Authority,* pp. 172–88 for the reading of Turretin as a rationalist.

"rational" arguments frequently rest on theological and biblical assumptions.

Not only is it necessary that God reveal himself by means of Word, it is also necessary that the Word be written. Thus, the Reformed, together with the Lutheran orthodox, affirm the "necessity of Scripture" or of the "written Word" *(verbum scriptum)* over against the contrary claims of Roman Catholic writers like Robert Bellarmine, who argue the usefulness of written Scriptures to the church but not their necessity and who assume that the church and its "unwritten traditions" could stand in the absence of Scripture.[106] In other words, the issue is not only the necessity of Scripture considered *materialiter,* in terms of the doctrines taught by the text, inasmuch as all count the doctrines to be necessary, but rather the necessity of Scripture considered *formaliter,* in terms of the writing, or, in terms of the manner according to which the teaching is conveyed *(modus tradendi).*[107]

In a material sense, in terms of the doctrines conveyed in the text, Scripture is necessary unconditionally and absolutely *(simpliciter et absolute)*—so that without this doctrine, the church itself could not exist. It is clear, also, that Scripture, considered formally as a written document, is not necessary with respect to God *(respectu Dei).* God can and did communicate with his people in a living voice *(viva voce)* apart from a written word; such was the form of his revelation before Moses. The point to be debated is the Protestant contention that the written Word is necessary *ex hypothesi* or as a consequence of the will of God. Granting that this is the will of God, the written Word is necessary not merely to the well-being *(bene esse)* but to the being *(esse)* of the church, so that the church would cease to exist without it: "Thus, God is in no way bound to Scripture *(alligatus Scripturae),* rather he binds us to Scripture *(nos alligavit Scripturae).*"[108]

Turretin can summarize the point by stating these several distinctions or divisions in a short definition of the question: "We do not therefore inquire, Whether the writing of the Word was absolutely or unconditionally necessary, but relatively *(secundum quid)* and as a consequence *(ex hypothesi);* not in all times, but in the present state of things; nor in terms of the power and freedom of God, but in

---

[106]Turretin, *Inst. theol. elencticae,* II.ii.1; cf. Bellarmine, *De verbo Dei,* IV.4.

[107]Turretin, *Inst. theol. elencticae,* II.ii.2.

[108]Turretin, *Inst. theol. elencticae,* II.ii.2; cf. Mastricht, *Theoretico-practica theol.,* I.ii.23; *Synopsis purioris theologiae,* II.vii.

terms of his wisdom and manner *(oeconomiam)* of working with human beings."[109] As we have already recognized in the Reformed prolegomena, and their focus on ectypal theology after the fall, Reformed theology emphasizes the accommodation of the divine will to human need and of divine revelation to the modes of human knowing.[110] Here Turretin quite pointedly directs attention away from the absolute power of God toward the power of God exercised according to the divine wisdom concerning the needs of human beings in this life. Thus, comments Turretin, in the natural pattern *(oeconomia naturali)* of human life, parents teach their children— first, with a living voice, when children are infants and are being given their initial formation, and then, later, with the voice of a teacher, through the use of books and reading, in order to inculcate, as with a strong rod, the teaching *(doctrina)* in those books. God has followed the same pattern in teaching his children.[111] Thus, in the infancy of the people of God, God spoke directly and in a living voice. This unwritten word could be properly conserved at that time because of the longevity of the patriarchs, the small number of people in the covenant, and the frequency of the revelations. In later times, however, the church was no longer confined to a few families and human life was shortened considerably. Oracles were fewer and, moreover, the establishment of the nation of Israel demanded not so much a living voice as written laws.[112]

Thus, too, the written word was necessary "that the church might have a certain and true rule and canon, whereby it might judge all questions, doubts and controversies of religion," and "that the faith of men in Christ which was to come, might better be confirmed, when they should see that written before their eyes which was done by the Messias, and see all things that were foretold of him verified in the event," and further, "that the purity of God's worship might be preserved from corruption and the truth propagated among all nations." Scripture is also given to take away excuse from those who would ignore the precepts of God.[113]

In all of these arguments, the necessity of Scripture rests on the special providence of God. The fact of the written Word and its central place in the work of salvation is referred to the order of grace. The argument rests not so much on Scripture as such as on the

[109]Turretin, *Inst. theol. elencticae*, II.ii.3.
[110]*PRRD*, I, 4.1, 4.4.
[111]Turretin, *Inst. theol. elencticae*, II.ii.3.
[112]Turretin, *Inst. theol. elencticae*, II.ii.7; cf. Leigh, *Treatise*, I.viii (p. 136).
[113]Leigh, *Treatise*, I.viii (p. 136); cf. *Synopsis purioris theologiae*, II.vi–xi.

logic of the *ordo salutis*. Thus, the orthodox will speak of Scripture as the *medium conversionis* on the basis of James 1:18; the *medium fidei et consolationis*, on the basis of Romans 10:17; and the *fundamentum ecclesiae, et omnis cultis eius*, on the basis of Ephesians 2:20. Scripture is the "Lydian stone" by which all things are measured (Isa. 8:20; Gal. 1:9) and the *lux splendens in obscuro* (2 Pet. 1:19) to be employed as a remedy against all errors.[114]

Against the "Enthusiasts and the Libertines," who claim that Scripture is necessary only for children and beginners in faith, whereas the more perfect and mature Christian can rest on the teaching of the Spirit, the Reformed pose the testimony of Scripture itself. Thus, Paul asks the Corinthians to come to a decision on the basis of what he writes to them (1 Cor. 10:15)—while the apostle John first states that he writes to Christians as "children" and then, subsequently, addresses instructions to Christian "fathers" (1 John 2:1, 12–14). Similarly, Paul addresses the perfect or mature—*adulti*—with advice (Phil. 3:15).[115] The Enthusiasts and Libertines draw on 1 John 2:27 in order to argue that the special anointing of the Spirit renders them superior to all human teachings. These words, Riissen argues, ought not to be understood "absolutely," as if the New Testament writings were no longer necessary, inasmuch as John's own epistle in which these words appear would then be quite unnecessary (!), but rather "relatively" insofar as the Spirit working through the New Testament has provided a fuller teaching than had been available under the previous dispensation. Similarly, the words of Paul that "the letter killeth, but the spirit giveth life" cannot be used to refute the orthodox claim of the necessity of Scripture inasmuch as "the letter" is not the letter of Scripture but the letter of the law that condemns sin.[116] Or again, the promise of the prophet Jeremiah of a covenant so inscribed on the heart as to make teaching unnecessary in no way sets aside the necessity of Scripture here and now—since it is a prophecy of the kingdom when with clear vision we will see God face to face and no longer need the ministry of either Scripture or human pastors.[117]

Neither does the fact that the faithful are *theodidaktoi*, taught by the inward working of the Spirit, render Scripture unnecessary. Word and Spirit cannot be separated (Isa. 59:21). The former is

---

[114]Riissen, *Summa theol.*, II.vii, controversia I, arg.

[115]Riissen, *Summa theol.*, II.vii, controversia II; cf. *Synopsis,* II.viii, x.

[116]Riissen, *Summa theol.*, II.vii, controversia 2, obj.1–2 and resp.

[117]Turretin, *Inst. theol. elencticae,* II.ii.9.

objective and extrinsic, the latter efficient and inward in the heart: "the Spirit is the teacher, Scripture the doctrine that he teaches us"— "Spiritus est Doctor, Scriptura est doctrina quam nos docet." The Spirit does not work through new revelations, but by impressing the written Word on the heart.[118]

Similarly, the fact, confessed by the Reformed, that "Christ is our sole teacher"—"Christus est unicus Doctor noster" (Matt. 23:8)—in no way excludes the ministry of Scripture, but necessarily implies it inasmuch as Christ now speaks to his people only in Scripture and instructs them through it. Christ must not, therefore, be set over against Scripture.[119] The point, profoundly related to the concept of Christ as the *scopus* and *fundamentum Scripturae*,[120] does indicate the subordination of Scripture to Christ—of the Word written to the Word incarnate—and does identify yet another parallel in the orthodox doctrine of Scripture to the teaching of the Reformers, but it ought not to be taken, in either case, as an exclusive identification of Christ as Word and Revelation over against a scriptural witness to the Word. As we will see in the following discussion, there is a continuity between the Reformation and the Protestant orthodox language of Word that does not look in the direction of the neo-orthodox usage or, indeed, the typical neo-orthodox interpretation of the Reformers' doctrine of Scripture.[121]

The underlying issue addressed by the orthodox in their discussion of the necessity of the written Word is the fundamental issue of the Reformation—the issue of authority. The claim that Scripture has grown out of the saving work of God in history and is necessary to the present economy of salvation stands over against the Roman Catholic claim that salvation is authoritatively dispensed by the church and that the church, from its position of authority, and on the basis of the unwritten word that it holds as tradition, can attest to the soteriological importance of Scripture as the fundamental truth of God. The orthodox echo the Reformers in pressing —albeit more formally and with more elaborate definition—the prior authority of Scripture and the secondary, derivative authority of the church. The orthodox equally echo the Reformers in setting aside the Anabaptist and Spiritualist claim of ongoing revelations by the Spirit. In short,

---

[118]Turretin, *Inst. theol. elencticae,* II.ii.9; *Synopsis purioris theologiae,* II.ix.
[119]Turretin, *Inst. theol. elencticae,* II.ii.12.
[120]See below, §3.5.
[121]Cf. Richard A. Muller, "Christ—the Revelation or the Revealer? Brunner and Reformed Orthodoxy on the Doctrine of the Word of God," in *Journal of the Evangelical Theological Society* 26/3 (Sept. 1983):307-19.

the basic argument of the orthodox concerning the necessity of Scripture is of a piece with the underlying thrust of the entire *locus de Scriptura* and is clearly reflected in and frequently paralleled by the arguments of the other subtopics.

3.3 The Word of God in the Reformation and Orthodoxy: Issues and Basic Definitions

The Reformed orthodox did not, as is commonly assumed, make a rigid equation of the Word of God with holy Scripture.[122] To be sure, they identified Scripture as the Word of God, but they also very clearly recognized that Word was, ultimately, the identity of the second person of the Trinity. They also recognized that the second person of the Trinity, as Word, was the agent of divine revelation throughout all ages. These basic doctrinal assumptions concerning the meaning of the term "Word of God" led the Protestant scholastics to a series of distinctions in their definition of Word. The Word was, first, either the essential Word of God or the Word of God sent forth in the work of creation, redemption, or revelation and, therefore, present in a knowable manner to the finite order. In addition to the Word incarnate, the Word could be understood in a series of three interrelated distinctions and definitions: the unwritten and the written Word, the immediate and the mediate Word, the external and the internal Word.

The historical and covenantal aspect of the Reformed doctrine of the necessity of a written Word, a Scripture, was connected, early in the Reformation, with a doctrine of the Word of divine revelation as unwritten *(agraphon)* and written *(engraphon)*. The Word was first heard and later recorded. This historical path of the Word from moment of revelation to written text not only appears in the ancient histories of the Bible that refer to the events that took place before Moses but also to the prophetic writings, where divine revelation to the prophet preceded the production of the text. The Reformers and their orthodox successors not only recognized this pattern in the production of Scripture, they viewed it as of utmost importance to their conception of Scripture as Word and to their doctrine of the authority of Scripture. Related to this point, particularly in view of the question of authority, is the problem of the way in which the Word operates—it is heard and written and, therefore, known both

---

[122]Cf. Heppe, *Reformed Dogmatics,* pp. 14–15; Brunner, *Dogmatics,* I, pp. 22–28; Laplanche, "Débats," in *BTT* 6, p. 120.

internally and externally, the former knowledge or impression having a profound impact on the individual and on the individual's ascription of authority to the Word. As a corollary of the doctrine of Scripture as Word, Protestantism must also include a discussion of the reading and hearing of the Word in the *locus de Scriptura sacra*.[123]

These considerations stand in some opposition to the view of orthodoxy as holding to a rigid definition of Scripture and Scripture alone as "Word" in distinction from the view of the Reformers, according to which Scripture "contains" the Word and "witnesses" to it. The Reformers are associated with a "dynamic" approach to Word and Scripture that allowed a distinction between the living Word or the Word incarnate in its revelatory work and the written text, while the orthodox are associated with a static view of Word that rigidly identified "Word" with "text."[124] Contrary to Brunner's assertions, the orthodox were not at all blind to the message of the Johannine prologue that Jesus is the Word of God. If they did not allow the words of the prologue to undermine their sense of Scripture as Word and as the source of revealed doctrine, this does not mean that they forgot the fact that in some sense Christ is himself the revelation of God or that he is the Word preeminently and immediately in a manner beyond the manner of Scripture. Whereas Brunner was led by his affirmation of Christ as Word to relativize the Scripture, the orthodox tread a fine doctrinal balance in their distinction between the essential, the unwritten and written, the external and internal Word.

A similar critique of the orthodox perspective is found in Althaus' characterization of Polanus' theory of knowledge as a variety of dualism. On the one hand Polanus holds Scripture to have an objective certainty reflected in the scientific character of theology and the self-authenticating nature of the scriptural revelation; on the other hand, Polanus insists on a subjective and inward working of the Spirit which confirms the truth of Scripture. Althaus describes the gift of revelation in Scripture as an "isolated supernatural act," set beside the event of the inward work of the Spirit.[125] But is this a genuine dualism and, therefore, a substantive departure from the thought of a Calvin or a Bullinger?

[123]Cf. below, §7.1.a.

[124]Cf. Brunner, *Dogmatics,* I, pp. 22–38, with Reid, *Authority of Scripture,* p. 86.

[125]Althaus, *Die Prinzipien,* p. 235.

Concerning the relationship of the divinity to the truth of Scripture, Polanus wrote, "Faith in the divinity of Scripture is by nature prior to faith in the truth of Scripture; we, however, first believe that it is true and subsequently believe that it is divine. Unless you believe first that Scripture is true, you will never believe that it is divine."[126] This argument, according to Althaus, is tantamount to an assertion that "all knowledge, faith, doctrine, and theological demonstration finally ends in some ultimate, immutable, and first truth ... which is some other than holy Scripture, the Word of God." Althaus sees this as a combination of a formal supernaturalism with an empirical attitude in theology.[127] But we must distinguish between an autonomous scientific empiricism and an empiricism of divine evidences, of the inward working of the Spirit, and of the revelatory working of God in his Word. In the latter, the conviction of the divinity of Scripture comes, via faith in the truth of Scripture, as a work of God rather than as a realization of man, with the result that the "formal revelatory character" and the "formal authority" of Scripture are not—as Althaus would have it—distinct from the content of the faith.[128] Indeed, the inseparability of the external Word of Scripture from the internally known Word was integral to the Reformed response to Roman Catholic emphasis on an internal Word of spiritual tradition known to the heart of believers.[129]

The contrast between the formal, self-evidencing character of Scripture as divine and the inward confirmation of Scripture's truth and divinity by the testimony of the Holy Spirit is created by the logical, rationalizing nature of Polanus' argument rather than by an real sense of rift between the objective truth of Scripture and its subjective apprehension. It is not as if the Spirit testifies inwardly to the truth of Scripture apart from actual encounter with the scriptural Word or as if the Spirit that, by the act of inspiring the original writers of Scripture, gives to the text its character as Word can be any other than the Spirit that testifies to the believer of his work and of the truth of his work. This interpretation follows from Polanus' insistence, in an Aristotelian fashion, upon the undemonstrable nature of all principles. As Althaus himself admits, the separation between *in se* and *quoad nos* breaks down at this point[130]—leading us to conclude that Althaus' insistence on "two souls" in Polanus'

---

[126]Polanus, *Syntagma theol.,* cited in Althaus, *Die Prinzipien,* p. 236.
[127]Althaus, *Die Prinzipien,* p. 236.
[128]Althaus, *Die Prinzipien,* p. 237.
[129]Cf. Tavard, "Tradition in Early Post-Tridentine Theology," pp. 385–87.
[130]Cf. Althaus, *Die Prinzipien,* p. 239.

doctrine of Scripture mistakes a logical, dichotomizing method of exposition for an objective dualism.

Much of the theological critique of orthodoxy on these points appears to rest on Heppe's discussion of the loss of a distinction between *verbum agraphon* and *verbum engraphon* as Protestantism passed from the Reformation into the era of orthodoxy. Heppe ascribed this change to the "later dogmaticians" who separated "the idea of inspiration from that of revelation"—and then, in virtual refutation of his own argument, finds the problem caused by "later dogmaticians" to have existed "as early as the *Confessio Helvetica [posterior]*."[131] Heppe argues that the "old Protestant" distinction between the Word of God and the holy Scriptures, based on the revelation of God's will to the patriarchs prior to the writing of the Scriptures, was lost to orthodoxy which strictly equated Scripture with the Word of God.[132] While he is correct that the rather fluid sense of canon found not only in Luther but also in Musculus was generally lost to later thinkers, he is misled in drawing the conclusion that a sense of the revealing Word under or in the Scriptures was somehow lost: the *Irish Articles,* for example, explicitly state that "the ground of our religion ... is the Word of God, contained in the holy Scripture."[133] And such phrases as "the word of God in Holy Scripture," indicating an ability to distinguish between as well as to identify Word and Scripture, appear frequently in the works of seventeenth-century Reformed theologians.[134]

What Heppe assumed to be the loss of a broad conception of the Word of God in later Reformed theology is better understood in terms of the formal separation of the prolegomena and the various subordinate *loci* within the doctrine of Scripture from one another. The specific hermeneutical and epistemological themes formerly present in a variety of *loci* become concentrated in one place. A distinction arises between Word as knowledge and Word as means of grace. In the former definition, Word is defined as Scripture, which is to say, as objective revelation; in the latter Word is presented as the living gift of salvation in preaching and in sacrament. Similarly,

---

[131]Heppe, *RD,* p. 15.

[132]Heppe, *RD,* pp. 14–15.

[133]*Irish Articles,* §1; cf. Ussher, *Body of Divinity,* p. 7.

[134]Cf. e.g., Dickson, *A Commentary on the Psalms,* I, p. 2; Ussher, *Body of Divinity,* pp. 6–7; Burmann, *Synopsis theologiae,* I.iii.1–12; iv.1–4; Marckius, *Christianae theologiae medulla,* II.1–3, and idem, *Compendium theologiae,* II.2–3; Pictet, *Theol. chr.,* I.iv.1–2.

a distinction between unwritten and written Word occupies one specific place in the larger *locus* rather than pervading the whole.

The assumption of a radical discontinuity between the Reformation and the orthodox doctrine of the Word, thus, rests on a profound historical and dogmatic misunderstanding that falsifies both the teaching of the Reformers and the doctrine of their orthodox successors. Whereas it is incorrect to claim, on the one side, that the Reformers so stressed the concept of Christ as the living Word witnessed by Scripture that they either lost or diminished the doctrine of Scripture as Word of God written, it is equally incorrect to claim, on the other side, that the orthodox, by developing a formal doctrine of Scripture as Word, lost the Reformers' conception of Scripture as living Word. Theologically, such claims arise out of a mistaken either/or approach to the problem, where Word of God is taken to indicate either Christ or Scripture but not both. A multilevel understanding of Word is, however, quite typical of both the Reformers and the post-Reformation orthodox.

A clear foundation for this multilevel definition of Word in the Protestant tradition is provided by the Reformers, notably by Bullinger in a series of sermons included in his *Decades,* by Calvin in the *Institutes,* and by Musculus in his *Loci communes.* Bullinger begins by defining the various meanings of *verbum* in its biblical usage. It can signify a "thing" as the term *rhema* does in Luke 1:37, "With God shall no word *(rhema)* be impossible." Beyond this and more typically, *verbum* signifies, quite simply, "a word uttered by the mouth of men," a sentence, a speech, a prophecy. "But," Bullinger continues, "when *verbum* is joined with another term, as in this place [with] *verbum Dei,* 'the Word of God,' it is not used in the same significance." The "significance" toward which Bullinger points is a rich, manifold, and profoundly interrelated series of usages:

> For *verbum Dei,* the Word of God, signifies the virtue and power of God; it also indicates the Son of God, who is the second person of the most reverend Trinity: for the saying of the evangelist, "the Word was made flesh," is clear to all. But in this treatise, the Word of God properly signifies the speech of God and the revelation of God's will; first of all uttered in a lively voice by the mouth of Christ, the prophets and the apostles; and after that registered in writings which are rightly called "holy and divine Scriptures."[135]

---

[135]Bullinger, *Decades,* I.i (p. 37).

Since a word reveals the mind of its speaker, the Word of God is to be recognized as the "declaration" of God—and since God himself is "just, good, pure, immortal, eternal" and, by nature, therefore, "speaks the truth," his Word also "is true, just, without deceit and guile, without error or evil affection, holy, pure, good, immortal, everlasting."[136] Bullinger, in short, draws a connection between the eternal Word of God and the written Word that reflects the attributes of God in the attributes of the written revelation—the pattern and force of the argument look directly toward orthodoxy.

The certainty of the Word, according to Bullinger, is intimately linked to its cause. He even offers the doctrinal point in a syllogistic form: "the Word of God is truth: but God is the only well-spring of truth: therefore God is the beginning and cause of the Word of God."[137] God himself spoke in a voice like a human voice in order to convey his will to the most ancient of the patriarchs. He also spoke by means of messengers, angels, and prophets. By the preaching and writing of the latter he made his Word available to the entire world. Even so, he revealed himself more fully in the teaching of his incarnate Son and then, by the inspiration of the Spirit, made the apostles into "elect vessels" of his Word in their preaching and writing.[138] A fairly strict doctrine of inspiration is implied here but not elaborated. Indeed, Bullinger appears to focus on the identity of Scripture as Word as the primary issue, with the question of the mode of production of the written Word as secondary.

Calvin, similarly, places the concept of Word at the center of his doctrine rather than derive the authority of Scripture solely from a formal doctrine of inspiration. Inspiration and authority appear as corollaries of the work of the Spirit in its relation to the Word both in producing Scripture and in mediating through Scripture the saving knowledge of God. Scripture, according to Calvin, is the Word because the Spirit of Christ imparted to the ancient authors the wisdom of God directly from its source, the eternal Wisdom or Word that resides in God: "the Word, understood as the order or mandate of the Son, who is himself the essential Word of the Father," is given in the Scriptures by "the Spirit of the Word."[139] The point is fundamentally trinitarian—the Spirit of God and the

---

[136]Bullinger, *Decades,* I.i (p. 37).
[137]Bullinger, *Decades,* I.i (p. 38).
[138]Bullinger, *Decades,* I.i (p. 38).
[139]Calvin, *Institutes,* I.xiii.7.

Spirit of Christ are terms for one and the same Spirit—and serves to identify the connection between the eternal and the written Word.

Bullinger and Musculus note that there are no writings from the time before Moses: Enoch may indeed have written the prophecy that is cited in the fourteenth and fifteenth verses of Jude and the Book of Job may be of exceeding antiquity but still, in agreement with the views of earlier ages of the church, Bullinger grants Moses priority of place among "the holy writers."[140] Musculus confirms the point: "For if it were otherwise, Christ, for the declaration of whom all of the Scriptures are ordained, would not have begun with Moses when he expounded all the holy Scriptures pertaining to him to the two disciples going to Emmaus."[141] The issue, here, is not so much to identify the limits of the written canon of Scripture—although, as we will argue below, Bullinger's theology stands on the boundary between the late medieval and early sixteenth-century sense of a somewhat fluid canon and the later assumption of the Reformers of the mid-sixteenth century of a strictly defined canon of Scripture[142] —as to identify the forms of the revelation of God's saving will from the earliest times onward:

> From the beginning of the world, therefore, God spoke to the holy fathers by his Spirit and by the ministry of angels; and they taught their children, and children's children, and all their posterity by word of mouth what they had learned from the mouth of God.... The fathers taught their children that God, of his natural goodness, wishing well to mankind, would have all men come to a knowledge of the truth, and to be like in nature to God himself, holy, happy, and absolutely blessed.[143]

In an exposition that adumbrates later orthodox discussions of the dispensations of the covenants of works and grace, Bullinger proceeds to describe this ancient tradition of divine revelation recorded in the early chapters of Genesis. The Old Testament patriarchs, Bullinger argues, taught of one God, Father, Son and Holy Ghost, who is the "maker and governor of ... all things," the creator of human beings in his own image, and the "loving Father and bountiful Lord" of his creation. They also taught of the temptation

---

[140]See further, below, §§6.1 and 6.2, on the problem of "lost books" and the integrity of the canon.

[141]Musculus, *Loci communes,* xxi (*Commonplaces,* p. 350, cols. 1–2).

[142]See below, §6.1.

[143]Bullinger, *Decades,* I.i (p. 49); cf. the identical point in Musculus, *Loci communes,* xxi (Commonplaces, p. 350, col. 2–351, col. 1).

and fall of the first pair, the entry of death and damnation into all the world, and the transmission of sin "so that all the children of Adam, even from Adam, are born the children of wrath and wretchedness."[144] They taught, in addition, of the grace and mercy of God who "did, of his mere grace, promise pardon for the offense, and did lay the weight of the punishment on his only Son, with the intent that he, when his heel was bruised by the serpent, might himself break the serpent's head ... and should bring the faithful sons of Adam out of bondage; ... and should by adoption make them sons of God and heirs of life everlasting."[145]

Indeed, the ancients were taught to have faith "in God, and in his son, the redeemer of the whole world; when in their very sacrifices they did present his death, as it were an unspotted sacrifice, wherewith he meant to wipe away and cleanse the sins of all the world."[146] Because of this, the patriarchs valued very highly their lineage and the inheritance of the promise. They describe the promise given to Adam, the transformation of the curse into blessing, the universalization of the promise in Abraham—"In thy seed shall all the nations of the earth be blessed"—and the transmission of the promise from Abraham to Isaac and Jacob, to Judah, and thence to the house of David. Bullinger further describes this promise of God as a pact or covenant: "God, by a certain agreement, has joined himself to mankind; he has most firmly bound himself to the faithful and the faithful likewise to himself."[147] The patriarchs also knew of the immortality of the soul and of the resurrection of the flesh, with the result that they "exhorted us all so to live in this temporal life, that we do not lose the life eternal." This summary of the earliest tradition of revelation, argues Bullinger, can easily be identified in Genesis, as delivered in ancient times by word of mouth and finally recorded by Moses."[148]

Moses' inscripturation of the Word marks the point in the history of revelation at which God universalized his message, speaking no longer to "private families" but now, through the agency of the written Word, offering "true knowledge and religion" to the whole world.[149] In Moses God chose "a singular man" and, through signs and wonders" bestowed on him great "authority and credit" in order

[144]Bullinger, *Decades,* I.i (p. 43).
[145]Bullinger, *Decades,* I.i (p. 43).
[146]Bullinger, *Decades,* I.i (p. 44).
[147]Bullinger, *Decades,* I.i (p. 44).
[148]Bullinger, *Decades,* I.i (p. 45).
[149]Musculus, *Loci communes,* xxi (*Commonplaces,* p. 351, col. 1).

that "the things he would write might be credited as things not imagined by man but inspired by God." Indeed, before his own work of writing Scripture, Moses delivered to the people of Israel the tables of the law written by "the fingers of God."[150]

The position of Moses as the first writer of Scripture and as the bearer of the law to Israel gives him a role of paramount importance in Bullinger's description of the Old Testament word. Moses' writings are said to contain a full revelation of God and, as such, are of sufficient authority unto themselves to be believed by all men. Such is the divine authority of the words written by Moses that Bullinger can write that God speaks to us by it and that "there is no difference between the word of God that is taught by the living voice of man and that which is written by the pen of man." The phrase "living voice of man" ought to be referred to Bullinger's earlier comments about the nature of the patriarchal revelation—that God spoke in an audible voice like the voice of a human being.[151] After Moses, the word was given with the same authority by the prophets, "to guide the people in the faith." Above all, the prophets must be regarded as expositors of the Torah, namely, of the law of Moses and the tradition of the patriarchs. Their words rest on "visions and revelations" and are given, as a supplement and continuation of the work of Moses, "with the intent that there should be no excuse for them that should come after."[152] Thus, Moses must be regarded as the central figure of the Old Testament revelation.[153]

Bullinger next comes to the New Testament, giving a summary of Christ's and the apostles' teaching. Christ taught that, in order to be saved, a man must be born again to life, regenerated by the Spirit, instructed in that Spirit in the faith that Christ "died for our sins and rose again for our justification"; and that in so doing Christ fulfilled the law and the prophets. Musculus finds significant the parallel between God's ratification of Moses and God's ratification of Christ. As in ancient times, so also was Christ's promulgation of the gospel attended by signs and wonders in confirmation of its truth. In order that this message be spread to all the world, Christ chose the apostles as his messengers. To these apostles "are joined two great lights of the world, John the Baptist ... and ... Paul, the great teacher of the Gentiles." All these messengers of the gospel, Bullinger adds,

---

[150]Musculus, *Loci communes,* xxi (*Commonplaces,* p. 351, col. 2).
[151]Bullinger, *Decades,* I.i (pp. 47–48, cf. pp. 38–39).
[152]Musculus, *Loci communes,* xxi (*Commonplaces,* p. 351, col. 2).
[153]Bullinger, *Decades,* I.i (pp. 49–50).

have a "great dignity and authority in the church" since, "being endued with the Spirit of God, they did nothing according to the judgment of their own minds."[154] On this authority, they converted the world to Christ and founded churches throughout the world, deeds "which, by man's counsel and words, surely, they could never have performed."[155] Very much as later writers would argue, the events of the New Testament history themselves indicate the divine authority of the apostolic word. Miracles continued for a time in the life of the church in order to confirm the truth of the apostolic message and to make clear that no further revelation of God's truth is needed.[156]

Bullinger offers a brief summary of the argument, beginning with the genealogy from Adam to Moses, stating that Moses compiled "the history and traditions of the holy patriarchs, to which he joined the written law, and the exposition of the law, together with a large and splendid history of his own lifetime." Next, in the writings of the prophets, we are given the truths which those men of God "had learned from the Lord." Then in the New Testament, in the coming of God's "only-begotten Son," we see the fulfillment of the entire Scripture:

> so that now we have from the patriarchs, the prophets, and the apostles, the word of God as it was preached and written. These writings had their beginning in one and the same Spirit of God, and tend to one end, that is, to teach us men how to live well and in holiness.[157]

As for the authors of these Scriptures, the patriarchs, the prophets and the apostles,

> such men are utterly without comparison. All the world cannot show us their like again, although it should be assembled in a thousand councils.... these are not so much as shadows when compared with them, from whom we have received the word of God. Let us therefore in all things believe the word of God delivered to us by the Scriptures.[158]

---

[154]Cf. Musculus, *Loci communes,* xxi (*Commonplaces,* p. 351, col. 1) with Bullinger, *Decades,* I.i (p. 53).

[155]Bullinger, *Decades,* I.i (pp. 53–54).

[156]Musculus, *Loci communes,* xxi (*Commonplaces,* p. 351, col. 2–352, col. 1).

[157]Bullinger, *Decades,* I.i (p. 56).

[158]Bullinger, *Decades,* I.i (p. 56).

Bullinger does allow a certain degree of separation or, perhaps better, distinction between the Word of God and its vehicle, the holy Scriptures. This is not for the sake of identifying the Scriptures as anything less than Word or in any way lower or lesser in authority than a prior speech of God to the human writers of the text, but rather to allow Scripture to be understood as the instrument of the *viva vox Dei*, the living word or speech of God: "Let us believe that the Lord himself, who is the very living and eternal God, speaks to us by the Scriptures."[159]

It is important that we place these comments into the context of the famous marginal title in the *Second Helvetic Confession,* "Praedicatio verbi Dei est verbum Dei"—"the preaching of the word of God is the word of God."[160] The statement is typically taken as an indication of the incredibly dynamic character of the Reformers' doctrine of Scripture and of their existential emphasis on preaching —and there is an element of truth in this reading of the words—but it is also clear that it in no way stands over against a fairly strict identification of the text of Scripture as Word of God and, indeed, rests on such an identification. Indeed, the previous marginal title reads, "Scriptura verbum Dei est."[161] Bullinger insists, in other words, that preaching the "words" was the Word because he was convinced that the text of Scripture was not merely a witness, but, because of the work of God and the Spirit of God, a form of Word itself. It was surely not the intention of the confession to claim either that every sermon ought to be regarded as divine Word or that the moment of revelation that produced the words of the text was some-how automatically re-presented in the pulpit through the activity of the clergy: the confession simply indicates the permanent and authoritative relation between the words of the text and the Word of God that they convey.[162]

A similar and more direct statement of the various meanings of Word in the history of revelation is found in Calvin's *Institutes.* On the one hand, Calvin assumes that Scripture expresses in a form accommodated to human understanding the "eternal and inviolable truth of God."[163] Thus, although given in a form suited to our

---

[159]Bullinger, *Decades,* I.i (p. 57).

[160]Cf. the text in Niemeyer, *Collectio confessionum,* p. 467; N.B., the version offered by Schaff in Creeds, III, p. 237, does not include the marginal title.

[161]See Niermeyer, *Collectio confessionum,* p. 467.

[162]Cf. the comments in Mildenberger, *Theology of the Lutheran Confessions,* pp. 229–30.

[163]On Calvin's doctrine of accommodation, see Ford Lewis Battles, "God

capacity, Scripture is hardly an imperfect witness. On the other hand, Calvin, like Bullinger and Musculus, acknowledges a logical and chronological distinction between the essential Word of God, the Word spoken, and the Word written. The Scripture is not Christ —rather it "clothes" Christ and communicates Christ's promise to us. Christ, the eternal and essential Word, is the ground and foundation, the underlying meaning of the Scriptures.[164] The entire revelation of God in the Old Testament depended on the mediation of Christ as Word of God—first in the form of "secret revelations" and oracles given to the patriarchs, later in forms of the written law, the prophecies, the histories, and the psalms that are also "to be accounted part of his Word."[165]

Finally, in confirmation and conclusion of all previous revelation, "the Wisdom of God was at length revealed in the flesh." This revelation of "the perfect radiance of divine truth" as preserved in the writings of the apostles, completes the scriptural word of God and provides the church with its norm for doctrine, beyond which there can be no authority. God "has so fulfilled all functions of teaching in his Son that we must regard this as the final and eternal testimony of him."[166]

This concept of a progressive revelation culminating in the Word made flesh both parallels the expositions of the doctrine of Scripture as Word found in the writings of Calvin's contemporaries and unites several of the elements in the early Reformed doctrine of Scripture. Here, as in his Christology, Calvin relates the form taken by the Word to the issue of knowledge. Like Luther, though not in as paradoxical a manner, Calvin holds that God is both hidden and revealed in his self-manifestation. Human forms of expression and, indeed, the human form of Christ, both reveal to us what is necessary for our salvation and hide from us the awesome and incomprehensible majesty of God. In Scripture, as in the incarnation, God gives himself wholly but is not fully contained or encapsulated by human forms. A profound connection, therefore, exists between the progressive revelation of the Scriptures and the work of Christ in his prophetic office. Indeed, Calvin even describes the anointing of the Mediator to the work of teaching in a manner that reflects his sense of the inspiration of Scripture and explains why the Spirit of the

Was Accommodating Himself to Human Capacity," in *Interpretation* 31/1 (1977):19–38.

[164]Calvin, *Institutes,* II.vi.2–4; x.4.
[165]Calvin, *Institutes,* IV.viii.5–6.
[166]Calvin, *Institutes,* IV.viii.7.

Word also testifies to the heart in confirmation of the message: "he received anointing not only for himself that he might carry out the office of teaching, but for his whole body that the power of the Spirit might be present in the continuing preaching of the gospel."[167]

This intimate relationship between the doctrines of Scripture and of Christ and the fundamental epistemological questions of theology does not function, as some writers have indicated,[168] to identify Christ as Word in such a way as to redefine Scripture as a witness to the Word rather than as Word or to identify revelation with Christ in an exclusive way—no more than it did for Bullinger or Musculus. The whole of Scripture is, indeed, directed toward Christ, teaching first of God as Creator and Ruler and then as Redeemer. In a sense, all of this teaching comes from Christ who, as the Word, is

> the everlasting Wisdom, residing with God, from which both all oracles and all prophecies go forth. For, as Peter testifies, the ancient prophets spoke by the Spirit of Christ just as much as the apostles did.[169]

These statements indicate a firm distinction between the revelation and the one who reveals—obviating the difficulty sometimes alleged against Calvin's thought of a discrepancy between faith as the acceptance of the revelation given in Scripture and faith as the personal acceptance of Christ: In the former the believer is led to Christ by a true knowledge of God and his work; in the latter the believer receives the Christ to whom he has been led by Scripture. Scripture is the place to which the faithful must go to learn of Christ, and through Christ to learn of the Father. The Word is the scepter by which Christ rules his kingdom.[170]

In very much the same vein, Bullinger argues that in the New Testament, the Word of God once revealed by the prophets was "in the last times set forth most clearly, simply, and abundantly by his Son to all the world."[171] The form of Bullinger's statement is important. Although he clearly identifies Jesus Christ as the Word incarnate, he does not propose any movement from that identification to the conclusion that the Old Testament Word of promise has, in Christ, been manifest as a person who, himself, is identical with

---

[167]Calvin, *Institutes,* II.xv.2.
[168]Cf. e.g., Niesel, *Theology of Calvin,* pp. 27–30.
[169]Calvin, *Institutes,* I.vi.1; xiii.7.
[170]Calvin, *Institutes,* IV.ii.4.
[171]Bullinger, *Decades,* I.i (p. 52).

the revelation. For Bullinger, as for Calvin and for virtually all of their contemporaries and, indeed, for the Protestant orthodox, the Word incarnate stands not as the revelation itself but as the final revealer of God. The doctrine of Scripture and Word, in short, reflects the Reformed doctrine of the prophetic office of Christ.

This approach to the identification of Word and the relation of Word to Scripture did not disappear from theology after the deaths of the second-generation Reformers. Indeed, contrary to the general impression given by much of the scholarship on the Protestant doctrine of Scripture, the orthodox theologians not only retained the concept of a multilevel definition of Word, they codified it, formalized it, and made it one of the central issues in their own doctrine of Scripture. Ursinus, following out the pattern of the early *Theses Bernenses,* argues the priority of Scripture over the church by first identifying the Word as the eternal wisdom of God, the "immortal seed of which the church is born." "Nor could the church exist," he continues, "unless the Word was before tradition": Scripture is not merely words in a book, but the "Word of God inscribed in letters."[172] Burmann, for example, would begin his discussion of Scripture with the distinction, and declare, as an integral part of his discussion of the necessity of a scriptural revelation, that "The Word of God existed before all things: it was, with God, invisible," that the Word was active in creation and was subsequently spoken audibly to Adam and Eve in paradise.[173]

Gomarus similarly identifies Scripture as the *sermo Dei* which is given both internally and externally to believers and which was first unwritten, later written.[174] A majority of post-Reformation Protestant theologians, whether early or high orthodox, echo these distinctions, not to the exclusion of one by the other but for their mutual relation and explanation.[175] When the distinctions are not offered, more probably out of a desire for different emphasis in argument rather than out of disagreement, it is not as if one set has replaced the other—rather both sets are simply lacking.[176] And

[172]Ursinus, *Loci theologici,* in *Opera,* I, col. 434.
[173]Burmann, *Synopsis theologiae,* I.iii.2.
[174]Gomarus, *Disputationes,* I.lii–lv.
[175]Cf. Polanus, *Syntagma theol.,* I.xv; Wendelin, *Christianae theologiae libri duo,* prol., III.viii; Maccovius, *Loci communes,* II (pp. 10–11); *Synopsis purioris theol.,* II.iv, viii–ix; Mastricht, *Theoretico-practica theol.,* I.ii.4, 6; Turretin, *Inst. theol. elencticae,* II.ii.4–7, 9.
[176]Cf. Ames, *Medulla,* I.xxxiv; Walaeus, *Loci communes,* II; Pictet, *Theol. chr.,* I.iv.2, where the latter issue is addressed, without explicit reference to the

although both sets of distinctions are, arguably, used more prominently with more architectonic implication by early orthodox theologians like Polanus and Gomarus, it would also be incorrect to view the distinctions as less important to the high than to the early orthodox. Perhaps the clearest statement of the paradigm appears in Riissen's carefully stylized summary of Turretin:

> I. The principium *essendi* or cause of theology is God himself. The principium *cognoscendi* is the Word of God *(Verbum Dei)*.
>
> II. *Verbum* indicates (1) the spoken Word, Heb. 13:7, "Remember those who rule over you, who have spoken unto you the word of God *(sermonem Dei)*." (2) The written Word, Rom. 3:2, "To them (the Jews) were committed *ta logia tou theou*." (3) *That which is received by the spirit, 1 John 2:14,* "the Word of God abides in you." (4) Christ himself, Rev. 19:13, "his name is the Word of God."[177]

As we noted in the context of the prolegomena to orthodox system, there is no problem of an overemphasis on the so-called *ordo essendi* to the exclusion of proper consideration of the *ordo cognoscendi*. The high orthodox dogmaticians strove to achieve a fine balance between these two aspects of system, recognizing not only that the one had to reflect the other but also that the doctrine of Scripture—specifically the doctrinal identification of Word—in its placement directly following the prolegomena offered the key to the epistemological or cognitive problem of theology: the Word, granting the multiple and interrelated levels of the meaning of the term, rightly reveals the nature and intention of God. The distinction between the *principium essendi* and the *principium cognoscendi*, moreover, is so widely noted in the seventeenth-century orthodox systems that it may be classed as a truism.

Having thus carefully defined the meaning of *verbum Dei*, the orthodox go on to focus their attention on the meaning of *verbum Dei* as *scriptura*, on the relationship between divine Word and written Word, and to note the various synonyms found in Scripture itself. Scripture, for example, calls itself *logia tou theou* (Rom. 3:2; 1 Pet. 4:11; Heb. 5:12) and *logos tou theou* (1 Thess. 11:13; Heb. 4:12). In addition, *verbum Dei*, when used as a synonym for *scriptura*, indicates those words which undoubtedly are from God, are

distinction.

[177]Riissen, *Summa theol.*, II.i–ii; cf. Turretin, *Inst. theol. elencticae*, I.i.7; II.i.1, 4–6.

concerned with God, and point toward God—"quod nimirum *a Deo sit, de Deo* agat, & *ad Deum* tendat"—which is to say the *lex Dei,* the divine judgments, commissions, mandates, statutes, and precepts that the New Testament identifies either as "the law and the prophets" or as Moses and the prophets" (cf. Matt 22:40; Luke 16:16). Even so the Greek word *biblia,* when used in the plural, is a synonym for "Scripture."[178] "Scripture," therefore, can be defined as

> the Word of God, written by inspired men in the canonical Old and New Testament, containing true religion and teaching *(doctrina),* in order to provide a perfect and perpetual standard *(norma)* for the church and in order to lead to their true salvation to the glory of God.[179]

As is true of many scholastic arguments, the process of defining Scripture here has followed a movement of definition from the larger concept to the smaller, namely, from Word of God to Scripture, and that even as it identifies Scripture as Word of God nonetheless continues to recognize that Word of God does not always indicate Scripture, indeed, that Word is foundational to Scripture. The Protestant orthodox definitions are designed, in particular, to recognize both an unwritten and a written form of Word but to exclude from the category of Word any traditions outside of the present canon of Scripture, especially those remaining unwritten into the present day.

3.4 Word as Essential, Unwritten and Written, Living and Inscripturated, External and Internal, Immediate and Mediate

Clarification of the doctrine of Scripture—particularly over the possible contradiction between the activity of the Word in the Old Testament and the idea of dictation by the Spirit—occurs in both the orthodox *locus de Scriptura sacra* and their treatment of the official work of the Mediator. Here, in their identification of Christ as eternal Word of God and, in the work of revelation as the *Logos asarkos* and *incarnandus,* the orthodox both relate the eternal, essential Word and Wisdom of God to the forms of revelation and pose a basic distinction between the eternal, essential Word and the various

---

[178]Mastricht, *Theoretico-practica theol.,* I.ii.7; cf. Marckius, *Compendium theologiae,* II.ii.
[179]Marckius, *Compendium theol.,* II.i.

forms in which the Word is revealed to the human race.[180] At the beginning of his *locus* on Scripture, Burmann poses the basic distinction between Word and Scripture: the *Verbum Dei,* absolutely so-called, existed before all things, invisible, the second person of the Trinity, through whom all things were made. And in the primeval condition of man, prior to the fall, this divine Word spoke directly to man.[181] So too, in his prophetic office, is Christ the Word from "the bosom of God" and "the principal author of prophecy."[182] By the "word of God" we also mean the revelation given by this principal author and preserved in "the canonical books of the Bible, whereunto ... is given the name of holy scripture."[183] We know this Bible to be the word of God, even though we also know it to have been written down by men, because

> the holy Ghost, which spake by them, nay whose instruments only they were, do engrave that faith in our hearts. Then, that assurance may be confirmed by observing the special excellency, which it is easy to perceive in those writings, as also the most holy effects which they work in us.[184]

Scripture, argues Leigh, is called the Word of God because of "the matter contained in it." He distinguishes in the usual orthodox manner between Scripture as "the written Word of God" and Christ as "the essential Word of God."[185] The written word, in all probability, begins with Moses. (Leigh discounts belief in books written by Enoch, particularly since Christ speaks of Moses as the primary author of ancient scriptures.)

> The Author of the Scriptures was God himself, they came from him in a speciall and peculiar manner, commonly called inspiration, which is an act of God's Spirit immediately imprinting or infusing those notions into their brains, and those phrases and words by which the notions were uttered. ... 'holy men spake as they were moved' or carried, 'by the Holy Ghost,' 2 Pet. 1.21.

---

[180]Cf. Riissen, *Summa theol.,* II.ii; Leigh, *System,* I.ii (p. 7); Heppe, *RD,* p. 455.

[181]Burmann, *Synopsis theologiae,* I.iii.2.

[182]Leigh, *System,* V.v (p. 585); cf. Heidegger, *Corpus theologiae,* XIX.28; *Synopsis purioris theologiae,* XXVI.xxxix; Poole, *Commentary,* III, p. 277 (John 1:1).

[183]Leigh, *Treatise,* I.i (p. 2).

[184]Leigh, *Treatise,* I.i (p. 3).

[185]Leigh, *System,* I.ii (p. 7).

They did not write these things of their own heads, but the Spirit of God did move and work them to it, and in it.[186]

Thus Scripture is called God's Word "because by it, Gods Will is manifested and made known, even as a man maketh known his mind and his will by his words." Further, God himself is the Author: "The principal Author of all Scriptures is God the Father in his Son by the Holy Ghost, Hos. 8.12. 2 Pet. 1. The Father hath revealed, the Sonne confirmed, and the Holy Ghost sealed them up in the hearts of the faithful."[187]

The "word," writes Pictet, "was the most appropriate *(aptissimum)* means of revealing God, and instructing men, to whom he had given the faculty of hearing and reasoning." God at first spoke to mankind without committing his word to writing because of "the longevity of the patriarchs, the small number of people, and the frequency of divine revelations."[188] The multiplication of the race, the shorter term allotted to human life, and the growth of evil made necessary the written preservation of God's word and the establishment of a "fixed rule of faith *(certus fidei Canon)*." To this end God wrote the Decalogue on stone tablets "with his own finger" and instructed both Moses and the prophets to put his words into writing.[189] Under the New Testament dispensation the Son of God revealed divine truth to his disciples, commanding them to "teach all nations." Pictet argues that the Christ of the Apocalypse expressly enjoined his church "to write the things which you have seen" (Rev. 1:11, 19).[190]

Contrary to the impression given by Heppe's presentation,[191] the orthodox dogmaticians do in fact draw out the interconnection of Word as *revelatio* with the concepts of *verbum agraphon* and *verbum engraphon*. Nor, as Heppe claims, were these latter two concepts replaced by a distinction between *verbum internum* and *verbum externum*. We are dealing, here, with entirely different distinctions with different functions in the system. The former distinction retains its "historical" interest and occupies a major place in the Reformed orthodox system. The latter concept binds Word and Spirit together by distinguishing between the historical external

[186]Leigh, *System,* I.ii (p. 7).
[187]Leigh, *System,* I.ii (p. 7, margin).
[188]Pictet, *Theol. chr.,* I.iv.1–2.
[189]Pictet, *Theol. chr.,* I.iv.2–3; cf. Weemes, *Exercitations Divine,* pp. 61–62.
[190]Pictet, *Theol. chr.,* I.iv.4.
[191]*RD,* pp. 14–17.

prophetic office of Christ as Word and the ongoing internal teaching office of Christ by means of his Spirit.

Echoing the teaching of the Reformers, and building on these basic definitions, the orthodox argue the historical, economical, dispensational pattern of revelation by the Word. It is not as if, Marckius argues, the Word exists now in two parts, one written *(scripta)* and the other unwritten *(non scripta),* or as if the church today, after the completion of the canonical Scriptures, possesses an authoritative unwritten Word such as was given to the prophets of the Old Testament. Rather there is one authoritative Word that was unwritten *(agraphon)* and given in an "enunciative" form, as a "living voice," to the patriarchs before Moses and which, after Moses, has been written for the edification of the church.[192] This unwritten Word given directly to the church in the ages prior to Moses is, moreover, the subject of the written Word set down by Moses and the other ancient writers of the Scripture. The unwritten Word is not, therefore, a different divine truth from that presented in the written Word: *verbum agraphon* is prior to *verbum engraphon,* in Turretin's terms, not as genus is prior to species but as a subject is prior to its accidents.[193]

Even so, God's revelation could and did take various forms during the course of the sacred history:

> The manner of revealing Gods will is threefold, according to the three instruments of our conceiving, viz. Understanding, Phantasie, and Senses; to the understanding God revealed his will by engraving it on the heart with his own finger, Jer. 31.33. by Divine Inspiration, 2 Pet. 1.21. 2 Chron. 15.1. Heb. 8.11. John 14.26. and by intellectual Visions, Numb. 12.6. To the phantasie God revealed his will by imaginary Visions to Prophets awake, and by dreams to Prophets asleep, Gen. 40.8 & 41.8, 9. Acts 26.10 & 10.3. Numb. 14.4. To the Senses God revealed his will, and that either by Vision to the Eye, or lively voice to the Ear, Gen. 3.9 & 4.6 & 15.4, 5. Exod. 20.1, 2 & 3.1, 2, 3. & 33.17. And lastly by writing. This Revelation was, sometimes immediate by God himself after an unspeakable manner, or by means, viz. Angels, *Urim* and *Thummin,* Prophets, Christ himself and his Apostles.[194]

---

[192]Cf. Marckius, *Compendium theol.,* II.iii with *Synopsis purioris theol.,* II.iv; Wendelin, *Christianae theologiae libri duo,* prol., III.viii; and Maccovius, *Loci communes,* II (p. 11).

[193]Turretin, *Inst. theol.,* II.ii.4; cf. Riissen, *Summa theol.,* II.iii; and Maccovius, *Loci communes,* ii (pp. 10–11).

[194]Leigh, *System,* I.ii (p. 6).

The written form of revelation, therefore, was neither intrinsic to the Word nor absolutely necessary; rather, the numbers of people on earth, the increase in wickedness, and the decrease in lifespan in the time of Moses led to the writing of the word by the "amanuenses."[195] The different modes of revelation correspond to the maturity of the church as it grew from infancy to adulthood. In the time of the church's infantile stammering the living voice of God came directly *(agraphon)*; later in the childhood of the church and under the guidance of the law the living voice taught and made to write even as adolescents are taught and given lessons by the voice of a teacher. Now in the adult age of the church, we have the written Word and its doctrines to lead us.[196] Thus, the written Word is necessary for the "instruction" of the church *ex hypothesi* or as a consequence of the divine will that the Scripture be the instrument of the church's instruction.[197]

In this change in the pattern of revelation over the course of history, the wisdom of God is manifest. In the childhood of the church, the *viva vox Dei* instructed her by means of the most simple mode of revelation *(simplicissimus revelationis modus)*. In her later childhood, still taught by the living voice of God, she was given the divine law in written form—so that in later times, the adolescence of God's church, she might be taught as by a school teacher, in and through the reading of the law. Finally, under the gospel, she was brought to adulthood, to her righteous and perfected state, in which her people might be taught by the reading and hearing of the teaching contained in the Scriptures.[198] In this historical sense, corresponding to the progress of revelation and to the forward movement and development of the people of God, Scripture can be identified as "the gathering of books ... concerning those things that human beings must know, believe and do for the glory of God and their salvation."[199]

Against these arguments concerning the necessity of the written word—and in favor of a concept of a *verbum non scriptum*—the Roman Catholics argue that Christ never commanded the apostles to

---

[195]Cf. Maccovius, *Loci communes,* II (p. 11); Marckius, *Compendium theol.,* II.iii.

[196]Turretin, *Inst. theol.,* II.ii.3; Riissen, *Summa theol.,* II.v; Burmann, *Synopsis theol.,* I.iii.5–9; Marckius, *Compendium,* II.iii.

[197]Wendelin, *Christianae theologiae libri duo,* prol., III.viii; cf. *Synopsis purioris theologiae,* II.vii.

[198]Riissen, *Summa theol.,* II.v.

[199]Riissen, *Summa theol.,* II.vi; cf. Marckius, *Compendium theol.,* II.ii.

write and that, therefore, a written word cannot be absolutely necessary to the church. On the contrary, notes Wendelin, Christ himself
did say to "search the Scriptures." Moreover, contrary to the Roman
Catholic claims that the writing of the New Testament, as that of the
Old, resulted from a decline of faith and observance rather than a
direct mandate, it is clear that the apostles, by the inspiration and
mandate of the Spirit of Christ, preserved the gospel in writing even
though Christ had not so commanded prior to his resurrection. In
addition, the apostles' writings serve to maintain their witness in the
church after their deaths.[200] Hence, Wendelin continues, Scripture
must be the fundamental rule of religion and the faith, to which all
symbols and confessions must be subject.[201]

This necessary movement from unwritten to written Word and
the consequent priority of the Scriptures as the norm for faith and
practice was taught in almost identical form by the English
Reformed theologians. On this point of doctrine, as on most others,
it is not possible to draw stark lines of distinction between the
English and the continental Reformed.[202] Just as Perkins and
Rollock in the late sixteenth century had distinguished between the
unwritten Word of God and the written Word, the Scriptures, while
at the same time affirming the continuity of revelation and the
necessity of Scripture, so Arrowsmith in the mid-seventeenth
century could write:

> The word since written agrees with that which in former times was
> delivered to the Patriarchs, and transmitted by word of mouth. As
> the word *God* is the same today, yesterday, and for ever, although
> not incarnate until the fullness of time came, and then *manifest*. So
> the *word of God,* although till *Moses* received command to put it in
> writing, there was wanted that kind of incarnation, was for sub-
> stance the same before and after. And as the *written word* agreed
> with the *unwritten,* so doth one part of that which is written
> harmonize with another.... So here, the different style of the his-
> toriographers from Prophets, of the Prophets from Evangelists, of
> the Evangelists from Apostles may make the truths of Scripture
> seem of different complexions till one look narrowly into them and

---

[200]Wendelin, *Christianae theologiae libri duo,* prol., III.viii; cf. Tavard,
"Tradition in Early Post-Tridentine Theology," pp. 392–93.

[201]Wendelin, *Christianae theologiae libri duo,* prol., III.viii.

[202]Contra Rogers and McKim, *Interpretation and Authority of Scripture,*
pp. 202–3, 204, 207, 220, 223.

taste of them advisedly, then will the identity both of colour and relish manifest itself.[203]

Thus, too,

In the epistle to the Hebrews those two phrases "the first principles of the oracles of God" (5:12) And "the principles of the doctrine of Christ" (6:1) import one and same thing, implying also that Scripture Records are the only Storehouse and Conservatory of Christian Religion.... books of Scripture are oracles of God.[204]

Such oracles, according to Arrowsmith, were either "vocal," like those given by the cherubim from the mercy-seat above the ark of the covenant, or "written," like the Law or the canonical books of Scripture. Paul speaks of the OT as "oracles of God" committed to the Jews (Rom. 3:2) and Peter appears to refer to the NT in similar terms, *os logia theou* (1 Pet. 4:11).[205] He proceeds to show how the "oracles" of Scripture agree in part with but also surpass in perspicuity, piety, veracity, duration, and authority all heathen oracles. The oracles are vague, impious, and false on occasion—they have favored certain individuals and therefore lack authority, and they were all relatively short-lived. Scripture, however, "is so framed, as to deliver all things necessary to salvation in a clear and perspicuous way," is godly throughout, and "is free ... from all degrees of falsehood."[206] Scripture is also most ancient and "of divine authority," its authors all being moved by the Holy Spirit.[207]

Three decades into the eighteenth century, Thomas Ridgley could make this same distinction, explaining that

There was no written word, from the beginning of the world, till Moses time, which was between two and three thousand years; and it was almost a thousand years longer before the canon of the old testament was completed by Malachi the last prophet, and some hundred years after that before the canon of the new testament was

[203]John Arrowsmith, *Armilla catechetica. A Chain of Principles; or an orderly Concatenation of Theological Aphorisms and Exercitations; wherein, the Chief Heads of Christian Religion are asserted and improved* (Cambridge, 1659), p. 104; cf. *Westminster Confession,* I.ii, "holy Scripture, or the Word of God written."

[204]Arrowsmith, *Armilla catechetica,* p. 84.

[205]Arrowsmith, *Armilla catechetica,* pp. 84–85.

[206]Arrowsmith, *Armilla catechetica,* pp. 96, 99.

[207]Arrowsmith, *Armilla catechetica,* pp. 101, 103.

given; so that God revealed his will, as the Apostle says, in the beginning of the Epistle to the Hebrews, at sundry times, as well as in divers manners, and by divers inspired writers.[208]

It is of some importance, Ridgley argues, to understand "how this Revelation was gradually enlarged" and how, prior to the written word the church was nevertheless "not destitute of a rule of faith and obedience, neither ... unacquainted with the way of salvation." There was mediation of revelation by the Son of God, by angels, and by men like Enoch led by "the spirit of prophecy." Only after a long period of wickedness and "when man's life was shortened and reduced ... as it now is" did a written word become necessary and did God "command Moses to write his law, as a standing rule of faith and obedience to his church."[209]

As already indicated, this distinction between the unwritten Word *(vebum agraphon)* and the written Word *(verbum engraphon)* arises out of the historical pattern of divine revelation. The orthodox argue that distinction is not, as the papists claim, the division of a genus into its species as if there were two kinds of Word. Rather it is the distinction of a single subject, the Word, according to its incidental properties *(accidentia)* belonging to it as different times. With the completion of the *verbum engraphon* or *verbum scriptum,* the living voice of the *verbum agraphon* ceased.[210] God has revealed himself differently at different times and in different places—in a clear voice and with a word sent forth *(sermo prophorikon);* in an inward whisper or internal word *(sermo endiatheton),* in dreams and visions, in human form through the ministry of angels, under various symbols. In all cases the teaching has remained unchanged.[211]

Contrary, then, to the impression given by Heppe's exposition,[212] the orthodox dogmaticians do in fact draw out the interconnection of Word as *revelatio* with the concepts of *verbum agraphon* and *verbum engraphon.* Nor, as Heppe claims, were these latter two concepts replaced by a distinction between *verbum internum* and *verbum externum.* We are dealing, here, with two entirely different

---

[208]Thomas Ridgley, *A Body of Divinity wherein the Doctrines of the Christian Religion are Enlarged and Defended* (London, 1731), p. 20.

[209]Ridgley, *Body of Divinity,* pp. 20–21; Also Riissen, *Summa theol,* II.ii–iii; vii, controversia 1, obj.1; and Mastricht, *Theoretico-practica theologia,* I.ii.6.

[210]Turretin, *Inst. theol. elencticas,* II.ii.4.

[211]Turretin, *Inst. theol. elencticae,* II.ii.5.

[212]Heppe, *RD,* pp. 14–17.

distinctions with rather different functions within the system. The former distinction retains its "historical" interest: *verbum agraphon* precedes *verbum engraphon,* in the view of Turretin and other orthodox, not as a genus is prior to a species but as a subject is prior to its accidents.[213] Perhaps even more important—and also contrary to the impression given by Heppe and others—there is no hint here of a confusion of revelation with text or of a tendency to fasten rigidly on an identification of Scripture with Word that renders the orthodox doctrine of Scripture somehow different from that of the Reformers. The doctrine noted here stands in direct continuity with the teaching of the second-generation codifiers and with the great mid-sixteenth-century confessions.

Indeed, the central issue addressed by the orthodox in these formulas concerning the unwritten and written Word is, once again, the issue of authority. Their point, echoing the Reformers and even early Reformation confessions like the *Theses Bernensis,* is that the historical economy of revelation and its relation to the written Word rule out the identification of the unwritten traditions of the church as *verbum agraphon* necessary, alongside of the written Word, to the salvation of believers. Whatever unwritten traditions may exist in the church, they do not exist as the continuation of the original *verbum agraphon:* that Word has been superseded in the economy of revelation by the Scriptures, which now hold an authority higher than any traditions or private revelations.[214] The term *scriptura* itself derives, writes Mastricht, from the ancient work of setting down the precious *verbum agraphon* in order to preserve it from the vicissitudes of time and memory. The inscripturation of the Word is itself a work of providence. Even as God had propagated and conserved the unwritten Word, he chose to have the Word committed to writing in the time of Moses, knowing full well that the "perversity of heretics" can and will bend the meaning of unwritten traditions to the service of false teaching.[215]

The tendency of Protestant orthodoxy to move toward a rigid and mechanical theory of the inspiration of Scripture as verbal dictation was frequently counterbalanced in the same systems with an emphasis on Scripture as Word, indeed, as the *viva vox Dei,* the living voice of God. It is in these formulations that orthodoxy retained

---

[213]Turretin, *Inst. theol. elencticae,* II.ii.4; cf. Riissen, *Summa theol.,* II.iii; and Maccovius, *Loci communes,* ii (pp. 10–11).

[214]Cf. Turretin, *Inst. theol. elencticae,* II,ii,1; with idem. II.i.6; Marckius, *Compendium theol.,* II.xxxix; and Burmann, *Synopsis theol.,* I.iii.10.

[215]Mastricht, *Theoretico-practica theol.,* I.ii.6.

much of the dynamism of the doctrine of the Reformers and, by manifesting several interrelated meanings of "word," drew out the connection between the soteriological and christological language of the *fundamentum sacrae Scripturae,* the text of Scripture, and the effect of Scripture in preaching and in hearing. There is a sense in which the structural constraints of dogmatic system drove apart the more rigid statement concerning the mode of inspiration and the more dynamic statements concerning Scripture as Word rather than permit them to cohere as they had in the less systematized writings of the Reformers—but this does not mean that the orthodox system should be viewed as lacking one or the other of these perspectives on Scripture or as lacking a balanced statement of doctrine.

In turning to the topic of "Word" as external and internal, the orthodox dogmatics comes full circle. The doctrine of Scripture as Word of God and as, necessarily, the *principium cognoscendi theologiae,* had led to the discussion of authorship and inspiration and that discussion led, in turn, back to a discussion of Word, external and internal. Whereas the former discussion of Word prepared the objective dogmatic ground for both theology itself and the concepts of inspiration and authority, this latter discussion formed the bridge between the objective dogmatic statement and the fact that Word, in order to be effective, must not only be objectively given but also subjectively received. This larger pattern of the discussion of Word and inspiration in fact sets the rigid systematic structuring of orthodoxy back into the dynamic context of Reformation preaching—of *fides ex auditu.* Here, once again, we can note a major element of continuity between the orthodox teaching and that of the Reformers.

If Calvin refuses to allow Scripture to become a static, rationalizable norm divorced from the living work of the Spirit, he also refuses to let the Spirit be considered as a sole norm of faith apart from the rule of Scripture. The Spirit has a genuine "teaching office" in the church, as promised by Christ in the Gospel of John, which consists not in "inventing new and unheard-of revelations, or ... forging a new kind of doctrine," but in "sealing our minds with that very doctrine which is commended by the Gospel."[216] The testimony of the Spirit can only confirm the gospel. "He is the Author of the Scriptures: he cannot vary and differ from himself." The Holy Spirit "inheres" in the truth of Scripture. Scripture, therefore, cannot be a temporary mode of revelation, nor can it be equated with the

[216]Calvin, *Institutes,* I.ix.i.

killing letter and contrasted with the living Spirit. Calvin denies successive dispensations, one of Word, a second of Spirit. After Pentecost God "sent down the same Spirit by whose power he had dispensed the Word, to complete his work by the efficacious confirmation of the Word."[217] This means that Word and Spirit are joined by a "mutual bond" to the end that the Word is confirmed by the Spirit and the Spirit "shows forth his power" when the Word receives its due recognition.

Christ's prophetic teaching office is twofold: internal and external. Externally, Christ taught "by the Ministry of his Prophets in the times before his coming into the world, whom he raised up for that end, that they might reveal so much of his will as was necessary for them to know."[218] He also taught externally in person, preaching the "Doctrine of the Kingdom," and by his apostles. These latter recorded the Scriptures of the New Testament, being moved by Christ to bestow on the church a "perfect rule of Faith and Obedience" which might "plainly and perfectly instruct the whole Church each and every member of it to the saving knowledge of God and Christ."[219] Anyone, continues Leigh, can come to a knowledge sufficient to salvation by a diligent study of Scripture and a humble reception of its truth. For this knowledge, he adds, Scripture may be read in a valid translation.[220] Internally, Christ instructs "the Pastors and Teachers of all ages" in the knowledge of his truth by means of his Spirit illuminating the mind.[221]

In the present life of the church, the Word of God is also given in a two-fold manner: immediately and mediately.

> I call that the immediate word of God that which doth proceed immediately out of God's own mouth; and that I call mediate which the Lord speaks by his preacher or minister. We hold, then, and avouch, that the holy Scripture is that immediate and primary word of God, and to be unto us instead of that first immediate and lively voice of God himself; yea, that it serves us in place not only of that lively voice of God, but also of the secret and unsearchable mind of God, and God's unspeakable mysteries.[222]

[217]Calvin, *Institutes,* I.ix.3.
[218]Leigh, *System,* V.v (p. 585).
[219]Leigh, *System,* V.v (p. 586).
[220]Leigh, *System,* V.v (p. 586).
[221]Leigh, *System,* V.v (p. 586).
[222]Rollock, *Treatise of Effectual Calling,* p. 64.

The distinction made here between the *viva vox Dei* and the Scriptures reflects the *agraphon/engraphon* distinction made earlier by Rollock and it stands in the way of a rigid equation of Scripture with the divine Word in its fullness. In short, it allows for a sense of the accommodation of "the secret and unsearchable word of God, and God's unspeakable mysteries" to the vehicle of the written word. Thus, it also conforms to the distinction between *theologia archtypa* and *theologia ectypa* which appears in several of the early orthodox prolegomena—a difference in degree but not in truth.

The distinction between Scripture as *immediate* and preaching as *mediate* word of God reflects the general Reformed tendency to view preaching as derivative, that is, as a result of the presence of God's Word in the church. This implies, of course, no derogation of preaching. "The mediate voice of God, we call the voice of the holy and true Church of God; for albeit men speak, yet the word spoken is the word of God himself."[223] We saw this sense of preaching in Bullinger also. It allows for a high sense of the ministry but also for the fallibility of the individual minister who may, if not attentive to the Spirit, cease to preach the Word.

The fact that Scripture is the immediate voice of God Rollock attempts to prove rationally; not once does he revert to the inner testimony of the Spirit. Scripture must be the word of God immediately because it is the statement of his will. Further,

> If we had nothing to supply the defect of the lively voice of God, then doubtless our state were worse than that of the old Church of the Jews, which had the oracles of God; but it against all light of reason so to affirm.[224]

As a third argument, Rollock puts forth that the primary ground of faith must "be either the lively voice of God, or the very mind and counsel of God, or something to supply [their] want." Since, against Roman Catholic identification of tradition as the living spiritual voice of God, we have neither the *viva vox Dei* once given to the writers of Scripture nor the secret counsel of the mind of God, we must necessarily have God's word in another form and some revelation of his secret counsel. This Scripture which must, therefore, be held as the "very voice" and "very mind or will of God himself manifested unto us."[225] And as a fourth reason:

[223]Rollock, *Treatise of Effectual Calling,* p. 65.
[224]Rollock, *Treatise of Effectual Calling,* p. 65.
[225]Rollock, *Treatise of Effectual Calling,* p. 65; cf. Tavard, "Tradition in

The Scripture contains all those things which God hath spoken in elder ages, and what God himself hath decreed in his secret counsel, so far as is meet for us to know, concerning our life and salvation.[226]

The "adversaries," writes Rollock, confound the immediate and mediate words of God by claiming "the voice or Testimony of the Church ought to be accounted the principal voice of God."[227] The testimony of the church, according to these writers,

is a lively voice, proceeding from the living heart of the Church, wherein God hath engraven all truth with the finger of his own Spirit; whereas the Scriptures of the Prophets and Apostles, albeit they were spoken and delivered by God himself, yet they were not written by God's own hand, but by the Prophets and Apostles which were the penmen. Again, they were not written in the living hearts of men, but in paper and books, or tables. Hence, it therefore followeth ... that the voice of the holy Church is that most excellent voice of God, and ought to be to us as the immediate voice of God, and instead of the secret counsel of God.[228]

Rollock counters with the assertion that the word of the church has been produced by the Spirit who instructs in the meaning of Scripture:

For the Holy Ghost teacheth the Church nothing now but that which is written, and doth by, the Scripture, after a sort, beget the Church; and the Scripture is the mother, the Church the daughter.[229]

We have heard this argument before. It returns us to the well-springs of the Reformed faith in the *Theses Bernenses* (1528).

As evidenced also by the discussions of the "foundation" or "scope" of Scripture and of the relationship between the two Testaments,[230] this multilevel definition of Word manifests elements of the hermeneutic underlying the Reformed doctrine of Scripture, elements that continued to inform the doctrine even after the formalization of system had transferred the arguments to the doctrine of

Early Post-Tridentine Theology," p. 393.

[226]Rollock, *Treatise of Effectual Calling*, p. 65.
[227]Rollock, *Treatise of Effectual Calling*, p. 65.
[228]Rollock, *Treatise of Effectual Calling*, pp. 65–66.
[229]Rollock, *Treatise of Effectual Calling*, p. 66.
[230]See below, §3.5.

covenant. The identification of Scripture as Word of God in the theology of the Reformers and, as we will argue immediately below, in the theology of their successors, the Protestant orthodox writers of the late sixteenth and the seventeenth centuries, rests as much on a sense of the christological unity of Scripture as it does on the related issue of inspiration. The authority of Scripture rests on both its identity as Word and its inspiration by the Spirit; and, equally so, the unity of the Testaments rests on both Christ, who is their scope and foundation, and on the inspiration of the prophets and the apostles by the same Spirit. Scripture is Word because, in its entirety, it rests on the redemptive Word and Wisdom of God finally and fully revealed in Christ.

The problem encountered in the Protestant orthodox doctrine of Word and Scripture as Word, then, is not that they lost sight of the perceptions of the Reformers and so radically and rigidly identified Word as Scripture that they understood revelation strictly and restrictively as text. Like the Reformers, the orthodox simply recognized that, whatever the possible forms of revelation, the saving revelation of Christ is now accessible only in Scripture. The problem, which we will encounter again and again in our review of post-Reformation doctrine, is that the hermeneutic on which rested the Reformers' sense of the unity of Scripture and the identity of all Scripture as the Word fulfilled in Christ was becoming less and less easily maintained as a viable hermeneutic. The farther that Protestantism moved away from the allegorical and typological models of late medieval exegesis toward strictly historical, literal, and grammatical models—indeed, toward the reconstruction and interpretation of texts by means of the comparative study of ancient versions and cognate languages—the more difficult it became to argue a unity and continuity of theology throughout Scripture and to maintain, on the basis of that unity, a consistent relation between the eternal Word, the second person of the Trinity and revelatory act of the Godhead, and all the words of the canonical Scriptures. In particular, the presence of trinitarian and christological motifs in the creation narratives and in the patriarchal history became, in the course of the seventeenth and early eighteenth centuries, almost impossible to maintain in the face of the substantially altered hermeneutic. An identical hermeneutical strain will be seen in the following discussion of Christ as the "scope" or "foundation" of Scripture and in the late orthodox discussion of the "marks or characteristics" *(notae seu characteres)* of Scripture.

3.5 The Foundation and Scope of Scripture

a. Fundamentum *and* scopus *in the Earlier Reformed Theology*

Unlike the rather attenuated versions of Protestant orthodoxy found today in conservative theological systems, Protestant theology of the sixteenth and seventeenth centuries typically saw the need, in the *locus de Scriptura sacra,* not only to discuss what Scripture is and how the text of Scripture is to be received and understood in the church, but also what Scripture as a whole means and signifies. This need, conveniently identified by many of the Reformers and orthodox in terms of the language of the foundation *(fundamentum)* and focus or center *(scopus)* of Scripture, serves to underscore the fact that the *locus de Scriptura,* as found in the older Protestant theology, bound together the problem of hermeneutics and exegesis with the problem of authority. It was not enough for the older Protestantism to confess that Scripture is the necessary saving revelation and the Word of God written—nor was it enough for the Reformers and the orthodox to discuss the relation of these terms, necessary revelation and Word of God written, to the concept of revelation in general and to the identity of Word both as *verbum agraphon* and second person of the Trinity. In addition, the doctrine of Scripture had to face the interpretive question of the ultimate meaning of the revelation and of the Word written and the further question of the relationship of Scripture thus broadly understood to the doctrines of the church. If the dogmatic language of Scripture as authoritative, self-authenticating, and self-interpreting was to be maintained, then the path from Scripture to the doctrine of the church would have to be argued not from the position of the church but from the text of Scripture itself. In other words, the Protestant understanding of Scripture as authoritative Word required a foundational hermeneutical discussion that could manifest the connection between the whole of Scripture and the body of Christian doctrine.

The concept of a *fundamentum Scripturae,* or of a "foundation of foundations,"[231] presupposes the prior authority of Scripture over tradition and the beginnings of the identification of Scripture as *principium cognoscendi theologiae.* The medieval doctors had used the term *principia theologiae* but had typically meant by it the fundamental theological articles held by the church.[232] Only with the

---

[231]Leigh, *System,* I.ix; cf. *PRRD,* I, 9.1
[232]Cf. *PRRD,* I, 9.3.

Reformation of the sixteenth century did the debate over authority become so intense that theologians altered the language of *principia* so as to indicate, restrictively, God and Scripture—and, equally so, only with the Reformation did the question of the canon so intertwine itself with the question of authority as to raise the issue of a rule, internal to the canon itself, a foundation of foundations, determinative of the contents of the canon. At the level of canon, the identification of the *fundamentum Scripturae* parallels the discussion of the self-authenticating character of Scripture.

The term *scopus* or *scopus Scripturae* has a close relationship to the concept of a *fundamentum Scripturae,* but evidences a greater variety of use and application. In one sense, *scopus* can indicate a general doctrinal center or focus not unlike the christologically determined *fundamentum*. In another application, however, it can be virtually synonymous with *argumentum,* indicating the basic thrust or intention, including the general authorial intention of a particular passage in Scripture. The generalized "scope" of all Scripture or of the gospel, therefore, is usually identified as Christ or as the revelation of God's mercy and goodness—while the specific "scope" of a passage in Scripture might be faith, sanctification, or a more historically determined theme like the return of Israel from its exile. The term was applied, with different implications by the Reformers and their orthodox successors to particular texts, to chapters, to entire books of Scripture, and to Scripture itself, considered as a whole.[233] It is worth noting in this context that the two meanings and uses of the term are often found in the same work—so that there can be no thought that the broad, christological usage belonged to some authors and the more narrowly focused, exegetical usage was typical of others.[234] Any given text or pericope must have a "scope" but, equally so, the entire body of God's revealed Word—granting that it bears witness to a unity of teaching—must also have its "scope." In other words, the basic meaning of the term does not change from usage to usage, but only the breadth of its hermeneutical application.

It would also be incorrect to claim that the issue or even the language of *fundamentum Scripturae* or of *scopus Scripturae* can be identified, with all of these dogmatic associations, entirely and

---

[233]On the exegetical implications of the term, see Gerald T. Sheppard, "Between Reformation and Modern Commentary: The Perception of the Scope of Biblical Books," in William Perkins, *A Commentary on Galatians,* ed. Sheppard, pp. 42–66; and see further below, §6.4.

[234]Cf., e.g., Zanchi, *Praefatiuncula,* col. 319, with idem., *In Mosen et universa Biblia, Prolegomena,* col. 16.

completely in the theology of the earliest Reformers. Extended dogmatic discussion of a *fundamentum* or *scopus Scripturae* began to appear only after the middle of the sixteenth century—just as the debate over the canon took shape after the Tridentine definition of 1546 and the concept of Scripture as self-authenticating appears as a deduction, in the writings of Calvin, Bullinger, and their contemporaries, from the early Reformation identification of Scripture as the absolute and therefore absolutely prior norm for all churchly doctrine. Nonetheless, this particular element of orthodox Protestant doctrine of Scripture, together with its relationships to the problems of canon and authority, is rooted in some of the earliest pronouncements of the Reformers.

Luther expressed this sense of the christological center of Scripture in his preface to the Epistle of James (1522) as part of his argument against the apostolicity of the epistle:

> as Christ himself says in John 15[:27], "You shall bear witness to me." All the genuine sacred books agree in this, that all of them preach and inculcate Christ. And that is the true test by which to judge all books, when we see whether or not they inculcate Christ. For all the Scriptures show us Christ, Romans 3[:21]; and St. Paul will know nothing but Christ, I Corinthians 2[:2]. Whatever does not teach Christ is not apostolic, even though St. Peter or St. Paul does the teaching. Again, whatever preaches Christ would be apostolic, even if Judas, Annas, Pilate and Herod were doing it.[235]

The center of Scripture—the rule by which the message of Scripture is known to be authoritative—is the redemptive significance of Christ at the very heart of God's saving revelation. Not only, then, is the work of Christ that grounds justification the doctrinal focus of Protestant preaching, it is also the heuristic key to the unity of the authoritative or canonical Scriptures. Luther returned to the point in the *Schmalkald Articles* of 1538, where he declared that "the first and chief article is this, that Jesus Christ, our God and Lord, 'was put to death for our trespasses and raised again for our justification' (Rom. 4:25)."[236] "On this article," Luther concluded, "rests all that we teach and practice."[237]

The term *scopus Scripturae* or "scope of Scripture" has been much used and much misunderstood in twentieth-century

---

[235]Luther, *Preface to the Epistles of St. James and St. Jude*, in *LW*, 35, p. 396.

[236]*Schmalkald Articles*, II.i, in *Concordia Triglotta*, p. 460.

[237]*Schmalkald Articles*, II.i, in *Concordia Triglotta*, p. 460.

discussions of the doctrine of Scripture. It is particularly important that the contemporary English meaning of "scope," the full extent, range, or intention of a thing, be excluded. The original Greek *(skopos)* and Latin *(scopus)* indicates the center or bull's eye of a target. Indeed, in the *First Helvetic Confession, scopus* translates *der Zweck* of the German original.[238] The term is rightly understood, therefore, *not* as the full extent, range, or intention of the meaning of Scripture, but as the aim, purpose, goal, and center, indeed, the "bull's eye" of the biblical target. The Latin title of the section is simply *"scopus Scripturae,"* but the German reads, at greater length and with a clearer definition of the issue, "What the center *(Zweck)* of Holy Scripture is, and toward what the Scripture ultimately points." The "entire Bible" *(die ganze biblische Schrift)* teaches "that God is gracious and benevolent" and that he has bestowed his grace upon mankind in the person of Christ, his Son, by means of faith.[239] Much as in Luther's statement concerning the canon and in the *Schmalkald Articles,* the center of Scripture is not merely Christ doctrinally understood, but Christ apprehended by faith as the focus of God's work of reconciliation. This larger sense of *scopus* as the divine work of reconciliation throughout Scripture is echoed in Bullinger's use of the term to indicate the covenant—a usage that will appear in the writings of some of the Protestant scholastic theologians.[240]

This language was not confined, in the early sixteenth century, to Protestant circles. Erasmus could declare that Christ was the *scopus* of true theology and that the believer ought to "set Christ before" him "as the only *scopus*" of his life and work.[241] Boyle argues that his use of *scopus* by Erasmus, both with reference to theology in general and with reference to the exegesis of Scripture, indicates a focus of interpretation in the sense of a navigational "sighting" of a star. All refers to Christ, who is the focus and goal of faith. "The true astrotheologian," Boyle comments,

> does not gawk at pagan deities frozen into constellations.... He fixes on Christ alone. Only this determined focus will restore Christendom through the method of true theology.[242]

[238]Cf. *Confessio Helvetica Prior,* v, xii in Schaff, *Creeds,* III, pp. 212, 217.
[239]*Confessio Helvetica Prior,* v.
[240]Heinrich Bullinger, *De testamento seu foedere Dei unico et aeterno brevis exopsitio* (Zürich, 1534), fol. 16r, 17v.
[241]Erasmus, *Enchiridion,* cited in Boyle, *Erasmus on Language and Method,* pp. 75–76.
[242]Boyle, *Erasmus on Language and Method,* p. 81; cf. pp. 78–79.

This can be so even in the exegesis of a text inasmuch Christ is the word—in Erasmus' rendition of *logos,* the *sermo*—who speaks through every line of Scripture, revealing the mind of God whose eternal Word he is.[243]

It is worth inquiring for a moment into the hermeneutical basis of Luther's comments on the identity of the apostolic writings as those that "convey Christ" and of the early sixteenth-century language of the *scopus Scripturae* and *scopus evangelium.* Such assumptions, particularly the more generalized ones of the confession, do not arise out of a literal, grammatical exegesis of the text of Scripture.

The stronger shift away from the *quadriga* and the christological spiritual-literal exegetical patterns of the later Middle Ages that is evidenced in both Calvin's and Bullinger's theology brought about, also, a shift in the Reformed discussion of the *scopus Scripturae.* For Calvin, Christ is so clearly and fully the focus of redemption that Christ's work of mediation was known in some sense throughout the Old Testament as well as in the new:

> apart from the Mediator, God never showed favor toward the ancient people, nor ever gave any hope of grace to them. I pass over the sacrifices of the law, which plainly and openly taught believers to seek salvation nowhere else than in the atonement that Christ alone carries out. I am only saying that the blessed and happy state of the church always had its foundation in the person of Christ. For even if God included all of Abraham's offspring in his covenant, Paul nevertheless wisely reasons that Christ was properly the seed in whom all the nations were to be blessed (Gal. 3:14).[244]

Calvin, thus, quite clearly argues a concept of Christ as *fundamentum* and accepts on one level the assumption that Christ can be identified as the meaning of God's promise throughout Scripture—to the point of declaring that Christ was revealed "plainly" in the sacrifices of the old covenant.[245] This assumption provides an important point of contact between Calvin's thought and the use of the concept of the *fundamentum Scripturae* by later Reformed theologians in

---

[243]Boyle, *Erasmus on Language and Method,* pp. 82–83.

[244]Calvin, *Institutes,* II.vi.2; cf. Calvin, Commentary on 1 Cor. 3:11 and note the discussion in John T. NcNeill, "Calvin as an Ecumenical Churchman," in *Church History* (1963):386.

[245]Calvin, *Institutes,* II.vi.2; cf. xi.1 on Christ as the "fundamentum" of both Testaments; see further, below, §5.4.

connection with the beginnings of covenant theology,[246] and it looks ahead to the lengthy discussions by seventeenth-century federal theologians of precisely the issues that Calvin here chose to "pass over" with a brief reference.[247]

Calvin also uses the term *scopus,* sometimes with reference to Christ, sometimes with reference to the focus or center of argument of a biblical book or a particular section of a biblical book,[248] although it is clearly not his favored term. Typically, Calvin will describe the "argument" or the "design" of a book of Scripture very much in the way that other exegetes would speak of its *scopus.* Indeed, his contemporary, Hyperius, used the terms as virtual synonyms in describing the proper approach to the study of the books of the Bible.[249] It may be in part due to Calvin's usage as much as to the usage of the German Reformed that *scopus* was more often associated with the theme of a book or chapter in Scripture, while *fundamentum* tended to be used with reference to Christ.

Calvin was, moreover, almost invariably restrained in his exegetical application of concepts like the *fundamentum Scripturae.* His Old Testament commentaries only rarely christologize passages that do not fall into the category of obvious messianic prophecy.[250] What is more, Calvin refused to apply the principle dogmatically beyond the bounds of the language of covenant and reconciliation. Thus, his influential concept of the *duplex cognitio Dei*[251] not only indicated that Scripture teaches of God as Creator and as Redeemer but also that the knowledge of God as Creator was generally given throughout Scripture while the knowledge of God as Redeemer was focused on Christ.[252] Despite, therefore, the intensity of Calvin's doctrinal emphasis on Christology, the entire exposition of doctrine running from *Institutes* I.v to II.v (with the *duplex cognitio* theme reappear-

---

[246]E.g., Hyperius, Boquinus, Olevian, and Ursinus as discussed below, this section.

[247]Cf. Cocceius, *Summa theol.,* and idem, *Summa de foed.,* with Burmann, *Synopsis theologiae,* IV.xxvii–xxix; Witsius, *De oeconomia foed. Dei,* IV.iv, vi, ix; and Heidegger, *Corpus theol.,* xii.x–xivp; xiii.xi–xiv.

[248]Cf. B. Engelbrecht, "Is Christ the Scopus of the Scriptures," in Calvinus Reformator, pp. 192–200, with T. F. Torrance, *The Hermeneutics of John Calvin* (Edinburgh: Scottish Academic Press, 1988), pp. 51–138.

[249]Hyperius, *De ratione studii theologici,* II.i (p. 91).

[250]See Parker, *Calvin's Old Testament Commentaries,* pp. 194–96, 202–4.

[251]Cf. Dowey, *Knowledge of God in Calvin's Theology,* pp. 3–17; Muller, "'Duplex cognitio dei' in the Theology of Early Reformed Orthodoxy," pp. 54–61; *PRRD,* I, 5.3.

[252]Calvin, *Institutes,* I.ii.i.

ing in II.vi) is essentially nonchristological. Creation, providence, the doctrine of human nature and sin, and even the doctrine of the Trinity fall outside of the doctrines of redemption governed specifically by the revelation of God in Christ.[253] Calvin observes quite strictly the distinction between *verbum asarkos* and *verbum ensarkos*. He explicitly states, in his discussion of the divinity and eternity of the Word, that he postpones discussion of "the person of the Mediator" until he reaches "the treatment of redemption."[254] Calvin includes at this point "testimonies affirming Christ's deity" only "because it ought to be agreed among all that Christ is that Word endued with flesh" and the clear biblical testimony to Christ's divinity belongs to the exposition of the divinity of the second person of the Trinity. Calvin studiously avoids discussion here of Christology strictly defined: There is no presentation of the humanity or of the redemptive work of Christ.[255] As for the other doctrines —creation, providence, and human nature—together with the discussion of Scripture and revelation, Calvin makes quite clear the point that these all refer to the work of the Word apart from the flesh.[256] These observations are in no way weakened in force by Calvin's frequent references to Christ and redemption in book 1 of the *Institutes*. These only serve to underline the interrelationship of doctrines, not to break down the distinction between the eternal or pre-incarnate and the incarnate Word.

Bullinger's discussion of Word, Scripture, and the work of interpretation leaves a similar impression. He makes a categorical distinction between the Word of God before Christ and the Word incarnate,[257] but he also argues that the Old Testament was not only given to the church for its edification by Christ and the apostles but also contains in it "worshippings and figurings of Christ" that we "must at this day interpret to the church."[258] Even so, Christ was preached in the law to the people of the Old Testament as "the only Saviour, in whom alone they were to be saved."[259] Since "they, whose doctrine is all one, must of necessity have all one faith" it is clear that the people of the Old Testament had faith in Christ,

---

[253]Cf. Calvin, *Institutes,* I.ii.i, n. 3 in the McNeill/Battles edition.

[254]Calvin, *Institutes,* I.xiii.9.

[255]Calvin, *Institutes,* I.xiii.9.

[256]Calvin, *Institutes,* I.vi.1–3; ix.3; xiii.17–18; xv.3–4; xvi.4; cf. II.xiii.4, ad fin.

[257]Bullinger, *Decades,* I.i (pp. 38–39, 51–52).

[258]Bullinger, *Decades,* I.i (p. 59).

[259]Bullinger, *Decades,* III.viii (p. 283).

believing in him as the "Messiah that was ... to come."[260] Thus the whole message of Scripture is united by its reference to Christ, above and beyond all the differences between the Testaments. Even the ceremonial law and the tabernacle, set aside in the New Testament, point toward Christ who is the scope of Scripture and the sole foundation of all salvation.[261] Nonetheless, Bullinger does not demand a thoroughgoing christological exegesis of Scripture and his views on interpretation tend away from the allegorical and typological toward a close conferring of text with text, a broad application of a credal *analogia fidei,* and a strong emphasis on the context of a given passage.[262] Even so, Bullinger can declare that "the perfect exposition of God's word doth differ nothing from the rule of true faith and the love of God and our neighbor."[263]

Thus, the Reformation era christocentrism that identified Christ as the *scopus Scripturae* never intended that Christ be understood as the interpretive principle in all points of doctrine, the heuristic key to the entire range or extent of doctrinal meaning. In particular, the Reformed concept of Christ as *scopus Scripturae* simply placed Christ at the doctrinal center of Scripture and, therefore, at the doctrinal and specifically soteriological center of Christian theology. Christ does not point out the meaning of all doctrine—instead all Scripture and all doctrine point toward the person and work of Christ as the core of the Christian message, the central soteriological truth but not the overarching meaning of all Scripture, confession, and system. Christology does not impinge interpretively on every exegetical issue or point of doctrine. We are reminded that angry Lutheran exegetes and theologians, most notably Aegidius Hunnius, would refer to *Calvinus judaizans,* judaizing Calvin, precisely because Calvin adamantly refused the wholesale christologizing of the Old Testament and the trinitarian reading of the plural form *Elohim.*[264]

---

[260]Bullinger, *Decades,* III.viii (pp. 284–85).

[261]Bullinger, *Decades,* III.v (p. 147); cf. Bullinger's discussion of Christ as *scopus* in his preface to the Zürich Latin Bible of 1543 with Hall, "Biblical Scholarship: Editions and Commentaries," in *CHB,* III:71.

[262]Bullinger, *Decades,* I.iii (pp. 75–78).

[263]Bullinger, *Decades,* I.iv (p. 81).

[264]Aegidius Hunnius, *Calvinus Judaizans, hoc est judaicae glossae et corruptelae, quibus J. Calvinus scriptura sacra loca, testimonia de gloriosa trinitate ...* (Wittenberg, 1593), angrily answered by David Paraeus, *Calvinus orthodoxus seu vindicatio Calvini de trinitate* (Heidelberg, 1594); and cf. Gass, *Geschichte der Protestantischen Dogmatik,* 2, pp. 42–43, with Basil Hall, "Biblical Scholarship," in CHB, III:87–88. On Calvin's approach to the text

Heppe quite rightly saw that "the distinction between a *fundamentum Scripturae* and the individual doctrine in it, and the conviction that the latter are essentially present in the former, is so essential not merely to the federal theology but to the Reformed system in general, that the latter cannot be understood at all without recognition of the former."[265] The concept of a *fundamentum Scripturae*, according to Heppe, particularly when it is understood in this intimate relationship to the entire body of doctrine, provides Reformed dogmatics with its "scientific" point of departure, its basic method. In German Reformed theology, moreover, this "fundamental concept of Revelation" was understood from the beginnings of the Reformation in terms of the covenant of God *(foedus Dei),* the kingdom of Christ *(regnum Christi),* and communion with Christ *(koinonia cum Christo).*[266] Granting that revelation itself could be conceived as summed up in these terms, revelation clearly focused on Christ whose relationship with believers is identical with the covenant and whose work is the sum of the law and the gospel. Heppe concludes, "thus the concept of the *foedus Dei* is the essence of all revealed truths."[267]

These arguments point in several directions. In the first place, they point away from the central-dogma theory inasmuch as they manifest Christ and covenant, rather, than the eternal decree, as the hermeneutical focus of the Reformed orthodox system and the "basis" of its "scientific nature, the method in principle of Reformed dogmatics."[268] Schneckenburger recognized that this covenantal or economic focus of the system on the historical *executio* of the divine plan in Christ does direct the attention of theology to the eternal decree—as a "speculative deduction" from the historical execution of the work of salvation—and manifests the Reformed system as resting on a "theological" rather than on an "anthropological" principle.[269] But he also saw that the christological and federal model argued by Reformed theology prevented this principle from being conceived as "an abstract divine decree" and instead focused attention on the "personhood of the Son."[270] Indeed, we see, in both the

see: A. J. Baumgartner, *Calvin Hébraïsant et interprète de l'Ancien Testament* (Paris: Fischbacher, 1889).

[265]Heppe, *RD,* p. 42.
[266]Heppe, *RD,* p. 42.
[267]Heppe, *RD,* p. 43.
[268]Heppe, *RD,* p. 42.
[269]Schneckenburger, "Die reformirte Dogmatik," pp. 75–76.
[270]Schneckenburger, "Die reformirte Dogmatik," pp. 610–11.

Confessio christianae fidei of Beza and the virtually identical *Compendium doctrinae christianae* of the Hungarian churches, an insistence that "Christ is the *scopus* of faith, indeed Christ, as he is presented to us in the Word of God."[271]

Although Heppe did not, in general, draw these conclusions, but rather assumed that Reformed theology took from Calvin "the stark supernaturalism" of predestination used as a "principle of necessity,"[272] he did recognize a possible alternative to predestinarianism in two early orthodox systems, the *Exegesis divinae atque humanae koinonias* (1561) of Petrus Boquinus and Andreas Hyperius' *Methodi theologiae* (1566).[273] Heppe believed that early German Reformed dogmatics, before the attenuation of Melanchthonian models in the era of scholastic development, Calvinist influence, and the rigidification of Lutheranism toward the end of the sixteenth century, used the concept of a *foedus Dei* or *regnum Christi* as the foundational principle and central truth of the work of creation and redemption. "The reality, substance and means" that verified and dispensed this covenant were described by German Reformed theology under the terms *unio essentialis cum Christo* and *insitio in Christum* or *in corpus Christi mysticum*.[274]

The federal model appears most clearly in Hyperius' *Methodi theologiae,* an incomplete system written at Marburg between 1554 and 1564. The concept of covenant does not appear, as in later Reformed covenant theology, as a central historical motif linking together the work of creation and redemption, but instead as a basic heuristic device used in construction of each *locus.* Thus the *locus* on creatures and human beings and the *locus* on the Christian doctrines of faith, hope, and love, which together occupy the central portion of the system between the doctrines of God and the last things, are both subdivided into discussions of the conditions before and after the fall. Hyperius discusses, under the topic of Christian love, *lex ante lapsum* and *lex post lapsum;* under the topic of faith, *evangelium ante lapsum* and *evangelium post lapsum*.[275]

---

[271]Cf. Beza, *Confessio christianae fidei,* IV.6; with the *Compendium doctrinae christianae,* IV.6 in Müller, *BRK,* p. 386; and cf. Muller, *Christ and the Decree,* pp. 79–96 on the christocentric character of Beza's theology as a whole.

[272]Cf. Heppe, *Geschichte des deutschen Protestanismus,* I, pp. 13–17, with idem, "Der Character," pp. 670–674.

[273]Heppe, *DDP,* I, pp. 143–48.

[274]Heppe, *DDP,* pp. 143–44.

[275]Cf. Hyperius, *Methodi theol.,* with Heppe, *DDP,* I, pp. 145–46.

Boquinus' theology carried forward a similar view of the foundation or scope of revelation. His *Exegesis divinae atque humanae koinonias* is a full system of doctrine organized around the principle of union with Christ. "The *foedus Dei*," Heppe argues, "gains its reality in this spiritual-corporeal union of mankind with Christ" described by Boquinus as *koinonia*.[276] This communion of human beings with God was for Boquinus "the principal focus *(scopus)* of the holy writings."[277] In other words, Boquinus makes explicit the point already given implicitly in Hyperius' arrangement of *loci:* there is an interpretive center in Scripture that can be identified by theology and used as an organizing principle—specifically the God-given relationship in reconciliation between God and man in Christ that can be identified variously under its different aspects as the *foedus Dei* or as *koinonia* or as *unio cum Christo.*

b. The Foundation and Scope of Scripture in Reformed Orthodox Theology

Boquinus' conviction that theology could identify the *fundamentum* or *scopus* of Scripture was shared by his younger colleagues at Heidelberg, Olevian and Ursinus. In their theology, the concept of a federal *scopus* linked to the communion or union of believers with Christ was both elaborated and, at the same time, pointed back toward the confessional language of the *scopus Scripturae*. Commenting on Olevian's teaching, Heppe writes, "Since the institution of a covenant relationship with man is the purpose of all God's revelations, the Christian must regard the separate revealed truths in the light of the covenant idea, in such a way as recognizes them as a whole only in relation to that idea and grasps them with believing trust precisely in their special validity and significance for his individual person."[278] Olevian's *Fester Grund* or *Firm Foundation* is a catechetical work that identifies the central issue of Christian faith as "the promise of Jesus Christ" to which a Christian ought to look as to a "plumb-line" or rule that shows forth "the unchangeable will and eternal counsel of God, on which we may confidently build."[279] In his exposition of the creed, Olevian drew together at considerably greater length this language of *promissio* with the concept of the *regnum Christi* under the overarching theme of covenant, the *foedus*

---

[276]Heppe, *DDP,* I, p. 148.
[277]Cited in Heppe, *DDP,* I, p. 148.
[278]Heppe, *RD,* p. 45.
[279]Heppe, *RD,* pp. 45–46.

Dei constituted by God and inscribed on the human heart by faith.[280] The concept appears again in Olevian's final and most important work, *De substantia foederis gratuiti inter Deum et electos* (1585). Here Olevian defines the "substance of the covenant" as the promise and gift of adoption as children of God and of the inheritance of eternal life in Christ.[281] The exposition of the administration of the covenant, although not a formal system of theology in the fullest sense, can be viewed as an adumbration of a large-scale system focused on the idea of covenant as the central theme of Scripture.[282]

If Olevian gave dogmatic elaboration to the covenant idea and to the collateral concept of the promise of God in Christ without specifically defining either doctrine as the *fundamentum Scripturae,* his colleague Ursinus—whose covenant theology is not nearly as elaborate as that of Olevian—provides the closure of argument and the definition that is lacking in Olevian's formulation. When Ursinus approached the problem of gathering and organizing his *Loci communes,* he not only set the doctrine of Scripture first in order, he also outlined the meaning and content of Scripture in such a way as to adumbrate the structure and justify the contents of his entire projected system. The Scriptures, Ursinus begins, are nowhere better summarized than in the Decalogue and the Creed and cannot be better understood than as consisting in law and gospel. All doctrine can be understood as teaching concerning God—his nature, his will, and his works.[283] What is more, these several ways of characterizing the whole of biblical and Christian teaching cohere one with the other. The will of God is discerned in precepts, warnings, and promises and, even so, the works of God consist in judgments and blessings by which God works his good in all things. Both the will and the works of God are summed up, therefore, in the law and the gospel. By implication, the Decalogue and the Creed can be defined also as law and gospel.[284]

Not content with this somewhat dichotomizing view of Scripture, Ursinus notes that the Lord himself, who is the focus of the gospel, taught the law—indeed, he taught the two great commandments that summarize the law and the prophets. It is also true, as Peter taught in Acts, that the prophets bear witness to the gift of forgiveness of sins

---

[280]Olevian, *Expositio symboli apostolici,* p. [12?]

[281]Olevian, *De substantia foederis,* p. 2.

[282]Cf. Heppe, *DDP,* I, p. 151, with Bierma, "The Covenant Theology of Caspar Olevian" (Ph.D. diss., Duke University, 1980), pp. 211–13.

[283]Ursinus, *Loci theologici,* col. 426.

[284]Ursinus, *Loci theologici,* cols. 426–27.

in and through the name of Christ to all who believe (cf. Acts 10:43). Law and gospel are not, therefore, parts of Scripture but are together taught throughout Scripture.[285] Thus, the new covenant is not peculiar to the New Testament: the books of the New Testament simply declare its fulfillment, even as the testimony of Christ and the apostles confirms the promises given in the books of the Old Testament. What is more, "Christ himself is the sum of doctrine" *(Christus ipse summam doctrinae),* as is testified and confirmed in many places in Scripture.[286]

The identification of the prophetic and apostolic writings as Old and New Testament, Ursinus continues, points in much the same direction as the argument concerning the presence of law and gospel throughout Scripture and as together summed up in Christ. "The word *testamentum* is known to signify *foedus,* covenant," specifically "the covenant between God and believers." This covenant is concerned with all that God promises and fulfills—"his grace, the remission of sins, the Holy Spirit, righteousness and life eternal, and the preservation of the church in this life by and through his Son our mediator" all of which we receive by faith.[287] This is the meaning of the covenant, but it is also the sum of all that is taught in the law and the gospel. The reason for this final unity of Scripture is that, as the Holy Spirit teaches, "Christ is taught in the whole of Scripture, and he alone is to be sought here": Christ is the *fundamentum doctrinae ecclesiasticae,* the foundation of the doctrine of the church, and the *summa & scopus Scripturae,* the summation and focal point of Scripture.[288] Theological system must therefore also discuss Christ, the work of redemption, and the doctrine of the church, and Christians must be taught to seek Christ throughout Scripture. Indeed, "the true and uncorrupted knowledge of Christ comprehends the whole of the Scripture and of the doctrine of the church."[289] Ursinus' views are echoed in the theology of his colleague and successor, Zanchi.[290]

A similar concept of *fundamentum* or "foundation" can be found in Perkins' *An Exposition of the Creede.* There Perkins writes that

---

[285]Ursinus, *Loci theologici,* col. 427.

[286]Ursinus, *Loci theologici,* col. 427.

[287]Ursinus, *Loci theologici,* col. 427.

[288]Ursinus, *Loci theologici,* cols. 427–28; and cf. *PRRD,* I, 9.1, for a full quotation of the passage in its relation to the preliminary question concerning fundamental articles.

[289]Ursinus, *Loci theologici,* col. 428.

[290]Zanchi, *In Mosen et universa Biblia, Prolegomena,* col. 16.

"the foundation and ground worke of the Covenant is Christ Jesus the Mediatour, in whome all the promises of God are yea and amen."[291] Inasmuch, moreover, as the covenant of grace comprehends, for Perkins, the entirety of the revelation of the promise in the Old and New Testaments, Christ and the redemption offered in him must be understood as the fundamental truth at the very center of the scriptural message. Perkins, like many of his contemporaries, can use the term "scope" both with reference to Christ as the center of Scripture and as a synonym for *argumentum*.[292]

The most elaborate discussion of the concept of *fundamentum Scripturae* in the era of orthodoxy is most probably to be found in Cocceius' *Summa theologiae ex Scriptura repetita*. In Cocceius' thought, the *fundamentum sacrae Scripturae* is the basic rule of interpretation, theologically understood, that enables the exegete to move from the text of Scripture to theological formulation. Scripture itself speaks of this *fundamentum*, defining it in two distinct ways: first the term indicates Christ, the one to whom we are joined, in whom we live and on whom we rest in faith;[293] and second, it indicates "a fundamental truth or a fundamental axiom" on the basis of which God can be known, his Word believed and understood.[294] The first definition rests upon Peter's identification of Christ as the cornerstone, the living stone in and through whom believers are built into a "spiritual house" (1 Pet. 2:4–6). Even so, Christ is the most firm foundation (*fundamentum fundatissimus*) in whom the righteousness servant of God has a foundation for all time (*fundamentum seculi*, cf. Prov. 10:25), who was called by the prophet a "precious" cornerstone and foundation laid in Zion (Isa. 28:16): Christ, indeed, is the very cornerstone of the foundation of the prophets and the apostles (Eph. 2:20).[295]

It is possible, Cocceius continues, to speak of the *fundamentum apostolarum*, the basis upon which the apostles were able to preach the gospel, or of the *fundamentum prophetarum*, the source of the gift of prophecy. It is even possible to speak of the foundations of

[291]Perkins, *Workes,* I, p. 165, col. 2C.

[292]E.g., Perkins, *Commentary on Galatians,* p. 47 and *A Clowd of Faithfull Witnesses,* in *Workes,* III, second pagination, p. 1; Whitaker, *Disputation,* IX.5 (p. 472); Arminius, *Analysis of the Ninth Chapter of St. Paul's Epistle to the Romans,* in *Works,* III, pp. 485–86; cf. Muller, "William Perkins and the Protestant Exegetical Tradition," pp. 79–81.

[293]Cocceius, *Summa Theol.,* I.vii.1–2.

[294]Cocceius, *Summa Theol.,* I.vii.15–16.

[295]Cocceius, *Summa Theol.,* I.vii.3–5.

the city that is to come, the New Jerusalem.[296] This does not mean that there are many foundations. The twelve foundations of the New Jerusalem (Rev. 21:19) do not indicate a plurality of foundations but a plurality of ornaments, just as there are twelve apostles and twelve (minor!) prophets, but a single foundation. The New Testament—the apostolic preaching—followed upon the preaching of the prophets and the substance of the New Testament is proven by the word of the prophets. The foundation is one: "who is a rock," Cocceius argues, with a reference to Psalm 18:31, "except our God."[297] There are many columns in the house of God, but only one foundation.[298]

Echoing the early German Reformed writers, Hyperius and Boquinus, Cocceius defines the second usage of *fundamentum*—the fundamental axioms or truths of Scripture—as the acceptation and approbation of believers in covenant with the result that they are the inheritors of life and participants in righteousness.[299] Since, moreover, God is one, his righteousness is one and the end ordained by God for all things is one, the fundamental truth given for all human beings in all times and all places must also be one: even so there is but one *veritas* and *axiom fundamentale* in both Old and New Testaments.[300]

Cocceius' successors in the Reformed federal tradition also emphasize the concept as a basic component of the *locus de Scriptura sacra*. Witsius can, in his discussion of fundamental doctrines, identify Christ specifically as the *fundamentum* (following 1 Cor. 3:11) and argue that, therefore, as "fundamental doctrine" can be "separate from the doctrine concerning Christ."[301] Even so, Witsius can argue that "the doctrine of Christ is the key of knowledge (Luke 11:42) without which nothing can be savingly understood in Moses and the prophets" and, citing Bisterfeld, declare that "the Lord Jesus Christ was the spirit and soul of the whole, both of the Old and New Testament."[302] A similar approach can be noted in Burmann's discussion of the prophetic office of Christ in the Old Testament, where the identity of Christ as Word incarnate allows Burmann to point all of the *verba Dei* toward Christ and, moreover, to view all of the Old

---

[296]Cocceius, *Summa Theol.*, I.vii.6–8.
[297]Cocceius, *Summa Theol.*, I.vii.8, 13.
[298]Cocceius, *Summa Theol.*, I.vii.14.
[299]Cocceius, *Summa Theol.*, I.vii.18, 38.
[300]Cocceius, *Summa Theol.*, I.vii.39–40.
[301]Witsius, *Exercitationes*, II.x.
[302]Witsius, *De oeconomia*, IV.vi.2, citing Bisterfeld, *De scripturae eminentia*, xl.

Testament *verbi Dei* as the work of the preincarnate Word. The Old Testament, therefore, reveals the office of Christ.[303]

This is not to say that the idea of a *fundamentum Scripturae* had no place outside of the federal school. The English dogmatician, Edward Leigh could argue that Scripture was, in its ultimate meaning and purpose, "the Revelation of Christ"—so that the "doctrinal foundation" of theology, Scripture, has at its heart a "foundation of foundations," Jesus Christ, who is "the end of the law and the substance of the Gospel" and therefore "the principal subject of the whole Bible" and "the summe of all divine revealed truths."[304] The point is little developed from the statements of Ursinus and it stands in full agreement with the early orthodox view. Turretin does not elaborate the point either—but he does declare, quite pointedly against any and all alternatives, that there is "no other foundation" than Jesus Christ.[305] Other elements of the early Reformed doctrine of Boquinus and his contemporaries also appear in Turretin's system: in contrasting natural and supernatural theology Turretin identifies the distinctive content of the necessary supernatural biblical revelation as the promises of God in Christ or "the mercy of God in Christ";[306] and Turretin can declare that "we are unable to believe in God except through Christ," who in the "incomplex and personal" sense of the term *fundamentum* is the "foundation of all salvation."[307]

At considerably greater length than either Leigh or Turretin, Owen raises the issue of the *fundamentum* or foundation of the church and its doctrines by way of a polemical note on the question of authority. The text of Matthew 16:18, "upon this Rock I will build my church," he argues, cannot indicate the primacy of the pope, but rather points back to Peter's confession of faith in Christ as the foundation of the church. Thus, the "person of Christ, the Son of the living God, as vested with his offices ... is the foundation of the Church, the rock whereon it is built."[308] Owen elaborates the point:

> The foundation of the Church is twofold: 1) Real; 2) Doctrinal. And in both ways, Christ alone is the foundation. The real foundation of the Church he is, by virtue of the mystical union of it unto

---

[303]Burmann, *Synopsis theol.,* V.xii.3–4.
[304]Leigh, *System,* I.ix, i.
[305]Turretin, *Inst. theol.,* I.xiv.6.
[306]Turretin, *Inst. theol. elencticae,* I.iv.7, 23; cf. II.i.5–6.
[307]Turretin, *Inst. theol. elencticae,* I.iv.20; xiv.4.
[308]Owen, *Christologia,* in *Works,* I, p. 34.

him, with all the benefits whereof, and whereby, it is made par-
taker.... And he is the doctrinal foundation of it, in that the faith or
doctrine concerning him and his offices is that divine truth which
in a peculiar manner animates and constitutes the Church of the
New Testament.[309]

The doctrinal point, as Owen states it, provides further evidence
against the "central-dogma" thesis—particularly inasmuch as Owen
connects his argument concerning Christ as *fundamentum doctrinae*
specifically with the problem of christological heterodoxy in the
early church and in the seventeenth century. Such heresies, Owen
declares, more than any other sort, strike at the very foundation of
Christianity.[310]

The term is also found, with a somewhat different connotation in
quite a few of the high and late orthodox systems, both Lutheran and
Reformed. The Lutheran tendency to discuss Scripture as Word in
the *locus* on the means of grace, particularly when held in relation to
the strong Lutheran emphasis on Christ as the *res significatum* of the
sacraments, led to a stress on the purpose and efficacy of the Word
and, by extension, on the central purpose, the *scopus* or *Zweck,* of
Scripture. Thus Rambach can declare that the *Zweck* of Scripture,
considered as *finis proximus,* is repentance and faith in Christ, considered as *finis ultimus,* life eternal.[311] Or, again, speaking of the
proximate goal of Scripture in terms of a standard definition of religion as right worship and obedience, Rambach can declare that the
finis ac scopus Scripturae sacrae is "that a godly man ... a member
of Christ be perfected wholly, in body and soul, in understanding
and will, to perform service to God and directed to all the good
works that the Word of God demands."[312]

Among the later Reformed dogmaticians, Mastricht favored this
definition with its identification of *scopus* as the *finis Scripturae
sacrae.* It is the goal of Scripture that believers be perfected before
God and perfectly instructed in all good works.[313] Scripture has,
therefore, a twofold *scopus* or *finis,* a *finis cui,* a goal to which it is

---

[309]Owen, *Christologia,* in *Works,* I, p. 34.

[310]Owen, *Christologia,* in *Works,* I, pp. 9–10; cf. Dewey D. Wallace, "The
Life and Thought of John Owen," pp. 276, 336; and Richard W. Daniels,
"Christology of John Owen," pp. 62–67.

[311]Rambach, *Schrifftmässige Erläuterung der Grundlegung der Theologie*
(Frankfurt, 1738), pp. 597, 598–599.

[312]Rambach, *Dogmatische: theologie oder christliche Glaubenslehre*
(Frankfurt and Leipzig, 1744), I, p. 205.

[313]Mastricht, *Theoretico-practica theologia,* I.ii.2.

directed in a material sense, which is the believer; and a *finis cuius,* a goal of which it enables the believer to partake, formally, as an outcome, which is the perfection or blessedness of the believer.[314] Heidegger, with a similar intent, identifies the *scopus Scripturae* as the redemptive covenant or testament of God given to the church in all ages.[315] At the purely exegetical level, the dogmaticians—even as late as Wyttenbach—continue to argue that attention to the scope of a biblical book or of a passage in a book is necessary to right understanding: thus Wyttenbach can note that the *scopus* of the Gospels is not the entire history of Christ's life, but the demonstration of the identity of Christ as the Messiah. On a much smaller scale, he could note that the *scopus* of the text is crucial to any understanding of parables, where the story is to be read for its underlying meaning—as in the case of the parable of the talents (Matt. 25:16ff.), where the scope of the passage concerns the proper use of God's gifts.[316]

Nor should one imagine that the concept of a *scopus Scripturae* is the exclusive property of dogmaticians. It often appears in exegetical works from the era of orthodoxy, frequently with reference to the relation of the scope or argument of a particular text to the scope of Scripture as a whole and, as in the case of Burroughs' commentary on Hosea, with a sense of the continuity between later Protestant exegetical interests and the approach of the Reformers. "I remember Luther saith," writes Burroughs,

> That the general scope of the Scripture is, to declare the Lord to be a God of mercy and goodness; the whole Scriptures, saith he, aim especially at this, that we should believe and be confident that God is a gracious and merciful God. And this is the scope of this chapter. Let us rather charge ourselves of wickedness, and ungrateful dealings with God, and let us forever justify God, and acknowledge him not only to be a righteous, but a gracious God.[317]

The "scope" of individual chapters or textual units continued, moreover, to be a primary interest of exegetes throughout the era of orthodoxy.[318]

---

[314]Mastricht, *Theoretico-practica theologia,* I.ii.2.

[315]Heidegger, *Corpus theol.,* IX.4, cited in Heppe, *RD,* p. 281.

[316]Wyttenbach, *Tentamen theologiae dogmaticae,* II, §§180, 183.

[317]Burroughs, *Exposition of Hosea,* pp. 461–62 (on chap. 11).

[318]Cf. Burroughs, *Exposition of Hosea,* pp. 54 (chap. 2), 181 (chap. 3), 261 (chap. 5, using "sum" instead of "scope"), 461–62 (chap. 11); with Poole,

Given its covenantal formulation at the hands of Hyperius, Boquinus, Olevianus, and Ursinus, the concept of the *fundamentum* or *scopus Scripturae* became an emphasis, although hardly the exclusive property of the federal theology of Cocceius and his followers. Both its emphasis in their theology and its deemphasis in the works of other seventeenth-century Reformed theologians can, moreover, be attributed to the rather different hermeneutic employed by the federal theologians—indeed, to their adherence to a typological hermeneutic at the same time that Protestant theology in general was wrestling with the difficulties of an increasingly literal, grammatical, and historical view of the text.

Heppe was quite correct to understand this language of *scopus Scripturae* with its covenantal and christocentric implications as a focal point in the theological interpretation of Scripture and as the basis for construction of dogmatic model that stood against the reading of Reformed theology as a predestinarian system. Where he was incorrect was in his hypothesis of two distinct Reformed models, a German federal model and a Swiss and Dutch predestinarian model —and, by extension, he was incorrect in his assumption that the decline in emphasis on the *scopus Scripturae* was the result of an eventual dominance of predestinarianism over federalism. This argument not only misunderstands the relationship between the doctrine of the decrees and the doctrine of the covenant by playing one doctrine off against another as if one had to be the central dogma of the system;[319] it also misunderstands the root of the concept of *scopus Scripturae* and the reasons for its decline as a theological motif.

As we have seen, the concept of a *fundamentum* or *scopus Scripturae* was present in the thought of federal and nonfederal thinkers and belonged as much to the thought of the Swiss Reformed as it did to the thought of the German Reformed. Indeed, it appeared first in early confessional theology of the Swiss Reformation. Beyond this, the concept appears to have been a fairly common feature of the early theology of the Reformation, traceable to such diverse sources as Erasmus, Luther, and the Swiss confessions, a concept, moreover, resting on hermeneutical as well as doctrinal considerations. Indeed, it is best explained in relation to the various late medieval and early

Commentary on the Whole Bible, II, p. 648 (the "scope" of Lamentations).

[319]On the problem of covenant theology, see Anthony Hoekema, "The Covenant of Grace in Calvin's Teaching," in Calvin Theological Journal 2 (1967):133-61; Lyle D. Bierma, "Federal Theology in the Sixteenth Century: Two Traditions?" in *Westminster Theological Journal* 45 (1983):304–21.

sixteenth-century hermeneutical models that made Christ the focal point of interpretation—whether Faber Stapulensis' spiritual literal sense, Luther's claim that Christ is, *litteraliter,* the speaker of Psalm 3, or the *caput-corpus-membra* pattern, also employed by Luther.

Once this hermeneutical basis of the *scopus Scripturae* idea is recognized, not only is it apparent why the idea was prominent longer among the federal theologians than among other Reformed writers, it is also clear why it gradually ceased to be of use to Reformed theology in general, despite the strong christological focus of Reformed doctrine. The federal theology, as taught by Cocceius and his followers was far more open to allegorical and typological exegesis than the other varieties of Reformed thought and, therefore, far more liable to have recourse to christological readings of the Old Testament. The development of hermeneutics in the late sixteenth and seventeenth centuries, moreover, was toward an increasingly literal, textual, and comparative linguistic method that increasingly excluded the allegorical and typological approach not only of the Middle Ages but also of the early Reformers. In this altered hermeneutical context, it became impossible to claim that the goal or direction of each text was Christ, but quite acceptable to affirm that the goal of Scripture in whole and in part was the redemption of believers. This reading of the issue corresponded not only with the increasingly literal or grammatical reading of the text but also with the emphasis on *praxis* found in much Reformed and in Lutheran theology.[320] The more purely exegetical usage of *scopus* as a virtual synonym of *argumentum,* accordingly, did not pass away as quickly and, indeed, remained characteristic of Protestant exegesis through the seventeenth and into the eighteenth centuries.[321]

---

[320]On *praxis* and the practical orientation of theology, see *PRRD,* I, 6.3.
[321]See further below, §6.4.

4

The Divinity of Scripture

4.1 The Divinity of Scripture: Causes and Ends

The divinity of Scripture, particularly with reference to the causality that produced the text and to the goal and purpose of that causality in its work of production, is a topic that enters Protestant theological system during the era of early orthodoxy, notably in such major systems as Polanus' *Syntagma theologiae,* Gomarus' *Disputationes,* and the *Synopsis purioris theologiae.*[1] On the one hand, this discussion, particularly from the formal point of view, is rather different from anything that can be found in the writings of the Reformers. (Nor is it universally present among the Reformed orthodox, although it is typically implied in their discussions of the properties of Scripture.) On the other hand, it ought to be clear that the Reformers assumed a divine power at work in the writing and preservation of Scripture that, in concert with the efforts of the human authors and with the scribal preservers of the text, had assured the availability of and authoritative Word of God in and for the life of the church. The scholastic causal argumentation was intended, by those of the Protestant orthodox who adopted the argument, to develop and explain the origin and preservation of the text with due respect to the many levels of causality, divine and human, at work in that series of historical events. The orthodox effort at once formalized and nuanced the discussion, providing a context within which the arguments concerning the inspiration,

---

[1]Polanus, *Syntagma theol.,* I.xv–xvi; Gomarus, *Disputationes,* II.xii–xxx; *Synopsis purioris theologiae,* II.xxiii–xxiv.

231

authority, self-authenticating nature, and canonical character of the text could be understood.

These considerations raise again for us the issue of the Protestant scholastic use of causal language. The all-too-frequent response of theologians and historians has been simply to dismiss the language as a symptom of excessive Aristotelianism or, in the case of the Reformed orthodox, to claim it as evidence of a metaphysical, predestinarian, and even deterministic interest. The latter claim does not, of course, extend to the Lutheran orthodox systems, despite their virtually identical use of causal categories to argue the doctrine of Scripture. What is more, the lines of causality that will be noted here do not give any impression of overarching determinism but rather of the application of a heuristic principle. The causality of Scripture and of the preservation of Scripture is presented by the orthodox as a way of understanding the relationship of Scripture to the other topics and issues addressed in the system of doctrine. Our recognition of this fact points us, in turn, beyond the facile statement that the causal categories bear witness to Aristotelianism—which, of course, they do—to the deeper question of the theological meaning conveyed by and, sometimes, because of the foreignness of these categories to our present-day modes of theological expression, hidden under the language of Protestant orthodoxy.

In addition, as virtually all of the Reformed orthodox systems examined here demonstrate, the causal language underlying and guiding the discussion of the divinity of Scripture draws directly on and, typically, reflects throughout the multilevel conception of Word developed by the orthodox in their doctrine of Scripture. Thus, Trelcatius can argue that the Word is the source of true knowledge of God, so that in some sense the revelatory Word must be known or at least known about before God can be truly known. In order, however, God precedes the Word as the one who speaks: God "mediately" speaks to us in the Word and the Word "immediately" brings us to the true knowledge of God. Obliging this order, theology must first speak of the Word as the immediate source of the knowledge of God.[2] This word is "enunciative," uttered by God and communicated to human beings as a revelation in "oracles, visions, or dreams," or it is known by means of an "instrument" which is to say by means of a "tradition of doctrine" or, more excellently, by means of Scripture. From the vantage point of this causal approach to the knowledge of God, Scripture may be defined as

---

[2]Trelcatius, *Schol. meth.,* I.i–ii (pp. 11–12).

a holy instrument concerning the truth necessary to salvation, faithfully and perfectly written in the canonical books by the prophets and the apostles, [acting as] the secretaries of God for the salvific instruction of the church.[3]

The "authority, perfection, perspicuity, and [proper] use" of Scripture is made evident by further "analysis" of its causes.[4] This definition of Scripture as an instrument, moreover, raises the issue of causality inasmuch as an instrument is never an efficient cause but is always a means used by an efficient cause—or, as must be the case with Scripture, a means produced by one activity and used in another. From this vantage point then, the basic question dealt with in the discussion of the divinity of Scripture is the origin, which is to say, the causality productive of Scripture as the authoritative ground of Christian doctrine.

The problem of the causality of Scripture, then, is—as far as the Protestant orthodox mind is concerned—the problem of revelation itself, the problem of the transmission of knowledge about God in finite, human forms, in the case of Scripture, in the form of human words. In describing this causality, the Protestant scholastics looked to both the medieval scholastic tradition and the works of the Reformers. From the medieval teachers they received the definition of God as the *auctor principalis sive primarius Scripturae* and of human beings, the prophets, and the apostles, as secondary authors or instruments.[5] From the Reformers they received no new language, but they did find confirmation of the point in the repeated identification of Scripture as God's Word, as given by God and, as Calvin could say, produced by the Spirit "dictating" to human "amanuenses."[6]

The scholastic definition is particularly clear as stated by Gomarus:

The efficient cause of Scripture is twofold: its author and his ministers or assistants *(auctor, & ministri illius)*.

The author is God the Father (Heb. 1:1; Lk. 1:70); the Son (1 Pet. 1:11); and Holy spirit (2 Pet. 1:21): and on that account we speak of a divine direction *(syntagma divinum)*: as, for example, the

[3]Trelcatius, *Schol. meth.*, I.i–ii (p. 12).
[4]Trelcatius, *Schol. meth.*, I.i–ii (p. 12).
[5]See above, §1.2.
[6]Calvin, *Inst.*, IV.viii.8, 9; and see further, below, §§2.1 and 2.1.b.

logia tou theou or deliverances of God *(eloquia Dei)* (Rom. 3:2), are so called on grounds of divine inspiration.

The assistants *(ministri)* are, to be sure, holy men, moved by God, called immediately by him and by the Holy Spirit, instructed in theology, and to that end, taught and directed to put it into words and teach it for the general good of the church (Heb. 1:1; 2 Pet 1:21; 3:2; 2 Tim 3:16; Jn. 14:16; 16:13).[7]

That the efficient cause of Scripture is "God the Father, in the Son, by the Spirit" is evident from the substance of the oracles of God themselves, from the testimony of the Son in the New Testament, and from the inward testimony of the Spirit in believers. The orthodox place particular emphasis on the work of the Spirit in their discussions of the causality of Scripture: The Spirit is the connection between the immediate divine and the mediate human efficiency— since the Spirit has not only used the prophets and the apostles as "amanuenses" but has also confirmed the "subject" and the "certainty" of the teaching of Scripture in works of grace and power and has "sealed" the public or outward testimony of Scripture by an inward witness "in the conscience of the godly."[8] Accordingly, Scripture can be considered as the ground and foundation of truth on the basis of efficient causality—inasmuch as it is written either "immediately" by God, as when with his finger he wrote the Decalogue, or "mediately" by the "actuaries" and "tabularies" of God.[9] As confirmation of this divine causality, we can look to the personal fitness and worthy ministry of the prophets and the apostles, and the conformity of God's Word with the truth. The testimony of the church also confirms the divine efficiency in the production of Scripture, but only in a secondary sense, granting that the continued existence, ministry, and discipline of the church is grounded in Scripture.[10]

The "material cause" of Scripture is the divine substance or material that has been "revealed for our salvation," delivered "according to our capacity, and registered in the canon."[11] God, therefore, is the proper subject, and as such, the material cause of

---

[7]Gomarus, *Disputationes,* II.xii–xiv.

[8]Trelcatius, *Schol. meth.,* I.ii (p. 15); cf. Junius, *Theses theologicae heidelbergenses,* IV.3–8.

[9]Junius, *Theses theologicae heidelbergenses,* IV.13–14; cf. Trelcatius, *Schol. meth.,* I.i (pp. 13–14).

[10]Trelcatius, *Schol. meth.,* I.ii (pp. 16–17).

[11]Trelcatius, *Schol. meth.,* I.ii (p. 17).

Scripture. The text of Scripture contains descriptions and statements about the nature of God, primarily in terms of the divine attributes rather than the divine essence, and offered in such a way as to permit comprehension by the human mind. The divine subject, moreover, is not universally presented in its ultimate proper sense—as God revealed in his attributes—but often in a secondary manner, as ordained by God for the sake of salvation. Thus, the subject and material of Scripture concern the activity of God among human beings and the duties of human beings toward God.[12]

Profoundly related to the material cause or subject of Scripture is the form or formal cause, "which God has impressed on [Scripture] to his glory and for our use."[13] Christ himself identified this form as "truth" (John 17:17). Scripture is, thus, to be recognized as fully divine—"there is nothing in Scripture that does not rest on divine truth."[14] More specifically,

> The formal cause of holy Scripture is twofold, inward and outward: by the former Scripture is proportionate both to divine truth and with each of its parts; by the latter, the exquisite language of holy Scripture, all things that are written in it have a style suitable to the dignity of the speaker, to the nature of the word spoken, and to the condition of those to whom it is spoken.[15]

The various attributes of Scripture discussed in the Reformed orthodox systems take their point of departure from this identification of the formal causality.

Finally, considered as to its *finis* or *telos* Scripture has a twofold purpose: the glory of God and the salvation of the elect. The church's present well-being and salvation leading to the final blessedness of God's servants is the secondary or subordinate goal, while the glory of God as manifest in the salvation of the elect is the primary and ultimate goal. Scripture is therefore perfectly suited to both the nurture of faith and the support and presentation of divine truth.[16] As in the cases of the other causal arguments, this discussion of the final causality of Scripture must be regarded as a heuristic device designed to ground a whole series of theological and

---

[12]Junius, *Theses theologicae heidelbergenses,* II.5–13.

[13]Junius, *Theses theologicae heidelbergenses,* III.1.

[14]Junius, *Theses theologicae heidelbergenses,* III.2–4.

[15]Trelcatius, *Schol. meth.,* I.ii (pp. 23–24).

[16]Cf. Gomarus, *Disputationes,* II.xxv–xxvi, with Junius, *Theses theologicae heidelbergenses,* V.5–7.

hermeneutical issues in the nature of the text itself. Once the basic identification of this final causality has been set forth, the orthodox, following out the a priori logic of the *locus,* can draw out attributes of Scripture and discuss the method of its interpretation.[17] The pattern of argument reflects the archetypal/ectypal structuring of theology discussed by the orthodox in their prolegomena.

Trelcatius makes the point simply in the Agricolan or Ramist style of early orthodoxy:

> The final cause, according to the consideration of the object, is twofold: the highest and most remote is the glory of God in the maintenance of his truth; the second and nearest ... is the instruction of his church unto salvation.[18]

A similar, though somewhat more elaborate and less clearly a priori, fourfold explanation is offered by Gomarus. The first *finis* or *telos* of Scripture is the "perpetual conservation and propagation, in the church and among both pastors and flock, in the face of all dangers of loss or corruption, of doctrine necessary to salvation." The second, which Gomarus describes as a "use" of Scripture, is to provide a rule in order that the church might possess a perfect and sufficient knowledge of God for both worship and Christian faith and life. Scripture is therefore called "canonical." The third purpose or end of Scripture is that the church be led by reading and hearing into the true knowledge of God, and into a right instruction and edification in matters of faith and love to the goal of eternal life.[19] These three proximate ends or uses, Gomarus concludes, are subordinated to the ultimate and foreordained goal *(finis ultimus ac praeordinatus)* of Scripture, the final glory of God's servants, as provided according to the mercy and immeasurable goodness of God.[20]

These arguments are developed at considerable length by later orthodox writers, who elaborate the discussion of the divine purpose in Scripture specifically for the sake of deducing the attributes of the text. In a sense, the entire argument proceeds on the assumption that Scripture not only reflects the being of its "primary author"—much as the creation mirrors the divine being, although in a far clearer manner—but that the divine character of Scripture, as self-evidencing, must be presented and argued in an a priori fashion.

---

[17]Cf. Leigh, *Treatise,* I.vii, ad fin. and viii (pp. 128–29; 130ff.).
[18]Trelcatius, *Schol. meth.,* I.ii (p. 27).
[19]Gomarus, *Disputationes,* II.xxvii–xxx.
[20]Gomarus, *Disputationes,* II.xxxi.

Thus, Leigh echoes the order not of Gomarus but of Trelcatius and places consideration of the ultimate goal first, prior to consideration of the proximate goals:

> The end of Scripture is considered, 1. In respect of God; 2. In respect of us. In respect of God, the end of the scripture is a glorifying of him; by it we may learn to know, love, and fear him, and so be blessed. The glory of God is the chiefe end of all things, Prov. 16:4.[21]

Leigh clarifies his definition of the primary end of Scripture by turning again to his christological theme: "God in Christ or God and Christ is the object of the Christian religion; without knowledge of Christ we cannot know God savingly." These words appear as a marginal gloss on the first part of the dichotomy, to be read in connection with "In respect of God." For Leigh, the God who offers Scripture and who ordains its "chief end" is not a *deus nudus absconditus* but the *deus revelatus in Christo*. The declaration of the great ends of the revelation in Scripture and, therefore, of Scripture itself returns us to the question of the foundation or scope of the whole of Scripture—identified by Reformed orthodoxy as Christ—and to the character of Scripture as Word, resting on the eternal Word and wisdom of God.

"In respect of us," Leigh continues, "the end of Scripture" is considered in two ways, "intermediate" or temporal and "ultimate and chiefest."[22] The intermediate and temporal end of Scripture is the edification of believers, which is to be considered, Leigh proposes, in five ways, corresponding with the configuration of the spiritual faculties of the human subject: "the two first respect the mind, the other three, the heart, will and affection":

> [1.] it is profitable for Doctrine, it serves to direct all saving truth; nothing is to be received as a truth necessary to salvation, but what is proved out of scripture.... 2. Reproof or Confutation, to refute all errors and heterodox opinions in divinity. By this sword of the Spirit, Christ vanquished Satan.... 3. Correction of iniquity, setting straight what is amiss in manners and life. 4. Instruction to righteousness.... 5. Comfort in all troubles...: the Greek word for Gospel signifieth glad-tidings ... as Gods Promises are the rule of

---

[21]Leigh, *Treatise,* I.vii (p. 128); cf. Venema, *Institutes of Theology,* p. 41.
[22]Leigh, *Treatise,* I.vii (pp. 128–29).

what we must pray for in faith, so are they the ground of what we must expect in comfort.[23]

The "ultimate and chiefest" end of Scripture, according to Leigh is,

> our Salvation and life Eternall, Iohn 5:39 and 20:31; II Tim. 3:15. It will shew us the right way of escaping Hell and attaining Heaven. It will shew us what to believe and practice, for our present and eternal happiness. This was Gods aim in causing the Scripture to be written, and we shall find it available and effectual for the ends for which it was ordained by God.[24]

The underlying point of the doctrine, thus, is to describe the causality of Scripture, granting the divine purpose of revelation and salvation and granting, also, what is known of the essence and attributes of God—in order to provide an a priori foundation for the discussion of the character of Scripture in bringing about the divine ends. As noted above, this is a somewhat circular pattern of argument that, in effect, moves from a general sense of the identity of Scripture as Word and of the redemptive scope and foundation of Scripture—all elicited from Scripture, following a fairly traditional doctrinal exegesis—to a discussion of the divine causality presupposed by the redemptive definitions and, from there, to the attributes of Scripture necessary to the redemptive ends, as defined by the causality. The underlying point of this approach is, clearly, to avoid the appearance either of an arbitrary declaration of the character of Scripture or of the implication that the authority and the attributes of Scripture are to be inferred from an extrascriptural source, as for example, the tradition of the church. The entire discussion appears to be an outgrowth of the language of Scripture as the self-authenticating and self-interpreting ultimate norm for faith and practice—and, therefore, the sole norm for the framing of a doctrine of Scripture.

Thus, in order to attain the nearer or proximate goals of Scripture, all doctrine given in Scripture must be plain and clear both in terms of "the matter delivered" and in terms of "the manner of delivering" the doctrine. Since, moreover, "dark and doubtful" teachings are wholly apart from the clear truth of God's Word, even those doctrines that seem obscure in their "dignity and majesty" are

---

[23]Leigh, *Treatise,* I.vii (pp. 128–29).
[24]Leigh, *Treatise,* I.vii (p. 129).

nevertheless plain in their truth.[25] Similarly, the sense of the words of the text must also be clear, signifying both "the intention of the speaker and the nature of the thing signified." By way of explaining his point, Trelcatius cites the scholastic maxim, *theologia symbolica non est argumentativa*—symbolical or figurative theology is not the basis of argument. Various allegorical readings, tropes, and anagoges may be useful to the hearer, but the literal and grammatical sense is unitary, entire, and the sole ground of legitimate theological interpretation.[26] The doctrine of the causality of Scripture, therefore, points to virtually all of the other topics in the *locus*.

4.2 The Inspiration of Scripture

The doctrine of the inspiration of Scripture, quite contrary to the impression given by much twentieth-century discussion, was not an issue elaborated at great length either by the Reformers or by the Protestant orthodox of the late sixteenth and early seventeenth centuries. The doctrine, whether "vaguely" or "dynamically," "formally" or "strictly" stated, tended to be presented quite briefly and without much argument. Only in the high orthodox era did the doctrine become a major focus of discussion, and even then it can hardly be said to have been the dominant issue in the *locus de Scriptura sacra*. The major Reformed scholastic systems—Polanus' *Syntagma*, Gomarus' *Disputationes*, the Leiden *Synopsis*, Walaeus' *Loci*, Maccovius' *Loci communes*, Burmann's *Synopsis theologiae*, Turretin's *Institutio*, Heidegger's *Corpus theologiae*, and Mastricht's *Theoretico-practica theologia*, just to name a few—all fail to single out inspiration as a separate topic. They tend to view inspiration either as a subtopic of the discussion of the divinity of Scripture,[27] or as a characteristic of the *forma scripturae* arising from the discussion of the efficient, formal, material, and final causality of Scripture,[28] or as part of the argument for the authority and authenticity of the text.[29] The major exegetical works of the era also

---

[25]Trelcatius, *Schol. meth.,* I.ii.

[26]Trelcatius, *Schol. meth.,* I.ii.

[27]Cf. Polanus, *Syntagma theol.,* I.xv–xvi; Gomarus, *Disputationes,* II.xiii–xiv; *Synopsis purioris theologiae,* II.iii, v; Walaeus, *Loci communes,* II; Maccovius, *Loci communes,* II (pp. 11–12); Burmann, *Synopsis theologiae,* I.iv.23–30; Turretin, *Inst. theol. elencticae,* II.iv.2; Mastricht, *Theoretico-practica theol.,* I.ii.2, 13.

[28]Cf. Gomarus, *Disputationes,* II.xix; Leigh, *System,* I.viii (p. 97).

[29]Cf. *Synopsis purioris theol.,* II.xxviii; Maccovius, *Loci communes,* IV;

assume the doctrine but make little effort to prove it or to argue it against possible counter-evidences in the text.[30] This is not to say that the doctrine of inspiration was unimportant to the Protestant thinkers of the sixteenth and seventeenth centuries. It is to say, however, that a right understanding of the old Protestant doctrine of inspiration arises out of a sense of its place and role in the larger doctrine of Scripture rather than out of a mistaken equation of the doctrine of inspiration with the doctrine of Scripture. The fundamental issue addressed by the Reformers and orthodox alike was the issue of authority and certainty.

The reason for this placement, function, and relative lack of emphasis on the doctrine of inspiration is that the doctrine was not a matter of debate between the Reformers and their chief adversaries, the Roman Catholics. As Mangenot pointed out, the first Roman Catholic polemicists addressed primarily the issue of the canon of Scripture and its authority and "did not treat directly of the nature of inspiration": Cochlaeus, Pighius, Eck, Driedo, and Alphonse de Castro all "strongly affirmed the inspiration [of Scripture] without elaborating on the concept." Indeed, Mangenot could conclude, with considerable justice, that neither the Renaissance nor the Reformation had a major influence on theological consideration of "the nature of inspiration." The tendency of these writers, like the tendency of many of the medieval doctors, had been to make little or no distinction between revelation and inspiration:

> [inspiration] was understood always as a particular kind of revelation, produced in the minds of the sacred writers by an infusion of supernatural light, capable of revealing immediately to them the otherwise unknown things of which they were supposed to write and of exerting an influence on their presentation of things known naturally by them. This revelation was the intellectual vision of which the scholastics had spoken.[31]

Turretin, *Inst. theol. elencticae,* II.iv–v, especially v.6 and II.xii.

[30]Cf. Ames, *An Analytical Exposition of I and II Peter,* 2 Pet. 1:21, in loc.; Diodati, *Pious and Learned Annotations,* and Tossanus, *Biblia,* IV:2 Tim. 3:16 and 2 Pet. 1:21, in loc.; Poole, *Commentary,* I, pp. 456, 513 on the authorship problems of Judges and 1–2 Samuel as not destructive of the authority of the books and ibid., III, pp. 797, 921, on the interpretation of the traditional *sedes doctrinae,* 2 Tim. 3:16 and 2 Pet. 1:21; with Henry, *Commentary on the Whole Bible,* III, pp. 1215–16, 1332–33; and, for a synopsis of Roman Catholic exegesis, see Lapide, *Commentarius,* 2 Tim. 3:16 and 2 Pet. 1:21, in loc.

[31]Mangenot, "Inspiration de l'Écriture," col. 2131.

Renaissance humanists, like Pico, Ficino, and Reuchlin, with their interest in the Cabala and the mystical senses of Scripture, in no way sought to diminish the influence of the Spirit on the writers of Scripture—and the Reformers, with their emphasis on the sole authority of Scripture, only reaffirmed the doctrine of inspiration: Mangenot notes that the concept of inspiration was "vague" in the writings of Luther and Zwingli, "more precise and firm" in the thought of Calvin and still "more systematic" in the work of Beza.[32] In any case, none of these writers were viewed by their Roman Catholic contemporaries as the cause of controversy over the doctrine of inspiration. In addition, the development of Protestant doctrine sketched out by Mangenot actually parallels, with little polemic, the development of Roman Catholic doctrine toward and beyond the Council of Trent.

Similarly, the doctrine of inspiration was not a matter of primary debate between the Reformed orthodox and their various adversaries, whether Arminian, Lutheran, or Roman Catholic:[33] it was only during the high orthodox era that the later Arminian and Socinian polemic against the notion of an utterly infallibly inspired text had a major impact on the Protestant orthodox polemic. Nor was the definition of inspiration, the question of the nature of the work of the Spirit in relation to the prophets and the apostles, a point in need of new formulation. The roots of the scholastic Protestant formulation lie deep in the tradition of the church, reaching back through the Reformation into the Middle Ages and even into the patristic period. Indeed, the movement toward a clearer definition of inspiration in relation to as well as distinction from the idea of revelation, and the eventual use of this distinction as a corollary and even buttress of the doctrine of the authority and infallibility of the text, was characteristic of many Roman Catholic as well as Protestant thinkers of the seventeenth century. What is important to an understanding of the old Protestant doctrine of inspiration, then, is not only the language of the doctrine itself, but the way in which this particular doctrinal point related to the great debated questions of the day—authority, canon, and interpretation—and the way in which these other questions both drew on and molded the doctrine of inspiration. In particular, the increasing stress of seventeenth-century orthodox

[32]Cf. Mangenot, "Inspiration de l'Écriture," col. 2131; with Köstlin, *Theology of Luther,* II, pp. 250–257; and François Wendel, *Calvin: The Origins and Development of His Religious Thought,* trans. Philip Mairét (New York: Harper and Row, 1963), pp. 156–60.

[33]Cf. Arminius, *Disputationes publicae,* II.iii–iv, xii, xxii.

theologians on the manner, mechanism, and extent of inspiration must be understood in relation to the pressures created by hermeneutical developments on the other questions of authority and canon. Our discussion will explore the historical development of these problems through the Reformation, early orthodox, and high orthodox eras, noting finally the transition to the troubled times of late orthodoxy.

Perhaps the most fundamental question to be answered in the discussion of the development of the Protestant concept of inspiration concerns the nature and character of the doctrine of the Reformers. We are already in a position to argue—on the basis of our outline of medieval teaching on the subject—that the rather formal doctrine of verbal inspiration argued by the Protestant scholastics was not an invention of the seventeenth century. Its basic premises are found in the formulations of the medieval scholastics. The question to be answered is, first, whether the doctrine of the Reformers differed significantly from the medieval conception of inspiration and then, second, whether the Protestant orthodox doctrine looked to the Middle Ages, to the Reformation, or to both eras for its form and contents—and how the doctrine itself developed in continuity and discontinuity with its past.

A major difficulty in addressing the Protestant doctrine of inspiration (as distinct from the other topics addressed in this study) arises from the number of scholars who have discussed the issue and with such varied results. The classic, orthodox reading of Luther as standing in continuity with medieval and post-Reformation Protestant views of inspiration has never lacked supporters.[34] Seeberg, Reu, Loofs, and Scheel all credit Luther with a theory of verbal inspiration, with Seeberg identifying some of Luther's language as drawn from the medieval theory of inspiration, but all four scholars making a distinction between Luther's view and the "mechanical" theory of the Lutheran orthodox.[35] Seeberg, however, far more than

---

[34]E.g., Wilhelm Rohnert, *Die Inspiration der heiligen Schrift und ihre Bestreiter. Eine biblisch-dogmengeschichtliche Studie* (Leipzig, 1889); Robert D. Preus, *The Inspiration of Scripture: A Study of the Theology of the Seventeenth Century Lutheran Dogmaticians* (Edinburgh: Oliver and Boyd, 1955); idem, "Luther and Biblical Infallibility," in *Inerrancy and the Church,* pp. 99–142; and idem, "The View of the Bible Held by the Church: The Early Church through Luther," in *Inerrancy,* pp. 357–82; Eugene F. Klug, *From Luther to Chemnitz; on Scripture and the Word* (Grand Rapids: Eerdmans, 1971).

[35]Seeberg, *Textbook,* II, pp. 298–99; Reu, *Luther and the Scriptures,* p. 131;

Reu, and somewhat after the manner of Köstlin's classic study, attempts to take into account Luther's many references to textual problems and "errors" in Scripture as well as Luther's questions about the full canonicity of Esther, Hebrews, James, Jude, and the Apocalypse, by arguing Luther's primary attention to the gospel of Christ and his work as the central truth in all Scripture and the fundamental issue in the identification of the canon. These considerations, according to Seeberg, resulted in "an entirely new conception of the authority and inspiration of the Scriptures."[36] Distinct from both Seeberg and Reu, Köstlin had argued that the different directions found in Luther's comments on the text of Scripture pointed away from the "idea that the Holy Scriptures are the result of a uniform divine inspiration, without the intervention of human individuality" toward the conclusion "that the Spirit did not exert His energy with equal strength and fullness in all the recipients of the Word and the authors of Sacred Scriptures."[37] Even more than Köstlin, several of the recent interpreters of Luther have argued, on christological grounds, the distinction between Luther's views and the Protestant orthodox view of verbal inspiration.[38] Nonetheless, several contemporary scholars, notably Davies and Gerrish, have echoed the classic, orthodox reading of Luther, arguing a strong emphasis on verbal inspiration in Luther, with Gerrish arguing a tension between arguments that rest authority of Scripture on its reference to Christ and arguments that rest authority on inspiration by the Spirit. Gerrish understands the former as looking toward the kind of doctrine of Scripture present in neo-orthodoxy and the latter toward the kind present in the older orthodoxy and in conservative Protestantism.[39]

Much of the difficulty in understanding Luther's view of inspiration—and Calvin's as well—arises from the absence of a formal statement of the doctrine in his works and from what appear to many

---

Ferdinand Loofs, *Dogmengeschichte,* IV, pp. 380–81, 412–14; Scheel, *Luther's Stellung zur Heiligen Schrift,* pp. 20–21, 66–73.

[36]Seeberg, *Textbook,* II, p. 301.

[37]Köstlin, *Theology of Luther,* II, p. 252.

[38]Cf. Wilhelm Pauck, *The Heritage of the Reformation* (Boston: Beacon, 1950), pp. 167–69; E. M. Carlson, *The Reinterpretation of Luther* (Philadelphia: Muhlenberg, 1948), pp. 117–19; Reid, *Authority of Scripture,* p. 86; Grant, *Short History,* pp. 97, 99; Ebeling, *Word and Faith,* pp. 82–83; Bainton, "The Bible in the Reformation," in *CHB,* III:12–16.

[39]Rupert Davies, *Problem of Authority in the Continental Reformers,* pp. 40–41; Gerrish, "Biblical Authority," pp. 342–44.

modern writers to be conflicting elements in his teaching that render impossible a fully developed concept of Scripture as verbally inspired Word. As we have already noted briefly in the introductory chapter and as adumbrated in the discussion of the concept of "Word" in the Reformation and orthodoxy,[40] there is no fundamental contradiction between the assumption that Scripture is authoritative because it is grounded and focused on Christ and the assumption that its authority can also be explained in terms of a doctrine of inspiration. Indeed, these two assumptions function as opposite sides of the same theological and hermeneutical coin, granting the identity of the Word incarnate in Christ with the essential Word or Wisdom of God underlying the message revealed to the writers of Scripture by the Spirit in its work of illumination and inspiration. In addition, the assumption of a christological focus, of the necessity of the testimony of the Spirit, and of an objective inspiration of the human authors of Scripture in no way stood opposed to the recognition of various discrepancies in the biblical narrative: Luther can be cited at length on all four of these points—and nowhere does he pose the one against the other.[41] It is also the case that the Reformers, as well as the orthodox, could argue directly from inspiration to authority.[42]

In addressing Calvin's view of inspiration, one finds the same division of interpretation between those who understand Calvin's doctrine as similar in implication to that of the post-Reformation Reformed theologians,[43] and those who argue a difference and deny that Calvin held a theory of dictation or verbal inspiration.[44] It is

[40]Cf. §§3.2, 3.3, and 3.4.

[41]Cf. Köstlin, *Theology of Luther,* II, pp. 223–61, with Reu, *Luther and the Scriptures,* pp. 38–102; and Gerrish, *"Biblical Authority,"* pp. 342–48.

[42]Cf. Vermigli, *Commonplaces,* I.vi.3; Bullinger, *Decades,* I.i (p. 50), iv (p. 93)

[43]E.g., Benjamin B. Warfield, "Calvin's Doctrine of the Knowledge of God," in *Calvin and Augustine,* pp. 29–130; Kenneth S. Kantzer, "Calvin and the Holy Scriptures," in *Inspiration and Interpretation,* pp. 115–55; Brian Gerrish, "Biblical Authority and the Continental Reformation," *Scottish Journal of Theology* 10 (1957): 337-60; John H. Gerstner, "The View of the Bible Held by the Church: Calvin and the Westminster Divines," in *Inerrancy,* pp. 385–410; H. Jack Forstman, *Word and Spirit: Calvin's Doctrine of Biblical Authority* (Stanford University Press, 1962); James I. Packer, "John Calvin and the Inerrancy of Holy Scripture," in *Inerrancy and the Church,* pp. 143–88.

[44]E.g., Émile Doumergue, *Jean Calvin, les hommes et les choses de son temps,* 7 vols. (Lausanne, 1899-1917), pp. 67, 73–75; John T. Mc Neill, "The Significance of the Word of God for Calvin," *Church History* 28/2 (June 1959):131-46; Ford Lewis Battles, "God Was Accommodating Himself to

instructive to note, first, that Calvin parallels the concept of the inward testimony of the Spirit to the authority of Scripture with the concept of the inspiration of Scripture by using the former as a fundamental principle of his argument in book I, and the latter doctrine as a fundamental principle of his discussion of Scripture in *Institutes,* book 4. Calvin speaks of the testimony of the Spirit in his main exposition of the content and authority of the scriptural revelation, and grounds the authority of the text not on externally visible evidences of divinity but in the Spirit's inward testimony to the Word. He has recourse to the doctrine of inspiration when he sets the authoritative Scripture against the authority of the church as the interpreter of Scripture. In both places, he joins Word and Spirit closely together in order to argue that the church cannot be elevated above Scripture—either, in the first instance, as a *locus* of authority or, in the second, as a source of doctrine.[45] The two issues—testimony of the Spirit and inspiration—are, therefore, intimately related in Calvin's theology despite their formal separation. They are also related by the rather categorical statement of Calvin in the former discussion: "When that which is set forth is acknowledged to be the Word of God, there is no one so deplorably insolent—unless devoid also both of common sense and of humanity itself—as to dare impugn the credibility of Him who speaks."[46] In connection, then, with the testimony of the Spirit, Christians must also recognize that Scripture, in some objective sense, is the Word of the divine speaker. The question, of course, is precisely how the text of a book comes to contain the living speech of God.

On the one hand, Calvin's writings bear ample testimony to his conviction that not simply the desire of the prophets and the apostles to witness but also the words of their written testimony derive from the ministry of the Spirit. Commenting on 1 Peter 1:11–12 he remarks that the continuity and consistency of the Testaments rest on the Spirit who speaks in both the prophetic and the apostolic writings. Both the ancient prophecies and the gospel were given by the "dictation and guidance" of the Spirit of God.[47] The word "dictated" also appears in the comment on 2 Timothy 3:16, where Calvin argues that "the prophets did not speak of themselves, but as

Human Capacity," in *Interpretation* 31/1 (January 1977):19–38; Reid, *Authority of Scripture,* pp. 35–45; Wendel, *Calvin,* pp. 159–60.

[45]Cf. Calvin, *Institutes,* I.vii–ix with IV.viii.

[46]Calvin, *Institutes,* I.vii.1.

[47]Calvin, *Commentary on 1 Peter,* 1 Pet. 1:11–12 (CTS, pp. 40, 42); cf. Warfield, "Calvin's Doctrine of the Knowledge of God," p. 67.

organs of the Holy Spirit" and that "we owe to the Scripture the same reverence as we owe to God, since it has its only source in him and has nothing of human origin mixed with it."[48]

On this point, there is no detectable difference between Calvin and Bullinger:

> the doctrine and writings of the prophets have always been of great authority ... for ... they did not take their origin from the prophets themselves as chief authors; but were inspired by God in heaven by the Holy Spirit of God: for it is God who, dwelling by his Spirit in the minds of the prophets speaks to us by their mouths.[49]

At least one writer has observed that Bullinger did not teach a doctrine of strict verbal inspiration,[50] but here Bullinger comes very close, echoing the traditional scholastic view of God as *auctor primarius*. Bullinger can also cite Christ's praise of the prophets and point toward the accuracy of the prophets in foretelling events of future history as evidence "that the doctrine and writings of the prophets are the very Word of God."[51]

This is the case even granting the fact that much of the work of the prophets and the apostles was the exposition of extant "Scripture." "Let this be a firm principle," writes Calvin,

> No other word is to be held as the Word of God, and given place as such in the church, than what is contained first in the Law and the Prophets, then in the writings of the apostles; and the only authorized way of teaching in the church is by the prescription and standard of his Word. From this we also infer that the only thing granted to the apostles was that which the prophets had of old. They were to expound the ancient Scripture and to show that what is taught there has been fulfilled in Christ. Yet they were not to do this except from the Lord, that is, with Christ's Spirit as precursor in a certain manner dictating the words.[52]

Even so, when commenting on the passage in Jeremiah in which the prophet is called upon to dictate to Baruch the words that he had

---

[48]Calvin, *Commentaries on the Second Epistle of Timothy,* 2 Tim. 3:16 (CTS, pp. 248–49); cf. Calvin, *Commentaries on the Second Epistle of Peter,* 2 Pet. 1:20–21 (CTS, pp. 389–91).

[49]Bullinger, *Decades,* I.i (p. 50).

[50]Neve, *History,* I, p. 318.

[51]Bullinger, *Decades,* I.i (p. 51).

[52]Calvin, *Institutes,* IV.viii.8.

previously spoken to Israel, Calvin argues that "there is no doubt that God suggested to the prophet at the time what might have been erased from his memory ... the greater part of so many words must have escaped the prophet, had not God dictated them again to him."[53] Calvin concludes that "the words which God dictated to his servant were called the words of Jeremiah; yet, properly speaking, they were not the words of man, for they did not proceed from a mortal man, but only from God":[54] this of words dictated by Jeremiah to Baruch.

The phrase, "in a certain manner *(quodammodo)* dictating the words," must be interpreted with a modicum of caution, granting the tendency of some historians and theologians to construe it as a highly qualified remark in which the concept of dictation is virtually denied. On the one hand, the words ought to be taken together with the sentiment expressed by Calvin in the next section of his exposition that "the difference between the apostles and their successors" was that the apostles were *"certi et authentici Spiritus sancti amanuenses"* —"sure and authentic secretaries of the Holy Spirit."[55] This interpretation also comports with the passages in the commentaries where Calvin refers to dictation. To claim that Calvin did not hold "any doctrine of exact verbal inspiration" is to ignore the plain sense of the words.[56] On the other hand, the qualifier, *quodammodo,* does indicate that Calvin was not interested in defining precisely how the biblical writers were to be considered as amanuenses or secretaries receiving dictation, although, granting the qualifiers placed on the analogy between divine and human dictation by medieval doctors like Aquinas and Tostatus and the similar view held by many later Protestants, Calvin's famous qualifier may simply be a reflection of a rather traditional approach to the problem.[57] Even so, very much like many of the later Reformed exegetes and theologians, Calvin assumed both that Scripture was "dictated" and

[53]Calvin, *Commentary on Jeremiah,* Jer. 36:4–6 (CTS, IV, p. 329).

[54]Calvin, *Commentary on Jeremiah,* Jer. 36:8 (CTS, IV, p. 334).; cf. Dowey, *Knowledge of God in Calvin's Theology,* pp. 92–93.

[55]Calvin, *Institutes,* IV.viii.9.

[56]Cf. *Institutes,* ed. McNeill, IV.vii.8, n.7, with Reid, *Authority,* pp. 44, 53–55, and McNeill, "Significance of the Word for Calvin," pp. 140–45; and note the strict reading of Calvin in Gerrish, "Biblical Authority and the Reformation," p. 355; and Kantzer, "Calvin and the Holy Scriptures," pp. 138–42.

[57]Cf. Calvin, *Commentaries on the Second Epistle of Peter,* 2 Pet. 1:20–21 (CTS, p. 391), with the analysis in Warfield, "Calvin's Doctrine of the Knowledge of God," pp. 63–64; also see above, §§1.2 and 1.3 and below, this section.

that it was reflective of the individual style and characteristic patterns of perception belonging to its human authors.[58] Thus, on the analogy of dictation, Calvin argues a verbal, but not a "mechanical" inspiration.[59]

As Musculus points out, the apostle Paul himself tells us that Scripture comes by inspiration and is profitable to doctrine, reproof, and correction. "Doctrine is an instrument to them that be ignorant ... a godly light" whereby they may learn of God.[60] This doctrine, moreover, is given in four parts: "of the knowledge of God, of Faith, of Godly love, and of Justice." Scripture first teaches of God and knowledge of him, "the order whereof we set forth in the beginning of the places." We are taught,

> First that there is a God, and that he is a rewarder of them that do seek him. Next that we do believe in Christ his only begotten Son, sent into this world for our salvation.[61]

This faith in turn teaches fear, obedience, and true worship. There is a general faith in God as creator and ruler of all things and a special faith in Christ as saviour and our instructor in the way of salvation.[62] The end or intention of Scripture is thus the wholeness and soundness of believers "in true faith, godly love, and justice."[63]

This high doctrine of inspiration must not be separated from the equally strong emphasis, found particularly in Calvin's writings, on the accommodated character of God's revelation. Scripture only reveals what serves to advance piety and its revelation is couched in terms accessible to the human intellect.[64] Thus, accommodation of

[58]Cf. Woudstra, "Calvin Interprets What 'Moses Reports,'" p. 154.

[59]Cf. Warfield, "Calvin's Doctrine of the Knowledge of God," pp. 63–67; Dowey, *Knowledge of God in Calvin's Theology,* pp. 100–102; and Murray, *Calvin on Scripture and Divine Sovereignty,* pp. 20–27.

[60]Musculus, *Loci communes,* xxi (*Commonplaces,* p. 381, col. 1).

[61]Musculus, *Loci communes,* xxi (*Commonplaces,* p. 381, col. 2).

[62]Musculus, *Loci communes,* xxi (*Commonplaces,* p. 382, col. 1).

[63]Musculus, *Loci communes,* xxi (*Commonplaces,* p. 382, col. 2).

[64]On Calvin's doctrine of accommodation, see David F. Wright, "Calvin's Pentateuchal Criticism: Equity, Hardness of Heart, and Divine Accommodation in the Mosaic Harmony Commentary," in *Calvin Theological Journal* 21 (1986):33–50; Martin I. Klauber and Glenn S. Sunshine, "Jean-Alphonse Turrettini on Biblical Accommodation: Calvinist or Socinian?" in *Calvin Theological Journal* 25/1 (1990):9–12; Ford Lewis Battles, "God Was Accommodating Himself to Human Capacity," in *Interpretation* 31 (1977):19–38; and Dirk W. Jellema, "God's 'Baby Talk': Calvin and the 'Errors' of the Bible," in *Reformed Journal* 30 (1970):25–47.

the message to the situation and to the needs of its recipients accounts for the differences between the Old and New Testaments.[65] Similarly, Calvin allows for a certain imprecision in usage and description within Scripture as an accommodation to the capacity of the "unlearned" reader and to the common forms of speech.[66] He also recognized and dealt with a wide variety of variant texts, emendations, and scribal errors in the conviction that the underlying inviolability and coherence of God's Word enabled the faithful exegete to penetrate to the meaning of the passages in question.[67]

Of the first group of major codifiers of the Reformed tradition, Vermigli appears to have been the theologian who most clearly tied the definition of Scripture to the issue of inspiration. At least this is the impression given by his posthumous *Loci communes* as they were arranged by Robert Masson. Vermigli defines the Scriptures as "a certain declaration of the wisdom of God, inspired by the Holy Spirit in godly men, and then set down in monuments and writings." These writings, moreover, are "inspired by the inward motion of the Holy Spirit for our salvation and restoration."[68]

The crucial issue for the Reformers, then, was not so much the mechanism of inspiration—although virtually all of them used such terms and phrases as "dictation," "amanuenses," "the Spirit's own writing," and so forth—but rather the fact that inspiration, in the strict sense of the term, belongs to the production of the canonical Scriptures and not to either the apocrypha or to the writings of the church's postbiblical tradition. Their doctrine of inspiration, even when generally or vaguely stated, was little different from the medieval doctrine. Where it differed radically was in its application to the question of authority. The authority of the inspired Scripture could be set above the authority of the holy and catholic, but uninspired, church and its tradition.

The absence of lengthy discussion of the actual manner of inspiration from the writings of the Reformers appears to have resulted on the one hand from the absence of controversy and, on the other, from the generally unsystematic character of their writings. Even the most fully systematized works of the early Reformed codifiers—

[65]Calvin, *Institutes,* II.xi.2, 5.

[66]Cf. e.g., Calvin, *Commentaries on the First Book of Moses,* Gen. 1:16; 2:8 (CTS, I, pp. 85–86, 113).

[67]Cf. Calvin, *Harmony of the Pentateuch,* (CTS, I, p. 304); with idem, *Commentary on Joshua,* Josh. 15:17 (CTS, pp. 206–7), and *Commentary on the Acts,* (CTS, pp. 263–64, 267).

[68]Vermigli, *Commonplaces,* I.vi.1 (p. 39).

Calvin's *Institutes,* Musculus' *Loci communes,* and Bullinger's *Decades*—fall short of the detail and the topical coverage of large-scale theological system. The theologians of the Reformation were content simply to state the basic definition: that the Scriptures were inspired, dictated by the Holy Spirit, the words of God. The definition needed little or no elaboration or logical buttressing in view of the ability of the Reformers to draw on long-standing hermeneutical assumptions about the christological foundation of all of Scripture and on trinitarian assumptions about the identity of the eternal Word and Wisdom of God with the Word incarnate and with the ultimate truth given in human forms by the work of the Spirit inspiring the prophets and apostles.

Heppe attempted to conceive the difference between the Reformers' view of Scripture and the noticeably more systematized and dogmatic view of the Bible propounded by the later scholastic Protestant writers in terms of a shift in the doctrine of inspiration:

> At the root of the original Reformed doctrine of inspiration lay the distinction *between,* at the root of the later Church doctrine the identification *of* the concepts "Word of God" and "H. Scripture." Hence for Calvin the authority of H. Scripture rested purely on the fact that it reports upon the real acts of God in revelation. In other words, it is the original document of revelations, which were followed before their recording and were for a time transmitted orally.... there is no word of a peculiar inspiration of the record.[69]

In other words, Heppe argues that Calvin and others of his generation assumed a divine act of revelation in the original unwritten communication of God to Adam, Noah, or Abraham, but no further divine assistance was required for the writing down of the revelation. Even Ursinus was "on the whole unacquainted with the mechanical theory of inspiration."[70] In Heppe's view, the authority of Scripture was guaranteed by its character as Word, not by a theory of inspiration or, as he stated the point,

> the ground upon which the infallibility of their narratives rests is not the operation of the Holy Spirit at the time of writing and the canonical Scriptures, but the abiding fellowship of the Spirit in which God kept the prophets and the apostles, the knowledge of

[69]Heppe, *RD,* p. 16, correcting the typographical error "'Word of God' and 'H. Spirit'."

[70]Heppe, *RD,* p. 16.

the truth which the Biblical authors enjoyed generally through the
illumination of the H. Spirit.[71]

Heppe argues that

> as early as the end of the sixteenth century the conception of inspi-
> ration had changed; it was now completely severed from the idea
> of revelation. Scripture was therefore now regarded as inspired,
> purely because it was dictated to the Biblical authors by God.[72]

Writings of early orthodox theologians like Zanchi, whose late
sixteenth-century efforts would probably fall into the era designated
by Heppe as the time at which the doctrine of Scripture was altered,
tend to evidence a much richer emphasis on the work of the Spirit
than Heppe indicates. They also give the impression that the infallibility of the text, albeit intimately connected with the inspiration of
the Spirit, ought not to be severed from the general illumination of
the biblical authors by the Spirit. In other words, the writers of this
period do not seem to press a choice between inspiration and illumination but to consider both in their teaching concerning the writing
of the Word. Indeed, there is a threefold distinction operative in their
thought between inspiration, illumination, and revelation—all of
which bear on the case of biblical authorship. Thus, Zanchi can
define revelation and inspiration as the basic modes of divine communication from the beginning: "the church, from the beginning of
the world, had in its possession the word of God (without which the
church could not exist) and that partly by inspiration and revelation
of God, partly by the tradition of the fathers preserved *agraphon* in
the church until Moses."[73] Later Protestant theologians, therefore,
neither equated revelation with inspiration as Brunner and various
neo-orthodox writers have argued, nor did they radically "sever"
revelation from inspiration. Rather they distinguished the concepts
as Aquinas had—"inspiration" and, sometimes, "illumination" refer
to the elevation of the mind and heart of the writer that enables him
to receive truths of God normally beyond his grasp; "revelation"
refers specifically to the impartation and reception of divine truths.[74]
"The former is the condition preparatory to prophecy, the latter is its

---

[71]Heppe, *RD,* p. 17.
[72]Heppe, *RD,* p. 17.
[73]Zanchi, *Praefatiuncula,* col. 353.
[74]Wyttenbach, *Tentamen theologiae dogmaticae,* II, §140.

accomplishment, when the veil of obscurity and ignorance that hides divine mysteries is removed."[75]

In so far as the problem of revelation is frequently dealt with, in the prolegomena, separately from the problem of inspiration, Heppe is formally correct—but the difference between the Protestant scholastics and earlier thinkers on this point cannot be stated quite so simply. Even in those cases in which the discussion of revelation is virtually confined to the prolegomena, the issue of revelation is discussed at length.[76] Nor was the connection between revelation and Scripture lost to the orthodox. Turretin, for example, begins his *locus de Scriptura sacra* with the question, "Whether revelation by means of the Word is necessary?" This question must be posed first of all because the Word of God alone is the principle of theology *(theologiae principium)*. After speaking of the limitations of human thought and of the limited usefulness of natural revelation, Turretin concludes that revelation by means of the Word is necessary if we are to know of God as Redeemer and to know of his work of redemption. The theme of the *duplex cognitio Dei* appears as the ground of the necessity of Scripture.[77] Similarly, among the late orthodox, Venema emphasizes the issue of revelation and the relationship of the "immediate" and "mediate" revelation of God to Scripture, while Stackhouse and Wyttenbach discourse at length on the necessity, character, and forms of revelation before their discussion of Scripture.[78] Wyttenbach, moreover, carefully relates and distinguishes revelation and inspiration.[79]

Two further considerations stand against the acceptance of Heppe's view. In the first place, generally, the doctrine of inspiration as strictly related to the writing of the text of Scripture was hardly unknown in the time of Calvin and Ursinus. As we have seen, it was standard fare in the patristic period and received considerable discussion at the hands of the medieval scholastics. In the second place, with specific reference to the thought of Calvin and Ursinus, the doctrine of inspiration that is absent from the passages cited by

[75]Benoit, "Revelation et inspiration selon la Bible, chez Saint Thomas et dans les discussions modernes," p. 321; and cf. the discussion above, §1.2

[76]E.g., de Moor, *Commentarius perpetuus in Joh. Marckii compendium,* I, i.27–34.

[77]Turretin, *Inst. theol. elencticae,* II.i.5–6; cf. II.ii.

[78]Venema, *Institutes of Theology,* III (pp. 44–50); Stackhouse, *Complete Body of Divinity,* I, pp. 26–71; Wyttenbach, *Tentamen theologiae dogmaticae,* I, §94–100, 101–22.

[79]Wyttenbach, *Tentamen theologiae dogmaticae,* II, §140.

Heppe appears quite clearly stated in other places. Heppe did recognize, however, without fully understanding his own point, that the early Protestant theologians had made little distinction between revelation and inspiration.[80] The point is not that the orthodox "severed" the concepts, but rather made a clearer distinction between them—as did the medieval tradition and the Roman Catholic theologians of the late sixteenth century.

The Roman Catholic doctrine of the verbal inspiration of the sacred authors—typical of Catholic theologians after Bañez—differed from the Protestant orthodox doctrine not so much in substance as in application. The Protestant doctrine was attached increasingly to Hebrew and Greek originals as representing the language of the *autographa* and, because of the language of the *autographa,* to the Masoretic Text of the Old Testament and to the oldest Greek manuscripts of the New Testament. Roman Catholic arguments concerning a plenary verbal inspiration, quite to the contrary, were less rooted in the Hebrew and Greek originals, more ready to acknowledge a late dating of the vowel points in the Hebrew text, and profoundly invested in the doctrinal and historical priority of the Vulgate over the Masoretic Text.

The problem that Heppe saw derives not from the loss of the basic category of revelation in the *locus de Scriptura sacra.* Revelation remains a primary issue—indeed, revelation of God's saving will provides the underlying necessity of Scripture. Rather, the problem derives from a scholastic separation and distinction of issues. Whereas the category of revelation relates to the issues of the character of Scripture as Word of God and to the necessity of Scripture, the category of inspiration relates to the issues of the authority and authenticity *as sacred Scripture* of words written down by the human hand. Even so, revelation is referred to the content and inspiration to the manner in which that content has been conveyed in writing. This separation of issues is clearly seen in Turretin's *Institutio* and a bit less obviously in Burmann's *Synopsis.*[81] This distinction between revelation and inspiration is also demanded by the Reformed assumption that, "considered essentially," Scripture proceeds from God while considered "accidentally" it was written by human beings.[82] Among the English Leigh approaches most

[80]But see Calvin, *Commentaries on the First Epistle of Peter,* 1 Pet. 1:11 (CTS, p. 39).

[81]Turretin, *Inst. theol. elencticae,* II.i–iv, and Burmann, *Synopsis theol.,* I.iii–v.

[82]Weemes, *Exercitations Divine,* p. 63.

closely to Heppe's description, yet even Leigh speaks of the "immediate" writing or inspiring of human writers by God as but one of the modes of revelation, and his definition, insofar as it remains bound to the exegetical tradition, maintains the soteriological emphasis found in the biblical *loci* or *sedes doctrinae,* 2 Timothy 3:16 and 2 Peter 1:21.[83]

Thus, although orthodox dogmatics do manifest a tendency to objectify the doctrine of the authority of Scripture by grounding it in a causal theory of origin by inspiration or dictation, we still encounter a richness of doctrine, drawing on the trinitarian foundation of all theology, and indicating the conjoint activity of Word and Spirit as they reveal the truth and perform the saving work of the God:

> Scripture ... is Divine. 1. In its Efficient cause and original, which is God the Father dictating, in his Son declaring and publishing, by his Holy Spirit confirming and sealing it in the hearts of the faithful. He wrote the Decalogue immediately with his own finger, and commanded the whole system, and all the parts of Scripture, to be written by his Servants the Prophets and Apostles, as the public actuaries and penmen thereof; therefore the authority of the Scripture is as great as that of the Holy Ghost, who did dictate both the matter and the words....[84]

The divinity of Scripture is also clearly shown in its subject matter "which is truth according to godliness ... joined with a sensible demonstration of the Spirit, and Divine Presence."[85] Throughout the Protestant orthodox discussion of Scripture a high degree of topical interrelationship and interpenetration is achieved despite the neat divisions of argument characteristic of Protestant scholastic method. The fact is that the orthodox, contrary to Heppe's view, were quite incapable of discussing revelation apart from Word or inspiration and authority in isolation from the concept of Scripture as revealed Word. The entire *locus* is bound together by threads of argument with the preliminary discussions of revelation, Word, divine causality, inspiration, and authority providing the fundamental rationale for the entire discussion.

---

[83]Leigh, *Treatise,* I.ii (p. 8).

[84]Leigh, *A System or Body of Divinity,* I.viii (p. 97); cf. idem, *Treatise,* I.ii (p. 8).

[85]Leigh, *A System or Body of Divinity,* I.viii (p. 97); cf. idem, *Treatise,* I.ii (p. 8).

The very order of these systems seems to predicate the inspiration of the text upon its divine, revelatory character as Word. Almost invariably the character of Scripture as Word of God and as revelation serves as the ground for the discussion of inspiration, even as inspiration serves as the ground for the authority of Scripture. Inspiration is the agency by which God's revelation takes form as Scripture. Thus, too, in a less systematic context, Perkins could, like Calvin, ground his certainty of the divinity of Scripture on the internal testimony of the Spirit and then argue the infallible authority of the text on the basis of its inspiration.[86]

God has established the Scriptures, Mastricht writes, in part by "revelation" and in part by "canonization." The work of revelation is accomplished in three ways: first, by direct writing, as in the case of the Decalogue; second, by the command to write (cf. Deut. 31:19; Rev. 1:19); and third, by "inspiration, which is to say, by suggesting the writing and by infallibly directing the writing." It appears, in the latter case, that God not only inspires the substance but also dictates the words: "non solum res inspiraverit; sed etiam singula verba dictarit."[87] The work of canonization assumes the existence of the inspired text and is accomplished when the Scriptures are carried forward in and sealed to the church as its rule of faith.[88]

Inspiration, according to the orthodox writers, was a matter of both substance and form—so that the entirety of Scripture is to be understood as inspired. Inspiration is, thus, "whole" or "entire" *(integra)* extending to both the meaning of the words and the words themselves, and consists in both "immediate revelation" and the "direction" of the biblical authors by the Spirit.[89] It is this inspired *forma Scripturae* to which the apostle refers, comments Gomarus, in 2 Timothy 3:16 by the term *theopneustos,* since both "the meaning *(res)* and the words *(voces)* were introduced by God into the minds of those holy men—or as it reads in II Peter 1:21, 'For the prophecy came not in old time by the will of man: but holy men of God spake *as they were* moved by the Holy Ghost.'" Nor should these texts be referred only to the speech of the prophets and the apostles, to the *verbum agraphon,* but to the *verbum engraphon* as well, according

[86]Cf. Perkins, *Cases of Conscience,* in *Workes,* II, p. 54–56, with idem, *A Clowd of Faithfull Witnesses,* in *Workes,* III, p. 184, and with Breward, "Life and Theology of William Perkins," pp. 38–41.

[87]Mastricht, *Theoretico-practica theol.,* I.ii.13.

[88]Mastricht, *Theoretico-practica theol.,* I.ii.13.

[89]Gomarus, *Disp. theol.,* II.xix; cf. Rollock, *Treatise of Effectual Calling,* pp. 94–95.

to the normal usage of the Scriptures.[90] In addition, the entire Bible is considered inspired—with the result that Mayer notes, before Grotius' work was published and therefore probably in response to the theories of Lessius and Bonfrère, "Some bookes of Scripture are historicall, and therefore may not seeme to have been inspired, but they are also said to be inspired, because they who wrote them, were infallibly guided by the Spirit, that they could not erre in any thing, and for the choice of the things written by them, others being omitted."[91]

This inspiration, granting that it extends to both substance and form, can be said to indicate three acts of the Spirit—as identified by the orthodox from various texts in the New Testament. The Spirit "roused" or "excited" the human authors of Scripture to the task of writing (2 Pet. 1:21); breathed into them the words, *verba inspiravit* (2 Tim. 3:16); and "preserved" the writers "from all error" (1 Pet. 2:2).[92] Such inspiration does not, of course, extend to the ancient superscriptions, marginalia, and the division of the text into chapters and verses, all of which are of human devising.[93]

In direct reflection of the medieval exegetical and theological tradition and its understanding of inspiration, the orthodox indicate that these men "are here called *holy,* not only because of their lives ... but because they were special instruments of the Holy Ghost, who sanctified them to the work of preaching, and penning what he dictated to them."[94] Even so, the words "Spake as they were moved" indicate that the prophets and apostles were "elevated above their own natural abilities," influenced and assisted by the Holy Spirit. Specifically, "this may imply the illumination of their minds with the knowledge of divine mysteries, the gift of infallibility, that they might not err, of prophecy, to foretell things to come, and a peculiar instinct *of the Holy Ghost,* whereby they were moved to preach or write."[95]

---

[90]Gomarus, *Disp theol.,* II.xx, citing Luke 24:25, 27 and Acts 2:31; 28:25.

[91]Mayer, *Commentarie upon the New Testament,* vol. II, p. 552; cf. Creehan, "The Bible in the Roman Catholic Church," in *CHB,* III:217–18.

[92]Riissen, *Summa theol.,* II.xvi.

[93]Riissen, *Summa theol.,* II.xvii.

[94]Poole, *Commentary,* III, p. 921. See also the discussion of the medieval background, above, §1.2.

[95]Poole, *Commentary,* III, p. 921; cf. *Annotations upon all the Books of the Old and New Testament* (1645), in. loc.: "Gods Spirit acquainting them with the things they knew not, directed them in the words that they might not erre. God shewed them things above nature, and gave them a will to publish them, though sometimes they were unwilling to do it"; and Henry, *Commentary on the Whole*

This inspiration of God, understood in terms of spiritual enlightenment and direction, could also be described as threefold—*antecedenter, per concomitantiam,* and *subsequenter.* Thus, antecedently, God revealed to the prophets "things to come ... and made them to write his prophesies." But God also "inspired them in writing the Histories and Actes ... *per concomitantiam*: for that which was done already, hee assisted them in so writing it downe; that they were able to discerne the relations which they had from others, to be true." This second form of divine assistance belongs particularly to the work of Luke and other evangelists "who saw not Christ" but who were guided by the Spirit in the production of a true narrative concerning Christ and his teaching. Finally, God assisted the prophets and the apostles in recounting things that had happened before the time at which they wrote by supporting their memory and making clear what they had seen in visions.[96]

The orthodox Reformed teaching, like that of the medieval doctors, resembles also the late patristic theory of inspiration as formulated largely against the ecstatic theory of the Montanists. While acknowledging that ecstasy was evidenced in the prophetic writings, the orthodox tended to follow Augustine and the medieval doctors both in defining ecstasy as *alienatio mentis a sensibus corporibus* and in denying that this phenomenon was an *alienatio a mente.* The mind might be abstracted from corporeal sense in the moment of inspiration, but not from itself or from its inherent rationality.[97] The mind and spirit of the prophet, argued Witsius, were indeed "agitated" by the will of God and, thereby cooperatively moved to consider an external object, but this was "alienation of the mind" understood as "the cessation of the external function of the senses" and the total concentration of the prophet on the knowledge revealed by the Spirit.[98] The biblical writers had, therefore, a freedom of exercise or operation *(libertas exercitii)* but not of specification *(libertas specificationis)*: "they were not like Blockes or Stones, but the Lord inclined their wills freely to write." Neither, therefore, were the prophets and apostles like "the Sibyls, and other Prophets of the

---

Bible, III, p. 1333.

[96]Weemes, *Exercitations Divine,* pp. 72–73.

[97]Cf. Augustine, *Enarrationes in Psalmos,* Psalm 68:34 *(PL* 36, col. 834) with *Ad Simplicianum,* II, q.1 *(PL* 40, cols. 129–30), and Gustav Friedrich Oehler, *Theology of the Old Testament,* trans. G. E. Day (Edinburgh: T. & T. Clark, 1873), p. 470.

[98]Witsius, *De prophetis et prophetia,* in *Miscellanea sacra,* I.iii.3 and iv.1 (pp. 16–17, 21–22).

Divell, who were blasted and distracted in their wits, when they prophesied."[99] Nonetheless, the prophets "had not *libertatem specificationis;* that is, they might not leave that subject which they were called to write, and write any other thing, as they pleased; they were necessitated onely to write that, although they wrote it freely ... without any paine or vexation of their spirit."[100] In Oehler's words, "the Protestant theologians assumed, in the case of prophets, both an entire passivity in the reception of revelation, and a continued state of rational consciousness, with at most but momentary intermissions," very unlike the emphasis on subjectivity and the interest in fully ecstatic experience found in eighteenth-century theories of prophecy and inspiration.[101]

The Protestant orthodox denial of an "alienation of mind," moreover, was frequently linked with a denial of the total passivity of the biblical writers in receiving the words of the text. Their emphasis on the inspiration of the individual words as well as the doctrinal substance or meaning relates directly to the orthodox assumption that the text communicates divine knowledge and not merely the grounds and forms of piety and observance. This view, however, does not amount to a denial either of the necessary agency or of the consciousness or of the individuality of the various human "amanuenses":

> The writers [of the Scriptures] did not always regard themselves as purely *pathetikos* or passive, but also *energetikos* or effective, as those who applied both skill and mental activity and discourse and memory, arrangement and order and their own style (whence the difference in manner of writing among them) ... presided over, however, perpetually by the Holy Spirit, who so guides and directs them, that they are preserved from all errors of mind, memory, language and pen.[102]

Voetius thus denied quite strenuously that "the writers of the New Testament thought in a different language (i.e., Syriac) from the one they wrote in (i.e., Greek or 'Hellenistic')." Indeed, he argues, "No one produces anything correctly or rationally, whether orally or in writing, unless he has first conceived it rightly."[103]

---

[99]Weemes, *Exercitations Divine,* p. 73.

[100]Weemes, *Exercitations Divine,* p. 74.

[101]Oehler, *Theology of the Old Testament,* p. 471.

[102]*Synopsis purioris theologiae,* III.7.

[103]Voetius, *Selectarum disputationum,* I.iii, problemata, 17 (I, p. 44).

Thus, although the prophets and apostles were immediately called by God, they were also gifted and learned as individual human beings: Moses was taught by the Egyptians and Daniel by the Chaldeans. The prophets studied in schools and their divinely given knowledge was carried forward in a life of reading and meditation. They retained their general knowledge of the world as a disposition or *habitus* of mind but were also given a distinct gift "of new illumination when they prophesied." Nor did this inspiration oppose or remove the individual wisdom and prudence of the biblical writers. It was, therefore, possible, for these "secretaries of the holy Ghost" to err "in some of their purposes, and in some circumstances of their calling," but not in doctrine, since "they spake not onely by their mouthes, but also they were his mouth."[104] Paul, accordingly, could write of his intention to go to Spain and never be able to go there, erring in "externall purposes and resolutions" but not in what he "wrote of Christ, and matters of salvation."[105]

Even so, the orthodox did not so emphasize the inspiration of the *words* that they lost sight of the teaching of the text or of the larger doctrinal significance so carefully outlined by them in their language of the "foundation" and "scope" of Scripture. The seventeenth-century thinkers make a distinction between the "essential" and the "accidental" or incidental form of Scripture: "Essential [form] indicates the entirety of doctrine necessary to salvation" prior even to the unwritten form of the revealed word while "accidental form" is the letters or written form of the text as distinguished from spoken words or signs. This distinction between substance *(materia)* and form *(forma)* also points to the priority of the inspired text over the church, inasmuch as it is the substance of Scripture that is the foundation of the church.[106]

This concept of inspiration also follows as a consequence from the doctrine of the divinity of Scripture. The divine knowledge that is contained in Scripture and the truth of biblical prophecy can only be explained by the influence of the Holy Spirit. Not only do these books exceed human comprehension, they appear also to be a "perpetual rule of faith and practice" held free from error: "it is contrary to our impression of reality to think that Galilean fishermen, or publicans, wrote so many excellent things without the

---

[104]Weemes, *Exercitations Divine,* pp. 67–68; cf. Witsius, *De prophetis et prophetia* in *Miscellanea sacra,* I.x.1–5 (pp. 75–78), and Witsius, *De Apostolorum in docendo infallibilitate,* in *Miscellanea sacra,* I.xxii.28 (p. 343).

[105]Weemes, *Exercitations Divine,* p. 69.

[106]Gomarus, *Disp. theol.,* II.xxiv.

guidance of the Holy Spirit."[107] What is more, Christ, in the Scriptures, explicitly tells his disciples that the Holy Spirit "will guide them into all truth" and the apostles themselves testify that they speak by the Holy Spirit and by the Word of God, not of men.[108]

Among the high orthodox writers, Mastricht offers one of the most careful and precise delineations of the doctrine of inspiration, including a rather strict statement of the theory of verbal dictation. "The origin [of the Scriptures], upon which their authority is founded," can be argued either "in terms of the penmen *(quantum ad Amanuenses),* who were called 'the hands of the Holy spirit' by Gregory the Great in his preface to Job" or "in terms of the author *(quantum ad Auctor),* who generally speaking, is God." These amanuenses can be identified, on the basis of 2 Peter 1:21, as the prophets and apostles, the "holy men of God." Even so, the church is said to be built "upon the foundation of the prophets and the apostles" (Eph. 11:20). As for evangelists like Mark and Luke, who might be distinguished from prophets and apostles and excluded from the definition, they ought to be understood as "prophets" or "apostles," granting the more general connotation of the terms in passages like 1 Corinthians 14:29, 32; Romans 14:7; and Philippians 2:25.[109] As Ames indicated, Mastricht argues, the Spirit has accomplished this work of inspiration with considerable variety. Thus,

> certain things have indeed been written that were unknown immediately before they were written, such as the history of the initial creation and the predictions of future events ... while certain other things were known before they were written down, as in the history of Christ, written by the apostles. In addition, some of these things were understood by natural, others by supernatural knowledge. Divine inspiration manifested the entirety of the hidden and unknown things by itself; whereas it enlivened the religious zeal of the writers concerning those things either already known to the writers or capable of being known by ordinary means, God assisting them in order that they might not err in writing. Moreover, the Holy Spirit influenced them in an appropriate and suitable manner in order that each writer might be able to use the manner of speaking most agreeable to his character *(persona)* and condition.[110]

---

[107]Pictet, *Theol. chr.,* I.vii.2, obs.5.
[108]Pictet, *Theol. chr.,* I.vii.2, obs.6, citing John 16:13.
[109]Mastricht, *Theoretico-practica theol.,* I.ii.12.
[110]Mastricht, *Theoretico-practica theol.,* I.ii.12.

The resultant Scripture is called the "Word of God" because God, its Author, "is said to speak in it: [the persons] singly, as God the Father, who spoke 'in sundry times and in divers manners' (Heb. 1:1); the Son, who not only sent the Apostles forth to teach, doubtless as the occasion demanded, but who ordered them to write (Rev. 1:19); and the Holy Spirit who has inspired those who are said to witness and to speak in the Scriptures." The authority of the Scriptures rests on the "principal cause" or primary author, God, who has superintended the writing of these sacred books by his amanuenses.[111]

The passage to high and late orthodoxy was marked by an increasing debate over the doctrine of inspiration and an increasing need to strengthen and clarify the doctrine itself through increasingly precise formulation and to elevate the doctrine to a more prominent place in the *locus de Scriptura*. The point must be made that the basic terms of the doctrine never changed appreciably: from the patristic period through the seventeenth century, theologians assumed divine superintendence over the writing of the words, not merely the ideas, of text. What changed was the detail and the intensity of the doctrinal statement and, above all, the importance of the doctrine of inspiration to the construction of the language of authority. These developments of the concept of inspiration reflected, thus, not only the ongoing polemic with Rome, the Socinians, and the Arminians, but also a Reformed biblical scholarship increasingly concerned with textual and contextual or historical questions. The variations that we see in Witsius, Poole, Pictet, and Venema indicate a greater receptivity to the textual and historical concerns, whereas those noted in Voetius and Mastricht indicate opposition to various adversaries on doctrinal grounds.

The movement of Reformed orthodox thought, thus, was not a uniform march toward increasingly strict or "rigid" notions of verbal inspiration. A very strict view of inspiration that could appear to exclude or even overrule human agency is found throughout the period of orthodoxy in the work of Perkins, Owen, Voetius, Mastricht, and Henry. Other writers, however, notably Rivetus, Cameron, Cocceius, Witsius, Pictet, and late orthodox thinkers like Venema and Stackhouse differed appreciably with this strict view, and moved toward a doctrine of inspired infallibility without the assumption of a divine dictation of every word of the text and, eventually without the assumption of a uniform inspiration of every

---

[111]Mastricht, *Theoretico-practica theol.*, I.ii.12.

portion of the text.[112] Still others, like Lightfoot and Poole, recognized that the inspiration of the text could be maintained in the same breath as a more text-critical approach.

Owen, perhaps because of the polemic in which he was involved, elaborated the doctrine of inspiration in a manner that emphasized the divine authorship of the text to the exclusion of the biblical writers' reliance on either their own knowledge or their own mental faculties. In his description of the revelation given to the prophets, Owen declares that

> the laws they made known, the doctrines they delivered, the instructions they gave, the stories they recorded, the promises of Christ, the prophecies of gospel times they gave out and revealed, were not their own, not conceived in their minds, not formed by their reasonings, not retained in their memories from what they heard, not by any means beforehand comprehended by them, (1 Pet. 1:10, 11), but were all of them immediately from God— there being only a passive concurrence of their rational faculties in their reception.[113]

As if to reinforce a point already so strongly made, Owen continues,

> God was so with them, and by the Holy Ghost so spake in them— as to their receiving of the Word from him, and their delivering of it unto others by speaking or writing—as that they were not themselves enabled, by any habitual light, knowledge, or conviction of truth, to declare his mind and will, but only acted as they were immediately moved by him.[114]

Owen did not deny that the prophets and apostles diligently studied the Word of God that had been given to their predecessors, and that they learned these truths through study and the illumination of the Holy Ghost, "even as we," but he insisted a prophet's or an apostle's own writings contained "nothing by study or meditation, by inquiry

---

[112]Cf. Rivetus, *Isagoge*, pp. 8–11; Cocceius, *Summa theol.*, I.iv.41; Pictet, *Theol chr.*, I.vii.3; Venema, *Institutes of Theology*, pp. 44–47; Stackhouse, *Complete Body of Divinity*, I.iv (pp. 76–78); on Cameron's theory of inspiration, see Laplanche, *L'Écriture*, pp. 205–8; and Diestel, *Geschichte des Alten Testamentes*, pp. 320–21.

[113]Owen, *Divine Original*, in *Works*, XVI, p. 298; cf. the almost identical view in Perkins, *Cases of Conscience*, in *Workes*, II. pp. 54–55; and Whitaker, *Disputation*, III.iii (pp. 296–97).

[114]Owen, *Divine Original*, in *Works*, XVI, p. 298.

or reading" and that in the composition of the books assigned to them in the canon they were purely instruments of the divine author.[115] Owen's motivation, in defining the doctrine so strictly, was clearly to rule out elements of human fallibility in the teachings of Scripture.[116]

By way of contrast, Pictet and late orthodox writers like Vitringa, Venema, Stackhouse, and Wyttenbach could argue a far less strict doctrine. Thus, Pictet can state that the biblical writers were not given all knowledge by the Spirit and that they were not necessarily preserved free from sin for the sake of the doctrinal purity of their message. Nor ought we to conclude that the Holy Spirit revealed to the disciples whatever they desired to know, but only those things necessary for faith. Venema and Stackhouse argue strict dictation of words on only a few occasions in Scripture and a general superintendence of the Spirit, inspiring and illuminating the biblical writers throughout the larger part of Scripture.[117] Pictet similarly offers a concept of plenary inspiration and full authority, without the assumption of thoroughgoing verbatim dictation.[118] On occasion, the prophets and apostles wrote of facts or events of which they already knew or they touched on personal issues. Thus, "Moses did not receive what is contained in Genesis by immediate revelation, but ... from the ancient monuments of the patriarchs."[119] Furthermore, the Spirit clearly allowed the apostles to draw conclusions from revelations and use "purely human patterns of speech" while at the same time preserving them from error as they wrote. In contrast to the view expressed by Owen, Pictet and Venema declare that it is not necessary to claim immediate revelation as the source of all truths in Scripture. Inspiration in no way indicates the loss of rational faculties on the part of the biblical writers, but rather an illumination of their rational faculties with a heavenly light and their preservation from error.[120] Portions of Pictet's and Wyttenbach's argument may reflect the theory of Grotius, which made a distinction between essential and unessential matters in Scripture, or those of Cameron

---

[115]Owen, *Divine Original,* in *Works,* XVI, p. 299.

[116]Owen, *Divine Original,* in *Works,* XVI, p. 300.

[117]Pictet, *Theol. chr.,* I.vii.6; Venema, *Institutes of Theology,* III (p. 45); Stackhouse, *Complete Body of Divinity,* I.iv (pp. 77–78).

[118]Pictet, *Theol. chr.,* I.vii.3.

[119]Venema, *Institutes of Theology,* III (p. 44), citing Campegius Vitringa, *Observationes sacrae,* iv.

[120]Pictet, *Theol. chr.,* I.vii.4; cf. Venema, *Institutes of Theology,* III (pp. 45–46); Wyttenbach, *Tentamen theologiae dogmaticae,* II, §141, scholion.

and Cocceius, which indicated varieties of inspiration both in both
nature and extent, depending on the character of the text, whether
prophetic or historical, though neither Pictet nor Wyttenbach
approves of a limitation of inspiration as did later Arminian proponents of the theory, like Limborch.[121]

In accord with this assumption that the biblical authors used their
rational faculties, Poole could argue that 1 and 2 Kings were a composite work drawn together from various older writings of "prophets" and "holy men of God" by an unknown "penman":

> But whoever was the penman, that these are a part of those Holy
> Scriptures which were divinely inspired is sufficiently evident,
> first, From the concurring testimony of the whole Jewish church in
> all ages, to whom *were committed the oracles of God*.... Christ and
> his apostles, who reproved [the Jews] freely for their several sins,
> never taxed them with this fault, of depraving the Holy Scriptures
> of the Old Testament. Secondly, Because this is manifest concern-
> ing divers parcels of them which were taken out of the records of
> the prophets Nathan, Ahijah, and Iddo, 2 Chron. ix.29, and out of
> the prophecies of Isaiah and Jeremiah.... Thirdly, From the appro-
> bation of these books by the New Testament, both generally, as
> 2 Tim. iii.16 ... and particularly, Rom. xi.2, 3, &c. where a passage
> out of these books is quoted and owned as a part of the Holy
> Scriptures.[122]

Inspiration and primary divine authorship do not, therefore,
remove the faculties of the human authors of Scripture. Lightfoot
can, for example, balance a strict view of inspiration with a strong
sense of human activity in the writing of Scripture. The earlier narratives of which Luke spoke in the first verses of his Gospel lacked
the Holy Spirit as a "guide of action" and a "director of [the] pen"
and did not evidence "that style wherein the Holy Spirit would ...
declare" God's truth. Nonetheless, the divine superintendence of the
canonical writings includes Luke's own critical activity: "Our evangelist ... takes care to weigh such kind of writings in such a balance
as that it may appear they are neither rejected by his as false or

---

[121]Pictet, *Theol. chr.,* I.vii.5; Wyttenbach, *Tentamen theologiae dogmaticae,*
II, §142; cf. Cocceius, *Summa theol.,* I.iv.41; Limborch, *Theol. chr.,* I.iv.10; and
note Laplanche, "Débats," in *BTT* 6, p. 128 on Cappel and Morus.

[122]Poole, *Commentary,* I, p. 645; cf. the similar comments in Poole's introductions to Joshua, Judges, Ruth, 1–2 Samuel, 1–2 Chronicles, and Nehemiah
in *Commentary,* I, pp. 408, 456, 507, 513, 774–75, 883; Stackhouse, *Complete
Body of Divinity,* I.iv (p. 79); and note the discussion, above §2.5.

heretical, nor yet received as divine and canonical."[123] Poole similarly states that Luke "undertakes (not without the direction of the Holy Spirit, as appeared afterward) to compile a history ... to which he was either encouraged by the example of others, or incited by the mistakes of those who had done it ill." Luke had the advantage, Poole continues, of a perfect understanding of the history arising from "his converse with the apostles and other ministers of Christ."[124]

It would be a mistake, therefore, to view the seventeenth-century orthodox theory of inspiration as utterly opposed to the results of a more critical and textual exegesis or as incapable of accommodation to the various problems of authorship and composition raised by the critical approach. Poole can state, for example, of 1–2 Samuel,

> It is not certainly known who was the penman of this Book, or whether it was written by one or more hands; nor is it of any great importance; for since there are sufficient evidences that God was the chief author of it, it matters not who was the instrument. As when it appears that such a thing was really an act of parliament, or of the council-table, it is not considerable who was the clerk or which was the pen that wrote it.[125]

And then, echoing the more flexible approach to inspiration found in Cameron and Cocceius, Poole could conclude that the lack of a single, identifiable author "is the less material in such historical books, wherein there is but little which concerns the foundation of faith and good life."[126] At very least, Poole's approach indicates that a strong doctrine of inspiration was not an altogether fragile perspective.

More remarkable, particularly granting his rather strict doctrine of inspiration, is the analysis of the text of Joshua through 2 Kings offered by Matthew Henry. Henry accepts the tradition that the historical books were, in large part composed by the prophets, but he assumes, also, a large-scale redaction of the history:

> It should seem that though the substance of the several histories was written when the events were fresh in memory, and written under a divine direction, yet that under the same direction, they were put into the form in which we now have them, by some other hand, long afterward, probably all by the same hand, or about the

---

[123]Lightfoot, *Horae hebraicae et talmudicae,* III, pp. 5–6.
[124]Poole, *Commentary,* III, p. 185 (on Luke 1:1–4).
[125]Poole, *Commentary,* I, p. 513.
[126]Poole, *Commentary,* I, p. 513.

same time. The grounds of the conjecture are, 1. Because former writings are so often referred to, as the Book of Jasher, Josh. X.13 and 2 Sam. 1.18, and the Chronicles of the Kings of Israel and Judah often; and the Books of Gad, Nathan, and Iddo. 2. Because the days when the things were done, are spoken of sometimes as days long since passed; as 1 Sam. ix.9, *He that is now called a prophet, was then called a seer.* And, 3. Because we so often read of things remaining *unto this day,* as stones, Josh. iv.9; vii.26; viii.29; x.27; 1 Sam. vi.18. Names of places, Josh. v.9; vii.26; Judg. i.26; xv.19; xviii.12; 2 Kings xiv.7. Rights and possessions, Judg. 1:21; 1 Sam. xxvii.6 Customs and usages, 1 Sam. v.5; 2 Kings xvii.41. Which clauses have been since added to the history by the inspired collectors, for the confirmation and illustration of it to those of their own age.[127]

Henry also offers a theory to explain the later prophetic gathering and editing of the materials:

if one may offer a mere conjecture, it is not unlikely that the historical books to the end of the Kings were put together by Jeremiah the prophet a little before the captivity, for it is said of Ziklag, 1 Sam. xxvii.6, it pertains to the *kings of Judah* (which style began after Solomon, and ended in the captivity) *unto this day:* And it is still more probable that those which follow, were put together by Ezra the scribe, sometime after the captivity. However, though we are in the dark concerning their authors, we are in no doubt concerning their authority; they were a part of the oracles of God, which were committed to the Jews, and were so received by our Saviour and the apostles.[128]

By "those which follow" Henry indicates 1–2 Chronicles, which he

---

[127]Henry, *Commentary on the Whole Bible,* I, p. 518; cf. the various comments in Poole, *Commentary, I:* on 1 Sam. 9:9, noting that these words might be "of some later sacred writer, which, after Samuel's death, inserted this verse" (p. 531); on Josh. 4:9, *"They are there unto this day:* this might be written either, 1. By Joshua, who wrote this book near twenty years after this was done; or, 2. By some other holy man, divinely inspired and approved of by the whole Jewish church, who inserted this and some such passages, both in this book, and in the writings of Moses"; on 1 Sam. 27:6, *"Unto this day:* this and some such clauses seem to have been added by some sacred writers after the main substance of the several books was written"; and cf. Stackhouse, *Complete Body of Divinity,* I.iv (pp. 78–80).

[128]Henry, *Commentary on the Whole Bible,* I, p. 518; cf. Poole, *Commentary, I,* 579, for a similar remark, in the commentary itself, on the phrase "unto this day."

associates with the gathering of the law by Ezra: "It is a groundless story," he writes, "of that apocryphal writer, 2 Esdr. xiv.21, &c. that, all the law being burnt, Ezra was divinely inspired to write it all over again, which might yet take rise from the books of Chronicles, where we find, though not all the same story repeated, yet the names of all who were the subjects of that story."[129] Poole similarly accepts the authorship of Ezra, on the basis of 2 Chronicles 36:20ff. and because of parallels with the Book of Ezra. He adds, "If one or two passages seem to be of a later date, those were added by some other prophets, there being some few such additional passages in the Books of Moses" as well. Poole also hypothesizes that the "sacred penman" who completed the histories took materials out of family genealogies and "public registers" of Israel.[130] It is quite clear from these examples, as well as numerous others that can be cited from the exegetical works of the Protestant orthodox, that the rise of textual criticism cannot be viewed as a phenomenon that took place alongside of orthodoxy and in antagonism to it, or that proponents of the traditional theory of a verbal inspiration were unable to deal with critical problems in the text of Scripture.

The doctrine and polemics of high orthodoxy, thus, looked in several directions. Against the claim of some Roman Catholic polemicists that not all of the Scriptures were written "by the express mandate of God" but were "occasional" writings transmitted within the tradition of the church, the orthodox continued to affirm the priority of the Word over the church and to insist on the pattern of progress from *verbum agraphon* to *verbum engraphon* that had been argued from the time of the Reformers onward. Riissen could argue that even "occasional" writings—occasional insofar as they address specific historical events or issues—can be commanded by God and can have a continuing significance and normative value.[131]

More important than this old polemic was the relatively new debate with third- and fourth-generation Socinians and Arminians who had moved beyond the early biblicism of their movements to a more rationalistic perspective and who substituted for the doctrine of plenary inspiration a concept of partial or limited inspiration that made allowances for error on the part of the biblical writers. In this position, the Reformed orthodox saw a deeper issue that the simple opposition of an error-free text with the fallibility of human authors.

---

[129]Henry, *Commentary on the Whole Bible,* I, p. 1001.
[130]Poole, *Commentary,* I, pp. 774–75.
[131]Riissen, *Summa theol.,* II.xvii, controversia 1.

They were quite willing to concede that the sacred writers, considered as human beings, could and did err. Apart from the sacred writings, any private works of the prophets and apostles (none of which, of course, survive) were neither inspired nor infallible. In the specific act of setting down the Scriptures, however, the prophets and the apostles "were moved and inspired by the Holy Spirit, in order that they might be preserved from error, both according to substance and according to word, and in order that their writings might be truly authentic and divine."[132]

Examination of the orthodox theory of the inspiration of Scripture, therefore, does not manifest a completely "rigid" or "mechanical" theory, but rather considerable variety of formulation and, often, an incomplete solution of the problem as it was then raised. The theory was designed to remain within the bounds of the long-held view of inspiration and to support the Protestant doctrine of the authority of Scripture, but not to answer in any depth either the question of the relationship of the divine and human wills in religious experience underlying the writing of Scripture or to deal with the recognition, found in many of the orthodox prolegomena, that theological statements and "theological certainty" do not function in the same way that mathematical and empirical statements and mathematical and empirical certainty function.[133] This latter problem is seen most clearly not in the writings of the seventeenth-century orthodox, but in the thought of eighteenth-century writers whose task it was to maintain "orthodoxy" in the context of an increasingly empirical and mathematical view of truth. At this point, the redacted nature of the text, already noted by Poole and Henry, *became* a problem where before it had not been seen as causing any great difficulty for doctrine.

There was, however, a series of problems that did confront the theory of verbal inspiration as it was taught in the seventeenth century. These are not primarily problems caused by any major departure from the thought of earlier periods, including the Reformation —rather they are problems caused by the encounter of this time-worn approach to inspiration with changing patterns of hermeneutics and with a set of new, critical approaches to the text of Scripture. Thus, the orthodox of the seventeenth century perceived the critical analysis of the origin of the vowel-points as an attack on the Protestant doctrine of the divinity and authority of Scripture (as indeed it

---

[132]Riissen, *Summa theol.,* II.xvii, controversia 2.
[133]Cf. *PRRD,* I, 6.2.

was in the hands of Roman Catholic polemicists) and countered by including the vocalization of the text in the work of divine dictation. The Reformers had used the language of dictation and amanuenses, but they had not encountered a critical polemic focused on the origin of the vowel points. The conjunction of the old theory with the new issue, in a writer like Owen, pressed the theory beyond its usefulness and application, and associated it with both a philological error and a polemically rigidified defense of both the text and the doctrine. Later orthodox writers, however, like Venema, Wyttenbach, and Stackhouse were able to adapt the theory of inspiration to the results of textual criticism and, at the same time, retain both the basic definition and the assumption of an infallible text.

The inspiration of Scripture appears in the debates of the seventeenth century not only as a doctrinal but also as a hermeneutical issue. An inspired text can—more easily and predictably than an uninspired one—point beyond itself and its original situation. When the human author of the text is an instrumental cause and God is identified as the *auctor primarius,* the historical situation of the human author cannot ultimately limit the doctrinal reference of the text. (It is worth noting that the hermeneutical corollary of this understanding of the implication of inspiration is a method which, like the *quadriga* and various patterns of typological interpretation, consistently points beyond the historical letter toward divine things, whether doctrinal, moral, or eschatological.)

The most important example of this extension of the meaning of an inspired text is surely prophecy—particularly since prophecy is a category of religious and theological teaching intrinsic to the text itself. But even apart from prophecy, an inspired text can be argued to point toward or to provide an indication of a doctrine presumably unknown or historically and culturally unattainable by a human author but known to God. The trinitarian nature of the Godhead, unknown to the Israelites and presumably unknown to Moses except by a special revelation, can be adumbrated in Genesis 1, not a prophecy, but simply because the text indicates the divine creative operation which is, by definition, trinitarian.[134] Moses, arguably, could not have been responsible for placing this doctrine into the text—but the *auctor primarius,* God, simply reflected his own nature in speaking, through Moses, about himself, his Spirit moving on the face of the waters and his creative word. The capability of an inspired text pointing beyond the historical letter is, therefore,

[134]Cf. Poole, *Commentary,* I, p. 2.

clearly an issue related to hermeneutics—specifically to the way in which a text is assumed to "work" in relation to the larger body of Christian doctrine.

The increasingly textual, grammatical, historical, and literal character of Protestant exegesis in the seventeenth century pressed against the doctrine of inspiration precisely because the doctrine, as originally conceived, belonged to a different hermeneutical context. What is usually identified as a rigidification of doctrine on the part of the orthodox is better characterized, therefore, as the attempt to place the traditional doctrine of inspiration into an altered interpretive context. This perspective on the problem of inspiration in the seventeenth century serves to explain not only the strong interest of the Protestant orthodox in the concepts of *analogia Scripturae* and *analogia fidei,* but also to explain why the exponents of a more critical method found themselves increasingly pressed both to redefine the doctrine of inspiration and to defend themselves against accusations of Arianism, Socianianism, and other heresies—heresies that it had not been their intention to advocate.

4.3 The Divinity of Scripture: Authority, Authenticity, and Evidences

a. The Reformers and the Early Orthodox: Problem of Divine Authority and Its Evidences

The doctrinal arguments concerning the necessity of revelation by the Word, the forms of the Word, and the causality of Scripture, including the doctrine of inspiration, led the Protestant orthodox to the rather obvious question of results. There must, in other words, be some evidence or imprint of the divine work of producing Scripture in the Scriptures themselves. Significantly, the order of the argument in the orthodox systems—reflecting still the approach of the Reformers even if in a far more dogmatic and formalized statement —is a priori, not a posteriori. The orthodox do not attempt to rise from effects to cause and to prove the divinity of Scripture by recourse to an evidentialistic argument—rather they move from cause to effect, arguing the divinity of Scripture first and foremost and then noting how the divine handiwork is evidenced in the text. This is not to say that the arguments adduced for the authority, authenticity, and evidences of divine handiwork in Scripture are viewed by the orthodox as unconvincing, but only to note that they are quite aware what kind of arguments these are and how the usefulness of such arguments is and must be limited. Typically, the self-evidencing character of biblical authority is paired with the testimony of the Spirit and set prior to the various signs of the truth of the text such as its majesty and sublimity.[135]

The place and importance of such rational argumentation concerning the divinity of Scripture in Protestant dogmatics have been a matter of debate at least since Barth declared that these "proofs," like rational arguments for the existence of God, had no place at all in the teachings of the Reformers.[136] This debate, like the general debate over the continuity or discontinuity between the teachings of the Reformers and the doctrine of the Protestant scholastics, arises in no small part because of the difficulty of making a formal comparison between the theology of the Reformers and that of the orthodox. It is quite true that the Reformers did not present lengthy, formal discussions of the divinity of Scripture, its evidences, causes, and ends—but it is also true, generally, that they did not write detailed systems of theology. The claim that such arguments as belong to more elaborate theological system have no place within the thought of the Reformers is, at best, a shallow argument from silence and, at worst, a statement of personal theological preference for the form and genre typical of theology in one period over the form and genre typical of theology in another period that has been put forth in the guise of a historical argument.

Calvin's views are, very frequently and quite wrongly, posed against the Reformed orthodox on this point. On the one hand, the orthodox, typically, did not give extrinsic evidences of the divinity of Scripture priority over the inward work of the Spirit, while, on the other, Calvin never claimed the *testimonium internum Spiritus Sancti* as the sole correct argument for the divinity of Scripture apart from the various external evidences. Indeed, it is Calvin who, in the second generation of the Reformation, formulated his doctrine of Scripture with a careful balance between the prior testimony of the Spirit and the secondary external evidence of divinity,[137] giving to the Protestant doctrine of Scripture both a subjective and an

---

[135]Cf. Wendelin, *Christianae theologiae libri duo,* prol., III.iv, with Cloppenburg, *Exercitationes super locos communes,* I.ii.1–16, and idem., *Aphorismi theologiae christianae,* II.ii.

[136]Karl Barth, *The Word of God and the Word of Man,* trans. Douglas Horton (Boston: Pilgrim Press, 1928; repr. New York: Harper and Row, 1957), pp. 242–44.

[137]Calvin, *Institutes,* I.vii–viii.

objective character as well as the form that would remain definitive for this particular point on into the era of orthodoxy.[138]

Calvin's arguments for the divinity and authority of Scripture are particularly instructive in view of both their content and somewhat less than fully systematized character and the relationship indicated by Calvin between the self-evidencing authority of Scripture and the internal testimony of the Spirit on the one hand and the so-called external evidences of the divinity of Scripture on the other.[139] Scripture, argues Calvin, is *autopiston,* self-authenticating, not subject to "proof and reasoning" and having no authority beyond its Word to which believers need turn for validation. Scripture, inasmuch as it is "unassailable truth," itself provides the norm for judgment:

> it is sealed upon our hearts through the Spirit. Therefore, illuminated by his power, we believe neither by our own nor by anyone else's judgment that Scripture is from God; but above human judgment we affirm with utter certainty (just as if we were gazing upon the majesty of God himself) that it has flowed to us from the very mouth of God by the ministry of men.[140]

This is no static deposit of revelation that Calvin describes, no past manifestation of God's will duly recorded and embalmed for posterity: Scripture, when read, preached, and heard in faith is the living voice of God speaking with divine authority—so clearly authoritative in its own words and by the Spirit's testimony in the reading that it is self-authenticating. Here, incidentally, is the link between Calvin's view of inspiration and his doctrine of the authority of Scripture. The same Spirit that first offered the Word by means of this "ministry of men" continues to work in and through the words upon the hearts of the readers and hearers. It is the same Spirit who "dictates" to his "amanuenses" who continues to testify of the truth of the Word to believers.[141] As the Reformed orthodox would later argue, Calvin indicates that inspiration is the ground of the authority of Scripture: "in order to uphold the authority of Scripture, [the

---

[138]Cf. Warfield, "Calvin's Doctrine of the Knowledge of God," pp. 82–93, 123–30

[139]Cf. Warfield, "Calvin's Doctrine of the Knowledge of God," pp. 82–93.

[140]Calvin, *Institutes,* I.vii.5.

[141]Cf. Calvin, *Institutes,* I.vii.5, with idem, *Commentaries on the Second Epistle to Timothy,* 2 Tim. 3:16 (CTS, p. 249), and idem, *Commentaries on the Second Epistle of Peter,* 2 Pet. 1:20–21 (CTS, pp. 390–91); and note the similarity with Zwingli's view as discussed in Stephens, *Theology of Zwingli,* p. 57.

apostle] declares that it is divinely inspired; for, if it be so, it is beyond all controversy that men ought to receive it with reverence."[142]

Calvin can, thus, speak objectively of the authority of Scripture, commenting on the apostle's words in 2 Timothy 3:16, "to assert its authority he teaches that it is inspired of God ... dictated by the Holy Spirit." He also, however, recognizes that this objective authority is not apprehended primarily by empirical analysis of the text as object: "if anyone ask how this can be known, my reply is that it is by the revelation of the same Spirit both to learners and to teachers that God is made known as its author."[143]

No amount of argument or testimony, Calvin was convinced, would be sufficient "to prove to unbelievers that Scripture is the Word of God ... for only by faith can this be made known."[144] Even so, "Scripture will ultimately suffice for a saving knowledge of God only when its certainty is founded upon the inward persuasion of the Holy Spirit."[145] The church, therefore, cannot be the guarantor of Scripture inasmuch as the church can only argue and testify to the truth of Scripture in an external way. Indeed, the church itself rests on "the writings of the prophets and the preaching of the apostles," with the result that the church may proclaim the Word but "the same Spirit ... who has spoken through the mouths of the prophets must penetrate into our hearts to persuade us that they faithfully proclaimed what has been divinely commanded."[146] Those who attempt to "build up faith in Scripture through disputation," comments Calvin, "are doing things backwards"—since even the successful vindication of Scripture from various attacks will not produce piety in the hearts of those defeated by argument.[147] True conviction of the authority and divinity of Scripture derives from a higher source than mere human argument, "the secret testimony of the Spirit."[148]

---

[142]Calvin, *Commentaries on the Second Epistle to Timothy,* 2 Tim. 3:16 (CTS, p. 248).

[143]Calvin, *Institutes,* I.vii.4; cf. idem, *Commentaries on the Second Epistle to Timothy,* 2 Tim. 3:16 (CTS, p. 249).

[144]Calvin, *Institutes,* I.viii.13. Note that this virtual paradox of the knowability of the objective evidences of the divine origin of Scripture only after and on the basis of the internal testimony of the Spirit mirrors closely the problem of natural revelation and natural theology: the revelation is objectively present, but can be known fully and truly only by the regenerate. Cf. *PRRD,* I, 5.2, 5.3.

[145]Calvin, *Institutes,* I.viii.13.

[146]Calvin, *Institutes,* I.vii.4.

[147]Calvin, *Institutes,* I.vii.4.

[148]Calvin, *Institutes,* I.vii.4; cf. III.i.1, 3–4; ii.15, 33–36.

Nevertheless, having once declared that no amount of external evidence and argumentation can suffice to persuade an unbeliever of the authority of Scripture, Calvin—almost paradoxically—devotes more space to a discussion of the external evidences of the divinity of Scripture than he had given to his discussion of why such evidences are unnecessary. There are, notes Calvin,

> manifest signs of God speaking in Scripture. From this it is clear that the teaching of Scripture is from heaven. And a little later we shall see that all the books of Sacred scripture far surpass all other writings. Yes, if we turn pure eyes and upright senses toward it, the majesty of God will immediately come to view, subdue our bold rejection and compel us to obey.[149]

The final sentence in the quotation not only indicates the strength of Calvin's valuation of the marks of divinity in Scripture, it also indicates an almost overriding sense of the power of those marks or attributes to convince the doubtful, despite Calvin's comments to the contrary. Calvin attempts to strike here what Reformed orthodoxy would find to be an increasingly difficult balance between the subjective and inward certainty resting on the Spirit and on faith alone and an external objective certainty resting on evidence. The former must be present if the Reformed emphasis on grace alone to the exclusion of works is to be maintained and paralleled at this crucial juncture, the doctrine of the self-authenticating authority of Scripture to the exclusion of individual human proof and of churchly testimony. But the latter must also be present if the subjective conviction is to be grounded in reality.

Thus, Calvin begins his discussion of the objective divinity of Scripture with the disclaimer that "unless this foundation is laid (i.e., the foundation provided by the work of the Spirit) its authority will always remain in doubt." Once this work of the Spirit is accomplished, however, Calvin knows of no bounds to the usefulness and the power of the evidences of divinity present in Scripture.

> What wonderful confirmation ensues when, with keener study, we ponder the economy of the divine wisdom, so well ordered and disposed; the completely heavenly character of its doctrine, savoring of nothing earthly; the beautiful agreement of the parts with one another.... But our hearts are more firmly grounded when we reflect that we are captivated with admiration for Scripture more

[149]Calvin, *Institutes,* I.vii.4.

by grandeur of subjects than by grace of language. For it was not without God's extraordinary providence that the sublime mysteries of the Kingdom of Heaven came to be expressed largely in mean and lowly words.... Consequently, it is easy to see that the Sacred Scriptures, which so far surpass all gifts and graces of human endeavour, breath something divine.[150]

Like the later orthodox writers, Calvin notes that the antiquity of Scripture is also an external mark of its divinity—Moses "devised no new god, but rather set forth what the Israelites had accepted concerning the eternal God handed down by the patriarchs age after age."[151] Even so, the record of miracles and of the fulfillment of prophecy is clear proof of the divinity of Scripture.[152] Granting also the vicissitudes of Israelite history, the providential preservation of the books of Scripture is also a profound testimony to their divinity.[153] Even so, the substance of the gospel testifies to the divinity of the New Testament, particularly given the humble origin of the disciples and the lowliness of literary style found in their writings. Beyond the New Testament, there is the testimony of the church which, Calvin, admits, has its place in the proofs of the divinity of Scripture. For Scripture has remained the "unassailable" standard of truth to the church despite the efforts of Satan and the world to destroy it. The preservation of the text is so marvelous that it cannot be merely the result of human effort, just as the steadfastness of the martyrs who died for its truths cannot be but a testimony to the divine power at work in and through the text of Scripture.[154]

These basic perspectives on the inspiration and authority of Scripture—including the balance between subjective and objective evidence of testimony—carry over directly into Reformed orthodox theology. One of the primary mediators of this view was Zanchi. That Scripture is truly *theopneuston,* he declares, we know neither from human testimony nor from the testimony of the church, but only from God: the Spirit alone enables us to discern the Word of God from other words.[155] Even the Scriptures themselves are unable to illuminate the mind when it is not moved by the Spirit. Similarly, all of the rational proofs of the inspiration of Scripture—such as its

[150]Calvin, *Institutes,* I.viii.1.
[151]Calvin, *Institutes,* I.viii.3.
[152]Calvin, *Institutes,* I.viii.5–8.
[153]Calvin, *Institutes,* I.viii.10.
[154]Calvin, *Institutes,* I.viii.11–13.
[155]Zanchi, *Praefatiuncula,* col. 332.

antiquity, its internal harmony and agreement, its confirmation through miracles, its revelations of otherwise unknowable truths—all fall short of proof and fail to sway the mind. Zanchi lists, but does not elaborate these arguments at length. How many philosophers and wise men, he asks, have been drawn to faith by such arguments—and how many, for the sake of knowing the Word of God, have become as common men and fools?[156]

This illumination of the Spirit, argues Zanchi, alone suffices to demonstrate to the mind that the Scriptures are *theopneustos*—and, he adds, it suffices without the testimony of the church.[157] Nonetheless, both the testimony of the church to the truth of the word preached and the hearing of the word preached are useful and, indeed, necessary. It is Scripture itself, as read and heard, that provides knowledge of God and not the internal testimony of the Spirit. Although the testimony of the church to the divinity of Scripture is neither the principle nor the effectual cause of our acceptance of the authority of Scripture, it does occur first in order, in the case of the church of the present day. (In the case of Moses and, arguably also, of the prophets and the apostles, the *verbum Dei* is both temporally and logically prior, inasmuch as the testimony of the church was lacking.) Zanchi thus accepts the statement of Augustine that he would not have believed the gospel apart from the church in the sense that the church is the place where the Word is preached and heard.[158]

Related to this necessity of the hearing of the word is what Zanchi calls "the other means *(alterum medium)*." This, he writes, "is the testimony of Scripture, or of God speaking to us in the Scriptures *(Dei in Scripturis nobis loquentis)*."[159] Zanchi compares the relationship of God to the Scriptures to that between the sun and its light. The light comes from another, but it is nonetheless objectively present. The only problem is our ability to receive the light. Scripture, considered as a medium of communication, remains ineffectual —"not in itself, but in relation to us"—apart from the work of the Spirit. With the aid of the Spirit, however, the voice of God can be heard when Scripture is preached in the church. This "other means," therefore, although subsequent in time to the church's testimony, is, granting the work of the Spirit, the most effective.[160]

---

[156]Zanchi, *Praefatiuncula,* col. 334.
[157]Zanchi, *Praefatiuncula,* col. 334.
[158]Zanchi, *Praefatiuncula,* col. 335.
[159]Zanchi, *Praefatiuncula,* col. 336.
[160]Zanchi, *Praefatiuncula,* cols. 335–37.

A fourth testimony to the inspiration and, therefore, to the authority of Scripture, is the demonstration, both within Scripture itself and external to it, by its "consequences," of its divinity. The substance and the quality of biblical teaching, the form of Scripture and its language, at once humble and enduring, the harmony or consonance of Scripture with itself, and the power of Scripture to regenerate human nature constitute internal proof of its divinity. Externally, Scripture is shown to be inspired by the fulfillment of its prophecies, by its miracles, by "the furor of Satan and Antichrist against it, by the conservation of its doctrine against the power of Satan," and by the evils that came upon the persecutors of the gospel.[161]

Following Zanchi and the writers of his generation, we encounter very little change in the doctrine of the authority, authenticity, and evidences of Scripture as it passed into the era of orthodoxy. In some writers, like Leigh, the discussion of evidences appears to be somewhat more elaborate, but the reader never has the impression that the arguments from evidences, either internal or external, ever predominate: The focus of the doctrine remains on the presence of the divine Word in Scripture as testified by the Spirit. Scripture, as inspired, is assumed to be authoritative—and although, like the Reformers, the orthodox never hesitate to call Scripture the *verbum Dei,* they also, following out the teaching of the Reformers, continue to assume the priority of the *materia* over the *forma,* the priority of the Word of saving doctrine mediated by the text over the text as such. Scripture, the orthodox can declare,

> is of Divine Authority, and so greater than all exception. It is Divine. 1. In its efficient cause and original, which is God the Father dictating, in his Son declaring and publishing, by his holy Spirit confirming and sealing it in the hearts of the faithful.... 2. In the subject matter, which is truth according to godliness, certain, powerful, of venerable antiquity, joined with a sensible demonstration of the Spirit and Divine presence.[162]

Note here the trinitarian formulation of the causality of Scripture and the consequent emphasis both on Christ as the center of revelation and on the Spirit as the source of internal testimony. Note also that the characterization of the subject matter of Scripture is designed to draw on those characteristics already treated under the arguments for

[161]Zanchi, *Praefatiuncula,* col. 338.
[162]Leigh, *Treatise,* I.viii (p. 130).

the divinity of Scripture. We see, in both instances, an example of the logic of the orthodox (here, Leigh's) system and of the necessary interpenetration of doctrinal topics. Similarly, the attributes of Scripture as Word cannot ultimately be severed from the attributes of the God whose Word has been inscripturated.[163]

The orthodox theologians are in accord that the divinity of Scripture results in the primary characteristic or attribute of authority.[164] In brief, authority is the characteristic that results from the nature of the author. In religious or theological matters, ultimate authority derives from God inasmuch as God is the ultimate source or author of all things religious, while relative and limited authority derives from human beings who, as authors of theological documents, command only limited respect. The issue, here, is a direct reflection of the language of the Reformed prolegomena.[165] The ultimate and therefore perfect archetypal theology is identical with the divine mind—all other theology is, at best, a reflection of this archetype, a form of ectypal theology. Ectypal theology in the human subject (in all systems of theology!) is not only finite and reflective but also limited by human sinfulness and by the mental capacities of the theologian. The human author of theology, thus, has little intrinsic authority. If theology is to be authoritative, its source (other than the mind of the theologian) must carry authority with it. That source cannot be the divine archetype, but it must stand in a more direct relation to that archetype than any utterly human effort.

Even so, the doctrine of inspiration leads, in many of the orthodox systems, directly to the doctrine of the authority of Scripture.[166] As such Scripture is the *fundamentum,* the sustaining power of Christian faith and life through which the Spirit works, having the authority to adjudicate all theological controversies and all disputes over morals: It is the "authentic norm" *(authentian norma)* which stands above and directs faith and life.[167]

---

[163]Heppe saw this in a rudimentary fashion, but viewed it not as a subtle interpenetration of *loci* but as a crass divinization of the text! Cf. *RD,* p. 26.

[164]Cf. *"authoritas divina duplex"* and *"authoritas Scripturae,"* s.v. in *DLGT.*

[165]Cf. *PRRD,* I, pp. 123–66.

[166]Cf., e.g., Mastricht, *Theoretico-practica theologia,* I.ii.13–14; Cocceius, *Summa theol.,* I.ii.3; Turretin, *Inst. theol. elencticae,* II.iv.2; Pictet, *Theol. chr.,* I.viii.2–3.

[167]Mastricht, *Theoretico-practica theol.,* I.ii.14.

Thus, the scholastic language of the essential divinity and authority of Scripture arises directly as a result of the discussions of *verbum agraphon* and *verbum engraphon, verbum internum* and *verbum externum.* Since Scripture arises from the unwritten Word of God being given written form or, more precisely, from the internal Word given to the prophets being externalized as proclamation and then written, the primary author *(author primarius)* of Scripture is God and Scripture, therefore, is in some sense divine *(divina)* or holy *(sacra).* Insofar as authority *(authoritas)* is a power of dignity deriving from the *author,* this divinity or holiness of the text can be summed up in the term *authority,* when that authority is considered *absolute in se.* Thus Turretin: "On the basis of the origin of Scripture ... its authority is judged: since it is indeed from God, it cannot be other than authentic *(authentica)* and divine."[168] (We reserve full discussion of the canonical or regulatory authority of Scripture *quoad nos* for subsequent discussion.)

The authority of Scripture, as considered and defined by Pictet following his treatment of inspiration,

> is nothing other than the right and dignity of the sacred books, according to which they are worthy of faith in what they set forth to be believed, and our obedience in whatever they prescribe to be done, or left undone. For having been proved to be of God, and not of men or of the devil, the necessary consequence is, that they should have the highest authority for us. For who would deny the authenticity of that which is divine? ... Even so, we ought to consider Scripture, which is the first principle of faith, as we view the principles of other bodies of knowledge, which do not derive their authority from any other source, but are known of themselves, and prove themselves.[169]

This authority of Scripture, arising out of the revelatory character of the Word as delivered by inspiration to the prophets and the apostles, can be defined in terms of the *authentia* or authenticity of Scripture. The written Word has authority if it is authentically divine —if it is authentically divine and, therefore, authoritative, it can stand as the *principium cognoscendi theologiae,* the cognitive foundation of all human theology that, in a mediate and derivative sense, to be authoritative. As noted in the introductory chapter, the question of authority is the central question addressed by both the

---

[168]Turretin, *Inst. theol. elencticae,* II.iv.1.
[169]Pictet, *Theol. chr.,* I.viii.2–3.

Reformers and the Protestant orthodox. All else is in some sense subsidiary, whether it is the doctrine of inspiration, the doctrine of the various properties of Scripture, or the argument concerning the use and interpretation of Scripture. Indeed, all of these subsidiary issues are addressed in terms of the relationship of the authoritative Word of Scripture to the various other authorities that participate in the formulation and exposition of Christian doctrine—the tradition, the church in the present day, the exegete or theologian, the relational capacity of human beings, and philosophy formally considered.

Polanus' *Syntagma* provides a representative synopsis of the doctrine:

> The authority of the Holy Scripture is twofold: divine *(divina)* and canonical or regulatory *(canonica)*.
>
> This authority is considered both absolutely in itself *(absolute in se)* and with respect to us *(quoad nos)*.
>
> Holy Scripture is established among us today as truly divine both in general and in particular, both on the basis of divine testimonies and arguments *(ex testimoniis & rationibus divinis)* as a criterion or norm of judgment; and on the basis of human testimonies.
>
> The divine testimonies or criteria are two: one internal, the other external; the former is Scripture itself as the voice of God *(vocis Dei)* making testimony to itself, the latter is truly the Holy Spirit in our hearts.
>
> Similarly the human testimonies are two: one, the true Church; the other, those who are outside of the Church.
>
> The testimonies of other men outside the Church of God are either of the Jews, or of the heretics or of the Pagans *(Gentilium)* themselves.[170]

Following out the logic of Polanus' divisions, we will confine ourselves in this section to the divine authority of Scripture considered absolutely in itself and discuss the canonical authority *quoad nos* at a later point.[171]

Polanus' neat doctrinal divisions, representative of the Ramist model frequently used by the early orthodox, provide a useful overview of the scholastic Protestant conception of the authority of

---

[170]Polanus, *Syntagma,* Synopsis libri I.
[171]See below, §5.5.

Scripture. The scholastic approach carefully and logically touches on all of the possible ways of considering the divine authority of Scripture—the general and the particular; divine testimony both internal and external to the text; human testimony both Christian and non-Christian. In his exposition of these points, as in the basic divisions, Polanus gives priority to the *vox Dei* speaking in Scripture and to the *testimonium Spiritus Sancti* in the heart of the believer without, however, neglecting the more empirical language of the marks of divinity that are observable in the text of Scripture.[172] In this balance, his exposition is typical of the orthodox systems, although we will be able to detect in the writings of the high and late orthodox eras an increasingly apologetic emphasis on the observable or empirical *notae divinitatis* in the text.

Like most of the seventeenth-century orthodox, Pictet takes opportunity to attack the Roman claim of the church's authority in testifying to the truth of Scripture. It is wrong, nay impious, he reasons, to place the authority of man above the authority of God as if the fallible voice of ecclesiastics could validate the truth of God. Indeed, no human being has infallibly preserved from error since the days of the apostles. The church can only judge the authority of Scripture on the grounds of Scripture—and, having recognized the truth of the Bible, rest all ecclesiastical authority on the Scriptures. To this must be added that the church taken either in whole or in part bears no such marks of divinity as do the Scriptures.[173]

> The Divine Authority of the Word may be defined, a certain dignity and excellency of the Scripture above all other sayings or writings whatsoever; whereby it is perfectly true in word and sense; it deserves credit in all sayings, narrations of things past, present and to come, threatenings and promises, and as superior doth bind to obedience, if it either forbid or command anything, ... though the thing in man's judgment seem unlike or incredible, or the Commandments hard and foolish to the carnal mind.[174]

These considerations led the orthodox to refer to Scripture as the *formale obiectum fidei* in so far as it was the written revelation of God—revelation itself in both unwritten and written forms being the proper formal object of faith and that Scripture, as such, is not to be

---

[172]Cf. Polanus, *Syntagma theol.,* I.xvii–xxii.

[173]Pictet, *Theol. chr.,* I.viii.4, arg. 2.

[174]Leigh, *System,* I.ii (p. 8), ellipses indicating omission of biblical references only.

identified as revelation in a reductionistic way but is nevertheless the only normative source of knowledge concerning revelation.[175]

The *authoritas* of Scripture can, thus, also be identified as *autopistia,* for

> the Scriptures are for themselves worthy to be believed; they have authority in and of themselves (not borrowed from any persons in the world) by which they bind the consciences of all men to receive them with faith and obedience.... And as Christ by himself could demonstrate that he was the Messias, so the Word by itself can prove that it is the Word of God.[176]

This is necessary logically, moreover, if Scripture is to be the first principle of theology:

> Every principle is known by itself. The scripture is the *primum credendum,* the first thing to be believed; we must believe it for itself, and all other things for their conformity with it.[177]

By extension, this argument also shows why the a priori order of theology among the orthodox does not reflect a speculative metaphysic. There is here no deduction of principles but only a reliance on the a priori of revelation.

b. Evidences of the Divinity and Authority of Scripture in Reformed Orthodox Theology

Just as Calvin and other Reformers assumed objective evidences of the divinity of Scripture to be visible in the text and in its history, so also do the Protestant orthodox assume these evidences or marks of divinity to be present. In addition, the orthodox generally preserved the same order and/or priority of discussion as was found in Calvin's *Institutes:* The testimony of the Spirit remains the primary key to the authority and divinity of Scripture, with the evidences standing as ancillary testimony and, more important, as the necessary result of the divine work performed in the inspiration and

---

[175]Cf. Robert Baron, *Disputatio theologica de formali objecto fidei* (Aberdeen, 1627): "Formale obiectum fidei generaliter & absolute consideratum est divina revelatio in tota sua amplitudine accepta, seu divinus authoritas cuiuslibet doctrinae a Deo revelata, sive ea scripta sit, sive non scripta. At formale objectum fidei illius quae creduntur ea quae in Scriptura credenda proponuntur, est ipsius Scripturae divina & canonica authoritas."

[176]Leigh, *Treatise,* I.ii (pp. 25–26; cf. margin, p. 25).

[177]Leigh, *Treatise,* p. 26, margin.

writing of the text.[178] Very much after the manner of Calvin, therefore, Owen could identify the connection between the original work of inspiration and the subsequent recognition by believers of the authority of Scripture:

> God speaking *in* the penmen of the Scripture, (Heb. 1:1) his voice to them was accompanied with its own evidence, which gave assurance unto them; and God speaking *by* them or their writings unto us, his word is accompanied by its own evidence, and gives assurance unto us.[179]

As with Calvin, so also with the Reformed orthodox, the primary evidence of the authority, divinity, and truth of Scripture is the internal testimony of the Spirit. Somewhat more pointedly, perhaps, than Calvin, the orthodox insist on the inseparability of Word and Spirit and deny that this testimony is a private revelation of any sort: The orthodox do not, of course, rest their doctrine of Scripture on some sort of private revelation: "we do not affirm," Owen argues,

> that the Spirit immediately, by himself, saith unto every individual believer, This book is, or contains, the word of God. We say not that this spirit ever speaks to us *of* the Word, but *by* the Word.[180]

The Spirit teaches our hearts to help us to "acknowledge the voice of God, and of Christ himself, speaking in the Scripture." In this work, the Spirit "gives no new light to Scripture" but "cleareth our understanding, to see the light of Scripture, by the very Scripture itself and by the light of the Scripture." The Spirit thus uses two means to convince us, an outward and an inward, the inward being the foremost and offered in and through the Scripture itself: "if the Holy Ghost, speaking in the Scripture, do not first of all inspire our minds, and open the eyes of our understanding ... all other means shall profit us nothing at all."[181]

This approach reminds us very strongly of Calvin's description of the testimony of the Spirit to the authority of Scripture and of the

---

[178]Contra Laplanche, "Débats," in *BTT* 6, p. 120.

[179]Owen, *Divine Original,* in *Works,* XVI, p. 307.

[180]Owen, *Divine Original,* in *Works,* XVI, pp. 325–26; cf. Henry Ainsworth, *The Trying Out of the Truth: Begunn and Prosequuted in Certayn Letters or Passages between Iohn Aynsworth and Henry Aynsworth; the one pleading for, the other against the present religion of the Church of Rome* (London, 1615), p. 59.

[181]Rollock, *Treatise of Effectual Calling,* pp. 69–70.

way Calvin describes Scripture as *autopiston*. Thus,

> we have no need simply of any other light, or of any one special
> evidence to demonstrate this matter, but that very light which is in
> Scripture. For the Scripture (being the first and immediate word of
> God) is of authority sufficient in itself (*autopistos*), and so likewise
> of itself most clear and evident.... For like as the light of the sun is
> not perceived nor to be seen by means of any other light, for that it
> so far exceeds all other bodily and external light, so, that spiritual
> light of the Scripture hath no need in itself of any other light ... for
> of all the spiritual lights that enlighten the mind withal, it is the
> most bright and most beautiful in the world.[182]

The Spirit accomplishes his work in part "by producing certain testimonies of Scripture" such as 2 Timothy 3:16, "All Scripture is given
by divine inspiration," in part by suggestion, admonition, and warning that we observe the commands and teachings of Scripture. Since,
however, we are so "blind by nature" and the causes of doubt concerning Scripture are in our minds rather than in the holy writ,
arguments of a collateral sort may be used by the Spirit as means in
order to open the eyes to the light of Scripture, to lead us "to behold
the divine majesty of God shining bright, and speaking to us in the
Holy Scripture."[183]

The primary testimony to the divinity of Scripture, therefore, is
from God—and it is twofold: "first, by the internall Testimony of his
Spirit; secondly, by his externall testimony." The secondary testimony is drawn from Scripture itself. At a third level, the church also
testifies to the authority of Scripture—and finally, even those outside of the church sometimes offer testimony.[184]

The continuity of the orthodox position with the Reformation is
nowhere more clear than in this presentation of evidences. Calvin's
list of arguments is echoed in Ursinus' discussion of indication of
divine origins belonging to biblical teaching. These two lists, in turn,
had a profound impact on the early orthodox doctrine of Scripture in
such documents as Polanus' *Syntagma* and the *Synopsis purioris
theologiae*. A half-century later, Owen would declare that "Scripture
hath all its authority from its Author, both in itself and in respect of
us," an almost verbatim reflection of Polanus' basic division of the
issue.[185] This relationship to Author and origin, moreover, "it

---

[182]Rollock, *Treatise of Effectual Calling*, p. 68.
[183]Rollock, *Treatise of Effectual Calling*, p. 69.
[184]Weemes, *Exercitations Divine*, p. 76.
[185]Owen, *Divine Original*, in *Works*, XVI, p. 309; cf. Polanus, *Syntagma*

declares itself, without any other assistance"—so that Scripture is recognized to be "self-authenticating" or trustworthy in itself, *autopistos*.[186] Nor does this pattern of argumentation disappear in late orthodoxy. Writers like Venema, Van Til, and Wyttenbach, who had moved more in the direction of rationalism than their high orthodox predecessors, and who had begun to adapt the doctrine of inspiration to some of the results of textual criticism, still held to the delineation of intrinsic and extrinsic evidences, in the case of Wyttenbach, at considerable length.[187]

Like most of the Reformed orthodox, Owen argues the self-authenticating character of Scripture both "by the way of testimony" and "by the way of deductions and inferences," which is to say, both intrinsically and extrinsically,[188] but he also provides a significant argument, a "general induction" based on the "three ways whereby God ... revealeth himself, his properties, his mind, and will to the sons of men."[189] This argument, moreover, both clarifies the notion of self-authentication and demonstrates an important relationship between the doctrine of Scripture as authoritative rule of faith and practice and the Reformed conception of the value and limitation of natural theology. Owen finds untenable the notion that Scripture, as Word of God, could fail to be self-authenticating or self-evidencing—but he finds equally untenable the notion that this self-evidencing character is peculiar to the scriptural form of God's self-revelation. Indeed, Owen believes that the self-evidencing character of all revelation is crucial to the Reformed teaching of the authority of Scripture. Authority "arises from relation"; there is no authority without relationship, no authority "in itself" apart from authority "in respect of others," and, certainly, no authority "in respect of others" apart from authority "in itself."[190] Authority arises out of relationship, even if it resides entirely in one of the parties in relation, and it needs no testimony of a party external to the relationship in order either to exist or to be known. The authority of God's written Word

---

theol., Synopsis libri I, as cited above p. 285.

[186]Owen, *Divine Original,* in *Works,* XVI, p. 309; cf. *"autopistos,"* s.v. in *DLGT.*

[187]Cf. Wyttenbach, *Tentamen theologiae dogmaticae,* II, §§115–23 (pp. 99–129); Venema, *Institutes of Theology,* pp. 47–62; Van Til, *Theologiae utriusque compendium ... revelatae,* IV (p. 11).

[188]Owen, *Divine Original,* p. 313; cf. p. 309.

[189]Owen, *Divine Original,* p. 309.

[190]Owen, *Divine Original,* p. 308.

must be, thus, an authority "in itself towards us"[191]—but such authority must necessarily belong to all divine revelation.

There are three ways that God reveals himself: in his works of creation and providence, by "the innate (or ingrafted) light of nature, and the principles of the consciences of men," and by his Word as preserved in the holy Scriptures.[192] It belongs to the essence of each of these three forms of revelation that they are self-authenticating. Thus,

> The works of God (as to what is his will to teach and reveal of himself by them) have that expression of God upon them—that stamp and character of his eternal power and Godhead—that evidence with them that they are his—that, wherever they are seen and considered, they undeniably evince that they are so, and that what they teach concerning him, they do it in his name and authority. There is no need of traditions, no need of miracles, no need of the authority of any churches, to convince a rational creature that the works of God are his, and his only; and that he is eternal and infinite in power that made them. They carry about with them their own authority. By being *what* they are, they declare *whose* they are.[193]

Similarly, the inward voice of nature and conscience "declares itself to be from God by its own light and authority ...: without further evidence or reasoning, without the advantage of any considerations but what are by itself supplied, it discovers its author, from whom it is, and in whose name it speaks."[194] *Koinai ennoiai* or "common notions" are "inlaid in the natures of rational creatures by the hand of God, to this end, that they might make a revelation of Him ..., are able to plead their own divine original, without the least contribution of strength or assistance from without."[195]

This view of the character of natural revelation, Owen recognizes, is held not only by the Reformed but also by their Roman Catholic and rationalist adversaries. If such a view of natural revelation is assumed, how much more ought its logic apply to Scripture!

---

[191]Owen, *Divine Original*, p. 309.

[192]Owen, *Divine Original*, pp. 309–10; and cf. the discussion of natural revelation in *PRRD*, I, pp. 167–93.

[193]Owen, *Divine Original*, pp. 310–11.

[194]Owen, *Divine Original*, p. 311.

[195]Owen, *Divine Original*, p. 311.

Now, it were very strange, that those low, dark, and obscure principles and means of the revelation of God and his will, which we
have mentioned, should be able to evince themselves to be from
him, without any external help, assistance, testimony or authority;
and that which is by God himself magnified above them ... should
lie dead, obscure, and have nothing in itself to reveal its Author,
until this or that superadded testimony be called to its assistance.[196]

It must be accepted, Owen concludes, "as a principle of truth" that
all of God's revelation, both general and special, has "such an
impression of his authority upon it, as undeniably to evince that it is
from him" and to leave all those who ignore its testimony "without
excuse."[197]

Defining Scripture as the Word of God indicates also that "the
holy Scriptures are that Divine instrument and means, by which we
are taught to believe what we ought touching God, and ourselves,
and all creatures, and how to please God in all things unto eternal
life."[198] Thus, the canonical authority of Scripture "is uniformly
divine" in all of the books of Scripture, although not all of the books
can be said uniformly to convey the contents of revelation. The
"idea of theology" is firmly and fully expressed "not in individual
books or in the separate words of the books, but in the integral
gathering of the canonical books (in librorum Canonicorum integro
syntagmate)."[199] As indicated above in the discussion of inspiration,
despite the insistence of the Reformed that the very words of the
original are inspired, the theological force of their argument falls in
the substance or res rather than on the individual words. Translations can be authoritative quoad res because the authority is not so
much in the words as in the entirety of the teaching as distributed
throughout the canon.

Scripture, then, broadly and canonically understood, in all its
parts but primarily in the whole, is divine and authentic in itself and
needs no human assent in order to be so—as the sun is light even if
all people were blind. The issue posed by the doctrine of authority,
however, is that Scripture also be acknowledged divine and authentic in the church and identified as the rule of faith and obedience.
Granting the polemic of the age concerning the ultimate locus of
religious authority, the orthodox fasten on a series of proofs of the

[196]Owen, Divine Original, p. 311.
[197]Owen, Divine Original, p. 312.
[198]Leigh, System, I.ii (p. 8).
[199]Cloppenburg, Exercitationes super locos communes, I.i.10.

divine authority of Scripture. Leigh divides the proofs of Scripture's divinity and authenticity into *intrinsic* and *extrinsic* categories.[200]

Intrinsically, Scripture appears to be divine from its heavenly subject matter, the "divine and supernatural" truth contained in it,

> which it was impossible for any man to counterfeit and feign, and which being told are so correspondent to reason, that no man can see just cause to call them into question; as the Doctrine of Creation of all things in six days; the Doctrine of the Fall of our first Parents; the Story of the Delivering of Israel out of Egypt, of the Delivering of the Law and ten Commandments; the Doctrine of the Incarnation of Christ Jesus, of the Resurrection of the dead, of the last Judgement, of the life to come, and of the Immortality of the Soul.[201]

Furthermore, Scripture

> teacheth the nature and excellency of God, and the works of God, more clearly and distinctly than any other writings, nay than any without God could have contrived, viz. that there are three persons and one God, that God is Infinite, Omniscient, Omnipotent, most Holy; that he created all things, that he doth by a particular Providence rule all things; that he observes all mens actions, and will call them to account, and give every man according to his works; that he alone is to be worshipped, and that he must be obeyed in his Word above all creatures.[202]

It can also be argued that, whereas "many histories" have shown the sins of mankind and the wrath of God, only the Scriptures "shew us *morbum, medicinam, & medicum* ... the sicknesse, the physicke, and the Physician to cure it." Even so, Scripture alone teaches what is necessary to salvation and offers "nothing for our curiosity": "the Scriptures are not given to passe the time with, but to redeeme the time."[203]

Similarly, Owen can declare that the divinity of Scripture is known from the fact that its teachings are often "sublimely glorious" and "so profound and mysterious an excellency, that at the first proposal of them, nature startles, shrinks, and is taken with horror, meting that which is above it, too great and too excellent for it."[204]

[200]Leigh, *System,* I.ii (p. 8).
[201]Leigh, *System,* I.ii (p. 9); cf. Weemes, *Exercitations Divine,* p. 83.
[202]Leigh, *System,* I.ii (p. 9); cf. Ussher, *Body of Divinity,* p. 9.
[203]Weemes, *Exercitations Divine,* p. 78.
[204]Owen, *Divine Original,* in *Works,* XVI, p. 339.

Nonetheless, further consideration of these otherwise unknowable truths allows "the eyes of reason" to be "a little confirmed" and manifests to our nature that these "unsearchable" truths are the foundation on which all other truth and our entire relationship to God rests. Thus, denial of revelations like the doctrines of the Trinity, of the incarnation of the Son of God, and of the resurrection of the dead, undermines the whole of faith and obedience:

> Take away, then, the doctrine of the Trinity, and both these are gone; there can be no purpose of grace by the Father in the Son— no covenant for the putting of that purpose in execution: and so the foundation of all fruits of love and goodness is lost to the soul.[205]

This argument concerning the importance of doctrines not otherwise available to the human race is, Owen comments, "not to be withstood."[206] If these remarks of Leigh and Owen are any index of the tone of Reformed orthodoxy, there is little evidence of any formative effect upon mid-seventeenth-century Reformed dogmatics of the rising tide of skeptical philosophy, Cartesian rationalism, or empiricism. What is present is the typical view, inherited from the older scholasticism that the doctrines given by revelation transcend reason, but ultimately do not demand an irrational or nonrational stance on the part of the believer. Over against the rationalistic perspective, orthodoxy held to a strong soteriological motive in the conservation of its doctrines and of the suprarational source from whence they came.

The divine origin of Scripture also appears clearly in the examination of the text. In the rather rustic words of "another herdsman, Jeremiah, and Zechariah" as much as in the refined language of David and Isaiah, the "majesty of the Spirit" is evident. Miracles and the fulfillment of prophecies also testify to the divine hand at work, as does the providential preservation of the text throughout history. Even more, the simplicity of style and spirituality of content of the New Testament require assent to the origin of Scripture in the instruction of the Spirit. All these evidences are confirmed by the "unvarying testimony of the Church" and the willingness of the martyrs to die for the doctrines of Scripture.[207] Scripture, furthermore,

---

[205]Owen, *Divine Original,* in *Works,* XVI, p. 341; cf. Ussher, *Body of Divinity,* p. 9.

[206]Owen, *Divine Original,* in *Works,* XVI, p. 342.

[207]Leigh, *Treatise,* I.viii; cf. Ursinus, *Explicationes catecheseos,* in *Opera,* I, col. 50 (Williard, p. 8); Ussher, *Body of Divinity,* pp. 9–10.

calls itself divine; the authors often testify that they speak not of themselves, nor by any human instinct, but from God's command with the Spirit inspiring.[208] Scripture also "is called a light, Psal. 119.105. because it discovers itself; the testimony, and the testimony of the Lord, because it bears witness to itself."[209] Even more important, both Peter (2 Pet. 1:19, 20; 3:15) and Paul (2 Tim. 3:16) give notice that Scripture is inspired of God.[210] Even so the condition of these amanuenses, collated with the contents of Scripture, testifies to its divinity: for they preach "with the majesty and sublimity of truth" about such things as the Trinity, original sin, the hypostatic union of the two natures in Christ, the redemption of humankind by the blood of the Son of God—and they do so not by inference as "the wisest of Philosophers," indeed "not in a human manner" given our fallenness. The only and most certain conclusion is that "these mysteries" could only be known if the Scriptures "were inspired by God."[211] Wyttenbach adds to this—indicating the rationalistic tendencies of his late orthodox approach—that the divinity of Scripture is seen in the congruence of its "theoretical truths" with right reason, even when they arise from beyond reason and its grasp.[212]

Next, Scripture manifests its excellence in its commands. For the divine requirement of "most exact and perfect goodness" is far beyond the ability of man to invent but in its particulars so confirms to "right reason" that all must acknowledge it both true and necessary—such as only God could propound. Thus the righteousness of the commandments, the generality and impartiality of the threatenings, and the comprehensive character of the promises testify to the divinity of Scripture.[213] Similarly the statements of Scripture that we must trust not in men but in God and look not for reward of merit but for grace by reason of "the merits and intercession of another" are beyond the powers of human invention.[214] Further,

---

[208]Leigh, *Treatise,* I.ii (p. 23, margin).

[209]Leigh, *Treatise,* I.ii (p. 23).

[210]Leigh, *Treatise,* I.ii (p. 23).

[211]Mastricht, *Theoretico-practica theol.,* I.ii.23; cf. Van Til, *Theologiae utriusque compendium ... revelatae,* IV (p. 11).

[212]Wyttenbach, *Tentamen theologiae dogmaticae,* II, §117.

[213]Leigh, *Treatise,* I.ii (p. 16); cf. Ursinus, *Explicationes catecheseos,* in *Opera,* I, col. 49 (Williard, p. 7).

[214]Leigh, *Treatise,* I.ii (p. 12); cf. Ursinus, *Explicationes catecheseos,* in *Opera,* I, col. 50 (Williard, p. 7); Wyttenbach, *Tentamen theologiae dogmaticae,* II, §118.

The end of the Scripture is Divine, viz. the glory of God shining in every syllable thereof, and the salvation of man, not temporal but eternal. These writings lead a man wholly out of himself, and out of the whole world, & from and above all the creatures to the Creator alone, to give him the glory of all victories: therefore they are from him and not from any creature, for he that is the Author of any writing will surely have most respect of himself in that writing. The scriptures manifest God's glory alone, Jerem. 9.23, 24].[215]

The simplicity and majesty of style and the truth of the words, their lack of human trick of persuasion and of flourishing speeches, their clarity in teaching God's truth, and their unvarying expression of the sovereign will and command of God also clearly denote him as author.[216]

Another argument is taken from the experience of the truth of the predictions and prophesies thereof. For seeing it is generally confessed, that only the Divine essence can certainly foresee things contingent which are to come many ages after, and which depend on no necessary cause in nature; therefore in what writings we meet with such things foretold and do find them fully and plainly accomplished, these writings we must confess to have their birth from Heaven and from God. Now in the Scriptures we have divers such predictions. The two principal and clearest ... are 1. the conversion of the Gentiles to the God of Israel by means of Christ.... Again [2], it was foretold that Christ should be a stone of offence to the Jews, and that they should reject him, and so be rejected by God from being a people; do we not see that to be performed? The accomplishment of these two main prophesies so long before delivered to the world by the Pen-men of holy writ, shows manifestly, that they were moved by the Holy Ghost.[217]

Even so the prophesies of the devil and of the heathen are "doubtful and ambiguous, but these are distinct and plain"—those of the heathen "for the most part false," these of God "most true and certain."[218]

---

[215]Leigh, *Treatise,* I.ii (p. 13); cf. Riissen, *Summa theol.,* II.vi, controversia, argumentum 1; Wyttenbach, *Tentamen theologiae dogmaticae,* II, §§115–116.

[216]Leigh, *Treatise,* I.ii (p. 13); cf. Ussher, *Body of Divinity,* p. 8; Weemes, *Exercitations Divine,* p. 79; Pictet, *Theol. chr.,* I.vi.16.

[217]Leigh, *Treatise,* I.ii (pp. 14–15); cf. Van Til, *Theologiae utriusque compendium ... revelatae,* IV (p. 11).

[218]Leigh, *Treatise,* I.ii (p. 15); Ussher, *Body of Divinity,* p. 9.

The orthodox also frequently point to the antiquity of Scripture, both in its "matter" or "substance" as "contained in the words and letters" and in its physical actuality, both substance and form. In the first instance, referring to the substance alone, the antiquity of Scripture is apparent, since it is the "substance of those divine oracles which not only the patriarchs and prophets have spoken, but also God himself uttered; which things also were hidden in God's mind from eternity," such as the plan of creation and salvation.[219] The antiquity of the documents themselves and its fidelity in recording ancient history also evidence divine supervision.[220] Rollock also notes in a brief excursus that Scripture is *theopneustos* and therefore in every "jot or prick" the truth of God—perhaps indicating an assumption of the Mosaic origins of the vowel points.[221] This argument from the substance of Scripture serves to defeat the "adversaries" who claim that the church of the patriarchs was prior to the Scripture as written down by Moses, for clearly the eternal will of God and even the *viva vox Dei* preceded the foundation of the church, indeed called it into being as testified by 1 Peter 1:23, which calls the church "born not of mortal seed, but of immortal, even by the word of God, who liveth and endureth forever."[222]

This divine word has been committed to writing only in the books of the Old and New Testaments, Pictet comments, as he proceeds to enumerate the books of the Bible and their major divisions.[223] That these books are divine can be demonstrated by the presence in them of certain "marks" or characteristic. A divine writing is intended:

> *The first* characteristic is to state nothing but the truth. *Second,* to reveal such mysteries as cannot arise from the human imagination, but which are nonetheless in accord with the natural ideas God has impressed upon the mind. *Third,* to direct our worship and our minds to the true God alone. *Fourth,* so to instruct the mind, as to satisfy and set at rest the most insatiable desire after knowledge.

---

[219]Rollock, *Treatise of Effectual Calling,* IX (p. 76); cf. Weemes, *Exercitations Divine,* pp. 77–78; Wyttenbach, *Tentamen theologiae dogmaticae,* II, §122.

[220]Leigh, *Treatise,* I.ii (p. 16), and Riissen, *Summa theol.,* II.vi, controversia, argumentum 1; cf. Ursinus, *Explicationes catecheseos,* in *Opera,* I, col. 49 (Williard, p. 7).

[221]Rollock, *Treatise of Effectual Calling,* p. 77.

[222]Rollock, *Treatise of Effectual Calling,* p. 77.

[223]Pictet, *Theol. chr.,* I.v.1; cf. Mastricht, *Theoretico practica theologia,* I.ii.8.

Fifth, to teach men by the most holy precepts to love God above all things, and to renounce all iniquities. *Sixth,* to be always consistent with itself, and to exhibit no contradiction. *Seventh,* to teach those things, which calm all the passions of the mind, and fill it with indescribable peace and joy, bringing it into such subjection, that it is compelled under a sweet, yet most powerful influence, to obey the laws of God. *Eighth,* to predict those things, which no human being could foreknow, and which were all fulfilled as predicted.[224]

In a final and summary argument concerning the intrinsic evidences of the divinity of Scripture, the orthodox point to the "design" and the internal consistency or "harmony" of the whole.[225] This consistency, particularly the consistency of the revealed purpose underlying the text, indicates that "the whole proceedeth from one and the same principle, and hath the same author, and he wise, discerning, able to comprehend the whole compass of what he intended to deliver and reveal."[226]

The wonderful content, singular harmony and agreement of the Scriptures shows that they came not from men but from God, John 5.46. each part sweetly agreeth with itself, with another, and with the whole, Acts 26.22 & 11.17. Luke 24.27. John 5.46. Matth. 4.4. what was foretold in the old is fulfilled in the New Testament. If there seem any contrariety either in the numbering of years, circumstance of time and place, or point of doctrine, the fault is in our apprehension or ignorance, not in the thing itself, and may easily be cleared.[227]

Since, moreover, the Scripture that reveals itself to be the "word of the living God" also throughout declares the goodness and the glory of God, its readers must acknowledge on the basis of this consistency and harmony of statement that either this word is true and God is indeed the author—or that this word is false and the author is a most evil being, indeed, the devil himself. The divinity of Scripture follows as a necessary conclusion:

[224]Pictet, *Theol. chr.,* I.vi.2.

[225]Owen, *Divine Original,* in *Works,* XVI, pp. 342–43; Ursinus, *Explicationes catecheseos,* in *Opera,* I, cols. 49–50 (Williard, p. 7).

[226]Owen, *Divine Original,* in *Works,* p. 343.

[227]Leigh, *Treatise,* I.ii (p. 18); cf. Ursinus, *Explicationes catecheseos,* in *Opera,* I, cols. 49–50 (Williard, p. 7); Rollock, *Treatise of Effectual Calling,* p. 70; Weemes, *Exercitations Divine,* p. 81.

it cannot fall upon the understanding of any man that that doctrine which is so holy and pure—so absolutely leading to the utmost improvement of whatever is good, just, commendable, and praise-worthy—so suitable to all the light of God, of good and evil, that remains in us—could proceed from anyone everlastingly hardened in evil, and that in the pursuit of the most wicked design that that wicked one could possibly be engaged in, namely, to enthrone himself, and maliciously to cheat, cozen, and ruin the souls of men; so that upon necessity the Scripture can own no author but him whose it is—even the living God.[228]

Thus also, Scripture expressly teaches the difference between the true God and idols.[229]

On a lesser level of significance but nonetheless useful to the defense of the text against its detractors are the *"extrinsic"* arguments, which are divided by Leigh and others into two basic categories: miracle and testimony.[230] The miracles can be miracles of "confirmation" as those performed by Christ and the apostles to manifest the truth of their words, or miracles of "preservation" like the providential care by which God preserved Scripture from all efforts of tyrants and evil men "to suppress and extinguish" the word.[231] Similarly the divinity of Scripture is attested by "the Church and the Saints of God in all ages."

The Church of the Jews professed the doctrine and received the books of the old Testament, and testified of them that they were divine; which invincible constancy remaineth still in the Jews of these days, who (though they be bitter enemies of the Christian Religion) do stiffly maintain and preserve the Canon of the old Testament pure, and uncorrupt, even in those places which do evidently confirm the truth of the Christian Religion.[232]

(Here, incidentally, we see the reason that Roman arguments con-

[228]Owen, *Divine Original,* in *Works,* XVI, p. 343; cf. Ussher, *Body of Divinity,* p. 8.

[229]Weemes, *Exercitations Divine,* p. 79.

[230]Leigh, *Treatise,* I.ii (pp. 19–23); cf. Ursinus, *Explicationes catecheseos,* in *Opera,* I, cols. 49–50 (Williard, pp. 7–8).

[231]Leigh, *Treatise,* I.ii (p. 19); cf. Rollock, *Treatise of Effectual Calling,* p. 71; Ussher, *Body of Divinity,* p. 10; Pictet, *Theol. chr.,* I.vi.16; Van Til, *Theologiae utriusque compendium ... revelatae,* IV (p. 11); Wyttenbach, *Tentamen theologiae dogmaticae,* II, §119.

[232]Leigh, *Treatise,* I.ii (p. 21); cf. Ussher, *Body of Divinity,* p. 11; Riissen, *Summa theol.,* II.xvii, cont. III, argumenta 3 & 4.

cerning the relative corruption of the text through malice of the Jews had little initial effect on the Reformed view of the Old Testament. This text handed on as divine by the Jews was received by the apostles "as a *depositum* and holy pledge of the Divine will."[233] We also see why the debate over the vowel points took on such broad doctrinal dimensions.)

Further, after the writing of the New Testament, external testimony to its divinity continued as the "worthy Martyrs" died for their faith. In this argument, not only the number of martyrs needs to be considered but also the "quality and condition of them which suffered"—all types and classes of men and women. Surely "all these could not suffer out of vain-glory, that stubbornly they might defend the opinion which they had taken up."[234] Moreover, the great torments to which they were subjected and the patience and constancy with which they endured their afflictions also testify to the divinity of their scriptural faith.[235] Even the heretics testify to the divinity of Scripture by their efforts to prove their doctrines scripturally.[236] Finally, the divinity of the Bible is assured by the "extraordinary propagation of the Christian faith throughout the world, by the instrumentality of mean and ignorant men ... in opposition to the very gates of hell."[237] Taken together all these characteristics of Scripture—found together in no other book— convince us of its divinity and confirm its own testimony (2 Tim. 3:16) that it is "given by inspiration of God."[238]

While it is clear that the use of Scripture as a criterion or norm of judgment in religion rests entirely upon divine origin and in no way arises out of human practice, the Protestant orthodox do develop a series of arguments concerning human testimony to the divinity of Scripture. These arguments are chiefly polemical or apologetic in nature and are intended to refute the claims both of Roman Catholics, who rest the authority of Scripture on the testimony of the church, and of the pagans, who deny the authority of Scripture. Thus, the "Papists demonstrate Scripture to be God's word" by "the testimony of the Church" and specifically the testimony of those

[233]Leigh, *Treatise,* I.ii (p. 21).

[234]Leigh, *Treatise,* I.ii (pp. 21–22); cf. Ursinus, *Explicationes catecheseos,* in *Opera,* I, col. 50 (Williard, p. 8); Rollock, *Treatise of Effectual Calling,* p. 71.

[235]Leigh, *Treatise,* I.II (p. 22).

[236]Weemes, *Exercitations Divine,* p. 84.

[237]Pictet, *Theol. chr.,* I.vi.15, obs.4; cf. Ussher, *Body of Divinity,* p. 10.

[238]Pictet, *Theol. chr.,* I.vi.16.

who have preserved the faith "by continued succession from the Apostles unto our times," that is to say, the popes. "These men will have the Church the judge and interpreter of all Scriptures, from whose judgment it may not be lawful for any man to depart for an appeal to any other judge." The voice of God in the church, according to the papists, is God's primary voice—and it sheds light on Scripture "not only in respect of us, but also in respect of the Scripture itself."[239] Against this claim of the "lying papistical synagogue," Rollock writes, "the voice of the Church is but as the voice of the handmaid, or as the voice of a crier, which is to publish and to proclaim that voice of God, full of excellency, speaking in the Scripture." The Word or Scripture that is expressed "in the heart of the Church" can only be a reflection of the written Word of God. Even so, the true church depends for its existence and its truth on the Scriptures.[240]

Following the apologetic pattern inaugurated by de Mornay's *De veritate religione christianae* Mastricht does not confine his polemic in the *locus de Scriptura sacra* to the defense of *sola Scriptura* against Christian adversaries. Mastricht also faces the problem of the Koran. Could it be true that Scripture is a partial or corrupt revelation that needs to be succeeded by the Koran? Is Mohammed a true prophet? Is the Koran true revelation, true Scripture? Mastricht also questions whether the Talmud is Scripture and the Cabala divine revelation.[241] In answer to the questions concerning the Koran, Mastricht comments that the Psalms frequently state the perfection of the law of God (Ps. 19:8), the damning imperfection of human doctrines (Matt. 15:9). Nothing, adds Mastricht, can be added to the gospel.[242] Beyond this, Mohammed was no true prophet: he revealed no mysteries of God, prophesied no future events, and worked no miracles. The mode of revelation claimed by Mohammed, moreover, is altogether different from the mode of scriptural revelation: He claimed no inspiration in writing but a visitation from the angel Gabriel. Finally, the morality of this revelation is suspect and it so frequently contradicts Scripture that it must be false.[243]

As for the Talmud and the question of its divine authority—it claims to be the oral tradition of interpretation of the law, but it hardly can be either of Mosaic or divine origin or authority, since in

---

[239]Rollock, *Treatise of Effectual Calling*, pp. 74–75.
[240]Rollock, *Treatise of Effectual Calling*, pp. 74–75.
[241]Mastricht, *Theoretico-practica theol.*, I.ii.24–27.
[242]Mastricht, *Theoretico-practica theol.*, I.ii.24.
[243]Mastricht, *Theoretico-practica theol.*, I.ii.25–26.

both its forms, the Jerusalem and the Babylonian Talmud, it exhibits not the characteristics of divine law but of scholarly disputation. The Talmud is a record of the teachings and arguments of the Jewish teachers and schools—of Hillel and Shammai. Nor do the Jews claim that the authors of the Talmud or the Mishnah were divinely inspired. Finally, the Talmud contains many things that are "false, perverse, and injurious to God, man and truth."[244] Similarly, the Cabala, which claims to be a universal oral law and to contain the mystical meaning of the Scriptures, cannot be of divine authority because of the falsehood and impiety of its rules, because even according to the Jews it rests on Scripture and is not *autopistos*.[245]

The great controversy with Judaism, however, is not so much over the Talmud and the Cabala as over the New Testament and "whether it is *theopneuston,* of an infallible truth and divine authority, equivalent to the Old Testament."[246] The question is complicated, Mastricht notes, by the Anabaptists who hold the abrogation of the Old Testament and declare that we are no longer under the law and by the Socinians who depreciate the Old Testament and claim an essential difference between its religion and that of the New Testament. The Reformed, however, declare against all these adversaries that the Old and the New Testaments possess "the same truth and authority."[247] This appears, according to Mastricht, from the fact that the very arguments used by the Jews to prove the truth of the Old Testament apply also to the New—in particular the argument that the accuracy of the narratives demonstrates the Scriptures to be characterized by *axiopistia,* worthiness for faith.

Nevertheless, like Calvin, the Reformed orthodox assume that, for all their persuasiveness, these arguments cannot fully prove the divinity of the Scripture:

> None of these arguments can undoubtedly persuade the heart *certitudine fidei,* that the holy Scripture, or any doctrine contained in it is the word of God, till we be taught it of God, till the holy Spirit of God have inwardly certified and assured us of it. This is called the Sealing of the Spirit of God, Ephes. 1.13. by this the Scripture is imprinted in our hearts as the sign of the Seal in the Way. Other arguments may convince, but this is absolutely necessary; this is alsufficient to persuade certainly, Matth. 11.25. The Holy Ghost is

---

[244]Mastricht, *Theoretico-practica theol.,* I.ii.28.
[245]Mastricht, *Theoretico-practica theol.,* I.ii.29.
[246]Mastricht, *Theoretico-practica theol.,* I.ii.30.
[247]Mastricht, *Theoretico-practica theol.,* I.ii.30.

the author of light, by which we understand the Scripture, and the persuader of the heart, by which we believe the things therein to be truly divine, 1 John 5.6. It is the Spirit that beareth witness, because the Spirit, (i.e. metonymically the doctrine delivered by the Spirit) is truth. So to prove that there is a God, reasons may be brought from nature and the testimony of the Church, but no man can believe it savingly but by the Holy Ghost.[248]

Pictet, like many of the orthodox, similarly sums up his list of evidences with the comment,

> we have proved the Scripture to be divine and to have various marks of divinity, and, consequently, to be authentic and to have its authority from no source beyond itself. However, we must not imagine that even these marks can be clearly understood, without the aid of Him who impressed them on the Scripture, and who is the author of Scripture, namely the Holy Spirit.[249]

Pictet observes that the marks of divinity in Scripture are so sure and its authenticity so certain that a person whose thoughts were pure would readily accept its authority; our sinfulness, however, stands in the way of such acceptance. He cites Augustine to the effect that we could not be convinced of the brightness of the sun if our sight were faulty. Even so, our minds are so blinded in spiritual matters that they require the aid of the Spirit to render them attentive, allay the passions, and to enlighten, convince, and convert us to godliness.[250]

---

[248]Leigh, *Treatise,* I.ii (pp. 23–24); cf. Ursinus, *Explicationes catecheseos,* in *Opera,* I, col. 50 (Williard, p. 9); Turretin, *Inst. theol. elencticae,* II.vi.6–7, 13–14; Maccovius, *Loci communes,* ii (pp. 25–26); Owen, *The Divine Original,* in *Works,* vol. 16, pp. 325–29; de Moor, *Commentarius perpetuus in Joh. Marckii compendium,* II.xxiv (I, pp. 332–38); contra Rogers and McKim, *Inspiration and Authority,* pp. 182, 186, 188, 220–21; specifically, they note that Turretin "omitted reference to the internal witness of the Spirit in developing the authority of Scripture" (p. 188) and held that the Spirit's work was primarily to enable people "to come to intellectual clarity about what the Bible said" (p. 182). Note that the references to the *testimonium internum Spiritus Sancti* cited above from Turretin are found in his discussion of how the authority of Scripture is known and that Turretin emphasizes the efficacy of the Spirit upon the human *"heart."* Turretin directly echoes Calvin in his statement that "the Spirit working in the hearts of the faithful, testifies that the teaching bestowed on the Evangelists by the Spirit is true and divine" (Turretin, *Inst. theol. elencticae,* II.vi.13; cf. Calvin, *Institutes,* I.vii.4, and idem, *Commentaries on the Second Epistle to Timothy,* 2 Tim. 3:16 [CTS, p. 249]).

[249]Pictet, *Theol. chr.,* I.x.1; cf. Ussher, *Body of Divinity,* pp. 11–12.

[250]Pictet, *Theol. chr.,* I.x.2.

The Spirit can lead a person into a godly life by means of the Scriptures, thus convincing him of their divinity, even though he may not discern all the marks of divinity there present. Knowledge, discernment, and power of expression are not the necessary marks of the true believer, only assent to the divine truth given in Scripture.[251] This final recourse to the Spirit remains even in that most rational of the late orthodox, Wyttenbach, who concludes that the evidences of divinity, despite their clarity and surety, can produce nothing more than *fides humana;* for *fides divina,* a divine and saving faith, to arise the inward testimony of the Spirit is necessary.[252] We have, therefore, not come very far from the view of Calvin and his contemporaries. The various arguments, intrinsic and extrinsic, for the divinity of Scripture have been set forth at far greater length by the scholastics than by the Reformers, but the caveat remains—argument alone will not suffice as proof of divinity and authenticity or for the final establishment of authority.

Whereas the Protestant orthodox manifest broad agreement in their definition and discussion of the themes of the intrinsic and extrinsic works of the authority of Scripture and of the authenticity of the text, they differ over the order and arrangement of these issues in discussion. Turretin and de Moor, for polemical as well as purely doctrinal reasons, take a more objectivist approach by dealing first with the grounds of biblical authority in the intrinsic and extrinsic indications of the authenticity of Scripture and arriving, only secondarily, at the discussion of the subjective apprehension of the authority of Scripture through the testimony of the Spirit.[253] Heidegger, however, approaches the authority of the text, like its inspiration, as a matter of doctrinal assent. He declares emphatically that the marks or *indicia* of the divinity of Scripture, like the light of the sun, are of no avail unless the eyes are opened and that, in the case of the authority of Scripture, the eyes of faith are opened not by empirical argument but by the Spirit.[254]

Each of these writers attempts to balance the objective authority of Scripture against the necessary work of the Spirit convincing the hearer or reader and against the work of the church conveying,

[251]Pictet, *Theol. chr.,* I.x.2.

[252]Wyttenbach, *Tentamen theologiae dogmaticae,* II, §130.

[253]Cf. Turretin, *Inst. theol.,* II.iv.3–6, with ibid., II.vi.6–9, 15; and note de Moor, *Commentarius perpetuus in Joh. Marckii compendium,* II.vi–xxiii (on the authority and authenticity of Scripture), xxiv (on the internal testimony of the Spirit).

[254]Heidegger, *Corpus theol.,* II.xii–xv.

preserving, and providing the text for the use of believers. Turretin, for example, indicates three causal grounds of the authority of Scripture, "the objective, the efficient and the instrumental or organic." There is, therefore, a threefold argument for the divinity of the text that begins with the objective argument offering the basis of "why and according to what" Scripture may be believed to be divine. This argument deals with the marks of divinity *(notae)* in the text. Next, there is the question concerning the efficient cause by which one is led to this belief—and this is the work of the Spirit leading a person to faith. Finally, there is the issue of the instrument or means by which this belief becomes possible, which is the church that bears and delivers the Scripture to believers.[255] Turretin thus sets forth the objective warrants for the authority of Scripture distinct, but not separate from the subjective ground for the discernment of those warrants, giving some writers the impression (a false one, even on the ground of his own theological presuppositions) that the *indicia* or *notae* stand independently as a ground of faith—as if the original-language texts *quoad res et quoad verba* and the various versions *quoad res* could be considered the authoritative Word of God prior to and apart from any personal apprehension.[256] The various intrinsic and extrinsic arguments for the authenticity and authority of Scripture, therefore, are useful primarily to the faithful and serve to reinforce faith rather than to demonstrate, apologetically, the authority of Scripture. Nonetheless, the intrinsic and extrinsic authority of Scripture is a matter of fact—of identifiable effect—not merely of opinion. In other words, the authority is objectively grounded but subjectively apprehended. The nature of this subjective apprehension, moreover, as determined by faith rather than by reason, creates a certain tension in the orthodox doctrine. Turretin, writing at the height of orthodoxy, attempts to resolve this tension by arguing three kinds of certainty: mathematical or metaphysical, moral, and theological, with the latter being grounded on faith.[257]

In the decline of orthodoxy, Venema seems to have given up the point. He assumes the authority of Scripture and maintains the intrinsic and extrinsic arguments at considerable length, but he recognizes that the third kind of certainty, the theological, cannot be argued of the tangible, external sources themselves, granting the

---

[255]Turretin, *Inst. theol.,* II.vi.6; cf. Burmann, *Synopsis,* I.iv.17.

[256]Cf. Rogers and McKim, *Interpretation and Authority of Scripture,* pp. 175–88.

[257]Turretin, *Inst. theol. elencticae,* II.iv.22; cf. *PRRD,* I, pp. 208–10.

inward and spiritual nature of the certainty of faith. He therefore argues,

> The proof which we adduce is not *mathematical,* but *moral,* which is such that, though it be sufficient to demonstrate the truth, when no opposition or prejudice exists against the truth, it does not at the same time force conviction upon a man, or compel him to receive the truth, but leaves him at liberty to assent to it or not. This kind of proof is sufficient for producing conviction. It does not infringe on man's liberty, for it does not extort assent, it does not compel him to the pursuit of virtue against his will.[258]

Such arguments cannot be "admitted in establishing the divinity of Scripture"; rather, they produce "conviction" in the heart of one disposed already to the truth of Christianity. When it is argued that the divinity of Scripture cannot be proved, Venema concludes, the argument is correct with reference to mathematical or rational proof that, by its nature "compels assent" but not with reference to the moral argument.[259]

Three points can be made concerning Venema's argument. First, we sense here the positive relationship that existed between Reformed federalism and pietism. Venema has taken seriously the Reformed argument that theology does not rest on rational evidence and has merged it with the more subjective tendency of pietism so as to make theological and moral conviction virtually indistinguishable. Second, he points directly toward the Kantian reduction of theology to ethics—which itself had roots in German pietism. Venema had allowed reason to attain the status of *principium cognoscendi theologiae*[260] alongside of Scripture and, in the light of this alliance of philosophy and theology, had set aside without argument the earlier concept of a distinctive theological certainty. Presumably the certainty of reason now reinforced the moral conviction of the text of Scripture. With the Kantian assault on rational metaphysics, only the moral conviction would be left to theology. Third, the critical atmosphere of the day, specifically the rational, historical address to the text of Scripture from the time of Semler onward, had rendered the so-called evidences of the divinity of Scripture empirically uncertain. Venema's recourse was not to

---

[258]Venema, *Institutes,* III (p. 47).
[259]Venema, *Institutes,* III (p. 47).
[260]Cf. Venema, *Institutes,* prolegomena (p. 8), with the discussion in *PRRD,* I, pp. 242, 305–8.

introduce a new empiricism but to retreat from the objectivizing model of the older orthodoxy. The doctrine, in its original form, could not survive the great shift in hermeneutics.

When skeptical or critical reason was applied to the *indicia,* these marks of divinity became vulnerable and fell away, as well the Protestant orthodox recognized. In the absence of faith and the Holy Spirit, the *principium* and *testimonium internum,* the *indicia* did not appear. We see the problem illustrated starkly in the late eighteenth century in Thomas Paine's *The Age of Reason.* Paine's work is useful because it is the synthesis of a century of critique, the popular distillate of the Enlightenment assault on fideistic orthodoxy. What had appeared as a hesitant and sometimes veiled criticism at the beginning of the century appears in the full light of day at the end. Moreover, inasmuch as British deism was the foundation not only of the critical method in England but also on the Continent,[261] Paine's late eighteenth-century deism is quite representative.

4.4 Faith and the Scriptural *principium*

The declaration of the prior authority of Scripture and its dogmatic corollary, the identification of Scripture as *principium cognoscendi theologiae,* occurred in close relation to the Reformers' and the Protestant orthodox theologians' affirmation of salvation by grace alone through faith. The saving message of God's revelation in Scripture could be appropriated directly by faith either hearing or reading the words of the gospel—apart from the mediation or intervention of the church and its sacramental system. It was not without justice, therefore, that the theologians and historians of the nineteenth century spoke of two basic principles of the teaching of the Reformation, the formal principle or Scripture, and the material principle or justification through faith, although both the rootage of the formula in the Reformation and its theological usefulness were questioned, most notably by Carl Beck and Albrecht Ritschl.[262]

The problem that Beck and Ritschl saw was that the actual

---

[261]Cf. Reventlow, *Authority of the Bible,* pp. 411–13.

[262]Cf. Heppe, *Geschichte des deutschen Protestantismus,* I, pp. 25–32; Dorner, *History,* I, pp. 220–64; Schaff, *History,* VII, pp. 16–26, adding a third principle, the social or ecclesiastical; Albrecht Ritschl, "Über die beiden Principien des Protestantismus," in *Zeitschrift für Kirchengeschichte* 1 (1876): 397–413; Karl Stange, "A Ritschls Urteil über die beiden Principien des Protestantismus," in *Theologische Studien und Kritiken* (1897):599–621; and O. Ritschl, *Dogmengeschichte,* I, pp. 42–64.

formula concerning a material and a formal principle could not be traced back any farther than the end of the seventeenth century—to the scholastic systems of Johann Wilhelm Baier and David Hollaz— and even there the formula was present only in germ or by implication and not in a direct statement.[263] The formula arose, Ritschl argued, out of the conflict between rationalism and positivistic orthodoxy in the eighteenth century and became more or less of a truism concerning the Reformation and its doctrines by the beginning of the nineteenth century.

As a perusal of Heppe's discussion of the formal and material principles shows,[264] there is an intimate, genetic relationship between this aspect of the nineteenth-century approach to the Reformation and orthodoxy and the development of the central dogma theory. Heppe, even before the appearance of Schweizer's *Die protestantischen Centraldogmen,* noted that the Lutheran and the Reformed traditions were in agreement in their affirmation of the material and formal principles of the Reformation, but that the Reformed tended to develop and to systematize the principles further than the Lutherans. On the one hand, the Reformed brought the formal or scriptural principle to confessional and dogmatic completion as an independent theological *locus* before the Lutherans did; and on the other, the Reformed drew out the logic of the material principle of justification through faith by grace alone into a strict doctrine of predestination, replacing the original material principle with its dogmatic rationalization. The result of this development is the creation of two central dogmas. The original material principle, justification, became the central dogma of Lutheranism, and the rationalized material principle, predestination, became the central dogma of Reformed theology.

If we cannot follow Heppe and his contemporaries in drawing this conclusion, it is nonetheless clear in the dogmatics of post-Reformation Protestantism that the scriptural *principium,* understood as an external, objective foundation for doctrine, stood in a close and necessary relationship to an internal, subjective foundation—faith as generated by the Word, by the *verbum internum* or *testimonium internum Spiritus Sancti.* Thus, in passing from his prolegomena on theology and Scripture to his doctrine of God, Mastricht saw fit to

---

[263]Ritschl, "Über die beiden Principien des Protestantismus," p. 600.

[264]Cf. Heppe, *Geschichte des deutschen Protestantismus,* I, pp. 25–32, with idem, "Der Charakter der deutsch-reformirten Kirche und das Verhältniss derselben zum Luthertum und zum Calvinismus," in *Theologische Studien und Kritiken* (1850):669–706.

make the transition via a discussion of saving faith.[265] His approach
is very nearly unique among the scholastic Protestant systems of the
seventeenth century, although it certainly has roots in the more catechetical models for system followed by the Reformers;[266] and it
reflects the Ramist division of theological system, also characteristic
of the early orthodox era, into the doctrines of faith and the doctrines
of obedience. Ames in particular moves from his definition of theology to his doctrine of God by way of faith. God is not only the
essential foundation of theology—God is also the ultimate object of
faith.[267] The use of a *locus de fide* as a point of transition from
prolegomena to the body of doctrine proper is also found in Witsius'
lectures on the Creed where, once again, the catechetical model
itself raises the issue of faith.[268]

Mastricht not only maintained a strong respect for the basic
Ramist division of theology into the doctrines concerning the faith
and the doctrines concerning obedience—a division that he received
from William Ames—he also held that the logical movement from
the doctrine of Scripture to the doctrine of God was impossible apart
from saving faith. The doctrine of God, he writes, in direct reliance
on Ames, must follow the *locus de fide salvifica* since God is the
obiectum primarium of faith, to whom we are drawn by Christ.[269]
By thus interposing the question of faith between the discussions of
Scripture and God, Mastricht reinforces the subjective emphasis of
his Ramist or Amesian definition of theology: theology as the *scientia* of living blessedly forever or of living before God. He also
echoes, although probably unconsciously, the model presented early
in the development of Reformed theology in Bullinger's *Decades*.

In moving from a catechetical toward a systematic model,
Bullinger had looked for a way to connect his discussion of Scripture as foundation of Christian teaching to his formal exposition

---

[265]Mastricht, *Theoretico-practica theol.*, II.i.

[266]E.g., Bullinger, *Decades*, I.iv (p. 93).

[267]Cf. Ames, *Medulla theologica*, I.iii, with Maccovius' identification of
God as the principal cause of our acquisition of theology and "diligent meditation on the divine Word" as the second or adjunctive cause in *Loci communes*, I
(p. 3).

[268]Cf. Mastricht, *Theoretico-practica theol.*, II.i.1, with Witsius, *Exercitationes*, I.ii; this particular orthodox model, most probably learned from
Mastricht, is also found in Louis Berkhof's *Introduction to Systematic Theology*
(Grand Rapids: Eerdmans, 1932; repr. Grand Rapids: Baker Book House,
1979), pp. 170–185.

[269]Mastricht, *Theoretico-practica theol.*, II.i.14–15.

of that teaching, beginning with sermons on the Creed and the Decalogue. That connecting link was the doctrine of faith, offered, in catechetical order, by the *credo* itself. It is faith by which believers apprehend the truths contained in God's Word and move from the Word to the God who uttered it. "God ... and the word of God is the object or foundation of true faith."[270]

In good scholastic fashion, Bullinger notes that there are several meanings that can be given to the term, "faith" or "belief." First, the term can mean "any kind of religion or honor done to God," as, Bullinger adds, "the Christian faith, the Jewish faith, the Turkish faith." In other words, faith can be considered objectively, as the faith that is believed *(fides quae creditur)*, that is, as a body of beliefs. Faith, Bullinger continues, can mean "a conceived opinion about anything that is told to us," even though what is believed is not a basis for hope: "this is that faith whereof St. James says that the devil believes and trembles."[271] In the scholastic definition of faith, this would be *fides historica,* historical faith, belief that a thing is, without any faithful apprehension of a saving truth.

Finally, in the positive sense given to the word in Scripture, "faith is commonly put for an assured and undoubted confidence in God and his word." The Hebrew word for faith, comments Bullinger, derives from a root that indicates "truth, certainty and assured constancy." In Latin, faith indicates, as Cicero had taught, a doing of what has been said *(fides, quod fiat, quod dicitur)*. Bullinger himself defines faith as "an undoubted belief, most firmly grounded in the mind" or "a settled and undoubted persuasion or belief leaning upon God and his word."[272]

Bullinger quotes as his first definition of faith from other sources of opinion the Epistle to the Hebrews: "Faith is the substance of things hoped for, the evidence of things not seen." This substance, in the original "hypostasis" is the *fundamentum* "which upholdeth us, and whereon we lean and lie without peril or danger."[273]

> touching the mysteries of God revealed in God's word, in themselves, or in their own nature, they cannot be seen with bodily eyes; and therefore are called things not seen. But this faith, by giving light to the mind, doth in the heart perceive them, even as they are set forth in the word of God. Faith, therefore, according to

[270]Bullinger, *Decades,* I.iv (p. 93).
[271]Bullinger, *Decades,* I.iv (p. 81).
[272]Bullinger, *Decades,* I.iv (pp. 81–82), citing Cicero, *De officiis,* I.vii.
[273]Bullinger, *Decades,* I.iv (p. 82).

the definition of St. Paul, is in the mind a most evident seeing, and in the heart a most certain perceiving of things invisible, that is, of things eternal; of God, I say, and all those things which he in his word setteth forth unto us concerning spiritual things.[274]

Bullinger next supports his interpretation of Paul by quotations from "another godly and learned man"—probably Calvin—and then cites yet another author, identified by the editor of the Parker Society edition of the *Decades* as Johann Gropper (1502–1559).[275]

These definitions enable Bullinger to define faith still more clearly as a heavenly *donum infusum:*

Faith is a gift of God, poured into man from heaven, whereby he is taught with an undoubted persuasion wholly to lean on God and his word; in which word God doth freely promise life and all good things in Christ, and wherein all truth necessary to be believed is plainly declared.[276]

Bullinger elucidates this definition: it indicates, first that the "cause or beginning of faith" is not in man but is God's gift, given by the inspiration of the Spirit who enables the heart to be faithful. God is "the well-spring and cause of all goodness." In several places Christ shows God to be the source of faith (John 6:44; Matt. 16:17).[277]

And yet we have to consider here, that God, in giving and inspiring faith, doth not use his absolute power, or miracles, in working, but a certain ordinary means agreeable to man's capacity: although he can indeed give faith without those means, to whom, when, and how it pleaseth him.... Whom he meaneth to bestow knowledge and faith on, to them he sendeth teachers, by the word of God to preach true faith unto them. Not because it lieth in man's power, will, or ministry, to give faith; nor because the outward word spoken by man's mouth is able of itself to bring faith: but the voice of man, and the preaching of God's word, do teach us what true faith is, or what God doth will and command us to believe. God himself alone, by sending his Holy Spirit into the hearts and minds of men, doth open our hearts, persuade our minds, and cause us

---

[274]Bullinger, *Decades,* I.iv (p. 82).

[275]Bullinger, *Decades,* I.iv (p. 83). The citation from Gropper's *Enchiridion* and *Institutio catholica,* if indeed it is from Gropper, is curious since Gropper was an Erasmian reformer who, after 1542, turned against the cause of reform.

[276]Bullinger, *Decades,* I.iv (p. 84).

[277]Bullinger, *Decades,* I.iv (p. 84).

with all our hearts to believe that which we by his word and teaching have learned to believe.[278]

Although Bullinger recognizes this established pattern for the working of faith in man, he realizes also that the fact of divine causality ought not to diminish our own personal zeal for faith:

> in hearing the word of God, we must pray for the gift of faith, that the Lord may open our hearts, convert our souls, break and beat down the hardness of our minds, and increase the measure of faith bestowed upon us.... true faith is the mere gift of God, which is by the Holy Spirit from heaven bestowed upon our minds, and is declared unto us in the word of truth by teachers sent of God, and is obtained by earnest prayers which cannot be tired.[279]

The result of faith must be "an undoubted persuasion": even though "the spot of original sin" that is in all of us does not fail to cloud faith or bring misgivings, ultimately "faith yieldeth not to temptation, neither is drowned nor sticketh in the mire of staggering; but, laying hold upon the promised word of truth, getteth up again by struggling, and is confirmed."[280] Nor does this faith accept "every great and impossible thing": "For faith is ruled and bound by the word of God; by the word of God ... rightly understood." Faith accepts only what God has truly revealed and promised.[281] "God, therefore, and the word of God, is the object or foundation of true faith."[282]

Although he does not develop a formal and structural relationship between faith and Scripture in his *Institutes,* Calvin does point toward a theological and, indeed, a profound religious relationship between faith and Scripture. This relationship, Calvin argues, is "permanent" and can no more be dissolved "than we could separate the rays from the sun from which they come."[283] The Word is the foundation of faith: if the Word is taken away, faith too will depart inasmuch as God "always represents himself through his Word to those whom he wills to draw to himself."[284] Nonetheless, Calvin recognizes a reciprocity between Word and faith. Not every word

---

[278]Bullinger, *Decades,* I.iv (pp. 84–85).
[279]Bullinger, *Decades,* I.iv (p. 87).
[280]Bullinger, *Decades,* I.iv (pp. 88–89).
[281]Bullinger, *Decades,* I.iv (pp. 90–91).
[282]Bullinger, *Decades,* I.iv (p. 93).
[283]Calvin, *Institutes,* III.ii.6.
[284]Calvin, *Institutes,* III.ii.6.

from God engenders faith. "God's word to Adam ... 'you shall surely die'" was not the cause of faith in Adam—rather faith is "founded upon the truth of the freely given promise in Christ, both revealed to our minds and sealed upon our hearts through the Holy Spirit" and this faith, regarded as "a preconceived conviction of God's truth" in turn receives the revelation in Scripture as authoritative.[285] What Calvin identifies as the inwardly authenticating witness of the Spirit in his basic exposition of the doctrine of Scripture,[286] he conjoins to his doctrine of faith when he outlines the relationship of faith to the Word. Calvin recognizes, in other words, the need to identify not only the objective authority of the Word and the testimony of the Spirit but also the human capacity to receive the Word as authoritative. That capacity is the graciously given capacity of faith.

A model similar to that of Bullinger is followed in the *Heidelberg Catechism* and, therefore, in Ursinus' catechetical lectures, albeit without the close association of a fully developed doctrine of Scripture with the credal articles. The catechism links the questions on the gospel (qq. 19–20) to the questions on the creed (qq. 22–58) with a question on faith (q. 21). The logic of the catechism is that the gospel promise of salvation is made available to all who are "ingrafted" into Christ "and receive all his benefits by a true faith." The answer to question 20 thus introduces the topic of faith—and the discussion of faith indicates that some truths about God must be known and believed. The catechism can then continue in question 22 by introducing the creed with the words, "What is then necessary for a Christian to believe."

In the high orthodox era, Mastricht denoted three meanings of the term "faith": first the *habitus* by which we believe or *fides qua;* second the *obiectum* in which we believe; and third the body of belief or *fides quam credimus.*[287] Saving faith, he continues, is nothing other than the *actus totius animae rationalis,* which God accepts as its highest end and because of which Christ, as the sole Mediator, communicates all his benefits.[288] Taken in its parts, faith could indicate *nudus assensus* or *fides historica,* but in larger theological sense *fides salvifica* indicates the "act of faith that is required for salvation" in which knowledge, assent, and faithful apprehension

---

[285]Cf. Calvin, *Institutes,* III.ii.6–7 with III.ii.21.
[286]Calvin, *Institutes,* I.vii.1, 4–5.
[287]Mastricht, *Theoretico-practica theol.,* II.i.1.
[288]Mastricht, *Theoretico-practica theol.,* II.i.3.

of God's truth conjoin.[289] Faith is thus an *actus* accepting God as the end *(finis)* and Christ as the Mediator—an act of the intellect, the will, and the affections.[290]

In the intellect faith means knowledge *(notitia)* of the promises of the gospel coupled with assent to the truth of these promises. Assent, moreover, must be explicit, not implicit, and be given to "the fundamental dogmas, especially to the promises of the Gospel: without which there no one could receive God or Christ." This proposition must above all be accepted, "Christ, is the Messiah promised of old, outside of whom, no hope of salvation remains." Finally, this assent cannot simply be a theoretical acceptance: "nor does a theoretical knowledge and assent suffice; rather, a practical [knowledge and assent is necessary], which brings about conviction and moves the will."[291] Thus, the will enters as profession of this faith and the affections are enjoyed in the love of God, the desire to participate in his promises, the praise of God, and the hate of all things contrary to his will.[292]

Receiving Christ and believing the gospel savingly are synonymous.[293] Therefore the object of theology in general is the *universum Dei verbum* and specifically Christ, *ipse Deus & Mediator,* the *theanthropos.*[294] This argument, which Mastricht relates to the sinful character of man, draws on both the *duplex cognitio Dei* and the view of theology as conformed to the nature of its subject found in the prolegomena, *theologia hominibus communicata* as *theologia revelata in subiecto post lapsum.* No man comes to the Father but by Christ, argues Mastricht, citing John 14:6—the first and highest object of faith is God, from whence comes the phrase so frequently seen in Scripture, *credere in Deum.* But the subordinate and secondary object is Christ the Mediator through whom we are enabled to believe in God. Thus we believe in God as the goal *(qua finis)* and in Christ as the means or mediator *(qua medium, aut Mediator).*[295]

Mastricht now proceeds in brief to set forth the *ordo salutis:* justification, adoption, sanctification, glorification, the end and fruit

---

[289]Mastricht, *Theoretico-practica theol.,* II.i.5.
[290]Mastricht, *Theoretico-practica theol.,* II.i.8–10.
[291]Mastricht, *Theoretico-practica theol.,* II.i.8.
[292]Mastricht, *Theoretico-practica theol.,* II.i.9–10.
[293]Mastricht, *Theoretico-practica theol.,* II.i.11.
[294]Mastricht, *Theoretico-practica theol.,* II.i.12, 14.
[295]Mastricht, *Theoretico-practica theol.,* II.i.15.

of which is union and communion with Christ.[296] He follows this by describing the various levels of faith as it moves from initial knowledge of Christ and the moment of regeneration, to assent and conversion, to acceptance of and submission to its truth in sanctification.[297] He will need to treat these topics at more length later on in his sixth book, *de redemptionis applicatiore,* but here they provide a sense of the purpose of the system and of the great difficulty in selecting a point of departure for discussion of doctrine.

This powerful sense of the central issue of faith as Christ and, considered individually or personally, the acceptance of Christ, was clearly linked by the Protestant orthodox to their sense of Christ as the center and "foundation" or "scope" of Scripture. John Baillie long ago recognized—at least in the case of the Puritan theologian, John Flavel—that this seventeenth-century conception of faith was hardly subject to the censures pressed by neo-orthodoxy generally and by Brunner in particular. He notes at length Brunner's claim that post-Reformation Protestantism moved away from the Reformers' conception of faith as "obedient trust" and revelation as "God's action in Jesus Christ" to an overly intellectualized sense of faith as acceptance of revealed doctrine.[298] Flavel, like other Reformed and Puritan writers of his time had asked rather pointedly the question of the "essence" or center of faith. He noted that "the Papists generally give the essence of saving faith to ... assent,"[299] and thereby recognized as problematic the very point of doctrine alleged by Brunner against older Protestantism. And he concluded that

> acceptance, which saith, I take Christ in all his offices to be mine, this fits it exactly, and belongs to all true believers, and to none but true believers, and to all true believers at all times. This therefore must be the justifying and saving act of faith.... By saving faith, Christ is said to dwell in our hearts.[300]

The point not only echoes precisely the language of the Reformers, most notably, Calvin, it also stands as quite typical of orthodoxy, whether of the English Puritan or of the continental variety.

---

[296]Mastricht, *Theoretico-practica theol.,* II.i.19.

[297]Mastricht, *Theoretico-practica theol.,* II.i.20–21.

[298]Baillie, *Idea of Revelation,* p. 97, citing Brunner, *Offenbarung und Vernunft,* pp. 10–11 (cf. Brunner, *Revelation and Reason,* pp. 10–11).

[299]Flavel, *The Method of Grace,* in *Works,* II:114.

[300]Flavel, *The Method of Grace,* in *Works,* vol. 2, p. 115.

As a concluding section to the final and practical part of his *locus de fide salvifica,* Mastricht presses four conclusions on his readers. First, study for the sake of increasing the faith is not the equal of faith itself but is only a means by which faith is strengthened. Study belongs to the practice of religion by those already persuaded of its truth. Second, exploration of the faith is not in itself saving, but presumes the power of God keeping us in faith unto salvation: Mastricht cites 1 Peter 1:5, 7. Third, we must be wary of obstacles to faith—be they errors concerning the nature of faith or the fullness of our persuasion, weaknesses or laziness of faith, perturbations of conscience over sins, or momentary spiritual lapses. Fourth, having understood the preceding, we may proceed to the well-conceived study of our faith, its arrangement, conservation, augmentation, and appropriation.[301]

> In saving faith, by which we desire and receive God, even as our highest end, it is altogether necessary that we be persuaded 1. that God is 2. that he is of such a kind that, for himself and for us, he perfectly suffices. Who 3. this his sufficiency, can and will communicate to us, by his efficiency or operations. And that this all-sufficiency of God leads to two conclusions: first concerning the essence of God and his essential perfections and second concerning his subsistence and persons, seeing that from the love of the Father, the grace of the Son, and the communion of the Holy Spirit all good redounds to us, 2 Cor. xiii.14. All the things concerning God, thus, flow forth from four topics. 1. of the existence and knowledge of God. 2. of his essence, names and essential attributes. 3. of his subsistence and persons. 4. of the efficiency and works of God.[302]

Thus does saving faith relate to the body of doctrine. As the fundamental scriptural text for this *locus,* Mastricht cites Hebrews 11:6, "for he that cometh to God must believe that he is, and that he is a rewarder of them that diligently seek him."[303]

Mastricht's insight into the faith that moves the mind from the *principium cognoscendi* to the *principium essendi* is counter-

---

[301]Mastricht, *Theoretico-practica theol.,* II.i.57.

[302]Mastricht, *Theoretico-practica theol.,* II.ii.1.

[303]Mastricht, *Theoretico-practica theol.,* II.ii.1—it is characteristic of Mastricht's exegetical interest that each dogmatic *locus* is prefaced by a scriptural citation, the interpretation of which underlies his doctrinal exposition. In this he echoes the origin of Protestant *loci communes* as exegetical handbooks of doctrine drawing on scriptural *sedes* doctrine.

balanced, however, by the relative brevity of his treatment of that crucial *principium cognoscendi*. The orthodox amplification of the *locus de Deo,* so evident in the *Theoretico-practica theologia* finds no reflection in the development of hermeneutical issues in the *locus de Scriptura sacra.* Indeed, at this juncture (c. 1700–1706) we begin to see in Mastricht's system an adumbration of the decline of prolegomena which would be symptomatic of the Wolffian phase of orthodoxy and would reach its extreme in the theology of Endemann. In the work of the latter the philosophical problem of knowledge of God would dominate to the extent that the *locus de Scriptura* would be displaced from the prolegomena or *principia* to an ancillary position—almost an after-thought—at the conclusion of the system. Much as in Mastricht's dogmatics, a deemphasis on the *principium cognoscendi* as a substantive, hermeneutical element in the preliminary stages of system is seen in the eighteenth-century English scholastic systems of Ridgley and Gill.

The presentation of a principial discussion of faith—not *fides quae* but *fides qua*—raises one of the great issues confronted by but only partially and perhaps not satisfactorily answered in the orthodox systems. Is *fides* a doctrinal issue that needs to be treated in the prolegomena to dogmatics prior to any movement from Scripture as the ground of theologizing to positive theology? Must we discuss faith between the *locus de sacra Scriptura* and the body of the theological system? Is in fact all theology a *theologia regenitorum* and how should system be accommodated to this realization? In the *Decades* Bullinger seems to have felt that a doctrine of faith was the necessary point of transition between Word and exposition of the Word. To the extent that later orthodoxy excluded this issue from its formal prolegomena it may be viewed as creating an atmosphere that, although hardly rationalist in a philosophical sense, was more conducive to the use of philosophical reason in an increasingly principial manner. As Weber rightly saw, orthodoxy was forced by the Hoffmann controversy to decide for or against *fideism.* We cannot follow Weber in viewing the choice as the beginning of rationalism in theology, but it was certainly the point at which Luther's antiphilosophical, *fideistic* stance became formally unacceptable.[304]

[304]Cf. H. E. Weber, *Reformation, Orthodoxie and Rationalismus,* I/2, pp. 268–71, 278–84 with Muller, *"Vera Philosophia,"* pp. 347–51, 361–65.

5

Scripture According to Its Properties

5.1 The Attributes or Properties of Scripture in the Protestant Tradition

Holy Scripture, considered according to its incidental properties, is to be discussed in terms of authority *(authoritas)*, necessity *(necessitas)*, the authentic edition, translation into vernacular languages, privilege of reading *(lectio)*, clarity *(perspicuitas)*, interpretation or exposition, and perfection.[1]

The dogmatic presentation of Scripture according to its attributes or incidental properties (accidents) occupies a central position in the Protestant orthodox doctrine of Scripture. Before we analyze these attributes, some discussion of the rationale behind the dogmatic presentation is in order, particularly insofar as this kind of presentation has become increasingly foreign to modern dogmatic theology and represents a point at which modern theological studies of the Protestant orthodox frequently argue a major breach with the theology of the Reformers. On a very rudimentary level, presentation of the properties of Scripture follows from the standard scholastic pattern of argumentation as given in the questions, *An sit, Quid sit,* and *Qualis sit.* That Scripture exists, no one denies—so discussion can proceed immediately to the question, *Quid sit?*—What is it? This question is answered in the scholastic discussion of Scripture

[1]Polanus, *Syntagma,* Synopsis libri I.

313

according to its essence or quiddity.[2] Once the question "What?" is answered, then discussion can proceed to the problem of description, that is, to the question, *Qualis sit?*—Of what sort is it?—which is to say, to the discussion of its properties.

The Protestant orthodox understand these properties of Scripture both formally and analogically. The list of properties indicates, on the one hand, the formal causes of Scripture and, on the other, as a catalogue of formal causes, it presents the marks of the divine architect of the scriptural revelation as they are evidenced in the text. The Protestant scholastics assume, thus, an *analogia entis* comparable to the analogy of the divine being found in the created order but, as indicated by their preliminary discussion of natural and supernatural revelation, a far clearer and surer analogy that, in its clarity and completeness, provides a salvific revelation not available in nature.[3] This analogy draws, of course, directly on the causal argumentation and the description of intrinsic and extrinsic marks of divine authorship discussed in the preceding chapter. The attributes of Scripture have an analogic relationship to some of the communicable attributes of God, because God is the cause or author of Scripture.

This view of the attributes of Scripture was certainly not part of an attempt on the part of the orthodox to divinize the text, any more than the claim that some of the divine attributes are known by analogy in nature was an attempt to divinize nature. Admittedly, the concept of "attributes of Scripture" could be carried to an extreme—to the point, indeed, of imparting an otherworldly, docetic character to Scripture and to the point of removing all finite, human qualities of the text from consideration. While this may have been a tendency of some of the orthodox polemic against both Roman Catholic and rationalistic adversaries, it was certainly not the intention of the positive statement of doctrine by the Protestant orthodox. The analogical identification of divine handiwork in the attributes of Scripture both establishes the likeness and recognizes the unlikeness of the attributes of Scripture to the attributes of its author. As the orthodox recognized explicitly in their prolegomena to theology, Scripture is a form of ectypal theology reflective of but not identical with the divine archetype.[4] In the context of the polemic with Rome and with the early modern rationalists, deists, and skeptics, this Protestant orthodox emphasis on the attributes of the text appears,

[2]Cf. above, §3.1.
[3]See *PRRD,* I, 5.2–5.3.
[4]Cf. *PRRD,* I, 4.1.

moreover, as an attempt to argue a positive, objective ground for the authority of the text beyond the problems of certainty raised by the *sola Scriptura,* the Protestant emphasis on the individual exegete, and the doctrine of the *testimonium internum Spiritus Sancti.*

The character of this discussion of attributes or properties of Scripture by the Protestant orthodox, moreover, partakes of the dogmatic, one might say "positivistic," approach found in the previous discussion of Scripture according to its essence. Virtually all of the attributes of Scripture noted by the orthodox are taken directly from biblical references to the Word of God or to "the Scriptures" as inspired writings—and are never elicited inductively or empirically by examination of the text either in whole or in part in order to determine whether, on rational or evidential grounds, it could be inferred to be authoritative, necessary, perfect, clear, sufficient for salvation, and so forth. As we will see particularly in the discussion of the clarity or perspicuity of the text, these are dogmatic assertions resting both on the prior assumption of divine agency in the writing of Scripture and of the necessity of such a divine work for the offer and effecting of salvation, both of which assumptions were held throughout the Middle Ages and the Reformation and could therefore be taken as a common ground in the argument with Roman Catholics.

In addition, the choice of terms like clarity, perspicuity, simplicity, majesty, and so forth, as attributes of the text reflects the movement and development of rhetorical theory during the sixteenth and seventeenth centuries and the effort of the Protestant orthodox to place Scripture and its language into the context of a rhetorical analysis of the proper mode of communication for the expression of sacred truths. Thus, the common ground of theological assumption about the significance of the text, drawn into a discussion of the technically understood "style" of the text, could, again, serve to undergird the quest for an authoritative ground for theology and, underlying that quest, the demand for certainty beyond the subjective status of the individual exegete possessed of the *testimonium internum Spiritus Sancti.*

The derivation of the attributes of Scripture from scriptural declarations concerning the Word of God is seen in Reformed dogmatics from the time of Calvin and Vermigli onward: "he that would know at more length the properties of Holy Scripture," comments Vermigli,

let him read Psalm 19: they are described there both with marvel-
lous brevity and with great elegance. First, the law of God is called
temima, that is, immaculate and perfect. Second, it is affirmed that
the law restores to soul and that it is not to be discovered in profane learning. Third, it is called a sure testimony of the Lord,
whereas man's counsels are evermore variable and inconstant.[5]

The law of God, moreover, is directed toward both the learned and
the simple—it is plain, clear, and just, having qualities that make the
heart glad. Even so, in its central declarations of the counsel or
covenant of God, Scripture is clear to all and ought to be commended to the "common people."[6] The command of the Lord is
"pure" and "sincerely made," devoid of human deceit and offering
an everlasting salvation beyond the transitory promises of a fallen
world: "the statutes of God endure forever."[7] What is more, the
commendations of the "law" found in the Psalmist's writings "ought
not to be understood as if the other parts of Scripture should be
excluded": "in commending the law," the Psalmist "includes all the
rest of the inspired writings" and intends them to be "the standard of
godliness" for all religion.[8]

The Reformers' views are reflected in the writings of seventeenth-
century exegetes and theologians, like Dickson, Ainsworth, Diodati,
the Westminster annotators, and Poole, who similarly understand the
Psalm 19 as referring to "the whole word of God" or the breadth of
revealed "doctrine" under the term "law,"[9] and as teaching the manner in which "the glory of the Lord" is "declared in his word and
Scripture."[10] Since the "light" of God's Word "is far more necessary
for our blessedness than the sun's light is for our bodies," the
Psalmist commends the Word for its "perfection, efficacy, infalli-

---

[5]Vermigli, *Commonplaces,* I.vi.4; cf. Calvin, *Commentary on the Psalms,*
Ps. 19:7–8, in loc. (CTS, I, pp. 317–20).

[6]Calvin, *Commentary on the Psalms,* Ps. 25:14, in loc. (CTS, I, p. 431).

[7]Vermigli, *Commonplaces,* I.vi.4; cf. Calvin, *Commentary on the Psalms,*
Ps. 19:9, in loc. (CTS, I, pp. 322–23).

[8]Calvin, *Commentary on the Psalms,* Ps. 1:2, in loc. (CTS, I, p. 4).

[9]Poole, *Commentary,* II, p. 29. Note also the comment on Psalm 1:2 in ibid.,
II, p. 1; Annotations upon all the Books of the Old and New Testament (1645),
in loc.: "V.7. The law of the Lord. That is, the word of God: for some effects
following belong to Gods promises. [law] or doctrine."; cf. Ainsworth, *Book of
Psalmes,* pp. 54–55, and note his annotation on Ps. 1:2 (p. 2), where, as with
Poole, "law" is understood as synonymous with "doctrine."

[10]Dickson, *Commentary on the Psalms,* I, p. 94; cf. Poole, *Commentary,* II,
pp. 29–30.

bility, and sundry other properties." From this commendation and from the identification of these specific attributes, believers can receive salutary counsel—and Dickson goes on to list thirteen lessons, reflecting various divinely given properties of the text. Thus, as Psalm 1 teaches, "the blessed man maketh the word of God in holy Scripture, to be his counsellor ... for the Scripture to him, for the obedience of faith, is a law, and that fenced with supreme authority."[11] Henry sums up the interpretation of Psalm 19:7–10 with his comment, "Here are six several titles of the word of God, to take in the whole of divine revelation, precepts and promises, and especially the gospel."[12] As in virtually any other instance of doctrinal application of a text that could be drawn from the writings of the Protestant orthodox, the citation of texts refers the reader of theological system to works of exegesis and, more important, to a tradition of interpretation that undergirded the theological conclusion drawn in the system or "body of divinity." What is more, the superficial discontinuity between the recitation of the attributes of Scripture found in the orthodox systems and the patterns of exposition found in the more systematic works of the Reformers, like Calvin's *Institutes,* is far outweighed by the continuity of the exegetical tradition, reaching back into the Reformation and the Middle Ages, on which the Protestant orthodox drew for their dogmatic formulations.[13]

The orthodox systems differ over the number and the designation of the properties belonging to Scripture and necessary to the achievement of its divinely ordained end. Polanus and Scharpius noted authority, perspicuity, necessity, and perfection,[14] while the high orthodox Riissen is content with three "principal" attributes, authority, perfection, and perspicuity.[15] Riissen here follows Turretin in considering other possible attributes of Scripture—such as its necessity—separately, without formally designating them as *proprietates* or *attributa*.[16] Burmann offers six separate *proprietates,* the

---

[11]Dickson, *Commentary on the Psalms,* I, p. 2 (Ps. 1:2), pp. 94–96 (Ps. 19:7–10).

[12]Henry, *Commentary on the Whole Bible,* II, p. 178; cf. Poole, *Commentary,* II, pp. 29–30; Dickson, *Commentary on the Psalms,* I, pp. 94–96; Diodati, *Pious and Learned Annotations,* in loc.; Tossanus, *Biblia,* II in loc.

[13]See further, below, §7.3.c, on the issue of *dicta probantia*.

[14]Cf. Polanus, *Syntagma* theol, I.xvi, xxxv, xliv, xlvi, with Scharpius, *Cursus theologicus,* col. 8.

[15]Riissen, *Summa theol.,* II.viii.

[16]Cf. Turretin, *Inst. theol.,* II.ii.

necessity, divinity, authority, integrity, perfection and perspicuity of Scripture.[17] Leigh argues seven attributes, arguing that Scripture is

> 1. Of Divine Authority. 2. True and Certain. 3. The rule of faith and manners [i.e., canonical authority]. 4. Necessary. 5. Pure and Holy. 6. Sufficient and Perfect. 7. Perspicuous and Plain.[18]

To these seven, Mastricht adds an eighth, the effectiveness or efficacy of Scripture.[19] Despite these differences in enumeration and classification, the orthodox stand in substantial agreement in their doctrine, with the Reformed and Lutherans virtually duplicating each other's discussions both in broad outline and in detail.[20] The differences, most frequently, appear as differences in organization—with those theologians whose systems contain shorter lists of attributes covering the other dogmatically-identified properties of Scripture either as sub-topics of one of the other attributes or as part of the general identification of the essence or nature of Scripture as the Word of God.

5.2 Truth, Certainty, and Infallibility[21]

a. The Reformers on the Truth, Certainty, and Infallibility of Scripture

The Reformed doctrine of the truth, certainty, and infallibility of Scripture belongs to a complex of statements all intended to explain and argue the authority of the text as above all human authority. The

[17]Burmann, *Synopsis theol.,* I.iii–v, vii, viii, x.

[18]Leigh, *Treatise,* I.viii (p. 130).

[19]Mastricht, *Theoretico-practica theol.,* I.ii.21.

[20]Cf. Schmid, *DTEL,* pp. 50–80, with Baier-Walther, *Compendium,* I: 118–143.

[21]Throughout this chapter, I have used the term "infallibility" rather than the term frequently used in modern conservative or evangelical discussion of Scripture, "inerrancy," because the Reformers and the Protestant orthodox typically use the noun infallibilitas as the attribute of Scripture, indicating that Scripture does not err (non errat). I have not encountered any attempt on their part to construct a noun out of the verb errare. In other words, the usage in this section, as throughout the volume, follows the descriptive and historical intention of the study and arises out of historical and linguistic considerations. Inasmuch as this is a historical study, I leave aside entirely all consideration of the modern debate over infallibility and "inerrancy" and refer to historical essays arising out of that debate only insofar as they are useful to the historical discussion of the doctrine of Scripture in the sixteenth and seventeenth centuries.

question of infallibility, therefore, represents a subsidiary doctrinal aspect of the larger problem of the text and its interpretation within the context of competing authorities—text, tradition, church, and inward witness. Here again, there is a strong continuity in the development of Reformed doctrine, particularly when the breadth of the problem is taken into consideration. We cannot state dogmatically, with Dowey and others, that "there is no hint anywhere in Calvin's writings that the original text contained any flaws at all."[22] Calvin was not in the habit of basing his doctrine of the authority and truth of Scripture on a distinction between error-free *autographa* and later scribal copies; and he does note, scrupulously, all errors in points of fact and all possibilities for emendation of the text. On the other hand, Calvin was certain that God had used the prophets and apostles as his instruments and, by them, had given the church an infallible rule of faith. This doctrine ought not to be seen through the glass of later orthodox attempts to guard the infallibility of the original text against Roman polemical references to historical and textual error. In Calvin's time we are not yet at that point in the controversy. What we have in Calvin's doctrine is the simple assertion of the absolute truth of Scripture, its dictation by the Spirit, and the inward testimony of the Spirit guaranteeing the authority of the written Word. We have, in short, the ground—a bit less rigid, less technical, and less insistent on small detail—of the later doctrine.

Calvin could view not only Scripture but also the humanity of Christ as both a channel or means of revelation and as a limitation and accommodation of divine knowledge to human abilities of perception. He very clearly argued that the language and meaning of Scripture are accommodated to the need and capacity of human beings. On the text of Isaiah 40:12, "Who has measured the waters in the hollow of his hand ... and weighed the mountains in scales, and the hills in a balance," Calvin writes,

> When he names "measures," which are used by men in very small matters, he accommodates himself to our ignorance; for thus does the Lord often prattle with us, and borrow comparisons from matters that are familiar to us, when he speaks of his majesty; that our ignorant and limited minds may better understand his greatness and excellence.[23]

---

[22]Dowey, *Knowledge of God in Calvin's Theology,* p. 100; cf. John Murray, *Calvin on Scripture and Divine Sovereignty* (Grand Rapids: Eerdmans, 1960), p. 11.

[23]Calvin, *Commentary on Isaiah,* in loc. (CTS, III, p. 218).

Calvin, thus, qualifies his language of the truth, certainty, and infallibility of Scripture with his sense of the distance between God and human beings. It is not that Scripture is any less true, less certain, or less infallible—rather its truth, certainty, and infallibility belong to the realm of human rather than divine knowing, and are therefore qualified by the finite character of the forms of revelation.[24]

Bullinger voices an almost identical position, based like Calvin's, on the majesty of God. "Holy Scripture teaches in plain words that God's majesty far exceeds the weakness of our mind," he writes, "wherefore in this life God's majesty can neither be expressed by us with words nor seen with the eyes. We ought therefore to be content with that knowledge of God which is declared to us in Christ by his servants."[25] "And even as God is true of word, and cannot lie, so is his word true and deceiveth no man. In the word of God is expressed the will and mind of God."[26] Thus, the Word of God is unchangeable and immoveable—no human effort can alter it or set it aside. It is a suitable ground for faith. All these points concerning the relationship of word and faith can be reduced to two principles: first, God promises us in his Word eternal life through Christ, which promise true faith receives as its chief article; and second, "that in the word of God there is set down all truth necessary to be believed; and that true faith doth believe all that is declared in the scriptures." This latter follows from the fact that, the word "telleth us, that God is; what manner one he is; what God's works are; what his judgments, his will, his commandments, his promises, and what his threatenings are."[27] Whatever cannot be drawn from Scripture or is contrary to Scripture ought not to be believed, "for the very nature of true faith is, not to believe that which conflicts with the word of God."[28]

Musculus writes of "the truth and the accomplishment of the holy

---

[24]Cf. Martin I. Klauber and Glenn S. Sunshine, "Jean-Alphonse Turrettini on Biblical Accommodation: Calvinist or Socinian?" in *Calvin Theological Journal* 25/1 (1990):9–12; with Ford Lewis Battles, "God Was Accommodating Himself to Human Capacity," in *Interpretation* 31 (1977):19–38; Dirk W. Jellema, "God's 'Baby Talk': Calvin and the 'Errors' of the Bible," in *Reformed Journal* 30 (1970):25–47; and Clinton M. Ashley, "John Calvin's Utilization of the Principle of Accommodation and Its Continuing Significance for an Understanding of Biblical Language" (Ph.D. diss., Southwestern Baptist Theological Seminary, 1972).

[25]Bullinger, *Commonplaces,* II.ii (fol. 34v).

[26]Bullinger, *Decades,* I.iv (p. 93).

[27]Bullinger, *Decades,* I.iv (p. 96).

[28]Bullinger, *Decades,* I.iv (p. 96).

Scriptures." The truth of Scripture, he argues, depends on the truth of God.[29] God can neither lie nor change—and anyone who is persuaded of the truth of God must be convinced of the "certainty and truth of the sayings of God."[30] Of greatest importance in the Scriptures, then, are the narrations, commendations, doctrines, prophecies, promises, and threatenings "and the commandments and forbiddings" which tell us what has been done or will be done by God and communicate his will. Of less importance, though no less true, are reports of fact contained in Scripture. The things told of the works of God and of Christ are of greatest necessity, as the goodness, love, and faithfulness of God and his eternal appointment of Christ to be the savior of those who believe.[31] Musculus emphasizes theologically and soteriologically the importance of recognizing and accepting Scripture and, specifically, its prophecies and promises as true:

> Take away the credit of truth from these things, although they never be so true of themselves, and must be fulfilled of necessity, yet they do not work with unbelievers but to their destruction. Wherefore this is the chief point of our religion, that we do give credit of truth to the holy Scripture, without any manner of doubt, whether it do declare, commend, teach, prophesy, or promise anything to believers, or threaten the unbelieving. Without this fact of truth, there is nothing in our religion that can stand.[32]

As indicated in the introductory chapters, the issue behind these declarations is the issue of certainty—of the foundation and basis for authoritative doctrinal and religious statement and practice. This issue, moreover, remained at the heart of the Protestant orthodox doctrine of Scripture, and the rigidification of formulation or increase in polemical emphasis that may sometimes be noted among the seventeenth-century writers is more a sign of the shifting grounds of polemic and of new hermeneutical and text-critical constraints rather than an indication of an alteration of basic doctrine.

b. The Reformed Orthodox Doctrine of Biblical Infallibility

The affirmation of Scripture's divine authority implies the infallibility of Scripture in all matters of faith and practice insofar as it allows no higher authority and, as such, is both self-authenticating

[29]Musculus, *Loci communes*, xxi (*Commonplaces,* p. 387, col. 2).
[30]Musculus, *Loci communes*, xxi (*Commonplaces,* p. 388, col. 1).
[31]Musculus, *Loci communes*, xxi (*Commonplaces,* p. 388, col. 2).
[32]Musculus, *Loci communes*, xxi (*Commonplaces,* p. 389, col. 1).

and intrinsically worthy of belief. Leigh, therefore, can argue that Scripture is,

> 1. Infallible *(Scriptura est autopiston kai axiopiston)* which expresseth the minde and will of God, to whom truth is essential and necessary. 2. Supreme and Independent into which all faith is resolved, from which it is not lawful to appeal.... As God is jehovah of himself, so is his word authoritative of itself, and is true and to be obeyed.[33]

Thus, *"Authoritas est divina eius eminentia, gui obligat hominem ad fidem & obedientiam."*[34]

Scripture is therefore in perfect agreement with the divine will and "just truth" "of which ... [it] is a symbol and lively Image." Scripture is true and certain, then, in its "essential parts": the "historical narrations" as those of creation, fall, and Christ's coming to earth; the "threatenings," as Leigh comments, "The eternal torments of hell are sure as if thou wast already in them"; and the promises of Scripture, the predictions, and the prophesies, are certain of accomplishment.[35] This material certainty of Scripture rests on the fact that Scripture is "truth itself" in a twofold sense: first a truth of assertion in that it contains no error, and second a truth of promise in that there "is no unfaithfulness in it."[36] Thus, in addition to these particular descriptions of the truth of Scripture, there is a truth or certitude which it has *generaliter,* since in no part or aspect is it fallible.[37]

"Truth of assertion" indicates the absolute truth of "the matter which is signified," whereas "truth of promise ... refers to the intention of the Speaker, which is properly called veracity or fidelity." This second type of truth appears in Psalm 19 in the phrase "thy testimonies are sure."[38] Thus,

> The essential form of the word is truth in forming the whole and every part; all divine truth is there set down.... There are two signs of truth in Scripture: (1) the particularity of it; it names particulars in genealogies, *dolosus versatur im generalibus.* (2) Impartiality

[33]Leigh, *Treatise,* I.viii (p. 131).
[34]Riissen, *Summa theol.,* II.xi.
[35]Leigh, *Treatise,* I.viii (p. 131, margin); cf. Mastricht, *Theoretico-practica theol.,* I.ii.15.
[36]Leigh, *Treatise,* I.viii (p. 132).
[37]Mastricht, *Theoretico-practica theol.,* I.ii.15.
[38]Leigh, *Treatise,* I.viii (p. 152).

toward friends and their adversaries; the most holy men have their faults described, they give due commendation to their adversaries.[39]

From these arguments it may be concluded,

The truth of Scripture is. (1) More than any human truth of sense or reason. (2) Above all natural reason, as the doctrine of the Trinity, the incarnation of Christ, justification by faith in Christ. (3) A truth which evidences itself. (4) The standard of all truth; nothing is true in doctrine or worship which is not agreeable to this.[40]

The orthodox definition of the truth of Scripture—like the orthodox definitions of infallibility and authority—treads a very narrow line. Scriptural truth is never allowed to rest upon empirical proof: truth depends upon divine authorship and can be defined as a "truth of promise" or as an intentional fidelity or veracity upon the part of God as author. The infallibility of the text, then, is bound up with the concept of inspiration and is identified not as a conclusion drawn by examination of the text, but as one of the gifts given to the biblical writers in the their inspiration by the Holy Spirit.[41] Thus, Twisse could declare categorically that those who say that "true knowledge is demonstrable" are correct with reference to natural knowledge, but "not of knowledge Christian, which is grounded only on God's word." To drive the point home, he adds, "it was never known that to prove a thing out of Scripture was called demonstration."[42]

If, moreover, Scripture is defined unequivocally as "the standard of all truth" the emphasis of definition is nevertheless upon truth in faith and practice, in other words, upon the truth of what God intends to convey to believers. On the other hand, the orthodox can also make a powerful empirical statement: Scripture is true "in assertion" and in its "particulars," and these truths of fact can be seen as evidences of the truth of Scripture. What prevents the orthodox doctrine from becoming utterly empirical is the priority of the truth of Scripture as a matter of confession to any empirical arguments and the clear distinction made, both in their theological

[39]Leigh, *Treatise,* I.viii (margin and text, p. 132).

[40]Leigh, *Treatise,* I.viii (p. 132).

[41]Cf. Poole, *Commentary,* III, p. 921 (2 Pet. 1:21), with Henry, *Commentary on the Whole Bible,* III, pp. 1215–16 (2 Tim. 3:16), 1332 (2 Pet. 1:21); and compare the discussion, above §4.2.

[42]Twisse, *Scriptures Sufficiency* (1795), p. 79.

prolegomena and in the doctrine of Scripture itself, between the infinite truth of God and the finite soteriological truth infallibly given in Scripture. Thus, Turretin saw fit to apply the distinction between archetypal and ectypal knowledge of God to the issue of the character of divine revelation in Scripture, declaring that, there, God speaks "not to himself" but "to us," which is to say—clearly echoing Calvin—*accomodate ad captum nostrum, qui finitus est,* "accommodated to our capacity, which is finite."[43]

When Turretin addresses the question of contradictions in Scripture, he very clearly excludes from his doctrinal point the problem of technical flaws in extant manuscripts. The extant text does indeed contain "irregularities of spelling and punctuation" and "variant readings." There are genuine problems in individual ancient codices —errors brought about by the negligence of scribes and, more recently, of typesetters. But there is no need for contemporary texts to be identical with original autographs. The question that needs to be addressed is whether the extant texts of Scripture have lost the "genuine meaning" of the originals and whether we no longer possess the meaning of the originals as our "rule of faith and practice" *(fidei et morum regula).*[44] There are difficult passages, but no "universal untruths" *(menda universalia),* no problems that cannot be dealt with by comparison of variants or collation of similar passages out of the whole text of Scripture.[45] Once again, the basic premise is virtually identical with that of the Reformers. What has changed is the intensity of the textual problems and issues, brought on as much by linguistic and text-critical advance on the part of the Protestants themselves as by polemic with various adversaries.

Against various attempts, notably by the Arminians, Episcopius, and Grotius, and by Socinus and his followers to argue levels of truth and authority in the text of Scripture, the Reformed argued a uniform authority of the text. Episcopius clearly held the revelation of the Old Testament to be inferior to that of the New and Socinus had argued that on minor issues and points of "no importance" the biblical authors could and did err.[46] The orthodox response was

---

[43]Turretin, *Inst. theol. elencticae,* II.xix.8.

[44]Turretin, *Inst. theol. elencticae,* II.v.4; cf. II.v.5.

[45]Turretin, *Inst. theol. elencticae,* II.v.5.

[46]Cf. Episcopius, *Institutiones theologicae,* III.v.1; IV.1.1; idem, Disputatio de auctoritate S. Scripturae, thesis 3, in *Opera theologica,* 2 vols. (Amsterdam, 1650), vol. I; Socinus, *De auctoritate sacrae Scripturae,* i, in *Bibliotheca fratrum polonorum quos unitarios vocant,* 6 vols. (Irenopolis [Amsterdam], 1656), vol. I, cols. 264–87.

directed toward the preservation of the entire canon—and it included the insistence that "there is nothing in Holy Scripture of no importance" and that even in relatively minor details, the Holy Spirit had preserved his "amanuenses" free from error, leading them "always and in all things ... into a most certain, unfailing, and constant truth."[47] Such, indeed, states Hoornbeeck, was the faith of the Reformed churches as taught in the *Second Helvetic Confession* and the *Belgic Confession*.[48]

Hoornbeeck goes on, in a highly polemical vein that approaches the stereotype of orthodoxy more closely than either its positive doctrinal statements or is exegetical works, to list eight arguments leading to the conclusion that Scripture contains no "disagreements or contradictions." First, there can be no errors inasmuch as the Holy Spirit has inspired all of the biblical writers in an immediate and infallible manner. In a syllogistic form, Hoornbeeck can justify his major proposition that an inspired writer cannot err on the basis of John 16:13: "the spirit of truth ... will guide you into all truth." The minor proposition, that the writers of holy Scripture were inspired, he finds clearly stated in 2 Timothy 3:16; and the further qualification that they were inspired "always and in all things," he finds by implication in 2 Peter 1:20: "*no* prophecy ... is of private interpretation"; and Romans 1:2, where "the gospel of God" is said to have been "promised afore by his prophets."[49] Second, "For the whole of Scripture to be pure, perfect, and divine, it is necessary that it be without error"—but, adds Hoornbeek, supplying the obvious minor proposition of a syllogism, the purity of Scripture is affirmed throughout by such texts as Psalm 12:6: "The words of Jehovah are pure words; as silver purified in a furnace of earth, cleansed seven times."[50]

Third, there is nothing in Scripture that is "trifling and of not importance," as Socinus claimed. The scriptural view of Scripture stands against such claims: 2 Timothy 3:16 not only states that "all Scripture is inspired by God," but goes on to indicate that all Scripture is "profitable for doctrine, for reproof, for correction, for instruction in righteousness"; similarly, Romans 15:4 teaches that "whatsoever things were written aforetime were written for our

[47]Hoornbeeck, *Socinianismus confutatus,* I, p. 6.

[48]Hoornbeeck, *Socinianismus confutatus,* I, p. 6, citing *Second Helvetic Confession,* ii, and *Belgic Confession,* v.

[49]Hoornbeeck, *Socinianismus confutatus,* I, p. 8.

[50]Hoornbeeck, *Socinianismus confutatus,* I, p. 12, citing in addition, Pss. 19:8, 9; 93:5; 119:140; Prov. 30:5; 1 Pet. 2:2; Rev. 19:9

learning."[51] Hoornbeeck's fourth point—a purely logical one—is related closely to the third: theories that jeopardize the whole of Scripture cannot be allowed among Christians; but to claim that Scripture contains errors and contradictions jeopardizes the whole of Scripture. Hoornbeeck appears to be particularly sensitive to the inability of Christians to limit the impact of an error. The error does not simply undermine a single passage, but the entire portion of Scripture in which it is claimed to exist.[52]

For his fifth point, Hoornbeeck raises an immediate soteriological issue: "If the Holy Scriptures err in some things ... our faith in Scripture can be neither certain nor divine." Error is, after all, a human, not a divine, characteristic. The result of Socinus' position for faith is far worse than the Roman Catholic alternative, which argued the authority of the pope, the church, and tradition, but which still assumed the formal object of faith to be the "ultimate truth" of "infallible divine revelation."[53] Clearly, the underlying issue throughout the discussion of infallibility is the authority of Scripture as the ground of certainty in matters pertaining to salvation. If the logic of Hoornbeeck's polemic fails in its near circularity to prove the infallibility of the text, it surely does indicate the state of the question in the seventeenth century. Certainty had to be grounded somewhere—and the options offered were the individual exegete, the church and its tradition, and the Bible. The first two options, represented by Socinianism and Roman Catholicism respectively, were clearly problematic. Hoornbeeck's sixth point drives the issue home: Socinus and his followers have not convincingly shown Scripture to err, but have only managed to identify difficult passages, none of which are impossible of explanation.[54] As a seventh argument, Hoornbeek notes the oddity and novelty of Socinus' view of Scripture. There is a "consensus of the Fathers and the theologians" of later ages concerning the infallibility of Scripture against the various adversaries of the faith. Augustine, Epiphanius, and even the Jesuits of Louvain condemn those who deny the truth of Scripture and who claim that it is not necessary for all of its words to be inspired by the Spirit. Finally, Hoornbeeck is able to cite passages from Socinus and his followers that speak of the authority and integrity of Scripture. Such self-contradiction is a final argument against their teaching![55]

---

[51]Hoornbeeck, *Socinianismus confutatus,* I, pp. 12–13.
[52]Hoornbeeck, *Socinianismus confutatus,* I, pp. 14–15.
[53]Hoornbeeck, *Socinianismus confutatus,* I, pp. 17–18.
[54]Hoornbeeck, *Socinianismus confutatus,* I, p. 18; cf. below, §6.3.b.
[55]Hoornbeeck, *Socinianismus confutatus,* I, pp. 18–19.

5.3 Purity, Holiness, Sufficiency, and Perfection

The related identification of Scripture as pure, holy, sufficient, and perfect—pure, holy, and sufficient in its teachings for the preaching of salvation and perfect or complete in its communication of those teachings—is a point of doctrine that marks out a major line of continuity between the medieval scholastics, the Reformers, and the Protestant orthodox. This particular element of the doctrine of Scripture had been developed in considerable detail in the later Middle Ages and was not altered at all in its basic statement. Whereas it is quite true that the concept of the purity, holiness, sufficiency, and perfection of Scripture did not, in its original medieval context, point ineluctably toward the Reformation, the Reformers, and the orthodox, Protestant thinkers were able to place the concept into the context of a different view of authority and interpretation and to use it as one of the foundations of their declaration of *sola Scriptura*. Indeed, the radically altered shape of the questions of interpretation and authority in the post-Reformation era placed the Roman Catholic polemicists in the somewhat unenviable position of arguing against the express statements of great medieval doctors like Aquinas and Scotus concerning the prior authority, sufficiency, and perfection of the text.

Bullinger, who offers one of the strongest statements of the point among the earlier Reformed writers, places the notion of the purity, holiness, sufficiency, and perfection of the Scriptures into the context of the identity of Scripture as Word and of the saving function of the scriptural Word:

> And to this end is the word of God revealed to men, that it may teach them concerning God and his will, and of what manner God is towards men; that he would have them to be saved; and that, by faith in Christ: what Christ is, and by what means salvation cometh: what becometh the true worshippers of God.... Neither is it sufficient to know the will of God, unless we do the same and be saved.[56]

Several issues came to the fore here. First, the type of questions that Bullinger poses, despite the informal, homiletical character of the *Decades,* springs out of the scholastic background—*quis* and *qualis.* Second, he here makes the distinction typical of the Reformers between historical and saving faith, a distinction which would carry

---

[56]Bullinger, *Decades,* I.ii (p. 60).

over into orthodoxy as that between *assensus* and *fiducia*. The Word
of God delivered by the prophets and apostles contained the entire
ground of piety *(pietatis rationem)*:[57]

> no man can deny that to be a most absolute doctrine, by which a
> man is so fully made perfect, that in this world he may be taken for
> a just man, and in the world to come be called forever to the com-
> pany of God. But he that believeth the word of God ... is called a
> just man, and heir of life everlasting, that doctrine therefore is an
> absolute doctrine.... perfect in all points.[58]

Scripture, thus, is perfect both in itself and in its effects.[59]

After having said this, Bullinger notes, "I am not so ignorant, but
that I know that the Lord Jesus both did and spake many things
which were not written by the apostles. But it followeth not therefore, that the doctrine of the word of God, taught by the apostles, is
not absolutely perfect."[60] For John, who testifies to this fact, writes
immediately afterward that what was written conduces to faith and
to life. Thus nothing was omitted that might have been necessary to
salvation and to the holy life. Furthermore, the Lord himself (John
16:12, 13) reveals that the truths he himself does not impart will be
given by the Spirit to the apostles and that they would be led into
"all truth." Paul's continual repetition of the same teaching also
testifies to this fact—had there been other truths, he would not have
repeated himself, but taught further.[61]

> As for those which do earnestly affirm, that all points of godliness
> were taught by the apostles to the posterity by word of mouth, and
> not by writing, their purpose is to set to sale their own, that is,
> men's ordinances instead of the word of God.[62]

Anything that deviates from the Scriptures, Bullinger asserts, is not
of God—for the apostles, infused with the Spirit of truth, would not
have written one thing and spoken another. "Furthermore, we must

[57]Bullinger, *Decades,* I.ii (p. 61).
[58]Bullinger, *Decades,* I.ii (p. 61).
[59]Bullinger, *Decades,* I.ii (pp. 61–62).
[60]Bullinger, *Decades,* I.ii (p. 62).
[61]Bullinger, *Decades,* I.ii (pp. 62–63); cf. Calvin, *Commentaries on the Gospel of John,* John 16:12–13; 21:25 (CTS, II:141–145, 299); and idem, *Commentaries on the Second Epistle of Timothy,* 2 Tim. 3:16 (CTS, p. 250).
[62]Bullinger, *Decades,* I.ii (p. 64).

diligently search, whether those traditions do set forth the glory of God, rather than of men; or the safety of the faithful, rather than the private advantage of the priests."[63]

Without any hesitation, Bullinger reduces his argument on the perfection of Scripture to a syllogism:

> [John] affirmeth by this doctrine, which he contained in writing (i.e. John 20:30–31), that faith is fully taught, and that through faith there is granted by God everlasting life. But the end of absolute doctrine is to be happy and perfectly blessed. Since then that cometh to man by the written doctrine of the gospel, undoubtedly that doctrine of the gospel is most absolutely perfect.[64]

A similar view, lacking the dogmatic character and the fullness of Bullinger's treatment, is expressed by Calvin, who argues that the fullness and completeness of the apostolic witness—granting that the apostles were "sure and certain amanuenses of the Holy Spirit" —excludes the invention of "any new doctrine."[65] Even so, the Scriptures are called holy in order to distinguish them from the profane "scriptures" or writings of men. "Profane matters," says Musculus, are those which relate not only to the things of this world and the conduct of men, "but any other superstitions also, false worshippings, wicked sacrifices, and erroneous opinions of God." Thus, profane writings include those which presume to be called holy but contain grave errors in religion "such as the Alkoran."[66]

We see these assumptions carried over directly into the thought of theologians of the next generation. Thus, Zanchius also maintains as a basic proposition that Scripture contains in itself all things necessary for a knowledge of salvation and for true worship of God—and contains them clearly.[67] Scripture provides, therefore, the ground of all doctrine, all actions, and all precepts in the church— and the church, by extension, cannot teach doctrines not contained in Scripture. That doctrine is necessary which gives knowledge of salvation and of eternal life. And this is the doctrine of Scripture.[68] Zanchius proceeds to refute arguments against the perfection of

---

[63]Bullinger, *Decades,* I.ii (p. 64).

[64]Bullinger, *Decades,* I.ii (p. 62).

[65]Calvin, *Institutes,* IV.viii.9.

[66]Musculus, *Loci communes,* xxi (*Commonplaces,* p. 349, col. 2–p. 350, col. 1).

[67]Zanchi, *Praefatiuncula,* cols. 369, 409.

[68]Zanchi, *Praefatiuncula,* cols. 370–71.

Scripture and to enlist the fathers of the church as supporters of his high view of Scripture and of his conception of the relation of the church to Scripture.[69]

The doctrine offered by later orthodox writers differs but little from the expression given to the point by Bullinger, Ursinus, and Zanchius. Scripture is "Pure and Holy" because "it commands all good, and forbids, reproves, and condemns all sin and filthiness; it restrains not only from evil words and actions, but thought and glances." Scripture is called holy,

> 1. From its efficient principal cause, God who is the holy of holies, holiness itself.... 2. In regard of the instrumental cause, the pen-men of it were holy men ... 3. From its matter, the holy will of God ... the Scripture contains holy and divine mysteries, holy precepts of life, holy promises, ... holy Histories. 4. From its end or effect, the holy Ghost by the reading and meditation of the Scripture sanc-tifieth us.[70]

Scripture is also called pure, "because God himself is pure."

> It is pure: 1) Formally in itself, there is no mixture of error, no cor-ruption or unfoundedness at all in it. Prov. 8.6, 7, 8. 2) Virtually so as to make others pure. ... It begets grace, ... and preserves and increases it.... The assertory part is pure; 1) what it affirms to be is; and what it denies to be is not.... 2) What it promiseth shall be performed, and what it threateneth shall be executed.... 3) What it commandeth is good, and what it forbiddeth is evil.[71]

Rollock similarly argues that Scripture is perfect inasmuch as it contains the knowledge necessary to salvation not only sufficiently but abundantly. Scripture not only testifies to this fact specifically, but the existence of the church depends upon it.

> As for the judgment of the adversaries in this matter, which affirm that the Scripture is lame and maimed, chiefly note Bellarmine and his arguments for this purpose. They teach the Scripture to be defective and weak, that we might give place to their traditions and forgeries.[72]

---

[69]Zanchi, *Praefatiuncula,* cols. 376–400.

[70]Leigh, *Treatise,* I.viii (p.137); very similarly, Mastricht, *Theoretico-practica theol.,* I.ii.17.

[71]Leigh, *Treatise,* I.viii (p. 137).

[72]Rollock, *Treatise of Effectual Calling,* pp. 92–93.

The papists, moreover, mistake the meaning of the word "tradition," calling it unwritten while both Scripture and the fathers know both written and unwritten traditions. There is no tradition, then, to be considered necessary, which conflicts with the express record of the Scriptures—since none of these things can bind men's consciences in the way which the Word of God binds the conscience.[73]

Scripture is also perfect in substance: essentially in terms of matter and form and also in an "integral" sense in terms of the absolute perfection of law and gospel and their perfection relative to one another. The substance of Scripture is considered perfect absolutely in that Scripture contains "either expressly or analogically all that doctrine concerning faith and manners, which is communicable." Clearly in divine matters, some knowledge is communicable, some not—and we affirm that Scripture contains all communicable knowledge of God which can be known and is profitable.[74] In contrast to this absolute perfection of "essence" Scripture may also be considered as perfect according to relation: Even as it has perfection as a whole, so does it have a perfection in its parts, of quantity as contrasted with essence.[75]

Similarly, Scripture can be called perfect according to its effect, "for it makes a man wise unto Salvation, instructs him to every good work, and makes him blessed by a beginning in this life and by perfection in the other."[76] This and the other perfections of Scripture may be taken in and of themselves, but also should be seen in contrast to the imperfection of all traditions. In other words, the doctrine "written by the Prophets and Apostles" is binding, while "Dogmatic," or "Historical," or "Ceremonial" traditions of the church make no final claim on faith and morals. Scripture alone and of itself contains all doctrine necessary to salvation.[77]

Perkins defines traditions as "doctrines delivered from hand to hand, either by word of mouth, or by writing, beside the written word of God."[78] According to this definition,

> The very word of God hath beene delivered by tradition. For first, God revealed his will to Adam by word of mouth: and renewed the same unto the Patriarkes, not by writing but by speech, by

---

[73]Rollock, *Treatise of Effectual Calling,* p. 93.
[74]Trelcatius, *Schol. meth.,* I.ii (p. 25).
[75]Trelcatius, *Schol. meth.,* I.ii (p. 25).
[76]Trelcatius, *Schol. meth.,* I.ii (p. 26).
[77]Trelcatius, *Schol. meth.,* I.ii (p. 27).
[78]Perkins, *Reformed Catholike,* in *Works,* I, p. 580, col. 2A.

> dreames, and other inspirations: and thus the word of God went
> from man to man, for the space of two thousand and foure hundred
> yeares, unto the time of Moses, who was the first pen-man of holy
> Scripture.[79]

The prophecy of Enoch is yet another example of early traditions
gotten by direct inspiration of God and written down subsequently:

> And the historie of the newe Testament (as some say) for eightie
> yeares, as some others thinke, for the space of twentie yeares and
> more, went from hand to hand by tradition, till penned by the
> Apostles, or being penned by others it was approoved by them.[80]

It is also true, continues Perkins, that the prophets and apostles
spoke things not recorded in Scripture but passed on by tradition. In
2 Timothy 3:8 we learn the names of the magicians who withstood
Moses; in Hebrews 12:21 we read words of Moses nowhere else
recorded; and in Jude we learn that the archangel Michael strove
with the devil over Moses' body. These are traditions, comments
Perkins, which the apostles learned by word of mouth "or by some
writings then extant among the Jewes."[81] It is also believed that
Isaiah was killed with a "fuller's club," that Mary "lived and died a
virgin." Similarly, the ancient writings of the church contain sayings
of the apostles not recorded in Scripture. These last things may be
believed if they do not go against the written word of God.[82]

> We hold that the Church of God hath power to prescribe ordi-
> nances, rules, or traditions, touching the time and place of Gods
> worship, and touching order and comelinesse to be used in the
> same.... And this kind of traditions, whether made by general
> Councels or particular Synods, wee have care to maintaine and
> observe: these caveats beeing remembered: first, that they pre-
> scribe nothing childish or absurd to bee done: secondly, that they
> be not imposed as any part of Gods worship: thirdly, that they be
> severed from superstition or opinion of merit: lastly, that the
> Church of God be not burdened with the multitude of them.[83]

This far Perkins can accept traditions, but he forever divides his
doctrine from that of Rome because

[79]Perkins, *Reformed Catholike*, p. 580, col. 2B.
[80]Perkins, *Reformed Catholike*, p. 580, col. 2C.
[81]Perkins, *Reformed Catholike*, p. 582, col. 2D.
[82]Perkins, *Reformed Catholike*, p. 582, col. 2D.
[83]Perkins, *Reformed Catholike*, p. 581, cols. 1A–B.

Papists teach, that beside the written word, there be certaine unwritten traditions, which must be beleeved as profitable and necessarie to salvation. And these they say are two-fold; Apostolicall, namely, such as were delivered by the Apostles, and not written: and Ecclesiasticall, which the Church decreeth as occasion is offered. We hold that the Scriptures are most perfect, containing in them all doctrines needfull to salvation, whether they concerne faith and manners: and therefore we acknowledge no such traditions beside the written word, which shall be necessarie to salvation: so as he which beleeveth them not cannot be saved.[84]

Perkins adduces several scriptural texts on the sole sufficiency of Scripture and cites both Tertullian and Vincent of Lerins. Rainolds was able to argue that Vincent's identification of two ways to avoid or refute heresy—first through the use of Scripture and second on the basis of the church's tradition—did not indicate two sources of authority, but instead pointed to Scripture itself and then, under the term "tradition of the Catholike Church," to "the true and right exposition of the scripture, made by faithfull pastors and teachers of the Church."[85] It was Vincent's express intention to not call upon unwritten traditions nor to "adde the tradition of the Church to the authoritie of the scriptures, as though that the scriptures were not themselves alone sufficient ... but to shew, that, bicause heretickes do wrest and misse-expound the scriptures, therefore we must learne their right sense and meaning, delivered to the godly by the ministrie of the Church."[86]

To these authorities Perkins and Rainolds add the arguments of reason. Even as the apostles never sought to prove doctrine from tradition but only from Scripture, neither should the church today, and further, if tradition were necessary to salvation we would have to view the writings of the ancient fathers as normative and on a level with Scripture despite the many errors contained in their books.[87] Opponents of this logic claim that the very trust we have in Scripture is conveyed to us by tradition. But it appears that, in point of fact, the value of Scripture can be determined by the inward testimony of the Spirit to the reader as well as by

[84]Perkins, *Reformed Catholike,* p. 581, col. 1C.

[85]Rainolds, *Summe of the Conference between Iohn Rainolds and Iohn Hart,* p. 147.

[86]Rainolds, *Summe of the Conference between Iohn Rainolds and Iohn Hart,* p. 147, citing Vincent, *Commonitorium,* ii, xli.

[87]Perkins, *Reformed Catholike,* p. 582, col. 1A–B; cf. Rainolds, *Summe of the Conference between Iohn Rainolds and Iohn Hart,* p. 149.

the matter therein contained, which is most divine and absolute truth full of pietie; the manner and forme of speech, which is full of majestie in the simplicity of words; the ende whereat they wholly aime, which is the honour and glory of God alone.... Thus Scripture proves itself to be Scripture: and yet we despise not the universal consent or tradition of the church, which though it does not persuade the conscience, yet it is a notable inducement to moove us to reverence and regard the writings of the Prophets and Apostles.[88]

This perfection or sufficiency, moreover, is not, as Cardinal Perronius argued, a "mediate" rather than an "immediate" perfection that remands us to the church where the defects or lacks in Scripture are supplied. Riissen comments that the whole idea of a "mediate sufficiency" is self-contradictory, inasmuch as something that is sufficient cannot and will not remand us to another authority—and, by implication, something that does so, is not sufficient: Scripture remains the rule to which nothing can be added and from which nothing can be taken away.[89]

Thus, Scripture is perfect "in respect of the matter" and "in respect of the form." In form, furthermore, Scripture is perfect both "absolutely in itself" in its principle and its subject and "as opposed to unwritten traditions, all which it excludes by its sufficiency."[90] First, then, Scripture is perfect,

In respect of the matter or the Books, in which the holy doctrine was written, all which (as many as were useful to our salvation) have been kept inviolable in the Church, so that out of them one most perfect and absolute Canon of faith and life was made, and this may be called the Integrity of the Scripture.[91]

Second, it is perfect,

In respect of the form, viz. of the sense or meaning of these Canonical Books, or of Divine Truth comprehended in them, which Books contain most fully and perfectly the whole truth necessary and sufficient for the salvation of the elect.[92]

[88]Perkins, *Reformed Catholike,* p. 582, col. 1D–2A.
[89]Riissen, *Summa theol.,* II.xi., controversia 1, obj.3.
[90]Leigh, *Treatise,* I.viii (pp. 138–39).
[91]Leigh, *Treatise,* I.viii (p. 138); cf. Mastricht, *Theoretico-practica theol.,* I.ii.16.
[92]Leigh, *Treatise,* I.viii (p. 138).

These two primary perfections can be considered as an "essential perfection" in doctrine and as an "integral or systematic" perfection in the books themselves, their succession, and their inclusion in the canon.[93]

By "essential perfection" the orthodox mean that nothing need be added and nothing may be taken away from Scripture: Scripture is the perfect foundation for all things to be believed and all things to be done *(credenda et facienda)* "inasmuch as it contains all of the dogmas and precepts that are necessary to salvation."[94] The formal perfection is considered in two ways, "absolutely in itself" and "as opposed to unwritten traditions." The absolute perfection of Scripture refers first to its regulative perfection as the *principium cognoscendi* and indicates neither a perfect communication of universal knowledge nor an absolute uniformity of statement throughout its many pages, but only in the communication of those things necessary to salvation either by direct statement or as a necessary consequence of a statement.[95] Thus,

> for every principle, whether of a thing or of knowledge, ought to be the perfect, since demonstration and true conclusions are not deduced from that which is imperfect, therefore it is necessary that the holy Scripture being the first only immediate principle of all true doctrine should be most perfect.[96]

Second, absolute perfection refers to

> the Subject, for it hath all Essential parts, matter and form; and integral, Law and Gospel, and is wholly perfect both 1. Absolutely, because of the substance ... [and] 2. Relatively, because it hath a perfection of the whole, so of the parts in the whole; that perfection is called essential, this quantitative. For ... although integrally they have not a sufficiency of the whole, but only of their own, yet so that at distinct times every part sufficed for their times; but all the parts in the whole are but sufficient for us.[97]

And, third, Scripture possesses an absolute perfection in "effect and operation," which is to say, in leading human beings toward the goal

[93] Mastricht, *Theoretico-practica theol.,* I.ii.19.

[94] Riissen, *Summa theol.,* II.xii, controversia, obj.2, resp.

[95] Turretin, *Inst. theol. elencticae,* II.xvi.2, 9.

[96] Leigh, *Treatise,* I.viii (p. 139); cf. the virtually identical formulation in Trelcatius, *Schol. meth.,* I.ii.

[97] Leigh, *Treatise,* I.viii (p. 139).

of salvation. This perfection indicates a specific adequacy of Scripture to its *finis,* rather than a universal adequacy to its divine *obiectum*: certain of the profound mysteries of the faith, like the doctrine of God in unity and trinity, are not fully explained.[98]

The formal perfection of Scripture "as opposed to unwritten traditions" appears in that Scripture, in its sufficiency, alone can bind the conscience.[99] By "tradition," Leigh indicates a doctrine "not written by Prophets or Apostles." Traditions exist as doctrine, as ceremonies, and as historical memory and are not to be rejected out of hand: "If traditions agree with the Scripture, they are confirmed by it; if they oppose it they are disproved by it."[100]

After having expounded at such length and in so many particulars on the perfection and divinity of Scripture, Leigh adds a note concerning the accommodated character of the scriptural revelation:

> The perfection of the Scriptures is not, First, Infinite and unlimited; that is an incommunicable property of God; everything which is from another as the efficient cause, is thereby limited both for the nature and qualities thereof. Secondly, we do not understand such a perfection as containeth all and singular such things as at any time have been by Divine inspiration revealed unto holy men, and by them delivered to the Church ... for all the Sermons of the Prophets, of Christ and his Apostles, are not set down in so many words as they used in the speaking of them; for of twelve Apostles seven wrote nothing which yet preached and did many things; neither are all the deeds of Christ and his Apostles written ... but we mean only a Relative perfection which for some certain ends sake agreeth to the Scripture as to an instrument, according to which it perfectly comprehendeth all things which have been, are or shall be necessary for the salvation of the Church.[101]

In this Mastricht concurs, defining Scripture as perfect *ad vivendum Dei* and *ad salutem creditu ac factu necessarium.*[102]

In the third place, the "perfection" of the individual books of Scripture is relative to the purpose of the book and does not imply that any book of itself "is sufficient to the common end" which is the salvation of the church. For example, "Paul speaketh much of Justification, and Predestination, in the Epistle to the Romans [yet

---

[98]Leigh, *Treatise,* I.viii (p. 139); Turretin, *Inst. theol. elencticae,* II.xvi.34.
[99]Leigh, *Treatise,* I.viii (p. 139).
[100]Leigh, *Treatise,* I.viii (p. 140).
[101]Leigh, *Treatise,* I.viii (p. 140).
[102]Mastricht, *Theoretico-practica theol.,* I.ii.19.

offers] nothing of the Eucharist or Resurrection."[103] Nevertheless—
and fourth—"those writings which by the Divine hand and providence were extant in the Church, were so sufficient for the Church
in that Age, that it needed not Tradition, neither was it lawful for
any human ... to add thereto or take therefrom; but when God did
reveal more unto it, the former only was not then sufficient without
the latter."[104] Thus, the relative incompleteness both of individual
books or of the canon at various stages of its composition is not a
barrier to the concept of Scripture's perfection, granting the "integral perfection" of the individual books themselves in and for the
sake of their several temporal or historical purposes.[105]

The perfection of Scripture is frequently defined by the Reformed
orthodox in terms of the principle "that the scriptures contain all
things necessary to salvation."[106] This fact is proved from the
inspired and authoritative word of Scripture itself, specifically
2 Timothy 3:15–16—

> we observe from this [text] that, 1. the scripture is profitable not
> only for some things, but for all things, for *instruction* in the truth,
> *conviction* of error, *correction* of evil, and *direction* in what is
> good; 2. it is pronounced able to make a man of God perfect, and
> completely furnished for every part of his office; and 3. it is capa-
> ble of rendering a man wise unto salvation.[107]

Similarly, as an integral part of argument on the nature and limits of
the perfection of Scripture, Leigh writes:

> The holy Scripture doth sufficiently contain and deliver all
> Doctrines which are necessary for us to eternal salvation, both in
> respect of Faith and good works, and most of these it delivereth to
> us expressly and in so many words, and the rest by good and nec-
> essary consequence. The Baptism of Infants, and the consubstan-
> tiality of the Father and of the Son, are not in those words
> expressed in Scripture, yet is the truth of both clearly taught in
> Scripture, and by evident proof may thence be deduced; that the
> Article of Christs descent into Hell, *totidem Verbis* is not in the
> Scripture, yet it may be deduced thence, Acts 2.[108]

---

[103]Leigh, *Treatise,* I.viii (pp. 140–41).
[104]Leigh, *Treatise,* I.viii (p. 141).
[105]Mastricht, *Theoretico-practica theol.,* I.ii.19.
[106]Pictet, *Theol. chr.,* I.xi.2.
[107]Pictet, *Theol. chr.,* I.xi.2.
[108]Leigh, *Treatise,* I.viii (p. 141); and cf. Riissen, *Summa theol.,* II.xii.

This basic definition led the orthodox to a series of conclusions that relate the sufficiency of Scripture to their sense of the unity of proclamation throughout the Bible. It follows that salvation was by grace in all ages of the church, never by the law either of nature or of Moses, and that this gracious salvation was sufficiently revealed throughout all time: Scripture thus declares concerning itself, "Ye shall not add unto the word which I command you neither shall ye diminish ought from it" (Deut. 4:2; 12:32). God in ancient times, therefore, "desired the people to be content with the one rule he had given them, adding nothing to it and removing nothing, since it was a perfect revelation for that age of the church." Even so, subsequent revelations in Scripture have augmented and fulfilled God's promises for the sake of successive ages of the church,[109] while "the substance of all things necessary to salvation, ever since the fall of Adam hath been, and is, one and the same, as the true Religion hath been one and unchangeable."[110]

This sense of the relation of the sufficiency of Scripture to its unity in ultimate doctrinal substance leads Leigh to a series of propositions that relate to the issue of the scope or foundation of Scripture and to the interpretive principle of the *analogia fidei*.[111] Since "the knowledge of God and Christ is the sum of all things necessary to salvation" and "this knowledge was ever necessary" we must infer the sufficiency of the Old Testament in these matters, even though "the Fathers indeed saw Christ more obscurely and enigmatically, we more clearly, distinctly and perspicuously." For indeed, "the Covenant of grace ... is an everlasting Covenant" even as God is "one and unchangeable, as in nature, so in will."[112] Thus also, the religion taught by Christ and the apostles was not a new religion, but the one true religion that was taught by God "before, under and after the Law since the fall of Adam."[113]

The perfection and sufficiency of the Scriptures may also be viewed cumulatively, in terms of their substance and tendency: the whole points to the Messiah and then reveals him fully. "Who also at his coming did establish that order in the Church of God, which was to continue therein forever." This appears most clearly in that

Christ was ordained of the Father to be the great Doctor of the

---

[109]Pictet, *Theol. chr.*, I.xi.2.
[110]Leigh, *Treatise,* I.viii (pp. 141–142).
[111]See above §3.5, on "scope" and below, §7.3, on the analogy of faith.
[112]Leigh, *Treatise,* I.viii (p. 142).
[113]Leigh, *Treatise,* I.viii (p. 142).

Church, a Prophet more excellent than the rest that were before him, both in respect of his Person, office, Manner of receiving his Doctrine, and the excellency of the Doctrine which he delivered.[114]

From this, in turn, it appears that

All things necessary in that manner as we have spoken were taught and inspired to the Apostles by our Saviour Christ, and there were no new inspirations after their times; nor are we to expect further hereafter.[115]

Even so, Christ himself saw to it that he omitted nothing needful from his teaching; he sent the Spirit into the church immediately upon his exaltation to the right hand of the Father; and the age of prophecy ceased.[116] Leigh's last three propositions simply continued this argument, moving from the sufficiency of the completed Scripture and the absence of any need of further revelation to the conclusion that "no new Revelation or Tradition beside those inspired, published and comprehended in the Scripture are necessary for the salvation of the Church."[117]

These arguments are strengthened by the further admonition of Scripture neither to add to nor take away from the words of the book (Rev. 22:18, 19) and the similar statement in Proverbs 30:6. Paul also pronounced "a curse upon those ... who should 'preach any other gospel than that which he had preached'" (Gal. 1:8). The apostles also point out that they declared "all the counsel of God" (Acts 20:20, 27) and that by their preaching men could obtain life eternal (John 20:31; 1 John 5:13).

Now if they had not written all things that were necessary for salvation, they could not have led men to eternal life. Nor is it likely that the apostles omitted necessary things, since they committed to writing so many things which were not necessary, and that for the purpose of more fully instructing us.

A third argument, then, may be stated as follows: if Scripture were imperfect, it would be so, either because God was unwilling that all things necessary to salvation should be written, or because the apostles were unwilling to write them, although God had

---

[114]Leigh, *Treatise,* I.viii (p. 143).
[115]Leigh, *Treatise,* I.viii (p. 144).
[116]Leigh, *Treatise,* I.viii (p. 145).
[117]Leigh, *Treatise,* I.viii (p. 146).

commanded them. The latter idea no one will assert; the former cannot be maintained; for no reason can be adduced, why God should have wished only a part of the things needful to salvation to be written, and the other part consigned to the uncertain tradition of men.[118]

Pictet, however, is aware that the category of "things necessary to salvation" needs to be explained further in relation to Scripture, its interpretation, and it use in the church. In the first place, there are things known naturally such as the existence of God and the immortality of the soul. These truths cannot be proven, but they are confirmed by Scripture in order to free us from doubt. Next there are things necessary to salvation "not taught in scripture in express words" but "deduced by fair and legitimate inferences" from the Scriptures. Nor is it necessary for Scripture to refute all heresies. It is sufficient for it to establish the truth without explicitly describing all possible errors. We also need to recognize that

the perfection of Scripture has not always been the same with respect to its degree, for revelation has increased according to the different ages of the church; not in regard to the substance of the truth, but in regard to their clearer manifestation.[119]

Finally, it should be observed that "A rule is no less perfect when a hand [i.e., an agent] is required to apply it." The perfection of Scripture notwithstanding, the "ministry of the church" and "the work of the Holy Spirit in conversion" are necessary parts of God's design. In addition, much is left to the general "prudence" of the church and its rulers, though not in things necessary to salvation.[120]

5.4 Plainness, Perspicuity, and Efficacy

The Reformed orthodox concept of the plainness and perspicuity or clarity of Scripture cannot be reduced to a grammatical point or restricted to a theological one. The grammatical and theological issues stand together in the context of the Protestant movement away from allegorical exegesis toward a literal-grammatical reading of the text. The doctrinal issues once addressed by means of the *quadriga* now had to be addressed not only on the basis of a more literal and grammatical reading of the text but also on the assumption that there

[118]Pictet, *Theol. chr.*, I.xi.2.
[119]Pictet, *Theol. chr.*, I.xi.3.
[120]Pictet, *Theol. chr.*, I.xi.3.

was no norm for interpretation other than the text itself. Grammatical meaning and theological clarity were thus bound closely together. If not the entirety of Scripture, then at least the crucial *loci,* would have to be grammatically clear in order that the difficult passages could be explained by readily understandable texts and the doctrinal content of Scripture be broadly and generally available without necessary recourse either to tradition or to church. Only in this way could the confessional and doctrinal norms of Protestant orthodoxy remain in their subordinate place under the *sola Scriptura.*

This grammatical as well as doctrinal point stands, moreover, at a place in the orthodox dogmatics prior both logically and in the typical order of system to the usually lengthy discussion of the interpretation of Scripture—so that, just as in the case of the orthodox doctrinal statement of the infallibility of Scripture, the doctrinal point does not rest on an empirical or rationally evidentialistic argument. Perspicuity is a doctrinal assumption, resting on the declaration of the inspiration, authority, and soteriological sufficiency of the biblical revelation. And, as such, it must be juxtaposed with the problem of the "obscurity" of Scripture in many of its individual texts. In other words, the Reformed doctrine of the *perspicuitas Scripturae sacrae* does not represent a denial of the difficulties of interpretation. Rather, the difficulties of interpretation, including the genuine and freely acknowledged obscurity of certain texts, are encountered in the context of the presupposition that whatever is needful for the preaching of the church and the teaching of its fundamental doctrines is somewhere stated clearly and plainly.

The Scriptures can, therefore, as Vermigli stated, be commended to the godly as "a candle lighted by God" and a guide into truth. The godly, moreover, have been so assured of this truth that they have been willing to die for it—as is seldom true among "natural philosophers and mathematicians."[121]

> For faithful and godly hearts, there is no lack of clarity in Scripture, such as the Greeks call *sapheneia* and the Latins perspicuity. For whatever the sounder theologians dispute, they always conclude with the testimony of Scripture as the common rule known by Christians which no one may rightly doubt.[122]

Vermigli qualifies his point by noting that this perspicuity comes not primarily to reason but to faith—and it is by faith that we are

[121]Vermigli, *Loci communes,* I.vi.2.
[122]Vermigli, *Loci communes,* I.vi.2.

persuaded of the truth of Scripture. Faith recognizes that this truth of Scripture rests on the Word of God and is eternal:

> "Thus says the Lord" *(Dominus dixit)* ought to be held as a first principle *(primum principium)* into which all true theology is resolved. This is not, moreover, an evidence derived from the light of human senses or from reason, but from the light of faith, by which we ought to be most fully persuaded, and which is contained in the sacred writings.... Christ himself teaches us, as it is said in Matthew 24, "heaven and earth shall pass away, but my words will never pass away": and it is repeated everywhere that "the Word of God stands forever."[123]

Echoing Vermigli, Musculus cites Chrysostom and Augustine at length as examples of the churchly use of Scripture as a clear and certain rule of faith. Against these examples, he notes, "the adversaries cry out that the Holy Scriptures are too obscure for us to gather any certain judgment out of them." The fathers, however, do not appear to have been at all daunted by difficulties of interpretation and have in fact testified that there is no point in Scripture which is not somewhere clearly expounded: "if anything is stated obscurely in one place in the Scriptures, it ought to be clarified from those places in which the same teaching is more plainly expressed."[124] This point is particularly true for those passages in the Old Testament that can only be understood in terms of their fulfillment in the New. The perspicuity of Scripture as a whole, therefore, points directly to the analogy of Scripture as an interpretive device and to the insistence that Scripture itself, not tradition or church, is the primary interpreter of Scripture.[125] By way of polemical warning to those who might be tempted to listen to the caveats of his adversaries, Musculus adds, "if the Gospel is dark, it is dark to those who are perishing."[126]

As Trelcatius declares for the early orthodox, the plainness or clarity of Scripture is necessary inasmuch as the Scriptures are our one "means and instrument of faith." Since faith moves from knowledge to assent, to full assurance, faith could not stand without the

---

[123]Vermigli, *Loci communes*, I.vi.2.

[124]Musculus, *Loci communes*, xxi *(Commonplaces*, p. 358, cols. 1–2).

[125]Cf. the Roman Catholic view in Tavard, "Tradition in Early Post-Tridentine Theology," pp. 393–96; and below, §7.3.a on the *analogia Scripturae*.

[126]Musculus, *Loci communes*, xxi *(Commonplaces*, p. 359, col. 1).

full and plain knowledge of God in Scripture. Neither could we be sure of the law in the heart were it not for the written confirmation of that law in God's Word. Although there are degrees of understanding, and although Scripture is plainer in meaning to some than to others,

> whence it is that neither all things are clear and perspicuous to each person alike, not each thing to all persons equally; yet to all and singular persons [Scripture is] sufficiently clear unto salvation, according to the measure of faith and divine illumination.[127]

The continuity between this early orthodox view of the perspicuity of Scripture and the view of the Reformers can be easily identified in Whitaker's *Disputatio* of 1610. After citing the opinions of numerous Roman Catholic writers concerning the obscurity of Scripture and the inadvisability of allowing laity to read Scripture, Whitaker presents the "state of the question." The Roman opponents labor to demonstrate the obscurity of the text while at the same time claiming that Protestants teach "that all things in scripture are so plain that they may be understood by any unlearned person, and need no exposition and interpretation."[128] This claim, replies Whitaker, is false. What Protestants teach is identical with the view of Luther in his *De servo arbitrio* in response to Erasmus. Whitaker paraphrases:

> in the scriptures, there is nothing abstruse, noting obscure, but ... *all* things are plain. And because this may seem a paradox, he afterwards explains himself thus: he confesses that many places of scripture are obscure, that there are many words and places shrouded in difficulty, but he affirms nevertheless that no dogma is obscure; as, for instance, that God is one and three, that Christ suffered, and will reign forever, and so forth. All of which is perfectly true: for although there is much obscurity in many words and passages, yet all of the articles of faith are plain.[129]

It is quite true, adds Whitaker, that anyone who is able to ascertain "the grammatical sense of scripture" will be able "best to explain and interpret the scriptures."[130]

---

[127]Trelcatius, *Schol. meth.*, I.ii.
[128]Whitaker, *Disputation,* IV.i (p. 361).
[129]Whitaker, *Disputation,* IV.i (pp. 361–62).
[130]Whitaker, *Disputation,* IV.i (p. 362).

Nonetheless, it is the grammatical meaning that is sometimes the most difficult to ascertain. "Luther adds besides," Whitaker continues,

> that the things themselves are manifest in scripture; and that there-fore we need not be put to much trouble, if the words be some-times in many places less manifest.... Luther is speaking of things, that is, of the doctrine and of the articles of the christian religion: the truth of which (though not of all, yet of those which are neces-sary to salvation...).[131]

We note briefly that the issue of "things" *(res)* and "words" *(verba)* broached by Whitaker is crucial to the Protestant doctrine of Scrip-ture and is, as many of the other elements of the Protestant doctrine, an element taken over from the medieval tradition and rooted in Augustine's hermeneutics. Whitaker is here attempting to draw out an issue that was bound in many ways to an older, fundamentally allegorical, pattern of interpretation and to raise it in the context of a more literal and grammatical approach to the text. Whitaker, thus, not only accepts Luther's position as normative for his own, he also continues to follow the Augustinian view of the text as espoused by Luther: the words of the text are signs pointing to the doctrinal "things." This distinction between *signa* and *res significata,* the sign and the thing signified, carries over into the language typical of scholastic Protestantism, of the words of the text and the substance of the text, of the authority of translations not strictly *quoad verba* but *quoad res,* according to the substance or meaning indicated by the original.[132]

The perspicuity of Scripture also receives extended treatment and reaches an even more precise definition in later orthodox systems, like those of Leigh, Riissen, and Mastricht. According to Leigh, "the perspicuity of the Scripture, is a clear and evident manifestation of the truth delivered in it, both in respect of itself and [of] us."[133] Mastricht similarly defines *perspicuitas* as "the clear and evident manifestation of the truth that is contained in [Scripture]," while Riissen comments that "the perspicuity of Scripture is its divine eminence that so presents the mystery of salvation that [its] true meaning can be gathered from its words."[134]

---

[131]Whitaker, *Disputation,* IV.i (pp. 362–63).
[132]See below, §6.4.a.
[133]Leigh, *Treatise,* I.viii (p. 161).
[134]Mastricht, *Theoretico-practica theol.,* I.ii.18; Riissen, *Summa ,* II.xiii.

In a manner typical of the scholastic argumentation of the age, Riissen can also elaborate and, to his mind, demonstrate the perspicuity of Scripture in a casual argument. He notes four grounds for assuming perspicuity. First, Scripture can be demonstrated perspicuous from its "efficient cause," God, who is the "father of light." If God is said to be either unable or unwilling to speak clearly, the contrary can be proven from his ultimate goodness and wisdom. Equally so, Scripture must be clear in view of its final cause or "end." It is intended to be the "canon and rule of faith and morals," which it could not be unless it were clear. From its materials or material causality, which is to say the law and the gospel, Scripture is also known to be clear inasmuch as these things can be easily understood by anyone who examines them. Lastly, the form of Scripture, which is a testament or covenant published and decreed for the church by its Lord, ought to be clear to all.[135] Efficiently, finally, materially, and formally, then, Scripture must be clear if, indeed, it is what it claims to be, the Word of God. If the logic of the argument appears to be circular and, therefore, lacking in genuine demonstration, that failing is somewhat ameliorated by the fact that the argument stands internal and not external to the theological system and that the basic premise, that Scripture is the Word of God sufficient in all things necessary to salvation, was held by virtually all of the adversaries in the sixteenth- and seventeenth-century debate. In addition, the "demonstration" provides at very least an outline of the theological components of the argument and evidences in a short and logical form the doctrinal grounding and the doctrinal elements to be included in the discussion of the clarity and perspicuity of Scripture.

Each of these definitions implies what Leigh spells out explicitly in his subsequent comments—the clarity or perspicuity of Scripture is a resident clarity that is not imported to the text or imposed upon it from without and it is also a clarity that directly relates the text to the reader or interpreter. Thus, "in respect of itself" (i.e., objectively) Scripture is perspicuous in the truths that it conveys and in the manner that it conveys them. For although some passages "seem obscure for their Majesty and dignity, yet they carry the light of truth before them" while at the same time, in both style and grammar, Scripture evidences "simplicity both in words, either proper or figurative; and in the clear sense and most perspicuous propriety of

---

[135]Riissen, *Summa theol.*, II.xiii, controversia, arg.3.

signification."[136] In all of the difficulties of Scripture, Leigh notes, a distinction must be made: "there are two things in God's revealed will, *verbum rei,* the word, and *res verbi,* the mystery." The *verbum rei,* literally, the word concerning the thing, is clear even if the thought or teaching it reveals, the *res verbi* or "thing" indicated by the word, is beyond human understanding.[137] Riissen similarly notes that the perspicuity of the text in no way removes the mystery from what has been revealed in the text: Scripture remains filled with sublime mysteries that far exceed the ability of our minds to grasp them. We can be certain only that God has given our minds the capability of knowing such things as are necessary to salvation, even while they remain in an ultimate sense mysterious to us.[138]

In a limited and soteriologically functional sense, Scripture is also clear subjectively, "in respect of us." This must be the case, Leigh argues, granting the purpose of Scripture. What Scripture teaches must have its subjective application in and for believers, in and for the church and its theology. The logic of the point is simple, and it rests on the nature of God and of God's intention for believers. Thus,

> God the Author of Scripture could speak perspicuously; for he is wisdom itself; and he would speak so because he causeth the Scripture to be written to instruct us to our eternal salvation, Rom. 15:4; and he commands us in the Scripture to seek eternal life.[139]

The point can also be made in terms of the principial status of Scripture. Scripture must be clear "in respect of us" if it is to function as

> the principle, means, and instrument of faith; every Principle ought to be by itself, and in its own nature known and most intelligible, and there being three degrees of faith—knowledge, assent, and full assurance—these cannot consist without the perspicuity of the Scripture; the divine promises also of writing the Law in our heart, and concerning the spreading abroad, and clear light of the Gospel, should be to no purpose, if the Scriptures should not be plain in things necessary to salvation.[140]

Thus, in a multitude of places, Scripture declares itself to us as

[136]Leigh, *Treatise,* I.viii (p. 162).
[137]Leigh, *Treatise,* I. viii (p. 162).
[138]Riissen, *Summa theol.,* II.xiii, controversia.
[139]Leigh, *Treatise,* I.viii (p. 162).
[140]Leigh, *Treatise,* I.viii (p. 164).

plain and simple in meaning, "both in regard to the law and to the gospel."[141] The apostle Paul confirms these texts when he declares (Rom. 15:4) that Scripture was written for edification. We cannot doubt but that God would fail in his purpose if the Scripture were unclear, and this is unthinkable. If, Pictet concludes, some of the passages of Scripture are hard to interpret and obscure in meaning, this must be for the purpose of increasing the diligence of the faithful, to "check pride" and to "remove any disdain" that might arise if the Scriptures were too simple to understand! Of course, none of these difficult passages are sole repositories of doctrines necessary to salvation.[142]

These arguments concerning the concept of the "perspicuity" of Scripture are intelligible only in the context of the debate over authority and interpretation. Against the Protestant position, Bellarmine could argue that Scripture, understood in and of itself and addressed by the individual interpreter, was not so clear and plain in its meaning "as to be sufficient, without any further interpretation, to determine controversies of the faith."[143] The absence of *perspicuitas* provided a fundamental rebuttal of the Protestant claim of the prior authority and self-interpreting character of Scripture. If Scripture were in fact unclear, then, whatever its divine status, the church's agency would be required not only for its interpretation but also for the declaration of its authoritative character on any particular point.

It is worth noting that the Roman Catholic denial of clarity and perspicuity, as much as the frequently bitter Protestant defense of the authority and sufficiency of the text, arose out of the travail of hermeneutics in the sixteenth and seventeenth centuries. Even though the Protestant *sola Scriptura* never intended the loss of the tradition—certainly not of dogmatic results of traditional exegesis, like the doctrines of the Trinity and the two natures of Christ—the combination of the Protestant insistence on Scripture as the absolute norm and the increasingly literal and grammatical tendencies of exegesis and interpretation had the result of weakening or at least changing permanently the nature of the hermeneutical link between text and dogma. The result of this change was that Protestants, holding to Scripture as the absolute norm, found it difficult to defend traditional dogmas against Socinian and rationalist claims—while the Catholics, looking critically from a dogmatic perspective at the

---

[141]Pictet, *Theol. chr.*, I.x.
[142]Pictet, *Theol. chr.*, I.x.
[143]Bellarmine, *De verbo Dei*, III.i.

results of the *sola Scriptura,* found it increasingly necessary to seek the grounds of dogma in tradition as opposed to a Scripture which, if no less clear in its exegetically derived meaning, was increasingly murky in its relation to the deposit of faith.

Bellarmine's refinement of the Roman Catholic polemic drew response from so large a number of early orthodox theologians that it is fair to say that the early orthodox *locus* on Scripture and its address to particular issues like the perspicuity of Scripture depended in no small measure on the systematizing efforts of Bellarmine. In addition to Whitaker, such writers as Ames, Rollock, Hommius, Trelcatius, and Scharipus all devoted lengthy attention to the refutation of Bellarmine and to the development of positive doctrine around the points addressed in debate. Rollock, for one, tried to balance the Protestant assumptions of clarity and of the availability of Scripture to laity with the genuine problem of obscure passages and with the need for some secondary, churchly norms of interpretation.

Thus, Rollock can insist on the one hand that the Word must be granted clear in itself—otherwise he notes, we offer insult to the Spirit. It is also certain, Rollock insists, echoing Calvin, that God has, in and through the words of Scripture, accommodated himself to our ability to understand. Even "the most unlettered among the people," therefore, can grasp the meaning of Scripture "for it is certain that the Lord in the Scriptures doth, as it were, lisp with us."[144]

It is also the case, however, that "natural and carnal" men cannot understand the things of God, Rollock argues, citing 1 Corinthians 2:14. Rather than follow Bellarmine and accuse Scripture of a lack of clarity in some places, we should berate ourselves for our remaining "corruption and blindness."[145] The point is, of course, polemical and serves to make a rhetorical point against anyone who would claim the Scriptures to be less than clear in their basic meaning. We see it repeated in the late orthodox era: "The Scripture not only contains all things necessary to salvation," writes Pictet, "but also contains them in so clear and perspicuous a form, that they may be discovered and known by any one whose eyes have not been blinded by the god of this world."[146]

Since, therefore, Scripture is clear both in itself and in respect to humanity, Leigh can declare that "All difficulty in understanding the

[144]Rollock, *Treatise of Effectual Calling,* ch. 10 (p. 78).
[145]Rollock, *Treatise of Effectual Calling,* ch. 10 (p. 81).
[146]Pictet, *Theol. chr.,* I.xiii.1.

Scripture ariseth not from the obscurity of it, but from the weakness of our understanding, corrupted by natural ignorance, or blinded by divine punishment and curse."[147] This no more lessens the value of Scripture as a rule of faith and life than an individual's inability to comprehend Euclid renders his books any less a standard in geometry. Thus, the fundamental plainness and the occasional obscurity of Scripture may be explained in several ways. First, the Scriptures

> are plain and easy to understand by all men in Fundamentals, and the Special points necessary to salvation, as the Decalogue, the Apostles' Creed, the Lord's Prayer, and the like; unless by those whose minds the god of this world hath blinded; if they be obscure in some less principal and circumstantial matters, there is need of interpretation, that the meaning may be more clearly unfolded.
>
> [Second] a difference of persons is to be considered ... as they are elect and regenerate, or reprobate and unregenerate; to those the Scripture is plain and perspicuous to whom alone it is destinated, and whose minds the Holy Ghost will enlighten.[148]

Similarly, the various conditions and vocations of men, their education and their individual inability to understand also relate to the ease or difficulty of reading Scripture.[149]

It is worth noting here the connections, implied in the foregoing quotation from Edward Leigh, with other doctrinal issues found in the prolegomena and in the doctrine of Scripture. Leigh, in the first place, registers the distinction between Scripture as *principium cognoscendi theologiae* and the "principles" of doctrine elicited from Scripture that can be described as "fundamentals" of the faith.[150] The Apostles' Creed appears here along with the Decalogue, not because the orthodox have obliged the legend of its apostolic authorship or have confused tradition with Scripture, but because the Creed is typically identified as a summary of the *articuli fundamentales*. The point concerning perspicuity, therefore, is bound closely to the ground established in the prolegomena concerning the nature of doctrine and its relation to the directly and readily understandable contents of Scripture. Fundamental doctrines appear

---

[147]Leigh, *Treatise,* I.viii (p. 162); cf. Mastricht, *Theoretico-practica theol,* I.ii.18: "Proinde, si quae in Scripturis, deprehenditur obscuritas; ea non tam a Scriptura est; quam quidem ab intellectus nostri imbecillitate."

[148]Leigh, *Treatise,* I.viii (p. 163).

[149]Leigh, *Treatise,* I.viii (pp. 163–64).

[150]See further, *PRRD,* I, 9.2.

readily upon reading of the text, even if the niceties of theological system do not. Leigh's comments concerning the doctrine of election relate directly to the question of the "efficacy" of Scripture in Christian calling—which is to say to the connection between the doctrine of Scripture and the Reformed teaching concerning the *ordo salutis* and the means of grace.[151]

It is true, then, that some places in Scripture are more difficult to understand than others—yet these places do not contain in any exclusive sense the knowledge that is necessary to salvation, nor do they prove impossible to interpret by means of the analogy of faith and the basic rules of grammatical interpretation. Indeed, Rollock concludes, the illumination of the Spirit, the comparison of Scripture with Scripture, the use of "the commonplaces of divinity" and "the testimony of the Church," the study of the grammar of the Hebrew and Greek languages, and a knowledge of logic and rhetoric all come to the aid of the interpreter. Commentaries and preaching are also aids to understanding, but of course cannot be deemed necessary to the interpretation of the text.[152]

Like most of the Reformed theologians of his generation and, indeed, like the majority of Reformers, Rollock's assertion of *sola Scriptura* and his assumption of the doctrinal and soteriological perspicuity of the text function in a churchly manner and stand in the interpretive model identified by Oberman as "Tradition I": *sola Scriptura* in no way negates the churchly tradition of doctrine and exegesis. Indeed, Rollock's comments on the various aids to interpretation identify tradition as a positive guide on a par with the other hermeneutical tools available to the theologian.

Here, again, we can note the continuity of argument between the Reformation, the early orthodox, and the high orthodox periods. The doctrinal point becomes, perhaps, more stylized in its formulation, if only by reason of repetition, but substantially, it remains the same. The points that we have drawn out of Whitaker, Rollock, and Leigh are summarized by Pictet in an argument for the perspicuity of the text, the need for concerted exegetical work to overcome difficulties, and the importance of the testimony of both the preaching church and the biblical commentator. Not all persons, comments Pictet, will find the text clear, but only those who are "in possession of their reason and implore the light of divine grace, and who are not neglectful and slothful, and who are neither blinded by preconceived

---

[151]See further, below, this section.
[152]Rollock, *Treatise of Effectual Calling,* pp. 80–81.

opinions, nor carried away by their passions, nor perverted by wilful sin."[153]

In addition to the perspicuity of the substance of the Scriptures, the Reformed orthodox argue also the plainness and purity of the words themselves:

> the sacred Scripture is of itself most simple and plain, void of all ambiguity and amphibology ... it containeth nothing doubtful in one place which is not expressed in another.... For the word of the Lord and his Spirit be ever single and sincere; neither doth God at any time speak to catch men with ambiguous and doubtful speeches, as do devils and sophisters; but to teach men his holy truth.[154]

This plainness and clarity of purpose is attested, moreover, by Christ who used Scripture to confute Satan, and also by the apostles, their successors, and the fathers of the church to refute heretics and to confirm the truth. Against such examples, "the adversaries" contend that Scripture has a "nose of wax" and is the well-spring of heresies!

> But these blasphemies are easily answered by that which is before showed. For this ambiguity and flexibility is not to be attributed to the Scripture, which is given by God by divine inspiration, and serveth us instead of God's own voice; but must be ascribed either to ignorance or malice, or malapertness of men, who either cannot apprehend the simple and true sense of Scripture, or maliciously pervert and turn the same into a strange sense.[155]

Nor does the further objection that Scripture is ambiguous because of "tropes, allegories, parables, words of divers significations, amphibological sentences [and] visions" carry any real weight. For this is a superficial ambiguity of words and not a real ambiguity of substance. These ambiguities of words can be reduces to "five principal heads":

> first, there be simple of common words of divers acceptations: secondly, there be tropical or figurative words: thirdly, there be whole speeches or sentences which carry a doubtful signification: fourthly, there be allegorical speeches consisting of the continuities of tropes: fifthly, there be also typical words and sentences

[153]Pictet, *Theol. chr.,* I.xiii.3, obs.4.
[154]Rollock, *Treatise of Effectual Calling,* ch. 11 (p. 82).
[155]Rollock, *Treatise of Effectual Calling,* ch. 11 (p. 83).

concerning types and figures. Of all these, this I say generally, that
in all such places the Holy Ghost hath but one only simple sense
and meaning.[156]

More specifically, these problems may be overcome by consideration of other passages in Scripture and of the general sense of
Scripture *(sensus plenior!),* or "by observation of grammatical acci-
dence, accents, points, or pricks, and such like."[157]

Even so, Pictet could argue that the writings of the Old
Testament frequently "are less clear than those of the New, for it
was clouded with various types, figures and shadows, but was sufficiently clear in its meaning *(in rebus)* that the patriarchs were not
ignorant."[158] It is worth noting the parallel between Pictet's argument and the language of the Reformers and early codifiers of the
sixteenth century. By way of example, Musculus had noted the
obscurity of many passages in the Old Testament and concluded,
that "after Christ, the light of the world, had appeared, he had dis-
pelled the shadows of the figures, fulfilled the truth, and gave such
clear light to the Scriptures" that there could be no question as to
their fundamental meaning.[159]

Thus, too, allegories and types are resident in the text and have
but a single significance. The doctrine of perspicuity is, thus, fundamentally a theological and hermeneutical issue, that is bound to
the problems of the relation of the Testaments, the method of
exegesis, the study of the rhetorical forms in the text, and the problems encountered by linguists and text-critics of the sixteenth and
seventeenth centuries. The concept of perspicuity, therefore, does
not stand in isolation from the other elements of the orthodox
doctrine of Scripture or from the ongoing work of exegesis—and it
is not a doctrinal point that ought to be viewed as an example of
"rigid" formulation taught in the face of theological and exegetical
problems.[160]

It is probably also true that the orthodox doctrine of perspicuity
developed both with sensitivity and in reaction to the increasingly
obvious difficulties encountered by theological exegesis in the
seventeenth century. There are far fewer textual and exegetical

[156]Rollock, *Treatise of Effectual Calling,* ch. 11 (p. 83).
[157]Rollock, *Treatise of Effectual Calling,* ch. 11 (p. 84).
[158]Pictet, *Theol. chr.,* I.xiii.3, obs. 5.
[159]Musculus, *Loci communes,* xxi (*Commonplaces,* p. 359. col. 1).
[160]Musculus, *Loci communes,* xxi (*Commonplaces,* p. 359. col. 1) and see
further, below, 7.2 and 7.3.

qualifications registered by thinkers of the late sixteenth and early seventeenth centuries than by the high orthodox writers. Of particular significance is the greater weight placed on exegesis, churchly teaching, and commentary by later writers, like Pictet, in their basic definitions of perspicuity:

> We argue for a perspicuity of the scriptures that does not exclude either attention of mind or necessary assistance of God (thus David prays for his eyes to be opened to understand the marvellous truths of the law) or the words and teaching ministry of the church, or the reading of commentaries. The only obscurity which we explode, is that which would drive the people from the pure fountains of Scripture and compel them to have recourse to the impure streams of human tradition.[161]

These final reflections on the clarity of Scripture relate also to the controversy between the Protestant orthodox and their Socinian and Remonstrant adversaries over the place of reason among the *principia theologiae* and within the structure and method of biblical hermeneutics. Riissen defines the debate with two questions: "Whether a person is able to understand Scripture without the grace of God?" and "Whether a special illumination of the Spirit and a renovation of the heart is required for a person rightly to understand Holy Scripture and, by means of it, to have faith and fulfill obedience?"[162] Once again indicating the connections between this and other *loci* in the system, Riissen notes that the answer depends—as already implied by the two questions—on the type of understanding that is sought. "It is one thing," he argues,

> to grasp the meaning of the words which the careful reader is easily able to do in the Decalogue, the histories and the Gospels. It is another thing to receive the truth of a historical faith, which the unregenerate are able to do, as in the case of King Agrippa, who believed Paul and the Prophets (Acts 26:17). It is still another thing to perceive and to receive for one's self the good and the salvation in Scripture, and [another] to enter into salvation by means of Scripture. The work of the Spirit illuminating and regenerating is required for these last two things.[163]

---

[161]Pictet, *Theol. chr.*, I.xiii.3, obs.6.
[162]Riissen, *Summa theol.*, II.xiv.
[163]Riissen, *Summa theol.*, II.xiv.

Thus it may be stated that "without the work of the Holy Spirit, a person can neither rightly understand Scripture nor duly subject himself to it." Some may object, Riissen continues, that eyes and ears have no need of spiritual renovation—but these, he counters, are merely instruments of the mind and the mind itself needs cleansing. Some may also object that this teaching stands in the way of the promulgation of the gospel, since the unregenerate cannot be expected to understand the text rightly when it is read and exposited to them. Riissen counters that "they are able to understand because, before Scripture is announced and proposed to them, God wills to bestow on them, powerfully and by this same means, the grace of conversion."[164]

These doctrinal arguments once again point toward the relationship of the concept of the perspicuity of Scripture to other elements of the orthodox theological system—in this case, to the doctrine of faith and to the related topic of the "efficacy of Scripture."[165] Word and Spirit are, in the orthodox dogmatics—as in the teaching of the Reformers—closely bound together, with the result that the perspicuity of Scripture is linked to the effective work of the Spirit and of grace that is mediated in and through the reading and preaching of the Word. The orthodox doctrine of the efficacy or efficiency of Scripture may well be the clearest example in the *locus de Scriptura sacra* of the balance and interrelationship between formalism and dynamism that is characteristic of the "baroque" era of Protestant theology. To describe Scripture in terms of a set of attributes is perhaps the height of formalism—yet, the formal attribution of "efficacy" to Scripture represents the attempt of orthodox dogmatics to state doctrinally the dynamic experience of the Word preached that is so fundamental to the Reformation and to Protestantism.

In terms that echo Calvin's teaching concerning the testimony of the Spirit, Rollock argues:

> This we say also concerning the sacred Scripture, that it is most effectual, most lively, and most vocal, sounding to every man an answer of all things necessary to salvation.[166]

The "life" of Scripture, Rollock continues, is not a "fleshly or carnal

---

[164]Riissen, *Summa theol.,* II.xiv, controversia, obj.2,3, and resp., citing 2 Tim. 2:25–26.

[165]On the doctrine of faith in its relation to both Scripture and the prolegomena to theology, see above, §4.4.

[166]Rollock, *Treatise of Effectual Calling,* ch. 12 (p. 85).

life" as that of human beings, but a spiritual life. Even so, the "lively voice" of Scripture is "a spiritual voice, speaking not so much to the ear as to the mind of man." The form and substance are, at this point of the argument, beyond controversy—Scripture is an inspired writing containing the Word of God, a written Word that mediates the living Word. Neither the church as a whole nor its pastors and teachers can be called "the voice of God," for they may err, but Scripture is both preserved from error and, by its own testimony (Rom. 9:17, 27), is a lively and present voice that provides the church with truths necessary to salvation. Even so, Christ himself, the apostles, the "primitive church," and the fathers all direct questions concerning salvation to the Scriptures.[167] Leigh summarizes the point:

> The Holy Ghost by means of this word works powerfully, so changing and reforming a man, that he finds himself transformed and renewed thereby. 1. It overmasters the soul. 2. It separates the heart from lusts, and the world. 3. Alters and changes the customs of men. 4. It keeps the heart up under the guilt of sins, against all power of the devil. It quickeneth the dull, Ps. 119:93, 107; comforteth the feeble, Rom. 15:4; giveth light to the simple, Ps. 119:7; convinceth the obstinate, I Cor. 12:3; 14:24; reproveth errors, rebuketh vices, II Tim. 3:16; is a discoverer of thoughts, I Cor. 14: 24–25; and aweth the conscience, James 4:12.[168]

Similarly, at the close of the high orthodox period, Mastricht could argue that the authority, truth, necessity, purity, perfection, and normative or regulatory character of Scripture all point by way of implication toward the efficacy or power of Scripture. Conferring Romans 1:16 on the power of God unto salvation with James 1:21 on "the engrafted word which is able to save your souls," Mastricht can speak of the *efficacia Scripturae* as a *dynamis* or, referring to 1 Thessalonians 2:13, of "the word of God which effectively works *(energeisthai)*." This efficacy is a power of Word and Spirit working together, not a physical but a "moral and instrumental power": *"nec in solo sermone esse, sed et in potentia et in Spiritu Sancto (I Thess. 1:5), quatenus Spiritus agit per verbum."*[169] Mastricht concludes with a list of ten effects of the Word of God that link his doctrine of Scripture definitively to his *ordo salutis:*

---

[167]Rollock, *Treatise of Effectual Calling,* ch. 12 (pp. 85–86).
[168]Leigh, *Treatise,* I.ii (p.17).
[169]Mastricht, *Theoretico-practica theol.,* I.ii.21.

It (1) penetrates directly to the heart, [Heb. 4:12–13]; and (2) un-
covers its mysteries and its often pondered secrets, [I Cor. 14:23–
25]. As experienced by the Samaritan woman [John 4:29], it
(3) marvellously influences the souls of human beings, sometimes
contending with them [Acts 2:37], sometimes terrifying them [Is.
66:2]. It (4) illuminates the mind [Ps. 19:8–8; Acts 26:17–18],
(5) converts the heart [James 1:2], (6) enkindles faith [Rom. 10:17;
Gal. 3:5], (7) sanctifies the whole person [John 17:17], (8) invigo-
rates even as it defeats the world [I John 2:14], (9) consoles the
believer [Rom. 15:4; Ps. 119:50, 92] and (10) provides eternal
salvation [Rom. 1:16; James 1:21].[170]

Scripture thus appears, in its perspicuity and efficacy, as the
present and necessary means to the end of faith, obedience, and
worship. In Scripture, God both demands our devotion and provides
the revelation of himself and the power of the Spirit required to
effect both the mode of and the inclination toward devotion. This
efficacy of Scripture is attested by "the candor and sincerity of the
Pen-men or amanuenses, respecting God's glory and not their own,"
who in the very style of their writing evidence the clarity of the
Word and power of God working in it.[171]

These arguments concerning clarity, perspicuity, plainness, and
efficacy, taken in their obvious relationship to the Reformed language of an order of salvation, raise the question of predestination as
a central dogma—particularly in view of Leigh's reference to election and reprobation in his discussion of the problem of the obscurity
of the text not only in certain places but generally to some people. It
is worth noting that, of the group of theological systems and treatises
examined in this study, his is the only one that presses the point back
toward the decrees for an answer and even Leigh does not discuss
the decrees at length under the topic of perspicuity, nor does he draw
out the point into his comments on the efficacy of Scripture. The
issue addressed by the majority of Reformed authors is not the
mechanics of the execution of the decree but rather the effective
power of the Word. The result of this emphasis, as noted in Rollock
and Mastricht in particular, is to underline the gracious calling of the
Word in and through its reading and preaching—and even to leave
the reader with the question of how, given this confession of power,
any are left unbelieving. Rollock, Riissen, Pictet, and Mastricht
speak of the problem of the obdurate heart rather than of an eternal

---

[170]Mastricht, *Theoretico-practica theol.,* I.ii.21.
[171]Leigh, *Treatise,* I. ii (p. 17).

divine decision to close the Scriptures to certain minds and hearts. In other words, we detect virtually nowhere in these systems any desire to focus this portion of the doctrine of Scripture around or to derive its contents from a doctrine of the eternal decrees.

Finally, we need to add a few comments on the fairly consistent reference by the theologians cited to the "plain" style of Scripture. This ought not to be taken as a reference to the so-called plain style of classical rhetoric—a style adapted to unadorned philosophical argument but not to the expression of wonder, sublimity, grandeur, and similar characteristics of religious literature. The Reformers and the orthodox here use "plainness" as a synonym for clarity and perspicuity—and in fact, as Shuger has demonstrated, the writers of the late sixteenth and seventeenth centuries would tend to understand the rhetorical style of both Scripture and Christian theology as a variant of the "grand style" of classical rhetoric.[172]

5.5 Scripture as Rule of Faith and Judge of Controversies: Canonical Authority

> The authority of Scripture is twofold: divine *(divina)* and canonical or regulatory *(canonica)*.[173]

We return now to the distinction noted previously between the divine and the regulatory authority of Scripture.[174] In the earlier discussion, we dealt with the *authoritas scripturae* considered as that essential genuineness, power, and dignity of the written Word of God that derives from God, the *author primarius* of Scripture. This discussion was elaborated by the orthodox in terms of the causes and ends of Scripture and the inspired *forma* of the scriptural materials. These doctrines and definitions, in turn, provide the basis for a definition of the authority of Scripture *quoad nos,* in respect of us, which is to say, the authority of Scripture considered as a property of the written Word according to which the Word has a canonical, normative, or regulatory function in all debates concerning Christian doctrine. This authority of Scripture *quoad nos* is the central issue of the orthodox Protestant doctrine of Scripture. It is grounded, by both the Reformers and the orthodox, in the nature of Scripture as

---

[172]Cf. Debora K. Shuger, *Sacred Rhetoric: The Christian Grand Style in the English Renaissance* (Princeton: Princeton University Press, 1988).

[173]Polanus, *Syntagma,* Synopsis Libri I.

[174]See above, p. 287.

inspired, living Word of God, but it is also, quite clearly the reason for the stress placed on these preceding definitions and the reason for the discussion of the attributes or properties of Scripture found in most of the orthodox Protestant theological systems.

The Reformation itself was rooted in the question of authority, which it answered with the language of *sola Scriptura* and of the priority of Scripture as the ultimate norm of doctrine over all other grounds of authority. The Protestant orthodox doctrine of Scripture is a codification of this answer—and the focus of the entire doctrinal exposition is clearly the character of Scripture as rule or norm and the way in which Scripture ought to be considered as prior to the church and its traditions. This issue, in other words, is the underlying reason for the form taken by the Protestant doctrine of Scripture in its development from the Reformation through the era of orthodoxy. There is some irony, therefore, in the fact that this elaborate doctrine, with its theological and hermeneutical stress on text and exegesis, could serve so well against the claims of churchly authority in the sixteenth and early seventeenth centuries—and then fare so poorly against the claims of reason and of the autonomous exegete advanced late in the seventeenth and in the eighteenth centuries. The great shield of Protestantism against popery would ultimately become a liability in the war against rationalism.

a. The Reformers and the Reformed Confessions on the Canonical Authority of Scripture

The strongly worded arguments of Protestant theologians of both the Reformation and orthodox eras against the idea of a co-equal authority of Scripture, tradition, and church, typically summarized by the phrase *sola Scriptura,* must never be taken as a condemnation of tradition or a denigration of the authority of the church as a confessing community of believers. The Reformation took as its point of departure the late medieval debate over the relation of Scripture to tradition and assumed that tradition stood as a subordinate norm under the authority of Scripture and derived its authority from Scripture. This assumption of the fundamental value and rectitude of the church's faith insofar as it was genuinely grounded on the biblical Word allowed place in the Protestant mind both for a use of tradition and for a churchly use of confessions and catechisms as standards of belief.

What we have already noted of the doctrine of Scripture is equally the case with the doctrine of tradition. It existed in a partially or almost completely formulated state within the body of

Christian doctrine during the Middle Ages but was not drawn out as an independent dogmatic *locus* until the sixteenth century. Just as the Reformation pressed Protestants toward the formal statement of a doctrine of Scripture, so did the Reformation press Roman Catholics to define more closely their own foundational principles and, at the time of the Council of Trent, to produce the first formal dogmatic treatise on tradition, such as probably Martin Perez de Ayala's *De divinis, apostolicis atque ecclesiasticis traditionibus* (Cologne, 1549).[175] As Congar comments, with reference to Chemnitz' *Examination of the Council of Trent* and *Loci theologici,* Protestants acknowledged a variety of forms of tradition and recognized their value in Christian instruction:

> the *principle* of tradition is not denied, but its *applications* are rigorously submitted to the sovereign criterion of Scripture, taken as much in its material aspect (the content) as in its formal aspect. A door remained open, or at least ajar. It remained so even after the Triden tine decree, but in an atmosphere getting progressively more and more awkward.[176]

Thus, the church's transmission of the message of Christ and the apostles and of Scripture generally, the ancient creeds, the development of dogmas from Scripture, the consensus of the fathers, and the practices and rites of the early church were all acknowledged as significant precedents for contemporary teaching.[177] Where the Protestant and the Roman Catholic views diverged, particularly in the wake of Trent, was over the council's identification of tradition as "a formal principle different from Scripture, if not autonomous."[178]

But the debate was not, as Congar characterizes it, "between the Protestants and the champions of the ancient faith."[179] Nor can we

[175]Cf. Congar, *Tradition and Traditions,* p. 296, with Tavard, "Tradition in Early Post-Tridentine Theology," p. 391.

[176]Congar, *Tradition and Traditions,* p. 145.

[177]Cf. Musculus, *Loci communes,* xxi; Bullinger, *Decades,* pp. 12–35; with A.N.S. Lane, "Scripture, Tradition and Church: An Historical Survey," in Vox *Evangelica* 9 (1975):37–55; and J. F. Peter, "The Place of Tradition in Reformed Theology," in *Scottish Journal of Theology* 18 (1965): 294–307.

[178]Congar, *Tradition and Traditions,* p. 145.

[179]Congar, *Tradition and Traditions,* p. 139; cf. J. N. Bakhuizen Van Den Brink, "La tradition dans l'Église primitive et au XVIe siècle," in *Revue d'histoire et de philosophie religieuses* 36 (1956):271–81, who understands the Reformers as returning to a view of tradition more like that of the early church than the Tridentine view.

follow him in his adaptation of Lortz' thesis—"the Reformers were doubtless victims of the bad formulation of the question prevalent in the fourteenth and fifteenth centuries, itself the fruit of excessive exaggeration of ecclesiastical machinery and especially of papal authority."[180] Rather, the debate was between two late medieval views of the relationship of Scripture and tradition which, in the era of the Reformation, became so strictly associated with Protestantism on the one side and Roman Catholicism on the other that they could no longer exist within the same ecclesial and confessional body.[181] To make the point in another way, the debate was between two groups, both nurtured within the medieval church catholic, over the question of which group and, indeed, which view of the relationship of Scripture and tradition, represented the "ancient faith" and was, therefore, truly catholic. As the Reformation passed over into the era of confessional orthodoxy, the positive reception of tradition by Protestants—noted by Congar in the case of Chemnitz, but easily documented from numerous other writers—became increasingly the trademark of a Protestant theology that claimed catholicity for itself.[182]

According to Vermigli, the balance of Scripture and tradition advocated by the Reformers was taught by both Paul and Augustine and also has "the firm consent and authority of the catholic church: yet not in such sort, that (as our adversaries endeavor to prove) all the judgment of the scriptures should depend thereon."[183] Neither the church nor a council of the church has the authority to set itself above Scripture as an arbiter of doctrine:

> Therefore when they interpret the word of God, it is their part to prove, that they have expounded such things, according to the consent and proportion of the other places of the scripture.

For the church does not give authority to Scripture:

> Whatsoever estimation or authority hath happened unto the church, all that hath come from the word of God. . . . And yet I urge not

[180]Congar, *Tradition and Traditions,* p. 146.

[181]Cf. Oberman, *Harvest,* pp. 365–412, with E. Flesseman-van Leer, "The Controversy about Scripture and Tradition between Thomas More and William Tyndale," in *Nederlands Archief voor Kerkgeschiedenis* 43 (1959):143–64.

[182]See Muller, "Vera Philosophia cum sacra Theologia nusquam pugnat," pp. 352–55, 361–65, and idem, "Scholasticism Protestant and Catholic," pp. 200–201, 204–5.

[183]Vermigli, *Commonplaces,* I.vi.7 (p. 42).

this much as though I despised or condemned the dignity of the church. For I attribute unto it three godly functions about the word of God. The first is that I grant she doth, as it were a witness, preserve the holy books.... Secondly, we doubt not, but that the churches part is, to preach and set forth the word of God committed unto it.... Thirdly, we also acknowledge it to be the function of the church, that seeing it is endued with the holy Ghost, it should decipher & discern the true and proper books of the heavenly word, from them that be not canonical.[184]

In no instance do these duties set the church above Scripture, for as the church preserves Scripture she does not pervert or alter its contents; as she preaches the Word she proclaims faithfully that which she has received and no more; and as she adjudges the canon only as she is taught so to do by the Spirit of Christ, her Teacher, and by the comparison of Scripture with Scripture—even as a counterfeit letter is proved by comparison with a genuine letter. The church is the "keeper of God's books" commanded to do as God himself in his Word has prescribed.[185] This is the true meaning of Augustine's statement that he would not have believed the gospel had it not been for the authority of the church moving him. The church here acts as an instrument of the Spirit and not as an authority in and of herself. Even so Augustine uses the word *commoveret* which means "to move with the authority of another thing" and not "to move of itself."[186] Moreover, the fathers of the church and the church in any age are liable to error; only the Scripture is of God and pure and therefore only the Scripture can be of first authority.[187]

From the very outset of the Reformation, the debate over authority looked to the early history of the church for precedent and Augustine's comment that he "would not have believed the gospel" had he not been moved by "the authority of the catholic church" became, as it had in the late Middle Ages, a focus of debate. The quotation appears, for example, in Tyndale's *An Answer to Sir Thomas More's Dialogue* (1530), where Tyndale attempts to turn back the claim of a prior authority of the church by arguing that his adversaries "abuse the saying of thay holy man" much as they abuse and distort the meaning of Scripture itself.[188] Before he converted to

---

[184]Vermigli, *Commonplaces,* I.vi.7 (p. 42).
[185]Vermigli, *Commonplaces,* I.vi.8 (pp. 42–43).
[186]Vermigli, *Commonplaces,* I.vi.9.
[187]Vermigli, *Commonplaces,* I.vi.10–11.
[188]Tyndale, *Answer,* pp. 49–50; cf. E. Flesseman-van Leer, "The Contro-

Christianity, Augustine "was an heathen man ... full of worldly wisdom, unto whom the preaching of Christ was foolishness," but he was moved by "the earnest living of the Christen ... and stirred ... to believe that it was no vain doctrine; but that it must needs be of God, in that it had such power in it."[189] Augustine was moved, therefore, not by a prior doctrinal authority of the church, but by the example of Christians, to examine their teaching and especially to examine their Scriptures with due seriousness.

Tyndale's argument, for all its rough vernacular English eloquence, was hardly new. We have encountered it already in the late medieval debate over Scripture and tradition, in Gansfort's reply to Hoeck. Tyndale also echoes Luther's interpretation of Augustine's famous maxim in the tract, *A Reply to the Texts Cited in Defense of the Doctrines of Men* (1522), inasmuch as Luther understood the *catholicae ecclesiae* of the original not as the institutional church but as "Christendom" *(Christenheyt)* and the *auctoritas* as an "external proof of faith, by which heretics are refuted and the weak are strengthened in faith" and not as an a priori ground for belief.[190] The ultimate basis of belief in Scripture is simply the fact that Scripture is "the word of God" and that the believer, recognizing this truth inwardly, "is convinced in his heart that it is true."[191]

The testimony of the church, according to Tyndale, functions differently than the testimony of Scripture. It is quite true that "they which come after receive the Scripture of them that go before," but it is quite another thing to claim that the primary reason for accepting Scripture as God's Word is the testimony of the church. "There are," Tyndale argues,

> two manner of faiths, an historical faith and a feeling faith. The historical faith hangeth of the truth and honesty of the teller, or of the common fame and consent of many.... So now with an historical faith I may believe that the Scripture is God's, by the teaching of them; and so I should have done, though they had told me that Robin Hood had been the Scripture of God: which faith is but an opinion, and therefore abideth fruitless.... But of a feeling faith it is written (John 6), "They shall all be taught of God." That is, God shall write it in their hearts with his Holy Spirit.... And this faith is

versy about Scripture and Tradition between Thomas More and William Tyndale," in *Nederlands Archief voor Kerkgeschiedenis* 43 (1959):143–64.
[189]Tyndale, *Answer,* p. 50.
[190]WA, 10.89; trans. in *LW*, 35, pp. 150–51.
[191]*LW,* 35, p. 151.

none opinion; but a sure feeling, and therefore fruitful. Neither
hangeth it of the honesty of the preacher, but of the power of
God.[192]

Tyndale does not, obviously, discount either the testimony of the
church or the "honesty of the preacher" entirely—and he would
probably not be averse to the idea of a tradition of interpretation,
provided that the Scripture be recognized as the sole authoritative
norm of doctrine. His polemic is not against testimony per se but
against churchly testimony elevated above the level of opinion and
used as the foundation of something more than *fides historica*. This
interpretation of Augustine's words is a typical focus of the
Reformers' teaching on the authority of Scripture and of the teaching of the post-Reformation orthodox. The argument is repeated by
generation after generation of Protestant writers—and it sounds so
typically Protestant that we all too easily neglect the fact that it is
evidence of continuity with the thought of the later Middle Ages.

The early Reformed confessional foundations of Reformed orthodoxy had made clear the priority of Word over the authority of its
recipients. Early in the Reformation, the confessions and theses of
the Zwinglian reform in German-speaking Switzerland had stressed
the living and life-giving character of Word, the priority of Word
over text, and the priority of the Word as presented in and by the
text over all human, including all churchly authorities.[193] The debate
was central to the life of the Reformation and it rapidly became
central not only to the confessions of the Reformed church but also
to the dogmatic systems of the first generation of codifiers—
Bullinger, Calvin, Musculus, and Vermigli.

Even so, the Reformed doctrine of the authority of Scripture
attained a fairly complete codification in the generation of Calvin,
Hyperius, Musculus, and Vermigli, and, therefore, in theological
summations written, for the most part, in the years between 1550
and 1564. Significantly, this is also the era of the Council of Trent.
Musculus' *Loci communes* offer a particularly full and developed
discussion that addresses the issue both formally and functionally,
first touching on "the authority and excellence of the canonical
Scriptures" and then on "the necessity and use" of that authority. It
cannot be denied, writes Musculus, "that those who are ignorant of
godly things" need to be "instructed in the knowledge of God to
their salvation." Yet, granting their condition, they may resist or fail

[192]Tyndale, *Answer,* pp. 50–51.
[193]See above, §2.1.b.

to be convinced. Thus,

> necessity requires that they first be moved by some authority to
> submit to teaching *(doctrina)*, the spirit and understanding of
> which they are not immediately able to grasp until their faculties
> are prepared to understand the things in which they should be
> instructed. Authority, therefore, ought to be viewed as the gate
> through which all must pass in order to attain the knowledge of
> those things that must be learned.[194]

Musculus' point is that knowledge cannot be gained unless one first
accepts the validity of certain truths and, indeed, of certain sources
of truth, on authority. This being the case, it is all the more important that scholars be wary of "false authority." For this reason, "the
first rulers of the church of God" gave highest authority to Scripture
—that it might guide the minds of the faithful as a "rule" preserving
them from error.[195]

A preliminary distinction must be made between "two kinds of
authorities," the former "everlasting and highest," the latter "temporal and lesser." The authority of God alone is everlasting and highest
—while the valid temporal, lesser authorities are those that have
been appointed by God, such as the rights of parents over children,
of magistrates over citizens, of preachers over congregations. These
lower authorities are derivative and must look to God in all things as
their source and sanction. Lower authorities are also bound to indicate in all of their actions their divine foundation "in order that the
authority of God might remain umblemished always and in all
places."[196] Noting that he passes over until a subsequent point the
character and forms of the dispensation of temporal authority, word
and deed, Musculus addresses these categories in God and God's
work:

> We must consider that higher and everlasting authority attributed
> to God and to God alone, not in respect to its manifestation in deed
> but in respect to its dispensation in the word of our salvation. For
> even as such great authority is attributed to his deeds ... so also is
> it fitting that we acknowledge the firm authority of his words,
> even when the wisdom and truth of them is not immediately
> understood.[197]

[194]Musculus, *Loci communes,* xxi (*Commonplaces,* p. 354, col. 2).
[195]Musculus, *Loci communes,* xxi (*Commonplaces,* p. 355, col. 1).
[196]Musculus, *Loci communes,* xxi (*Commonplaces,* p. 355, col. 2).
[197]Musculus, *Loci communes,* xxi (*Commonplaces,* p. 356, col. 1).

The Scriptures have this higher and everlasting authority inasmuch as they "were not brought forth by man's will and wisdom, but were given by God for our salvation and contain not the word of men but of God."[198] The relationship between this point and the Protestant doctrine of inspiration ought to be obvious. It is only on the basis of a strong doctrine of inspiration that the divine authority of Scripture can be opposed to the human authority of church and tradition. The Holy Spirit worked both to communicate and to teach this heavenly wisdom and to lead into a godly life those "men in whom he set forth [this wisdom] as the interpreters of God's oracles." From this relationship of the Spirit to the written Word, it appears that the "Holy Scriptures are from God and have sufficient authority in the church of God." Even so, the apostles Peter and Paul have written that Scripture is "inspired by God"—or, as Christ himself told his disciples, "it is not you who speak, but the Spirit of your Father speaking through you" (Matt. 10:20). So also the prophets announce the Word of God and testify that the words are not their own but the Word of the Lord speaking in them. Thus, the apostles and all who heard their words,

> believed that God is the author of Holy Scripture, that Scripture comes by the inspiration of the Holy Spirit, that it surpasses the wisdom of the world, that it exceeds the capacity of human reason, and that it contains perfect teaching.[199]

In his own times, Musculus continues, "doubts have arisen in the church of Christ on many matters" and a clear canon or rule of faith is necessary. By way of example, he notes that some defend the authority of "the see of Rome" while others argue the rectitude of ideas "drawn from the philosophy of Plato and Aristotle." Those whose concern, however, is for the salvation of the faithful willingly set aside these other standards and, indeed, their own prerogative to act as authorities and, following the counsel of the Spirit and the example of the early church, look to the "rule of Holy Scripture."[200] Indeed, adds Musculus, the writings of the fathers add nothing to the biblical Word and ought to be followed only insofar as they agree with the canon of Scripture.[201]

---

[198]Musculus, *Loci communes,* xxi (*Commonplaces,* p. 356, col. 1).
[199]Musculus, *Loci communes,* xxi (*Commonplaces,* p. 357, col. 1).
[200]Musculus, *Loci communes,* xxi (*Commonplaces,* p. 357, col. 2).
[201]Musculus, *Loci communes,* xxi (*Commonplaces,* pp. 360–62).

Musculus next encounters the argument that, since the church of the apostles precedes the writing of Scripture, Scripture depends for its authority on the church. Christ himself, Musculus notes, never argued in this way about the authority of the Old Testament—and well he might have since the people of God existed long before Moses wrote the books of the law. Quite to the contrary, Musculus argues,

> In the church of Christ the issue is not antiquity but the truth of doctrine: the authority of Christian doctrine does not arise because of great antiquity but because of its essential truth and because of its source in God.[202]

If this were not so, we should have to follow the Jews in preferring the Old Testament to the New, on grounds of antiquity. While it is true that the canonical authors wrote as members of the church, both the church and the Scriptures receive their authority from God. The biblical writers "were not moved to write by the church but by the inspiration of the Holy Spirit."[203] Since, moreover, Scripture is the Word of God given as a rule to the church, the authority of doctrine and of the church comes from God only indirectly by way of the Scriptures. Indeed, it is the Scriptures that, as the Word of God, "bring faith and authority to the church."[204]

Musculus offers, by way of elaboration of the point, a long excursus on Augustine's statement, "I would not have believed the gospel were it not for the church," that follows out the arguments we have already encountered in Tyndale and Luther. The debate has progressed to the point, however, that Musculus can use the statement as a set-piece for illustrating the precise way in which the church actually derives its authority from Scripture even as the church testifies to the centrality of Scripture and its message.[205] Calvin, similarly, addresses the "context" of Augustine's words: Augustine does not teach "that the faith of godly men is founded on the authority of the church" but only that unbelievers, who have no knowledge of Scripture, would not be drawn to the Word or "rendered teachable" if it were not for the testimony of the whole church.[206] This is a matter of suasion and example, not of prior

---

[202]Musculus, *Loci communes,* xxi (*Commonplaces,* p. 363, col. 2).

[203]Musculus, *Loci communes,* xxi (*Commonplaces,* p. 364, col. 1).

[204]Musculus, *Loci communes,* xxi (*Commonplaces,* p. 367, col. 2).

[205]Musculus, *Loci communes,* xxi (*Commonplaces,* pp. 365, col. 1–367, col. 2)

[206]Calvin, *Institutes,* I.vii.3.

authority—to borrow Oberman's words, a "practical authority" rather than a "metaphysical priority."[207]

Even so, no human tradition not grounded firmly on Scripture can be necessary to salvation. Vermigli points out that Christ himself, our best teacher, expressly tells the church to search the Scriptures. "Moreover," Vermigli argues,

> every rational faculty and intellectual discipline derives its worthiness from the subject matter with which it deals.... Wherefore, since our [theological] *scientia* treats of nothing other than Christ, it ought all the more to be acknowledged as the highest knowledge, since Christ is most excellent above all things. I suppose no one doubts that the New Testament speaks chiefly of Christ; but because some doubt that the Old Testament does likewise, let them attend to Paul writing in the tenth chapter of Romans: "Christ is the end of the law"; and in the fifth chapter of John, when the Lord said ... "Search the Scriptures," he added ... "For they bear witness of me"; and in the same chapter it is said of Moses, "He has written of me."[208]

Vermigli also cites the various New Testament texts (2 Tim. 3:16, 17; Rom. 15:4), which speak of the inspiration of Scripture and its authority in doctrine and morals: "which things, seeing they are spoken of in the Old Testament, (for while this was written, the new Testament was not yet published) what shall we now think, having the monuments both of the Apostles and of the Evangelists added thereunto?"[209] Even so, in 1 Timothy 4:13 the power to save is attributed to the Scriptures "by the Holy Ghost." Augustine is an example of this, having been converted by the reading of Scripture.

> the decrees of the Christian faith can be confirmed by no other means, than by authority of the holy scriptures. Therefore as the ecclesiastical history declares: *Constantine* the great, in the council of *Nice,* exhorted the fathers of the church, that by the oracles of the holy scriptures, they would appease the controversies sprung up in religion.[210]

Significantly, at the same time that the first great Protestant codifiers were formulating their doctrine of the priority of Scripture over

---

[207]Oberman, *Forerunners,* p. 56.
[208]Vermigli, *Commonplaces,* I.vi.1 (p. 39).
[209]Vermigli, *Commonplaces,* I.vi.3.
[210]Vermigli, *Commonplaces,* I.vi.3,

tradition and resting it on the assumption of the sole sufficiency of
Scripture in those teachings necessary to salvation, Roman Catholic
theologians were in the process of deemphasizing the patristic and
medieval tradition concerning the sufficiency of Scripture: "post-
Tridentine theology," writes Congar, "lost sight of this almost
entirely, since it was interested less in the content, the *quod* of dogmas, than in the formal aspect of truth become dogma, in the *quo,*
the formal motive, the light or authority which transforms a particular statement into an obligatory *dogma.*"[211] Whereas the language of
the sufficiency of Scripture could subsist together with a strong
traditionalism in the medieval period—because of the already noted
hermeneutical possibility of moving with ease, by means of the
quadriga, from scriptural teaching to traditional dogma and back
again—in the new hermeneutical context of the early sixteenth century and, after Trent, granting the precise definition of the canon of
Scripture on both sides of the argument, emphasis on the sufficiency
of Scripture tended to become a Protestant possession while emphasis on the equality of Scripture and tradition and on the ability of
tradition to "speak in the silence of Scripture" became an almost
exclusive property of Roman Catholicism. (Just as, of course,
Protestantism retained tradition as a support of interpretation, secondary in status to the text of Scripture, so also did several Roman
Catholic theologians of the time, notably John Driedo in the era of
Trent and Robert Bellarmine after Trent, retain the doctrine of the
sufficiency of Scripture.[212])

The brief "argument" prefacing Book I of Bullinger's *Compendium* is a fairly representative statement of the doctrine of the
Reformed churches, already at a rather early stage buttressing the
teaching of *sola Scriptura* with statements concerning the divine
authorship, inspiration, and authority of the text:

> It behoveth all and every faithful Christian to know, that without
> all gainsaying, they ought to believe the holy Scriptures of the
> Bible contained in the old and new Testament. Forasmuch as they
> are the true word of God, inspired by God, and have of themselves
> authority and credit, so that it is not needful that they should be
> made authentic by the Church, or of men. Furthermore, we ought

[211]Congar, *Tradition and Traditions,* p. 167.
[212]Cf. Murphy, *Notion of Tradition,* pp. 76, 89, 122–23, 133–35 with
Congar, *Tradition and Traditions,* pp. 116–17, 167–168, citing Driedo, *De
ecclesiast. Scripturis et dogmat.* (Louvain, 1556), IV.6, and Bellarmine, *De
verbo Dei,* IV.11.

to know, that the said Scripture was truly and uncorruptly written and set forth unto the world, by the holy Prophets and Apostles: and that it doth fully and plainly comprehend, and teach all these things, which are necessary to godliness and salvation: also that the holy Scripture ought to be read, and heard of all men. All causes and controversies of Religion ought to be determined and approved by the holy Scriptures. But such as agree not with these, either are contrary hereunto, of them we ought to beware, whether they be named Traditions or Decrees of Elders, or what name soever they have else. Although the same are either set forth or received by many of few: of learned or of unlearned: although they have been by common consent and custom ever so long received. For the word of God ought by right to be preferred before all other things, inasmuch as the Author thereof is the truth itself, the very eternal and almighty God.[213]

These considerations in no way stand against the use of creeds and confessions in the church as derivative or secondary norms nor do they in any way indicate a perceived discontinuity on the part of the Reformers between their doctrine and the great tradition of Christian orthodoxy. Thus, Bullinger's *Decades* contain a preliminary section, set prior to the first decade of sermons, in which the results of Nicaea, Constantinople, Ephesus, and Chalcedon are exposited and complete texts of their creeds provided together with the creeds from two synods of Toledo, the rules of faith from Ireneus' *Against Heresies* and Tertullian's *On the Praescription of Heretics,* the *Athanasian Creed,* the creed of Damasus, bishop of Rome (ca. 376), and the imperial decree concerning the catholic faith from the *Tripartite History*. Bullinger states in his preface that he has included these works in his theological summation in order to show that Protestant doctrine is indeed the historic teaching of the church.[214] Even so, Bullinger's *Decades* and his related *Compendium christianiae religionis,* plus Calvin's *Institutes* and the *Heidelberg Catechism,* all follow out the catechetical practice of basing their primary doctrinal exposition on the articles of the Apostle's Creed.

In a similar manner, somewhat later in the sixteenth century, Virel could set forth a discussion of the standard signs or proofs of the divinity of Scripture and then move on to discuss what he identified as the primary effect of this divine work, "that the church hath

---

[213]Bullinger, *Commonplaces,* bk. I, argument, p. 1 r–v.
[214]Bullinger, *Decades,* pp. 12–35; cf. p. 12, n. 1.

always (as it is at this day) been gathered together by the authority of the holy Scripture" and that its worship proceeds along the lines instituted by God and Christ in Scripture.[215] The special or personal effects of Scripture are the reverence it instills in the heart and the desire for the heavenly and higher life as well as a contempt for the world. Even so, it follows that the church depends on Scripture and not the authority of Scripture on the testimony of the church. The church's witness may well move people to embrace the Scripture, but faith is generated by the Spirit—so that the very witness of the church depends on the doctrine originally witnessed by the Spirit in the Scriptures and by the Spirit moving the church to faith.[216]

The priority of Scripture over tradition, therefore, is argued by the early Reformed systematicians, on much the same grounds as the identification of Scripture as Word. Not only do the Reformed insist on divine agency in the production of Scripture, but they also relate that divine agency and the resultant concept of authority to the saving purpose behind all of the revelation in Scripture and, granting that saving purpose, to the "foundation" or "scope" of Scripture which is Christ himself. In other words, Scripture bears and conveys Christ in a way that tradition cannot: tradition only knows of Christ and of God's saving purpose in Christ because of the biblical witness. In a parallel and complementary sense, the church exists only because it has been called by the Word—and the Word is found in Scripture. It is also worth noting at this point that the relationship between the Christ-center of Scripture and of the Reformed doctrine of Scripture and the language of divine causality so evident throughout the Reformed exposition of the doctrine of Scripture reflects the balance and relationship between divine decree and christological focus that can be identified in the doctrines of predestination and the Person of Christ in the theology of the Reformed theologians of the early sixteenth century and of the early orthodox era.[217]

b. The Canonical Authority of the Old and New Testaments According to Reformed Orthodoxy

The Reformed orthodox stand in accord with the Reformers in their assertion that "Scripture is the rule of faith and manners" or of "faith and life" and has, for this reason, been called "canonical"

---

[215]Virel, *Treatise,* I.i (pp. 3–4).

[216]Virel, *Treatise,* I.i (pp. 4–5).

[217]Cf. Muller, *Christ and the Decree,* pp. 7–11, 69–75, 108–24, 171–73, 179–82; *PRRD,* I, pp. 82–87.

since the time of the fathers.[218] Scripture must be this rule inasmuch as "the ground of our religion and the rule of faith and of all saving truth is the Word of God, contained in the holy Scripture."[219] Even so, writes Leigh, Scripture is a "worthy" canon or "rule of religion, faith and godliness, according whereunto the building of the house of God may be fitted."[220]

This identity of the authority of the text with its claim on faith is noted by Cloppenburg as the first and foremost element of his definition: "The faith by which Scripture is believed [fides qua Scripturis creditur] (which the Papists are pleased to call auctoritatem quoad nos) is that conviction of mind and conscience that acknowledges the divine authority of sacred Scripture, requiring the obedience of our intellect and our will."[221] This faith, moreover, does not arise "without the illumination of the intellect, which those who believe the Scriptures have in themselves by the internal testimony of the Spirit." The content of this illumination is simply the testimony that "the Spirit speaking in Scripture is the truth."[222]

These definitions serve to clarify several points made previously concerning the Reformed approach to theology and religion. In the first place, the Reformed orthodox—despite their extensive discussion of the theme of "religion"—had no interest in the question of "religion in general" and of Christianity as a specific instance or a "species" of religion.[223] The Protestant orthodox interest in religion is parallel to their interest in Scripture as the sole ground of religion. Their stress is on the right relationship between God and humanity and on the way in which Scripture and faith in the truth of Scripture offer a foundation not for religion in general but for right religion, the Christian religion.

By way of further example, the prolegomenon to Ursinus' catechetical lectures[224] contains an initial definition of religion that seems to address this question, but his discussion soon demonstrates that his concern is not for the general religion in the world but rather

---

[218]Leigh, *Treatise,* I.viii (p. 132); *Westminster Confession,* I.ii.
[219]*Irish Articles,* §1.
[220]Leigh, *Treatise,* I.viii (p. 132).
[221]Cloppenburg, *Exercitationes super locos communes,* I.ii.1.
[222]Cloppenburg, *Exercitationes super locos communes,* I.ii.2.
[223]Cf. *PRRD,* I, 3.3.
[224]Drawn largely from his *Loci theologici,* in *Opera,* I, cols. 426–55 and incorporated into early editions and translations of the catechetical lectures: e.g., Zacharias Ursinus, *Doctrinae christianae compendium* (Oxford, 1585), translated as *The Summe of Christian Religion* (Oxford, 1587; 1591).

for the divisions within Christianity and with the character of proper religious observance. Similarly his comment concerning the forms of religious thought and observance drawn "from nature herself" is soon forgotten in the presence of the greater issue, that of diverging interpretations of God's revelation and of the falsity of those doctrines not grounded on the scriptural deposit of revelation.[225] Rather than making a distinction between religion in general and religion in specific instances or between natural and revealed religion, Ursinus simply makes a distinction between true and false religion that serves as a transition and an introduction to his central theme, the scriptural foundation of Christian religion, the true religion and its theology.

Arguing with an intentional circularity—seeing, that is, no reason to step outside of the circle of the church to argue either the truth of Christianity or relative falsity of other faiths—Ursinus moves from the identification of Christianity with *religio vera* to the identification of Scripture alone as authoritative: "Whence it may appear that this religion alone was delivered by God, which is contained in the Scripture."[226] Since the creation of the world—and in the explicit statements of the prophets of old—God has forbidden that any of his words be called into question or disobeyed.

> Since, therefore, it appears that the books of the Old and New Testament are the words of God, there is no room left for doubt whether the religion and doctrine contained in them is true. But whether these books were written by divine inspiration, and by what proofs and testimonies we are certain of so great a matter ... is a consideration worthy of those, who are desirous of the word of God, and do seek for sure comfort.[227]

The arguments and proofs for the authority of Scripture, therefore, contain an element of piety. Knowledge of the word and comfort in it are made available in and through the discussion of the grounds of the authority of the text.

Having stated these principles, Ursinus sets a pattern for many of the orthodox theologies by turning to the Roman argument that the authority of Scripture is grounded on the testimony of the church. This would make "the authority of God's word" depend on "the Testimony of man" and in so doing make "man's voice ... greater

---

[225]Ursinus, *Loci theologici*, in *Opera*, I, cols. 428–29.
[226]Ursinus, *Loci theologici*, in *Opera*, I, col. 433.
[227]Ursinus, *Loci theologici*, in *Opera*, I, col. 433.

than the voice of God," all of which argument is "unworthy of the majesty of God," indeed, a blasphemy. In addition this argument, in effect, reduces Scripture to a document of uncertain value in view of the "ignorance, error, and vanity" of humankind.[228]

The only means, therefore, of determining the truth of religion definitively, is showing not that it has the approbation of men but that its origin is in God. Scripture itself testifies to this and refutes the Roman theory of ecclesiastical ratification of scriptural authority. Christ himself in the Gospel of John testifies to the divine origin of his word and Paul, in 1 Corinthians 2 grounds his preaching on the power of God rather than the wisdom of men.[229] The church is built on the foundation of the prophets and apostles, as it is written in Ephesians 2: Therefore "the certainty of Scripture cannot depend on the Church's witness." Even so the soundness and incorruptibility of the text rest not on the church's testimony but on God's own testimony "both in Scripture and in the hearts of his Saints." The canonicity of the scriptural books is similarly guaranteed not by the church but by the testimony of the prophets and apostles themselves: either by the identity of the author as a man inspired of God or by the manner of speech of the book.[230]

The Word of God is both temporally and regulatively prior to the church. Even if the church existed when any particular book of Scripture was written down, nevertheless "the sum of the Law and Gospel was the same forever" and precedes the church as "the immortal seed of which the church was born." Since "the word of God is the everlasting wisdom of God himself,"[231] the Roman Church's *magisterium* cannot hold any value over against the authority of Scripture. The argument here has advanced somewhat in the several decades since Musculus stated it. The emphasis falls not simply on the priority of the Word as a norm but on the essential identity of the eternal Word of truth, the sum of law and gospel, with the biblical revelation. The argument now excludes the post-Tridentine approach of Cano's *De locis theologicis* which had acknowledged Scripture as the "foundation of sacred letters" but had also inferred, from the temporal priority of church over Scripture, that "faith and religion" could stand "without Scripture," as indeed they once had—by resting on unwritten tradition.[232] Ursinus'

---

[228]Ursinus, *Loci theologici*, in *Opera,* I, col. 433.
[229]Ursinus, *Loci theologici*, in *Opera,* I, cols. 433–34.
[230]Ursinus, *Loci theologici*, in *Opera,* I, col. 434.
[231]Ursinus, *Loci theologici*, in *Opera,* I, col. 434.
[232]Cano, *De locis theologicis,* III.3 (cols. 502–3, 243); cf. Tavard,

response focuses on the revelatory Word of God and follows out the historical distinction between unwritten and written Word, opposing Cano's argument that the unwritten traditions continue. parallel to the written, but with a different content.[233]

Scripture itself lays down the rule that no words be added to or subtracted from true doctrine. No creature, therefore, can determine what we are to think of God and God's will. Even so, faith is grounded on the Word alone and must be if doctrine and worship are to be certain; the doctrines that are held by faith cannot be of human origin.[234] Nothing which is foreign to the scriptural Word can be binding on worship or belief. All teachers in the church are, therefore, subordinate to the preeminent teachers, the prophets and the apostles who communicate to us the Word of God. What is more, declares Ursinus, the whole ancient church submitted itself to the authority of Scripture notwithstanding the greatness of many of its teachers—and recognized that its task was the exposition of Scripture. Against this manifold witness, "the adversaries of the truth" claim in addition to Scripture certain decrees of the church as necessary to salvation. They argue that Scripture is incomplete by its own testimony; it mentions books of the ancient people of Israel and Pauline epistles which we no longer possess. The lack, they conclude, must be supplied by the church. Yet it seems clear from Scripture itself and from the goodness of God that what is necessary to salvation has been preserved for us.[235]

Cloppenburg, with noticeable anger, writes of the "double impiety, on account of hypocrisy" resident in the canons of Trent and in the writings of Bellarmine when they distinguish among divine, apostolic, and ecclesiastical traditions, written and unwritten.[236] This

"Tradition in Early Post-Tridentine Theology," pp. 380–81; also see Albert Lang, *Die Loci theologici des Melchior Cano und die Methode des dogmatischen Beweises. Ein Beitrag zur theologischen Methodologie und ihrer Geschichte* (Munich: Kösel and Pustet, 1925). Cano argued a fundamental and necessary authority of the divinely inspired and "dictated" Scriptures and of an unwritten apostolic tradition in the church, followed by a carefully argued hierarchy of authorities—the catholic church, the councils, the Roman church, the tradition of the fathers of the earliest centuries, and the teaching of the doctors of the church and the canonists.

[233]Cano, *De locis theologicis,* III.3 (cols. 245–46, 252–53); cf. Tavard, "Tradition in Early Post-Tridentine Theology," p. 382.

[234]Ursinus, *Loci theologici,* in *Opera,* I, cols. 445–46, citing Deut. 4:2; Rev. 22:18–19.

[235]Ursinus, *Loci theologici,* in *Opera,* I, cols. 446–47.

[236]Cloppenburg, *Exercitationes super locos communes,* I.iii.1, citing the

division is a great mystery with its three classes of written and unwritten traditions, each with its own level of authority —such a mystery that it requires a diagram in order to be understood! The highest authority, they claim, belongs to divine traditions, written and unwritten; a mediate authority to apostolic traditions, written and unwritten; and a lower authority to ecclesiastical traditions, written and unwritten. The entire dispute over these traditions, argues Cloppenburg, is concerned with the authority and office of the church *circa Scripturam sacram* and whether tradition, both written and unwritten, is necessary in view of the purported uncertainty and obscurity of the meaning of the text of Scripture.[237]

Rollock similarly argues that "the knowledge of the truth which is in the heart of the Church by means of the Scripture, is not so perfect nor so absolute as is the Holy Scripture." The church is "enlightened and renewed but in part"—and may err in the most weighty matters. Indeed the church can and does err "so often as it forsakes the canon and rule of the Sacred Scripture."[238] The voice even of the true church—excluding "that whorish church of Rome"—falls short of the truth of Scripture and is a "testimony of man" even as was the testimony of John the Baptist to Christ. Scripture, however, has been preserved from error since its authors, though human, were "instruments" of God. Scripture is a human testimony in the sense that its authors were human—but it is God's word in terms of the "matter" contained within it.[239] Rollock also seems, here, to emphasize again the dynamic quality of the Scripture, since he admits that the actual writing of Scripture by the prophets and apostles is not to be "compared with the lively voice of God" but insists that "the voice of Scripture is God's own voice."[240] Rollock, like the early Protestants and like Owen in the next century, demonstrates the perpetuation in English Reformed Theology into the orthodox period and despite the emphasis on the doctrine of inspiration, a strong sense of Scripture as the Word of God because there God speaks—so that not so much the process of inscripturating the Word but the presence of the Word in power receives emphasis.

This binding character of Scripture as rule of doctrine correlates with various properties of Scripture previously argued by the

canons and decrees of Trent, session 4; and Bellarmine, *De verbo Dei*, IV.2; cf. Tavard, "Tradition in Early Post-Tridentine Theology," p. 382.

[237]Cloppenburg, *Exercitationes super locos communes,* I.iii.1–2.

[238]Rollock, *Treatise of Effectual Calling,* p. 66.

[239]Rollock, *Treatise of Effectual Calling,* p. 67.

[240]Rollock, *Treatise of Effectual Calling,* p. 68.

orthodox, particularly with the attributes of sufficiency and plainness. Indeed, Pictet could argue that the identification of Scripture as "the true and only rule of faith and practice" followed as a logical conclusion from the divinity, inspiration, authority, and perspicuity of Scripture.[241] Leigh similarly notes that:

> Whatsoever is needful to be believed or do to please God, and save our souls, is found here; whatsoever is not here found, is not needful to believe and practice for felicity.... The Heads of the Creed and Decalogue are plainly laid down in Scripture.... When we say all matters of doctrine and faith are contained in the Scripture, we understand as the Ancient Fathers did, not that all things literally and verbally, contained in the Scripture, but that all are either expressed therein, or by necessary consequence may be drawn from thence.[242]

All religious and theological controversies, therefore, are to be decided with primary reference to Scripture.

This view of Scripture as, in Mastricht's words, "the perfect rule of living before God," can also be confirmed by rational derivation from the character of worship and righteous living. In the first place, Mastricht argues, since we recognize God to be the *ens primum* and *ultimus finis* of all things, as the one who is above all things and contains all things, we must also acknowledge that he must be worshiped. We recognize, moreover, "that this worship of God is not a work of nature like seeing, hearing, or walking, none of which require rules, but a kind of occupation or skill *(artificium)* governed by certain rules."[243] The rule of religion cannot be our "corrupt reason" inasmuch as that could never function as an ultimate "measure of rectitude." Nor can it be human wisdom *(sapientia)* because it too, since it rests on reason, must also fall short of absolute authority. So too, comments Mastricht, the writings of the church fathers fall short, granting that they are fallible and, indeed, sometimes false in their ideas. The "Jewish Talmud," identified as a religious tradition carried forward in unwritten form from Moses to later Judaism, is also, Mastricht comments, "of uncertain worth" and full of fables and falsehoods. Much less could the "Muhammedan Alcoran" be a rule of faith, as is manifest from its "senile and scurrilous trifles," amounting to old wives' tales. Scripture alone satis-

---

[241]Pictet, *Theol. chr.,* I.xiv.1.
[242]Leigh, *Treatise,* I.viii (pp. 133–34).
[243]Mastricht, *Theoretico-practica theol.,* I.ii.4.

fies the requisite conditions of a rule of life and worship before almighty God.[244]

Clearly, Mastricht continues, this claim can be confirmed from a comparison of the nature and requirements for such a rule with Scripture itself. A rule of living before God ought to prescribe obedience to God alone. Scripture not only, therefore, demands obedience to God alone (Deut. 12:32; Matt. 15:9), it also clearly condemns other allegiances and is alone designated by God as a rule (2 Tim. 3:16; 2 Pet. 1:21).

By extension, with reference to the attributes or properties of Scripture, the orthodox can declare that the Scripture is not a "partial or insufficient rule, as the Papists make it; as God is a perfect God, so is his word a perfect word"—or, as Whitaker argued, "Regula fidei debet esse adaequata fidei, aut regula non erit."[245] In order, moreover, for Scripture to be an adequate rule, it must oblige the basic "properties" acknowledged to belong to all proper rules. Leigh draws his list of these properties from Suárez: a rule must first, "be known and easy," second, "first in its kind and so the measure of all the rest," third, "inflexible," and fourth "universal." Mastricht similarly indicates that Scripture has all the *notae* required for it to be a perfect rule: clear and perspicuous, constant and firm, always and everywhere self-consistent, indivisible and capable neither of augmentation or diminution.[246] Pictet also makes the point that we readily acknowledge as a rule that which is "perfect in all its parts, needing neither addition nor diminution ... certain and unchangeable.... For Scripture is such that its truth is of the unchangeable God, and cannot lie."[247] As a final property, Mastricht adds that a rule of faith and life must be public and must be received by all as standing beyond controversy.[248] Since Scripture obliges all of these properties—all of which, to a certain extent, reflect the attributes argued of Scripture by the orthodox—it must be recognized as "a perfect rule of faith and obedience," which "directs our faith and conduct in such a manner, that the very least deviation from it renders us guilty of error."[249] The prophets, the apostles, and Christ himself appeal to Scripture as just such a rule—and Scripture refers to itself as a "rule" in Galatians 6:16.

[244]Mastricht, *Theoretico-practica theol.*, I.ii.4.
[245]Leigh, *Treatise*, I.viii (p. 134).
[246]Mastricht, *Theoretico-practica theol.*, I.ii.5.
[247]Pictet, *Theol. chr.*, I.xiv.2.
[248]Mastricht, *Theoretico-practica theol.*, I.ii.5.
[249]Leigh, *Treatise*, I.viii (p. 132); cf. Pictet, *Theol. chr.*, I.xiv.2.

This point, as in the case of other aspects of the orthodox doctrine of Scripture that we have examined, is somewhat circular:
Scripture is declared to have certain attributes such as clarity,
perspicuity, perfection, and so forth, on grounds of its divine origin
and the divine doctrines contained in it—and, subsequently, it is
declared to be a perfect rule, because it obliges this set of characteristics elicited from it by dogmatic and rational argument. Whether
the structure of argument is ultimately acceptable, the dogmatic
issue and intention underlying the point is clearly the formal
identification of Scripture, via its attributes, as so conforming to the
character of an ultimate rule that no other rule—particularly such
candidates as the tradition of the early church and the church's
magisterium—can be deemed either necessary or desirable. What is
more, the fundamental issue underlying the entirety of the orthodox
doctrine of Scripture, is once again clearly the issue of authority and,
indeed, the whole course of the argument running from the discussion of the essential divinity of Scripture to the attributes assumed to
belong to such a divinely inspired and providentially preserved book
is seen to be directed toward and to conclude in the discussion of
Scripture as the canonical rule of doctrine and in the discussion of
the proper attributes of such a rule.

In other words, the internal logic of the orthodox doctrine of
Scripture is, throughout, directed toward the dogmatic and logical
affirmation of *sola Scriptura* and, in particular, of the identity of
Scripture as the *principium unicum cognoscendi theologiae.* The
discussion of the divine authority of Scripture was intended as the
objective basis for a statement of canonical authority. Thus,

> From the Divine flows the Canonical authority of the Scripture.
> The books of Scripture are called Canonical books (say some)
> from the word *kanon* ... because they were put into this Canon by
> the Universal Church & acknowledged to be divinely inspired by
> it, and are also made a perfect Canon or rule of all doctrine con-
> cerning religion, *credendorum & agendorum,* of faith and man-
> ners, of all things which are to be believed or done toward
> salvation.[250]

Even so, Scripture is a "universal and perpetual rule both in
regard of time and person; ever since Scripture hath been, it hath

---

[250]Leigh, *Treatise,* I.iii (pp. 42–43); cf. almost identically, Riissen, *Summa
theol.,* II.xv: "Ex his attributis Scripturae [i.e., authoritas, perfectio, perspicui-
tas] sequitur, eam nobis esse canonem & normam credendorum & agendorum."

been the only rule."[251] The objection that Scripture cannot be the "rule of faith" inasmuch as faith existed before Scripture leads the orthodox back to the distinction between *verbum agraphon* and *verbum engraphon*: "The word of God is twofold: 1. Revealed, that preceded faith; 2. Written, that did not."[252] Since Scripture is the present form of the Word of God—the only present form—it can and must be the rule of faith: "Prayer, Preaching, the knowledge of tongues, and the Ministry of the Church, these are the means to use the rule and subordinate to it."[253]

From the context of these remarks, it can easily be inferred that the entirety of Scripture and not just certain sections function as our rule:

> Not only the Scripture of the New, but also of the Old Testament, is the rule of our faith and practice, although we are no longer under the old dispensation, which has been abrogated. "For whatever things," says Paul (Rom. 15:4), "have been written aforetime, were written for our instruction, that we, through patience and comfort of the Scriptures, might have hope." Both testaments contain the same doctrinal substance; they propose the same objects of faith *(credenda)*, and command the same moral life *(agenda)*, and each testament belongs to the foundation of the church *(Ecclesiae fundamentum)*.[254]

The problem of the relationship of the two Testaments, associated in the Reformed debates of the seventeenth century with problems in Cocceian or federal hermeneutics and with polemic against the Anabaptists and the Socinians, also affected the Reformed understanding of the canon and, specifically, the authority of the Old Testament. The federalism of Cocceius and his followers raised a peculiar hermeneutical problem. The orthodox had consistently affirmed the authority of the entire Scripture and, like Calvin, had drawn their theology from both the Old and the New Testaments. In the federalist hermeneutic, however, the Old Testament was more clearly subordinated to the New on grounds of the historical development of revealed truth, the gradual abrogation of the covenant of works and gradual inauguration of the covenant of grace, and the typological character of Old Testament revelation, to the point that

[251]Leigh, *Treatise,* I.viii (p. 134).
[252]Leigh, *Treatise,* I.viii (p. 135).
[253]Leigh, *Treatise,* I.viii (p. 135).
[254]Pictet, *Theol. chr.,* I.xiv.4.

many of the Reformed orthodox feared that Cocceian theology represented the Old Testament as a less than adequate source of doctrine, and even flirted with the Socinian rejection of its authority.[255] Cocceius had so emphasized the *historiam sequentium temporum* in the biblical books, the gradual abrogation of the covenant of works throughout the Old Testament, and presence in the gospel of a full revelation of what had been foreshadowed "in the words of Moses and the Prophets,"[256] that he viewed many aspects of the Old Testament revelation as vague, as offered in the form of figures and types, and as superseded by the New.[257] Cocceius' approach to the distinction of the Testaments became an object of controversy when he argued that the Decalogue could not be used as a basis for commanding Sabbath worship, granting that the Decalogue here stood as part of the covenant of works.[258]

This problem, moreover, carried over into the thought of the more strictly orthodox of the federal theologians. Witsius, for example, comments on "defects" in the Old Testament mode of revelation. In the first place, the Old Testament fathers did not have present to them the cause of their salvation. Rather than the fullness of Christ, they had only "the figure of Christ in various appearances, preludes to the coming incarnation."[259] Second, revelation under the Old Testament dispensation was clothed in obscurity and characterized by a legalistic rigor and severity. The promises of grace are therefore infrequent and obscure throughout most of the Old Testament.[260] What is more, the Old Testament was subject to the *elementa mundi*, as Paul calls them (Gal. 4:3, 9) with specific reference to the ceremonial law, and is therefore superseded by the New Testament as the "shadows of night" are by the dawn of a new day. Unlike Cocceius, who had viewed even the Decalogue, particularly in its "law of the Sabbath," as accommodated to the circumstances of Israel, Witsius fully excepted from this generalization the immutable moral law revealed in the Old Testament.[261]

---

[255]Cf. Diestel, "Studien zur Föderaltheologie," pp. 237, 239–44 with Gass, *Geschichte der protestantischen Dogmatik*, II, pp. 297–98.

[256]Cocceius, *Ultima Mosis, in Opera*, III, p. 3.

[257]Cocceius, *Summa theol.*, I.ii, §388.

[258]Cf. Cocceius, *Indagatio naturae Sabbati et quietis Novi Testamenti*, vi–x (in Opera, VII), with the discussion in Van der Flier, *De Johanne Cocceijo antischolastico*, pp. 154–61.

[259]Witsius, *De oeconomia foederum*, IV.xiii.2.

[260]Witsius, *De oeconomia foederum*, IV.xiii.5, 9.

[261]Cf. Witsius, *De oeconomia foederum*, IV.xiii.10; xiv–xv with Cocceius,

A similar problem was faced by the Reformed in their polemic against the Anabaptists and Socinians, a fact which certainly sharpened the worry over Cocceian hermeneutics. The difficulty was for the Reformed to maintain, in their theological use and application of Scripture, their insistence on the unity and integrity of the whole canon while at the same time allowing for different administrations of the covenant and differing forms of expression. Thus, we find various orthodox writers defending the canonicity and authority of the Old Testament against both the Socinian and the Anabaptist concentration on the New Testament and their insistence on a difference in "substance" rather than simply in "dispensation."[262] The dispensation or economy of the Old Testament is superseded, declares Riissen, but not the teaching *(doctrina)*. Even so, as we learn from Luke 16:29 and 2 Peter 1:19–21, Christ and the apostles commended the Old Testament to the faithful. Paul specifically declared that "the church of the New Testament was built on the foundation of the Prophets and the Apostles, Eph. 2:20" and the "scripture" to which Paul referred (Rom. 15:4) was clearly the Old Testament. Indeed, Riissen and other orthodox were quite willing to recognize that, historically, in the absence of a completed New Testament canon, the standard proof-text for the inspiration and authority of Scripture, 2 Timothy 3:15–16, was a reference to the sufficiency of the Old Testament revelation in matters of faith and morals.[263]

In his two final arguments for the doctrinal equality of the Testaments, Riissen points to the continuity of the divine promise and specifically to the identity of Christ as the promised Messiah—if the Old Testament was not authoritative for the church, Christians would be incapable of arguing against the Jews that Christ was indeed the Messiah! Indeed, the historical basis of Christianity would be erased.[264] Thus, when Scripture says that the law and the prophets came to an end with John (Luke 16:16), it does not mean the end of the authority of the books of the Old Testament, but the end of the Old Testament *oeconomia*. And, although the law was given by Moses, it continues to have a place under the gospel, "since

---

Summa de foed., XI, §338.

[262]Riissen, *Summa theol.,* II.xv, controversia; Turretin, *Inst. theol. elencticae,* II.viii; Mastricht, *Theoretico-practica theol.,* I.ii.35–36; Van Til, *Theologiae utriusque compendium ... revelatae,* appendix, pp. 216, 220–221.

[263]Riissen, *Summa theol.,* II.xv, argumenta 1–4; Maccovius, *Loci communes,* II (p. 18); Mastricht, *Theoretico-practica theol.,* I.ii.35; Turretin, *Inst. theol. elencticae,* II.viii.6–8.

[264]Riissen, *Summa theol.,* II.xv, argumenta 5–6.

Moses is not opposed to Christ, but subordinate, as a servant of his Lord."[265]

Leigh concludes his arguments with a rhetorical flourish: if, he notes, human beings are permitted to declare Scripture to be a "partial rule," then human beings "are bound to be wise above that which is written, that is, above the Law and Gospel."[266] Nor is it the case that the technique of drawing conclusions from Scripture places human reason higher than the text. A distinction must be made between *scientia* and *fides,* between the "theological conclusions" drawn from the rule and faith in the rule itself. Nonetheless, such conclusions, when rightly drawn, contain the efficacy and excellence of the Word of God and must, therefore, be regarded as the Word of God.[267]

c. The Authority of Canon and Church According to Reformed Orthodoxy

In their polemics, early orthodox Reformed theologians were quick to point out that there had been major differences between Roman Catholic theologians on the authority of Scripture. In his debate with Hart, Rainolds had taunted his Catholic opponent by noting that

> the flower of your Cardinals, the Cardinall *Caietan,* beginning to expound the scriptures, doeth set it downe as a principle, that *God hath not tied the exposition of the scriptures unto the senses of the fathers*. Wherefore if he fall upon *a newe sense agreeable to the text, though it go against the streame of the Fathers:* he doth advise the reader not to mislike of it.[268]

And to Hart's rebuttal that "the flower of our Bishops, Bishop Melchior Canus," had rebuked Cajetan for his rashness, Rainolds was able to cite the eminent Roman Catholic exegete Andradius, who had noted that the fathers frequently fail to interpret the Scriptures literally and that in such cases, "we may leave their allegories and expound them literally"; and even when the fathers have sought the "literal senses ... they doe not alwaies find them, but give divers senses one unlike the other."[269]

[265]Riissen, *Summa theol.,* II.xv, obj.1.

[266]Leigh, *Treatise,* I.viii (p. 135).

[267]Riissen, *Summa theol.,* II.xii, controversia.

[268]Rainolds, *Summe of the Conference between Iohn Rainolds and Iohn Hart,* p. 38, citing Cajetan, *Comment. in libros Mosis,* praef.

[269]Rainolds, *Summe of the Conference between Iohn Rainolds and Iohn*

The high orthodox systems recognize that the definitions of the authority of Scripture immediately raise the question of the necessity of ecclesial testimony to the authority of Scripture and, by direct implication, of the relationship of the authority of the church to the authority of the Bible. It must be asked, therefore, "whether Holy Scripture has its authority or power of placing under religious obligation *(vim obligandi)* from the church, that is, whether it ought to be received as canonical inasmuch as the church declares it so, and whether it neither can nor ought to be received unless the church so orders."[270] Thus, Riissen argues, the Roman Church claims that, without the *testimonium ecclesiae,* Scripture would have no more authority than Aesop's fables. Catholics do not, of course, deny "that Scripture is authentic absolutely and in itself," but only that it is, by itself, capable of being recognized as having authority "in relation and as far as we are concerned." He responds that, certainly, the church must be understood to have a number of "duties" concerning or "surrounding" Scripture *(officia circa Scripturam):* it serves as "custodian, guide, defender, herald, interpreter." Nonetheless, the authority of Scripture does not depend on these duties that lie around *(circa)* it but on various *notae* and *criteria* placed in *(insita)* the text. Since, moreover, "the authority of the church is founded on Scripture, Eph. 2:20, and all of its authority derives from Scripture," the church "is not capable of confirming the authority of Scripture either in itself or in relation to us."[271]

There are in fact, eight rightful duties of the church *circa Scripturam*:

> 1) to approve and receive the Scriptures; 2) to commend publically the approved and received Scriptures; 3) to draw up a catalogue of the canonical books, rejecting apocryphal writings; 4) to preserve the authentic codices of holy Scripture; 5) to furnish translations faithful to Scripture; 6) to write creeds, catechisms, and summaries of doctrine grounded on Scripture; 7) to interpret and explain the obscure and difficult passages of Scripture; 8) to adjudicate controversies in faith and morals on the basis of Scripture.[272]

The "Papists," however, "prevaricate" about the office of the church in equal measure with the "Libertines and Enthusiasts" by

---

Hart, p. 38.

[270]Riissen, *Summa theol.,* II.ix, controversia.

[271]Riissen, *Summa theol.,* II.ix, controversia, arg.1.

[272]Cloppenburg, *Exercitationes super locos communes,* I.iii.3.

claiming the uncertainty of the text and relinquishing the concept of Scripture as self-authenticating *(autopistos)*.[273]

It is also inadmissable, continues Riissen, to argue in a circle as the Church of Rome does when it claims that the authority of the church is proven from Scripture and the authority of Scripture grounded on the church. One of these authorities must be prior.[274] In addition, he notes, these circular arguments offer no clear understanding of the meaning of "church": does the term indicate the church today or the ancient church, the church collectively or representatively? And whichever of these forms of church is indicated by the term, the fact remains that the church's testimony is human and, consequently, fallible.[275]

The church is an "object" rather than a "principle" of theology. The debate over the relative authority of church and Scripture, thus, ultimately returns the orthodox to the question of *principia*. Only God and God's revelation are entitled to be identified as *principia;* the church is a body defined doctrinally by Scripture and, therefore, an object of theological discussion and not one of the foundation of the discussion. "The church," comments Leigh, "ought to be subject to Christ, Eph. 5:24." and "the Scripture is the word of Christ, Col. 3:16."[276] Even so, the Scriptures, as Word of God, always speak the truth, while the church may err and, indeed, has at times erred and spoken falsely. Faith must always seek "a divine foundation, for every human testimony is uncertain."[277] Like Riissen, Leigh argues that Rome argues against itself by arguing the authority of the church from the text of Scripture:

> The authority of proving is greater, more certain, and more known, than the conclusion proved by the same. *Authoritas probans* is greater than *probata.* The Papists to prove the authority of the Church fly to the Scriptures.[278]

Nor comments Leigh, echoing the Reformed doctrine of unwritten

[273]Cloppenburg, *Exercitationes super locos communes,* I.iii.5.

[274]Riissen, *Summa theol.,* II.ix, controversia, arg.3; cf. Cloppenburg, *Exercitationes super locos communes,* I.iii.8.

[275]Riissen, *Summa theol.,* II.ix, controversia, arg.4–5.

[276]Leigh, *Treatise,* I.ii (p. 26).

[277]Leigh, *Treatise,* I.ii (p. 26); cf. Rainolds, *Sex theses de sacra scriptura et ecclesia,* III.xi, as cited by Leigh: "Spiritus sanctus Spiritus veritatis, loquitur semper in Scriptura; in ecclesia vero quandoque spiritus humanus, spiritus erroris."

[278]Leigh, *Treatise,* I.ii (p. 27).

and written Word, can the Roman objection that the church is more ancient than Scripture be conceded, since this priority is true only *quoad formale externum. Quoad formale internum,* according to "the matter and sense or meaning ... Scripture was more ancient than the Church, because the Church is gathered and governed by it." The "thing itself, the being and substance of the word" preceded the church with only the outward "circumstance" of the written form following the historical constitution of the believing community.[279] Similarly, the argument that the ground upon which something is proven must itself be proven by another higher ground or principle —so that Scripture as the ground of doctrine still needs further proof—fails inasmuch as Scripture is the first principle beyond which no regress is necessary or, indeed, possible in this life.[280]

The orthodox also place themselves in the tradition of Luther, Tyndale, Vermigli, Calvin, Musculus, and, explicitly, Whitaker, by raising the issue of authority in terms of the debate over Augustine's famous words (cited here from Leigh), "Non crederem evangelio, nisi me commoveret ecclesiae catholicae authoritas":

> These words (saith Whitaker) are so well known to the Papists that one can hardly exchange three words with them, but they will produce them. It is true indeed, that we may at the first be much moved to receive and hearken to the Scriptures, because the Church gives testimony of them.... When [Augustine] was a Manichee he was first moved by the authority of the church to believe the Gospel. His meaning is, that he had never believed the Gospel, if the authority of the Church had not been an introduction unto him, not that his faith rested on it as a final stay, but that it caused him so far to respect the word of the Gospel to listen unto it.... We deny not the ministry of the Church as an external means to move us to embrace the word of God, but we deny the authority of the Church as the principal means.[281]

Much like Riissen and Cloppenburg, Leigh offers a maxim defining the relation of church to Scripture as "around" and not "above," as concerned with "ministry" or "service" rather than with "directorship" or teaching office: "ecclesia non habet magisterium supra

[279]Cf. Leigh, *Treatise,* I.ii (p. 28). Cf. with Riissen, *Summa theol.,* I.ix, controversia, obj.5: "[Ecclesia] est antiquior formaliter, quoad modum scriptionis, non materialiter, quoad substantiam doctrinae."

[280]Riissen, *Summa theol.,* I.ix, controversia, obj.6; cf. Cloppenburg, *Exercitationes super locos communes,* I.iii.14.

[281]Leigh, *Treatise,* I.ii (p.28).

Scripturas, sed ministerium circa Scripturas."[282] Thus, despite this qualification and definition of its authority, the church retains an office concerning Scripture and a grave responsibility to preserve the canon of Scripture, "to be a faithful keeper of those books which are inspired by God, like a notary keepeth public writings," "to publish, declare and teach the truth" of the Scriptures, and "to interpret Scripture by Scripture" for the sake of believers.[283]

That this point of the priority of Scripture in matters of controversy is not only a hermeneutical point relating to the self-authenticating character of the text and to the necessity of a churchly recourse to the *analogia Scripturae,* but also a point relating to the more "existential" identification of Scripture as Word becomes clear from Rollock's comments on the canonical authority of Scripture. He notes that "the adversaries" claim, against both the internal evidence and the ancient testimonies, that

> the sacred Scripture is but a dead letter, mute, and not able to give answer to any man, not able to decide questions and controversies in religion: and, contrarily, they glory that the voice of the church, which proceeds from the Scripture (as they speak), which is graven by God's own Spirit in the hearts of men; they boast, I say, that this is vocal, and able to answer all the demanders of all questions appertaining to salvation.[284]

When Scripture fails to decide a controversy, Rollock replies, this is not due to any fault of the text but to the perversity of men who will not listen to "the Scriptures speaking and answering, yea, crying in their ears." Against their own conscience, these adversaries "wrest the voice of Scripture into another sense, and that to their own perdition!"[285] The Scripture stands unchangeable. Its truth cannot be altered. Thus, careful study, attended by the effectual working of the Spirit opening hearts and minds, is sufficient to answer all controversy and, indeed, is the foundation of the church and of the church's word.[286]

The orthodox approach to these doctrinal points involved, in addition to the basic arguments that we have just reviewed, a discussion of the several passages in Scripture used by the Roman Church

---

[282]Leigh, *Treatise,* I.ii (p.28, margin); cf. Cloppenburg, *Exercitationes super locos communes,* I.iii.6.

[283]Leigh, *Treatise,* I.ii (p. 29).

[284]Rollock, *Treatise of Effectual Calling,* p. 87.

[285]Rollock, *Treatise of Effectual Calling,* p. 87.

[286]Rollock, *Treatise of Effectual Calling,* pp. 87–88.

to support its claims. From 1 Timothy 3:15, "the house of God, which is the church of the living God, the pillar and ground of the truth," Roman Catholic theologians argued that, since the church was the "pillar" or "support" of the truth understood generally, it must also be the pillar and support of the truth of Scripture. The question, Riissen notes in rebuttal, granting that Scripture is true and the church must be recognized as a pillar of truth, concerns the kind of pillar indicated by the text. We ought not to understand the church as a pillar *"in sensu architectonico,"* as if it were a pillar sustaining an edifice, but rather *"in sensu forensi,"* like the magistrates who are often termed "the pillars of the law," insofar as they set it forth. The church, so far as this text of Scripture is concerned, is "a pillar by reason of the promulgation and safeguarding *(custodia)*" of the text and message of Scripture.[287] By Riissen's time, the point could readily be drawn from the Protestant exegetical tradition: "The church holds forth the scripture and the doctrine of Christ, as the pillar to which a proclamation is affixed, holds forth the proclamation."[288]

If Protestants were able to identify the circularity of the Roman recourse to Scripture as a ground of the prior authority of the church over the text, they were also able to see the problem of the potential circularity of their own arguments and to attempt to defend against it. Have the Reformed in fact argued, in circular fashion, that Scripture is proven divine by the Spirit and that the testimony of the Spirit is understood from Scripture? Riissen notes in response that there are, in fact, three separate aspects to the Reformed affirmation of the authority of Scripture as rule of faith, rather than a single, potentially circular argument.[289]

First, there is "the proof *(argumentum)* on account of which *(propter quod)* I believe"; second, "the foundation *(principium),* or efficient cause because of which *(a qua)* I believe"; and third, "the means and instruments through which *(per quod)* I believe." In the first case, Scripture itself demonstrates by its marks or qualities, "such as light and splendor," that it is worthy of belief; in the second, it is the Spirit who, as noted in Luke 24:45, "opened" the understanding of the disciples and who, by implication, opens the understanding of believers to the truth of the Scriptures; in the third, it is the church, used by God in the preservation and communication

---

[287]Riissen, *Summa theol.,* I.ix, controversia, obj.1.
[288]Henry, *Commentary on the Whole Bible,* in loc.; and see below, §7.3.c.
[289]Riissen, *Summa theol.,* I.ix, controversia, obj.3.

of the truths of the Scriptures.[290] If, therefore, Scripture is said to be proven worthy of belief by the Spirit, the statement refers to the Spirit as the efficient cause of belief. If, however, we ask on what ground we believe that the Spirit testifying within us is the Holy Spirit, the answer is that we know by the marks of the Spirit revealed in Scripture. As for the objective authority of Scripture, it is to be grounded on the Scripture itself, understood as self-authenticating.[291] Nor, comments Riissen, does it hold against the Protestant argument to claim that the church is the authority that indicates which books are canonical and which are not—for John the Baptist indicated the identity of the Messiah, but the Messiah's authority surely did not rest on John the Baptist!—"it is one thing to discern and declare the canon, quite another to constitute it and to make it authentic."[292]

This Roman Catholic claim that only the church can have final authority to determine the canon was made and answered in considerable detail. It is impossible, they noted, to prove from the Scriptures themselves that the Gospel of Matthew is by Matthew but the Gospel of Thomas not by Thomas. Since this is the case, Scripture cannot be sufficient in itself and does not contain all things necessary to salvation. The antecedent in the argument is not strictly true, responds Wendelin. It is indeed possible to prove from Scripture that the Gospel of Thomas is not the work of the apostle Thomas, inasmuch as it dissents from the truth offered in the known canonical Scriptures. As for the consequence, it is simply false—it is not necessary to salvation to prove that the Gospel of Matthew is indeed by Matthew, nor does it interfere with the canonical and divine status of the gospel history if the identity of the author is not absolutely established, granting that there are many books in the canon of unknown authorship.[293] The papists also impugn the canon and argue the prior authority of the church on the ground that books have been lost, but it ought to be clear that the canon as it now exists contains all that is necessary to salvation.[294]

[290]Riissen, *Summa theol.,* I.ix, controversia, obj.3.

[291]Riissen, *Summa theol.,* I.ix, controversia, obj.3.

[292]Riissen, *Summa theol.,* I.ix, controversia, obj.4.

[293]Wendelin, *Christianae theologiae libri duo, prol.,* III.vii.2; cf. above, §2.5, for discussion of this issue as raised by Poole in the context of exegesis.

[294]Wendelin, *Christianae theologiae libri duo, prol.,* I.iii.7, and see further §§6.1–6.2 for a more detailed discussion of the perfection of Scripture and the problem of lost books.

6

The Canon of Scripture and Its Integrity

Protestant orthodoxy was a biblical, exegetical, and homiletical phenomenon as much as it was a dogmatic and confessional phenomenon. A vast amount, if not all, of its dogmatic energy was directed toward the establishment and protection of a biblical preaching of salvation in and for the church. For all its formalization and, indeed, confessional and dogmatic definition of Protestantism, scholastic orthodoxy seldom lost sight of the Reformers' sense of the life and the power of the living Word of God. Even the most strictly defined of the dogmatic definitions of Scripture found in the orthodox period manifest this interest in the dynamic character of God's Word and thereby bear witness to the fact that dogmatic definition was intended to hedge the biblical witness and keep it safe for the church's use.[1] In addition, a large number of the orthodox dogmaticians, after the pattern established in the Middle Ages and modified considerably under the impact of the Reformation and Renaissance humanist emphasis on languages, began their careers as exegetes and biblical theologians. Their careers began in the service of the text and their dogmatic writings built on that biblical and exegetical foundation. We should also note that a majority of the orthodox theologians were involved in the life of the church as pastors and preachers during the years of their tenure as professors.

The situation of the Protestant orthodox differed, however, from that of the Reformers in the character of the critique they experienced as they attempted to defend their doctrine of the biblical

[1]Cf. Beardslee, *Reformed Dogmatics,* pp. 9–10, 14; and note Beardslee's comments in Turretin, *Scripture,* pp. 11–13.

Word against its adversaries. Whereas the Reformers experienced humanism and its emphasis on the sources in their original languages as a strong ally in the debate both with Rome and with the Radicals and Anabaptists, the orthodox began to feel the sting of textual criticism as practiced by the seventeenth-century heirs of Renaissance humanism, the technical linguists and orientalists—many of whom belonged to the orthodox or confessional churches. The high orthodox doctrine of Scripture was framed by debate over the critical approach to the text and the canon of Scripture—with the result that discussion of the canon, the text, the various "authentic" editions, the ancient translations and the modern vernacular versions, and even the history of exegesis, became an integral part of the orthodox doctrine of Scripture. Far more than their predecessors, the high orthodox were faced with the problem of maintaining the doctrine of the Reformation and its orthodox codification in the face of a new and critical view of the text—a perception of text and of interpretation quite different from the perceptions that had originally fostered the Protestant view of Scripture. This problem accounts, in large measure, for the differences in emphasis and the discontinuities between the Reformers' teaching and the dogmatic pronouncements of the last of the high orthodox writers.

Intervening between the early Reformation and the high orthodox era, moreover, during the second confessional phase of the Reformation, as the theological leadership of Protestantism passed from the hands of the first codifiers in the generation of Calvin, Bullinger, Vermigli, and Musculus to the hand of their early orthodox successors in the generation of Beza, Ursinus, Zanchi, and Olevian, a major event occurred that changed forever the church's approach to Scripture. Beginning with the fourth session of the Council of Trent in 1546 and continuing on through the era of the *Gallican* and *Belgic Confessions* and the *Thirty-Nine Articles*—for the first time in the history of the church—the canon of Scripture received not only clear identification and enumeration but also confessional and dogmatic definition.

6.1 The Problem of the Canon in the Reformation

The Protestant identification of Scripture as inspired Word, true, certain, infallible, pure, holy, sufficient, efficacious, as *principium cognoscendi theologiae* and sole final rule of faith and practice, was applied only to the canonical books of the Old and New Testaments. Thus Bullinger commented in the *Second Helvetic Confession,* "we do not deny that certain books of the Old Testament were by the ancient authors called *Apocryphal* ... such as they would have to be read in the churches, but not alleged to avouch or confirm the authority of faith by them."[2] Both the *Gallican* and *Belgic Confessions* list the books of the canonical Scripture, a pattern followed also by the *Thirty-Nine Articles*—the *Belgic Confession* and the *Thirty-Nine Articles,* moreover, list the apocryphal books and pronounce them edifying, particularly for "example of life and instruction of manners" but pointedly exclude them from the rule of faith.[3]

This very strict identification of the canon, found in several of the major Reformed confessions of the sixteenth century and in the scholastic Reformed theological systems of the early and high orthodox eras was clearly the product of a new confluence of doctrinal and text-critical issues. Although the early church had developed a relatively clear sense of the canon of the New Testament against Marcion and the Gnostics, it had not provided either a definitive listing of the doctrinally normative books of the Bible or an absolutely firm rule for excluding books belonging to the orthodox tradition of the church but not to either the Hebrew canon of the Old Testament or the confirmed list of "apostolic" writings. Specifically, the difference between the Hebrew Old Testament and the Septuagint was not an issue that troubled the church greatly before the sixteenth century—early on the church lost its contact with Hebrew and accepted the larger list of the Septuagint as standard, despite some continuing reservations concerning those books utterly lacking Hebrew originals.[4]

Thus, the early Reformed confessions and at least one Lutheran confessional document written before the *Formula of Concord* make a point of enunciating in a general fashion the principle of the canon and its authority without, however, offering either a dogmatic definition or an enumeration of the books in the canon. Zwingli's *Sixty-Seven Articles* (1523) do not offer a specific article on Scripture, but consistently invoke Scripture as the sole norm for Christian

---

[2]*Second Helvetic Confession,* I.9 in CC, III, pp. 238, 833.

[3]Cf. *Gallican Confession,* IV; *Belgic Confession,* VI; *Thirty-Nine Articles,* VI, in CC, III, pp. 361–62, 387, 490–91.

[4]On the history of the canon, see Edward Reuss, *History of the Canon of the Holy Scriptures in the Christian Church,* trans. David Hunter (Edinburgh: R. W. Hunter, 1891); idem, *History of the Sacred Scriptures of the New Testament,* 5th ed., trans. E. L. Houghton (Edinburgh: T. and T. Clark, 1884); and Brooke Foss Westcott, *A General Survey of the History of the Canon of the New Testament,* 6th ed. (1889; repr. Grand Rapids: Baker Book House, 1980).

doctrine—nor do his two other essays in confessional form, the *Fidei ratio* (1530) and *Christianae fidei expositio* (1531), contain a formal article on Scripture.[5] The first movement toward Reformed confessional articulation of the canonical principle occurs in the *Ten Theses of Bern* (1528) and the *First Confession of Basel* (1534). The former document begins with a statement of the priority of the Word of God over the church and the latter document closes with a statement of the priority of the Word of God over the church and a submission of the confession to the prior authority of Scripture. For the actual statement of the canonical authority of Scripture, we must look to the *Confession of Bohemia* (1535) and the *Second Confession of Basel* or *First Helvetic Confession* (1536). The first of these documents declares that "the Holy Scriptures which are contained in the Bible and which are by the Fathers received and given canonical authority, are to be held as unshaken, true, and most certain."[6] The second declares simply and forcefully, "the canonical Scriptures, the Word of God conveyed by the Holy Spirit and set forth to the world by the prophets and apostles, contains the most perfect and most ancient philosophy and piety, and the only perfect rule *(ratio)* of life."[7]

The Lutheran confession noted above is the *Confessio Würtembergica* or *Confessio piae doctrinae* (1551) of Johannes Brenz. Here we read that "We identify *(vocamus)* as Holy Scripture those canonical books of the Old and New Testaments the authority of which has never been doubted in the church."[8] Brenz' confession, like Melanchthon's *Confessio doctrinae saxonicarum ecclesiarum* of the same year, was written in response to Charles V's invitation to the Protestant princes of Germany to send delegates to the Council of Trent.[9] Melanchthon had stated, perhaps in a hope for dialogue, that "the voice of true doctrine" was heard in "the prophetic and apostolic writings and the creeds *(symbola)*."[10] Brenz, surely in

---

[5]Cf. *Articuli sive Conclusiones LXVII,* especially art. I, V, XV, XVI on the priority and salvific character of the gospel, and art. LVII, LXII where the scriptural norm is used to argue against purgatory and elders or priests not invested with the preaching of the Word, in Niemeyer, *Collectio,* pars. I, pp. 3, 5, 13; with the *Fidei ratio,* in Niemeyer, *Collectio,* pars. I, pp. 16–35; and the *Christianae fidei brevis et clara expositio,* in Niemeyer, *Collectio,* pars. I, pp. 36–64.

[6]*Confessio Bohemica,* I, in Niemeyer, *Collectio,* pars II, p. 787.

[7]*Conf. Helv. prior,* I (Schaff, *Creeds,* III, p. 211).

[8]Cited in Heppe, *DDP,* I, p. 211.

[9]See Schaff, *Creeds,* I, pp. 341–44.

[10]Cited in Heppe, *DDP,* I, pp. 233–34.

response to the decisions of the fourth session of Trent concerning norms and authorities for doctrine, had pointedly reiterated the *sola Scriptura,* now in the form of a distinctly Protestant identification of the canon.

The contrast between Luther's views and those of other early sixteenth-century thinkers, whether Roman Catholic or Protestant, on the one hand, and later Protestants on the other, also points to an issue in the development of the Protestant doctrine of Scripture and to a difference between the teaching of the earliest Reformers and the orthodox dogmaticians. As Heppe's analysis of the problem of canon in sixteenth-century Protestantism indicates, even in the somewhat truncated form offered in his *Reformed Dogmatics,*[11] the point of transition came with the second-generation codifiers of the Reformation and the beginning of early Protestant orthodoxy. Heppe notes both the disagreement among Protestant theologians concerning the boundaries of the canon and their debate over its "integral perfection." Not only did some of the Protestant authors allow anti-legomena or "apocryphal" books in the New Testament, they also allowed the possibility that some canonical books had been lost, either in whole or in part.

Musculus registered this latter debate in his comments on the "prophecies of Enoch" (cf. Gen. 5:22)—certain antediluvian histories and prophecies may have been lost. Vermigli, similarly, had noted that ancient books referred to in the Old Testament, like the "book of the Wars of the Lord" (Num. 21:14) or the "book of Jasher" (2 Sam. 1:18), were lost, although probably of canonical worth. Nevertheless, both Musculus and Vermigli asserted that providence has preserved those books as canon that were necessary to salvation, and Musculus expressed the conviction that the Old Testament history of the earliest periods contained the essence of the earliest revelations, preserved and presented in a form suited to the needs of the postdiluvian world.[12] Heppe incorrectly assumed that these queries about the canon and the problem that they evidence concerning the so-called integral perfection of Scripture indicated a distinction between the "Word of God" and "Holy Scripture" not found among the later orthodox, but the orthodox not only

[11]Heppe, *RD,* pp. 12–15, 29–30. Heppe treated the issue in much greater detail and offered a more nuanced interpretation in *DDP,* I, pp. 218–22, 226–29, 243–44, 246–48, 254; also note his *Geschichte des deutschen Protestantismus,* I, pp. 28–31.

[12]Musculus, *Loci communes,* xxi (*Commonplaces,* pp. 350, col. 2–351, col. 1; cf. p. 352, col.2); Vermigli, *Loci communes,* cited in *RD,* p. 29.

maintained the distinction in the "historical" form noted by Heppe, they also raised these and other critical questions about the text, without in any way impugning their view of its authority.[13] The issue is not so much the relative rigidity of the doctrine of inspiration as the way in which the critical issue came to have an increasingly negative and disruptive effect on that doctrine during the later decades of the high orthodox era.

Even so, after describing the contents of the canon of Scripture, Musculus notes that the apocryphal or "hidden" books belong outside the canon, inasmuch as they contain teachings arising from "the spirit of man" more than from the Spirit of God—and they also include "some points not fully in agreement with the canonical Scriptures." His comment is directed toward the Old Testament Apocrypha, but he quickly adds that the ancient canon of the Council of Laodicaea did not include 2 Peter, 2 and 3 John, Jude, Hebrews, or the Apocalypse of John. Some recent authors, he continues, in a probable reference to Luther, would also exclude the Epistle of James. He concludes:

> It is not for me to pronounce judgment concerning [these books] whether or not they are from those under whose names they are found. The judgment of the elders, however, renders me less bound to these than to the other Scriptures, though I do not think that all of the things that can be read in them ought to be condemned out of hand.[14]

What is significant about this passage is its date: Musculus' *Loci communes* were published in 1560, more than a decade after the beginning of the Council of Trent. Not only is it reasonably certain that this particular *locus* was written earlier and left unchanged when incorporated into the larger work, it is also the case that Musculus was one of the older members of the group loosely called second-generation reformers. Born in 1497, he was a dozen years Calvin's senior and, at least on this point, formed more by the experience of the early than the later years of the Reformation. Absolute closure of the canon and its integral perfection were issues that came to be of doctrinal importance only when the bounds of the canon and its relation to the authoritative tradition and magisterium of the church became a matter of faith—a confessional or credal issue.

The starting point of debate, then, for the theologians of the

---

[13]Cf. Heppe, *RD*, pp. 14–15 with the §§2.5 and 3.3–3.4.
[14]Musculus, *Loci communes,* xxi (*Commonplaces,* p. 353, cols. 1–2).

second generation of the Reformation and of early Protestant orthodoxy was the teaching of the Council of Trent expounded at the
fourth session of the council on 8 April 1546. The council stated
first that it received and venerated

> with an equal affection of piety and reverence, all the books both
> of the Old and of the New Testament—seeing that one God is the
> author of both—as also the said traditions, as well those appertain-
> ing to faith as to morals, as having been dictated *(dictatas)* either
> by Christ's own word of mouth, or by the Holy Ghost, and pre-
> served in the Catholic Church by a continuous succession.[15]

Appended to this statement, "so that none may doubt which are [the
books] that are received by this Synod" as canonical, is a list of the
canon of the Old and New Testaments including those singled out as
apocryphal or deuterocanonical by the Protestants: Tobit, Judith,
Wisdom, Ecclesiasticus, Baruch, and 1 and 2 Maccabees.[16] The
decree concludes that anyone who refuses to receive the entire list as
"sacred and canonical" or who refuses to receive all of the books
"entire *(integros)* with all their parts," as set forth in the Latin
Vulgate, is anathema.[17]

The language of the decree implied that not only the seven
disputed books explicitly mentioned—Tobit, Judith, Wisdom, Ecclesiasticus, Baruch, and 1 and 2 Maccabees—but also certain disputed
parts of or additions to books were canonical as well: the "Hymn" or
"Song of the Three Children" and the stories of Susannah and "Bel
and the Dragon" (three additions to Daniel), and the additions to the
Book of Esther, all of which (like the other deuterocanonical books)
are absent from the Hebrew Old Testament but present in the
Septuagint and, therefore, in the Vulgate. The term "Apocrypha"
was reserved by the Roman Catholic writers for such works as 3 and
4 Ezra, 3 and 4 Maccabees, the Prayer of Manasseh, and Psalm
151.[18] Trent offered, for the first time in the history of the church, an
absolutely clear and determinate canon—and offered it, on the
authority of the church as a matter of the faith.

---

[15]*Canones et decreta dogmatica concilii Tridentini*, IV, in Schaff, *Creeds*,
II, p. 80.

[16]*Canones et decreta dogmatica concilii Tridentini*, IV, in Schaff, *Creeds*,
II, p. 81.

[17]*Canones et decreta dogmatica concilii Tridentini*, IV, in Schaff, *Creeds*,
II, p. 82.

[18]Cf. *Canones et decreta*, in Schaff, *Creeds*, II, p. 82 with *Synopsis purioris
theol.*, III.36–37; Turretin, *Inst. theol.*, II.ix.2.

Calvin, like Luther, argued canonicity on theological rather than historical grounds but, quite unlike Luther, he was unwilling to acknowledge doubtful books or antilegomena in the New Testament. Thus Calvin quite firmly argues on both textual and historical grounds that Paul was not the author of Hebrews and expresses keen doubts about the authorship of James and 2 Peter. Yet he nonetheless advocated the canonicity of Hebrews, James, and 2 Peter on the grounds of their doctrinal content and what he believed to be the agreement between the teaching of these books and the message of the rest of the New Testament.[19] Calvin can state that not Paul but "another apostle" wrote Hebrews[20] and that 2 Peter was probably written by a disciple of Peter.[21] The latter conclusion seems to have led Calvin to place the Johannine epistles and James between 1 and 2 Peter.[22]

The *Institutes* contains no full discussion of the canon of Scripture even in the 1559 edition, but it does give Calvin's readers a clear sense of non-normative status to which the Apocrypha had been relegated. In his discussion of free will, Calvin notes the use of a passage from Ecclesiasticus to overturn his position. Here, he comments, is "a writer whose authority is known to be in doubt." Calvin takes up the argument, even though he notes his "perfect right" simply to reject the opinion of Ecclesiasticus, in order to argue against this writer "whoever he may be."[23] As for the use of 2 Maccabees 12:43 to support the doctrine of purgatory, Calvin writes, "what they bring forward ... I deem unworthy of reply, lest I seem to include that work among the canon of the sacred books."[24]

Calvin does, however, very clearly identify the theological issue underlying the question of the canon is posed in the sixteenth century: his Roman Catholic opponents give to the church the right to determine "what reverence is due Scripture and what books ought to be reckoned within its canon."[25] Calvin specifically argues against a normative churchly tradition concerning the delimitation

---

[19]Cf. Calvin, *Commentary on Hebrews,* pp. xxvi–xxvii (CTS); with Calvin, *Commentary on James,* pp. 276–77 (CTS); and Calvin, *Commentary on II Peter,* pp. 363–64 (CTS).

[20]Calvin, *Institutes,* II.xvi.6; cf. Calvin, *Commentary on Hebrews,* p. xxvii (CTS).

[21]Calvin, *Commentary on II Peter,* p. 363 (CTS).

[22]Cf. Reuss, *History of the Canon,* p. 318.

[23]Calvin, *Institutes,* II.v.18.

[24]Calvin, *Institutes,* III.v.8.

[25]Calvin, *Institutes,* I.vii.1.

of the canon:

> If the authority of Scripture is grounded in the approval of the church, the decree of which council will they cite on this point? They have none. I believe....They bring forward as evidence an ancient list, called "canon," which they say came from the judgment of the church. But I ask once more, in what council was that canon ever promulgated? Here they must remain mute. However, I should like to know furthermore what sort of canon they think it is. For I see that it was little agreed on among ancient writers. And if what Jerome says ought to have weight, the books of Maccabees, Tobit, Ecclesiasticus, and the like, are to be thrown into the rank of Apocrypha. This the Romanists cannot bear to do.[26]

This does not mean that Calvin invariably scorned the Apocrypha. He could cite with strong agreement "the very true and holy words" written by an "unknown author" and "attributed" to Baruch on the subject of prayer.[27] He could cite Tobit in passing to find the name of the angel Raphael—although, admittedly, the point was of little value to him.[28] The picture that Calvin paints of the peace of God's kingdom in his famous "Meditation on the Future Life" contains a positive citation from Ecclesiasticus,[29] and Calvin may even refer to the author of Ecclesiasticus as Solomon in his discussions of the eternal or pretemporal begetting of the divine Word or Wisdom.[30] At very least, Calvin assumed that the Apocrypha might be read for edification—and he may, at times, have been willing to support doctrinal conclusions with particular texts from the Apocrypha. As Reuss recognized, the testimony of the Spirit and the exegetically gained conviction of the validity or, indeed, apostolicity of the message of the book, rather than ascertainment of prophetic or apostolic authorship was Calvin's primary criterion for canonicity. The eventual rigidification of the canon to the virtual exclusion of reference to the Apocrypha was not always reflected in Calvin's usage even though it was clearly echoed in his polemics.[31]

Thus, in his response to Trent, Calvin offers a far clearer demarcation of the canon than is available in the *Institutes* and provides evidence of the profound impact of the *Canons and Decrees*

[26]Calvin, *Institutes,* IV.ix.14.
[27]Calvin, *Institutes,* III.xx.8.
[28]Calvin, *Institutes,* I.xiv.8.
[29]Calvin, *Institutes,* III.ix.6.
[30]Calvin, *Institutes,* I.xiii.7; II.xiv.8.
[31]Reuss, *History of the Canon,* p. 317.

on Protestant conceptions of Scripture. Rome, Calvin argues, merely provides itself with new support for its doctrinal errors and abuses by bestowing "full authority" on the Apocrypha.

> Out of the second of the Maccabees they will prove Purgatory and the worship of saints; out of Tobit satisfactions, exorcisms, and what not. From Ecclesiasticus they will borrow not a little. From whence could they better draw their dregs? I am not one of those, however, who would entirely disapprove the reading of those books; but in giving them *an authority which they never before possessed,* what end was sought but just to have the use of spurious paint in coloring their errors?[32]

The Apocrypha were, after all, counted of doubtful authority by Jerome and Rufinus. Augustine followed the Council of Carthage in accepting the Apocrypha, but he noted disagreement over the issue in his own time. Not only the fathers, continues Calvin, but the documents themselves testify to their own lack of authority:

> Not to mention other things, whoever it was who wrote the history of the Maccabees expressed a wish, at the end, that he may have written well and congruously; but if not, he asks pardon. How very alien this acknowledgment from the majesty of the Holy Spirit.[33]

Not only does Calvin argue against the Apocrypha, but he demonstrates the theological ground of his argument. The testimony of the Spirit is absent from the Apocrypha and—presumably related to this underlying problem—the Apocrypha teach unacceptable doctrines such as purgatory and satisfactions, that is, a doctrine of penance. The historical argument is clearly secondary.

For Calvin, as for Luther, the question of the canon was a question of authority and, given the prior authority of Scripture, the question had to be answered theologically rather than ecclesially. He was perfectly willing to use the tradition of the church negatively, citing its disagreement over the identity of the canonical books—and unwittingly preparing the way for a far more detailed polemic with his queries about ancient lists and councils. Calvin avoids, however, Luther's christological criterion for canonicity and looks both to a broader harmony of biblical teaching and toward the criterion of the testimony of the Spirit and to the related concept of the self-

[32]Calvin, *Antidote,* in *Tracts and Treatises,* III, p. 68.
[33]Calvin, *Antidote,* in *Tracts and Treatises,* III, pp. 70–71.

authenticating character of Scripture.[34] In this, he points the way both toward the Reformed confessions and toward the perspective of early orthodoxy.

The theological ground of canonicity—in clear opposition to the argument made a decade earlier in the *Canons and Decrees of the Council of Trent*—is summed up in the *Gallican Confession* of 1559:

> We know these books to be canonical, and the utterly certain rule of our faith, not so much by the universal agreement and consent of the church as by the testimony and the inward persuasion of the Holy Spirit, who enables us to discern them from other churchly books on which, however useful they may be, we are not able to found a single article of faith.[35]

A virtually identical statement appears in the *Belgic Confession* while the *Second Helvetic Confession* explicitly links canonicity with the speaking of the living Word of God in and through the text.[36] The basic issue, from the point of view of the Reformed confessions, is the religious or theological import of the books as guaranteed by the presence of Word and Spirit—issues of authorship and historical usage are secondary, very much as the divine authority of Scripture is prior to all collateral argumentation from internal and external evidences.[37] In other words, the argument always proceeds from the theological principle to the logical and empirical proofs. Neither the Reformers themselves, nor the Reformed confessions, nor the Protestant orthodox were willing to reverse the pattern of argument and present historical or rational proofs as the foundation for a doctrinal point, whether the basic point of the prior authority of Scripture or the related point of the limitation and identification of the canon of Scripture.

The fully developed Protestant doctrine of the canon, defined theologically in its integral perfection, is offered by Bullinger in the *Decades* following an enumeration of the canonical books:

> Therefore in these few and reasonable, not immeasurable, these plain and simple, not dark and rude books, the entire doctrine of godliness is contained, which is the very word of the true, living, and eternal God.

[34]Calvin, *Institutes,* I.vii; and see above, §§4.3 and 5.5.
[35]*Conf. Gall.,* iv.
[36]*Conf. Belg.,* v; *Conf. Helv. Post.,* I.i.
[37]See above, §§4.1 and 4.3.

The books of Moses and the prophets were, moreover, preserved sound and uncorrupted through so many ages, perils, captivities, until the time of Christ and the apostles. For the Lord and the apostles used these books as true and authentic. This they undoubtedly neither would nor could have done, if [the books of Moses and the prophets] had been corrupted or had altogether perished. The books also, which the apostles of Christ added and which are one with the law and the prophets, were throughout all persecutions kept in the church safe and uncorrupted, and are come sound and uncorrupted into our hands, on whom the ends of the ages are fallen *(in quos fines saeculorum inciderunt)*. For by the vigilant care and unspeakable goodness of God our Father, it is brought to pass, that no age at any time has lacked or will lack so great a treasure.[38]

6.2 The Reformed Orthodox Doctrine of the Canon

The Reformed orthodox doctrine of Scripture followed closely the model established by the codifiers of the mid-sixteenth century and by the great Reformed confessions of the same period in its inclusion of a doctrinal discussion of the canon of Scripture within the formal theological *locus de Scriptura sacra*. Granting both the issues raised by the Council of Trent and the Protestant confessional response of mid-sixteenth century, the orthodox systems evidence none of the flexibility of the documents of the early Reformation in their definition of the canon. The Old Testament apocrypha are clearly excluded from the normative canon and the antilegomena of the New Testament are, typically, incorporated into the canon as on a par with the unquestioned books without much discussion. The high orthodox writers, in particular, viewed the discussion of the canon as occupying a place of fundamental importance in the *locus de Scriptura sacra*. There we see the polemics of the Reformers and of the early orthodox drawn together and codified, with the problem of authority holding an explicit and prominent place in the discussion and the problem of hermeneutics hovering implicitly in the background of the argument. Of course, Protestant theologians and exegetes continued to refer to the apocrypha "for edification" and even cited them occasionally in their theological writings,[39] and commentators continued to note questions concerning the authorship

---

[38]Bullinger, *Decades,* I.i (p. 55).
[39]Cf. Keckermann, *Praecognitorum philosophicorum,* col. 69H, citing Sirach.

of the antilegomena—but the doctrinal stance assumed a strictly defined canon and usually led to an acceptance of apostolic authorship.[40]

Further development and solidification of the Protestant position took place under the impact of polemic. Roman Catholic theologians were quick to point out that heretics in all ages of the church had denied the normative status of entire books of Scripture or had attempted to excise portions of books for the sake of supporting their doctrinal errors. Gregory Martin noted that this had been the practice of Ebion, who set aside all of the Pauline epistles; of Manichaens, who disavowed the Acts; of the Alogoi, who attacked the Gospel of John; of Marcion, who excised parts of the Gospel of Luke; and in recent times of Luther, who had called the work of St. James "an epistle of straw" unworthy of the spirit of the apostles.[41] On no more authority than Luther had in his attack on James, Protestants in general reject Tobit, Ecclesiasticus, and the Books of Maccabees. The Calvinists, notes Martin, accept James while rejecting the rest, for no more reason than it pleased Calvin to do so—even though Tobit, Ecclesiasticus, and the Books of Maccabees "were allowed and received for canonical by the same authority that St. James' epistle was."[42]

Orthodox Protestant response came in minute detail. The various heretical assaults on the canon of Scripture were examined and distinguished from the Protestant position. The general claim of Trent and the Roman Catholic theologians that their canon of the Old and New Testaments was the authoritative canon accepted by the ecumenical councils of the whole church and, therefore, the true canon of Scripture is examined point for point and refuted. And, finally, each of the disputed books is examined and reasons are given for its exclusion from the canon.[43] In response to the comment that Luther had disputed certain books of the New Testament and therefore differed with subsequent Protestant declarations, Whitaker could note his own disagreement with Luther and then easily place Luther into the context of patristic and late medieval distinctions between homologoumena and antilegomena and, indeed, into the company of Cajetan.[44]

---

[40]E.g., Owen's lengthy discourse on the probability of Pauline authorship of Hebrews in *Exposition of the Epistle to the Hebrews,* in *Works,* 18, pp. 65–92.

[41]Martin, *Discourse,* cited in Fulke, *Defense,* pp. 7, 14.

[42]Fulke, *Defense,* p. 18.

[43]Cf. Cloppenburg, *Exercitationes super locos communes,* I.iv–v.

[44]Whitaker, *Disputation,* I.xvi (p. 105).

The Protestant orthodox debate over the canon of Scripture continually returns to the issue of certain writings normative for the church's teaching both for faith and for life. The question of the canon involves issues of language, authorship, inspiration, and so forth, but primarily it is a question of doctrinally normative status: the canon is the *regula fidei*. Thus Whitaker begins his disputation on the canon of Scripture:

> The books of scripture are called *canonical,* because they contain the standard and rule of our faith and morals. For the scripture is in the church what the law is in a state, which Aristotle in his *Politics* calls a canon or rule. As all citizens are bound to live and behave agreeable to the public laws, so Christians should square their faith and conduct by the rule and law of scripture. So, in Eusebius, the holy fathers accuse Paul of Samosata of departing from this rule, and becoming the author of an heretical opinion.[45]

Whitaker goes on to cite a series of other patristic sources—Tertullian, Cyprian, Chrysostom, Augustine, Basil, and Rufinus—in support of his position. He adds also a citation from Aquinas' lectures on 1 Timothy to support his argument.[46] The church stands in agreement *that* there is a biblical canon of faith and morals. The debate "between us and the papists is, what books are to be esteemed canonical and testamentary."[47]

The centrality of doctrinal concerns to the definition of the canon is clearly seen in Trelcatius' doctrinal summary. He points out that inasmuch as the "material cause" of Scripture is "the divine matters revealed to our salvation, according to our capacity, and registered in the canon," the canon is in turn to be defined by the doctrine it contains—which is to say, Trelcatius adds, by "the unchangeable truth of God."[48] The truth of God is the "internal form," while the Scripture itself, as found in the canon, is the "external form" and "absolute symbol" of God's truth. God has, in other words, used Scripture as an index or guide to the "essential canon" or rule of his truth and has provided the external canonical form as "a measure both whole and perfect" of Christian "faith and life." This scriptural canon functions in the church just as the laws of a republic function

---

[45]Whitaker, *Disputation,* I.ii (p. 27), citing Eusebius, *Hist. eccl.,* VII.30 (which, most probably, is a reference to the creed as *regula fidei* and not to the canon of Scripture.)

[46]Whitaker, *Disputation,* I.ii (pp. 27–28).

[47]Whitaker, *Disputation,* I.ii (pp. 28–29).

[48]Trelcatius, *Schol. meth.,* I.ii.

as a "canon" or rule by which its citizens are governed. In the church, this scriptural canon has two basic functions: it is the rule of all true teaching, and the norm by which all controversies in religion are to be decided.[49]

The early orthodox also, typically, note that the church recognizes two canons, the "divine" and the "ecclesiastical." The divine canon consists in the books of Scripture which, by reason of their time of composition, are divided into the Old and New Testaments. Once this has been said, however, the Reformed orthodox adopt a variety of descriptions of the contents of the canon. According to Scharipus, the books of the Old Testament are divided into three classes: law, prophets, and hagiographa; the books of the New Testament into two classes: the historical and the dogmatic. To these, the "ecclesiastical canon" adds the apocryphal books of the Old Testament which are edifying works not entirely sound in their doctrine.[50] Gomarus, more simply, offers two divisions in each Testament: Moses and the Prophets, the Evangelists, and the Apostles.[51] A detailed account, more sensitive to the genre of the various books and organized into Agricolan or Ramist bifurcations, is offered by Ussher. On the basis of the New Testament, Ussher writes, the Old is properly divided into "the books of Moses (otherwise called the Law) and the Prophets." Ussher notes, however, that the Psalms do not fit precisely into this division and that the Prophets are subject to a further distinction into "historical and doctrinal" works, and the doctrinal works into "poetical and prosaical." The poetical he defines broadly as "such as are written in Metre or Poesie, containing principally wise and holy sentences, whence they may also be called Sentential"—i.e., Job, Psalms, Proverbs, Ecclesiastes and Song of Songs. The "prosaical" are the books strictly identified as prophetic.[52] Ussher also offers a division, this time accompanied by a Ramist chart, of the New Testament canon. After a basic division into books that concern past revelation and the one book that concerns the future, the Apocalypse, he distinguishes the New Testament into historical and doctrinal works—the four Gospels and the Acts on the one hand and the twenty-one epistles on the other.[53]

---

[49]Trelcatius, *Schol. meth.,* I.ii; Scharpius, *Cursus theol.,* I.i (cols. 8–9).

[50]Cf. Scharpius, *Cursus theol.,* I.i (cols. 9–10).

[51]Gomarus, *Disp. theol.,* II.xxxvi, xxxviii.

[52]Ussher, *Body of Divinity,* p. 13.

[53]Ussher, *Body of Divinity,* p. 17.

The canon of Scripture, moreover, can be considered as an article of faith. Weemes notes that articles of faith are considered either as *de fide* or as *de verbo fidei*—as belonging to the faith or as directly from the Word of faith. The identity of Christ as Emmanuel is both *de fide* and *de verbo fidei*, since it is an article of faith that is delivered in the Word—but the fact that Paul "left his cloak at Troas" is *de verbo fidei* but not *de fide*. A third category—to which belong a great number of Christian doctrines—includes things not directly stated in Scripture *(non de verbo fidei)* but drawn as proper conclusions from the text and necessary to faith, such as the doctrine *"that the Scriptures are the word of God;* for this is evident from the whole word generally, and although this be a principle in it selfe, which ought to be first beleeved; yet in my conception, and manner of taking it up, it is a conclusion arising from that majesty and Divine character which is in the word it selfe, or the particular conclusions drawn from the word."[54] As for the identification of the canon or word as written, this is not an article of faith in the most general sense—since the identity of the books in the canon is neither, strictly speaking, a doctrine contained in Scripture nor a doctrine deduced from Scripture. In a special or particular sense, however, the articles of the faith are "that which is contained in the Creed; for the Creed is the substance of that which is contained in the Scripture; and then it is an article of our faith to beleeve the Canon of the Scriptures."[55] The credal *analogia fidei,* therefore, looks to the canonical books for Scripture in its identification of a canon or rule—so that the summary of the faith in turn identifies the canon of Scripture as a primary article of faith.

Having offered these strict definitions of the canon, the orthodox devote some space to the enumeration of the books belonging to it. Here, Trelcatius pays some attention to the historical formation of the canon, but the doctrinal issue remains foremost in his mind. Thus, the canon of the Old Testament was "received from God by the ancient church of the Jews ... and delivered hand to hand to their posterity by God's appointment."[56] The "New Canon" that follows the Old is the peculiar possession of the Christian church,

> the substance of which canon is the word uttered by Christ, and the things that he did: the most faithful history of which is contained

---

[54] Weemes, *Exercitations Divine,* pp. 62–63.
[55] Weemes, *Exercitations Divine,* p. 63.
[56] Trelcatius, *Schol. meth.,* I.ii.

in the four Evangelists; the examples in the Acts; the exposition in twenty-one Epistles; the prophecy in the book of Revelation.[57]

Although "the manner of delivery of both canons varied according to the times of the church and the persons" to whom the revelations were given, the "internal form, ... the unchangeable Word of God" has remained ever the same. By way of example, Trelcatius notes that Moses provided a rule for the church and, although later canonical books have supplemented and aided in the interpretation of the law, no revelation has ever supplanted it.[58]

Robert Rollock, writing in the same era, manifests an interest in the diversity of the materials in Scripture, and like Trelcatius, makes a distinction between the essential truth of God underlying and guaranteeing the Scriptures and the external or "accidental" form of the Scriptures,[59] but he pays considerable attention to the accidents or incidental properties of the biblical books. He notes that, in the first place, the Bible contains two kinds of books, the canonical and the apocryphal, the former alone being given as "the rule or direction touching faith and manners."[60]

A similar, but more precisely defined theological view of the canon, containing a significant covenantal motif is offered by Gomarus:

> The Canon, conformable to the theological verity and wisdom of saving revelation [Heb. 1:1; Rom. 1:2; Eph. 2:20], is one (as is frequently said) in substance *(substantia);* but twofold in its circumstances *(circumstantiis);* the old and the new.[61]

The definition, in its contrast of *substantia* with *circumstantia,* echoes clearly and intentionally the basic Reformed definition of the covenant of grace as one in substance but diverse in the manner of its administration.[62] There is, in other words, a strong interrelationship at this point between the Reformed doctrine of Scripture and the Reformed doctrine of the covenants. Not only does the doctrine of Scripture draw on the federal perspective, but the federal

[57]Trelcatius, *Schol. meth.,* I.ii.

[58]Trelcatius, *Schol. meth.,* I.ii.

[59]Rollock, *Treatise of Effectual Calling,* ch. xvii (pp. 99–110).

[60]Rollock, *Treatise of Effectual Calling,* ch. xvii (pp. 99–110).

[61]Gomarus, *Disp. theol.,* II.xxxv.

[62]Cf. Calvin, *Institutes,* II.x.2: "Patrum omnium foedus adeo substantia et re ipsa nihil a nostro differt.... Administratio tamen variat"; cf. Calvin, *Institutes,* II.xi.1.

approach so becomes a part of the doctrine of Scripture that it brings with it profound hermeneutical and doctrinal implications.[63]

We also see, both in the thought of Gomarus and of Rollock why, from a canonical perspective on the problem of authority, the generally Mosaic authorship of the Pentateuch was so jealously guarded by Protestant orthodoxy and so hotly debated by both the late orthodox on the one side and the deists on the other:

> The Old is that which, in times past, before Christ, was for the Church of the Hebrews, in Hebrew, by Moses in the Pentateuch, fully established and first set forth as a foundation *(plenè constitutus, ac primo propositus);* then, more clearly exposited *(clarius expositus)* in subsequent writings of the Prophets.... For that reason, [the Old Testament] is referred to as "Moses and the prophets" [Lk. 19:29], by metonymy as "the writings of the Prophets" [Matt. 26:56], "the words of the Prophets" [Acts 15:15], or the "prophetic words" [II Pet. 1:19].[64]

> Which canon, because of its object, the Church of the Hebrews, is called "the Canon of the Hebrews," since to them the oracles of God *(eloquia Dei)* were entrusted [Rom. 3:2; Psal. 147:13, 19, 20]: and which because of its material expression *(à materiae modo),* is identified economically as the covenant of grace but more fully as the Law, the covenant of works, or the old testament, and preeminently, in Scripture itself, is called by metonymy, the Law [Prov. 6:23; Rom. 3:19]; and commonly, the Old Testament.[65]

The Mosaic revelation, therefore, provides an anchor for the canon. It is the objective foundation, firm in and of itself, by which subsequent books are judged to be canonical.

This is not to say that the orthodox ignored textual problems or denied that editorial hands had been at work in the composition of the Pentateuch and the subsequent histories. Much more than the Reformers, they were aware of the edited nature of the text and the authorial anonymity of much of the material. They did, however, root the text in the actual words of "Moses and the prophets," arguing that the signs of editorial work in no way set aside the assumption that the larger part of the material in the books came from the mouths or, indeed, the pens, of Moses, Joshua, Samuel, and the prophets.[66]

[63] See above, §2.3.
[64] Gomarus, *Disp. theol.,* II.xxxvi.
[65] Gomarus, *Disp. theol.,* II.xxxvii.
[66] See the extended discussion of Matthew Poole's and Matthew Henry's

Rollock offers a parallel argument, even more explicit in its cumulative and developmental view of canonicity. Like Trelcatius, Scharpius, and other of the early orthodox, he makes no attempt to rule the Apocrypha out of the "ecclesiastical canon" of the Bible, but only out of the normative or "divine" canon, by arguing, in a pattern similar to that noted by Gomarus, but somewhat more theologized, a covenantal or salvation-historical path toward the formation of the canon, resting on the primordial written Word given to Moses. Rollock notes that, in addition to and confirming the distinction between canonical and apocryphal books, there is a threefold division of the text of Scripture, indeed, there are three distinct and interrelated canons that make up the larger canon of Scripture.

Thus, "the books of Moses are the first canon or precedent sent from God, which may not be judged or tried by any other external canon whatsoever."[67] The absoluteness and self-sufficiency of this first canon stand on two foundations. In the first place, there were no books given by God before Moses by which the books of Moses and their teachings might be tested; in the second place, the "authority of the writer," the "evidence of the Spirit" in the teaching of the books, and the "holiness of the books" themselves are so great as not to be impugned. "The books of the prophets," Rollock continues, "make up the second canon." Since they were preceded by the divinely given books of Moses, they have been "adjudged canonical by that external standard of the Mosaical books" and also recognized as God's revelation because "they were, and are discerned of such as be taught of God inwardly by the Holy Ghost, by the great evidence of God's Spirit which is manifested in them both in words and matter."[68]

In the New Testament documents, the orthodox point to a rule that is both temporally and logically final, the culmination of the revelatory history in which the canon was formed:

The New *(Novus),* which was written by the Evangelists and Apostles after the old, and after the last of its authors, is truly the last *(novissimus)* Canon and the edifice of salvation for the church in all the world [Eph. 2:21; John. 20:31].[69]

Which gathering of authors, not only illuminates the older Canon of Scripture, but also perfects it [in two ways]: first, thetically

views above, §2.5.
[67]Rollock, *Treatise of Effectual Calling,* p. 100.
[68]Rollock, *Treatise of Effectual Calling,* p. 100.
[69]Gomarus, *Disp. theol.,* II.xxxviii.

(thetikos), in the four Evangelists; second, interpretively *(ek-thetikos)*, in the remainder of its writings. And so, because of its primary material or substance, it is called the Gospel *(Evangelium)* and the New Testament.[70]

Rollock argues similarly, and, in the parallel construction of his argument, manifests the New Testament as gathering together and concluding in a cumulative sense the criteria of canonicity—rendering the New Testament both final but nonetheless historically contingent on the preceding patterns of revelation:

> The third canon are the apostolical books of the New Testament, which are adjudged and approved as canonical, partly by the canonical books of Moses, partly by the books of the Prophets, partly by the spiritual evidence they carry in themselves.[71]

From a doctrinal point of view, Rollock's argument both allows the historical development of the canon and excludes authority of the postcanonical church from the process. The canon, although identified historically and formulated in the church over centuries, bears in itself the grounds of its authority. Thus, the self-evidencing character of the "divine authority" of Scripture finds a doctrinal analogue in the self-evidencing character of the "canonical authority" that is derived from it.

Gomarus concludes, consciously reiterating the doctrine declared in the prolegomena from a dogmatically a priori perspective—Scripture is the cognitive foundation of theology—but now, he can make the argument in an a posteriori form, as a conclusion drawn from his definitions of the canon:

> The whole Canon, because of its object, the Church or gathering of Christians from both the Jews and the Gentiles, is called the Canon of the Christians *(Canon Christianorum):* and, after the time of the Apostles, granting the absence of an immediate revelation of saving doctrine, it is the self-evidencing, organic or instrumental cognitive foundation of Christian theology *(cognitionis theologia Christianae principium organicum autopiston)*, from which doctrine first arises and in which it is ultimately reconciled. To its author, God, be the glory.[72]

Very much like Trelcatius' and Gomarus' definitions and some-

[70]Gomarus, *Disp. theol.*, II.xxxix.
[71]Rollock, *Treatise of Effectual Calling*, p. 100.
[72]Gomarus, *Disp. theol.*, II.xl.

what more representative of orthodox doctrine than Rollock's three-fold salvation-historical paradigm are the basic definitions of canon offered later in the seventeenth century by Leigh and Riissen. Leigh, for example, maintains both the sense of the canon as a reflection of ectype of the divine truth noted in Trelcatius' thought and the related idea we cited earlier from Polanus of a twofold authority, divine and canonical, belonging to Scripture. Thus, his definition:

> From the Divine flows the Canonical authority of the Scripture. The books of Scripture are called Canonical books (say some) from the word *kanon* ... because they were put into the Canon by the Universal Church and acknowledged to be divinely inspired by it, and are also a perfect Canon or rule of all doctrine concerning religion, *credendorum et agendorum,* of faith and manners, of all things which are to be believed or done toward salvation.[73]

This canon obliges two fundamental conditions for such a rule: first, it contains the image of the truth of the divine mind; and second, it is "commended sanctified and confirmed by Divine authority" as a rule to the church.[74] Riissen similarly understands canonical authority as a deduction, not directly from divinity or divine authority but from several of the "attributes" of Scripture: "From these attributes of Scripture [authority, perfection, and perspicuity] it follows that it is a canon and norm of the things to be believed and things to be done by us, and on the basis of which all controversies of religion ought to be settled."[75] This canon, despite the common usage dividing the Old Testament into the Law and the Prophets and Rollock's rather interesting precedent, is usually divided by the orthodox into two Testaments or covenants, as commonly acknowledged by Christians.[76]

Typically, the orthodox systems, whether early or high orthodox, follow out the confessional pattern of listing the books belonging to the canon. Leigh goes so far as to devote the larger portion of two chapters—one on the Old Testament, one on the New—to a discussion not only of the books of Scripture but of the best commentaries on them.[77] It is also at this point that issues concerning authorship were usually raised and settled. Even granting the stricter post-

---

[73]Leigh, *Treatise,* I.iii (pp. 42–43).

[74]Leigh, *Treatise,* I.iii (p. 43).

[75]Riissen, *Summa theol.,* II.xv.

[76]Leigh, *Treatise,* I.iii (p.44); Maccovius, *Loci communes,* ii (pp. 16–18); Turretin, *Inst. theol. elencticae,* II.viii.

[77]Cf. Leigh, *Treatise,* I.iii–iv (pp. 42–83).

Tridentine approach to the canon characteristic of the Protestant orthodox, a certain level of doubt about certain books still can be noted. Solomonic authorship of the Song of Songs was doubted and Proverbs understood to be a compilation, in part by Solomon.[78] Thus, too, after listing the canonical books of both Testaments, Rollock and others note that the authenticity of Hebrews, James, 2 Peter, 2 and 3 John, Jude, and the Apocalypse had been doubted by some theologians and exegetes but had never been "utterly rejected." They raised, therefore, the issue of the antilegomena and of a "canon within the canon" but give no evidence of any great controversy over the doubted books. They make no allusion at all to the views of Luther, Musculus, and other earlier Protestant thinkers who had relegated the books to a secondary status. They also note that some of the books in the canon have no clearly stated or identifiable author—but, again, unlike the earlier writers who saw some fluidity in the canon, they comment somewhat dogmatically that the absence of ascription to a human author ought to be understood as an indication of the authorship of the Holy Spirit and the instrumentality of the human writer (whoever it was) rather than a sign of the doubtfulness of the book. These works are, therefore, to be considered canonical and not relegated to the category of apocrypha.[79] Even, therefore, in authors like Rollock and Poole, who maintained in the era of orthodoxy a rather "dynamic" language of the living Word speaking in Scripture, the approach to the text as rule or canon has solidified considerably and the problems noted fairly widely in the early sixteenth century are no longer registered.

The apocryphal books of the Old Testament, the orthodox uniformly declare, are "so called because the church would have kept them hid, and not to be read or taught publicly in the churches; only the private reading of them was permitted."[80] Leigh dismisses one and hypothesizes two possible reasons for the designation "apocryphal": the books are called "secret" or "hidden," he comments, "not because the names of the writers are unknown ... but because they were not wont to be read openly in the Church of God as Canonical books ... or because their authority was obscure or doubt-

---

[78]Poole, *Commentary,* II, pp. 213, 307–308.

[79]Rollock, *Treatise,* pp. 101–2; cf. Poole, *Commentary,* III, pp. 808 (Hebrews), 917 (2 Peter), 928 (2 and 3 John), and 943–44 (Jude); Turretin, *Inst. theol. elencticae,* II.ix.13.

[80]Rollock, *Treatise,* p. 102; cf. Whitaker, *Disputation,* I.iv–xv; *Synopsis purioris theologiae,* III.xxxvi–xxxix; Turretin, *Inst. theol. elencticae,* II.ix.

ful with the Ancients."[81] It was clear to Rollock that the apocryphal books do not have the same historical warrant as the canonical books of the Old Testament. None of them was first written in Hebrew and they were unknown in the time of Ezra. Riissen summarizes the argument tersely: "their authors were not prophets or inspired men *(viri theopneustoi);* moreover, they were written after Malachi, the last of the prophets; nor were they inscribed in the Hebrew tongue like the books of the Old Testament, but in Greek."[82]

In confirmation of their absence from the classical canon of the Hebrew Scriptures, it is also the case that the apocryphal books were rejected by the Jews and were not cited as Scripture either by Christ or by the apostles.[83] Many of the fathers of the church, moreover, raised objections to these books, and Jerome in particular viewed them as less than canonical.[84] Furthermore, they are easily recognized as containing teachings contrary to the contents of the canonical books, such as a doctrine of purgatory (cf. 2 Macc. 12:42–45).[85] Mastricht rehearses the same arguments and cites what he considers, even in his time, to be the best discussions of the problem of the apocrypha: Rainolds' essay on the Apocrypha, Whitaker's *Disputation on Sacred Scripture,* and Alsted's *Praecognita,* all works from the era of early orthodoxy.[86]

The Protestant orthodox also assert that the apocryphal books also lack the evidences of divinity found in the canonical books— indeed, in the place of the marks of divinity characteristic of the authoritative Scriptures, the Apocrypha abound in "human" characteristics: "The style and substance of these books cry out that they are human," writes Riissen:

> for not only does the style fail to reflect the majesty and simplicity of the divine style, but it smells of the weaknesses and infirmities of the human imagination, of vanity, flattery, curiosity, affectation of wisdom and eloquence, which occur not infrequently in them; many things are found in them that are frivolous, absurd, false, superstitious and contradictory.[87]

---

[81]Leigh, *Treatise,* I.v (p.85).
[82]Riissen, *Summa theol.,* II.vii, controversia iii, arg.2.
[83]Cf. Leigh, *Treatise,* I.v (p. 88).
[84]Cf. Whitaker, *Disputation,* I.vii–xv (pp. 67–105), *passim.*
[85]Leigh, *Treatise,* I.v (pp. 103–4).
[86]Mastricht, *Theoretico-practica theol.,* I.ii.9.
[87]Riissen, *Summa theol.,* II.vii, controversia, arg.2.

For example, Riissen notes that the Book of Tobit attributes lies to an angel: Raphael states (Tob. 5:15) that his name is Azarias the son of Ananias; in the sixth chapter of the same book (vv. 13–17) Raphael gives Tobit a magic spell to drive away demons, but Christ himself tells us, in the Gospel of Matthew (17:21), that this kind of being is cast off only through prayer and fasting. Even so, Judith praises Simeon (9:3), the very son who was cursed by his father Jacob for his ruthlessness (cf. Gen. 49:5–7). The fraud and mendacity of Judith are praised (ch. 11)![88] The identification of Holofernes as an emissary sent in the thirteenth year of the reign of Nebuchadnezzar is a fable, as is the claim that nearly one hundred years of peace followed the encounter of Judith with Holofernes. Indeed, none of the Roman Catholic exegetes and apologists are able to account for the tale in relation to the known chronology of the Old Testament![89] The author of the so-called Book of Wisdom falsely identifies himself as Solomon, king of Israel—and then alludes to athletic games of the Greeks not practiced in the time of Solomon (4:2). Beyond that, Riissen comments, the book teaches a Pythagorean doctrine of the transmigration of souls (8:19–20).[90] Whitaker notes that the simple fact that Greek is the original language of the Wisdom of Solomon excludes it from the canon as, in Jerome's words, "pseudepigraphal." This, Whitaker adds, is also the opinion of Roman Catholic scholars like John Driedo—and it must be remembered that Bonaventure said much the same thing and, in fact, attributed Wisdom to Philo.[91] The Book of Baruch has its author writing from Babylon, when we learn from Jeremiah 40 that Baruch was with Jeremiah in Egypt. The book also speaks of the offering of sacrifices by the Jews in Babylon—but there never was either a temple or an altar for such purposes in Babylon![92] In the Books of Maccabees suicide is praised (1 Macc. 1:16; 9:5, 28) and sacrifices are offered for the dead (2 Macc. 12:42).[93] Obviously such books

---

[88]Riissen, *Summa theol.,* II.vii, controversia, arg.2.

[89]Cloppenburg, *Exercitationes super locos communes,* I.iv.2; Whitaker, *Disputation,* I.xi (pp. 83–86).

[90]Riissen, *Summa theol.,* II.vii, controversia, arg.2; Cloppenburg, *Exercitationes super locos communes,* I.iv.3. *N.B.* Most commentators view the doctrine of Wisd. 8:19–20 as a Platonic doctrine of the preexistence of souls, but the theological point, disputing the canonicity of the text as containing anachronistic and nonbiblical concepts, remains unchanged.

[91]Whitaker, *Disputation,* I.xii (pp. 87–89).

[92]Cloppenburg, *Exercitationes super locos communes,* I.iv.5.

[93]Cloppenburg, *Exercitationes super locos communes,* I.iv.5.

cannot be considered divine.

The orthodox argue further that the fathers and the ancient councils of the church—and even many of the medieval doctors—rejected the authority of the Apocrypha. Only several suspect councils affirm the canonicity of these books and, as Rollock notes with a touch of polemical irony, even Cajetan spoke at Trent for a distinction between the canon and the antilegomena.[94] Nonetheless, despite the firm doctrinal line drawn between the normative canon and the Apocrypha, and despite the presence of problematic doctrinal points in the apocrypha, many of the Protestant writers register respect for this ancient collection of books: Trelcatius referred to them as belonging to an "Ecclesiastical Canon" and Leigh calls than a "second canon."[95] The apocryphal books, Leigh comments, do not contain "an infallible truth, out of which firm arguments may be drawn," but they are "good and profitable" for study beyond the value of more recently written books.[96]

These books are called "Apocrypha," that is, secret or hidden, "not because the names of the writers are unknown ... but because they were not wont to be read openly in the Church of God as the Canonical books ... or because their authority was obscure and doubtful with the Ancients."[97] These books were, moreover, written after the time of Malachi, the last of the prophets. Whereas the prophets all wrote in Hebrew, these books exist only in Greek. Furthermore, they were rejected by the ancient Jews and were never commended by Christ and the apostles; rightly so, inasmuch as they contain teachings contrary to the rest of Scripture.[98] Mastricht concurs in these arguments and cites as standard works on the subject Rainolds' study of the Apocrypha, Whitaker's disputation on Scripture, and Alsted's *Praecognita,* all significantly, works of the early orthodox period.[99]

The doctrinal conclusion drawn by the orthodox from their definition and delimitation of the canon is the issue already raised in the discussion of the early Reformation approach to the lost books of the Old Testament and antilegomena of the New: the doctrine of a *perfectio integralis* of the canon or of the *integritas Scripturae*

---

[94]Whitaker, *Disputation,* I.vi (pp. 54–66); Rollock, *Treatise,* pp. 106–110.

[95]Trelcatius, *Schol. meth.,* I.ii; Leigh, *Treatise,* I.v (p.84).

[96]Leigh, *Treatise,* I.v.

[97]Leigh, *Treatise,* I.v (p. 84).

[98]Riissen, *Summa theol.,* II.vii, controversia 3; Leigh, *Treatise,* I.v (pp. 88, 90–91).

[99]Mastricht, *Theoretico-practica theol.,* I.ii.9.

sacrae. The dogmatic assertion looks back to the discussions of the external evidences of the divinity of Scripture and of the perfection of Scripture and applies what had been argued there in general to the specific issue of the canon:[100] the divine providence that preserved the text of Scripture through so many vicissitudes can be seen, in the light of the discussion of the canon, to have preserved Scripture from corruption both in the whole and in each of its parts.[101]

The adaptation of this argument to the needs of the doctrine of the canon raised for Protestant orthodoxy, at a dogmatic level, the problem of the lost books of the Old Testament and the issue not only of the antilegomena of the New Testament but also of the possible existence of other New Testament books, like the Pauline Epistle to the Laodicaeans, the text of which was available in some medieval Bibles. Does the loss or absence of such works prejudice the overall integrity of the canon? The question gains its importance from the situation, in which the Roman Catholics on the one side and the Protestant "Spiritualists" on the other were ready to argue the need for norms other than the canon of Scripture—in the case of the Catholic argument, a churchly norm capable of identifying and defining the canon and capable, also, of supplying the doctrinal lacks of a textually imperfect canon. From a somewhat different perspective, the Socinians argued the loss of books from the Old Testament and the imperfection of its revelation over against the New Testament revelation. Against such arguments, the orthodox insist that the books presently found in the canon provide all the truths necessary for salvation, so that no other books are needed. There is no lost book that was either an essential or an integral part of Scripture.[102]

Riissen offers a two-point summary of the argument, noting that his views rest on the arguments of Musculus and Whitaker who, in turn, had drawn their views from Chrysostom. In the first place, the lost books mentioned in the Old Testament are not affirmed as canon by the New Testament; and in the second place, the perfection of Scripture "is not measured by the number of books, but by the fullness of the teaching."[103] Thus, the integrity of the Old Testament

---

[100]Cf. above, §§4.3 and 5.3, with Whitaker, *Disputation,* I.xvi; Pictet, *Theol. chr.,* I.x–xi; de Moor, *Commentarius perpetuus in Joh. Marckii compendium,* II.xvi (pp. 281–85).

[101]Mastricht, *Theoretico-practica theol.,* I.ii.16; cf. Burmann, *Synopsis theol.,* I.vii.

[102]Weemes, *Exercitations Divine,* pp. 117–118.

[103]Riissen, *Summa theol.,* II.xvii, controversia 4; cf. Hoornbeeck, *Summa*

may be inferred from the words of Christ himself (Matt. 5:18; Luke 16:17) to the effect that heaven and earth may pass away but not a jot or tittle be taken from the law. The providence of God and the office of the church, moreover, do not allow that Scripture could be lacking in its substantial or doctrinal integrity. Indeed, the intent of Scripture, argues Riissen, which is to be the rule of faith and life to the church, could not be furthered by the Scripture if the canon were imperfect.[104]

What then of "the book of the wars of Jehovah" (Num. 21:14), or "the book of the Upright" (Josh. 10:13; 2 Sam. 1:18), or "the history of the kings of Judah and Israel" (1 Kings 14:19; 15:23)? "These books," comments Riissen, "did not contain the teaching of religion, but were either political annals in which the public business of the Israelites *(res gestae Israëlitarum)* was recorded, or contained either registers of events or of civil statutes."[105] There may also have been books written by the prophets as private writings—such as Solomon's reported books of herbs and plants (1 Kings 4:33), but such works were not written for "the edification of the Church."[106] As for the so-called chronicles of Samuel, Nathan, and Gad (1 Chron. 29:29), the "visions of Iddo" (2 Chron. 9:29), and the "chronicles of Shemaiah" (2 Chron. 12:15) these are parts of the present books of Samuel, Kings, and Chronicles, as even Roman Catholic scholars like Sixtus Senensis and Paulus Burgensis had admitted.[107]

The Reformed writers also hypothesize that other writings of the apostles might have existed, but were not preserved because they were not specifically related to the teaching of the gospel. As de Moor notes, the arguments drawn from the fathers concerning the possible existence of a second epistle to the Philippians and a third epistle to the Corinthians are inconclusive and, in any case, do not point toward works destined for the canon.[108] The one extant book

controversiarum, p. 449 and idem, *Socinianismus confutatus,* I, pp. 48–53.

[104]Riissen, *Summa theol.,* II.xvii, controversia 2, arg.1–4.

[105]Riissen, *Summa theol.,* II.xvii, controversia 4, obj.1 and resp.; cf. Weemes, *Exercitations Divine,* p. 120. *N.B.:* Riissen's comments about the public records and the political annals of ancient Israel reflect a major interest of the federal theology, which typically discussed these topics at length under the historical analysis of the Old Covenant: see e.g., Heidegger, *Corpus theol.,* locus XVI: "De lege judiciali Mosis."

[106]Weemes, *Exercitations Divine,* p. 120.

[107]Riissen, *Summa theol.,* II.xvii, controversia 4, obj.2 & resp; cf. Weemes, *Exercitations Divine,* p. 121.

[108]De Moor, *Commentarius perpetuus in Joh. Marckii compendium,* II.xvi (pp. 287–88).

that exemplifies this problem is the so-called *Epistle to the Laodicaeans*. Not only is the book extant and attributed to Paul, there is also a possible indication in the text of the Epistle to the Colossians that Paul had actually written such a work (Col. 4:16). Cloppenburg views this document as posing a significant problem for the doctrine of canon, specifically, of the integrity of the ancient codices. The problem is caused, he argues, by the text of some Latin codices that indicates an epistle *ad Laodicenses* rather than correctly rendering the Greek as *ex Laodicea*. Theophylact, Cloppenburg notes, had identified this work as the first epistle to Timothy—a view that is confirmed by the reference in the following verse to Archippus, to whom Paul and Timothy sent greetings in the Epistle to Philemon.[109] In confirmation of this interpretation, Riissen notes that some ancient texts of 1 Timothy conclude with the inscription, "The first to Timothy was written from Laodicaea, which is the chief city of Phrygia Pacatiana."[110] The other option, taken by Calvin and by a majority of the orthodox is that the epistle "from Laodicaea" was not a letter by Paul but an epistle by a now unknown writer of the church of Laodicaea recommended by Paul to the Colossians as edifying.[111] In any case, the extant writing known as the *Epistle to the Laodicaeans* is a forgery and cannot be used as the foundation of an argument against the integrity of the canon. We can be certain, the orthodox argue, that the books in the canon are those that God willed to be consecrated to the public use of the church of the old and new covenants. All these books were providentially preserved in their integrity—and we even learn from Scripture that "when any booke which was necessary for the use of the Church was lost; the Lord had a care that that booke should be found againe, as the booke of the law found by *Hilkiah, 2 Kings 22:8*."[112] With all of the objections thus set aside, the orthodox conclude that the canon possesses the integrity or integral perfection suitable to a rule of faith.

[109]Cloppenburg, *Exercitationes super locos communes,* I.v.5; cf. Burmann, *Synopsis theologiae,* I.vii.7.

[110]Riissen, *Summa theol.,* II.xvii, controversia 4, obj.3, cf. the inscription still found in the KJV at the conclusion of 1 Timothy.

[111]Cf. Calvin, commentary on Col. 4:16, with Whitaker, *Disputation,* I.xvi (p. 108); Gataker et al., *Annotations upon all the Books of the Old and New Testament,* in loc.; and with the extended discussions in Poole, *Commentary,* III, pp. 729–30 and de Moor, *Commentarius perpetuus in Joh. Marckii compendium,* II.xvi (pp. 285–87).

[112]Cf. Cloppenburg, *Exercitationes super locos communes,* I.v.3, 6, with Weemes, *Exercitations Divine,* pp. 118–19, citing also the story of Jeremiah's second dictation of the lost Lamentations to Baruch (Jer. 36:32).

Granting the relative openness and fluidity of the canon in the Middle Ages and the willingness of the writers, Protestant and Roman Catholic alike, of the early sixteenth century to open the question of the canon on doctrinal and critical grounds, some explanation must be provided, by way of conclusion to this section, for the increasingly rigid approach to the canon of Scripture found in the confessional writings of the Reformed and in the theology of the Reformed orthodox. The point taken up by Heppe as a central dogmatic issue and also suggested by Reuss that the orthodox set aside an earlier Protestant distinction between Holy Scripture and the Word of God, cannot be accepted. The distinction, rightly understood, remained in use throughout the period of orthodoxy.[113]

The early Reformers were more able than their successors to allow for an unevenness of quality in Scripture—for a clearer and fuller communication of the Word in some places than in others. Insofar as Luther's successors, notably Flacius, maintained Luther's distinction of books within the canon as well as the distinction between canonical and apocryphal books, and inasmuch as Lutheranism felt no immediate need to follow the Reformed in defining the canon with precision in its confessions, it may be possible to argue the maintenance of the early Reformation concept of the canon and, therefore, a subtly different resolution of the question of authority in the context of the believing church on the Lutheran side of the Reformation longer than on the Reformed or Calvinistic side. Heinrich Heppe noted, with some justice, that "Calvinism held fast to the authority of the biblical Word inasmuch as it was for the community of believers on earth precisely what the eternally uttered Word of God is once and for all," while "German Protestantism confessed the authority of the biblical Word because it needed an authority on the basis of which traditional structures of churchly knowing would be confirmed and standardized *(normiert)* in their integrity."[114] It is true that the Reformed systems, even in the era of early orthodoxy, draw the distinction between archetypal and ectypal theology into the discussion of the canon and postulate a strict relationship between the eternal and the temporal Word as lodged in the canonical books of Scripture.

Whereas it would be unwise to follow Heppe in his extrapolation

[113]Cf. Reuss, *History of the Canon,* pp. 354–55; Heppe, *RD,* pp. 14–16, with the discussion above, §§2.1–2.2, and in Muller, "Christ—the Revelation or the Revealer?" pp. 311–15.

[114]Heppe, *Geschichte des deutschen Protestantismus,* I, p. 28.

from the Reformed sense of a direct relation between the scriptural and the eternal Word to an identification of the eternal Word with the *decretum absolutum* of a predestinarian system and, hence, of the scriptural Word as a "divinely effected evidence of the eternal decree,"[115] his basic point is well taken. The Lutheran use of the canon as a standardizing norm *(norma normans)* above the confessional, standardized norm *(norma normata)* marked out a path that was somewhat more open to traditional usages and somewhat more respectful of churchly authority than the Reformed perspective. Even when, in the seventeenth century, the Lutheran approach to Scripture became virtually identical with the high orthodox Reformed approach, Lutheran orthodoxy retained the balance of Scripture and churchly confession and, indeed, was more firmly bound to a unitary confessional model than were the Reformed churches. (This latter confessional point was, of course, a political as well as a doctrinal issue, but the doctrinal significance must not be underestimated because of the political reality.)

6.3 The Authentic Editions and the Text of Scripture

a. The Hebrew and Greek Texts

At the beginning of the sixteenth century, Protestant exegetes and theologians, in alliance with humanist classical scholarship, could easily assert the priority of the Greek New Testament and of the Hebrew Old Testament over ancient translations like the Septuagint and the Vulgate—and, indeed, find general agreement among biblical scholars, both Protestant and Catholic.[116] As the sixteenth century progressed, however, use of the Hebrew and Greek texts, given the difficulty of interpreting certain passages, was questioned by Roman Catholic defenders of the Vulgate, some of whom were themselves eminent exegetes and textual scholars.[117] And as the seventeenth century dawned, the linguistic field broadened considerably. Whereas the early Reformers could easily accept the Masoretic Text of the Old Testament and Erasmus' Greek New Testament as definitive, with little or no argument, later generations of Protestants

[115]Heppe, *Geschichte des deutschen Protestantismus,* I, p. 28; and see above, §3.5.

[116]Cf. Bainton, "The Bible in the Reformation," in *CHB,* III:10–11, with Hall, "Biblical Scholarship: Editions and Commentaries," in *CHB,* III:38–69.

[117]Cf. Montgomery, "Sixtus of Siena and Roman Catholic Biblical Scholarship," p. 227, with Creehan, "The Bible in the Roman Catholic Church," in *CHB,* III:202–5.

became acquainted with textual problems in both of these sources. Ancient versions other than the Septuagint and the Vulgate became available as the humanist passion for classical languages moved on from Latin, Greek, and Hebrew to Arabic, Aramaic, and Syriac—and the seventeenth century became the great era of linguistic and textual study.[118] Variant readings multiplied, text-traditions appeared, the Masoretes were seen to be divided into at least two schools (Ben Asher and Ben Naphtali) and their system of pointing was argued to be postcanonical in its origins, indeed, more recent than several of the ancient versions, notably the Septuagint and the Vulgate.[119] These philological problems of the seventeenth century are also doctrinal problems inasmuch as they could become barriers to the early dogmatic assertion of the Greek text of the New Testament and of the Masoretic Hebrew text of the Old Testament as the authentic and therefore absolutely authoritative text of inspired Scripture. Seventeenth-century orthodoxy was hard put to maintain the once simple argument of the Reformers in the face of the complexity of the textual problem.

[118]Cf. Diestel, *Geschichte des Alten Testaments,* pp. 442–50, with Peter T. van Rooden, *Theology, Biblical Scholarship and Rabbinical Studies in the Seventeenth Century: Constantijn L'Empereur (1591–1648), Professor of Hebrew and Theology at Leiden,* trans. J. C. Grayson (Leiden: Brill, 1989); Emil Kautsch, *Johannes Buxtorf der Ältere* (Basel: Detloff, 1879); G. Lloyd Jones, *The Discovery of Hebrew in Tudor England: A Third Language* (Manchester: University of Manchester Press, 1983); J.H.C. Lebram, "Hebräische Studien zwischen Ideal und Wirklichkeit an der Universität Leiden in den Jahren 1575–1619," in *Nederlands Archief voor Kerkgeschiedenis* 56 (1975): 317–57; Roger Zuber, "De Scaliger à Saumaise: Leyde et les grands 'Critiques' français," in *Bulletin de la Société de l'Histoire du Protestantisme français* 126 (1980):461–88; Moshe Goshen-Gottstein, "The Textual Criticism of the Old Testament: Rise, Decline, Rebirth," in *Journal of Biblical Literature* 102 (1983):365–99; and idem, "Foundations of Biblical Philology in the Seventeenth Century: Christian and Jewish Dimensions," in *Jewish Thought in the Sevententh Century,* ed. Isadore Tweersky and Bernard Septimus (Cambridge, Mass.: Harvard University Press, 1987), pp. 77–94.

[119]The great study of the Masorah in the seventeenth century was Johannes Buxtorf (the elder), *Tiberias sive commentarius Masorethicus triplex: historicus, didacticus, criticus.* Recognitus ... a Johanne Buxtorfio Fil. (Basel, 1665); note Owen's acknowledgment of the two Masoretic traditions in *The Divine Original of Scripture,* in *Works,* 16, p. 301; and, similarly, de Moor, *Commentarius perpetuus in Joh. Marckii compendium,* II.ix (I, p. 194); also see Richard A. Muller, "The Debate over the Vowel Points and the Crisis in Orthodox Hermeneutics," in *Journal of Medieval and Renaissance Studies* 10/1 (1980):53-72.

In addition, the complexity of the textual problem together with the problem of a clearly and closely defined canon, led the orthodox to worry more deeply than the Reformers over the integrity of the canon itself and over the integrity of the various books placed in the canon. These problems were complicated further by polemic with the Roman Catholics, who could not only argue for the canonicity of the Apocrypha, but who could also argue for the crucial role of the churchly tradition and magisterium in identifying and determining the canon.

As a codicil to its first decree—virtually as a gloss on the statement that the canon of Scripture should be received as given in the Vulgate—the fourth session of Trent pronounced on the normative status of the Vulgate. The decree is carefully worded and in no way argues an absolute priority of the Vulgate as a translation, over the Greek and Hebrew text, but it does define the authority of the Vulgate in such a way that none of its renditions of the original languages could be superseded as norms for theological statement by new translations and that the Vulgate could be regarded as the basis for all further translation into the vernacular:[120]

> the ... sacred and holy Synod ... ordains and declares that this old and common *(vetus et vulgata)* edition, which has been approved in the church by the sustained use of so many ages, be owned as authentic *(authentica)* in public lectures, disputations, sermons, and expositions, and that no one dare or presume to reject it on any pretext.[121]

Since, of course, the apocryphal books are found in the Vulgate, this definition has implications for both text and canon. On the basis of this dogmatic decision, later Roman Catholic writers, like Bellarmine and Bannez, would argue that discrepancies between the Vulgate and the extant Hebrew and Greek texts of Scripture, particularly in parts of the Old Testament where Jerome had followed the Septuagint, were to be explained as problems in the Hebrew and the Greek caused by copyists who worked after the time of Jerome.[122]

The problem of the authentic edition of the Scriptures enters

---

[120]Cf. Creehan, "The Bible in the Roman Catholic Church from Trent to the Present Day," in *CHB*, III:203–4.

[121]*Canones et decreta dogmatica concilii Tridentini, IV,* in Schaff, *Creeds,* II, p. 82.

[122]Bellarmine, *De verbo Dei,* II.ii; cf. Creehan, "Bible in the Roman Catholic Church from Trent to the Present Day," 205.

Reformed theology, then, by way of the polemic with Rome. At the beginning of the Reformation, humanists and linguists on both sides were generally united in their emphasis on the sources—on the Hebrew and Greek originals of Scripture. As doctrinal debate intensified, however, the version of the Scripture employed in deciding theological matters became a matter of increasing importance. Early on Erasmus and Luther had easily shown the error of the Vulgate in translating *metanoiete* as "do penance."[123] By mid-century, in response to Protestant arguments based on the Greek and Hebrew texts, the Council of Trent declared the Vulgate "authentic" and definitive for exposition, preaching, and theological debate. Roman Catholic polemicists like Cano, Lindanus, and Andradius proclaimed that points of theology could not be determined by appeal from the Vulgate to the Hebrew and Greek.[124]

Reformed response, in defense of the authenticity of the Hebrew and Greek text, came in the form of a multitude of tracts and treatises, the arguments of which were ultimately incorporated into the fully developed orthodox dogmatic systems. The point had become of considerable dogmatic importance in view not only of the continued Roman Catholic insistence on the authority of the Vulgate but also in view of developments in linguistic and textual study that took place during the seventeenth century. Not only did biblical scholars address the problem of differences between the Greek and Hebrew "originals" of Scripture and the translations offered in the Vulgate and Septuagint, they were also faced with the problem of other ancient versions, like the Syriac, and the potential use of these versions to solve textual problems in the Greek and the Hebrew. From the vantage-point of a Protestant church founded radically on the text of Scripture, the problem of the ancient versions became a theological issue of almost equal weight with the problem of the canon.

Understandably, therefore, the topic treated by many of the Reformed orthodox immediately after their discussions of the canon and the Apocrypha is the debate over "the authentic edition of the Scripture" and the "integrity" of its text.[125] The contents of these

---

[123]Cf. Bainton, "The Bible in the Reformation," in *CHB*, III:11.

[124]Cf. Whitaker, *Disputation*, II.i (pp. 110–111).

[125]Cf., e.g., Alsted, *Theologia didactica*, I.iv.5; Polanus, *Syntagma theol.*, I.xxxvi–xxxix; Maccovius, *Loci communes*, III; Burmann, *Synopsis theologiae*, I.vii; Maresius, *Collegium theologicum*, I.xl; Heidanus, *Corpus theol.*, I (pp. 33–34); Leigh, *Treatise*, I.vi (pp. 91–119) and I.vii (pp. 119–29); Turretin, *Inst. theol. elencticae*, III.x–xii; Mastricht, *Theoretico-practica theol.*, I.ii.10; de

disputations and theological *loci,* moreover, provide evidence of the immersion of the dogmaticians of the seventeenth century in textual and exegetical issues. This is not dogmatics divorced from exegesis, but dogmatics framed by the exegetical debates of the day. Leigh comments at length on the "great diversity of editions of Holy Scripture" and shows the need to distinguish between them.

> There is a question betwixt the Church of Rome and the reformed Churches about the authentic edition of Scripture; they say, that the edition of the Bible in Hebrew and Greek is not authentic, but rather the vulgar Latin. We hold that the vulgar Latin is very corrupt and false; that the Hebrew for the Old Testament and the Greek for the New is the sincere and authentic writing of God; therefore that all other things are to be determined by them; and that the other versions are so far to be approved of, as they agree with these fountains.[126]

Riissen states the dogmatic point succinctly, with a clear reliance on the concept of a verbal dictation of the text by the Spirit:

> The authentic edition [of Scripture] is, that which is due the full allegiance of faith, and which has sprung forth from immediate divine inspiration. Such authenticity only the Hebrew and Greek editions have.[127]

He also supports the doctrinal point with the a series of arguments. In the first place, "only the sources are inspired *(theopneustoi)* both according to their substance *(quoad res)* and according to their words *(quoad verba)*." This must be the case, since "holy men of God spake as they were moved by the Holy Spirit, 2 Pet. 1.21, who dictated to them not only the substance *(res)* but also the very words *(verba)*." For the same reason, the Hebrew and the Greek are the norms and rules by which the various versions are examined and evaluated.[128] This claim, Leigh indicates, does not deny canonicity and authenticity to those parts of Daniel and Ezra which appear in the Chaldee. It seems that in these instances "the Lord was pleased that in that language as well as Hebrew some of his divine truth

---

Moor, *Commentarius perpetuus in Joh. Marckii compendium,* II.viii (vol. I, p. 160).

[126]Leigh, *Treatise,* I.vi (p. 92).

[127]Riissen, *Summa theol.,* II.xix, controversia I.

[128]Riissen, *Summa theol.,* II.xix, controversia 1.

should originally be written."[129] The question is, thus, not of the language per se but of the original language of the text. Similarly, the Reformed writers of the seventeenth century were aware that ancient remains of Israel indicated two forms of the letters of the Old Testament—an earlier "Samaritan" form, so called because the Samaritans retain it after the Jews turned to the later or "Chaldee Character," developed in response to the needs of Israel after the exile and credited by the seventeenth-century linguists to Ezra. This linguistic problem of exilic and postexilic Israel also explains why some portions of Daniel are in "Chaldee" or Aramaic.[130] It is fairly clear, given this and related points, not that the doctrine of Scripture had changed radically in the transition to orthodoxy, but that the polemic had altered the focus and emphasis of the doctrine, and had placed a greater burden on the language of the text and, by extension, on the concept of plenary, verbal inspiration by means of dictation.

Following his initial argument that the Hebrew and the Greek alone are authentic and "all other editions must be approved so far as they agree with these" is representative of the orthodox Reformed position, Rollock offered a typical breakdown of subsidiary issues to be addressed: the Hebrew language and its antiquity; the writing of the Old Testament in Hebrew; and the preservation of the Hebrew text.[131] Against claims of the priority of other texts, the younger Buxtorf followed earlier writers like Whitaker and Rollock in arguing that Hebrew was the most ancient language, the mother tongue of all languages, the single tongue spoken before the confusion of tongues at Babel, and alone preserved intact at the tower of Babel. Indeed, "Hebrew" takes its name from Heber, the descendant of Noah who lived at the time of Babel and who passed on the pure original language to his descendants in the line of Abraham. This teaching was, the Reformed note against Roman polemicists, the opinion of Augustine and Jerome. Hebrew was, moreover, the language in which Moses first wrote the word of God and, therefore, the first written language, and it remained the language of all the prophets, so that nearly all of Scripture was written in Hebrew— with the exception of Daniel and Ezra, who also used "the Chaldee tongue"—until the time of the New Testament. The letters used by Moses, moreover, were retained as the original form of the written

---

[129]Leigh, *Treatise,* I.vi (p. 93).
[130]Weemes, *Exercitations Divine,* pp. 88–89.
[131]Rollock, *Treatise of Effectual Calling,* XVIII (p. 110).

Hebrew language, despite various corruptions of practice during the time of the first temple, and were restored to their purity by Ezra.[132] According to God's gracious providence, then, all these holy books have been preserved in their integrity despite the great persecutions and devastating wars which took place in ancient times.[133]

Against Roman Catholic polemicists like Stapleton, Lindanus, Cano, Cotton, and Morin, the Protestant orthodox could cite as many Roman Catholic Hebraists who had accepted the verdict of Augustine and Jerome and had either assumed or defended the purity of the Hebrew and Greek texts, notably, Sixtus Senensis, Andradius, Driedo, Arias Montanus, Bonfrerius, and Simon de Muis.[134] Whitaker took time to refute the opinion of medieval thinkers like Isidore and Rabanus Maurus that Scripture either perished or was much damaged in the Babylonian captivity and only "restored to its integrity by Ezra, instructed and inspired ... by the direct agency of God," although he admitted the possibility that Ezra did correct errors in the text and, as Jerome believed, invented simpler forms of the letters, superior to those used by the Samaritans.[135] Rollock also notes that some writers in the church have believed that the Old Testament was lost in the destruction of Jerusalem and the exile of Israel—and that Ezra was specially called for the purpose of rewriting the Scriptures as dictated by God. This, he observes, is a story based on the apocryphal Book of Ezra and should be rejected. The canonical Book of Nehemiah testifies that Ezra "brought forth"

[132]Cf. the first four disputations in Johannes Buxtorf (the younger), *Dissertationes philologico-theologicae. I. De linguae hebraeae origine, antiquitate et sanctitate. II. De linguae hebraeae confusione et plurium linguarum originae. III. De linguae hebraeae conservatione, propagatione et duratione. IV. De litterarum hebraicarum genuina antiquitate. V. De nominibus Dei hebraicis. VI. De Decalogo. VII. De primae coena Dominicae ritibus et forma* (Basel, 1645); with Whitaker, *Disputation*, II.ii (pp. 112–14); Rollock, *Treatise of Effectual Calling*, XVIII (pp. 110–11); Lightfoot, *Horae hebraicae et talmudicae*, II, pp. 104–5; de Moor, *Commentarius perpetuus in Joh. Marckii compendium*, II.viii (vol. I, pp. 162–63).

[133]Cf. Calvin, *Institutes*, I.viii.10; Rollock, *Treatise of Effectual Calling*, XVIII (p. 111); Leigh, *Treatise*, I.ii (p. 19); Turretin, *Inst. theol. elencticae*, II.iv.8; Pictet, *Theol. chr.*, I.vi.15, obs.4.

[134]De Moor, *Commentarius perpetuus in Joh. Marckii compendium*, II.ix (vol. I, p. 182); cf the similar comments in Mastricht, *Theoretico-practica theol.*, I.ii.40.

[135]Whitaker, *Disputation*, II.ii (pp. 115–16); cf. Owen, *Divine Original of Scripture*, in *Works*, 16, p. 297; Wyttenbach, *Tentamen theologiae dogmaticae*, XI, §1378, scholion 1.

and read the law of Moses—not that he read what he had himself written. Ezra, it seems, "did revise the books of Moses and the Prophets" and "digested them into one volume, and set them down in this certain order."[136]

> We must hold, therefore, that we have now those very ancient scriptures which Moses and the other prophets published, although we have not, perhaps, precisely the same forms and shapes of the letters.[137]

Here, without any reference to the vowel points, which were already a point of issue in Whitaker's time, is the ground of the early orthodox doctrine of the authority of Scripture—which doctrine would very soon be thought to stand or fall with the integrity of the vowel points.

Having argued to their satisfaction that Hebrew is the original language of the text, Reformed theologians moved on to the problem of possible corruption in the text and to the Roman contention that, because of the corruption of the Hebrew, the Vulgate is to be esteemed prior to the Hebrew text.[138] Their adversary is often specifically Bellarmine, who, unlike his more polemical predecessors cites only five places where the Hebrew is uncertain—and cites them with the polemical advantage that none other than Calvin approved the Vulgate or a similar reading in these instances. Rollock shows in detail that the variations offer little if any changes of meaning, and in one instance that the variant text was already known, in Hebrew, to the Masoretes. He concludes that Bellarmine's arguments do not constitute a proof of the corruption of the text.[139] There was surely no such corruption before Christ's time, or he would not have stressed the necessity for believers to search the Scriptures and, as the arguments against Bellarmine show, no such corruption has taken place since that time.[140]

---

[136]Rollock, *Treatise of Effectual Calling,* XVIII (pp. 112–13).

[137]Whitaker, *Disputation,* II.ii (p. 117).

[138]Rollock, *Treatise of Effectual Calling,* XVIII (p. 114).

[139]Rollock, *Treatise of Effectual Calling,* XVIII (pp. 115–18); for examples of Calvin's use and, by implication, appreciation of the Vulgate, see Richard A. Muller, "Calvin, Beza and the Exegetical History of Romans 13," in *Proceedings of the Calvin Studies Society* (1991); and cf. T. H. L. Parker, *Calvin's New Testament Commentaries* (London: SCM/Grand Rapids: Eerdmans, 1971), pp. 93–151.

[140]Rollock, *Treatise of Effectual Calling,* XVIII (pp. 118–19).

As for the Greek text of the New Testament, the Reformed could argue that Greek was both the common language of the time of Christ and the foundational language of philosophy—and therefore obviously a suitable vehicle for divine revelation:

> The Greek copies of the New Testament are also from God immediately, the very dialect wherein these Prototypes were, which the Pens of the Evangelists and Apostles did write.[141]

The old question of Syriac, Latin, and Hebrew originals for the Gospel of Matthew, the Gospel of Luke, and the Epistle to the Hebrews gained a dogmatic dimension: if Greek was not the original language of these writings, then there might well be a reason to doubt the authority and authenticity of the Greek New Testament. Rollock cites Athanasius, Irenaeus, Nazianzen, and Jerome to the effect that Matthew wrote in Hebrew and Jerome to the effect that he had seen a copy of the original Hebrew of Matthew. Athanasius believed that the apostle James made the translation while the others assumed that Matthew translated the work himself. The Protestant orthodox generally discount these traditions and note that, in any event, the Hebrew of Matthew, if it ever existed, is not extant. As for the Epistle to the Hebrews, Jerome thought that the original was in Hebrew, but this theory appears to be even more uncertain than the previous, granting the idiomatic character of the Greek of the Epistle. And there is an utter lack of evidence for a Latin original of Luke.[142]

The problem of the vowel points, noted tangentially in several of the previously offered examples of debate over the purity and perfection of the text of the Old Testament, occupied the Protestant orthodox during the whole course of the seventeenth century. Not only was this debate of enormous proportions, it was also characteristic of the textual and hermeneutical problems confronting the Protestant doctrine of Scripture as it passed into its orthodox or scholastic phase. From the beginnings of the problem in the writings of the Reformers to the very end of the seventeenth century, moreover, Hebraists and exegetes were in disagreement both as to its

[141]Leigh, *Treatise*, I.vi (p. 93).
[142]Rollock, *Treatise of Effectual Calling*, XIX (pp. 119–22); cf. Voetius, *Disputationes selectae*, V, pp. 28–31; Leigh, *Treatise*, I.vi (p. 94); Glassius, *Philologia sacra*, I.iv.2; and the discussion of the language of Hebrews in Owen, *Exercitations on the Epistle to the Hebrews*, in *Works*, 18, pp. 102–5.

significance and its solution.[143] Both Luther and Zwingli, for example, assumed that the points were of comparatively late origin—after the time of Jerome's translation of the Vulgate—and were aids to interpretation rather than an integral part of the text. At a somewhat later date, Calvin could argue differences between the Hebrew and the Septuagint on the assumption of different readings possible before the pointing of the text.[144]

In this context, the findings of Elias Levita's erudite study of the Masorah (1538) would hardly have offered difficulties for the Protestant view of Scripture. There is, certainly, some irony in the fact that linguists on both sides of the debate, Protestant and Roman Catholic alike, recognized that the vowel points were not necessary to the understanding of the text, and that eminent Protestant theologians and apologists like John Jewel had maintained that the date of the origin of the points had no bearing on the authority of the text in theological matters.[145]

It was the polemic between Protestant and Catholic following the Council of Trent, particularly as it developed in the latter half of the sixteenth century, together with an alteration or even a rigidification of the approach to language and interpretation on the part of some major Protestant and Roman Catholic thinkers, that altered Protestant reaction to the problem of the vowel points and turned a textual issue into a highly charged doctrinal one.[146] Roman Catholic exegetes and polemicists noted that the late dating of origin of the system of vowel points in the seventh and eighth centuries A.D. and well after the writing of the canonical Scriptures both refuted the Protestant claim of the divinity of Scripture and justified the Roman Catholic claim of normative status for the Vulgate, which had been translated before the problem of the vowel points had arisen. As

---

[143]Cf. Richard A. Muller, "The Debate over the Vowel Points and the Crisis in Orthodox Hermeneutics," pp. 53-72, with Diestel, *Geschichte,* pp. 334–41 for accounts of the historical progress of the debate; Diestel offers discussion of the Lutheran side of the debate.

[144]Cf. Luther, *Enarratio in Genesin,* in WA, 44, 683 (commenting on 47:31) with Zwingli in *CR,* 101, pp. 98–101 and Calvin in *CO,* 44, cols. 305–6 and idem, *Ad Hebraeos,* in *CO,* vol. 55, col. 159.

[145]Cf. e.g., Gilbertus Genebrardus, *EISAGOGE: Ad legenda et intelligenda Hebraeae et orientalium sine punctis scripta* (Paris, 1587); and on the Protestant side, note Jewell, *A Replie Unto M. Harding's Answer,* in *Works,* II, pp. 678–79.

[146]Cf. Faulenbach, *Die Struktur der Theologie des Amandus Polanus,* pp. 106–10, with Preus, *Theology of Post-Reformation Lutheranism,* I, p. 308, and Burnett, "Christian Hebraism of Johann Buxtorf," pp. 246–49.

Bellarmine, Lindanus, and Cano argued, the readings offered by the Vulgate might, therefore, be preferable to the later interpretations offered by the Masoretes.[147]

In the second half of the sixteenth century, moreover, basic assumptions about the necessity of the vowel points were altered in polemic. Rather than argue, as had Jewel, that the text was intelligible without the points and that the problem of their origin was theologically inconsequential, Protestant theologians began to follow the approach of Johannes Isaac, a convert from Judaism to Roman Catholicism and a professor of Hebrew in Cologne, who held that the vowel points were necessary to the understanding of the text. In the hands of Protestant exegetes and theologians like Junius, Polanus, Chevallier (Cevallerius), and Buxtorf the elder, Isaac's argument became the keystone in a defense of the antiquity of the vowel points and their codification by the "men of the great synagogue" in the time of Ezra. In the middle of the next century, Owen still viewed the arguments of these thinkers as definitive:

> Junius, in the close of his animadversions on Bell[armine] *De Verbo Dei,* lib. ii, cap. ii, commends the saying of Johannes Isaac against Lindanus, "He that reads the Scriptures without points is like a man that rides a horse *achalinos,* without a bridle; he may be carried he knows not whither." Radulphus Cevallerius goes further: *Rudiment. Ling. Heb.* cap. iv., "As for the antiquity of the vowels and accents, I am of their opinion who maintain the Hebrew language, as the exact pattern of all others, to have been plainly written with them from the beginning; seeing that they who are otherwise minded do not only make doubtful the authority of the Scriptures, but, in my judgment, wholly pluck it up by the roots, for without the vowels and notes of distinction it hath nothing form and certain."[148]

Protestant theologians and polemicists were barely accustomed to this answer to the Roman Catholic argument against the authenticity and authority of the Hebrew and Greek texts when a noted Protestant exegete and text-critic, Louis Cappell, advocated at great length and in vast detail the views of Levita, against the views of Johann Buxtorf, the elder—the most noted Protestant Hebraist and the great

---

[147]Cf. Bellarmine, *De verbo Dei,* ii; Genebrardus, *In Ps. XXI;* Cano, *De locis theol.,* II.xiii.

[148]Owen, *The Integrity and Purity of the Hebrew and Greek Text,* in *Works,* XVI, p. 371; cf. Polanus, *Syntagma theol.,* I.xxxvii.

Masoretic and Talmudic scholar of the day.[149]

As Burnett has ably argued, a most telling feature of the debate over Cappell's work is that it did not arise suddenly. The elder Buxtorf did not rise to the occasion with a refutation of Cappell, nor did he see fit to respond to other scholars who (with due respect to his mastery of the Masora), had dissented from his conclusions about the vowel points and various other issues of textual criticism. Indeed, although he gathered materials for a refutation, he remained immersed in other projects and even maintained a cordial relationship with Cappell—who had, after all, consulted him before publication and who had never attacked him openly.[150] What is more, Cappell's *Arcanum punctationis revelatum* (1623) had the clear theological purpose of returning the debate over the vowel points to the place at which Jewel and other earlier Protestant apologists had left it, albeit by way of a different hermeneutic. The late dating of the vowel points, he argued, did not indicate a problem for the theological use of the text, which had always been and still remained clear in its meaning in its purely consonantal form.[151]

Significantly, Cappel's theological reasonings found few Protestant supporters, even among Hebraists and orientalists. Thomas Erpenius, who wrote the introduction, offered high praise. Rivetus, at first worried over the effects of Levita's arguments, eventually became positive. The English Hebraist, John Weemes, also changed his views and over the course of a decade came to advocate the position of Cappel.[152] The elder Buxtorf was asked to respond by several major scholarly colleagues but other projects caused a postponement of his answer and, in 1629, death intervened. The task of gathering and organizing the refutation of Cappel devolved on his son, Johann Buxtorf, the younger, whose massive rebuttal included a series of dissertations on the Hebrew language and its antiquity published in 1645, a refutation of the *Arcanum punctationis* in 1648, and a refutation of Cappel's *Critica Sacra* in 1653.[153]

---

[149]Cf. Muller, "Debate over the Vowel Points," pp. 59–62, with the extensive discussion of Cappel's work and its reception in Laplanche, *L'Écriture, le sacré, et l'historie,* pp. 212–14.

[150]Burnett, "Christian Hebraism of Johann Buxtorf," pp. 271–83.

[151]Cf. Cappel, *Arcanum punctationis revelatum,* II.xxii, at length; with Cappel's later, similar, arguments in the *Critica sacra,* VI.v.11; and with Muller, "Debate over the Vowel Points," pp. 60–62, 70–72.

[152]Cf. Laplanche, *L'Écriture,* pp. 220–21; Muller, "Debate over the Vowel Points," pp. 63–65.

[153]Johannes Buxtorf, II. *Dissertationes philologico-theologicae. I. De lin-*

Nor ought it to be assumed that advocacy of the late origin of the vowel points can be connected with a lower view of the text. Weemes, for example, argued that "every letter in the Hebrew hath [its] owne valor naturally" so that the actual work of pointing was simply a declaration of the sound already implied by the letter. This, he notes, can be proved from the other languages of the ancient world: neither Arabic, nor Syriac, nor Chaldee originally had vowel points—and, he continues, to this day, neither Ethiopic nor Persian have vowels. These languages are easily understood by those trained in them—and the vowels only provide a guide to those less schooled. For Weemes, the examination of the text for correct pointing, granting the occasional errors and variants found in the Masora, became a part of the work of the exegete.[154]

The Buxtorfs, however, had no lack of defenders both from among the Hebraists and from among the dogmaticians—and it must be noted that a majority of Jewish scholars and, by the beginning of the seventeenth century, a goodly number of respected Protestant exegetes, assumed an early dating of the points, at least within the canonical period of Scripture.[155] Some of the dogmaticians were content to assume that the argument for a late origin of the vowel points was a ploy of Roman Catholic polemic and that the debate could be ended with a reference to Christ's words concerning the indefectability even of the jots and tittles of the law;[156] others like

---

guae hebraeae origine, antiquitate et sanctitate. II. De linguae hebraeae confusione et plurium linguarum originae. III. De linguae hebraeae conservatione, propagatione et duratione. IV. De litterarum hebraicarum genuina antiquitate. V. De nominibus Dei hebraicis. VI. De Decalogo. VII. De primae coena Dominicae ritibus et forma (Basel, 1645); Tractatus de punctorum vocalium, et accentum, in libris Veteris Testamenti hebraicis, origine, antiquitate, et authoritate: oppositus arcano punctationis revelato Ludovici Cappelli (Basel, 1648); Anticritica seu vindiciae veritatis hebraica adversus Ludovici Cappelli criticam quam vocat sacram eiusque defensionem. Basel, 1653.

[154]Weemes, Christian Synagogue, pp. 49–50; cf. Weemes, Exercitations Divine, pp. 124–30.

[155]E.g., Junius, Theses theologicae, in Opera, I, cols. 1592ff.; Polanus, Syntagma theol., I.xxxvii (pp. 74–75); Flacius Illyricus, Clavis Scripturae Sacrae, vi; Broughton, Daniel his Chaldie Visions and His Ebrew (London, 1596), folio k2recto–k4verso; Weemes, Christian Synagogue (1623), p. 38; Owen, Vindication of the Purity and Integrity of the Hebrew and Greek Texts, in Works, 16, pp. 370–401; cf. Schnedermann, Die Controverse mit Ludovicus Cappelus, pp. 28–32; on the Jewish scholarship, see Burnett, "Christian Hebraism of Johann Buxtorf," pp. 246–48, 253, 256–57.

[156]Ussher, Body of Divinity, p. 13; Maresius, Collegium theologicum, I.xl.

Voetius and Owen continued to argue at length for a codification and finalization of the points within the canonical period of Scripture by Ezra and the "men of the great synagogue." Following the elder Buxtorf, they argued that the canon of the Old Testament had been gathered and edited, frequently from surviving *autographa,* by Ezra and his associates, who then supplied a basic division of the text into its chapters and who, inspired by the Holy Spirit, determined the correct vocalization and provided the text with the system of pointing. In other words, the Masoretic Text of the Old Testament was understood as rooted in the work of Ezra, long prior to the editorial efforts of the Tiberian Masoretes.[157]

The philological debate over the vowel points, which set linguists of the caliber of Walton and Lightfoot against one another, did not resolve in the era of orthodoxy.[158] The theological conclusion of the debate, the short-lived *Formula Consensus Helvetica* of 1675, although it disapproved of Cappel's arguments and, by implication, favored the Mosaic origin of the vowel points, nonetheless included the qualifier "either the vowel points themselves, or at least the power of the points"—in other words, if not the actual vowel points, then surely the sounds implied by the points, and therefore the words as such, are both definite and ancient. After the *Formula,* the theological debate lessened considerably and most theologians were willing to leave the issue to the philologists. Indeed, even the authors of the *Formula Consensus Helvetica,* Turretin and Heidegger, had passed well beyond Owen's angry denunciation of the Masoretes to a positive appreciation of their work in the preservation of the *apographa.*[159] At the beginning of the next century, Bentley could remark, in his defense of Christianity against free-thinking,

---

[157]Voetius, *Disputationes,* vol. I, iv (pp. 52–63, passim); Owen, *Integrity and Purity of the Hebrew and Greek Text,* in *Works,* XVI, pp. 358, 371, 391; and cf. Burnett, "Christian Hebraism of Johannes Buxtorf," pp. 265–69.

[158]In the first half of the eighteenth century, Schultens and Michaelis could still hold the view that some of the points antedated the Masoretes, and even the great synagogue. Eichhorn placed the origin of the points after Ezra, but before the Talmud, Jerome, and the Masoretes, and credited the latter only with finalization and codification. It appears to have been left to Gesenius and Hupfeld— as late as 1830—to settle the argument finally in favor of a Masoretic origin of the vowel points. See Diestel, *Geschichte des Alten Testamentes,* pp. 595–96.

[159]Cf. Muller, "Debate over the Vowel Points," pp. 69–71, with Turretin, *Inst. theol. elencticae,* II.xi.11–13; Marckius, *Compendium theologiae,* II.viii; Heidegger, *Corpus theologiae,* II.xliii–xlvi.

> What an uproar once was there, as if All were ruin'd and undone,
> when *Cappellus* wrote one Book against the Antiquity of the
> *Hebrew Points,* and Another for *Various Lections* in the Hebrew
> Text it selfe? And yet Time and Experience has cur'd them of
> those imaginary Fears.[160]

The point also needs to be made that those who contrast the
Reformers' views on the vowel points with the views of high orthodox writers like Owen, Turretin, and Heidegger, in order to argue
that Protestant orthodoxy deviated from the Reformation and produced a more rigid view of inspiration and infallibility have typically failed to examine the historical debate, its course, and its result.
The high orthodox up to the time of the *Formula* not only were
standing on what appeared to be reasonably solid philological
ground—and doing so for the sake of maintaining the Reformers'
hermeneutic of the *analogia Scripturae*[161]—but also the trajectory
of orthodoxy both contained the debate and a certain degree of resolution. In addition, the exegetes and philologists who argued the
Masoretic origin of the vowel points were seldom, if ever, beyond
the pale of orthodoxy in their general doctrine of Scripture. We have
already noted that Cappel's *Arcanum punctationis* had, as part of its
purpose, the defense of the Reformed doctrine of Scripture against
Roman Catholic attack. It is also the case that Walton, whose views
on the late origin of the vowel points was so angrily disputed by
Owen in the name of the doctrine of Scripture, was himself an advocate of a high doctrine of scriptural inspiration and authority: "the
Original Texts," he wrote, "are not corrupted, ... are of Supream
authority in all matters," and "the copies we now have are the true
transcripts of the first *autographa* written by the sacred Pen-
men."[162] Orthodox writers in the era after the *Formula* were able to
move past the philological problem and, like Marckius, Venema, de
Moor, and Vitringa, to offer clear affirmations of the authority and
infallibility of Scripture that echoed the views of Calvin and Jewel,
and assumed the pre-Masoretic origin of some vowel points and the
Masoretic origin of the fully developed pointing system.[163]

---

[160]Bentley, *Remarks Upon a late Discourse,* p. 63.

[161]Cf. Muller, "Debate over the Vowel Points," pp. 70–72, with Rogers and
McKim, *Authority and Interpretation of the Bible,* pp. 183–87, 223.

[162]Walton, *Considerator Considered,* p. 14.

[163]Cf. Marckius, *Compendium theologiae,* II.viii; idem, *Exercitationes text,*
V.xxviii; Venema, *Institutes of Theology,* pp. 37–39; Vitringa, *Doctrina christianae religionis,* I.ii.51 (vol. I, p. 93); with the lengthy summary of the debate,

By "original and authentic" text, the Protestant orthodox do not mean the *autographa* which no one can possess but the *apographa* in the original tongue which are the source of all versions. The Jews throughout history and the church in the time of Christ regarded the Hebrew of the Old Testament as authentic and for nearly six centuries after Christ, the Greek of the New Testament was viewed as authentic without dispute.[164] It is important to note that the Reformed orthodox insistence on the identification of the Hebrew and Greek texts as alone authentic does not demand direct reference to *autographa* in those languages; the "original and authentic text" of Scripture means, beyond the autograph copies, the legitimate tradition of Hebrew and Greek *apographa*. The case for Scripture as an infallible rule of faith and practice and the separate arguments for a received text free from major (i.e., non-scribal) errors rests on an examination of *apographa* and does not seek the infinite regress of the lost *autographa* as a prop for textual infallibility.[165]

The central issue for the orthodox was the establishment of an authentic and accurate text of the Hebrew and Greek originals, despite the loss of the *autographa:*

> We ... receive the Scripture in these languages only [i.e., Hebrew and Greek] as canonical and authentic. And what is more, not only

with citations of Marckius and Schultens in de Moor, *Commentarius perpetuus in Joh. Marckii compendium,* I, II.viii (pp. 163–69).

[164]Leigh, *Treatise,* I.vi (p. 102); cf. Owen, *Divine Original,* in *Works,* vol. 16, pp. 300–301.

[165]Cf. Turretin, *Inst. theol.,* II.xi.3–4, with Mastricht, *Theoretico-practica theol.,* I.ii.10. A rather sharp contrast must be drawn, therefore, between the Protestant orthodox arguments concerning the *autographa* and the views of Archibald Alexander Hodge and Benjamin Breckinridge Warfield. This issue must be raised because of the tendency in many recent essays to confuse the two views. Like virtually all exegetes and theologians before and after them, they recognized that the text of Scripture as we now have it contains contradictory and historically problematic statements. They also recognized the futility of harmonizations of the text—but they insisted that all such difficult or erroneous passages ought to be understood as the result of scribal errors. Those who claim an errant text, against the orthodox consensus to the contrary, must prove their case. To claim errors in the scribal copies, the *apographa,* is hardly a proof. The claim must be proven true of the *autographa.* The point made by Hodge and Warfield is a logical trap, a rhetorical flourish, a conundrum designed to confound the critics—who can only prove their case for genuine errancy by recourse to a text they do not (and surely *cannot*) have. See Archibald A. Hodge and Benjamin B. Warfield, *Inspiration* (1881; repr. Grand Rapids: Baker Book House, 1979), pp. 33–36.

the *Autographa,* which for many reasons belonging to the most wise counsel of divine providence, were allowed to perish: but in the *Apographa* as well.[166]

The orthodox discussion of *autographa* and *apographa* was designed, therefore, to point toward a continuity of text-tradition between the original authors and the present-day texts. The theory functioned primarily as a hermeneutical lever designed to assert the priority of the Hebrew and Greek over the ancient versions and to provide a methodological basis for the critical collation and comparison of the texts in their original tongues. The orthodox of the seventeenth century had, after all, no archaeological hopes for the discovery of ever-more-ancient manuscripts. For them, the *autographa* were not a concrete point of regress for the future critical examination of the text but rather a touchstone employed in gaining a proper perspective on current textual problems. Over against the more radical proposals of Louis Cappel concerning the critical alteration of the text of the Old Testament in the light of ancient versions, the orthodox took solace in the fact that Hebrew, not Syriac or Greek, was the actual language of the prophets and that variant readings of the text seldom, if ever, caused problems for the substance of Christian doctrine.[167] The versions could never be anything more than versions and could never represent the thoughts of the prophets *quoad verba.* The orthodox tended to address the issue of infallibility of Scripture in matters of faith and practice from an entirely different vantage point.

The orthodox, moreover, tend not to deal with the problem of error in Scripture as a facet of their argument on authority, inspiration, or infallibility, but rather in their discussion of the "purity" of the Hebrew and Greek texts or in their analysis of the "perfection" of Scripture. Their conclusions, therefore, are either on the hermeneutic level and couched in terms of the failure of "corruptions" to undercut the overall superiority and accuracy of the original language-texts, or on the dogmatic level and stated in terms of the preservation of Scripture in its doctrinal integrity. The perfection of

---

[166]Mastricht, *Theoretica-practica theologia,* I.ii.10; cf. Marckius, *Compendium,* II.ix: according to Marckius, *"Apographa in eadem lingua proximè ad Autographa accedant"* which dictum lies at the base of the orthodox insistence on critical exegesis and at the base, also, of the famous Princeton theory of the *autographa* held by the Hodges and brought to fruition by Warfield.

[167]Owen, *Divine Original,* in *Works,* vol. 16, p. 301; cf. Buxtorf, *Anticritica,* ii.14.

Scripture is not infinite and unlimited, like the divine perfection, but relative to the end of conveying those things necessary to salvation.

Even so, Turretin and other high and late orthodox writers argued that the authenticity and infallibility of Scripture must be identified in and of the *apographa,* not in and of lost *autographa.* The *autographa* figure in Turretin's argument only insofar as they were written in Hebrew and Greek and are, therefore, best represented *quoad verba* and *quoad res* in the extant Hebrew and Greek *apographa.* The issue raised by the Protestant scholastic discussion of the relation of *autographa* and *apographa* is, in other words, one of linguistic continuity rather than one of verbal inerrancy.[168] The orthodox do, of course, assume that the text is free of substantive error and, typically, view textual problems as of scribal origin,[169] but they mount their argument for authenticity and infallibility without recourse to a logical device like that employed by Hodge and Warfield.

As a rule summing up the argument for the purity of the Hebrew and Greek texts as the "original and authentic" Word of Scripture, Leigh could state:

> If the authority of the authentical copies in Hebrew, Chaldee, and Greek fall, then there is no pure Scripture in the Church of God, there is no high court of appeal where controversies (rising upon the diversity of translations, or otherwise) may be ended. The exhortations of having recourse unto the *Law and to the Prophets,* and of our Saviour Christ asking *how it is written,* and *how readest thou,* is now either of none effect, or not sufficient.[170]

This is, of course, precisely the claim of Rome: That Scripture, although truly the Word of God and contributing to the church's rule of faith and practice, could not stand as authoritative outside of the church's *magisterium.*[171]

Several of the orthodox cite in confirmation of this argument Augustine's rule of interpretation (*De doctrina christiana,* II.11;

---

[168]Cf. Turretin, *Inst. theol.,* II.xi.3–4; xii.10–12; Marckius, *Compendium theologiae,* II.ix; Mastricht, *Theoretico-practica theol.,* I.ii.10; de Moor, *Commentarius perpetuus in Joh. Marckii compendium,* II.viii (pp. 161–62); Wyttenbach, *Tentamen theologiae dogmaticae,* II, §145–48.

[169]Cf. Turretin, *Inst. theol. elencticae,* II.v; Burmann, *Synopsis theologiae,* I.vii.13; Marckius, *Compendium theologiae,* II.xxiii–xxiv; and see above, §§5.2 and 5.3.

[170]Leigh, *Treatise,* I.vi (pp. 102–3).

[171]Cf. Bellarmine, *De verbo Dei,* I.i.

XV.3) and the similar comments of Jerome in his *Contra Helvidium.*
Riissen and Leigh also note, with some relish, that

> Bellarmine himself, *De Verbo Dei,* II.xi, confesses that in certain
> cases one must return to the sources: a. when an error of the copy-
> ists is noted in the Latin codices; b. when there are different read-
> ings; c. when there is something ambiguous or uncertain; d. when
> the meaning of a word appears not to have been satisfactorily
> expressed.[172]

These declarations all indicate, despite Bellarmine's protests to the
contrary, a distinction between authenticity and authorship *quoad
verba* which belongs only to the Hebrew and Greek originals and
authenticity and authority *quoad res* which inhere in valid translations.[173] Bellarmine, in fact, took a more positive attitude toward the
Hebrew and Greek originals than many other Roman writers of the
period. It was his opinion that the originals were not generally corrupted but, in view of their partial impurity, could not be used as a
necessary rule in correcting variants in ancient versions like the
Septuagint and the Vulgate.[174]

More harsh than the judgment of Bellarmine was that of
Melchior Cano in his ground-breaking study of theological method,
De locis theologicis. Together with Lindanus, Cano argued that
the Jews, out of hatred for the Christian church, had corrupted the
text.[175] This view was opposed by nearly all of the renowned
Protestant libraists—Buxtorf, Rivetus, Erpenius, Walton—all of
whom noted the care of the Masoretes in preserving the text accurately, even when they differed over the origin of the vowel
points.[176] Cano and Lindanus are easily refuted. If the Jews corrupted the text of the Old Testament, they must have done this either
before or after Christ. They could not have done it before Christ,
since Christ himself testifies to the authenticity of the Scriptures. It
is highly unlikely that the Jews did this following Christ since all the

---

[172]Riissen, *Summa theol.,* II.xix, arg. 1–3; cf. Leigh, *Treatise,* I.vi (p. 102):
"*Bellarmine* grants that sometimes we must have recourse to Hebrew & Greek
fountaines, 1. When in the Latine Edition there be any errors of the Scribe.
2. When there are divers readings. 3. When there is anything doubtful in the
words or sentence. 4. To understand the force and Energy of the word, because
all things are more emphatical in the original."
[173]Marckius, *Compendium,* II.viii.
[174]Bellarmine, *De verbo Dei,* II.vii.
[175]Cano, *De locis theologicis,* I.ii.
[176]Cf. Muller, "Debate over the Vowel-Points," pp. 58–66.

testimonies cited by Christ and the apostles remain in the text as do the many special prophecies of the Messiah. Indeed, adds Riissen, if the Jews had engaged in such acts against the text that they had so diligently guarded, why is it that Origen and Jerome, both "most skilled in the sacred languages, absolve the Jews of this crime?" There are over two hundred arguments, comments Leigh, which show Christ to be the Messiah "more evident and express in the Hebrew text of the Old Testament, than there be in the Latin translation."[177]

b. The Problem of Corruptions in the Text

The Reformed theologians of the seventeenth century devoted much space in commentaries, in treatises on the text and language of Scripture, and in dogmatic treatises to the refutation not only of the general arguments of Roman Catholic and Socinian polemicists and linguists against the purity and authenticity of the Hebrew and the Greek but also to their claims against particular texts:

> For albeit some of them, the ... better learned, as Bellarmine, do not say that the Greek edition of the New Testament is altogether corrupt, as some of them have blasphemed, yet they say it is not so pure, that they can grant it to be authentical, because in some places it is corrupt.[178]

Against such claims, the Reformed orthodox insisted on the providential preservation of Scripture in its integrity and the consistent care taken by the church throughout history to care for the text. This assumption of integrity refers, moreover, not to the versions but to the Hebrew and Greek sources on which all versions must be based. As for the text itself, it is not without textual problems and minor corruptions of certain texts in some codices, but it must be asked whether the corruption is found in all codices or only in some, whether in the most ancient and best or in the more recent and common, whether the corruptions are a result of negligence and ignorance or of malice, and finally whether such corruptions are corrigible or incorrigible, and if corrigible, whether the corrections

---

[177]Leigh, *Treatise,* I.vi (p. 104); Riissen, *Summa theol.,* II.xvii, controversia III, arg.6.

[178]Rollock, *Treatise of Effectual Calling,* XIX (p. 123); cf. the almost identical characterization of Socinian arguments in Hoornbeeck, *Socinianismus confutatus,* I, pp. 28–29, citing Socinus, *De auctoritate Scripturae,* i and Volkelius, *De religione,* V.v.

can be made on the basis of the text itself or only on the basis of supposition.[179]

Polemicists like Hoornbeeck typically offered logical and theological arguments—such as have given Protestant orthodoxy its reputation for rigid, proof-texting biblicism—and left the technical exegetical arguments to the exegetes. Thus Hoornbeeck begins his defense of the integrity of the text by citing Matthew 5:18 ("Till heaven and earth pass, one jot or tittle shall in no wise pass for the law") and 1 Peter 1:25 ("The word of the Lord endures to eternity"), texts which could just as easily be used to argue the Mosaic origin of the vowel points as the general integrity of the text. Similarly, he adds, the providence of God itself, which even his Socinian adversaries acknowledge to be operative in the preservation of Scripture, would prevent such corruption from occurring—and if providence is operative in the preservation of certain texts, why not all texts?[180] The preservation of the text in its integrity is also a necessary corollary of its status as the canon or rule of faith and practice, and it remains the case that a few corruptions in some of the codices in no way prejudice the authoritative and normative use of Scripture as a whole.[181]

The orthodox also approached the question of corruptions textually and exegetically in great detail. Indeed, a close concern for problematic texts and possible corruptions is found not only in the works of dogmaticians, but also of the Protestant exegetes and linguists. The noted Protestant Hebraist, Solomon Glassius, for example, argued the accuracy of seventy-two disputed texts in the Old and twenty in the New Testament in his *Philologia sacra*. Rivetus' *Isagoge,* similarly, devotes many pages to the subject, while Lightfoot and Owen reviewed most of the textual problems concerned with the pointing of the Hebrew Old Testament in their responses to the critical apparatus of Walton's great London Polyglott Bible.[182] We must content ourselves here with a few of the

[179]Hoornbeeck, *Socinianismus confutatus,* I, p. 32.
[180]Hoornbeeck, *Socinianismus confutatus,* I, pp. 32–33.
[181]Hoornbeeck, *Socinianismus confutatus,* I, pp. 34–35, 39.
[182]So also, John Rainolds, *The Summe of the Conference between Iohn Rainolds and Iohn Hart: Touching the Head and Faith of the Church. Wherein are handled sundry points, of the sufficiency and right expounding of the Scriptures, the ministrie of the church ...* (London, 1598); Edward Kellet, *Miscellanies of Divinitie* (Cambridge, 1635), II.viii; Voetius, *Selectarum disputationum theologicarum,* I, iv (pp. 47–63).

most common textual problems cited in debate during the seventeenth century.

First, the traditional Christian reading of Psalm 22:16, "They have pierced my hands and my feet," rests on the reading, *karu,* "pierce," and on the Septuagint, which assumed *karu* when it rendered the Hebrew as *oryxan*—whereas most of the extant Hebrew texts, particularly as found in the Jewish Bibles of the sixteenth and seventeenth centuries, had, *ka ari,* "like a lion." Was this a corruption or an error in the text? The dispute between Christians and Jews over the messianic significance of the text almost paled before the debate between Protestants and Catholics over the question of textual purity. This, the orthodox note, is the only place that can be alleged as a valid corruption—but even it can be explained as a simple scribal error. The Masoretes note the *karu* variant—so that the supposed error is nothing but an example of *kethibh* (uncorrected error in the text) and *kere* (marginal correction).[183] Several writers note that the Chaldee paraphrase joins the readings together thus: "They have digged or pierced my hands and my feet as a lion is wont to dig with his teeth."[184]

Second, the Hebrew of Psalm 19:4 reads "Their line is gone forth in all the earth," while the Septuagint reads "their sound" or "their voice." Paul (Rom. 10:8) cites the Septuagint—thus certifying the Septuagint as correct and showing, according to several Roman Catholic authors, the Hebrew to be in error. In answer Leigh echoes the exegetical tradition, arguing that both the Septuagint and Paul's citation of the text represent an interpretation of the Hebrew to manifest the final extension of the "line" of the promise by the "word" of the gospel. This is a legitimate interpretation insofar as the Psalm (v. 7) shows how the Jews were instructed by the works of God:

> The Apostle alledgeth this Psalm to prove that the Jews might come to know God by his word, and thereby might have faith in Christ Jesus; the sense therefore is not only the delineation and constitution of things created, but also the word of God, and the doctrine of the Gospel, long since propounded to the Jews, and so propounded as they could not but hear, because it was published

---

[183]Cf. Calvin, *Commentary on the Psalms,* in loc. (CTS, I, pp. 373–74); Whitaker, *Disputation,* ix (p. 159); Ainsworth, *Book of Psalmes,* p. 64; Owen, *Integrity and Purity,* pp. 361–62; and Cloppenburg, *Exercitationes super locos communes,* I.v.8.

[184]Leigh, *Treatise,* I.vi (p. 108); cf. Whitaker, *Disputation,* ix (p. 159); Voetius, *Selectarum disputationum theologicarum,* I.iv (pp. 52–53).

openly to all the world by the ministry of the holy Apostles out of the predictions of the Prophets.[185]

As a third example of the corruption of the Hebrew text of the Old Testament, we can note the issue raised by Bellarmine among others, that the extant Hebrew texts lack an entire sentence at Exodus 2:22, "He begat another also, and called his name Eliezer, saying, 'The God of my father hath helped me, and delivered me of the hand of Pharaoh.'" Here, responds Whitaker, the problem is not a corruption of the Hebrew but the addition of a line, unsubstantiated by ancient texts, to the Latin—as even Roman Catholic exegetes, like Cajetan have recognized. Ainsworth and Willet, more precisely, note the presence of the variant in the Septuagint and the Vulgate and hypothesize that it is an augmentation of the text based on Exodus 18:4.[186] Willet comments that "neither is the Hebrew here thought to be wanting, expressing onely one of Moses sons, seeing that the other is supplied, chap. 18.2" and he noted that, similarly, in Exodus 6:19, "the Latine and the Septuagint put unto *Moses* and *Aaron Miriam,* which is not in the Hebrew; this rather sheweth great boldnesse in these translators, to adde that which the spirit of God passeth over in silence."[187]

A fourth example: also alleged against the purity and perfection of the Old Testament is Matthew 2:23, "he shall be called a Nazarene." Since the text refers to an Old Testament prophecy but there is no such text in the Old Testament, the Hebrew original must be corrupt. Of course, this argument weighs equally against the ancient versions, none of which contain the reference. Several solutions are proposed: Maldonatus, Junius, Piscator, Taylor, and Dod felt that "Nazarene" is a reference to "Netzer," "a branch," and therefore a citation of Isaiah 11:1.[188] Bucer, Calvin, Marlorat, Beza, Scultetus, and Perkins view the text as a reference to Judges 15:5, where Samson is, as a redeemer, a type of Christ. The Book of Judges is thus referred to by Matthew as composed by prophets.[189]

---

[185]Leigh, *Treatise,* I.vi (pp. 108–9); cf. Calvin, *Commentary on the Psalms,* in loc. (CTS, I, pp. 312–15); Ainsworth, *Book of Psalmes,* p. 54.

[186]Whitaker, *Disputation,* ix (p. 160), citing Cajetan, *In Pentateuchum* (Rome, 1531), p. 82, col. 2; cf. Ainsworth, *Annotations upon ... Exodus,* in loc.; Willet, *Hexapla in Exodum,* p. 14.

[187]Willet, *Hexapla in Exodum,* p. 24.

[188]Leigh, *Treatise,* I.vi (pp. 109–10).

[189]Leigh, *Treatise,* I.vi (pp. 109–10); cf. *Annotations upon all the Books of the Old and New Testament* (1645), in. loc., offering both explanations.

Fifth, in Matthew 27:9, the evangelist cites a passage from the Old Testament, claiming it to be a citation from Jeremiah—whereas it is clearly taken from Zechariah. A fairly lengthy series of explanations is offered: The citation of Zechariah is conflated with Jeremiah 18:1–3; the citation is from a lost book of Jeremiah; a copyist erred and substituted "Jeremiah" for the "Zechariah" of the original; the text says "spoken" by Jeremiah, not written—and Zechariah here simply delivers to his readers a tradition he received from Jeremiah; or, finally, Zechariah had in fact two names and was sometimes called Jeremiah, just as Solomon was called Jedidiah, Jehoiachim called Jeconias and Coniah, Simon called Peter and Cephas, Matthew called Levi. This latter hypothesis is supported by the fact that the names are similar in meaning, Jeremiah signifying "the commendation of God" and Zechariah "the exaltation of God."[190] Another possibility is that Matthew did not name the prophet and that the name was incorrectly inserted by a scribe—for, as some of the orthodox commentators note, the name of the prophet is not given in the ancient Syriac version.[191] The suggestion of Erasmus that Matthew suffered a lapse of memory is rejected on the ground that it neglects the fact that the Holy Spirit's authorship underlies that of Matthew.[192]

Sixth, Romans 12:11 is often said to be corrupt, the Greek text giving *kairo* rather than *kyrio*—"serving *the time*" rather than "serving *the Lord*." In response, Leigh clearly indicates the close interrelationship of dogmatic argument with the exegetical and textual studies of the age:

Many of the ancient Greek copies and scholiasts have also *kyrio* as Salmerond the Jesuit confesseth, "serving the Lord," and it appeareth in the Syriack translation: and who seeth not that it might rather be an oversight of the writer taking one word for another, rather than a fault in the text; and the cause of the mistake (saith Beza) was the short writing of the word, *ko,* which was taken by some for *kairo* whereas they should have taken it for *kurio.* If we should admit the other reading, we must not understand the Apostle as if he meant us to be *temporizers,* or to apply ourselves to the corrupt customs and manners of the times, but to keep time

---

[190]Cf. Leigh, *Treatise,* I.vi (pp. 110–11), with Voetius, *Selectarum disputationum theologicarum,* I.iv (pp. 59–60).

[191]*Annotations upon all the Books of the Old and New Testament* (1645), in loc.

[192]Leigh, *Treatise,* I.vi (p. 110).

in all our actions, and do them in the fittest season, as Col. 4:5; Ephes. 5:16.[193]

Seventh and last, the doxology at the conclusion of the Matthean version of the Lord's Prayer, "for thine is the kingdom, and the power, and the glory forever" (Matt. 6:13), does not appear either in the Vulgate or in the expositions of the prayer by Tertullian, Cyprian, Ambrose, Jerome, and Augustine. Beza referred to it as *magnificam illam quidam & sanctificam* but had also to admit that the text did not appear in the ancient codices he had examined. Is this a corruption of the text? Cartwright in his reply to the preface and glosses of the Rheims translation argued that the words were hardly a nonscriptural corruption but were a citation, abridged slightly and peculiar to Matthew, of 1 Chronicles 29:11, that renders the prayer more suitable for public worship.[194] Lightfoot had similarly argued, on the basis of talmudic sources, two forms of prayer, a public and a private, and explained the shorter, Lucan version of the prayer as the result of a second request on the part of the disciples. The rabbinic sources indicated the use of doxologies, like "for thine is the kingdom, and the power, and the glory for ever and ever," and a final "Amen" in public worship.[195] Leigh's dogmatic resolution reflects the exegesis:

> that cannot be superfluous without the which we should not have had a perfect form of Prayer; for since Prayer standeth as well in praising God and thanksgiving, as in petitions and requests to be made unto him; it is evident that if this conclusion had been wanting, there had wanted a form of that Prayer which standeth in praise and thanksgiving.[196]

Moreover, in addition to several of the Greek copies, the Syriac also has this doxology, as do the expositions of the prayer by Chrysostom, Theophylact, and Euthemius. It is also true that Matthew contains many words and phrases not in Luke.[197]

---

[193]Leigh, *Treatise,* I.vi (p. 112); Grotius, *Annotationes in Novum Testamentum,* in *Opera,* 2, p. 748, simply accepts *kyrio* as correct without comment.

[194]Cartwright, *Answere to the Preface of the Rhemish Testament,* pp. 153–54.

[195]Lightfoot, *Horae hebraicae et talmudicae,* II, vi.13; but cf. Grotius, *Annotationes in Novum Testamentum,* in *Opera,* 2, p. 81, where the doxology is noted as absent from the Greek and explained as a later liturgical addition—and the "Amen," in particular is singled out as not one of the words of Christ.

[196]Leigh, *Treatise,* I.vi (p. 115).

[197]Leigh, *Treatise,* I.vi (p. 116).

The Reformed orthodox do, thus, engage in a concerted textual effort to maintain their doctrine of the purity and perfection of the text of Scripture. They do not, however, assume that the doctrine of the authority of Scripture can be proven by such arguments—only defended. In addition and more important, many of these arguments must be regarded as evidences and elements of the enormous hermeneutical struggle of the seventeenth century, brought on by advances in textual criticism and by a new and detailed development of critical apparatus based on the collation not only of numerous manuscripts of the Hebrew and the Greek texts but also of the ancient versions. If the sixteenth century was the era of humanistic return to the sources, the seventeenth century was surely the great era of Protestant "oriental" linguistics and comparative textual study. It is very difficult, given the historical context of this florescence of linguistic study together with the relative stability of doctrinal orthodoxy and its forms of expression, to label the Protestant orthodox as rigid and obscurantistic. All of the arguments that we have examined evidence a careful use of linguistic tools, a survey of the opinions of commentators and critics, and a desire to address the textual problems accurately—granting the entirely legitimate historical as well as doctrinal assumption of the priority of the Hebrew and Greek texts as reflecting the language of the original authors of Scripture. The orthodox, moreover, were hardly incapable of recognizing problems in the text and differences of detail between parallel accounts—such as the differences between the four evangelists. Their conclusion was simply that such problems and differences seldom, if ever, touch on doctrinal issues.

Finally, we note two somewhat different textual problems that plagued orthodox Protestantism at the end of the seventeenth century—again, not because they had not been noted previously, and not because the doctrine of the inspiration and authority of Scripture had changed appreciably since the later Middle Ages or since the Reformation, but because the context of debate had changed considerably and critical, textual study, once the weapon of Protestants against excesses and abuses of doctrine and practice, had become the weapon of Socinians, deists, rationalists, and semi-Arians against primary dogmas of the church.

Many of the Bibles printed in the sixteenth and seventeenth centuries, whether in the original languages, in Latin, or in a vernacular translation, gave the following reading as the text of 1 John 5:5–8:

5. Who is he that overcometh the world, but he that believeth that Jesus is the Son of God?

6. This is he that came by water and blood, even Jesus Christ; not by water only, but by water and blood. And it is because the Spirit beareth witness, because the Spirit is truth.

7. For there are three that bear record in heaven, the Father, the Word, and the Holy Ghost: and these three are one.

8. And there are three that bear witness in earth, the spirit, and the water, and the blood: and these three agree in one.

The phrase at issue, verse 7, the so-called Johannine comma, is certainly the clearest and most convincing trinitarian text in the whole of Scripture and would be of considerable use in the debate with antitrinitarians. The problem, however, was the poor attestation of the verse, noted by scholars of the Renaissance and early Reformation virtually as soon as they passed beyond the bounds of the Vulgate. Accordingly, of the early sixteenth-century editions of the Greek text of the New Testament, the *Complutensian Polyglott* (1504–14) includes the phrase, while Erasmus' first and second editions (1516, 1519) omits it as does the edition prepared by Aldus Manutius (1518). On the basis of a single codex found in Dublin and most probably in the hope of silencing some of his "carping and uneducated" critics, Erasmus restored the phrase in his translation (1521) and in his third edition of the Greek text (1522). Later editions (1527 and 1536) also include the "comma." Erasmus' third edition was followed on this point by both Stephanus (1546, 1549, 1550) and Beza (1565; with annotations, 1582)—with the Bezan text setting the stage for heated debate in the seventeenth century, at least among the Reformed.

Lutheran commentaries on the epistle reflect the changes in Erasmus' text: Luther had argued that phrase was spurious while his associates, after Erasmus altered his text, simply explained the verse without comment on its authenticity—although Luther never did include the "comma" in those editions of his translation of the New Testament that were superintended by him. Some of the mid-sixteenth-century Swiss vernacular Bibles, based on Luther, include the phrase often in small print or in brackets, whereas late sixteenth- and seventeenth-century Bibles tend to include the "comma" and the exegetes of the seventeenth century, most surely because of the intensity of the polemic with anti-trinitarians, defend the "comma" as genuine.

Reformed theologians, following out the line of Erasmus, Stephanus, and Beza, tended to accept the text as genuine and, indeed, to use it as an integral part of their trinitarian theology. Thus,

Calvin argued the inseparable relationship between the work of Christ and the work of the Spirit by noting the parallelism of the "comma," "for, as three witnesses in heaven are named—the Father, the Word, and the Spirit—so are there three on earth: the water, the blood, and the spirit." The Spirit, therefore, not only is known as the witness to Christ but, as divine, "is the bond by which Christ effectually unites himself to us."[198]

In the theological works of the seventeenth-century orthodox— on the model provided by Calvin and Beza—the Johannine "comma" appears frequently, without question or comment, as one Johannine text among others cited in a catena of texts from the Gospel, the Apocalypse, and the epistles as grounds of the doctrine of the Trinity.[199] Often the phrase is simply cited without comment as a supporting text, while some of the high orthodox writers note that is was cited by Cyprian—thus, by implication, refuting the arguments concerning its extremely late date. Pictet even goes so far as to argue, almost to the refutation of the orthodox doctrine of the providential preservation of the text, that the heretics had long succeeded in deleting the passage but that, thanks to the citation from Cyprian, the orthodox had received warrant to reinsert it.[200] Cyprian does indeed state, "Dicit Dominus: 'Ego et Pater unum sumus.' Et iterum de Patre et Filio et Spiritu Sancto scriptum est: 'Et tres unum sunt.'"[201] Turretin noted that Erasmus had located the passage in a "most ancient British codex" and that "most praiseworthy editions, the Complutensian, the Antwerp, Arias Montanus, R. Stephanus, and Walton, which have all utilized the best codices, have the phrase."[202] Cloppenburg argues that the criticism of John 5:7 as not belonging to the original Greek has arisen largely as a result of the efforts of antitrinitarian heretics. Indeed, he comments, Luther's omission of the text from the first edition of his commentary led the Jesuits to accuse him of Arian tendencies![203] The theologians of the seventeenth century were reasonably secure in their use of the "comma," granting the rather illustrious proponents it had found both during the Reformation and the era of early orthodoxy and

---

[198]Calvin, *Institutes,* III.i.1.

[199]Maccovius, *Loci communes,* xxx (p. 245); cf. *Synopsis purioris theologiae, VII.49;* Mastricht, *Theoretico-practica theol.,* II.xxiv.9, 17; Riissen, *Summa theol.,* III.iii, controversia 1.

[200]Pictet, *Theol. chr.,* II.xiii.v.

[201]Cyprian, *De unitate ecclesiae,* vi (PL 4, cols. 503–4).

[202]Turretin, *Inst. theol. elencticae,* III.xxv.9.

[203]Cloppenburg, *Exercitationes super locos communes,* I.v.8.

granting the polemic associated with the critical examination of the text.

For the text to become genuinely troublesome and a focus of massive polemic it was necessary for major textual scholars who were not adherents of antitrinitarian views to dismiss it as a spurious addition to the epistle—the case is quite analogous to the uproar caused by Cappel's work on the late origin of the vowel points. As noted by Richard Simon and critical scholars as well as many theologians after him like Thomas Emlyn, Samuel Clarke, Richard Bentley, J. J. Wetstein, Michaelis, and J. S. Semler, only three Greek codices, all of them very late, attest to the phrase, and two of the three omit the words, "and these three are one." Neither the Greek nor the Latin fathers up to Augustine cite the phrase, although they all would have found it extremely useful in debating with the Arians. The first known use of the "comma" occurs in the writings of the Latin fathers of the fifth and sixth centuries—leading to the assumption that the few Greek codices in which the phrase does occur were augmented on the basis of medieval Latin texts. The polemic against the textual criticism of Simon and the others on this point became intense. To deny the text on whatever grounds appeared to support the Socinian claim, whereas what had actually happened was yet another severance of traditional theological result (achieved by older models of exegesis, prior to the rise of textual criticism and the great hermeneutical revolution of the sixteenth and seventeenth centuries) from exegetical practice.

A similar point can be made with reference to J. J. Wetstein's critical examination of 1 Timothy 3:16. On a trip to Cambridge in 1715 to visit with Richard Bentley, Wetstein examined the *Codex Alexandrinus* and concluded, after having scrutinized the text of 1 Timothy 3:16 with a magnifying glass, that the *theos* in the phrase, "God was manifested in the flesh" was a misreading and that the text actually had *hos,* "who," and that the phrase ought to read "who was manifested in the flesh."[204] Coming so soon on the heels of Bentley's arguments against the Johannine "comma," Wetstein's views on 1 Timothy 3:16 were viewed as profoundly antitrinitarian —and, indeed, they did argue against one of the texts favored by orthodoxy as a proof of the divinity of Christ.

[204]The misreading is quite understandable, given the standard abbreviation of *theos* in the uncial manuscripts as a *theta* and a *sigma:* see Metzger, *Text of the New Testament,* p. 187.

c. The Ancient Versions

The authentic editions of Scripture are, thus, the Hebrew and the Greek texts, which represent the language of the original authors. In this assertion, coupled with the recognition that the church possessed no original copies of the text, orthodoxy manifested the necessity of textual criticism and, indeed, fostered the detailed technical analysis of the ancient text and versions that would produce such works as the great London Polyglott Bible edited by Brian Walton.[205] Yet, in this process of critical establishment of text, orthodoxy could not—for obvious theological reasons—allow a priority of the ancient versions. Ainsworth, thus, quite carefully argues the importance of the use of ancient versions in the work of translation and interpretation. The versions, particularly the Chaldee paraphrase and the Septuagint, offer significant interpretations of difficult texts. Late in the seventeenth century, the eminent orientalist, Pocock, could similarly comment that the Hebrew text was illuminated by inquiry "into such other languages of neere affinity to it, in which the same words are in use, as the Syriacke and Arabick." Nonetheless, the Hebrew text remains prior.[206] Their seeming authoritative use by Cappel, therefore, generated a controversy over their use within the ranks of Protestantism, particularly in view of the polemic against Rome. The "Papists" did not, after all, oppose the idea of Hebrew and Greek originals—they merely contend that the extant Hebrew and Greek texts were corruptions of the original and therefore not authentic. If, moreover, the Septuagint and the Vulgate were translated before the entrance of these corruptions—as, for example, corruptions caused by the work of the Masoretes in the fifth and sixth centuries, they are authoritative. The Reformed churches controvert all these claims concerning the authority and, in the case of the Septuagint, the inspiration of the ancient translations.[207]

Even so, the Protestant orthodox hermeneutic identified even the Septuagint, which was cited by the apostles, to be a less than authentic and authoritative text. The Septuagint, comment the orthodox, was a laudable effort and it has the value of great antiquity, but since it was conceived and accomplished through the study and work of

---

[205]Brian Walton, ed., *Biblia Sacra Polyglotta,* 6 vols. (London, 1657) and *Biblicus apparatus, chronologico-topographico-philologicus: prout ille tomo praeliminari operis eximii polyglotti* (London, 1658).

[206]Ainsworth, *Psalmes,* fol. 2 verso; Edward Pocock, *Commentary on the Prophecy of Hosea* (Oxford, 1685).

[207]Leigh, *Treatise,* I.vi (pp. 100–101).

men alone it cannot merit the title *theopneustos,* nor can its authors be considered inspired. This fact is proven by the account of Aristeas which records disputes and conferences between the translators. Where there is inspiration and the work of the Spirit, there is no disagreement. Furthermore, the Septuagint, for all its value, does frequently differ from the Hebrew—so much, indeed, that Whitaker was led to argue that the original version of the "Seventy," said by Aristeas to conform to the Hebrew, had been lost or highly corrupted in its transmission.[208] Not even Jerome held it to be pure and authoritative! Nonetheless, the Septuagint, like other ancient versions and paraphrases, may be useful to the interpreter in determining the meaning of difficult Hebrew passages.[209] To the argument that its authenticity is shown by apostolic use, Riissen replies that such use hardly indicates the inspiration of the "Seventy" but only that certain of their words have been sanctified by their use in the New Testament—certain texts in the Septuagint, therefore, are authoritative according to their words in addition to being authoritative according to substance, but that authority is not *per se* but rather *per accidens.*[210]

Even more strenuous are the objections leveled against the Vulgate—which had been declared the authentic and dogmatically normative text by the Council of Trent. Many of the Reformed were quite willing to admit the quality of Jerome's work, the value of later corrections made in the Vulgate, and the general utility of this particular Latin translation throughout many centuries of the history of the church and even that "the fundamental points of the faith are preserved in tact in this Latin edition, if not everywhere, yet in very many places," but its authenticity as a rule of faith they denied.[211] Neither Jerome nor the subsequent editors, either Sixtus V or Clement VIII, were inspired, as is demonstrated by their editorial work. In addition, many scholars of the Roman church have suggested emendations on the basis of the Hebrew and Greek originals:

[208]Whitaker, *Disputation,* II.iii (p. 121); cf. Maccovius, *Loci communes,* III (p. 21).

[209]Riissen, *Summa theol.,* II.xx, controversia I, argumenta; cf. the positive comments on the use of the Septuagint and the Chaldee paraphrase in the work of translation and interpretation in Ainsworth, *The Book of Psalmes ... with Annotations,* preface, fol. 2 verso; Wyttenbach, *Tentamen theologiae dogmaticae,* II, §165, scholion 1.

[210]Riissen, *Summa theol.,* II.xx, controversia I, objectio & resp.

[211]Whitaker, *Disputation,* II.vii (p. 136); cf. Riissen, *Summa theol.,* II.xx, controversia II.

Erasmus, Valla, Paginus, Cajetanus, Sixtus Senensis, Bellarmine, Cano, and the Louvain editors of the Vulgate—which would seem to undermine the Catholic case for the authenticity of the Vulgate and, indeed, contradict the mandate of the Council of Trent.[212]

Thus translations can be used, but with the reservation that only the Hebrew Old Testament and Greek New Testament are the authentic norms of doctrine and the rule by which doctrinal controversy is to be decided:

> Versions that are congruent with the sources are indeed authentic according to substance *(quoad res);* for the Word of God [may be] translated into other languages: the Word of God is not to be limited, since whether it is thought or spoken or written, it remains the Word of God. Nonetheless they are not authentic according to the idiom or word, inasmuch as the words have been explained in French or Dutch.[213]

In relation to all translations, therefore, the Hebrew and Greek texts stand as *antiquissimus, originalis,* and *archetypos.*[214] Thus, translations are the Word of God insofar as they permit the Word of God to address the reader or hearer: for Scripture is most certainly the Word of God in the things it teaches and to the extent that in and by means of it the power of God touches the conscience. Even so, in translations as well as in the original the testimony of the Holy Spirit demonstrates the graciousness of God toward us.[215]

All translations have divine authority insofar as they correctly render the original: "the tongue and dialect is but an accident, and as it were an argument of divine truth, which remains one and the same in all Idioms."[216] As for the Chaldee, it is not a translation but a paraphrase and is of great usefulness as an exposition of the Hebrew.[217] The Greek of the "Seventy-two Interpreters," comments Leigh, had great authority among the Hellenistic Jews and was used by the Evangelists, "when they might do it without swerving from the sense of the prophets."[218] The Syriac and Arabic versions of the

---

[212]Riissen, *Summa theol.,* II.xx, controversia II, argumenta; cf. Whitaker, *Disputation,* II.ix (pp. 146–55).

[213]Riissen, *Summa theol.,* II.xix.

[214]Marckius, *Compendium,* II.viii.

[215]Riissen, *Summa theol.,* II.xxi.

[216]Leigh, *Treatise,* I.vi (p. 94); cf. Mastricht, *Theoretico-practica theologia,* I.ii.11, citing Ames, *Medulla,* I.XXXIV.32–33.

[217]Leigh, *Treatise,* I.vi (p. 95).

[218]Leigh, *Treatise,* I.vi (p. 97).

New Testament are ancient and "very profitable for understanding the Greek."[219] Leigh finally turns to the Latin translations, commenting that Tremellius' and Junius' version is best for the Old Testament while Erasmus and Beza are to be favored for the New.[220]

6.4 Vernacular Translations and Their Significance

In the face of Roman Catholic polemic against the Protestant translations and the massive emphasis placed by Protestant orthodoxy on the authority of the Hebrew and Greek originals over against such translations as the Septuagint, the Vulgate, and contemporary efforts like the Rheims-Douay version, the orthodox theologians were pressed by their own arguments to deal with the question of the legitimacy of translation and, granting the legitimacy, the value of translation. Wendelin actually presents as a theological thesis the definition of "vernacular version" as "a translation of holy Scripture into a commonly known language indigenous to a nation" and then proceeds to "prove" in several arguments that Holy Writ ought to be translated into the common tongues.[221] In the first place, the prophets and apostles themselves spoke and wrote in the vernacular in order that their hearers might understand. Translation thus enables the Scriptures to be read by all, as the prophets and apostles themselves intended. Second, the Scriptures are the "weapons of the faithful" for defense "against Satan and the heretics." Even so, third, all believers are commanded to read and study the Scriptures (John 5:39; Deut. 31:11) as, indeed, the apostle praised the Bereans (Acts 17:11).[222] Beyond this, the command to preach to all nations implies the need to translate Scripture, as does the great effort of the early church to produce translations in all of the languages of believers—such as the Syriac, the Chaldee paraphrase, the Septuagint, the many Latin versions, and even the Hexapla of Origen.[223]

The "Papists," writes Wendelin, claim the contrary, that Scripture ought not to be translated into vernacular languages—and that the common people ought not to be allowed to read the text, on the ground that access to Scripture is dangerous to the faith. The com-

[219]Leigh, *Treatise,* I.vi (p. 98).
[220]Leigh, *Treatise,* I.vi (p. 99).
[221]Wendelin, *Christianae theologiae libri duo,* prol., III.iii.
[222]Wendelin, *Christianae theologiae libri duo,* prol., III.iii.
[223]Riissen, *Summa theol.,* II.xviii, controversia 2.

mon people will misunderstand the meaning of the text and create new heresies. The answer to these arguments is simple, writes Wendelin: the abuse of a good and necessary thing provides no argument against its proper use. Indeed, the abuse notwithstanding, the prophets and the apostles delivered their truths in the vernacular. What is more, the clergy themselves can and do mistake the meaning of the text, and the "Papists" do not intend to prevent clergy from reading! And finally, the reputed misinterpretations, such as the identification of God as the author of sin, can easily be overcome by careful reading.[224] Translation, thus, is good, necessary, and in fact mandated by Scripture itself. The problems of obscurities in the text and of right interpretation remain—but these too will be addressed by the orthodox in their proper place.

a. The Authority of Translations

The controversy of the sixteenth and seventeenth centuries over the Vulgate and various contemporary translations of Scripture was considerably more subtle than an argument over the legitimacy of translations. Prohibitions of vernacular translations had occurred throughout the later Middle Ages. The early fifteenth-century constitutions promulgated in England usually addressed specific problems, such as the problem of nominally heretical Wycliffites or Lollard translations and not the work of translation in general:

> We resolve therefore and ordain that no one henceforth on his own authority translate any text of Holy Scripture into English or any other language by way of a book, pamphlet or tract, and that no book, pamphlet or tract of this kind, whether already recently composed in the time of the said John Wyclif or since, or to be composed in the future, be read in part or in whole, publicly or privately, under pain of the greater excommunication, until the translation be approved by the diocesan of the place, or if need be by a provincial council.[225]

The issue addressed by the prohibitions, in other words, was not translation per se—the issue was one of ecclesial authority in matters of doctrine. A similar perspective is reflected by the views of fifteenth-century censors in Germany—while in Italy, vernacular

---

[224]Wendelin, *Christianae theologiae libri duo,* prol., III.iii; cf. the discussion of the problem of vernacular bibles in McNally, "Council of Trent and Vernacular Bibles," pp. 226–27.

[225]Cited in *CHB,* II:393–94.

Bibles were used and sponsored by the Dominican and Franciscan orders.[226]

The problem, then, concerned the normative use of the theological conclusions expressed about the meaning of the text by the translations themselves and the tradition of the association of the Latin *sacra pagina* with the very essence of *sacra theologia* as formulated in Latin. On the Roman Catholic side, there was concern to retain the normative status of the Vulgate and to indicate the danger of Protestant efforts to use the Hebrew and Greek originals as the foundation for new and potentially heretical versions of the Bible. On the Protestant side, there was—precisely because of the structure and import of Roman Catholic polemic—a profound interest in affirming that the Hebrew and Greek originals of the Bible were the only foundation for correct doctrine and that the best translations, indeed, the only translations that could stand as norms for doctrine, would necessarily rest on these originals.

Virtually all positions on the advisability and use of translations were represented at the Council of Trent. The council recognized the need to press reform in four areas related to Scripture: *circa editionem, circa interpretatinem, circa impressionem,* and *circa praedicationem*—corruptions needed to be removed from the basic text of Scripture; false interpretations had to be identified and removed; only uncorrupt Bibles ought to be owned and read; and preaching ought to be reformed along genuinely biblical and churchly lines.[227] In the center of this desire to reform text and practice stood the problem of vernacular Bibles. Some of the bishops held that reading and interpretation ought to be reserved to the clergy because of the danger of vernacular Bibles—while Cardinal Madruzzo, the Prince-Bishop of Trent, argued eloquently for the need to make the Bible available in all languages for the progress of the gospel. The decision of the council, ultimately, was to refrain from speaking directly to the problem of the vernacular Bibles while at the same time identifying the Vulgate as the authentic and authoritative translation. Nor did the council disparage the Greek and

---

[226]Cf. Stephen Runciman, *The Medieval Manichee: A Study of the Christian Dualist Heresy* (Cambridge: Cambridge University Press, 1947; reissued, 1982), pp. 83–87, 167–68.

[227]R. E. McNally, "The Council of Trent and Vernacular Bibles," in *Theological Studies* 27 (1966):208–9; on the recognition of tridentine reformers that the study of Scripture ought to be the basis for theology, see Louis B. Pascoe, "The Council of Trent and Bible Study: Humanism and Scripture," in *Catholic Historical Review* 52 (1966-67):18-38.

Hebrew originals—it only argued the authority of the Vulgate in doctrinal matters. It was only after the accession of Pope Paul IV that vernacular Bibles lacking the authorization of the Roman Inquisition were forbidden.[228]

Characteristic of post-Tridentine Roman Catholic efforts at translation was an interpretive movement from the original languages through the Vulgate to the contemporary vernacular, as evidenced in the Rheims-Douay version. On the Protestant side, as evidenced preeminently by the Geneva Bible (1560), the theologically interpretive power of the translator and annotator rendered the text of Scripture itself a weapon against Rome. Tridentine and post-Tridentine denials of the right of translation and of lay reading must be understood in this context.

Late sixteenth-century debate over the character and quality of vernacular translations moved on two fronts: the problem of the relationship of ancient versions, principally the Septuagint, the Samaritan Pentateuch, the Chaldee paraphrase, and the Vulgate, to the Hebrew and in the case of the New Testament, the Greek originals concerned the integrity of the text itself and the character of the biblical foundation on which theology was to be established; whereas the problem of the modern versions, whether Luther's or various other German translations, Olivetan's French, or the several English versions was more an issue of the degree to which the actual substance *(res)* or meaning of the text could be communicated in words other than those of the original author and therefore of the degree to which any translation could function as an authoritative ground for contemporary theology.

Many of the late sixteenth- and seventeenth-century Protestant writers devoted considerable space to the refutation of claims made by Roman theologians and polemicists concerning the inspiration of the Septuagint and the normative status of the Vulgate.[229] The claim of inspiration for the Septuagint rests, according to the orthodox, on two arguments—first there is the fable of the miraculous agreement of the seventy translators who worked separately but who came to exactly the same conclusions regarding the meaning of the text. Bellarmine had argued that the Holy Spirit had so assisted the

---

[228]McNally, "Council of Trent and Vernacular Bibles," pp. 211–216, 225–226; cf. Creehan, "The Bible in the Roman Catholic Church," in *CHB* III, p. 204.

[229]Cf. Leigh, *Treatise,* I.vii (pp. 119–28), with Turretin, *Inst. theol. elencticae,* II.xiv; Mastricht, *Theoretico-practica theol.,* I.ii.40; Pictet, *Theol. chr.,* I.xvii.3–6.

"Seventy" that they ought to be "viewed as prophets, not as interpreters."[230]

Protestant response noted that Jerome himself countered the point by calling the "seventy" "interpreters" and not "prophets" and by calling attention to corruptions and errors in the translation. Leigh comments, with some sarcasm, that if the original of the Septuagint had been without error, surely it would have belonged to the providence of God to preserve it as well as the Hebrew original had been preserved,[231] and he notes that Sixtus Amama, Spanheim, and Heinsius conjectured that the story of the miraculous agreement of the ancient translators was adapted from the story of the seventy elders of Israel in Exodus 24 Walton had noted that the "Seventy" had conferred with one another about the translation—which in itself was an indication that they were not inspired—while de Moor commented on the rabbinic assumption of the conclusion of prophecy with Malachi and the absence of prophecy between the close of the Old Testament canon and the beginning of the New Testament revelation.[232] In any case, the Septuagint can only be viewed as worthy of belief when it offers a literal reflection of the Hebrew original: whatever authenticity it possesses, the Protestant orthodox argue, rests not on the character of the seventy per se but rather on their ability to convey the meaning of the original—as must be the case with all translations.[233]

The second, more profound, problem concerning the Septuagint encountered by Protestant exegetes and theologians was the normative use of the Septuagint, rather than the Hebrew text of the Old Testament, by the New Testament writers, despite the frequent differences in meaning between the Septuagint and the Hebrew. How could the Protestant orthodox claim the superiority of the Hebrew when this particular ancient version had been used—ostensibly instead of the Hebrew—by the inspired and infallible authors of the New Testament? Did not the use of the Septuagint by inspired authors indicate its inspiration and infallibility as well? Or did the

[230]Bellarmine, De verbo Dei, vi.

[231]De Moor, Commentarius perpetuus in Joh. Marckii compendium, II.xi (vol. I, p. 207); Leigh, Treatise, I.vii.

[232]Leigh, Systeme or Body of Divinity, I.vii (p. 89), citing Spanheim, Dub. evangel., I.23; Sixtus Amama, Antibarbarus, ii and Heinsius, Aristarchus; Vossius, De septuaginta interpretibus eorumque translatione et chronologia dissertationes (London, 1665); de Moor, Commentarius perpetuus in Joh. Marckii compendium, II.xi (vol. I, p. 209).

[233]Cf. Leigh, Treatise, I.viii (p. 122).

apostolic use of the Septuagint, like the Latin fathers' and medieval doctors' use of the Vulgate, simply indicate the authority of the church in ascertaining the theologically normative text of Scripture? These arguments are used rather pointedly by the annotators of the Rheims New Testament in their comments on Protestant recourse to the Hebrew and emendations of the text.[234]

Argument concerning the normative character of the Vulgate was, of course, uncomplicated by any canonical use of Jerome's readings, but it was made difficult for Protestants during the debate over the origin of the vowel points in the Masoretic Text of the Old Testament. If, as several scholars had claimed in the sixteenth and early seventeenth centuries, the vowel points were not merely used and standardized but also invented by the Masoretes, then a pre-Masoretic, unpointed Hebrew would have been used by Jerome and Jerome's variant readings might, arguably, be superior to the extant Masoretic Hebrew text. Thus, notes Wendelin, the *"Pontificii"* argue the authority of the Vulgate on the ground that it is the most ancient text used by the church—but of course "antiquity of itself does not make an edition authentic"—and, indeed, the Hebrew and Greek originals are far more ancient, and authentic in their own right.[235] Nor is it the case, as some of the papists claim, that just as New Testament usage indicates that the authority of the Septuagint Greek superseded the Hebrew text of the Old Testament, so also does ecclesial usage indicate the supersession of the Greek texts by the Latin.[236] Nor, indeed, as Voetius points out, is it at all legitimate to assume that the New Testament was written in another language —Hebrew or Aramaic—before it appeared in Greek.[237]

Apart from the problem of the vowel points, Protestant theologians had, then, a relatively easy task refuting the claims of authority for the Vulgate. Leigh comments:

> It was not Divinely inspired in respect of matter, form, or speech, as the Hebrew of the Old Testament, and the Greek of the New were, but was translated by human endeavour, and therefore it is against both religion and reason to say it is authentic; a work of

---

[234]*The New Testament of Iesus Christ,* translated faithfully into English, out of the authentical Latin ... in the English College of Rhemes.... (Rheims, 1582), annotation on Hcb. 11:21 (p. 633).

[235]Wendelin, *Christianae theologiae libri duo,* prol., III.ii.3.

[236]Wendelin, *Christianae theologiae libri duo,* prol., III.ii.3.

[237]Voetius, *Selectarum disputationum theologicarum,* V, pp. 28–31.

man cannot in perfection be equal with a work of God; for as Jerome saith, *aliud est esse vatum, aliud est esse Interpretem.*

It is the office of an interpreter, to translate the authentical Scripture, not to make his translation authentical; for both Jerome and every other Interpreter might err, so did not the Prophets and Apostles; the Council of Trent first decreed that this translation should be authenticall, [whereas] before it many learned Papists themselves did disallow that translation, as *Paulus Brugensis, Valla, Engubinus, Isidorus Clarius, Iohannes Isaacus, Cajetan, Erasmus, Iacobus Faber, Ludovicus Vives,* and divers others.[238]

Against the Roman contention that the Hebrew and Greek were sometimes inferior to the ancient versions, particularly to the Vulgate, the Protestant orthodox came to a determination based both on the logic of doctrine and the results of exegesis and of historical study. On the doctrinal level, Riissen could declare, "the providence of God proves irresistibly that the sources *(fontes)* are not corrupt, inasmuch as it is inconsistent that he would have willed books to have been written for the salvation of mankind, thus known to be false, and incapable of attaining this end."[239] On the basis of history, he could point to the diligence of the Jews generally and the Masoretes in particular in preserving the text—the latter going so far as "to have counted not only the words and letters, but also the points."[240] (In the context of such arguments over the relationship of the text to the ancient versions as well as the dispute over the divinity of Scripture and its authority in relation to that of the church, the debate over the vowel points took on a considerably greater significance than a mere historical and philological debate.)

b. Textual, Hermeneutical, and Theological Problems in the Work of Translation

The hermeneutical problems confronting the builders of a specifically Protestant orthodoxy as the post-Reformation era dawned are nowhere more apparent than in the work of biblical translation. Here, the more sophisticated linguistic and textual scholarship together with an increasing emphasis on the literal and grammatical meaning of the text, understood in an ever more historical manner, raised doctrinal issues in a far more pointed and pressing manner than ever before in the history of doctrine. Texts that had, tradition-

---

[238]Leigh, *Treatise,* I.vii (p. 122).
[239]Riissen, *Summa theol.,* II.xvii, controversia III, arg.1.
[240]Riissen, *Summa theol.,* II.xvii, controversia III, arg.3–4.

ally, been bearers of specific dogmatic meanings, when translated in the light of new insights into the text and into the implications of the biblical languages and their cognates, could cease to offer support for cherished doctrinal assumptions.

Beza, for example, worried textually and linguistically over the problem of the citation of Psalm 16:8–11 in Acts 2:25–28. Specifically, verse 10 of the psalm (Acts 2:27) had been used in the church as one of the biblical foundations for the doctrine of Christ's descent into hell. Since the meaning of the phrase was much debated during the sixteenth century, particularly between the Reformed and the Lutherans, as a major christological issue belonging to the problem of the two states of Christ,[241] Beza's new translation of the passage had considerable doctrinal significance. Beza raised the question of whether the Hebrew original of the psalm ought to determine the meaning of the Greek in Acts: for, if the Hebrew were brought to bear on the text, then *psyche,* soul, in the phrase, "thou wilt not abandon my soul to Hades," was a rendering of *nepesh* and Hades of *sheol.* Beza was very much aware that *nepesh* did not indicate an immortal, intellective form separable from the body and that *sheol* did not indicate hell. He therefore rejected the traditional equivalencies of *anima* for *psyche (nepesh)* and *infernus* for *hades (sheol),* rendering the phrase as "thou shalt not leave my body *(cadaver)* in the grave" *(sepulchrum)*—much to the dismay of his Reformed colleagues who needed *anima* in order to interpret the credal "descent into hell" in their accustomed manner, and much to the polemical grist of Roman Catholics, who understood *infernus* in Acts 2:27 with reference to 1 Peter 3:19–20 as a reference to the *limbus patrum.*[242]

Beza subsequently modified his usage and restored *anima* to the translation of Acts 2:27, but not before Roman Catholic polemicists like Gregory Martin had seized on the problem. Against Beza, they

---

[241]Cf. Bente, *Historical Introductions to the Book of Concord,* pp. 192–95, with Schaff, *Creeds,* I, pp. 296–98 and Muller, *Christ and the Decree,* pp. 103–4, 139, 148. It was typical of the Lutheran theologians to understand the *descensus* as the first act of the exalted Christ, immediately prior to the resurrection, when Christ, as the God-man, in body and soul descended into hell itself to announce his victory to Satan and to destroy the powers of darkness. Johannes Aepinus generated a controversy within Lutheranism by teaching the *descensus* was the suffering of Christ's soul in separation from the body and that the descent was, therefore, the final act of Christ's state of humiliation. Aepinus' views, attacked in their day (1544–54) and ultimately set aside in the *Formula of Concord,* were virtually identical with the Reformed position.

[242]Beza, *Annotationes in N.T.,* in loc.

claimed not only the normative status of the Vulgate translation of
the Greek New Testament, but also the inspiration of the Septuagint,
where *nepesh* had already, long before the writing of Acts, been
rendered as *psyche*. For Martin, Beza's treatment of the text was but
one more example of the heretical "wilfulness" of Protestant
exegesis.[243]

An example of a different order is the exegesis of Hosea 6:7,
where the medieval tradition had rested unquestioningly on the
Vulgate rendering, "ipsi autem sicut Adam transgressi sunt pactum."
The text indicated, as virtually all of the patristic and medieval
commentators concluded, a prelapsarian covenant made by God
with Adam and broken in the fall. The tradition of interpretation was
rather neatly summed up for the post-Reformation exegetes in the
massive commentary of the early seventeenth-century Jesuit scholar,
Cornelius à Lapide. Lapide first glosses the text, "IPSI AUTEM
SICUT ADAM (primus parens in paradisio violans pactum cum
Deo, eiusque conditionem et legem de non comedendo pomo vetito)
TRANSGRESSI SUNT PACTUM," and then cites by way of con-
firmation Jerome, Cyril, Rupert of Deutz, Hugh of St. Victor, and
Nicolas of Lyra.[244] The Septuagint, he adds, understood *adam* as a
universal rather than as a proper name, and was followed in this by
Vatable and Clarius, as indicating a general covenant with humanity.
Lapide renders the Septuagint as "Ipsi vero sunt sicut homo prae-
varicans testamentum, *vel* foedus" and notes Theodoret's variant,
"Ipsi autem transgressi sunt foedus meum sicut hominis."[245]

Many Protestant exegetes of the sixteenth and seventeenth centuries followed the exegetical tradition while others increasingly
understood the alternative rendering of the Hebrew as "sicut homo"
as the preferable reading. It is an incredible oversimplification of a
complex hermeneutical problem to assume, as has one recent study,
that the failure of Vulgate rendering to carry over into the King
James Bible of 1611 indicates that "the Protestant tradition did not
regard this verse as a reference to a prelapsarian covenant with
Adam at all."[246]

Had Zacharias Ursinus, for example, used a vernacular bible

[243]Martin, *Discourse,* cited in Fulke, *Defense,* p. 81.

[244]Lapide, *Commentarius,* Hosea 6:7, in loc.

[245]Lapide, *Commentarius,* Hosea 6:7, in loc.

[246]Weir, *Origins,* pp. 14–15. Weir appears to assume that the text was never
associated with the doctrine of the covenant of works until the nineteenth-
century American edition of the Westminster Confession added Hosea 6:7 to
the confession's proof-texts.

either during his studies in Wittenberg or during his time in the Rhenish Palatinate, he would most surely have examined Luther's version (1522–34; revised, 1539–41), in which Hosea 6:7 was rendered, "Aber sie übertreten den Bund, wie Adam; darin verachten sie mich." Protestant vernacular bibles of the first half of the sixteenth century echoed the Vulgate and Luther, retaining the reference to Adam and rendering *berith* not as a "pact" or "testament," but as a "covenant" or *foedus,* a shift of significance for the federal theology. Thus, Coverdale (1535)—evidencing, as in many other places, his reliance on Luther: "But even like as Adam dyd, so have they broken my covenaunt, and set me at naught."[247] The Zürich Bible of 1524–29 (in which the prophetic books were independent of Luther's German) offers, "Sy aber habend minen pundt gebrochen wie der Adam und mich übersehen."[248]

Also of considerable significance to a clarification of the role of Hosea 6:7 in the development of covenant theology are the editions of Luther's translation of the Bible prepared with Reformed prefaces and glosses by David Paraeus and Paulus Tossanus—the former a student of Ursinus and Olevianus, the latter the son of one of their colleagues. Tossanus' commentary uses Luther's translation ("Aber sie übertreten den Bund, wie Adam") and notes both possible meanings—that Adam, who was first blessed in the presence of God fell away and ate the forbidden fruit; or, that Israel transgressed her covenant with God as people often transgress a human pact *(eines menschen bund).*[249] Likewise, Grotius' annotation on the passage accepts the primary reading of the text as a reference to Adam and notes the generic understanding indicated by the Chaldee paraphrase, but finally paraphrases the verse as "Just as Adam, who violated my covenant, was expelled from Eden, so too shall you be expelled from your land."[250] Even so, later Latin readings of the text evidence a shift away from the Vulgate ("Sicut Adam transgressi

---

[247]On the relationship between Coverdale and Luther, see Heinz Bluhm, "Martin Luther and the English Bible: Tyndale and Coverdale," in *The Martin Luther Quincentennial,* ed. Gerhard Dünnhaupt (Detroit: Wayne State University Press, 1985), pp. 116–25.

[248]*Das Alt Testament dütsch der ursprünglichen Ebreischen waarheytnach uff das aller trüwlichest verdütschet* (Zürich: Froschauer, 1524–29), in loc.

[249]Tossanus, *Biblia,* vol. 3, in. loc.: "Der ob er wol reichlich von mir begabt und gesegnet gewesen dannoch von mir abgefallen und von der verbottenen frucht gessen hat. Vergl. Iob.31.33 und Eas.43.27. And. gebens: Sie übertreten den bund (den ich mit ihnen gemacht hab) wie eines menschen bund...."

[250]Grotius, *Annotationes ad Vetus Testamentum,* in *Opera,* 1, p. 493.

sunt pactum, ibi praevaricati sunt in me") toward a language more conformable to that of the Reformed federal tradition, specifically from a rendition of *berith* as *pactum* to its translation as *foedus*—as in the case of Cocceius, "Et illi, ut Adam, transgressi sunt foedus; ibi perfidè egerunt mecum."[251]

As a perusal of lengthier discussions of the covenant of works— notably those of Cocceius—makes clear, Hosea 6:7 was not viewed as crucial to the establishment of the basic doctrine of a prelapsarian covenant, but was nevertheless almost invariably cited as an indication that the fall into sin was the abrogation of a primal covenant.[252] Since, moreover, Protestant exegetes understood that the text could be translated equally well as "like man" as "like Adam," they refused to view it as an absolute or sole proof of the prelapsarian covenant: that they found in the Pauline Adam-Christ, first Adam-second Adam language and in the problem of law and gospel. Nonetheless, many of the Reformed did look to Hosea 6:7 as providing part of biblical basis for a covenant with Adam.[253] The history of the translation and exegesis of the text, moreover, reflects the development of the vocabulary of covenant theology; and the text, if not the exegetically sure foundation of the federal edifice, certainly functioned as a bearer of meaning and of vocabulary for the federal tradition.

The tradition of the Geneva Bible (1560), as it moved toward the King James Version, agreed with Calvin that the text was not a reference to Adam—and probably served to diminish the importance of the text in the English Reformed federal tradition. The Geneva Bible offers, "But they like men have transgressed the covenant: there have they trespassed against me"; and the King James, "But they like men have transgressed the covenant: there have they dealt treacherously with me." This approach, which identified the Hebrew *adam* as a generic reference to humanity in general, is also found in Tremellius' Latin translation of the Old Testament.[254] A similar interpretation appears in the London Polyglott Bible, where the Latin translations of the various ancient versions all point toward the

---

[251]Cocceius, *Summa theol.,* VIII.xxxi.1.

[252]Cf. Cocceius, *Summa theol.,* VII.xxxi.1, with Burmann, *Synopsis theologiae,* II.ii.vi and Marckius, *Compendium,* XIV.xiv.

[253]Cf. Cocceius, *Summa theol.,* VII.xxxi.1, with Burmann, *Synopsis theologiae,* II.ii.vi, and Marckius, *Compendium,* XIV.xiv.

[254]*Testamentis Veteris Biblia Sacra sive libri canonici priscae Iudaeorum ecclesiae a Deo traditi, Latini recens ex Hebraeo facti ... ab Immanuele Tremellio & Francisco Iunio* (London, 1585), in loc.

generic understanding.[255] Nonetheless, this weight of translation did not entirely abolish English Reformed interest in the text of Hosea 6:7 as an element in the formulation of the doctrine of the *foedus operum* or *foedus naturae*.

The Reformed exegetes and theologians of the seventeenth century—including English exegetes like Poole and Henry, who based their vernacular text on the King James Version—were aware of the older tradition of translation and of the patterns of interpretation found in the works of their continental contemporaries, and therefore of the possibility of reading Hosea 6:7 as "they like Adam have transgressed the covenant." Poole simply notes the possible readings: "*Like men;* or, like Adam: some take it for a proper name, and so refer it unto the first man, and his breaking of the covenant; and, for aught I see, it may well refer to him, who forgot or slighted the threat."[256] Poole, however, makes no direct reference here to the text of Genesis 2–3, nor does he, in his exposition of Genesis 2–3 discuss the covenant of works.[257] Similarly, in his comment on Job 31:33 ("If I covered my transgressions as Adam ..."), Poole notes two possible readings:

> *As Adam;* either, 1. As Adam did in Paradise; which history is recorded by Moses in Gen. 3:7 &c., and was doubtless imparted to the godly patriarchs to their children before Moses' time. Or, 2. *Like a man,* or after the manner of men in their corrupt state. Compare Hos. 6:7.[258]

Very similar is the comment in the Westminster divines' *Annotations:*

> V.7. *like men]* Heb. *like Adam,* the first sinner of all, who brake Gods first Covenant with mankinde, whence followed the generall curse upon all men. See Job 31.33. Isa. 43.27. Or, as if it had been the Covenant of some mean man.[259]

This use of the text, with some qualification, in the English covenant theology of the mid-seventeenth century may indicate the ongoing relationship of English to Dutch and German Reformed theology,

[255]Cf. *Biblia Sacra Polyglotta,* in loc.
[256]Poole, *Commentary,* II, p. 865.
[257]Cf. Poole, *Commentary,* I, pp. 7–12.
[258]Poole, *Commentary,* I, p. 1000.
[259]*Annotations upon all the Books of the Old and New Testament* (1645), in loc.

where the tradition of translation had long favored the translation "like Adam"; and it may offer evidence of the influence of the so-called *The Dutch Annotations upon the Whole Bible,* published at the time of the Westminster Assembly, in which "like Adam" was offered as the primary reading.[260]

A somewhat different approach to Hosea 6:7 is found in Matthew Henry's commentary, where the typological and allegorizing tendencies of the federal school allow the exegete to offer a double interpretation of the text. He writes first of the disobedience of Israel in the context of Hosea's revelation that God "desired mercy, not sacrifice." But he then elaborates the point,

> they trod in the steps of our first parents; they *like* Adam, have transgressed the covenant; (so might it very well be read;) as he transgressed the covenant of innocency, so they transgressed the covenant of grace; so treacherously, so foolishly; *there* in paradise he violated his engagements to God, and there in Canaan, another paradise, they violated their engagements. And by their *treacherous dealing* they, like Adam, have ruined themselves and theirs. Note, Sin is so much the worse, the more there is in it of the *similitude of Adam's transgression.*[261]

Even so, Henry draws out a covenant theme in his discussion of Genesis 2 and understands Job 31:33 as a reference to Adam without any qualification like that found in Poole.[262]

The generally cautious approach of the exegetes to the text is mirrored in the works of the high and late orthodox dogmaticians, who recognize that the text of Hosea 6:7 is of interest in the formulation of a doctrine of the *foedus naturae* or *foedus operum,* but neither necessary to its formulation nor definitive as a proof-text. Thus, Pictet could state that the creation of man according to the image of God clearly indicated a covenantal relationship even though this was not expressly stated by Scripture, "unless we wish to

---

[260] *The Dutch Annotations upon the Whole Bible,* in loc.: "7 *But they have transgressed the Covenant,* [Which I made with them and they with me, the sacrifices coming between ...] *like Adam:* [following the footsteps of their first fore-father, who notwithstanding he was so abundantly endowed and blessed by me, yet transgressed my Command, and revolted from me. Compare *Job.* 31.33. and *Isa.* 43.27.... Oth. *as men, i.e.* as vain men use to do, or *as a mans, viz.* covenant, *i.e.* as if they had to do with a meer man, not with me the Almighty and righteous God."

[261] Henry, *Commentary on the Whole Bible,* II, p. 1317.

[262] Henry, *Commentary on the Whole Bible,* I, pp. 10–11, 100–101.

refer to the *locus* Hosea 6:7, where it is said of the Israelites, 'ipsos sicut Adam violasse foedus,' but the phrase can be interpreted differently."[263] Van Til notes the text and simply states that it needs to be collated with Job 31:33, "If I covered my transgressions as Adam...."[264] Wyttenbach, writing in 1747, continued to use the text as a basic testimony to the prelapsarian covenant, albeit with considerable caution: Hosea 6:7 "is to be understood of Adam, but not however in an apellative manner, nor should it be interpreted to read 'they have transgressed my covenant as a human covenant *(ut foedus hominis)'*," but rather in view of Job 31:33 and Isaiah 43:27. In other words, "Adam" does not indicate either the first human being in a restrictive sense or a pure generic—rather it indicates Adam as the federal head of humanity, and speaks of a covenant made with him and, in him, with all his posterity. The parallel between God's covenant and "a human covenant" denied by Wyttenbach, may indicate an exegetical difference of opinion with Tossanus' commentary—*foedus hominis* standing as a translation of *menschen bund*.[265]

Further examples might easily be adduced. When examined from the perspective of dogmatic formulation, moreover, the difficulties caused by the increasingly sophisticated textual and linguistic scholarship of the seventeenth century serve to identify more clearly the great problem of Protestant orthodoxy in its effort to produce a churchly orthodoxy in continuity with the insights of the Reformers. The Protestant orthodox strove to support traditional dogmas, including and in particular those dogmas held firmly by the Reformers, even as the traditional exegetical grounds of the dogmas were lost to critical, textual investigation and literal reading of texts. It was not a very great step—as the Roman Catholic polemicists consistently noted—from the textual emendations of a Beza or of a Grotius to the heretical readings of the antitrinitarians.

---

[263]Pictet, *Theol. chr.,* IV.vii.1.

[264]Van Til, *Theologiae utriusque compendium ... revelatae,* II.ii (p. 81).

[265]Wyttenbach, *Tentamen theologiae dogmaticae,* VII, §792; cf. Tossanus, *Biblia,* as cited above, n. 249; and also cf. *Dutch Annotations upon the Whole Bible,* in loc., as cited above, n. 260.

7

The Interpretation of Scripture

If the question of the authority of Scripture was the principal dogmatic focus of the Reformation and post-Reformation doctrine of Scripture, the great problem confronting Protestantism and its authoritative, self-authenticating Scripture was the problem of interpretation. As the medieval doctors of the thirteenth and fourteenth centuries had recognized, a distinction had to be made between *sacra pagina* and *sacra theologia,* particularly when the latter was defined as an organized *scientia* or *sapientia.* This distinction not only identified the province of scholastic theology—whether polemical, didactic, or constructive—it also announced the difficulty of the theological task. The reading and exposition of Scripture is not theology, not in the technical doctrinal or dogmatic sense of the term. Doctrines and dogmas, presented in polemical, didactic, or large-scale positive systematic constructions, are a large step beyond exposition. In their work of interpretation, specifically, the interpretation of Scripture leading from *sacra pagina* to *sacra theologia,* the medieval doctors had a wide range of tools at their disposal. They had the church's tradition of doctrinal interpretation, they had philosophy in a somewhat uneasy alliance with theology, they had the teaching office of the church, and, most important as a means of bridging the gap between the text and the doctrinal language of the present, they had the *quadriga* or fourfold pattern of exegesis, loosely called the "allegorical method."

Developments in hermeneutics during the Renaissance and Reformation together with the rise of polemic between Protestants and Catholics over the nature of biblical interpretation and its relationship to the doctrines of the church deprived the Protestant orthodox of the *quadriga* as a path from *sacra pagina* to *sacra theologia*. The doctrinal meaning of Scripture would now have to be found in the literal sense of the text. Even so, the authority of the text for faith and life, previously distributed across the spectrum of literal, allegorical, tropological, and anagogical senses or across the similar spectrum of late medieval models like the twofold literal-spiritual or threefold *caput-corpus-membra* hermeneutic, was now focused on the literal meaning of Scripture as discerned by the grammatical study of the text and accomplished by the individual Christian exegete.

Whereas the movement away from the *quadriga* toward an increasingly critical access to the literal meaning of the text in its original languages served as an admirable weapon in the Reformation polemic against ecclesiastical abuses and doctrinal accretions or excesses, it proved to be a major challenge to Protestantism as the era of orthodoxy dawned. The Reformers, operating at least initially in the context of traditional Catholicism were able to adjust and revise certain key doctrinal points—like the doctrines of justification and the sacraments—by recourse to exegesis, while at the same time assuming the churchly stability of the larger body of doctrine. (It was one of the functions of the radical Reformation, perhaps most forcefully in its antitrinitarian moments, to test this assumption and to demonstrate the impossibility of holding on to the larger body of traditional dogmatic formulations when the tradition as a whole was set aside.) The Protestant orthodox, however, were left with the task of reconstructing a churchly and confessionally governed dogmatics in the context of a hermeneutical revolution. Doctrines like the Trinity, the Person of Christ, the fall, and original sin, which had developed over centuries and with the assistance of an easy mingling of theological and exegetical traditions and of an exegetical method designed to find more in a text that what was given directly by a grammatical reading, would now have to be exposited and exegetically justified—all in the face of a Roman Catholic polemic against the sole authority of Scripture as defined by the Reformers over against the tradition and the churchly magisterium, a polemic made all the more telling by the presence of the teachings of the radicals.

The development of the Protestant orthodox doctrine of the interpretation of Scripture can be divided into three phases, each with its own hermeneutical struggle, corresponding with the three basic periods of Protestant orthodoxy. In the early orthodox period (ca.

1565–1640), Protestant theologians faced major problems of developing a biblically and exegetically grounded system of doctrine, chiefly through the completion and arrangement of doctrinal *loci* into largescale dogmatic systems.[1] In many cases, most notably in the theological systems of Musculus and Vermigli, these *loci* were originally doctrinal expositions written as portions of commentaries on Scripture. A similar technique, although on a much larger scale, is to be found in the dogmatic treatises of Zanchi. On a hermeneutical level, the chief problem confronted by these writers was the explanation of the "literal sense" of the text in such a way as to facilitate the movement from the text of Scripture to a traditional and, therefore, orthodox dogmatics. The exegetical works of such writers as Andrew Willet and John Mayer manifest an extensive understanding and use of the exegetical tradition: Mayer explicitly cited and analyzed "divers expositions" of the text "out of the workes of the most learned , both ancient Fathers, and moderne Writers" in order to address the meaning of the text.[2] Indeed, much of the work of the exegetes and theologians of the early orthodox era was the establishment of a method in which the *sola Scriptura* of the Reformers was clearly identified as the declaration of Scripture as the prior norm of theology in the context of a churchly tradition of interpretation. Their success in this work may be measured in terms of the wide proliferation of defensible theological systems constructed biblically and exegetically out of a burgeoning Protestant tradition of commentary, biblically grounded confessional documents, and exegetically grounded theological systems.

A second era in the development of Protestant orthodox hermeneutics coincides roughly with the high orthodox era (ca. 1640–1700). During these years, Protestant scholarship made great advances not only in the study of the basic biblical languages, Hebrew and Greek, but also in the study of languages cognate to

[1]Cf. *PRRD*, I, 8.1 on the *locus* method with the discussion in Robert Kolb, "Teaching the Text: The Commonplace Method in Sixteenth Century Lutheran Biblical Commentary," in *Bibliothèque d'Humanisme et Renaissance* 49 (1987): 571–85.

[2]Cf. John Mayer, *A Commentarie upon the New Testament. Representing the divers expositions thereof, out of the workes of the most learned, both ancient Fathers, and moderne Writers,* 3 vols. (London, 1631), and idem, *A Commentary upon all the Prophets both Great and Small: wherein the divers Translations and Expositions both Literal and Mystical of all the most famous Commentators both Ancient and Modern are propounded* (London, 1652), with Andrew Willet, *Hexapla in Genesin* (Cambridge, 1605; 2d ed., enlarged, 1608); and idem, *Hexapla in Exodum* (London, 1608).

Hebrew—notably Syriac and Arabic—and in the close examination of variant Greek texts both of the Old and the New Testaments. The centerpieces of this advance are surely the studies made of the Masoretic Text by the Buxtorffs and Cappel, the great London Polyglott Bible edited by Brian Walton, and the philological studies of John Lightfoot. In the cases of Cappel and the London Polyglott, technical philological study not only led to greater knowledge of the history of the text of Scripture but to pressure on the orthodox Protestant hermeneutic and, by extension, on orthodox dogmatics—as witnessed in the controversy over the dating of the "vowel points."[3]

From the beginning of the seventeenth century onward, particularly in the era of high orthodoxy, the biblical-confessional system of Protestant orthodoxy was subjected, thus, to a strain brought on by the late-Renaissance or early modern development of "oriental" studies in relation to the textual criticism of Scripture and of an increasing sense of the cultural as well as historical distance between the text in its original languages and the dogmatic theologian. The seventeenth century, following out the line of the Renaissance interest in original languages, took the mastery of Hebrew, Greek, and Latin for granted and moved on to the study of Aramaic, Syriac, and Arabic, together with a broader interest in the development of Hebrew that directed Protestant exegetes toward Talmudic studies. The text-critical work of this generation of Protestant exegetes and orientalists—as evidenced by the intense philological and doctrinal debate over the origin of the vowel points in the Hebrew text—created an enormous pressure upon the still precritical understanding of the "literal sense" advocated by early orthodoxy and upon the use of such churchly, dogmatic tools as the analogy of Scripture and the analogy of faith in the interpretation of Scripture.[4] Toward the end of the high orthodox era, the historical understanding of the text, argued by such writers as Benedict de Spinoza and Richard Simon, created further difficulties for the dogmatic understanding of the text and adumbrated the critical developments of the next century and their disastrous impact on traditional dogmatics.[5]

The third period corresponds with late orthodoxy (ca. 1700–1790) and witnesses the rise of the historical-critical approach to the

[3]See above, §§4.2 and 4.4.

[4]Cf. Gerald T. Sheppard, "Between Reformation and Modern Commentary: The Perception of the Scope of Biblical Books," pp. 44–45, 54–57.

[5]Cf. *CHB,* III: 218–21, 239, with Kümmel, *New Testament,* pp. 40–47, and Farrar, *History,* pp. 383–84, 397–98.

text as well as the demise of Protestant orthodoxy as a dominant theological pattern and a genuinely productive intellectual movement. During this era, pressure was brought to bear on traditional dogmatics and dogmatic exegesis not only by the Socinian, rationalist, and deist critics of orthodoxy, but by the nominally orthodox or at least orthodox-trained exegetes, like Bentley, Wetstein, and Semler, whose work did not have as its fundamental intention the destruction of orthodox dogmatics, but whose application of text-critical and historical-critical methods resulted in conclusions about the meaning of the text that were incompatible with the older results of grammatical, theological exegesis, whether of the Reformers or of the orthodox.

The quandry of theology during and, especially, at the very end of the late orthodox era is well summed up in Gabler's famous distinction between biblical and dogmatic theology. The former describes the theology of ancient Israel or of earliest Christianity in a purely historical manner, unprejudiced by the tradition of Christian doctrine or by contemporary theological system; the latter speaks to the church of the present. Biblical theology, according to this view, is a purely historical exercise intended to discover the religion and theology past. Its entire enterprise would be forfeit if dogmatic categories intruded upon the work of the exegete.[6]

On one level, of course, Gabler stood on firm exegetical and solid Protestant ground. The meaning of Scripture must be identified without prejudice from the potentially erroneous theologizings of generation upon generation of churchmen—particularly granting the difference between methods of interpretation developed in the sixteenth, seventeenth, and eighteenth centuries and the methods used during the preceding fourteen centuries of the life of the church. On the other hand, the separation of biblical from dogmatic theology placed in jeopardy the very doctrines held by orthodoxy to be the core of the biblical message—such as Trinity and Christology—since all of these doctrines had been developed over the course of centuries, on the basis, at least initially, of exegetical methods no longer espoused. In addition, this separation of the disciplines, usually discussed from the perspective of its importance to the development of biblical interpretation and biblical theology, also

---

[6]Gabler, "On the Proper Distinction between Biblical and Dogmatic Theology," p. 137; cf. Rudolf Smend, "Johann Gablers Begründung der biblischen Theologie," in *Evangelische Theologie* 22 (1962):345–57; with Kümmel, *New Testament,* pp. 98–101.

had an effect on the development of systematic or dogmatic theology that was not nearly as positive. Whereas Gabler's distinction opened the way for an independent biblical theology far less prejudiced by the postbiblical dogmas of the church, it also served to undermine the alliance between exegesis and dogmatics and to open the way for an increasingly independent dogmatic theology far less influenced by the results of exegesis, even as it reinforced the removal of exegesis from the theological patterning of the exegetical tradition of the fathers, the medieval doctors, and the interpreters of the Reformation and post-Reformation eras. This latter point is of particular importance, granting that the loss of impact of the older exegetical tradition on the practice of exegesis has led to the increasing but erroneous impression that the older dogmatics was not based on careful exegesis and frequently read texts out of their biblical context.

The history of interpretation in the seventeenth and early eighteenth centuries, therefore, is bound to the historical problem of Protestant orthodoxy. The difficulty that historians and theologians alike have had in both the nineteenth and the twentieth centuries in approaching the phenomenon of Protestant orthodoxy have arisen, in no small measure, because of the hermeneutical and exegetical barrier that stands between that era and our own—and because of the tenuous similarities that can be sketched out between the more existential pronouncements of the Reformers and the interpretive patterns of the modern era. In addition, an uncritical understanding of the Reformers' demands for a literal exegesis has often left historians and theologians with the impression that the Reformation was a prelude to modern exegesis and hermeneutics.[7] Even as the development of textual criticism and historical method caused increasing difficulties for the exegesis of Protestant orthodoxy, so also did the gradual separation of dogmatic from biblical theology cause a distancing of orthodox theological system from the results of exegesis.

---

[7]Cf. Farrar, *History of Interpretation,* pp. 307–48, passim; Hans Joachim Kraus, "Calvin's Exegetical Principles," in *Interpretation* 31 (1977):329–41; and note the significant corrective to this view in Brevard S. Childs, "The Sensus Literalis of Scripture: An Ancient and Modern Problem," in *Beiträge zur alttestamentlichen Theologie,* ed. Donner, Hanhart, and Smend (Göttingen: Vandenhoeck and Ruprecht, 1977), pp. 80–93; also see Muller, "Hermeneutics of Promise and Fulfillment," pp. 75–76, 81–82.

7.1 The Interpretation of Scripture in the Reformation and Orthodoxy: Development and Codification

The distinction between unwritten and written Word, crucial to the Reformers' and the orthodox theologians' argument against the Roman Catholic view of the priority of church over Scripture, also served to undergird the Protestant case for the present right of Christians to interpret Scripture and, if necessary, to bring the contemporary results of exegesis to bear critically and, indeed, negatively, on traditionary interpretations. As Bullinger argued in his *Decades,* God intended not only to teach the fathers by the "lively voice" of the apostles but also to provide, in the writing of the apostles, the means of teaching future generations—to preserve them in the truth of his Word and to save them from seductive but false traditions of men. Our attention must be given to the Word that we profit from it and be enabled to ward off the plagues of falsehood.[8] For all this, there remain dangers even to those who intend to hear the Word of God for the world abounds in false interpreters.

> For some there are which do suppose that the scriptures, that is, the very word of God, is of itself so dark, that it cannot be read with any profit at all. And again some other affirm, that the word plainly delivered by God to mankind doth stand in need of no exposition. And therefore they say, that the scriptures ought indeed to be read of all men, but so that every man may lawfully invent and choose to himself such a sense as every one shall be persuaded in himself to be the most convenient.[9]

a. The Reading and Exposition of Scripture, Public and Private

Musculus had clearly linked the necessity of studying the Scriptures in the original languages and in the vernacular to the question of the public and private reading of the Scriptures, and Musculus notes a series of reasons for public reading: (1) the general edification of Christians; (2) the maintenance of "the purity of public doctrine" against the errors caused by ignorance; (3) the aid of others who cannot read and who, unless others read publicly for them, might be shut out from the light of Scripture; (4) preparation for and support of godly preaching; and (5) the establishment of a basic rule for the mind and heart more useful in a single verse than a

[8]Bullinger, *Decades,* I.ii (p. 69).
[9]Bullinger, *Decades,* I.iii (p. 70).

"whole sermon of a Doctor [who] intends to demonstrate his learning and eloquence more than to instruct simple folk plainly in the
knowledge of God."[10] Musculus also recommends the private reading of Scripture for much the same reasons. The individual Christian
needs constant instruction and support in the regulation of life and
the way of salvation.[11] Neither, he writes, should the laity be
restrained from reading Scripture—for the truth of Scripture will
more surely preserve them from heresy than lead them to it.[12] This
regular public and private reading of Scripture, Musculus asserts, is
that "reading of Holy Scripture without which all the diligence of
the Holy Spirit directed toward the writing of the Word of God for
the use of the faithful is void and to no purpose."[13]

There is great "profit," moreover, from the right exposition of
Scripture. The Scripture conveys to Christians "the mind of God,"
inasmuch as it is a record of "the sayings of God" and of "the works
of God's providence," in both the creation and governance of the
world and in the promise of blessings to come before the end.
Indeed, Musculus continues, those who in the past received the revelations of God and who are now dead have preserved their knowledge of divine teachings in the writings of Scripture, with the result
that,

> as far as their doctrine is concerned, they are neither dead nor
> departed from us, but by means of Scripture they continue to speak
> with us as truly and sufficiently ... as they once spoke with others
> in the flesh.... to hear their writings is to hear the writers them-
> selves.... Therefore we ought to be thankful to the Holy Scriptures
> for the continual remembrance of the works of God and for the
> everlasting voice that comes to us with the sayings of God.[14]

Bullinger, in one of the transitions between sermons in the
Decades, very similarly evidences a concern to link the past history
of the Word with its present-day use:

> in the last sermon you learned what the word of God is; from
> whence it came; by whom it was chiefly revealed; what increase it
> had; and of what dignity and certainty it is. Now ... I will declare to
> you ... to whom, and to what end the Word of God is revealed; in

[10]Musculus,*Loci communes,* xxi (*Commonplaces,* p.373, col. 1–374, col. 2).
[11]Musculus,*Loci communes,* xxi(*Commonplaces,* p.374, col. 2–375, col. 2).
[12]Musculus,*Loci communes,* xxi(*Commonplaces,* p.375, col. 2–379, col. 1).
[13]Musculus, *Loci communes,* xxi (*Commonplaces,* p. 379, col. 2, margin).
[14]Musculus, *Loci communes,* xxi (*Commonplaces,* p. 380, cols. 1–2).

what manner it is to be heard; and what the force thereof is, or the effect.[15]

Scripture itself tells us (1 Tim. 2:4) that God "would have all men to be saved, and to come to a knowledge of the truth." Thus we understand that the revelation of his word was for the sake of all mankind. Similarly, Christ (Matt 28:19; Mark 16:15) told his disciples to teach all nations and to preach to all creatures. Likewise, Peter was given to understand (Acts 10) that the message was not to be restricted to the Jews. Bullinger concludes from these examples that "the word of God and the Holy Scriptures are revealed to all men, to all ages, sexes, degrees, and states, throughout the world."[16] What is equally clear to Bullinger is that the Scriptures ought not simply to be read —they must also be expounded and interpreted. This, notes Bullinger, is clear from the example of Scripture itself, which not only recounts the giving of the law by God to Moses and the Israelites, but also manifests the need for the exposition of the law in the words of the prophets: Scripture itself, in other words, contains the exposition of Scripture and makes clear, in that exposition as in the history of Israel's disobedience, the continuing need for exposition and interpretation.[17]

Thus, the entirety of Scripture is given for the edification of all by means of right exposition in the church. Indeed, granting the historical unity of the proclamation in law, prophets, and gospel, Christians must attend not only to the New but also to the Old Testament.[18] In both Testaments, the Word of God enjoins a pure and obedient life both on the ministers of the Word and on its hearers. It demands "sincere belief" and a desire to live according to its precepts; it forbids excessive curiosity but commands attention to "all things profitable to salvation."[19] Those who receive the Word of God find that it has

a mighty force and wonderful effect. For it driveth away the misty darkness of errors, it openeth our eyes, it converteth and enlighteneth our minds, and instructeth us most fully and absolutely in truth and godliness.[20]

---

[15]Bullinger, *Decades,* I.ii (p. 57).
[16]Bullinger, *Decades,* I.ii (p. 58).
[17]Bullinger, *Decades,* I.ii (pp. 72–73, 80).
[18]Bullinger, *Decades,* I.ii (pp. 57–59, 72–73, 80).
[19]Bullinger, *Decades,* I.ii (p. 65).
[20]Bullinger, *Decades,* I.ii (p. 67).

The Word of God ought to be "heard with great reverence" and with due attention to its contents, "with continual prayers." It ought, moreover, to be heard "soberly to our profit, that by it we may become the better, that God by us may be glorified." Such hearing does not give anyone license to seek out the hidden counsels of God or to be "counted skillful and expert in many matters"; rather, a right hearing of the Word, by both ministers and laity, results in faith and salvation to the glory of God and in a pure and obedient life.[21]

It is not, however, the case, that all texts were received as equally enlightening. We have already seen that Reformers like Luther and Musculus made distinctions within the canon of Scripture and clearly viewed certain books—like 2 Peter and James—as less than central to the proclamation of the gospel. A similar view, attuned not to the problem of canon but to the specific issue of preaching and interpretation, is found in Bucer's treatise on Scripture and preaching.[22] Bucer not only places a priority on preaching from the Gospels, he views the interpretation of the Synoptics as a necessary prerequisite to the interpretation of John. He next assumes the priority of Romans and Galatians, but argues that simpler epistles ought to be exposited first, by way of introduction and preparation. The exposition of the Acts, he notes, must follow the presentation of the history of the gospel. Significantly, he omits mention of the non-Pauline epistles entirely. When he approaches the Old Testament, he recommends extreme caution in preaching on such texts as the Song of Songs and the visionary passages in Ezekiel and Zechariah.[23]

Similar approaches to text and interpretation, coupled with counsels concerning the relationship of Scripture to salvation, appear throughout the writings of the Protestant orthodox, despite the shift in genre from basic instruction in the faith and sermonic exposition —as in the cases of Calvin and Bullinger's works—to technical theological system.[24] Rollock concluded his discussion of the Scriptures by examining the qualities of translations ancient and modern and by entering the debate over the public reading of Scriptures and

---

[21]Bullinger, *Decades,* I.ii (p. 64).

[22]Martin Bucer, *Quomodo S. Literae pro Concionibus tractandae sint Instructio,* text, with intro. and trans. by François Wendel and Pierre Scherding, in *Revue d'histoire et de philosophie religieuses* 26 (1946):32–75; cf. the discussion of Luther's and Musculus' views on the canon of Scripture, above, §6.1.

[23]Bucer, *Quomodo S. Literae pro Concionibus tractandae sint Instructio,* pp. 50–52.

[24]Cf. Burmann, *Synopsis theologiae,* I.iii.10–12; Pictet, *Theol. chr.,* I.xvi. 1–3; Mastricht, *Theoretico-practica theol.,* I.ii.45, 61–84.

their use by the laity. He favored translating the text, viewed no translation as a final authoritative text, but at the same time insisted that translation, the basis of public and private reading, is essential to the perpetuation of the Christian faith and its preservation in the hearts of believers.[25] Perkins stressed the necessity of some basic knowledge of salvation and fundamental articles of the faith to right interpretation.[26] Poole and Henry echo Bucer's concern for care in the examination of the Song of Songs and prophecy.[27] Mastricht could teach the importance of cultivating a "love for the Word of God" and a pattern of daily meditation on the Scriptures—indeed, Mastricht discusses at length the importance of reading, hearing, interpreting, gathering, and practicing the teachings of Scripture.[28]

Against the claim of the "Rhemists" that the translation and reading of Scripture were not necessary and that their efforts were "upon speciall consideration of the present time" and the needs of the church, Cartwright had asserted that "it is absolutely necessary that all men should use all good meanes and helpes, whereby to know Christ more perfectly" and that the Scriptures certainly belonged to the category of "meanes and helpes": indeed, "to this stayre of clyming up to the knowledge of Christ by reading, doth our S. Christ lift up his hearers, when he willeth them to search the scriptures."[29] Even so, the example of the Bereans (Acts 17:11) indicates the necessity of reading Scripture in order that believers "by conference of the scripture" might "confirme themselves in the faith whereinto they are entered."[30]

It is, therefore, unjust for the Church of Rome to keep the Scriptures from the people and to read them publicly only in Latin which few understand. Scripture ought to be translated into the vernacular and read by all, in order that the commands of God might be known and obeyed. Indeed, argues Leigh, God intended that people read his Word, as is witnessed by the fact that it was written down: "the Epistles of the Romans, Corinthians, Galatians and Ephesians were

---

[25]Rollock, *Treatise of Effectual Calling,* chs. 20–23 (pp. 127–60).

[26]Cf. Perkins, *The Art of Prophecying,* in *Workes,* II, p. 650, with idem, *A Godly and Learned Exposition ... of Revelation* and *Godly and Learned Exposition ... of Jude,* in *Workes,* III, pp. 214, 498.

[27]Poole, *Commentary,* II, pp. 307–8; Henry, *Commentary on the Whole Bible,* II, pp. 625, 1081.

[28]Mastricht, *Theoretico-practica theol.,* I.ii.62, 69, 73.

[29]Cartwright, *Confutation of the Rhemists,* fol. B2r, citing John 5:39.

[30]Cartwright, *Confutation of the Rhemists,* fol. B2r.

written to the people, therefore to be read by them."[31] Further, that there is great profit in reading the Scriptures was recognized by the fathers of the church, to whom the Roman Catholics give so much authority. Indeed, the fathers by unanimous consent urge the careful study of Scripture by believers. Jerome, the translator of the Vulgate, and Augustine both made the point that Scripture ought not only to be heard, but also read and studied for comfort and edification.[32] As evidence of this patristic recommendation of Scripture to all, Leigh notes the early translation of Scripture not only into Latin, but also into Syriac, Arabic, and Ethiopic, for the use of the people.[33] Even so, mere reading and understanding do not complete the relationship or, indeed, the duty, of Christians toward Scripture. Upon reading and understanding, Christians should "give thanks to God for the right understanding, and pray to him to imprint the true knowledge of it in [their] hearts." Beyond this, believers ought to meditate on the knowledge of God as conveyed by Scripture and then, finally, apply "the precepts and examples of the Law to instruct [their] life, the promises and comforts of the Gospel to confirm [their] faith."[34] Riissen similarly argues that "Scripture ought to be read ... 1. with attentiveness and understanding (Matt. 24:15); 2. in faith (Heb. 4:2); 3. in good order (Col. 2:5); 4. throughout all of life (Deut. 17:19); 5. earnestly (Heb. 2:1); and 6. with obedience (I Thess. 2:13)."[35]

Against the Roman objections that lay reading of the vernacular Scriptures is detrimental to the life and teaching of the church and that such reading is hardly necessary to salvation, the Reformed respond that the problem of abuse in no way undermines the command of God to read and study the Scriptures. Of course, such reading is not necessary to salvation. Baptized infants are considered saved, as are those who only hear and do not read. Nonetheless, the reading of Scripture is enjoined on those who are able, for the sake of strengthening them in their faith and shielding them against the enemies of God.[36] What is more, the Roman claim that the reading

[31]Leigh, *Treatise,* I.ii (p. 33); cf. Cartwright, *Confutation of the Rhemists,* fol. B2r.

[32]Cartwright, *Confutation of the Rhemists,* fol. B2v, citing Jerome, *In Eccles.,* x, and Augustine, *In Psalm.,* 33.2.

[33]Leigh, *Treatise,* I.ii (pp. 34–35).

[34]Leigh, *Treatise,* I.ii (p. 38).

[35]Riissen, *Summa theol.,* II.xviii.

[36]Riissen, *Summa theol.,* II.xvii; cf. Mastricht, *Theoretico-practica theol.,* I.ii.45, 69–84.

of the Scripture by laity breeds heresy falls short of the mark inasmuch as heresy is founded not on reading per se, but on mistaken reading—and the careful, informed, and reverent reading of Scripture will preserve the faithful from the errors of the heretics. As for the argument that "holy things are not given to dogs," is quite clear from the text (Matt. 7:6) that Christ does not here refer to the reading of Scripture and does not intend to designate the children of God as dogs—rather he means that the symbols of divine grace are not to be given to the unfaithful.[37]

b. The Authority to Expound Scripture

The Protestant insistence on the availability of Scripture to all not only called forth a pointed response from the Roman Catholics, on the ground that access to the Scriptures in the vernacular by the laity was a cause of heresy, it also created a churchly problem internal to Protestantism over the right and authority to expound Scripture in public for the edification of the church. Particularly in view of the Protestant teaching of the priesthood of all believers and in view of the extent to which this teaching was understood as a basis for action by the radical Reformation in its reinterpretation of church and doctrine, both the Reformers themselves and their Protestant orthodox successors argued a limitation of the right and authority of public or churchly exposition even as they insisted on the universal right of access by all Christians to the text of Scripture.

Heppe singles out, with some justice, the *Synopsis purioris theologiae* as perhaps the "most penetrating discussion" of the question of the authority to expound or interpret Scripture.[38] There is, the *Synposis* states, "a twofold power or authority *(potestas duplex)* of interpretation or judgment, either public or private: and both rest on calling *(vocatione)* and a specific gift" for the task.[39] Both aspects of this authority and the gifts that support them are always subordinate "to the Word of God and to the Holy Spirit speaking in Scripture *(in Scriptura loquenti)*," with the result that faithful interpretation will not distort the meaning of the biblical Word, but will form its judgments on the basis and in the service of the Scriptures.[40]

The private authority to interpret and adjudicate the meaning of Scripture in matters concerning salvation belongs to all of the faithful—who are given gifts of interpretation in an acceptable measure

[37]Riissen, *Summa theol.*, II.xvii, controversia.
[38]Heppe, *RD*, p. 35.
[39]*Synopsis purioris theologiae,* V.xxviii.
[40]*Synopsis purioris theologiae,* V.xxxvi.

and who follow various callings. Such authority to interpret exists for the sake of confirming one's own faith and for the edification of others in a spirit of Christian love. This private authority of interpretation, the *Synopsis* continues, rests on what the apostle Paul terms the right of judgment or discretion.[41] It is the case, however, that faithful people are not given this gift in equal measure—some being like adults, others like children in their abilities: these, at least, should rely on Christ and on the teaching of rightly appointed pastors while avoiding those who rest their teaching not on the Word of God but on human testimony.[42]

"The right of public interpretation of Scripture and of adjudging the truth of interpretation in public do not belong to all, but only to those who have been supplied with both the gifts and the calling to the task." The apostle Paul, moreover, identifies these gifts—the first is the gift of prophecy or teaching, and the second (which, the *Synopsis* carefully notes, is included in the first) is the gift of discretion and of the testing of spirits.[43] Scripture testifies, moreover, in many places to this special calling—so that we need not doubt the presence of sound interpretation, grounded on the diligent reading and meditation on Scripture, in all ages of the church. Although it remains the case that all teaching must be measured against the biblical Word itself and the witness of the Spirit in and through Scripture, and that false teachers who distort the Word must be rejected on the basis of the Christian right to discern and adjudicate the spirit of teachers and their words.[44] Authority, therefore, is always measured by the veracity of the interpretation.

c. The Character and Place of Right Interpretation

"Interpretation," writes Wendelin, "is the genuine explication of topics in controversy, according to the standard of the Holy Spirit speaking in Scripture."[45] Scripture, after all, is "the voice of the highest and universal judge," God himself; the Spirit alone creates faith and teaches utter truth; Christ himself identifies Scripture as the judge of controversies (John 12:48) and used Scripture in his own debates; and Scripture, as Deuteronomy 5:38 testifies, is deflected

---

[41]*Synopsis purioris theologiae,* V.xix–xx, citing 1 Cor. 2:15.

[42]*Synopsis purioris theologiae,* V.xxxi.

[43]*Synopsis purioris theologiae,* V.xxxii–xxxiv, citing Rom. 12:6 and 1 Cor. 14:3.

[44]*Synopsis purioris theologiae,* V.xxxv–vi.

[45]Wendelin, *Christianae theologiae libri duo,* prol., III.vi.

neither to the right nor the left of the way of truth.[46] Both this sense of the importance of right interpretation and the basic view of the character and place of right interpretation carried over with considerable continuity from the Reformation into the era of orthodoxy.

The right interpretation of Scripture, Bullinger had argued, necessarily becomes an issue once the propriety of preaching and hearing the Word is established. God wills to have his Word understood that readers and hearers might profit by it. The prophets and apostles spoke not in strange or difficult speech but in language intelligible to the common man. Such difficulties as there are in the Scriptures may be easily overcome through "study, diligence, faith, and the means of skillful interpreters." Knowledge of the original languages, therefore, is necessary for the minister or teacher.[47] Uncertain and doubtful places are interpreted by the more certain and evident. As a whole, "the scriptures are evident, plain, and most assuredly certain."[48] Even so the Scriptures need exposition and explanation—as Moses himself explained the law at length to Israel and as Ezra did following the exile.[49] The Lord himself read and explained the Scriptures in synagogues and the apostles everywhere follow his example.[50] Those who would not have the Scriptures interpreted would subvert the ordinance of God.

If the Scriptures must be interpreted, they must also be interpreted properly in such a way that their meaning is not "corrupted with foreign expositions." Some who claim to interpret Scripture follow "their own affections," setting forth "their own inventions and not the word of God."[51] Of old, in the time of Ezekiel, this sin was already present—and the Lord punished it "most sharply":

> We, therefore, the interpreters of God's holy word, and faithful ministers of the church of Christ, must have a diligent regard to keep the scriptures sound and perfect, and to teach the people of Christ the word of God sincerely; made plain, I mean, and not corrupted or darkened by foolish and wrong expositions of our own invention.[52]

The surest way to attain this goal is to look to those places in

[46]Wendelin, *Christianae theologiae libri duo,* prol., III.vi.
[47]Bullinger, *Decades,* I.iii (p. 71).
[48]Bullinger, *Decades,* I.iii (p. 72).
[49]Bullinger, *Decades,* I.iii (pp. 72–73).
[50]Bullinger, *Decades,* I.iii (pp. 73–74).
[51]Bullinger, *Decades,* I.iii (p. 74).
[52]Bullinger, *Decades,* I.iii (pp. 74–75).

Scripture first which state the Word of God "so plainly ... that they have no need of interpretation," and to recognize that here the mind of God is revealed: "The true and proper sense of God's word must be taken out of the scriptures themselves, and not forcibly thrust upon the scriptures, as we ourselves would have it to be." Bullinger here cites 2 Peter 1:20—"No prophecy of scripture is of any private interpretation."[53] The point carries over in virtually identical form into the era of orthodoxy: "no man or company of men, no church nor public officers, are to interpret the Scripture of their own heads, according to their own minds, so as to make their private sense to be the sense of the Scripture, but to seek understanding of it from God, who shows them the meaning of the word in the word itself."[54]

Bullinger next sets down several rules to insure right interpretation of the text:

> First, since the apostle Paul would have the exposition of the scriptures to agree fitly, and in every point proportionally with our faith; as it is to be seen in the twelfth to the Romans (v. 6) ... let it therefore be taken for a point of catholic religion, not to bring in or admit anything in our expositions which others have alleged against the received articles of our faith, contained in the Apostles' Creed and other confessions of the ancient fathers. For saith the apostle: "In defense of the truth we can say somewhat, but against the truth we are able to say nothing."[55]

As examples of this pattern of interpretation Bullinger argues that we must not interpret the words "this is my body" to conflict with the reality of the Lord's body risen to heaven and sitting at the right hand of God; nor should we take such a verse as "Flesh and blood cannot inherit the kingdom of God" to deny the credal affirmation, "I believe in the resurrection of the body."[56]

Next, we must take seriously our Lord's summation of all the law and the prophets in the two great commandments and recognize that no interpretation of Scripture can "be repugnant to the love of God and our neighbor." Just so, notes Bullinger, had Augustine argued in his *De doctrina Christiana*: Any reading of Scripture which does not

---

[53]Bullinger, *Decades,* I.iii (p. 75).
[54]Poole, *Commentary,* III, p. 921 (on 2 Pet. 1:20); cf. Hottinger, *Cursus theologicus,* II.iii. canon B; Wyttenbach, *Tentamen theologiae dogmaticae,* II, §157.
[55]Bullinger, *Decades,* I.iii (pp. 75–76).
[56]Bullinger, *Decades,* I.iii (p. 76).

work charity toward God and neighbor is of necessity an imperfect reading.[57] Third,

> it is requisite in expounding the scriptures, and searching out the true sense of God's word, that we mark upon what occasion every thing is spoken, what goeth before, what followeth after, at what season, in what order, and of what person any thing is spoken.[58]

Even so, similar passages should be compared for mutual enlightenment; difficult and obscure passages be interpreted by the simple and clear.[59]

> And finally, the most effectual rule of all, whereby to expound the word of God, is an heart that loveth God and his glory, not puffed up with pride, not desirous of vain-glory, not corrupted with heresies and evil affections; but which doth continually pray to God for his Holy Spirit, that, as by it the scripture was revealed and inspired, so also by the same Spirit it may be expounded to the glory of God and safeguard of the faithful.[60]

Vermigli's discussion of the "sense" of Scripture parallels Bullinger's with its concentration on the necessity of a churchly, believing context for interpretation and its emphasis on the priority of Scripture over all other norms of interpretation, as argued under the doctrine of the self-authentication and self-evidencing nature of the text. Concerning this question, he comments, there are two issues to be noted "by which the truth of divine scripture may be perceived; namely, the holy Ghost, and the word of God itself."[61] As Christ said (John 8:47), "If you have God as your father, why do you not acknowledge my word?" We have God as Father by the work of the Spirit in us—and thus by the Spirit also do we discern the Word of God. Paul also testifies to this (1 Cor. 2:24), "A natural man doth not perceive those things that be of God, neither is he able to do them, because they be but foolishness unto him. But the spiritual man judgeth all things."[62] All Christians have the Spirit in such portion that they can "gather & judge out of the holy Scriptures, such things

---

[57]Cf. Augustine, *De doctrina Christiana,* I.36.
[58]Bullinger, *Decades,* I.iii (pp. 77–78).
[59]Bullinger, *Decades,* I.iii (p. 78).
[60]Bullinger, *Decades,* I.iii (p. 79).
[61]Vermigli, *Commonplaces,* I.vi.5.
[62]Vermigli, *Commonplaces,* I.vi.5.

as be necessary to salvation."[63] Even so, when reading and attempting to interpret Scriptures, the Christian ought not to go to them with "a hardened and prejudicate opinion" but ought to "lay aside all affectations, let thy coming be wholly to learn" in order that "out of the plain and unpolished speech of the holy scriptures, is brought to light the most sincere and manifest knowledge of the truth."[64]

> The second note, and sure token, by which we may thoroughly search out the truth of the holy scriptures, is the very scriptures themselves. For it is requisite, that we should determine that piece of scripture which is hard and dark, by another part which is more plain and easy. Christ hath given unto his Church the old testament; the authority whereof (let the Manichees, the Marcionites, and other such pestilent heresies fret thereat never so much) is most stable and sure: insomuch as by it, the old Christians also have judged of the new testament. It is written in the 17 chapter of the Acts, that the Thessalonians having heard *Paul,* repaired to the scriptures to see whether things were as Paul declared or otherwise. And Augustine *De doctrina christiana,* teaching what manner of man a preacher should be, willeth him to confer the places of scripture together, and doth not send him to search out the opinions of the fathers, or to seek out the determinations of the Church, or the canons, or the traditions of men.[65]

The opponents of an open Scripture complain that there are so many dark and difficult places in the text that the untutored cannot understand. Vermigli answers that no place is of such great difficulty that it cannot be understood by conferring with another passage. Indeed, far from causing great trouble, these difficulties prove of great aid to the faithful who by them are stirred to search the Scriptures.[66] Indeed, "in such things as are incident to salvation, the scriptures want no plainness nor perspicuity."[67]

> whatsoever is contained in the holy scriptures should be referred to these two chief points; I mean the law and the gospell. For everywhere, either God's commandments to live well are set forth unto us; or else when we are found to swerve from them either of weakness, or of some certain maliciousness, the gospel is shewed,

63Vermigli, *Commonplaces,* I.vi.5.
64Vermigli, *Commonplaces,* I.vi.12.
65Vermigli, *Commonplaces,* I.vi.6 (entire).
66Vermigli, *Commonplaces,* I.vi.15.
67Vermigli, *Commonplaces,* I.vi.16.

whereby through Christ we are pardoned of our trespasses, and are promised the power and strength of the holy spirit, to restore us again to the image of Christ which we have lost. These two things may be seen in all the books of Moses, in the histories, in the prophets, in the books of wisdom, and throughout the whole testament, old and new. Surely they are not separated from one another by books and leaves; but by that way, which we have now declared.[68]

We must underestimate neither the importance and the interrelation of these tools nor the difficulty caused for the theological system when these tools were questioned, subordinated, or set aside by the Reformers. Melanchthon, in the early editions of his *Loci,* could, on exegetical and "evangelical" grounds, exclude discussion not only of the proofs of God's existence and of the language of divine essence and attributes but also (and quite polemically) of the doctrines of Trinity and incarnation as discussed in traditional dogmatics.[69] None of the terms—person, nature, essence, coinherence, and so forth—were scriptural nor did exegesis of the New Testament result directly or immediately in theological situations and problems requiring the use of such terms for their solution. And if Scripture alone were the norm of doctrine, perhaps such terms could be dispensed with.[70] Even so, Ursinus, like Melanchthon, Bucer, and Calvin in the generation of thinkers who preceded him and very much unlike the later orthodox, still asks, following a discussion of the terms "essence," "person," and "trinity" the crucial theological question generated by the *sola Scriptura,* "whether these terms ought to be used"—although, like Calvin, Ursinus assumes that the terms are necessary in order to express and preserve the meaning of Scripture against the heretics.[71]

The problem of interpretation faced by Protestant orthodoxy, therefore, was not merely the problem of moving from the text to contemporary preaching but also the problem of moving from the

[68]Vermigli, *Commonplaces,* I.vi.19.

[69]Melanchthon, *Loci communes* (1521), in *CR* 21, cols. 84–85.

[70]Melanchthon, *Loci communes* (1521), in *CR* 21, col. 85; but note the non-speculative, highly biblical return of the doctrine of the Trinity in *Loci communes* (1535), *CR* 21, cols. 258–69, and *Loci communes* (1543), *CR* 21, cols. 613–37, where the texts used are largely from the New Testament, with the Psalms and the prophets, particularly Isaiah, being used to argue the divinity of Christ.

[71]Ursinus, *Explicationes catecheseos,* in *Opera,* I, cols. 118–19 (Williard, p. 132).

text to doctrinal statement and even to theological system without the battery of tools readily available to the medieval doctors. This is a fundamental point of divergence between medieval and post-Reformation Protestant scholasticism—and it is also the fundamental problematic of Protestant scholastic theological system. As we have seen previously, the success of the Reformation—its institutionalization both confessionally and ecclesially—demanded an orthodoxy, a catholic or churchly right teaching, and, therefore, the development of a theological system. The doctrine of the interpretation of Scripture was intended, in no small part, to make that system possible, to ground the system in Scripture despite the changed relationship of Protestantism to the traditional tools of interpretation.

The task was lightened to a certain degree by the fact that the major opponents of the Reformed orthodox—whether Roman Catholic or Lutheran—were quite willing to agree that traditional language of Trinity and Christology, not to mention divine essence and attributes, was eminently biblical. Initially, only the Socinians refused to acknowledge the point. The task was also determined by the gradual alteration of exegetical method. As noted in the introductory chapter, the fourfold exegesis was challenged already in the fifteenth century by several alternative patterns. The late Middle Ages and the Renaissance brought new emphases on the literal, grammatical meaning of the text and on simpler or more elegant approaches to the spiritual sense of Scripture. In addition, the literal, historical emphasis of the Reformation was hardly the modern historical-critical method. The Reformers and, indeed, the Protestant orthodox all assumed that the living Word addressed the church directly in and from the text. In other words, they advocated a spiritual and eccesial exegesis that participated in the same dynamic as patristic and medieval exegesis. The step from exposition to churchly dogma was not, therefore, ruled out on hermeneutical grounds. (This degree of hermeneutical continuity between the Middle Ages and the Reformation not only made possible the dogmatic enterprise of Protestant orthodoxy in the late sixteenth century, it also rendered that enterprise suspect as the patterns of interpretation continued to change and a historical-critical method was introduced, under the impact of rationalism and deism, in the eighteenth century.)

Whitaker well sums up both the content and the tone or implication of the *status quaestionis* during the era of early orthodoxy:

> It is written, John 5:39, "Search the Scriptures." Christ our Saviour said this to excite the Jews, and all of us also, to investigate the

true sense of Scripture. For Scripture consists not in the bare words, but in the sense, interpretation and meaning of the words. This is plain from Basil, in his second book against Eunomius, where he says, that "piety is not in the sound of the air, but in the force and meaning of the thing denoted." The same appears also from Jerome's commentary upon the first chapter of Genesis, where he writes thus: "Let us not think that the Gospel is in the words of scripture, but in the sense; not on the surface, but in the marrow; not in the leaves of speech *(sermonum foliis)*, but in the root of reason *(radice rationis)*." Since Scripture therefore is not concerned merely with the words, but the true sense of the words, which we may rightly call the very life and soul of scripture; it is plain that this precept of Christ, wherein he bids us "search the scriptures," is to be understood of the sense and meaning of the scriptures, and not of the bare words alone. Hence arises this question, concerning which we dispute with the papists,—Whence the true interpretation of scripture is to be sought?[72]

Here, as in the dogmatic discussion of Word, the orthodox understand a distinction, but no strict separation, between the living Word addressed to the church and the words of the text. Just as in the dogmatic discussion, the words of the text are identified as Word because they bear the meaning offered through revelation by the eternal Word and Wisdom of God, so also here, the intention of the exegete is to penetrate the surface of the words in order to encounter their theological significance. This character of Scripture is made clear by the orthodox, moreover, in the recurring themes of the analogy of Scripture and the analogy of faith.

Once this question of theological significance is asked, the controversy over interpretation becomes clear, granting that there are differences between Protestant and Catholic over the determination and the determiners of contemporary significance. The Council of Trent, continues Whitaker, decreed that "no one shall dare to interpret holy scripture contrary to that sense which holy mother church hath held, and holds, to whom (as they say) it belongs to judge of the true sense and interpretation of scripture."[73] The true sense, therefore, would agree both with the church in its present-day teaching office and with the consensus of the fathers. This decision, Whitaker argues, settles nothing, "For we inquire further, what is this church; and who are these fathers?"[74] Granting this further problem, the

[72]Whitaker, *Disputation,* V.i (p. 402).
[73]Whitaker, *Disputation,* V.i (p. 403).
[74]Whitaker, *Disputation,* V.i (p. 403).

"true state of the question" can be identified only by consulting the "papists," most notably, Bellarmine and Stapleton.[75]

There are, of course, certain obscurities in the text, but these are to be overcome by study of the text, not by recourse to tradition or to the magisterium. Leigh notes the obscurity of prophecy, which can only be interpreted by the identification of the event foretold; and the obscurity of ancient rites and customs, which can be surmounted by further study of the historical circumstances of the text.[76] These problems in no way detract from the perspicuity of Scripture but lead to the general analysis of methods of interpreting the text.[77]

> The interpretation of the Scripture is necessary in the Church of God. 1. because it is commanded by Christ John 5.39. I Cor. 4.1, 39. 2. It is commended to the faithful by the Holy Ghost. I Thess. 5.19, 20. 3. It conduceth much to the edification of the Church. I Cor. 14.3. 4. It was used by Christ and his Apostles Luke 4.16. and 24.27. Mark. 4.34.[78]

> This question [of the interpretation of Scripture] divides itself into three parts.

> First, concerning the divers senses of the Scripture.

> Secondly, to whom the chief authority to expound the Scripture is committed.

> Thirdly, what means must be used in the interpretation of Scripture.[79]

> The vehicle or means *(medium)* of the clarity of Holy Scripture, as far as we are concerned, is its interpretation. The interpretation of Scripture is either verbal, when Scripture is translated from one language into another; or real, which is the correct explication of difficult places in the text, their genuine sense and implication, in clear terms, set down for the glory of God and for the edification of the Church, Neh. 8:9; Luke 4:17ff; 24:27; I Cor. 14:3–5; 26:31.

> Interpretation is to be considered either according to its causes or its means *(media)*. The cause [of interpretation] is either principal or instrumental: the principal cause is the Holy Spirit himself

---

[75]Whitaker, *Disputation,* V.i (p. 403).

[76]Leigh, *Treatise,* I.viii (p. 165).

[77]Leigh, *Treatise,* I.ix (pp. 171–192); cf. Riissen, *Summa,* II.xiii, controversia, obj.4; on the perspicuity of Scripture, see above, §5.4.

[78]Leigh, *Treatise,* I.ix (p. 171, margin).

[79]Leigh, *Treatise,* I.ix (p. 171); on the interpretation of Scripture, see below, chap. 7.

speaking in Scripture; the instrumental cause is 1) the church, 2) anyone of the faithful *(quilibet fidelis)*, who may always weigh true interpretation by the standard of the Scripture, inasmuch as the church is capable of error. ...

We recognize, further that there are means [of interpretation]: these are either external or internal. The external are ardent prayer to God that he, by his Spirit might illuminate and teach the true meaning of Scripture. The internal are both languages and things or concepts *(res)*. Concerning the words themselves, we must consider which are to be taken properly, which figuratively, which of them are more obscure and which clearer: the analogy of faith *(analogia fidei)* and context of the passage *(contextus)* in turn govern these issues of interpretation.[80]

These summary divisions of the topic taken from Maccovius' *Loci communes,* although the subject of considerable elaboration in their original context, already provide us with a clear perception of the Reformed orthodox view of interpretation and of the relationship between the task of interpretation and their doctrine of Scripture. In the first place, the comment we made earlier[81] to the effect that the attributes or properties of Scripture denoted by the orthodox are not to be viewed either as the empirical results of an inductive process or as static dogmatic categories in no relation to the claims of theology to be a praxis, finds direct illustration in the causal language of Maccovius' argument. The *perspicuitas sacrae Scripturae* stands here as a dogmatic category to be worked out and presented in the efforts of the churchly interpreter. Insofar as Scripture is declared a priori to be clear or perspicuous in matters of faith, that dogmatically declared clarity can be regarded causally as the ground for clear interpretation.

7.2 The "Divers Senses" of Scripture

The Reformation and its sometime ally, Renaissance humanism, brought new tools and new attitudes to the study of the text of Scripture. The changing patterns of hermeneutics characteristic of the fifteenth and sixteenth centuries, the concentration on the Hebrew and Greek texts, and the emphasis on a single meaning, springing from study of the grammar and syntax of the original languages, fueled the fires of the Reformation—particularly its critique of

[80]Maccovius, *Loci communes,* vii (pp. 45–48).
[81]Cf. above, ch. 2, introductory remarks.

doctrines that rested either on a problematic rendering in the Vulgate or on the allegorical, tropological, and anagogical meanings of the text. In addition, concentration on the original languages of the text created a more pronounced division between the canonical Old Testament and the Apocrypha than had been experienced when the Vulgate functioned as the primary foundation for exegesis. As the Reformation progressed, however, from rebellion and critique to institutional church and confessional orthodoxy, its theologians were forced, both by Roman Catholic polemic and by the burden of positive theological formulation, to deal with the problem of interpretive movement from exegesis to doctrine and preaching. Medieval exegesis was no longer possible or desirable given the state of hermeneutics and of Protestant doctrine—but the question of the spiritual and churchly reading of the text of Scripture remained, indeed, was heightened in importance in view of the increased distance between the text, now in Hebrew and Greek rather than churchly Latin, and the complex doctrinal formulae of traditional theological system. Whereas the Reformers rejected the *quadriga* and many of the results of medieval exegesis, they did not reject hermeneutical devices like the movement from promise or shadow in the Old Testament to fulfillment or reality in the New Testament, nor did they set aside a typological understanding of the relation of the Old to the New Covenant.[82]

It is typical, therefore, for the Reformed orthodox to insist on a single literal and grammatical meaning of the text of Scripture and to argue that no extrapolated allegorical, tropological, or anagogical sense of the text can ever be a firm basis for theological formulation —no matter how edifying or spiritually invigorating it may appear to be. Nonetheless, the canonical character of the whole of Scripture and the assumption that the canon, as such was inspired and the infallible rule of faith and practice, led back to the problem of the spiritual meaning of Scripture according to which the whole of the

[82]Cf. Muller, "Hermeneutics of Promise and Fulfillment," pp. 70–81, with Bornkamm, *Luther and the Old Testament,* pp. 89–114. And note the studies by Erwin R. Gane, "The Exegetical Methods of Some Sixteenth-Century Anglican Preachers: Latimer, Jewel, Hooker, and Andrews," in *Andrews University Seminary Studies* 17 (1979):23–38, 169–88; "The Exegetical Methods of Some Sixteenth-Century Puritan Preachers: Hooper, Cartwright, and Perkins," in *Andrews University Seminary Studies* 19 (1981):21–36, 99–114; "The Exegetical Methods of Some Sixteenth-Century Roman Catholic Preachers: Fisher, Peryn, Bonner, and Watson," in *Andrews University Seminary Studies* 23 (1985):161–80, 259–75.

Bible belonged to the church for its doctrinal and practical edification. Symbolic meanings were not rejected, but the old scholastic maxim, *theologia symbolica non est argumentativa,* was strictly applied, even in preaching:

> Let [allegories] be used sparingly and soberly. Let them not be far fetched, but fitting to the matter in hand. They must be quickly dispatched. They are to be used for the instruction of the life, and not to prove any point of faith.[83]

The movement from text to contemporary statement, even without the modern, historical-critical approach to the original life-situation of a pericope, required a means of bridging the historical gap between the first century and Reformation-era Europe. The means of bridging that gap was an approach to the literal reading of the text that recognized within and in profound relation to the grammatically controlled letter "divers senses" of the text.[84] This is a point, not of easy or rigid formulation, but of hermeneutical struggle and theological tension in the orthodox Protestant system.

It is important to recognize the continuity of this struggle with the late medieval and Reformation development. From Nicholas of Lyra onward there was, at least on the part of many exegetes, a movement away from the *quadriga* toward a more grammatically controlled method. This movement was slow and fraught with difficulties, not the least of which was the precise determination of what was "literal." A case in point is the hermeneutic of the French humanist, Jacques Lefèvre d'Étaples, argued in his *Quincuplex Psalterium* of 1509. Lefèvre defined the "literal sense" as representing "the intention of the prophet and of the Holy Spirit speaking in him" or as the sense "that agrees with the Spirit and which the Holy Spirit shows forth."[85] According to this definition, Lefèvre could argue that the *literal* meaning of the Psalter is "Christ the Lord," as is made clear by the apostolic interpretation of Psalms 1, 2, 17, 18 and 20.[86]

The problem encountered by Lefèvre—which is, simply stated, the problem of finding the churchly and doctrinal significance of an

[83]Perkins, *Art of Prophesying,* in *Workes,* II, p. 664; cf. Breward, "The Life and Theology of William Perkins," p. 49, where this rule is wrongly viewed as a departure from medieval models.

[84]Cf. Leigh, *Treatise,* I.ix, pp. 171–75.

[85]Lefèvre d'Étaples, *Quincuplex Psalterium,* preface, as cited in Preus, *From Shadow to Promise,* p. 137 and p. 139, n. 22.

[86]Preus, *From Shadow to Promise,* p. 141.

ancient Israelite text while at the same time affirming a single literal meaning—was not confined to late medieval and humanist exegesis. It is a problem at the heart of the exegesis of the Reformers. Like Lefèvre, Martin Luther returned to the original languages, and also like Lefèvre, Luther found Christ in the Psalms. Indeed, Luther had no difficulty in claiming that the Psalter must be interpreted in terms of the New Testament fulfillment of prophecy and that, therefore, Christ's speech in the New Testament established Christ definitively as the speaker in the Psalter.[87] Even in his later years, Luther retained this emphasis on a christological reading of the Old Testament and, in addition, retained a powerful affinity for the tropological reading of the text, as witnessed throughout his lectures on Genesis.[88]

In Calvin's exegetical works we do find an increasing emphasis on literal, grammatical meaning and even on a genuinely historical reading of the Old Testament, at least in terms of Calvin's unwillingness to do christological exegesis. Lutheran exegetes of the day viewed Calvin's interpretations of the Old Testament as "Judaizing."[89] Nonetheless, Calvin's interpretations evidence a continuing difficulty with the "literal sense" and with the precise identification of what is in fact "literal." Granting that the New Testament is understood as the fulfillment of the promises of the Old Testament and therefore, as a final statement of the meaning of prophecy, there is little difficulty in accepting Calvin's assertions that his exegesis is literal and grammatical with reference to his commentaries on the Gospels and Epistles. There is, surely, a great deal of theological interpretation in Calvin's New Testament commentaries, but virtually nothing that could be viewed as allegorical. In his commentaries and lectures on the Old Testament, however, despite his unwillingness to christologize the text, Calvin does put considerable strain on the "letter" and the grammar of the text. Prophecies of the kingdom, for example, can refer equally well to the postexilic reestablishment of Israel, to Christ's bringing of the kingdom in the preaching of the New Testament, to the establishment of true Christianity in Geneva, and to the consummation of the kingdom of God at the final judgment.[90]

[87]Preus, *From Shadow to Promise,* pp. 143–44.

[88]Cf. Luther, *Lectures on Genesis,* in *LW,* vols. 1–8, and note e.g., Gen. 3:18 (v.I, pp. 219–10); Gen. 9:3 (II, pp. 134–37); Gen. 22:1–2 (IV, pp. 91–4); Gen. 27:21–22 (V, pp. 127–33).

[89]See above, ch. three, n. 264.

[90]Cf. Muller, "Hermeneutic of Promise and Fulfillment," pp. 68–82; and

These difficulties with the literal sense of text carried over into Protestant orthodoxy as an aspect of the movement of hermeneutics from the era of the Renaissance and Reformation toward the beginnings of modern critical exegesis in the eighteenth century. The Protestant orthodox early on addressed the problem of the various senses of Scripture with a view to showing the rootage of sound doctrine in a broadly defined literal sense and to manifesting the source of Roman Catholic abuses and errors in an allegorizing approach to Scripture. Whitaker's *Disputation* thus reflects both the Protestant view of the *quadriga* as a source and justification of error and the continuing quandary over the literal sense. "We concede," he writes,

> such things as allegory, anagoge, and tropology in scripture; but meanwhile we deny that there are many and various senses. We affirm that there is but one true, proper, and genuine sense of scripture, arising from the words rightly understood, which we call the literal: and we contend that allegories, tropologies, and anagoges are not various senses, but various collections from one sense, or various applications and accommodations of that one meaning.[91]

"Various collections" and "divers senses" can be identified in a text, but only when they arise directly from the literal grammatical meaning of the text. There is one genuine sense but there are various theological directions in which that sense points, particularly those directions indicated by the fulfillment of prophecy or by figures and types in the text. Words, the orthodox insist, can have only a single sense in any particular place—otherwise there is an ambiguity of meaning and ambiguity breeds errors in interpretation.[92]

note the discussion of Protestant hermeneutics in general in Joseph Lecler, "Littéralisme biblique et typologie au XVIᵉ siècle: l'Ancien Testament dans les controverses protestantes sur la liberté religieuse," in *Recherches de Science Religieuse* 51 (1953):76–95.

[91]Whitaker, *Disputation,* V.ii, p. 404; cf. Maccovius, *Loci communes,* cap. vii (pp. 50–51); William Bridge, *Scripture-Light the Most Sure Light* (London, 1656)., pp. 48–49; and note Charles K. Cannon, "William Whitaker's *Disputatio de Sacra Scriptura:* A Sixteenth-Century Theory of Allegory," in *Huntington Library Quarterly* 25 (1962):129–38; and Victor Harris, "Allegory to Analogy in the Interpretation of Scripture," in *Philological Quarterly* 45 (1966):1–23.

[92]Maccovius, *Loci communes,* cap. vii (pp. 50–51); cf. Pictet, *Theol. chr.,* I.xviii.2; and note the discussion of Benjamin Keach's similar views of allegory in Harris, "Allegory to Analogy in the Interpretation of Scriptures," p. 11.

In dealing with this problem of "divers senses of scripture" Leigh and others among the orthodox argue a basic distinction between the primary exegetical work related to translation and the subsequent work of exposition: "explication" or "the finding out of the meaning of any place, ... is more theological, the other (translation) being rather grammatical." Nevertheless, the explication of the meaning of Scripture attends closely to the grammatical and philological problems of the text as the only way to elicit theological implications:

> The Scripture hath often two senses, one of which the latter Divines call Literal, Grammatical, or Historical, another mystical or Spiritual. The sense of the Scripture is that which God the Author of the Scripture in and by the Scriptures gives men to know and understand. The right expounding of Scripture consists in two things. 1. In giving the right sense. 2. In a right application of the same I.Cor. 14.3.[93]

Turretin similarly rejects the fourfold exegesis and states categorically that "Holy Scripture has only one true and genuine sense." Nonetheless, this one sense can either be "simple" or "composite," which is to say, either the historical sense of the text "which contains the declaration of one thing only, whether a precept, a doctrine, or a historical event" or a "mixed sense" such as is found in prophecy, where part of the sense lies in the type and part in the antitype.[94] The simple sense, moreover, itself is twofold, either "proper and grammatical" or "figurative or tropical." In the former case, the literal sense is indicated by the words themselves, in the latter it lies in what the words signify. In no case, however, is there more than one sense of the text, because these several levels of meaning belong to the single intention of the Spirit.[95]

Two important elements of the orthodox hermeneutic appear in these definitions. In the first place, this dictum, "the sense of the

---

[93]Leigh, *Treatise,* I.ix (p. 171), citing Chamier, "Literalis senus est is, quem Sp. Sanctus autor Scripturae intendit"; cf. Pictet, *Theol. chr.,* I.xviii.2; Maccovius, *Loci communes,* cap. vii (pp. 50–51).

[94]Turretin, *Inst. theol. elencticae,* II.xix.2; cf. Weemes, *Christian Synagogue,* p. 230.

[95]Turretin, *Inst. theol. elencticae,* II.xix.2, 6; also Perkins, *Commentary on Galatians,* pp. 304–6. cf. citation of Glassius and the rather negative reading of this material in Fullerton, *Prophecy and Authority,* pp. 173–82, and note Donald R. Dickson, "The Complexities of Biblical Typology in the Seventeenth Century," in *Renaissance and Reformation/ Renaissance et Réforme* n.s. 3 (1987):258–59.

Scripture is that which God the Author of the Scripture in and by the Scriptures gives men to know and understand," is a measured statement of the rule *scriptura sui interpres* along with its underlying rationale. Scripture interprets itself and must necessarily give its own meaning since it is there and only there that God, its Author, speaks. An opening is left, however, in this statement for various types and figures, on the ground that these were intended by God and can be identified from the wider context of meaning in the sacred history. The *quadriga* is gone, the letter has triumphed, but it is the letter of the larger sense of the text, much as Aquinas had indicated centuries before. In the second place, the orthodox hermeneutic allows no gap between the "right sense" and the "right application" of the text. Grammatical meaning and meanings *pro nobis* cannot be divorced—the reason being that there, in the text, is no past voice of God speaking to the past but the *viva vox Dei* addressing the present.

The assumption that each text of Scripture has but one meaning relates directly to the orthodox Protestant doctrine of the clarity and self-evidencing light of the text. If Scripture is to be regarded as self-evidencing and self-authenticating—which is to say in no need of the authority of church or pope to guarantee its meaning—then its meaning must be clear and readily available. This could only be so if there were "only one meaning for every place in Scripture."[96] Ames makes the connection between clarity and unity of meaning quite forcefully: "Otherwise the meaning of Scripture would not only be unclear and uncertain, but there would be no meaning at all—for anything which does not mean one thing surely means nothing."[97]

"The Literal sense," Leigh continues

is that which the letter itself, or the words taken in their genuine signification carry. And because the genuine signification of the words is that, in which the Author useth them, whether speaking properly or figuratively, therefore the literal sense is divided into plain and simple, and figurative which ariseth from the words translated from their natural signification into another, as where Christ saith John 10.16. *I have other sheep which are not of this fold;* whereby he understandeth other people besides the Jews.[98]

---

[96]Ames, *Marrow,* I.xxxiv.2; cf. Maccovius, *Loci communes,* cap. vii (p. 50).
[97]Ames, *Marrow,* I.xxxiv.2
[98]Leigh, *Treatise,* I.ix (pp. 171–72), citing Sixtus Amama, "Est ille literalis sensus qui proxime per ipsa verba sive propria sive figurata sunt, significatur, vel ut Glassius, quem intendit proxime Spiritus Sanctus."

Leigh's central point is, after all, not very far from the definition of Aquinas—"the literal sense is that which the author intends, and the author of Scripture is God."[99] Even so, the "mystical or spiritual sense" of the text must also be firmly grounded in the literal reading: "The mystical or spiritual sense is that in which the thing expressed in the literal sense signifieth another thing in a mystery, for the shadowing out of which it was used by God." As an example Leigh states, "the waters of the Flood, with which the ark was upheld, signified Baptism, by which the church is saved under the New Covenant."[100] This leads to the dictum, "Not the Letter but the right sense and meaning of the Scripture is God's word."[101] By extension, then, the Scripture really has but one sense: "Verus sensus Scripturae S. est unicus, qui cum mente Spiritus S. circumstantiis loci, & analogia fidei convenit."[102]

These definitions bring Leigh into controversy with "the Papists" who

> say the literal sense is that which is gathered immediately out of the words, the spiritual which hath another reference than to that which the words do properly signify. This last they divide into Allegorical, Tropological, Anagogical; they say that Scripture beside the literal sense, may have these also.[103]

After defining the threefold spiritual sense and, in some cases, citing the medieval rhyming definition,[104] the Reformed pass on to criticism. There are three errors in the Roman pattern of interpretation; first, in the definition of the literal sense as "that which the words immediately present" which frequently in the Old Testament ignores

---

[99]Aquinas, *Summa theologiae,* Ia, q.1, a.10; and cf. the discussion above, §1.2.

[100]Leigh, *Treatise,* I.xi (p. 172); cf. Dickson, "Complexities of Biblical Typology," pp. 253–72.

[101]Leigh, *Treatise,* I.xi (p. 172, margin).

[102]Riissen, *Summa,* II.xxiii; cf. Weemes, *Christian Synagogue,* p. 229.

[103]Leigh, *Treatise,* I.iv (p. 172); also Riissen, *Summa,* II.xxiii, controversia: "An omni in loco sint quatuor diversi sensus; literalis, allegoricus, anagogicus, tropologicus? Neg. cont. Pontif."

[104]Turretin, *Inst. theol. elencticae,* II.xix.1; Leigh, *Treatise,* I.iv (p. 172, margin): "Litera gesta docet, quid credas allegoria; Moralis quid agas, quo tendas anagogia." Leigh also notes the association of the three spiritual senses with the three Christian virtues:
> *allegoria – fides – credenda*
> *tropologica – charitas – agenda*
> *anagogica – spes – speranda* (cf. pp. 172–73).

the primarily figurative significance of the words; second, in the claim that there may be several literal senses of a text; and third, in the "division of the mystical sense into Allegorical, Tropological, Anagogical."[105]

To the first claim, that the literal sense is that which the words directly or immediately provide in and of themselves, the Reformed orthodox reply that the definition is false—and, indeed, that the false definition becomes an excuse to develop allegories from texts that appear, in themselves, to be meaningless or absurd. For example, the prophetic statement in Psalm 91:13, "Thou shalt go upon the adder and the basilisk; the lion and the dragon thou shalt trample under foot?" either has no literal sense at all, or the literal sense of the text is something other than the words immediately provide, inasmuch as Christ, to whom the text ultimately refers, never trampled on adders, basilisks, lions, or dragons. Or, again, Christ's command in Matthew 5:29–30, "If thy right eye offend thee, pluck it out; if thy right hand offend thee, cut it off," is absurd taken literally in terms of the superficial meaning of the words themselves. There is, however, no reason to allegorize the text in order to make it meaningful. Rather, the exegete must recognize that "the literal sense is not that which the words immediately suggest ... but rather that which arises from the words themselves, whether they be taken strictly or figuratively."[106] In the case of the passage from Matthew, the *literal* meaning of the text is *figurative.*

If Bellarmine's claim that the literal sense must be the immediate significance of the words were correct—as opposed to this alternate definition—then there would be meaningless or absurd passages in Scripture, a conclusion that even Bellarmine would not allow![107]

> We hold that there is but one true proper and genuine sense of Scripture viz. the literal or grammatical, whether it arise from the words properly taken, or figuratively understood, or both. For that there should be divers literal senses of one and the same place, is against the truth, the Text, and reason. ...The literal sense can then be but one in one place, though a man may draw sundry consequences, *à contrariis, à similibus.*[108]

Once again, the principle offered in argument against allegorization

---

[105]Leigh, *Treatise,* I.ix (p. 173); Whitaker, *Disputation,* V.ii (pp. 403–6).
[106]Whitaker, *A Disputation,* V.ii (pp. 404–5).
[107]Whitaker, *A Disputation,* V.ii (p. 404).
[108]Leigh, *Treatise,* I.ix (pp. 173–74).

looks almost as much to Thomas Aquinas' insistence on the *univoc-ity* of the literal sense as it does to the Reformers' insistence on literal-grammatical exegesis.[109] Thomas had recognized the impossibility of drawing a theological conclusion if the text were equivocal—and Protestant scholasticism with its doctrine of *sola Scriptura* and its concomitant rejection of tradition and the church's *magisterium* as equivalent norms of doctrine had even greater need of the principle than Thomas.[110] The Protestant orthodox do not entirely reject the allegorical, tropological, and anagogical interpretations of the text; they exist as valid applications of or conclusions drawn from the literal sense.

> So we conclude that those are not divers senses, but one sense diversely applied. The literal sense is the only sense of the place, because out of that sense only may an argument be framed. ... It is manifest that is always the sense of the Holy Ghost, which is drawn from the very words.[111]

Thus, there are allegories in the text, according to the intention of the Spirit, but allegories of human invention, brought to the text from without, must be excluded.[112]

Citing the medieval scholastic dictum, Leigh notes in favor of the literal sense as the ground of all meaning, *"theologia symbolica non est argumentativa."*[113] This dictum, of course, applies only to human allegories and not to parabolic or spiritual implications of the text itself, placed there by the divine hand.[114] Thus, the *sensus mysticus* can serve as a ground of doctrine, but only when it is the sense "offered by the Holy Spirit by means of the sacred writers," as distinct from the added sense, not inherent in the text, "employed by churchly writers either for the sake of illustration or for the delight of [God's] grace." Whereas the ecclesiastical sense has no absolutely normative value, the "mystical sense," as bestowed by the Spirit, is normative inasmuch as it is the interpretation of the figures

[109]Cf. Aquinas, *Summa theologiae,* Ia, q.1, a.10; with Van der Ploeg, "Place of Holy Scripture in the Theology of St. Thomas," p. 415.

[110]Aquinas, *Summa theologiae,* Ia, q.1, a.10; cf. Van der Ploeg, "Place of Holy Scripture in the Theology of St. Thomas," pp. 416–17.

[111]Leigh, *Treatise,* I.ix (pp. 174–75); cf. Whitaker, *Disputation,* V.ii (p. 406); Turretin, *Inst. theol. elencticae,* II.xix.6.

[112]Turretin, *Inst. theol. elencticae,* II.xix.7.

[113]Leigh, *Treatise,* p. 175.

[114]Riissen, *Summa,* II.xxiv.

placed into the text by God.[115] This mystical sense, however, can always be understood from the larger context of Scripture and it does not appear in all texts. Thus we know from John 3:14 that the serpent in the wilderness prefigured Christ and from 1 Corinthians 10:1–4 that the pillar of cloud and the Red Sea were signs of baptism and the food and drink given to Israel in the desert were spiritual, prefiguring the Lord's supper.[116]

Pictet also states a rule to be followed when a text of Scripture seems to present a double meaning and to have both a literal and a figurative or mystical aspect to its intended import:

> in the interpretation of scripture, allegories are not to be sought everywhere, ... [we] must not hastily depart from the literal sense, but only when it is contrary to the analogy of faith, and offers an absurd meaning.[117]

By the same token, figurative or typological meanings must be indicated by the text itself, particularly as identified through the *analogia Scripturae* in such references as the bronze serpent or the high priest, Melchizedek.[118] Thus, more precisely, the text has a single, "simple" sense, resting on the words understood either "properly or improperly." Superficially absurd statements or statements that cannot be taken at their "literal" or face value are often figures in need of interpretation, but nonetheless still "simple" in meaning.[119]

Even so, it is a basic rule of interpretation that subjects and predicates must be suitable to one another. In cases where a biblical text juxtaposes a subject with an unsuitable predicate, the interpreter must inquire into the manner in which the predicate has been applied and by attending closely "to the nature of the thing" or subject come to a better understanding of the text. Thus, Scripture will often attribute "human members to God" (such as a face, a mouth, arms, hands, and feet), or indicate that God descends, hears, sees, and so forth), even though it is clear that God, by nature, cannot have such attributes. Such sayings must be understood as containing anthropomorphisms or anthropopathisms.[120] Indeed, Wyttenbach comments, "oriental" usage was given to various kinds of improper predications

---

[115]Riissen, *Summa,* II.xxiv.
[116]Turretin, *Inst. theol. elencticae,* II.xix.15.
[117]Pictet, *Theol chr.,* I.xviii.3; also Riissen, *Summa,* II.xxv.
[118]Pictet, *Theol. chr.,* I.xviii.3.
[119]Wyttenbach, *Tentamen theologiae dogmaticae,* II, §173.
[120]Wyttenbach, *Tentamen theologiae dogmaticae,* II, §171.

(figura), literary exaggerations *(hyperbole),* and the attribution of personal characteristics to inanimate objects *(prosopopoeia),* an example of the latter device being "the heavens declare the glory of God" (Ps. 19:1).[121]

The extent to which these formulae concerning the one sense of Scripture "diversely applied" or allowing "various inferences ... applications and accommodations" or concerning the "mystical sense" are evidences of the same difficulty in identifying the *sensus literalis* that had confronted Lefèvre and Luther barely a century before becomes clear the moment that we examine specific examples of these inferences, accommodations, or instances of the *sensus mysticus* and *analogia fidei.* Whitaker can argue, for example, that

> the literal sense of the words, "The seed of the woman shall crush the serpent's head," is this, that Christ shall beat down Satan, and break and crush all his force and power; although the devil neither is a serpent, nor hath a head.[122]

Indeed, there are two distinct kinds of spiritual or allegorical readings of a text. On the one hand,

> tropology, allegory, and anagoge, if they are real meanings, are literal ones. Now the reason why sound arguments are always derived from the literal sense is this, because it is certain that that which is derived from the words themselves is ever the sense of the Holy Spirit; but we are not so certain of any mystical sense unless the Holy Spirit himself so teaches us.[123]

Thus, such texts as Hosea 11:1, "Out of Egypt have I called my son," and Exodus 12:46, "Thou shalt not break a bone of him," are not unclear in their historical context, but they also have a prophetic referent:

> It is sufficiently plain that the former is to be understood of the people of Israel, and the latter of the paschal lamb. Who, now, would dare to transfer and accommodate these to Christ, if the Holy Spirit had not done it first, and declared to us his mind and intention?—namely that the *Son* in the former passage denotes not only the people of Israel, but Christ also; and the *bone* in the latter, is to be understood of Christ as well as of the paschal lamb. They

---

[121]Wyttenbach, *Tentamen theologiae dogmaticae,* II, §172.
[122]Whitaker, *Disputation,* V.ii (p. 405).
[123]Whitaker, *Disputation,* V.ii (p. 409).

who interpret these places merely of the people of Israel or the paschal lamb, bring only part of the meaning, not the whole: because the entire sense is to be understood of the sign and the thing itself together, and consists in the accommodation of the sign to the thing signified. Hereupon emerge not different senses, but one entire sense.[124]

The term "mystical sense," then, is typically used by the Reformed orthodox to indicate an issue of prophecy and fulfillment or of the Old Testament types of New Testament realities and, in the context of the concepts of the analogy of Scripture and the analogy of faith, does not indicate a departure from the *sensus literalis,* at least as understood by the Reformers and the orthodox. Other allegories or figures, not indicated directly by the Spirit in another text, such as the use of the story of David and Goliath to indicate Christ's victory over the devil or to point to the war in our members and the need to overcome our passions, these, comments Whitaker, are "true and may be fitly said: but it would be absurd to say that either the one or the other was the sense of the history."[125] Such figurative readings are applications of the text made by the interpreter.

7.3 Methods of Interpretation

If the Reformed orthodox doctrine of Scripture offers the impression of an almost unbroken uniformity of perspective from the time of early orthodoxy to the very end of the era of orthodox or scholastic Protestantism, the application of that doctrinal perspective in the actual work of exegesis manifests considerable diversity both of method and of specific result. Although the exegetical examination of the text of Scripture took place within a confessional context and the larger doctrinal implications of exegesis seldom strayed beyond the bounds of orthodox theological system, the diversity of approach and result in the examination and use of individual texts was quite remarkable. The exegesis of the orthodox era can be highly textual and grammatical, immersed in the original languages, or it can provide a biblical-theological reading of the text, with reference to extant translations;[126] it can favor a comparative linguistic approach

---

[124]Whitaker, *Disputation,* V.ii (p. 409).

[125]Whitaker, *Disputation,* V.ii (p. 406).

[126]Cf. William Perkins, *A Clowd of Faithfull Witnesses ... a Commentarie Upon the Eleventh Chapter to the Hebrews* [and] *A Commentarie Upon Part of the Twelfth Chapter to the Hebrews,* in *Workes,* vol. III, for a biblical-

involving the use of ancient versions or it may insist upon the use of the Masoretic Text of the Old Testament and the received Greek text of the New; it can manifest an interest in the relationship between talmudic scholarship and biblical exegesis or totally ignore Jewish interpretations of the text;[127] it may utilize typological readings of biblical themes or reject such readings out of hand;[128] it can favor a grammatical, historical approach or it can emphasize the theological debates concerning a text; it may emphasize problems of interpretation and translation with reference to the history of exegesis from Erasmus and Reuchlin onward or it may seek primarily to develop doctrinal and homiletical *loci* out of the text.

Even a cursory examination of these and other commentaries in their methodological and substantial variety is sufficient to refute the parody of the seventeenth-century history of interpretation offered by Farrar—who characterized the orthodox as reading "the Bible by the unnatural glare of theological hatred," of reducing "science to impotence," and of making the analogy of faith and the analogy of Scripture "the pretext for regarding the Bible as a sort of quartz-bed, in which was to be found the occasional gold of a proof-text."[129] Such statements reflect, unfortunately, a reading of the polemical theological systems of the seventeenth century and little or no examination of actual exegetical works.

a. Biblical Interpretation, Methods of Exposition, and Dogmatics

The exegesis, the larger framework of interpretation leading toward exposition, and the dogmatic methods advocated by

theological commentary that is highly literal but rests primarily on extant translations; and note the highly technical work of comparative translation and exegesis in Andrew Willet, *Hexapla in Genesin* (Cambridge, 1605; 2d ed., enlarged, 1608) and John Mayer, *A Commentary upon all the Prophets both Great and Small: wherein the divers Translations and Expositions both Literal and Mystical of all the most famous Commentators both Ancient and Modern are propounded* (London, 1652).

[127]John Owen, *An Exposition of the Epistle to the Hebrews,* ed. William H. Goold, 7 vols. (London and Edinburgh: Johnstone and Hunter, 1855) manifests the talmudic interest, as does Ainsworth, *Annotations upon the Five Books of Moses* ... (London, 1626–27); Diodati, *Pious and Learned Annotations* (London, 1648) and Tossanus, *Biblia* (Frankfurt, 1668) largely ignore Jewish interpretation.

[128]Johannes Piscator, *Commentarii in omnes libros Novi Testamenti* (Herborn, 1613; anr. edition, 1658) favors typology.

[129]Farrar, *History of Interpretation,* pp. 363–65.

Reformed orthodoxy were profoundly and organically interrelated. The assumption of the orthodox, much like that of the Reformers, was that exegesis functioned not as a disciplinary end in itself but as the ground and foundation of a path—a *methodus*—leading to theological formulation on all matters of doctrine and of practice. That formulation, moreover, could take the form of preaching, of catechesis, or of didactic, scholastic, or polemical theology.

Ursinus adumbrates the standard interpretive rule of later orthodoxy as given, for example, in the *Westminster Confession*. In the fourth division of his prolegomenon, he writes:

> we believe and confess that no doctrine may be taught in the church that is either repugnant to Holy Scripture or not contained in it. And whatever is either not conveyed by the express testimony of the Holy Scripture, or does not follow from a right understanding of the words of Scripture, may be believed or not believed, changed, abrogated, or omitted without violation of conscience. ... We do not, therefore, reject the doctrine and labors of others in the Church; but giving them in their proper place, we are subject to the rule of God's word.[130]

Ursinus here states the foundational issue of Reformed hermeneutics—granting that Scripture itself must be used and justified as in some sense self-interpreting, both in its direct doctrinal statements and in conclusions drawn from the text.

Similarly, Zanchi's discussion of the method of biblical interpretation indicates the intimate relationship established by the Reformation and continued by orthodoxy between the pattern of interpretation and the formulation of Christian doctrine. There are, he comments, two methods of teaching, the synthetic and the analytic. Following out the model taught at Padua by Zabaralla, Zanchi notes that the synthetic or compositive method is properly used in the collection and teaching of *loci communes* while the analytical or resolutive method is properly applied to the explication of the text of Scripture. The analytic study of the text demands, first, a demonstration of the "scope" of the author's argument in the particular place under examination, then a presentation of the arguments springing from the scope of the passage, and finally the formulation of questions or propositions that arise from the context of the discussion. Finally, the method calls for the formulation of *loci communes* out of the doctrinal issues set forth in the questions and propositions.

---

[130]Ursinus, *Loci theologici,* col. 445.

Zanchi's carefully defined approach, inherited from Bucer, Hyperius, and Musculus among others, was designed to produce theological results—indeed, to create methodologically the connecting link between grammatical interpretation of the text and the formulation of doctrines for the sake of proclamation and systematization.

Zanchi further distinguishes between the doctrine or doctrinal description of Scripture and the exposition of interpretive rules. He first reviews the case for the priority of the Hebrew and Greek texts of the Bible over ancient versions,[131] he next argues the necessity of vernacular translations, and then notes the general clarity of Scripture that permits its use by the people.[132] These lengthy and basically doctrinal comments provide the context for Zanchi's extended discussion of interpretation. Seeming obscurities in the gospel, he argues, are in fact obscurities belonging not to the gospel itself but to the clouded minds of the unregenerate and to the delusions of carnal philosophy. The rule, therefore, of interpreting Scripture consists in renouncing human wisdom and reason and, as children, submitting ourselves to the teaching of God in Scripture and making our thoughts subject to Christ.[133]

Another cause of the seeming obscurity of Scripture are various preconceptions or "prejudgments" held by the reader, such as are held by the impious and characterize the writings of "Papists and other heretics," or, indeed, of otherwise pious people whose thoughts have been twisted by the doctrinal "hallucinations" of the day. The study of Scripture must, therefore, be undertaken without preconceptions, without doctrinal presumption, and with a pure and open mind.[134] As a corollary to this point, Zanchi argues that the interpreter of Scripture must be converted to God, detesting his earlier sinfulness, and proficient in piety. The study of Scripture, thus, must accord with the end or goal of Scripture, which is not our wisdom but our belief in Christ and, proceeding from that, the sanctification of our lives.[135]

Apart from his polemic against claims of obscurity in the basic message of the gospel, Zanchi did recognize that certain texts were difficult to interpret and that obscurities did result from the use of figures by the writers of Scripture. He therefore also offered, in his *Prolegomena* to the Bible, a more extensive discussion of the actual

[131]Zanchi, *Praefatiuncula,* cols. 400–404.
[132]Zanchi, *Praefatiuncula,* cols. 404–15.
[133]Zanchi, *Praefatiuncula,* col. 416.
[134]Zanchi, *Praefatiuncula,* col. 417.
[135]Zanchi, *Praefatiuncula,* cols. 417–18.

method of interpretation, followed by a set of twelve basic rules.[136] Texts that are, in and of themselves, difficult to interpret must be examined in their original texts after a careful study of the ancient languages. In addition, lexical and historical difficulties demand use of reliable commentators and study of ancient histories. Zanchi singles out Beza's *Annotationes* as a reliable aid to the exegesis of the New Testament. Beyond the simple difficulties of the meaning of words lie problems of grammar and phraseology which can also be surmounted through study.[137]

As for the difficulties caused for interpretation by the figures in the text, these can be overcome by discernment of the thing signified by the figure. An aid to the discernment of signification is the *regula fidei*. The Old Testament, for example, often speaks of God anthropomorphically, but we recognize the figures since we know as a fundamental truth that God is a spirit. If a word or phrase tells of a shameful act or wicked deed—as Augustine teaches—it is figurative if it seems to have no use or benefit, not figurative if, as stated, it has a use or benefit. Finally, comments Zanchi, some of the figures of the Old Testament point to the advent of Christ and must be interpreted as adumbrations of Christian doctrine. Thus, circumcision ought to be understood as literal and not figurative in its own time and context in the Old Testament, but as figurative in and for the time of the New Testament, granting that it was given new significance in Christ.[138]

As in the briefer discussion found in the *Praefatiuncula,* the hermeneutics of Zanchi's *Prolegomena* evidences a strong emphasis on Christ-centered piety. The first rule for reading and interpreting Scripture is that all such endeavors must be preceded by the invocation of Christ Jesus who regenerates our souls and leads us to the right understanding of God's Word. Second, Zanchi argues, in clear reliance on Augustine's *De doctrina Christiana,* interpretation must be undertaken in the fear of God, inasmuch as the fear of God is the beginning of wisdom. Even so, third, we must study the will of God as revealed in Scripture—and fourth, we need to recognize that Christ is the *scopus* toward which all the Scriptures tend: Christ is the substance of the whole of Scripture. Fifth, again strongly echoing Augustine, we must look to the end of all the doctrine taught in

---

[136]Zanchi, *In Mosen et universa Biblia, Prolegomena,* in *Opera,* VIII, cols. 15–18.

[137]Zanchi, *In Mosen ... Prolegomena,* col. 18.

[138]Zanchi, *In Mosen ... Prolegomena,* col. 119, citing Augustine, *De doctrina Christiana,* III.10, 16, 18.

Scripture, which is the love of God to which are conjoined faith and hope.[139]

Is his sixth point, Zanchi turns to the rule of faith. As a preparation for all interpretation, the reader must know and understand all of the heads of doctrine stated in the Decalogue, the Lord's Prayer, and the Apostles' Creed. The Nicene and Athanasian Creeds, also, are of importance to interpretation. If all else fails, Zanchi comments, then the "testimonies and interpretations" of the best commentators ought to be consulted, particularly those of the "ancient and more pure Church." This is not to say, he adds, that an interpreter ought to fall back simplistically on the consensus of the ancient fathers.[140] There is nothing in Scripture which cannot be understood either by means of these symbols or through a diligent use of the *analogia fidei,* which Zanchi proceeds to address in rules seven through twelve.

In his seventh rule, he counsels a frequent reading and hearing of Scripture for the sake of drawing the attention of the reader to texts that state clearly those things left obscure in other places. Similarly, eighth, the New Testament may be understood as the interpreter of the Old.[141] More specifically, ninth, the scope of the individual books of Scripture (as distinct from Christ, the scope of the whole) should be noted as an aid to the interpretation of verses within the books; the intention of the author clarifies obscure passages. Tenth, the context of a verse is, therefore, also important—and attention ought to be given to the thoughts immediately preceding and following any given text.

As his eleventh rule, Zanchi notes the broader implications of the *analogia fidei:* Scripture does not contradict Scripture. Thus, if we wish to know whether Jacob or Abraham was justified by works, we must look not only to the Book of Genesis and to the context of the passage, but also to the statements of Paul on this issue. Therefore, twelfth, and by way of summary, "the Scriptures are explained by the Scriptures, obscure places by clear." All difficult places are explained in clear passages, with the result that nothing pertaining to our salvation remains obscure in Scripture.[142]

---

[139]Zanchi, *In Mosen ... Prolegomena,* col. 16: "Tendenus est scopus, in quem omnes scripturae tendunt: Hic est Iesus Christus. ... Est igitur semper in scripturis quaerendus in primis Christus: qouniam is est substantia, ut vocant, omnium scripturarum."

[140]Zanchi, *In Mosen ... Prolegomena,* col. 18.

[141]Zanchi, *In Mosen ... Prolegomena,* cols. 16–17.

[142]Zanchi, *In Mosen ... Prolegomena,* cols. 17–18.

Trelcatius offers a succinct statement of the early orthodox approach to the interpretation of Scripture that distinguishes between the importance of a basic knowledge of the truths of Scripture and the exegetical and theological study of the text: the former is "instruction," the latter, strictly speaking, "interpretation." Both instruction and interpretation are necessary. Instruction must take place for the sake of the communication and inculcation of the precepts contained in the Scriptures and for the sake of the offering of truths necessary to salvation to believers. It provides a general edification in the rules of life and doctrine. Interpretation follows on instruction—beginning with the Holy Spirit leading the reader in all truth toward Christian charity.[143] It is noteworthy that the Protestant orthodox approach to interpretation assumes the testimony of the Spirit in and through the text and recognizes, as did the Reformers, the necessity for interpretation to take place in the context of belief and salvation and, indeed, for interpretation to arise out of the work of salvation itself. Trelcatius' point, echoing Zanchi, is not unlike that made by Augustine in his *De doctrina Christiana* that the interpretation of Scripture proceeds from an initial fear of God, through meditation on the text, to faith and hope and, finally, to the genuine love of God.[144] The *De doctrina Christiana* remained an important point of reference for Protestant exegesis throughout the era of orthodoxy.

Indeed, we discern in the early orthodox approach to the doctrinal and theological interpretation of Scripture a continuity of intention binding the method not only to the work of the Reformers but also to the older exegetical tradition. Indeed, if there is a distinction to be made between the hermeneutic of a Zanchi or a Trelcatius and that of Calvin, it has less to do with a scholastic rigidification of doctrine or a predestinarian principle than with a broader catholicity of approach, clearer ties to the tradition, and given those ties, a stronger accent on interpretation as a spiritual exercise. Accordingly, there are two aspects of the method that would cause increasing tension over the shape and meaning of the doctrine of Scripture during the seventeenth century—the textual, grammatical approach to exegesis and the churchly, catholic, or traditional approach to the doctrines that were assumed to be grounded on the text. Thus, Trelcatius argues that the interpretation of Scripture consists in the "collation

[143]Trelcatius, *Schol. meth.*, I.ii.
[144]Augustine, *De doctrina Christiana*, I.22–36; II.6–7, in *PL* 34, cols. 26–34, 38–40.

of Scripture with Scripture; the consideration of the essential points of a place *(locus)*, both according to the intention of the speaker and of the nature of the word spoken."[145] Beyond this basic exegesis, moreover, the interpreter must be mindful of "the analogy of faith" and expound all of Scripture according to the truth of its basic principles and intention. And second, the interpreter should be aware of the "practice of the church, the decrees of the sounder councils, and the expositions of the fathers," as long as they "consent with Scripture and with the analogy of faith."[146]

The last point made by Trelcatius is, clearly, the point of stress on the Protestant model of interpretation. Orthodoxy, following out the views of the Reformers and the great Protestant confessions of the sixteenth century, stood consciously in the central tradition of the Latin church in its assumption of the rectitude of patristic theological decisions, not merely the trinitarian and christological views of the councils but also a myriad of minor theological points belonging to the exegetical tradition of the church. Even more than the basic analogy of Scripture, in other words, an extended analogy of faith placed into a framework of the application of logic and the drawing of conclusions from the text is what made orthodox theological system exegetically possible.[147] The *analogia fidei* permitted the orthodox to approach Scripture credally and confessionally on the assumption that the creeds and confessions had arisen out of a churchly meditation on Scripture and were therefore to be understood as biblically standardized norms *(norma normata)*.

Blench has distinguished three forms of styles of the construction of Protestant sermons in the sixteenth century and although his study was based on primarily on British sources, his model also serves to describe the continental Protestant sources quite well. He notes an "ancient" form of simple hortatory exposition, characteristic of early English Protestants like Richard Taverner, Roger Edgeworth, and Thomas Becon. The sermons are often brief and tend to emphasize moral applications of the text,[148] in other words, an essentially tropological approach to Scripture. When they are of considerable length, they tend to be organized into topical sections, each with a distinct hortatory message. Second, there is what Blench calls "the

---

[145]Trelcatius, *Schol. meth.*, I.ii.

[146]Trelactius, *Schol. meth.*, I.ii.

[147]Cf. Dudley Fenner, *The Arts of Logic and Rhetoric ... for ... the Resolution or Opening of certain Parts of Scripture* (Middelburg, 1584), with the discussion in *PRRD*, I, 7.2–7.3.

[148]Blench, *Preaching in England,* pp. 74, 100.

new Reformed method," found in the sermons of Bishop Hooper, mediated by the exegetical style of continental theologians like Musculus, and described as the approved method by Perkins in his *The Art of Prophecying*.[149] Third, there is what Blench identifies as the "modern style," conceived as resting on classical forms and allied to Renaissance and humanist models. This style has been taught by Reuchlin and Erasmus and it was the style taught in the influential manuals of Andreas Hyperius of Marburg.[150] These latter two forms tend to dominate Reformed exposition and demand extended comment.

Hyperius' approach argued the necessity of identifying the "argument" or "scope" of the biblical books. The difficulties of language, particularly of rendering the words of an ancient tongue into contemporary terms, multiple meanings of words, tropes, and figures, and the accommodation of speech to particular places and persons must be properly understood.[151] The interpreter must also respect the "mind of the writer," the various dialectical or rhetorical devices used in a particular text, its antecedents and consequences, and its "circumstances"—its physical, intellectual, and textual environment, identified by Hyperius in terms of "person, time, manner *(modus)*, cause, place, and equipment *(instrumenta)*."[152] By way of example: does a prophet speak in or for his own "person" or for another—for God, for another human being, and if the latter, for a pious or impious human being? Or again, the "equipment" or "instruments" used by a person may have significance for the interpretation of the text: Sampson's and David's equipment—the jawbone of an ass to slay a thousand Philistines and a sling to fell a giant—point to the wisdom of God that appears foolish to the world.[153] This method would be echoed in Whitaker's *Disputatio de sacra Scriptura* and in the work of many of the Protestant orthodox exegetes of the seventeenth century.

---

[149]William Perkins, *Art of Prophecying, a Treatise Concerning the Sacred and Onely True Manner and Methode of Preaching* (London, 1607), also in *Workes*, II, pp. 643–73; cf. Blench, *Preaching in England*, p. 101.

[150]Andreas Gerardus Hyperius, *De theologo seu de ratione studii theologici* (Basel, 1559) and idem, *The Practis of Preaching* (London, 1577), translated from the author's *De formandis concionibus sacris* (1553); cf. Blench, *Preaching in England*, p. 102.

[151]Hyperius, *De theologo*, II.viii (pp. 91, 110–20).

[152]Hyperius, *De theologo*, II.xi (pp. 146, 148, 151–53); cf. Whitaker, *Disputation*, V.ix (pp. 470–72); and Bridge, *Scripture-Light*, p. 50.

[153]Hyperius, *De theologo*, II.xi (pp. 153, 161–62).

The "new Reformed method" is of particular theological importance inasmuch as it rested on the *locus* method of the exposition of
Scripture and, therefore, both paralleled and contributed to the
writing of theological treatises and systems in the era of Protestant
orthodoxy. Its popularity, particularly in England, demonstrates the
close interrelationship among developing Protestant hermeneutics,
the exegesis of Scripture, the construction of theological system, and
the daily practice of Christian piety, as focused on the sermon. In
Perkins' model, the sermon was to fall into four parts. First, the
preacher is called upon "to reade the Texte distinctly out of the
Canonicall Scriptures" and then, second, to offer an exposition—"to
give the sense and understanding of it being read, by the Scripture it
selfe."[154] Perkins insists that "the supreme and absolute mean of
interpretation, is the scripture itselfe."[155] The sermon, in other
words, obliges the doctrinally identified normative canon. It cannot
be based on the Apocrypha or on any other text. And the pattern of
interpretation, the clarification of Scripture with Scripture, obliges
the *sola Scriptura* of the Reformation by accepting only the clearly
stated contents of the canon as a rule for interpreting the difficult
passages. Similarly, third, Perkins assumes a movement from the
basic grammatical and literal sense of the text to Christian doctrine.
The preacher is "to collect a few and profitable points of doctrine out
of the naturall sense" of the text. Allegory, trope, and anagoge are
discouraged, while use of the analogy of faith, a close analysis of the
"circumstances" of a particular text, and the comparison of various
texts are presented as the best means of clarifying difficult passages.[156] On the second point, the analysis of circumstances, Perkins
notes at some length that the identity of the author, the time, place,
purpose, historical context, and immediate occasion of the writing,
the person or persons to whom it is addressed, ought to be considered as a basis for explanation. The profitableness of the teaching
of Scripture is, finally, to be made clear: the preacher is instructed
"to apply (if he have the gifte) these doctrines ... to the life and
manners of men in a simple and plaine speech."[157]

---

[154]Perkins, *Art of Prophecying,* in *Workes,* II, p. 673; and cf. on Perkin's
exegetical method, Muller, "William Perkins and the Protestant Exegetical
Tradition: Interpretation, Style and Method in the Commentary on Hebrews
11," pp. 71–94.

[155]Perkins, *Art of Prophecying,* in *Workes,* II, p. 651.

[156]Perkins, *Art of Prophecying,* in *Workes,* II, pp. 652, 673; cf. Breward,
"Life and Theology of William Perkins," p. 52.

[157]Perkins, *Art of Prophecying,* in *Workes,* II, pp. 652, 673.

This approach to the text is little more than a development of the *locus* method of exegesis—which was already geared to a statement of the text, an exegetical examination of the text according to principles like those enunciated by Perkins, and a topical discussion of the doctrines presented or implied by the text. What the Reformed preachers added was a concluding hortatory section, describing the "use" or "uses" of the biblical doctrines. In many cases, particularly during the seventeenth century, Puritan preachers obliged the scholastic method of their theology still further by adding to their (already incredibly long!) doctrinal sermons sections, either following the doctrinal exposition or interspersed among the uses, in which objections to homiletical points were raised and answered, echoing the scholastic *quaestio*. This latter, extended scholastic style is evidenced, by way of example, in the sermons of John Owen, Stephen Charnock, John Flavel, and Thomas Manton—in their published form, literary and theological efforts hardly distinguishable from dogmatic theology.

The impact of Ramism on methods of interpretation is also of considerable importance to the development of early orthodox Reformed exegesis, particularly in its relation to the formulation of Christian doctrine. The Ramist method of definition of the component parts of a topic and of the progress of an argument by bifurcation was used by many Reformed theologians in the late sixteenth and early seventeenth centuries not only as a structural device in theological systems and treatises;[158] it was also employed in varying degrees as a logical tool for the exposition of Scripture. Thus, Daneau, Junius, and Perkins used Ramist or, in the case of Daneau, Agricolan, bifurcations at various points in their argument and occasionally introduced Ramist charts into their commentaries.[159] Temple, Turnbull, and Piscator introduced what can only be regarded as the extreme application—the reduction of entire books

[158]E.g., Ames, *Medulla theologica;* Polanus, *Syntagma theol.,* synopsis; idem, *Partitiones theologicae;* Perkins, *Golden Chaine.*

[159]Lambert Daneau, *A Fruitfull Commentarie upon the Twelve Small Prophets* (Cambridge, 1594), p. 270; Francis Junius, *The Apoclayps, or Revelation of S. John with a Brief Exposition* (London, 1596). p. 26; Perkins, *A Clowd of Faithfull Witnesses,* in *Workes,* III, pp. 1, 14; and note the Ramist charts in Perkins, *An Exposition upon the whole Epistle of Jude,* in *Workes,* III, p. 479; cf. Donald K. McKim, "William Perkins' Use of Ramism as an Exegetical Tool," in William Perkins, *A Cloud of Faithful Witnesses: Commentary on Hebrews 11,* ed. Gerald T. Sheppard, *Pilgrim Classic Commentaries,* vol. 3 (New York: Pilgrim Press, 1990), pp. 32–45.

of the Bible to a series of analytical divisions.[160] Hall used Ramist logic as a way of topically organizing and expositing the wisdom literature.[161]

b. The Practice of Exegesis

As for the actual practice of exegesis—the approach to the text— we have from Whitaker a lengthy statement on the ascertainment of the "true sense" of the text. First, he comments, following out the line of patristic and medieval as well as early Protestant advice on approach to Scripture, "prayer is necessary" for understanding—as Origen had well argued, "we must not only apply study in order to learn the sacred word, but also supplicate God and entreat him night and day, that the lamb of the tribe of Juda may come, and, taking himself the sealed book, vouchsafe to open it." A similar point, Whitaker continues, is made by Augustine and by Jerome.[162]

Second, granting that the very words of the text have been chosen by the Spirit, it behooves the exegete to master the words themselves in the original languages. "We should consult the Hebrew text in the old Testament, the Greek in the new: we should approach the very fountain-heads of the scriptures, and not stay beside the derived streams of versions."[163] Ignorance of the original languages of the text has been a major source of error in interpretation and theology. Indeed, without recourse to the originals, certain "mistakes" will be "unavoidable." Thus, Augustine "exhorts all students of theology to the study of these languages"—and the "otherwise superstitious" Council of Vienna in 1311 insisted on having professors of the biblical languages in all universities.[164] The Reformers, too, had argued that the study of the original languages

---

[160]William Temple, *A Logicall Analysis of Twentie Select Psalms* (London, 1605; Latin edition, 1611); Richard Turnbull, *An Exposition Upon the Canonicall Epistle of Saint James* (London, 1591); Johannes Piscator, *Analysis logica evangelii secundum Lucam* (London, 1596); *Analysis logica evangelii secundum Marcum* (London, 1595); *Analysis logica evangelii secundum Mattheum* (London, 1594); *Analysis logica in epistolarum Pauli* (London, 1591); *Analysis logica libri S. Lucae qui inscribitur Acta Apostolorum* (London, 1597); *Analysis logica septem epistolarum apostolicarum* (London, 1593).

[161]Joseph Hall, *Solomon's Divine Arts,* ed. by Gerald T. Sheppard; *Pilgrim Classic Commentaries,* vol. IV (Cleveland: Pilgrim Press, 1991), pp. 1, 2, 5, etc.; cf. Muller, "Joseph Hall as Rhetor, Theologian, and Exegete," pp. 17–18.

[162]Whitaker, *Disputation,* IX.5 (pp. 467–468).

[163]Whitaker, *Disputation,* IX.5 (p. 468).

[164]Whitaker, *Disputation,* IX.5 (p. 468).

of Scripture was necessary for the sake of salvation.[165]

In one of the more detailed discussions of method offered by a seventeenth-century exegete, Weemes argued that the first step in exegesis was the examination of the marginal and line readings of the text, followed by the correct pointing of the Hebrew. He is particularly concerned to offer rules for the use of the Masoretic marginal apparatus. When a marginal reading in one place appears as the line reading in another, Weemes argues, it may be used as a correct reading of the text. Thus in 2 Samuel 23:30, the text identifies Bennaija as "a lively man" while the margin has "a strong man" —but in 1 Chronicles 11:22, the marginal reading is "made a line reading," allowing us to read 2 Samuel 23:30 as "a lively strong man." So also, when the Holy Spirit has made an Old Testament marginal reading a line reading in a New Testament citation, the marginal reading may be accepted. In cases where the marginal readings do not oblige either of these two rules, but are not contrary to Scripture, "we may use them for illustration ... although wee may not make them line reading."[166] There are, it must be noted, few important differences between the margin and the line—but the marginalia must be examined for the occasional illuminating difference and for the occasional contrary reading.[167] "Where," therefore, Weemes adds, "the Mazorite notes sccme to impaire the credit of the Text, there we are not to follow them." It is often the case that the Masoretes

> will seeme to be more modest than the Text, and to put the Holy Ghost to schoole as it were, to teach him to speak. *2 King. 18:27. They shall drinke their own pisse.* but in the margnall, they will put it in more modest termes, *They shall drinke the water of their own feete:* but, *to the cleane, all things are cleane, Tit.1.11.*[168]

Once these issues are resolved, then the exegete must take care of the right pointing of the text—recognizing that "the points in valor were from the beginning," but that the actual sigla present in the text were devised by the Masoretes. Weemes notes, from the Zohar, that one who reads the text without points is like a horseman without a bridle. The right pointing is to be decided from the reading and

---

[165]Musculus,*Loci communes,*xxi (*Commonplaces,*p. 368, col. 2–372, col. 2).
[166]Weemes, *Christian Synagogue,* pp. 42–43.
[167]Weemes, *Exercitations Divine,* p. 127.
[168]Weemes, *Christian Synagogue,* p. 46.

collation of the text in its proper context in Scripture.[169]

Even so, errors are both avoided and refuted by study of the languages:

> For example, Luke 2:14, the Rhemists make out the freedom of the will from the Vulgate Latin version, which is this: *Pax in terra hominibus bonae voluntatis.* But they are easily refuted by the original: for in the Greek it is *eudokia,* which never denotes the free will of man, as the Rhemists absurdly explain it, but the gratuitous goodness of God toward men: and this, indeed, some of the papists themselves concede.[170]

Similarly, the Vulgate of Ephesians 2:10 reads *Creati in Christo Jesu in operibus bonis,* from which "some papists" conclude that justification is by or in our works—but the original Greek *"epi"* does not indicate *"in"* but *"ad,"* "for" or "toward."[171] Other examples, as Whittaker attests at length, are easily adduced.

This importance of the actual words of the text carries over into Whitaker's third point—that the meaning of the word in its actual use and context must also be noted. The exegete must understand whether the word is understood in its "proper" sense or in a "figurative and modified" sense. Figurative usages cannot be "expounded strictly." Just such a problem of interpretation underlies the debate between the Reformed and the "papists" over the words of institution of the Lord's supper: Rome understands the words "strictly," the Reformed take them figuratively.

A question arises, therefore, concerning the identification of figurative or strictly literal meanings. Here Whitaker comes to what must be considered the fundamental literal and grammatical procedure of Protestant exegesis: the right understanding of the actual use of a word in a particular text comes from consideration of "the occasion, scope, preceding and following context, and the other circumstances of [the] passage" or, otherwise stated, "the scope, end, matter, circumstances (that is, as Augustine says, the persons, place, and time), the antecedents and consequents of each passage" and

---

[169]Weemes, *Christian Synagogue,* pp. 48–49.

[170]Whitaker, *Disputation,* IX.5 (p. 468); cf. Calvin, *Commentary on a Harmony of the Evangelists,* in loc. (CTS I, p. 121; Diodati, *Pious and Learned Annotations,* in loc.; Poole, *Commentary,* III, p. 195: "the Vulgar Latin is most corrupt, that rendereth these words, *peace to men of good will.*"

[171]Whitaker, *Disputation,* IX.5 (p. 468); cf. Calvin, *Commentaries on the Epistle to the Ephesians,* in loc. (CTS, p. 230); Poole, *Commentary,* III, p. 667.

"the series and connection of the text."[172] By way of example, the "Rhemists" argue that 1 Peter 4:8, "charity covers the multitude of sins," teaches a means of justification before God other than by faith; charity or love takes away sin. The "occasion, scope, and ... context" of the passage, however, indicate that the subject of the discourse is not justification before God but the "fraternal love which represses many occasions of offense, inasmuch as the apostle speaks, in the verse immediately preceding of "sincere love one towards another." Thus the "context itself" indicates that the subject of the text is not justification before God but "the love wherewith we should embrace and respect our brethren." It is, moreover, the case that the words of Peter here reflect Proverbs 10:12, and that the conference of Scripture with Scripture also refutes the Rhemists' interpretation.[173]

Examination of occasion and context also led the annotators of the Geneva Bible to recognize that the Pauline statement, "Everie man praying or prophecying having any thing on his head, dishonoreth his head" (1 Cor. 11:4), as reflecting a customary rather than an apodictic standard. The annotation reads, "This tradition was observed according to the time and place that all things might be done in comelines and edification."[174] A similar annotation is found in the previous chapter with reference to the eating of meat previously dedicated for sacrifice. The text refers to a practice of the time.[175] Nor was the importance of the historical context of these verses forgotten in the seventeenth century: Poole comments on the problem of covering the head in prayer and prophecy indicated by 1 Corinthians 11:4 that "this and the following verses are to be interpreted from the customs of countries" and that the Christian practice of uncovering the head during prayer probably originated, as Lightfoot had argued, as an alternative to the Jewish custom of covering the head. Poole also notes the variety of customs in his own time and indicates that, even in the case of the following verses

---

[172]Whitaker, *Disputation,* IX.5 (pp. 470–71); cf. Maccovius, *Loci communes,* cap. vii (p. 48).

[173]Whitaker, *Disputation,* XI.5 (p. 470); cf. Calvin, *Commentary on I Peter,* 1 Pet. 4.8 (CTS, pp. 128–30); and Poole, *Commentary,* III, p. 913; Diodati, *Pious and Learned Annotations,* in loc., p. 416, does not cite Prov. 10:12, but his explanation conforms to the Protestant model.

[174]*The Bible and Holy Scriptures conteyned in the Olde and Newe Testament* (Geneva, 1560), in loc.

[175]*The Bible and Holy Scriptures conteyned in the Olde and Newe Testament* (Geneva, 1560), 1 Cor. 10:25, in loc.

concerning the covering of a woman's head, that the Pauline text so reflects a historical situation that it cannot provide a rule for contemporary practice.[176]

Attention to the words of the text and their various relationships also includes such issues as "the veritie or falsehood," the "propriety," and the "spirituality" of a text. How the text affirms or negates a statement must be closely examined, with attention to the way in which the languages of the text form their arguments. For example, "when the Scripture affirmes a thing earnestly," it uses "a double affirmation": "so they say, *Amen, Amen; Matthew* hath *alethos, verely, Math 5.26* and the other Evangelist *kai, indeede, Mark 9.1. Luk. 9.27* this they did that they might be beleeved the more."[177] Or, further, affirmations must be distinguished from hypothetical or conditional propositions. Thus, Matthew 11:21–22, "If the miracles which were wrought in thee, had been done in Tyre and Sidon, they had repented long ago," does not indicate "some inclination to repentance in Tyre and Sidon to repentance."[178] Negatives also must be interpreted with care, inasmuch as they are often not simple negatives: "proverbiall speeches deny a thing commonly, but not alwayes," as in the case of the statement in Matt. 10:24, "the disciple is not above the master." David, after all "excelled all his teachers."[179]

So also, close attention must be given to the "proprietie or manner of speech in the Scripture":

1. When a speech is spoaken *metaphorikos,* borrowing a word from one think to another. 2. When it speakes *emphatikos,* by way of excellency. 3. When it speakes *elliptikos,* suppressing something. 4. When it speakes *euschemonos,* when in modest tearmes, it utters uncommon things. 5. *schleuasmos, ioculariter dictum,* when by a taunte or mocke, it vilifies a thing. 6. When it speakes or utters a thing *per euphemismon,* buy a comly sort of speech. 7. When it utters a thing *per metaschematikon,* by representation of a thing. 8. When it speakes *pathetikos,* in passion. 9. When it speakes *hyperdolikos,* excessively. 10. *Per eutelismon,* abjectly of a thing.[180]

---

[176]Poole, *Commentary,* III, p. 577; cf. Lightfoot, *Horae hebraicae et talmudicae,* 1 Cor. 11:4, in loc. (IV, pp. 229–31).

[177]Weemes, *The Christian Synagogue,* pp. 236–37.

[178]Weemes, *The Christian Synagogue,* p. 237.

[179]Weemes, *The Christian Synagogue,* p. 239.

[180]Weemes, *The Christian Synagogue,* p. 243.

The humanistic reading of texts in terms of rhetorical forms not only had considerable impact on Protestant exegesis, it also became one of the paths to the elicitation of right doctrine in the era of orthodoxy. Thus, the exegete must be attentive to anthropomorphisms and anthropopathisms.[181]

Granting the necessity of understanding the "series and connection" of a given text, not only the immediate but also the extended context of a passage needs to be recognized and (fifth) "one place must be compared and collated with another; the obscurer places with the plainer and less obscure." Thus, it is true that the *Epistle of James* states that Abraham was justified by his works (2:21): "the place," comments Whitaker, "is obscure, and seems to favour the papists."[182] This obscurity is, however, cleared by comparison of the text with the fourth chapter of Paul's *Epistle to the Romans,* where the apostle "expresly" declares that Abraham was not justified by the works that followed his call. We know this from the text for several reasons—first, since Paul says,

"Abraham believed God, and it was counted unto him for righteousness;" which every body knows to have taken place after his call: secondly, because afterwards he proceeds to the example of David, whom all know to have been a holy man, regenerated by the Spirit of God, and called by God. We must needs therefore confess that the term "justification" is taken in different senses, unless we choose to suppose that the apostles are at variance, and pronounce contradictory declarations. In James, therefore, *to be justified* means to be declared and shewn to be just, as Thomas Aquinas himself confesses upon that place; but, in Paul, *to be justified* denotes the same as to be absolved from all sins, and accounted righteous with God.[183]

This "comparison of places," moreover, entails not only the comparison of "similar," but also (sixth in Whitaker's list of means of

[181]Weemes, *The Christian Synagogue,* pp. 243–44.
[182]Whitaker, *Disputation,* IX.5 (p. 471).
[183]Whitaker, *Disputation,* IX.5 (pp. 471–72); cf. Poole, *Commentary,* III, p. 887, for an exegesis of the text using the method noted by Whitaker. Poole concludes, like Whitaker, "that Abraham's justification here was not the absolution of a sinner, but the solemn approbation of a believer; not a justifying him as ungodly, but a commending him for his godliness," i.e., not a contradiction of Paul in Romans 4. Also note Calvin, *Commentary on James,* in loc. (CTS, pp. 309–13) and cf. Calvin, *Institutes,* III.xvii.11–12 and the marginalia in *The Bible and Holy Scriptures conteyned in the Olde and Newe Testament* (Geneva, 1560), at James 2:14.

interpretation), the comparison of "dissimilar passages." Granting the fundamental attention paid by the exegete to strict and figurative meanings of texts and to the "occasion, scope, and context" of passages, the exegete will need to have a sense of which texts state similar issues and which treat of dissimilar topics; the comparison or "conference" of texts stands as an integral part of the logic of this exegetical method, sometimes resting on a similarity or dissimilarity discovered by the analysis of text and grammar, sometimes determining whether a text ought to be read strictly or figuratively on the basis of clear similarities or dissimilarities.

Nonetheless, seventeenth-century theologians and exegetes recognized dangers and difficulties in the method. Weemes, for example, cautions against allowing the marginal readings to govern the readings of lines of the text and warns that "from wrong Analogy or Collation of Scripture with Scripture, wrong Doctrine is gathered." By way of example, a traditional Jewish collation of 1 Kings 4:30, "Salomon was wiser than all those of the East," with Isaiah 2:26, "thou art full of the manners of the East," led to the erroneous assumption that Solomon was a magician.[184]

In a correct use of analogy or collation, John 6:53 and John 4:14 are, theologically considered, similar passages. The former, "Unless ye eat the flesh of the Son of Man, and drink his blood, ye have no life in you," and the latter, "Whosoever shall drink of that water that I will give him, shall never thirst ...," both tell of the spiritual nourishment of believers by Christ. Rather than read the former text in a fleshly way, the interpreter ought to attend to an unlike passage, like the sixth precept of the Decalogue, "thou shalt do no murder." Whitaker comments, "for if it be a crime, yea, an enormity, to slay a man, it is certainly a far deeper crime to eat and devour a man; hence Augustine concludes, *de doct. christ.* Lib. iii. c.16, that these words must be understood and explained figuratively, because they otherwise would command a flagitious crime."[185] This kind of comparison or conference of texts rests, logically and hermeneutically, on an assumption of overarching harmony of meaning and message. Beyond this "analogy of Scripture" strictly defined stands the analogy of faith, according to which the fundamental articles of faith enunciated in the basic catechetical topics of Creed, Lord's Prayer, and Decalogue operate as interpretive safeguards upon the interpretation of particularly difficult texts. The negative interpretive use of

---

[184]Weemes, *Christian Synagogue,* pp. 269.
[185]Whitaker, *Disputation,* IX.5 (p. 472).

the Decalogue as a key to understanding John 6:53, therefore, also represents an integral element of the method—a logical step granting the character of the *analogia fidei*.[186]

The analogy of faith, moreover, was justified and safeguarded hermeneutically by the dogmatic recognition by the Protestant orthodox that the objective marks and attributes of the divinity of Scripture, for all that they could be rationally set forth, could not be proven rationally or empirically. Assurance of the divine authority of Scripture was given by faith—and faith, doctrinally considered, provided the bridge between the preliminary discussions in theological system (prolegomena and the doctrine of Scripture) and the doctrine of God.[187] The analogy of faith stands, therefore, as the hermeneutical parallel to the discussion of faith as *principium cognoscendi internum*.

This view of the role of faith—not only *fides qua* but also *fides quae creditur*—sets the stage for the Roman Catholic rejoinder that the tradition must be normative. Perkins noted the problem in his *A Reformed Catholike* and offered the orthodox solution in which the analogy of faith is limited by definition to a broad sense of Scripture as a whole, but still corresponding roughly with the church's theology, at least in its so-called fundamental articles:[188]

> Sundry places of Scripture bee doubtful, and every religion hath his severall expositions of them, as the Papists have theirs, and the Protestants theirs. Now then seeing there can be but one trueth, when question is of the interpretation of Scripture, recourse must bee had to the tradition of the Church, that the true sense may bee determined and the question ended.[189]

Perkins replies,

> It is not so: but in doubtful places Scripture itselfe is sufficient to declare his owne meaning: first, by the analogie of faith, which is the summe of religion gathered out of the clearest places of Scripture: second, by the circumstance of the place, the nature and signification of the words: thirdly, by conference of place with place. ... Scripture itselfe is the text and the best glosse. And the Scripture is falsely tearmed the matter of strife, it being not so by itselfe, but by the abuse of men.[190]

[186]On the analogy of faith, see above, §6.4.a.
[187]Cf. Mastricht, *Theoretico-practica theol.*, II.i.1.
[188]On fundamental articles, see *PRRD*, I, 9.2.
[189]Perkins, *Reformed Catholike*, p. 583, col. 1D.
[190]Perkins, *Reformed Catholike*, p. 583, col. 1D–2A.

In this definition, the analogy of faith indicates not the interpretation of Scripture by means of the tradition of Christian doctrine, but an extended analogy of Scripture. It functions similarly, in other words, to the broader meaning of *scopus* noted above.[191] The Protestant orthodox were certain of the unity and coherence of the biblical message—and they were also convinced of an intimate relationship between the various forms and levels of theology, from the basic exegesis of the sacred page, to the exposition of its fundamental articles in catechesis, to the more elaborate forms of positive, polemical, and scholastic theology.[192] The analogy of faith is connected, explicitly, with the identification of fundamental articles of faith and, therefore, also with the doctrinal truths identified for the whole church in basic catechesis:

> Now the analogy of faith is nothing else but the constant sense of the general tenour of scripture in those clear passages of scripture, where the meaning labours under no obscurity; such as the articles of faith in the Creed, the contents of the Lord's Prayer, the Decalogue, and the whole Catechism: for every part of the Catechism may be confirmed by plain passages of scripture.[193]

This "general tenour" of Scripture can, of course, be subject to rather broad application and, as Reformed orthodox exegesis shows, include not only teachings elicited directly from the text by exegesis but also doctrines drawn as logical conclusions from the text, with the result that arguments based on the analogy of faith can appear somewhat rationalizing.

Thus, Whitaker can offer as his primary example of the use of the analogy of faith a refutation of the Roman Catholic and Lutheran doctrines of sacramental presence:

> the papists elicit transubstantiation from the words, "This is my body," making the meaning of them this, This bread is transformed into my body. The Lutherans adopt another interpretation, namely, The body of Christ is under this bread; and hence infer their doctrine of consubstantiation. Both expositions are at variance with the analogy of faith.[194]

The analogy of faith, in this case, begins by noting of conclusions

---

[191]Cf. above, §3.4.
[192]Cf. *PRRD*, I, 8.1.
[193]Whitaker, *Disputation,* IX.5 (p. 472).
[194]Whitaker, *Disputation,* IX.5 (pp. 472–73).

legitimately drawn from the larger body of New Testament writings. There are three conclusions that weigh against Roman Catholic and Lutheran views:

> first, the analogy of faith teaches that Christ hath a body like to ours: now such a body can neither lie hid under the accidents of bread, nor be along with the bread. Secondly, the analogy of faith teaches that Christ is in heaven; therefore he is not in the bread or with the bread. Thirdly, the analogy of faith teaches that Christ will come to judgment from heaven, not from the pix.[195]

The logic of biblical argument, here, follows the principle frequently enunciated in Reformed prolegomena that mixed syllogisms using rational principles or rationally known truths in the major and the biblical text in the minor are legitimate in theology: in short, Christ's body must be like other human bodies.[196]

The theological meaning of the words, however, appears fully only from the analogy of Scripture, specifically, from the conference of the text with other similar texts, and from the subsequent examination of the linguistic forms in the text—the grammatical structures and the figures—on grounds provided by the analogy. In the first place, 1 Corinthians 11:26 offers the apostle Paul's exposition of Christ's words, "This is my body" and "this is my blood of the new testament, which is shed for many for the remission of sins" as indicating a act of remembrance "showing forth *the Lord's death till he come*." Applying the analogy and examining the grammar and the figure, Poole can argue:

> Christ's taking of the cup, and giving of thanks were actions of the same nature with those he used with a relation to the bread. ... Let the papists and Lutherans say what they can, here must be two figueres acknowledged in these words. The *cup* is put here for the wine in the cup; and the meaning of these words, *this is my blood of the new testament,* must be, this wine is the sign of the new covenant. Why they should not as readily acknowledge a figure in those words, *This is my body,* I cannot understand; the pronoun *this,* in the Greek, is in the neuter gender, and applicable to the term *cup,* or to the term *blood;* but it is most reasonable to interpret it, This cup, that is, the wine in this cup, is the blood of the new covenant, or testament, that is, the blood by which the new covenant is confirmed and established. Thus *the blood of the new*

---

[195]Whitaker, *Disputation,* IX.5 (p. 473).
[196]Cf. *PRRD,* I, 7.3.

covenant signifieth in several texts, Exod. xxiv.8; Zech ix.11; Heb. ix.20; x.29.[197]

The analogy of Scripture, understood in its larger sense and read in the context of a hermeneutic of promise and fulfillment is evident in Poole's exegesis of the other texts noted in the preceding citation: by way of example, the exegesis of Zechariah 9:11, "as for thee also, by the blood of thy covenant I have sent forth thy prisoners out of the pit wherein is no water." These words, comments Poole, are "Christ's words" to the "Jewish church." It is of course historically the case that the edict of Cyrus had "sent the Jews home, but in this he was Christ's servant, and Christ was mindful of the covenant, and to perform this brought them up *Out of the pit wherein is no water;* Babylon, compared to a pit in which no water was, wherein the Jews must have perished, had not mercy from Christ visited them."[198]

The other Old Testament text cited in the exposition of the words of institution, Exodus 24:8, "And Moses took the blood, and sprinkled it on the people, and said, Behold, the blood of the covenant, which the Lord hath made with you concerning all these words," serves as an example of the way in which, under the principle of analogy and granting models of prophecy and fulfillment, type and antitype, resting on the unity and distinction of the Testaments, the literally interpreted text can still point in several directions. Poole notes that this sprinkling of blood on the people indicated both "their ratification of the covenant on their parts, and their secret willing of the effusion of their own blood if they did not keep it" and "their sprinkling of their consciences with the blood of Christ, and their obtaining redemption, justification, and access to God through it alone," the latter meaning being confirmed by reference to Hebrews 9:20, 22; 13:20 and Luke 22:20.[199]

The exegetical method described here is neither a medieval nor a modern method. It has deemphasized and discouraged frequent use of the various allegorical and spiritual approaches to the text, and it has concentrated meaning in the grammatical, literal, textual, and contextual understanding of a given passage, but it has not moved

---

[197]Poole, *Commentary,* III, p. 127.

[198]Poole, *Commentary,* II, p. 1006; cf. Gataker et al. *Annotations upon all the Books of the Old and New Testament,* in loc. (Zech. 9:9–11) and *The Dutch Annotations upon the Whole bible,* in loc.

[199]Poole, *Commentary,* I, p. 171; cf. Willet, *Hexapla in Exodum,* pp. 466–67; Gataker et al., *Annotations upon all the Books of the Old and New Testament,* in loc.

toward a primarily "historical" model in the modern sense of that term. In common with medieval models, it retains a strong sense of the churchly character of exegesis—and its emphases on the occasion, scope, and context of the passage are, accordingly, directed toward the specifically *theological* occasion, the *dogmatic* scope, the *doctrinal* context. The focus or center of gravity of the method, as represented by these textual-theological concerns, is clearly on the literal meaning, and usually on a "strict" or nonfigurative understanding of "literal," unless a figurative construction appears to be demanded by the occasion, scope, or context of a passage. Unlike modern exegesis and in continuity with the various patristic and medieval methods, however, this Protestant exegesis not only does not focus on the original historical situation of the text as its primary *locus* of meaning, it also assumes that the alteration of historical context between the time of the writing of the text and the time of the exegete—even when that alteration is noted as a part of the interpretive exercise—in no way stands as a barrier to the address of the Word in the text to the churchly readers, interpreters, and hearers of that Word.

We have not come very far, in the era of Reformed orthodox exegesis, from the marginal head of the *Second Helvetic Confession,* "the preaching of the Word of God is the Word of God." Not only did this famous phrase imply a strict definition of Scripture as Word and a traditional theory of detailed, verbal inspiration, it also assumed—in continuity with medieval and later Reformed exegesis that (to borrow and abuse a phrase from modern hermeneutics) that the "two horizons," the horizon of meaning of the text and the horizon of meaning of the exegete, were potentially one and the same.[200] The point of exegesis was not to offer a totally new historical horizon of meaning but to offer a broader, clearer, and more precise vista upon the biblical-churchly horizon of the one community of faith. Or, to put the matter in an older language, the issue, for the Protestant orthodox, as for the medieval doctor and the sixteenth-century Reformer, remains the elucidation of *sacra pagina* for the sake of the declaration of *doctrina* and the formulation of *sacra theologia.* The distinction between the page and the theology is, moreover, not understood so much in historical and in formal terms—as the movement from the Word as given to the various accepted forms of its proclamation and declaration.

---

[200]Cf. Anthony C. Thiselton, *The Two Horizons: New Testament Hermeneutics and Philosophical Description* (Grand Rapids: Eerdmans, 1980).

This understanding of the underlying tenor of Protestant orthodox exegesis manifests, also, the intimate connection between the
more textual and grammatical work done by the Protestant exegete,
the element of older Protestant work sometimes viewed as
"modern," and the doctrinal and logical work of the orthodox
exegete, typically seen as problematic and as not genuinely related
to textual interpretation in histories of exegesis.[201] Quite to the contrary, the drawing of logical conclusions from the text is an integral
part of the method that serves the basic intention of the method—the
intention to draw *sacra doctrina* and *sacra theologia* out of the
sacra pagina. Indeed, the drawing of logical conclusions appears as
one of the final hermeneutical steps in the method, closely related to
the application of the *analogia Scripturae* and the *analogia fidei.*

Riissen offers a series of arguments to prove legitimate the use of
logic to draw doctrinal consequences in matters of faith. First, he
notes that such a logical procedure conforms to the known goals of
Scripture itself: "the goal of Scripture *(finis scripturae)* is instruction, debate, correction, training, and perfection in righteousness,
2 Tim. 3:16" while Romans 15:4, where Paul's correspondents are
identified as "filled with all knowledge and able to instruct one
another" certainly implies the importance of drawing conclusions
based on the fundamental instruction offered in the text.[202] (It is
worth noting both that Riissen's argument itself rests on the use of
logic to draw conclusions from juxtaposed texts and that it moves in
the realm identified by Congar's characterization of medieval biblicism, that questions concerning a "non-scriptural doctrinal formulation" could be answered with a "scriptural reference that was at least
equivalent or indirect."[203])

Furthermore, Riissen comments, it is not the nature of human
beings to be irrational blockheads—theirs is the desire and ability to
"penetrate to the marrow and sense of the words."[204] It is also the
case, declares Riissen, that the wisdom of God is such that God fully
understands the consequences of all that he says—and unlike human
beings, must surely wish that people might understand his word to

---

[201]Cf. Farrar, *History of Interpretation,* pp. 357–79; Grant, *Short History of
the Interpretation of the Bible,* p. 97; Hayes and Prussner, *Old Testament
Theology,* pp. 6–19.

[202]Riissen, *Summa theol.,* II.xii, controversia, arg.1.

[203]Congar, *Tradition and Traditions,* p. 87.

[204]Riissen, *Summa theol.,* II.xii, controversia, art.2: "Natura hominis, qui
non est truncus, sed creatura rationalis; adeo debet ad medullam & sensum
verborum penetrare."

include all that can be legitimately gathered from his pronouncements! This is, moreover, the only way to test out and refute the consequences erroneously drawn from the text by heretics and papists.[205] If more proof of the legitimacy of the practice is needed, Riissen concludes, one need only look to the example of Christ and the apostles: Christ, after all, refuted the Sadducees by proving the doctrine of the resurrection of the dead as a consequence of the doctrine of the covenant; and the apostles consistently argue Jesus to be the Messiah by drawing conclusions from the Old Testament.[206]

This drawing of logical conclusions, like the comparison and collation of texts, involves both positive and negative proof, inasmuch as some articles of doctrine are positive, containing dogmas that are to be believed, and others are negative, containing rejections of error: "the former, which are the proper objects of faith, ought to be demonstrated clearly and certainly from Scripture; as for the latter, they can easily be shown to be false because no mention is made of them in Scripture."[207] The burden of proof falls upon those who would affirm a theological article as biblical and true. Thus, "the adversaries" must prove their doctrines of the Mass and purgatory from the text of Scripture.[208]

Nor does the objection hold that such logical procedures make the faith inaccessible to the simple: "It must be allowed," Riissen comments, "that a theologian has a more perfect knowledge of the consequences [of the application of logic], there is however no reason that the most ignorant of persons, entirely lacking in knowledge of logic and metaphysics, should not possess according to his capacity enough light of reason and natural logic to grasp natural consequences."[209] Reason and even some ratiocination play a necessary part in faith, even though reason is capable of error. Faith, after all, implies some knowledge on the part of the believer and faith itself is characteristic only of rational beings. "Reason," argues Riissen, "does not err always and in all things; and if it occasionally falls into error, faith is in no way related to this—nor is all knowledge and certainty removed from the world and Pyrrhonism introduced."[210] (As in the case of Protestant orthodox apologetics and the orthodox use of the proofs of God's existence, the context of the

---

[205]Riissen, *Summa theol.,* II.xii, controversia, arg.3–5.

[206]Riissen, *Summa theol.,* II.xii, controversia, arg.6.

[207]Riissen, *Summa theol.,* II.xvii, controversia.

[208]Riissen, *Summa theol.,* II.xvii, controversia.

[209]Riissen, *Summa theol.,* II.xii, controversia, obj.1 & resp.

[210]Riissen, *Summa theol.,* II,xii, controversia, obj 1 & resp.

remark is almost as important as its content. From the late sixteenth century to the close of the seventeenth, philosophical skepticism, as evidenced by a revival of interest in the thought of Sextus Empiricus and, to a certain extent, by Descartes' search for a new method through doubt, led Protestant theology to the affirmation of the validity of rational judgment, within limits.[211] Riissen's statement that reason "occasionally falls into error," made at the transition between high orthodoxy and the eighteenth century does manifest a far greater trust in the instrumental function of reason than can be found among the Reformers. The statement should, at very least be placed into the context of Riissen's rather careful delimitation of the use of reason in his prolegomenon.[212])

The limited focus and application of Riissen's statement concerning the use of reason in drawing conclusions is seen from the next objection that he notes. The fact the disciples were unable to "bear" the entirety of the Lord's teaching (John 16:12) does not prevent the use of what doctrine we possess or stand in the way of drawing logical conclusions from it. Surely the Lord did not mean that new dogmas, different in substance from those he had previously taught were to be revealed in the future, but only that a fuller declaration and more certain persuasion concerning the same doctrines would be made possible through the work of the Spirit.[213] Nor is it acceptable to assume that there are many doctrines neither contained in nor capable of being concluded from Scripture—granting that those put forth by the "papists," such as the perpetual virginity of Mary, the local descent of Christ into hell, purgatory, and the Mass, are either unnecessary or false.[214]

Just as in the prolegomena, so too in the doctrine of Scripture, Protestant orthodoxy treaded the narrow line between fideism and rationalism. The line was difficult to draw and, in the seventeenth century, the balance increasingly difficult to maintain, more difficult at least than it had been for the medieval scholastics, because of the relative independence of the exegete from the tradition and from the churchly *magisterium*—and more difficult also than it had been for the Reformers, because of the increasing tension caused for doctrinal theology by the diverse results of exegesis, particularly as done by

---

[211]Cf. Popkin, *History of Scepticism,* pp. 17–43, 175–84. This issue will be discussed at some length in volume 3 under the theme of the proofs of the existence of God.

[212]Cf. Riissen, *Summa theol.,* I.vii; with the discussion in *PRRD,* I, 7.2.

[213]Riissen, *Summa theol.,* I.xi, controversia 1, obj.1.

[214]Riissen, *Summa theol.,* I.xi, controversia 1, obj.2.

Socinian and deistic exegetes, and because of the stresses and strains placed on Protestant theological system by the forward movement of textual criticism. Nonetheless, the prominence of faith as an element in the doctrine of Scripture and of the *analogia fidei* in the discussion of interpretation, brought about a confessional and churchly model for exegesis and maintained the spiritual and ecclesial reading of the text necessary to the existence of orthodox dogmatic system. Faith, both *fides qua* and *fides quae,* rather than reason remained the norm for interpretation even granting the powerful and necessary role played by the rationality of the individual Protestant exegete.

Whitaker's eighth means of interpretation, following the analogy of faith and subordinate to it, is consultation with other exegetes, specifically through the reading of commentaries. All such works are to be used with care, of course, inasmuch as they have no ultimate authority in themselves, but rest on the authority of Scripture and the exercise of reason.[215] The specifically Protestant exegetical tradition, therefore, insofar as it rests on Scripture and the right use of reason, will have equal weight with the "authorities" of the past. (Significantly, the one element of the medieval *quaestio* that all but drops out of Protestant use of that method of exposition is the *"sed contra,"* where the medieval doctor would offer an initial rebuttal from an "authority" prior to stating his own opinion. The Protestant exegetical method allows, indeed, recommends recourse to the theological tradition, but it refuses to grant it the same authoritative status as it held in the older scholasticism.)

c. Dicta probantia *and the Protestant Exegetical Tradition*

Some comment is needed here concerning the scholastic use of scriptural proofs and the absence of exposition of texts within the scholastic systems themselves. Frequently this technique has been labeled proof-texting—but it is something quite different than the rank citation of texts apart from their context and apart from any consideration of the results of exegesis that is typically identified as "proof-texting." Preus says of the Lutherans that they "were possessed of a naive and winsome confidence in the clarity of Scripture and in the power of *nuda Scriptura* to convince."[216] This is true, but it is not a full explanation of the technique of citation in the scholastic systems. The systems arose out of a context of normative, established exegesis. Frequently the dogmatic theologians had spent

---

[215]Whitaker, *Disputation,* IX.5 (p. 473).
[216]Preus, *Theology,* I, p. 42.

long portions of their careers as exegetes and had viewed study of the Old or New Testament as the proper preparation for the dogmatician.

The work of Johannes Marckius serves as an excellent example of this movement. Marckius not only began his teaching career as an exegete and later passed over into the field of dogmatics, but also left behind him a large corpus of exegetical works together with two theological systems—a fairly large *compendium* and a shorter *medulla*—both of which have the appearance of rank "proof-texting," inasmuch as Marckius offers brief, propositional definitions of doctrine followed by series of citations of Scripture by chapter and verse, accompanied by no exegetical warrant. Granting, however, the progress of Marckius' career, it easily appears that his citations of texts point back to the work of an exegetical tradition in which he was an active participant.[217] Similar observations can be made of theologians like Polanus, who first served as professor of Old Testament and who produced a number of commentaries on the prophets; Gomarus, whose writings are largely exegetical; Leigh, who wrote on New Testament philology before approaching his larger theological work.[218]

In the cases in which the writers of the system were not themselves exegetes and commentators, there was, by the seventeenth century, a tradition of Protestant exegesis on which to draw. System presents not exegesis but dogmatic result. To accuse the result of proof-texting is to ignore division of labor and to fail to respect careful distinction of topic—this latter being a characteristic of ortho-

---

[217]N.B., Johannes Marckius, *Analysis exegetica capitis LIII. Jesaiae in qua alia complura vaticina de Messia illustrantur; accedit Mantissa observationum textualium* (Groningen, 1687); idem, *In apocalypsin Johannis commentarius seu analysis exegetica* (Amsterdam, 1689); idem, *In canticum Salomonis commentarius, seu analysis exegetica ... annexa est etiam analysis exegetica Psalmi XLV* (Amsterdam, 1703); idem, *In Haggaeum, Zecharjam, & Malachiam commentarius seu analysis exegetica,* 2 vols. (Amsterdam, 1701); idem, *Sylloge dissertationum philologico-theologicarum, ad selectos quosdam textus Veteris Testamenti* (Leiden, 1717); *Scripturariae exercitationes ad quinque & viginti selecta loca Novi Testamenti* (Amsterdam, 1742).

[218]Cf. e.g, Amandus Polanus, *Analysis libelli prophetae Malachiae* (Basel, 1597); *In Danielem Prophetam visionum amplitudine difficillimum ... commentarius* (Basel, 1599); *Analysis libri Hoseae prophetae* (Basel, 1601); *In librum Prophetiarum Ezechielis commentarii* (Basel, 1608); Franciscus Gomarus, *Opera omnia,* 2 vols. (Amsterdam, 1644); and Edward Leigh, *Critica sacra: or Philologicall Observations upon all the Greek Words of the New Testament* (London, 1639).

doxy. Leigh's list, by biblical book, of recommended commentators manifests the background of established exegesis. Other scholastics, like Turretin, frequently cite the works of major exegetes and philologists. Indeed, the continuity between the theology of the Reformers and that of the Protestant orthodox is arguably better measured according to the exegetical tradition than according to pattern of theological system. A good case may be made that Calvin's greatest influence was normative exegesis—his Scripture commentaries—and not his *Institutes* which, as a system rooted in the style and the polemic of its day, was soon out of date.

When we enter the world of Reformation era and of orthodox Protestant exegesis, we enter a world of hermeneutical pattern and exegetical result that is quite different from the world of the twentieth-century or "postcritical" theologian and exegete. We enter a world in which there was an intimate connection between exegesis and theology, particularly in view of the centuries-long reading of certain *loci classici* or *sedes doctrinae* as sources for particular doctrinal perspectives. Even the more philosophical issues addressed in the doctrine of the divine essence were often directly related to the exegesis of certain texts in Scripture.

The exegetical and controversial literature of the early orthodox era occupied an important position both in the actual historical construction of Protestant scholastic dogmatics and in the modern analysis of the phenomenon of scholastic or orthodox Protestant theology. Both the exegetical and the controversial works of Protestant theologians provided materials and arguments that were incorporated into theological systems—often directly, by the authors of the commentaries and polemical treatises as they sought to codify their arguments in full-scale dogmatic works. The *locus*-method of theological argumentation in commentaries lent itself directly to the development of dogmatic *loci communes,* the typical form of scholastic Protestant system. Similarly, the topical approach of polemics was not only capable of easy adaptation to dogmatic statement—as has been the case throughout the history of the church— but was also conducive to the development and augmentation of already extant dogmatic topics. Beyond this general impact, moreover, the exegetical and controversial literature contains a wealth of detailed and substantive argumentation, frequently resting upon an examination of textual and syntactical problems in the original languages of Scripture, that provides an underlying rationale for the direction taken in Protestant dogmatics. A text merely cited in the dogmatic systems may point toward a massive exegetical labor in commentaries and polemical treatises.

The third and fourth chapters of Edward Leigh's *A Treatise of Divinity* (1646), for example, offer—as part of a theological system —an exhaustive book by book description of the canon of the Old and New Testaments, giving the names of the best commentators on each book.[219] We need not review in detail Leigh's catalogue of Scripture—but only remark that his knowledge of commentators, like his use of theologians, shows a vast knowledge of continental thought and that the presence of such a catalogue in a theological system (in addition to the exhortations to the careful study of Scripture we have already noted) demonstrate the close bond even in the period of orthodoxy between systematic theology and exegesis. We need, thus, to be wary of viewing persistent citation of chapter and verse of Scripture in these systems as mere "proof-texting"; rather it is a sign that reading of Scripture has contributed to the system and is recommended to the readers of the system.

The failure of much contemporary discussion of late sixteenth- and seventeenth-century theology and exegesis is nowhere more apparent than in Hayes' study *Old Testament Theology; Its History and Development*. Commenting specifically on the methodology of Sebastian Schmid's *Collegium biblicum,* but also clearly attempting to characterize Protestant orthodoxy in general, Hayes argues that "the flaws in this method cry out from every side," and are evidenced in "its superficiality and its totally inadequate view of the significance of the Bible."[220] Rather than deal with the text of Scripture on its own terms, Schmid collected a series of *dicta probantia* or *dicta classica* out of their original contexts and arranged them according to the topics of orthodox Protestant theological system, not for the sake of providing what to Hayes' mind, was a genuine exegetical interpretation of the texts, but for the sake of buttressing a particular system of doctrine. The division of the book into sections dealing with the Old Testament and the New Testament "was actually one of convenience and not one based on any recognition of deep-seated differences between the two testaments." The result of such dogmatic efforts was a failure to do "justice to all the religious ideas of the Old Testament," a frequently "fallacious exegesis," and

---

[219]*A Treatise,* I.iii–iv (pp. 42–83). Chapter 5 (pp. 83–91) on the Apocrypha also deals with the question of canon.

[220]Hayes and Prussner, *Old Testament Theology,* p. 19; and cf. the more balanced approach in Gerhard Ebeling, "The Meaning of 'Biblical Theology,'" in *Word and Faith,* pp. 79–97.

a "naive and superficial reading of biblical theology" based on an "extraneous doctrinal theology."[221]

Orthodoxy, to be sure, did view Scripture as infallible or inerrant and did tend to assume an ultimate harmony of the biblical message. It also assumed that its own theological systems could be developed directly on the basis of Scripture and, conversely (to borrow the words of the old Presbyterian ordination vow), that its confessions and, by extension, its confessionally grounded systems, contained the doctrine taught in Scripture. The medieval identification of the teachings of Scripture as *principia theologiae* remained an important element in the Protestant formulation of doctrine, specifically in the assumption that doctrines could be formulated as conclusions drawn from arguments based on the text. In its specific claims, however, Hayes' discussion is erroneous in the extreme, particularly because it refuses to oblige its own internal cautions and judges the whole of a past age on the basis of hermeneutical considerations and even of terminological distinctions taken from the present. Hayes assumes, without any examination of curricula or of discussions of useful commentaries such as provided in Leigh's *A Systeme or Body of Divinity* and Buddaeus' *Isagoge,* that whereas in the sixteenth century, biblical studies had been given first place in the theological curriculum, this emphasis was replaced, in the seventeenth century, with the study of "doctrines" as set forth in confessional books and theological systems. The Bible was then, Hayes concludes, viewed as an infallible and harmonious whole, without any elements of "historic development, of divine accommodation in revelation, or of progression in revelation."[222] Of course, the exegetes of the seventeenth century were only beginning to understand the problem of historical context and development—but they fully recognized the accommodated nature of the text and the progress of revelation. The nature of accommodation was a matter of extensive debate and the hermeneutics of most orthodox Protestant theology assumed a movement from promise to fulfillment.

Granting the polemical context of the times and the need to defend Protestantism against the Counter-Reformation, Anabaptist subjectivism, and Socinian rationalism, as well as against the critique leveled by the new philosophy and new science, the orthodox Protestant stance is historically understandable. The result of this polemic, was—according to Hayes—the subordination of

---

[221]Hayes and Prussner, *Old Testament Theology,* pp. 6, 19.
[222]Hayes and Prussner, *Old Testament Theology,* pp. 8, 14.

Scripture to doctrinal and confessional orthodoxy and the relegation of biblical theology so-called to the task of collecting proof-texts, *dicta probantia*.[223] In making this assertion, however, Hayes entirely ignores the strong emphasis of orthodoxy on exegesis and commentary—and, quite significantly, ignores the larger portion of Schmid's own work, which, as Diestel and Jacob remind us, was the literal-grammatical exegesis of the text of the Old Testament, with close attention to its religious significance, both for the formulation of doctrine and, as Spener's appreciation of Schmid testifies, for the formation of piety. Schmid wrote annotations on Genesis, Joshua 1–7, Ruth, and Kings and produced commentaries on Judges, Samuel, Job, Ecclesiastes, Jeremiah, Hosea, Isaiah, Romans 1–6, Galatians, 1–2 Corinthians, Colossians, and Hebrews and paraphrases of the prophetic Psalms, Titus, and Jude.[224] In addition, Schmid translated the entire Bible into Latin, evidencing what Jacob calls a "litteralism" and a "scrupulous faithfulness to the Hebrew and Greek text"—so intent on occasion, on rendering plurals as plurals and so forth that it could arguably even "border on error," but in sum a considerable advance on previous Latin translations.[225] Hayes' comment that Schmid's "*Collegium biblicum* and similar works were essentially designed to expound Christian doctrines instead of the religious thought of the Old Testament or the Bible,"[226] simply fails to recognize the relationship between the *Collegium* and the larger part of Schmid's work—and the way in which the *Collegium* and the various other works like it not only point toward theological system but also point from the theological system to the exegesis that had been done, elsewhere, at great length and with considerable knowledge of the language and content of the Bible.

As we have noted in other places in the present essay, the great divide in the history of exegesis and hermeneutics was not the Reformation but the eighteenth century, specifically the period from Semler to Gabler, in which historical method was brought to bear upon the exegesis of the text. That in itself is not a radical statement in the context of the various extant studies of the history of interpre-

---

[223]Hayes and Prussner, *Old Testament Theology,* p. 14.

[224]Diestel, *Geschichte des Alten Testamentes,* pp. 400–401, 410; Edmond Jacob, "L'Oeuvre exégétique d'un théologien strasbourgeois du 17ᵉ siècle: Sébastien Schmid," in *Revue d'histoire et de philosophie religieuses* 66 (1986):71–78.

[225]Jacob, "L'Oeuvre exégétique ... Sébastien Schmid," p. 74.

[226]Hayes and Prussner, *Old Testament Theology,* p. 18.

tation and of the history of Old and New Testament theology.[227] It is, however, a point that has seldom crossed over the disciplinary line into the modern study of Protestantism and the history of its theology—and it is a point that has typically passed unnoticed by the writers who have attempted to juxtapose the theology of the Reformers with that of their orthodox successors. Before the dawn of this radically historical method, the overriding concerns of the exegete were grammar and theological meaning, not historical context (even when the historical context was noted as an element in the understanding of the text), and the underlying assumption of hermeneutics was the lively address of the inscripturated Word to the present-day life of the church, not the problem of a religious "truth" lodged in the alien culture and strange thought-forms of long-dead peoples.

Schmid's *Collegium biblicum* and similar works, for all their division of the subject into Old and New Testaments, were not "biblical theologies" in the modern sense of the term.[228] Indeed, the idea of a "biblical theology" that reconstructed historically the religion of long-dead Israelites, with no reference to the life of the present-day religious community, would have seemed just as absurd and incongruous to Sebastian Schmid and his contemporaries as the *Collegium biblicum* and its *dicta probantia* seem to modern biblical theologians. The full title of Schmid's work, *Collegium biblicum prius, in quo dicta V.T., et collegium biblicum posterius, in quo dicta N.T. iuxta seriem locorum communium theologicarum explicantur,* when properly understood, explains its purpose—a purpose rather different from that of "biblical theologies" of the Old and New Testaments: "A first biblical gathering, in which sayings from the Old Testament, and a second biblical gathering in which sayings from the New Testament are explained relative to the series of theological commonplaces."

A bit of exegesis is in order. A *collegium* is a body or gathering—usually of people but, by extension of any series a set of like objects, even biblical texts. Schmid's choice of the term may echo the title frequently given to systems of theology in the sixteenth and seventeenth centuries, *corpus doctrinae,* a "body of doctrine." Schmid's *collegium* is also a "body" but not one as fully integrated

---

[227]Cf. Diestel, *Geschichte des Alten Testamentes,* pp. 555–63, 601–12, 708–713; Kümmel, *The New Testament: The History of the Investigation of its Problems,* pp. 62–107; Hayes and Prussner, *Old Testament Theology,* pp. 60–66.

[228]Cf. Jacob, "L'Oeuvre exégétique ... Sébastien Schmid," pp. 74, 78.

as a typical theological *corpus.* Indeed, the *collegium,* as the latter portion of the title indicates, is a preparation for or basic step toward a *corpus doctrinae.* Another, and even more usual, title of theological system in the sixteenth and seventeenth centuries was *loci communes theologiae,* common places or, better, universal topics of theology. Schmid's "gathering" of texts is for the purpose of placing them *iuxta,* close by or in immediate relation to the series of commonplaces or universal topics of theology.

Even so, the various seventeenth-century works entitled *Theologia biblica* or some variant thereof are not evidence—as some of the writers on the subject would have it—of dogmatizing predecessors of the biblical theologies of the late eighteenth and nineteenth centuries.[229] Rather these works are gatherings of texts, usually arranged by theological topic and often accompanied with exegetical comments. They are, in short, works designed as a bridge between the *locus* method of biblical interpretation and dogmatic theology. Such works extract the theological *loci,* together with some interpretation, for the sake of grounding the dogmatics. This exercise, moreover, was hermeneutically justifiable in the seventeenth century given the patterns of exegesis and the long history of understanding texts as bearers of a particular theological significance.

Conversely, the universal topics of theological system themselves stood in relation to the exegetical practice of many of the Reformers and of the Protestant orthodox. Far from representing the imposition of a dogmatic grid on the text, the various dogmatic *loci* stand as topics gathered, in the first instance, from the text and only subsequently arranged into the form of a theological system. Beginning with the exegetical work of Martin Bucer (1491–1551) and Wolfgang Musculus (1497–1563), Protestants had consistently echoed the medieval method of developing extended *scholia* on key texts in the Scriptures—*loci theologici* or *sedes doctrinae*—and had elaborated doctrinal topics, *loci,* within the structure of the commentary. The relationship among text, exegetical examination, theological discussion, and doctrinal system was not only easily established but was also assumed as an underlying principle of interpretation itself. As we have already seen, the rise of Protestant theological system was intimately bound up with the *locus* method of exegesis and with the extraction of these doctrinal *loci* from the commentary. In an intimate and technical sense, the theological systems of the

---

[229]E.g., Ebeling, *Word and Faith,* pp. 85–86, and Hayes and Prussner, *Old Testament Theology,* pp. 17–19.

orthodox rested directly on the exegetical task as understood by many of the Reformers and by their successors.[230]

The *locus* method did not disappear in the seventeenth century nor was it practiced to the exclusion of textual and exegetical study. This interpenetration of exegetical and theological approaches, with its fundamental interest in rising from a critical examination and establishment of the text through exegesis to doctrinal and homiletical statements useful in the church appears clearly in the pentateuchal work of Andrew Willet. Willet's method was distinguished by its "sixfold" approach to a text, a pattern that he followed in virtually all of his commentaries.[231] The method called for an introductory discussion identified by Willet as the "Analysis," "Method," or "Logicall resolution," corresponding to the "argument" placed by many commentators of the age at the beginning of commentaries and chapters. This he followed with "the Genesis or Grammaticall construction where the translations differ." Here Willet very briefly offers a verse by verse synopsis of the differences between translations noting all of the variant rendering of the Hebrew together with additions found in the Septuagint and the Chaldee paraphrase. "The Exegesis, or theologicall explication of doubtful questions and obscure places," Willet's third section, is constructed as a series of questions and answers—sometimes quite lengthy, as the thirty-five such questions and answers on the first chapter of Genesis. Here, Willet typically returns to the issues raised by the text, variants, and various translations in order to offer explanations of problems and resolutions based, typically, on comparison with other biblical texts and citation of the church fathers, rabbinic commentators, and various other translators and scholars. The fourth section, "the didactica" or "places of doctrine observed out of [the] chapter," follows the "locus" method of exegesis found in the works of earlier Reformed exegetes like Bucer, Musculus, and Zanchi by offering positive theological statement. Thus, in the discussion of Genesis 1,

---

[230]The examples that follow could be multiplied indefinitely; for other examples of the continuity of the exegetical tradition see above, §5.1 (on the properties or attributes of Scripture), §6.4.b (on the reading of Hos. 6:7 as a basis for the covenant of works); in addition to the examples adduced in this volume, the orthodox doctrine of God in volume 3 will follow a similar pattern of examining the history of exegesis.

[231]E.g., Andrew Willet, *Hexapla in Genesin* (Cambridge, 1605; 2d ed., enlarged, 1608); *Hexapla in Exodum* (London, 1608); *Hexapla in Leviticum* (London, 1631); *Hexapla in Danielem* (Cambridge, 1610); and *Hexapla: That is, a Six Fold Commentarie upon the Epistle to the Romans* (Cambridge, 1620).

Willet offers "places" on the Trinity, on the doctrine of creation out of nothing, on the eternity of the Word, and so forth—as raised by the exegetical tradition. The fifth section, "places of confutation," handles points of theological debate that relate to the doctrinal *loci* drawn out of the chapter. "The places of exhortation and comfort" offer moral and spiritual, one is tempted to say tropological meditations on the text. For example, commenting on the text of Genesis 1, Willet can note that "As God commanded light to shine out of darknesse, so we should pray to God to illuminate our minds with the knowledge of Christ, 2 Cor. 4.6."[232]

An excellent example of the orthodox Protestant use of Scripture —to which we will return in the third volume for its doctrinal argumentation—is Stephen Charnock's *Discourses Upon the Existence and Attributes of God* (1682), first delivered as sermons in the year of Charnock's death, 1680. Each discourse sets forth a single doctrinal point belonging to the dogmatic *locus* "God"—with the larger number of discourses focusing on an attribute as identified by a text from the Bible. For his discourse on the goodness of God, Charnock selected—with solid grounding in the exegetical tradition —the text of Mark 10:18 ("And Jesus said unto him, Why callest thou me good? There is none good but one, that is, God").[233] Rather than simply abstract from the text the idea of the goodness of God— as ratified by a dominical saying—Charnock both examines the text, noting differences between the Matthean and the Lucan versions, and discusses the views of various commentators on the implication of Jesus' reply to the questioner, prior to their application to the doctrinal problem at hand.

Thus Charnock notes the greater specificity of Luke's identification of the questioner: "a certain man" in Mark, "a certain ruler," according to Luke, one, notes Charnock, "of authority among the Jews." This man imagined "that eternal felicity was to be purchased

---

[232]Andrew Willet, *Hexapla in Genesin & Exodum: that is, A sixfold commentary upon the two first Bookes of Moses ... wherein these translations are compared together: 1. The Chalde. 2. The Septuagint. 3. The vulgar latine. 4. Pagnine. 5. Montanus. 6. Iunius. 7. Vatablus. 8. The great english Bible. 9. The Geneva edition. And 10. The Hebrew originall. Together with a sixfold use of every Chapter, shewing 1. The Method or Argument: 2. The divers readings: 3. The explanation of difficult places and doubtfull places: 4. The places of doctrine: 5. Places of confutation: 6. Morall observations,* 4th ed. (London, 1633), pp. 16, 18.

[233]Stephen Charnock, *Discourses Upon the Existence and Attributes of God* (1682; reissued, New York: Carter, 1853), vol. II, pp. 209–355.

by the works of the law" and required clarification of his duties. He did "not seen to have any ill, or hypocritical intent in his address to Christ" but "seems to come with an ardent desire, to be satisfied in his demand." Indeed, Charnock adds, Christ is said to "love" his questioner—a highly unlikely statement had the man been a hypocrite.[234]

What was at issue in the interpretation of the text, as Charnock's comments and references indicate, was the precise meaning of Jesus' "first reply," the reply based not on the man's question, but on his salutation, "Good Master." Some writers of the day, including the great talmudic scholar, John Lightfoot, assume that the response, "Why callest thou me good ...," is intended to draw the man toward a confession of Christ's divinity, granting that God alone can rightly be called good: "If you take me for a common man," Charnock paraphrases, "with what conscience can you salute me in a manner proper to God." This interpretation is supported—in Lightfoot's argument—by the fact that the title, "Good Master," *"Rabbi bone,"* does not occur in the Talmud and appears to be a unique title. On the other side of the point, Charnock notes that the "Arians" use the text in support of their view of Christ, arguing that its words amount to a denial, on the part of Christ, that he deserves to be addressed with a word that ought to be applied only to God.[235] As Erasmus had pointed out, however, the Arian reading does not follow, inasmuch as Jesus reproved the man for calling him good "when he had not yet confessed him to be more than a man." Had he meant to exclude himself from the divine goodness, Jesus would have said, "there is none 'good' but the Father."[236]

Other commentators, in particular Calvin, see in the text "no intention" on Christ's part to draw forth "an acknowledgment of his Deity," but only to assert "his divine authority or mission from God." This, Charnock notes, has led Maldonatus to call Calvin an Arianizer. In this view, the text can be paraphrased, "You do without ground give me the title 'good,' unless you believe I have a Divine commission for what I declare and act."[237] Charnock doubts the justification of an interpretation that would claim even the apostles did not yet know Christ's divinit y at the time of this incident, since Peter had not yet uttered his confession: after all, both a devil

---

[234]Charnock, *Discourses,* p. 209; cf. Poole, *Commentary,* III, p. 90.

[235]Charnock, *Discourses,* p. 209; cf. Lightfoot, *A Commentary on the New Testament,* III, p. 189 (Luke 18:19).

[236]Charnock, *Discourses,* p. 210.

[237]Charnock, *Discourses,* p. 210.

(Luke 4:34) and John the Baptist (John 1:32, 34) had previously stated it. Nonetheless, Charnock does accept the basic reading of Calvin and Paraeus that the text is not an argument for the divinity of Christ:

> why do you call me "good," and make bold to fix so great a title upon one you have no higher thoughts of than a mere man? Christ takes occasion from hence, to assert God to be only and sovereignly "good": "there is none good but God." God only hath the honor of absolute goodness, and none but God merits the name "good." ... He is "good" in a more excellent way than any creature can be denominated "good."[238]

Charnock then proceeds to offer four statements, each with exposition, defining the divine goodness which, he comments, is the "chief scope of the words":

1. God is only originally good, good of himself.
2. God only is infinitely good.
3. God is only perfectly good, because only infinitely good.
4. God only is immutably good.[239]

The reference to "scope" here is significant. The term indicates not so much a doctrinal or dogmatic as a hermeneutical concern.[240] Charnock, like the Reformers and various early orthodox exegetes, assumed that the fundamental issue to be addressed in identifying the meaning of a biblical passage was the focus, center, or "scope" of the passage, as defined both by its larger context in a chapter or pericope and by its own grammar and syntax. Exegetically, hermeneutically, and theologically, Charnock was working in the context of a tradition of interpretation—a tradition that he referenced closely in his effort to grasp the meaning of the text of Mark 10:18 and to move from the text to theological formulation. When, therefore, a brief compendium of doctrine, like Marckius' *Medulla,* cites Matthew 19:17, without elaboration, as one of several texts that prove

---

[238]Charnock, *Discourses,* p. 210.

[239]Charnock, *Discourses,* pp. 210–212.

[240]See Gerald T. Sheppard, "Between Reformation and Modern Commentary: The Perception of the Scope of the Biblical Books," in William Perkins, *A Commentary on Galatians,* ed. Gerald T. Sheppard, with introductory essays by Brevard S. Childs, Gerald T. Sheppard, and John Augustine (New York: Pilgrim Press, 1989), pp. 42–71.

the divine *bonitas*,[241] it ought not to be assumed that the text has been wrenched out of its context or the tradition and trajectory of Protestant exegesis has been ignored.

Other instances of this intimate relationship between the dogmatic use of *dicta probantia* and the tradition of Protestant exegesis can easily be identified: Riissen's use of 1 Timothy 3:15, "thou mayest know how thou oughtest to behave thyself in the house of God, which is the church of the living God, the pillar and ground of the truth," appears, on the surface to be a blatant case of "proof-texting," particularly because it engages in a rather technical dispute over the way in which "pillar" ought to be interpreted, rather than in an examination of the text and its language as they might have been understood by the author of 1 Timothy.[242] The text appears to have been wrenched out of its context by Catholic and Protestant alike and pressed into dogmatic service, almost despite the intentions of the apostolic author, as the basis of a discussion of the relative authority of Scripture and church.

It is, however, fairly easy to demonstrate that Riissen was drawing on a lengthy exegetical tradition that had, throughout its history, worked very carefully with the Greek text of the epistle—admittedly, on the basis of a hermeneutic quite different in its assumptions and intentions from the modern historical-critical method. The issue, here, however, is that the so-called *dicta probantia* arose not out of an arbitrary "eisegetical" procedure, but out of the accepted exegetical and theological methods of the time—and, indeed, the phrase "pillar and ground" *(tylos kai edraioma)* was carefully scrutinized in the Greek exegesis of the day.

Indeed, Riissen's argument stands in a profound and close relationship with the Reformed exegetical tradition reaching back to Calvin, Musculus, and Beza. Calvin had commented at great length on 1 Timothy 3:15, not only noting how the apostle "adorns the church with so magnificent a title" but also how the text indicates both the "greatness" of the pastoral office and the "dreadful ... vengeance that awaits" those allow "the light of the world, and the salvation of men" to be obscured. Thus "the Papists" apply the text to the church of Rome even as they trample truth underfoot! The church is called "pillar of truth" not because she is an infallible arbiter, but because she is enjoined to defend and to spread the truth of the gospel. "The office of administering doctrine, which God

241Marckius, *Christianae theologiae medulla,* iv.41.
242Riisen, *Summa theol.,* II.xv, argumenta 1–4 and cf. above, §5.4.

hath placed in her hands, is the only instrument of preserving the truth, that it may not perish from the remembrance of men."[243] Musculus included similar comments on 1 Timothy 3:15 in his *Loci communes*.[244]

Beza notes that the church is called *columna et stabliementum veritatis,* rejecting Jerome's translation as *columna et firmamentum,* lest anyone assume that the church, like Christ, could be identified as the "cornerstone" *(fundamentum)* of the faith—after all, he comments, there have been superstitions, darkness, lies, and errors as well as the right preaching of the word and the example of good works in the church! And beyond this, the church, here called a "pillar," itself rests on a foundation, which is Christ alone. Even so, Beza notes, those who would take this text as an assertion of the church as the final norm of truth are in error and are guilty of setting human traditions above the Word of God.[245]

With an obvious echo from the positive portion of Calvin's commentary, Diodati argues briefly that the apostle "adornes" the church "with two glorious Titles, *viz. 1. The house of God ... 2. The Pillar and ground of Truth."*[246] The latter title indicates that the church is the institution "By whose Ministry the authority, dignity, knowledge, virtue, and use of the truth of the Gospel ought to bee preserved in the world, and maintained against all errours."[247] There is no polemic against Rome, but the church is clearly identified as bearer and preserver rather than as arbiter and ultimate rule of truth.

Poole comments that English lacks a proper word to translate *edraioma* and that the absence of a true equivalent has been the cause of controversy. The Greek noun derives, he comments, from *edra* which can mean a "seat" or even, according to some, "the place ... in which the idol was set in pagan temples." The meaning, in fact, is much the same as that of *tylos*—"the firm basis upon which a thing standeth or leaneth." Thus, the church is a pillar or ground in the sense of a foundation or a base; but, Poole adds, "pillars also were of ancient use to fasten on them any public edicts ... hence the

---

[243]Calvin, *Commentaries on the First Epistle to Timothy,* 3:15 (CTS, pp. 90–91).

[244]Musculus, *Loci communes,* xxi.

[245]Beza, *Annotationes in Novum Testamentum,* 1 Tim. 3:15 (p. 632, cols. 1–2).

[246]Diodati, *Pious and Learned Annotations,* 1 Tim. 3:14–15, analysis (p. 317).

[247]Diodati, *Pious and Learned Annotations,* 1 Tim. 3:15, annotations (p. 325, col. 1).

church is called, *the pillar* and basis, or seal, *of truth,* because by it the truths of God are published, supported, and defended."[248] Thus, contrary to what the "Romanists" claim, "the church discovers and recommends the truth, but the testimony it gives is not the foundation of its credibility."[249] Poole offers almost identical arguments in the larger *Synopsis criticorum,* to the effect that Christ alone is the ultimate foundation, whereas the church is as a column setting forth and sustaining the faith.[250]

This intimate relationship between exegetical method and theological system was paralleled by the frequent movement of Protestant theologians in the sixteenth and seventeenth centuries among the several fields of theological endeavor. It was not the norm for a theologian to begin his career as a dogmatician. Typically —as in the cases of Musculus, Polanus, and Marckius—a Protestant theologian began his career as an exegete and, after years of work as a commentator, became a professor of dogmatic theology. In many cases, large portions of the dogmatic works of these writers were drawn out of the theological *loci* that belonged to their work as commentators—and the *dicta probantia* that they employed were argued exegetically either in their own commentaries or in the works of various exegetes with which they were familiar. There is, in other words, a relationship between the *dicta probantia* and the exegetical tradition that mirrors and in fact indicates a technique opposite to and based on the movement from exegesis to *locus theologicus* to theological system.

In other words, the gathered *dicta probantia* point from the theological topic back to the text from which the theological topic was elicited and, in effect, complete a hermeneutical circle linking the text with the practice of formulating theological system. The methodological link between text and system, both in the initial formulation of the locus out of the exegesis of the text and in the gathering of *dicta* for the sake of pointing the theological system toward the text and grounding it on the authority of Scripture, was the technique noted above of drawing logical conclusions from the text after the basic exegetical work had been completed. The assumption of the Protestant exegete was that the properly drawn conclusion carried with it the same authority as the text itself. While, in the general sense, Scripture was the *principium cognoscendi*

---

[248]Poole, *Commentary,* III, p. 781, col. 1.
[249]Poole, *Commentary,* III, p. 781, col. 1.
[250]Poole, *Synopsis criticorum,* 1 Tim. 3:15 (col. 1045–46).

theologiae, in the more specific and proximate sense, the individual *dicta, loci,* or *sedes doctrinae* provided the first principles of theology in the oldest sense of the identification of theology as *scientia:* a body of knowledge consisting in first principles and the conclusions that may be drawn from them. Granting this premise, the *dicta* become grounds for logical argumentation—both for the sake of establishing positive formulae and for the sake of demonstrating the fallacies of various forms of heterodoxy. Thus, Owen could declare, "that when the Scripture revealeth the Father, Son, and Holy Ghost to be one God, seeing it necessarily and unavoidably follows thereon that they are one in essence (wherein alone it is possible they can be three),—this is no less of divine revelation than the first principle from whence these things follow."[251]

7.4 Epilogue

If this study has demonstrated nothing else, it has demonstrated that the doctrine of Scripture taught in the era of Protestant orthodoxy, stood in substantial continuity with the views of the medieval doctors and the Reformers, and that, like the teaching of the medieval doctors and the Reformers, it was characterized by a fundamental doctrinal intentionality different not only in general from the intentionality that can be identified with modern exegesis and modern biblical theology, but also different in its specific hermeneutical implications. Beyond this basic doctrinal continuity, the study has also demonstrated a large-scale continuity in development of biblical interpretation in the western exegetical tradition: it is not, as some have suggested, as if the Protestant scholastics returned to medieval methods of allegory or that they failed to understand the ground gained for literal and grammatical interpretation by the Reformation.[252] Rather, the Protestant orthodox discussions of the "divers senses" of Scripture, given their fundamental emphasis on the unitary character of the literal sense, the recognition of allegorical or tropological meanings only when they belong to literal intention of the passage itself, and the control of typology by means of a hermeneutic of promise and fulfillment, so far from departing from the Reformers, ought to be seen as the full codification, in Protestant form, of the emphasis on the letter as the source of meaning that began with such exegetes as Andrew of St. Victor and

[251]Owen, "Brief ... Doctrine of the Trinity," in *Works,* II, p. 379.
[252]Cf. Fullerton, *Prophecy and Authority,* pp. 180–85; Farrar, *History of Interpretation,* pp. 357–71.

Thomas Aquinas and grew to maturity in the sixteenth century in the hands of the Reformers.

The problem of the Protestant orthodox doctrine of Scripture is not that it evidences a radical discontinuity with the doctrine of the Reformers but that it expresses in a strictly argued and scholastic form a view of Scripture which, like the view expressed by the Reformers, does not oblige the historical and hermeneutical criteria of biblical study from the eighteenth century onward. All too much discussion of the Reformers' methods has attempted to turn them into precursors of the modern critical method, when in fact, the developments of exegesis and hermeneutics in the sixteenth and seventeenth centuries both precede and, frequently conflict with (as well as occasionally adumbrate) the methods of the modern era. The doctrine and exegesis of the Protestant orthodox were supported by a theological, linguistic, and logical apparatus which, although both more intricate and more technical than that of the Reformers, was nonetheless a result of the ongoing development of methods of teaching and linguistic study characteristic of the sixteenth-century Renaissance and Reformation.

As for the doctrine of inspiration, which has received so much attention in earlier studies, our examination of the Reformed orthodox exegetes and theologians has offered a variegated picture rather than a monolithic presence. A very strict dictation theology was promulgated, to be sure, by a large group of Protestant orthodox thinkers—but it is also clear that the various subtleties of earlier doctrine were not lost to the seventeenth century and that both before and after major debates, such as the debate over the vowel points, a less rigid view of inspiration capable of being related to critical advances was also characteristic of many of the orthodox writers. And even the most rigid inspiration theory, as set forth by Voetius and Owen, was intended to support the authority of Scripture as taught by the Reformers.

In addition, this study has argued a consistent and intimate relationship between the theology of Protestant orthodoxy and the best exegetical results of the age. Over against what can only be called "the Whig interpretation" of the history of exegesis, we have not singled out the moments and insights in the sixteenth- and seventeenth-century history of exegesis that seem most to resemble the critical exegesis of the present day and then posed these moments and insights against the orthodox or scholastic exegesis. We must refuse that historical gambit if only because, as in the case of John Lightfoot, the forward-looking exegete is also one of the defenders of "scholastic orthodoxy"—or, in the case of Louis Cappel, the hermeneutical rebel had intended his work as a contribution to the orthodox polemic against Roman Catholicism. More important, we have detected an interrelationship between the exegetical results of the age and the contents of theological system. The critical insights fed the theological polemic and the exegetical tradition remained of extreme importance to dogmatic formulation even as it increasingly brought pressure to bear on time-worn dogmatic formulae.

Much of the extant discussion of the Protestant orthodox doctrine of Scripture, instead of attempting to enter the conceptuality of the sixteenth- and seventeenth-century writers and to exposit without prejudice *their* theological or doctrinal intention, has pretended to find difficulties in the Protestant orthodox approach to the text, not on the basis of sixteenth- and seventeenth-century issues and problems, but on the assumption that Reformation and Protestant scholastic teaching ought somehow to oblige the criteria and satisfy the theological needs of the present. As Steinmetz has commented of "precritical" exegesis, "its principal value ... is that it is not modern exegesis."[253] The importance, if not the value, of the Protestant orthodox doctrine of Scripture lies precisely in the difference between it and the various modern approaches to Scripture. In particular, unlike modern concepts of the nature and character of Scripture, the Protestant orthodox doctrine, for all of its formal and occasional substantial differences with the doctrine of the Reformers, was, like the Reformation view of Scripture, directed toward the exposition of the text in and for the church as the fundamental rule of faith and practice. For all of the difficulty caused for dogmatics by changing hermeneutical and critical methods in the seventeenth century, the connection between exegesis and dogmatics remained fundamental to the theological task of orthodoxy.

In retrospect, we must affirm what several historians of exegesis and interpretation have argued from a rather different vantage point. The great divide in the early modern history of theology was the movement leading up to J. P. Gabler's distinction between biblical and dogmatic theology. Contrary to the perspective of Ebeling and Hayes, it has become impossible for us to understand the biblical compendia of the orthodox era as poor and uncomprehending ancestors of later "biblical theology." Rather they are gatherings of traditionary exegesis that assumed the connection between exegesis and

---

[253]Steinmetz, "John Calvin on Isaiah 6," p. 170.

dogmatics as it had been established by the *locus* method of interpretation in the sixteenth century and by the creation of dogmatic systems by the gathering of theological *loci* out of the texts of commentaries. All of these works, like the *locus* method on which they were based, assumed a positive and necessary relationship between text and dogma, despite the increasing difficulty caused for those who made the connection by a more literal and grammatical method of exegesis.

As the Roman Catholic polemicists intimated in their declaration that Scripture alone, without the testimony of the church, was both unclear and, in that sense, insufficient for the salvation of believers —and, equally so, as the Protestant orthodox dogmaticians intimated in their massive and increasingly rationalizing encounter with the problems caused by the text for traditional dogmas—the alteration of approach to the text brought on by the combination of the Renaissance and Reformation mastery of ancient languages with the loss, over many centuries, of the *quadriga* and related "allegorical" patterns of exegesis pressed hard against the received doctrine of the inspiration and authority of Scripture, granting that perception's inspiration and authority were tied to a particular set of dogmas, dogmas that had often been elicited from the text through the use of allegorical method and had been taught with considerable ease when the language of the text, Latin, and the language of theology were identical. The great divide identified in Gabler's address was the historical dimension that the late seventeenth and early eighteenth centuries added to the critical dimension of Reformation and post-Reformation exegesis.